THE TOUR[ISM HOS]PITALITY AND EVENTS STUDENT'S GUIDE TO STUDY & EMPLOYABILITY

Sara Miller McCune founded SAGE Publishing in 1965 to support the dissemination of usable knowledge and educate a global community. SAGE publishes more than 1000 journals and over 800 new books each year, spanning a wide range of subject areas. Our growing selection of library products includes archives, data, case studies and video. SAGE remains majority owned by our founder and after her lifetime will become owned by a charitable trust that secures the company's continued independence.

Los Angeles | London | New Delhi | Singapore | Washington DC | Melbourne

THE TOURISM, HOSPITALITY AND EVENTS STUDENT'S GUIDE TO STUDY & EMPLOYABILITY

SALLY EVERETT, NICOLA CADE, ABIGAIL HUNT, DEBORAH LOCK, KATIE LUPTON & STEVE MCDONALD

Los Angeles | London | New Delhi
Singapore | Washington DC | Melbourne

Los Angeles | London | New Delhi
Singapore | Washington DC | Melbourne

SAGE Publications Ltd
1 Oliver's Yard
55 City Road
London EC1Y 1SP

SAGE Publications Inc.
2455 Teller Road
Thousand Oaks, California 91320

SAGE Publications India Pvt Ltd
B 1/I 1 Mohan Cooperative Industrial Area
Mathura Road
New Delhi 110 044

SAGE Publications Asia-Pacific Pte Ltd
3 Church Street
#10-04 Samsung Hub
Singapore 049483

Editor: Matthew Waters
Assistant editor: Jasleen Kaur
Assistant editor, digital: Sunita Patel
Production editor: Sarah Cooke
Copyeditor: Christine Bitten
Proofreader: Martin Noble
Indexer: Jess Farr-Cox
Marketing manager: Abigail Sparks
Cover design: Francis Kenney
Typeset by: C&M Digitals (P) Ltd, Chennai, India
Printed in the UK

Library of Congress Control Number: 2020936579

British Library Cataloguing in Publication data

A catalogue record for this book is available from the British Library

ISBN 978-1-5264-3645-0
ISBN 978-1-5264-3646-7 (pbk)

At SAGE we take sustainability seriously. Most of our products are printed in the UK using responsibly sourced papers and boards. When we print overseas we ensure sustainable papers are used as measured by the PREPS grading system. We undertake an annual audit to monitor our sustainability.

CONTENTS

ABOUT THE AUTHORS

PROFESSOR SALLY EVERETT, NTF, PFHEA, PHD, CMBE, MA, BA (HONS)

Sally is Professor of Business Education and Vice Dean (Education) at King's Business School, King's College London. Sally was previously a Deputy Dean at Anglia Ruskin University (ARU) and led their work on inclusive learning and teaching. She is a National Teaching Fellow and a Principal Fellow of the Higher Education Academy. Before her time at ARU, Sally was the Head of Department for Tourism and Marketing at the University of Bedfordshire, and previously worked for a large heritage visitor attraction in Bristol. Sally's research interests include cultural tourism and inclusive education. Her publications include *Food Tourism: Principles and Practices* with Sage Publications and numerous articles on tourism, community resistance and inclusive teaching.

NICOLA CADE, MPHIL, BA (HONS)

Nicola is a full-time PhD candidate at King's College London exploring the socio-cultural effects of mega-events on Rio's favela communities and tourism initiatives. She is an Associate Lecturer at Anglia Ruskin University in Marketing, Enterprise and Tourism. Nicola completed her Master of Philosophy (MPhil) focusing on a creative social legacy project for marginalised young people from Rio's favelas. She completed her Tourism Management degree in 2016 and was awarded a prize by The Association for Tourism in Higher Education (ATHE) as the 'Best Undergraduate Student in Tourism 2016'. She has two published co-authored articles in *Tourism Geographies*.

DR ABIGAIL HUNT, PHD, MED, PGCE, PGDIP, BA (HONS), PFHEA

Abi is Associate Professor of Heritage and Identity in the Department for Marketing and Tourism in Lincoln International Business School. Abi worked in the heritage industry before moving into Higher Education. Her academic expertise is in how the past is represented in written and object-based historical narratives. Her pedagogic expertise is in assessment, particularly the assessment literacy of students and staff. She regularly undertakes consultancy, involving students as partners in the work as a means of developing their employability skills.

PROFESSOR DEBORAH LOCK, PHD, MA, PFHEA

Deborah is an academic leader with more than 20 years of strategic-level experience in higher education. She has led numerous change management programmes including the re-development of curricula, re-branding of a Business School, the re-alignment of a centralised business development function and the creation of a distributed work-based learning infrastructure. In her roles as Professor of Inclusivity & Innovation in Teaching and Director of Education at the University of Lincoln, she is responsible for the internationalisation of the curriculum, online and flexible employer-led provision and student employability. Her PhD was on identity construction amongst KT staff in UK universities with specific attention on their career motives, educational practices and relationship management skills.

DR KATIE LUPTON, PHD, MSC, FHEA

Katie is a tourism academic with a PhD in the field of tourism and environmental psychology, currently working at Leeds Trinity University. Passionate about tourism for sustainability, her research interests include the role of tourism in developing ethical behaviour, social responsibility in tourism, and the relationship between tourism and social marketing. With a previous background in hospitality management, she is passionate about career opportunities within the industries and in lecturing to develop employable graduates across tourism, hospitality and events, that is, those who are prepared and equipped to take on the sustainability challenge and be industry innovators of the future.

DR STEVE MCDONALD, PHD, MA, BA, PGCE, CMBE, SFHEA

Before joining the Faculty of Business and Law at Anglia Ruskin University, Steve worked in industry in a variety of management positions. Additionally, he has worked as a consultant for SMEs, specifically in the hospitality area and the building area. He has experience in setting up and developing small businesses. Steve has been teaching for over 14 years, receiving awards and recognition for his teaching. He has been actively involved in the last five years in developing and implementing new teaching approaches, such as team-based learning and activity-based learning to engage students in their learning and development. Steve is currently working on supporting students to develop their emotional intelligence, professional resilience and wellbeing through his cognitive intervention approach to teaching.

ACKNOWLEDGEMENTS

A book of this size, complexity and breadth does not happen easily and we would like to acknowledge the wonderful colleagues and students who have helped us by contributing their ideas and insights. It has been a true team effort. We want to especially thank our families and friends for their patience and good humour. They have shown us great love and understanding when many of us have spent evenings, nights and weekends pulling together ideas, resources and activities.

We have been fortunate to have been joined by some amazing colleagues throughout the writing process. As co-authors, we have been blessed with input from friends who have written and contributed to several key chapters. We particularly acknowledge and extend our thanks to Dr Steven Rhoden, Dr Bartek Buczkowski, Alessandro Pesaro, Rosy Jones, Maryvonne Lumley and Dr Lyn Collier-Greaves.

We also want to thank our students, employers in our network and other colleagues. This book contains many employer and industry 'insights' and it is almost impossible to name every business, contact and contributor we have included, but we acknowledge them in the relevant chapters and extend our gratitude to them all. We would especially like to thank Natalie Brimecome-Mills, Monica Emmanuelli, Robin Evans, Jessica Neilson and Peter Schulze for their input into the digital and ICT chapter; Erick Robert Rombano Carandang and Cristina Ionita (second year BSc Tourism Management students at Anglia Ruskin University) and many others who were happy for their photos and stories to be reproduced. We extend our thanks to Marcus Hanwell (Anglia Ruskin University), who helped design some of the images, and to Dr Faye Taylor for her wisdom and input on the chapter on Social Responsibility and Sustainability and to her colleagues, Rachel Welton and Ian Gregson from Nottingham Business School, for their case study contribution.

Finally, we want to thank Jess and Steph, our amazing proofreaders. Jess (*aka* https://thefilthy comma.co.uk) not only helped tidy up all our chapters, but brought insight, wise suggestions and transformed our chapter drafts with lightning speed and incredible accuracy. We can't thank her enough. Highly recommended!

At the time of finalising this book, the world was gripped by the COVID-19 global pandemic and extensive bans were in place on travel, events and the wider hospitality industry. If nothing else, the crisis has illustrated just how unpredictable the world is and that you need to be prepared for whatever the future throws your way. At times in the writing journey we have felt overwhelmed as we have juggled teaching, responding to the crisis, supporting students and colleagues and progressing with our writing. We hope you find this labour of love both helpful and enlightening as you forge a career in the incredibly rich and diverse sectors of tourism, hospitality and events. It is a sector that needs excellent graduates. It needs you.

INTRODUCTION

━━ CHAPTER LEARNING OBJECTIVES ━━━━━━━━━━━━━━

By the end of this chapter you should be able to:

* Use this book to support your studies and career planning.
* Use the different activities, tools, reflection boxes and insights in this book to support your professional development.
* Understand how this book is structured and feel confident locating chapters and topics that are of most value to you at key stages of your studies and job search.

THE PURPOSE OF THIS BOOK

This guide to study skills and employability for tourism, hospitality, and event management students has been a labour of love for the authors. We very much hope that it is a helpful and engaging resource as you progress from starting a university or college programme; through to applying for graduate level jobs; and then finally, as you enter the world of work or establish your own business. When we started planning this book, it was very clear to us that there were very few resources available that specifically supported students interested in the tourism, hospitality and event management sectors, and even fewer that provided a structured guide that could take a student through all stages of the academic and skills development life cycle. There are many textbooks available for business students, covering core study skills, career management advice, personal development and employability, but we found very few focused on this distinct industry area (one very recent example is Firth, 2019). Rather than a generic textbook, we were keen to write something that directly supports an employability agenda by providing potential opportunities in tourism, hospitality and events and introducing students to a range of career opportunities.

We hope you find the content and guidance useful as you develop your own study skills, think about your personal development and assess your career and future. This introduction outlines the various educational features we have incorporated into each chapter of this book and how you might want to use the exercises and examples in conjunction with your studies. We have taught these subjects for many years and many of us have also worked in tourism, hospitality, leisure and events, so we know that it is an incredibly exciting sector in which to study and build a career. We hope our enthusiasm for these rich and diverse areas of work and study comes through in each chapter. In addition to unique insights from employers, industry contacts, our colleagues and students, we also offer our own personal reflections because we are keen to show that this journey is a deeply individual one. We wish you every success in your studies and hope this guide can help you along the path.

STANDING OUT FROM THE CROWD AND YOUR PART IN THE INDUSTRY

With this book, we want to help instil confidence in you as you consider embarking on a career in the tourism, hospitality and events industries. In the UK in 2018/19 there were 1.65 million under-graduate students doing their first degree (bachelor's) with a total of 2.38 million students on all types of degree (foundation, professional certificates and diplomas) and 585,730 postgraduate students (Higher Education Statistics Agency HESA, 16 January 2020). In 2018/19, the number of qualifications achieved was 496,110 at undergraduate and 305,025 at postgraduate level (including doctorates). The total number of qualifications achieved in 2018/19 was 801,135, an increase of 3% compared to 2017/18 (HESA, 2020). In the US, 3.97 million people graduated with a Higher Education (HE) qualification in 2019/20 (associate, bachelor's, master's and doctorate) (EducationData.Org, 2020). According to China's *People Daily* newspaper, a record 8.34 million people graduated from Chinese universities in summer 2019 (ICEF Monitor, 2019), up from 8.2 million in 2018 – that's more than double the figures in the US.

To say the global employment market is competitive is an understatement. Of course, these figures do not relate solely to hospitality, tourism and events students, but it is important to remember that job roles rarely specify a specific discipline and therefore you will not only be competing with those of a similar specialism. Your industry-related degree may well give you a competitive edge, but you will not be alone in applying within these industries. The World Travel and Tourism Council (WTTC, 2019b) found that the global travel and tourism sector grew at a rate of 3.9% and contributed a record $8.8 trillion and 319 million jobs to the world economy in 2018, which represents one in ten of all jobs globally. It is responsible for one in five of all new jobs created in the world in the last five years and is the second-fastest-growing sector in the world, ahead of healthcare (+3.1%), IT (+1.7%) and financial services (+1.7%). It is only behind manufacturing, which grew by 4%. Tourism and hospitality are responsible for around 9% of the world's GDP and constitute approximately 260 million jobs, which is about 9% of total global employment. In short, the THE sector is one of the biggest industries in the world.

Given the industry is around 10% of global GDP, it also means that global crisis and shocks can affect it more than many other economic areas. As we were finalising this textbook in 2020, the world was in the grip of a global pandemic. We hope by the time you are reading this that the COVID-19 virus is under control and that the world is recovering; however, the crisis highlights how important the tourism, hospitality and events industry is in terms of global employment, international stability and economic growth. The World Travel and Tourism Council forecasts that the COVID-19 pandemic could lead to the loss of over 50 million jobs worldwide in the travel and tourism industry (and more indirect losses) and it could take up to a year for the industry to recover (Faus, 2020). The United Nations World Tourism Organisation (UNWTO, 2020a) estimated that global international tourist arrivals could decline up to 3%, down from an estimated growth of around 4% (a rate predicated in early January 2020). We have seen far-reaching restrictive measures placed on international travel, public events and hospitality businesses across the globe. We have witnessed airlines grounded and collapse, cruise ships being placed in quarantine, and city lockdowns across the world which have directly affected restaurants and hotels, as well as visitor attractions and all public events. It is hard to know at the time of writing this book how the world will deal with the crisis and address the aftermath. The full impact of the crisis will depend on how long the epidemic lasts. However, there is hope because the world will need graduates like you who have the skills, knowledge and attitude to help rebuild the industry. In the wake of the COVID-19 crisis, your role as a graduate is going to be fundamental in rebuilding these key industries.

It is vital that you develop the transferable skills and reflective abilities that will help you secure a graduate-level career and make a difference to a fast-changing world. We hope this book will support you in your studies and to build a personal brand that will ensure you stand out in a crowded graduate marketplace. This book acknowledges the multi-faceted nature and complexity of the tourism, hospitality and events industries. Its specific focus on study skills, employability, career management resources, advice and support aims to provide a thorough and research-informed approach. We have endeavoured to reflect an international mindset, ensuring all students feel supported in their own career development. Although we provide several examples from the UK (where we are based as authors), we have sought to draw on examples, ideas and insights from a range of different country contexts.

THE STRUCTURE OF THE BOOK

We have structured this book in line with the key stages of a first tourism, hospitality or events degree by linking chapters to different levels and years of study. In the UK, Level 4 is equivalent to the first year of a bachelor's degree; Level 5 is the second year; and Level 6 the final year. We have aimed to make the book relevant to postgraduate students seeking promotion or those returning to study after a long break from study. Our hope is to support students of tourism, hospitality, event and leisure management, who are currently required to use more generic business texts that provide little or no relevant industry context. By focusing on the service industries, in addition to the more generic skills and guidance increasingly expected at university level, we hope you gain specific skills demanded in customer-facing, international and service-orientated career paths.

We are grateful to our students and colleagues we have consulted as this book has developed. They have provided incredibly helpful insights and feedback. As a result of their suggestions, we have included a lot of elements not usually found in similar study skills texts. Some of the additional areas we felt were important include digital literacy (Chapter 9), cultural sensitivity and language (Chapter 16), sustainability and social responsibility (Chapter 17), project management (Chapter 18), postgraduate studies and pursuing an academic career (Chapter 28), and developing new ideas as an entrepreneur (Chapter 34).

We have drawn on a multiplicity of academic fields, such as organisational behaviour, psychology, sociology technology and business, whilst integrating examples from current tourism, events and hospitality practice and policy. Coupled with industry-specific case studies ('industry insights') and employer cases ('employer insights'), we hope that you find the book both interactive and relevant. Practical educational features include:

- A glossary, provided at the beginning of each chapter
- Practical, accessible and inclusive reflection exercises and activities that help you evaluate your own skills, attributes and strengths/weaknesses
- Overarching skills audits where you can track your own development
- 'Test yourself' sections, including some examples of psychometric tests commonly used at assessment centres
- Think points designed to encourage you to pause as you are reading the chapters and reflect on what the content means for you
- Further reading and useful web resources at the end of each chapter if you wish to take your learning further
- Bulleted chapter learning objectives at the start of each chapter and conclusion points at the end summarise what has been covered in each chapter
- Resource ideas, including examples of initiatives used at different universities
- Figures, graphs, and images to help illustrate key skills, ideas and research
- Useful templates for you to adapt and use, e.g. covering letters, CVs, online profiles and so forth.

By drawing on some of the latest approaches and thinking in terms of how you maximise your social media presence, build your personal brand, work with big data in tourism, take advantage of new opportunities, network successfully, engage with recruitment processes and approach psychometric testing and online selection, we have written for today's graduates. We wish you every success as you progress through your studies and hope this book helps you leave university or college feeling ready, equipped and confident to pursue opportunities and succeed in the vibrant, creative and global industries of tourism, hospitality and events.

SECTION A

STUDY SKILLS FOR TOURISM, HOSPITALITY AND EVENTS

Level: 4

1

A GIANT LEAP? THE TRANSITION TO UNIVERSITY

CHAPTER LEARNING OBJECTIVES

By the end of this chapter you should be able to:

- Explain how a university works, what it is and how it is regulated.
- Describe the differences between types of universities, their approaches and how they are categorised.
- Manage and enjoy your first few days and weeks at university.
- Explain how universities support different populations of students.
- Articulate the value of a tourism, hospitality, or events degree.

GLOSSARY

- **Culture shock:** a sense of shock in moving from a familiar culture to one that is unfamiliar. Describes a sense of disorientation when someone is suddenly subjected to an unfamiliar place, culture or way of life such as university.
- **Degree algorithm:** the calculation that universities use to determine your final degree classification based on module results (differs from university to university).
- **Self-efficacy:** the level of personal confidence in your ability to succeed. It is one's belief in one's ability to do well with a task or deal with specific situations.
- **Social phobia:** this is also known as 'social anxiety disorder' and is a long-lasting and overwhelming fear of social situations. It is different from, and far more acute than, shyness.

INTRODUCTION

This chapter provides a brief history of universities and outlines what a university is, how they are generally regulated and the value of a university experience, as well as the importance of gaining a degree. The chapter covers some of the sources of student support you should use and addresses some of the questions you might be asking about university life and how best to deal with the transition into this new environment. Some of the issues and concerns you may have will probably include coping with being away from home, the importance of engagement and belonging, how to work within a university culture and getting used to some of the new and different processes that you come across in a university.

This chapter discusses the importance of seeking support and getting involved in the first few weeks of your university life. Research indicates that engagement is key in good student performance and outcomes. It will also look at some recent research on specific topics and student profiles including first-generation students, flexible mode students (part-time and online) and those from ethnic and minority backgrounds. This chapter should provide reassurance and an opportunity for you to assess your own motivations, expectations and plans for university and your future career.

Finally, this chapter will help you think about why a tourism, hospitality, events or degree might be useful and valuable to you. By offering examples of other students studying similar subjects and providing stories from their college or school, this chapter should help outline why a degree is important, and so often, life-changing.

WHAT IS A UNIVERSITY?

In Latin, the word *universitas* means 'a whole' where people come together. Our understanding of what a university is also comes from the Latin *universitas magistrorum et scholarium*, which roughly means 'a community of teachers and scholars'. The word 'university' has a long and detailed history and even today its definition remains highly contentious and debated (Denman, 2009). For the German philosopher Humboldt, a university was about a 'whole' community of scholars and students engaged in a common search for truth and meaning. Others see their role as teaching universal knowledge. However, if you read or watch the news, you will have noticed that universities are being discussed, debated and critiqued almost daily. The perceived role and status of universities seems to be in a constant cycle of change and this pace of change is perhaps faster than it has ever been – whether this is about how they are funded, what fees should be charged, what their leaders (Vice Chancellors and Principals) are paid, the value of a degree, what kinds of courses and degrees they should offer, and indeed how they are regulated.

THE HISTORY OF UNIVERSITIES

Aside from the origin of the word itself, another aspect people cannot agree on is which institution was the first university. It is commonly accepted that the first university in Europe was the University of Bologna, Italy which was founded in 1088 AD. This was followed by the formation of the University of Paris around 1150 AD (see Anderson, 2006). It is certainly true that these European medieval universities evolved from Catholic cathedral or monastic schools, which had been established for the clergy to offer Biblical teaching and promote the word of God.

Despite claims about their origins being in Europe, some writers suggest that the birth of the university was elsewhere, and much earlier than the twelfth century. It is claimed the Sumerians had scribal schools or *É-Dub-ba* around 3500 BC which bore close resemblance to what we would understand to be a university. According to UNESCO and the Guinness World Records, the oldest existing and continually operating educational institution in the world is the University of Karueein, also known as the Al Quaraouyine University, which was founded by Fatima al-Fihri in 859 AD in Fes, Morocco. However, whatever their history, the main thing today is to recognise the vast diversity of institutions that are now referred to with the term 'university' in terms of size, scope, priorities, mission and relationship to the general public and external world.

You might wonder what the difference is between a college and university. Briefly, a college educates people (often up to foundation degree level), while universities are focused on creating knowledge through research, and are committed to investigating and producing new ideas, concepts and ways of thinking. A university aims to develop and build the knowledge of those who come to learn there, but also aims to provide experience and encourages people to think and challenge their own views of the world, and indeed the views of others in an open environment, which should encourage and support free speech and free thought. Universities fundamentally promote research (thinking about thinking), followed by action and impact wherein work and thinking should make a difference to the world and to the lives of others. In addition to developing new knowledge, a university also has a role in disseminating and advancing knowledge through scholarship and research, and through its students and graduates. University research should make a difference to society and the wider world.

TYPES OF UNIVERSITY

There are many types of university, all with their own history, values and focus. For example, universities in the United Kingdom have a very long history and have been categorised in various ways, although all of them focus on helping students to learn and in developing knowledge through research. Oxford University is the UK's oldest higher education institution (founded in 1096 AD), followed by Cambridge University in 1209. In Scotland, the oldest universities are St. Andrews, Glasgow, Aberdeen and Edinburgh. There are also what are called 'red brick' universities (or civic universities), which were developed during the nineteenth century and are mainly city-based institutions in old industrial cities like Sheffield, Manchester, Leeds and Birmingham.

A significant expansion of universities in UK Higher Education in 1992 saw previous polytechnics, further education colleges, teacher training colleges, or university colleges being granted university status. It has meant that most of UK's larger towns and cities now have more than one university and many of these newer universities have developed an excellent reputation for the quality of their courses in tourism, hospitality, events, leisure and other service sectors. More recently, a small number of privately owned institutions (i.e. places that do not receive state funding) have become universities.

There are also other ways in which UK universities are categorised, with terms such as the Russell Group (https://russellgroup.ac.uk) which represents 24 UK research-intensive universities. Its member universities range from newer universities of 50 years to Oxford and Cambridge which have almost 1,000 year histories. Founded in 1994 with the aim of ensuring its member universities 'flourish and continue to make social, economic and cultural impacts through their world-leading research and teaching', its members include Bristol, Cardiff, Edinburgh, Glasgow, Imperial College, London, King's College London, Nottingham, Queen's University, Belfast, Oxford, and Warwick.

There are also groupings such as the Million+ Group who present themselves as 'the Association for Modern Universities in the UK, and the voice of 21st-century higher education' (www.millionplus. ac.uk). They 'champion, promote and raise awareness of the essential role played by modern universities in a world-leading higher education'. Members include Bedfordshire, Bolton, Sunderland, Cumbria and London Metropolitan. In addition to these, the Alliance Universities (www.unialliance. ac.uk) claim to be 'leaders in technical and professional education since the industrial revolution … we educate the professional workforce of the future, provide flexible and responsive R&D to businesses of all sizes and solve the problems facing society locally, nationally and across the globe'. Its members include Brighton, Central Lancashire, Coventry, Greenwich, Hertfordshire, Huddersfield and Kingston University. Finally, there is the Guild HE (www.guildhe.ac.uk) who focus on developing a more inclusive and diverse section and this association includes the universities of Falmouth, Bath Spa, Abertay and Harper Adams.

In terms of tourism, hospitality and events, some of the most highly regarded universities are those established in the last few decades and include institutions such as Lincoln, Sunderland, Bournemouth, Coventry and Surrey. However, always do your research and be wary of league tables as there are many, all using different (and sometimes questionable) metrics and changing every year. You need to choose the university that is right for you, rather than being led by the views of others. Some universities that you might not otherwise have considered might have the work placements you want, enterprise education initiatives, employer links or student experience opportunities.

The US has research-intensive universities that lead the world rankings, including institutions such as the California Institute of Technology, Stanford University, Massachusetts Institute of Technology and Harvard University (*Times Higher Education*, 2019). There are also public (state) universities that receive some government funding, and are part of a state university system housed in different locations around a state; for example, the State University System of New York (SUNY) comprises more than 60 campuses spread across the whole state of New York. There are also junior colleges (also known as community colleges) which are state-funded and offer an undergraduate-level qualification called an 'associate degree'; the largest is the California Community Colleges System (CCCS) with over 100 community colleges.

In addition to the state universities in the US, there are private universities where fees are higher but which include many of the country's most reputable institutions (e.g. MIT, Harvard, Yale, Princeton, Stanford, Caltech, Columbia and Cornell). Finally, there are also liberal arts colleges, which tend to specialise in undergraduate-level courses in the liberal arts and sciences. For example, the California university system has three types of university: community colleges, state universities and research-focused institutes. Each has its role, but they are all connected and feed into each other. Institutions with a specific reputation for tourism and event management are plentiful but include Arizona State, George Mason, Indiana, Florida International and George Washington.

In terms of the global picture, most countries have a wide range of universities, with many competing for the top rankings. Some of the leading universities in hospitality are in Switzerland, such as the ETH Zurich (Swiss Federal Institute of Technology) and the EHL (Ecole hôtelière de Lausanne), alongside the Hong Kong Polytechnic University in Hong Kong. In terms of the QS world rankings 2019 (QS, 2019), Russia is climbing up quickly and China now has several universities in the top 100. Furthermore, Europe (France, Germany, Italy) continue to do well, and in South East Asia the Nanyang Technological Institute recently overtook the National University of Singapore. You may be interested in studying overseas, so do also look at less obvious parts of the world. For example, Argentina and Brazil have highly regarded universities (e.g. Argentina's Universidad de Buenos Aires and Universidade de São Paulo in Brazil), as do New Zealand and Australia (e.g. Griffith in Australia is regularly rated highly for its hospitality subjects).

THINK POINT

What kind of university might suit you and your interests and way of learning? Why? You might need to do some research to be able to answer this with confidence and insight.

HOW ARE UNIVERSITIES REGULATED?

Universities around the world all have quality codes and policies that regulate teaching and research. For example, in the UK, there are nearly 200 universities with degree-awarding powers, most of which are members of Universities UK, so it is important there is accountability for the public in terms of protecting the interests of students (you!) and safeguarding the reputation of British higher education. Various bodies do this, although the Industry Insight of the UK outlines the most recent changes to regulation of universities.

INDUSTRY INSIGHT

The Office for Students, United Kingdom

In terms of regulation in the UK, the Office for Students was introduced in 2017 as part of the Higher Education and Research Act (HM Government, 2017). In brief, this was a significant change for universities. It marked the most significant sector legislation in 25 years for universities since the passage of the 1992 Further and Higher Education Act. In brief, the Act enacted the following things:

- It set up the Office for Students, which replaced the Higher Education Funding Council for England (or HEFCE). It works alongside the UK Research and Innovation (UKRI) as the main watchdog.
- It opened opportunities for new universities, allowing more institutions to gain degree-awarding powers.
- It introduced the controversial Teaching Excellence Framework (TEF), a medal-like rating system of gold, silver and bronze that assesses universities' teaching quality, although some argue the metrics used just provide proxy measures and the TEF remains under review.

In 2019, the Augar Review was undertaken, a post-18 review of education and funding that made several recommendations about fees and how universities should be funded. The Review was criticised because, despite reducing annual fees, the longer period to pay off a student load will disadvantage those on lower wages and women in particular. Government changes in the UK have meant its recommendations remain on hold (at time of publishing).

Source: Universities UK (2018)

WHAT IS A DEGREE?

Most degree awards comprise a number of units or modules attached to a certain number of credits, which then make up a programme of study. In the UK, a standard bachelor's degree requires you to pass 360 credits over three years, although increasingly many are introducing additional placement or 'sandwich' years. At the time of writing there is also debate about how two-year accelerated degrees might work. British degrees are awarded by universities or other degree-awarding bodies and these institutions are formally recognised by the UK government.

American universities and some British institutions use the term 'minor' and 'major' and generally have four-year bachelor's degrees. The major is the main area of study, including all the core classes in the relevant subject area. This is sometimes called a 'major concentration', and minor are the classes that form the foundation of the degree. These terms refer to the main/primary area of study (e.g. Tourism) and a secondary area (e.g. Tourism Marketing).

In the UK, modules are usually weighted with anything from 10–60 credits. Whether you need to pass all the modules in all the years will depend on the rules and regulations at the university you choose. Most institutions require you to pass all modules (120 credits/year) but many may just require you to pass the first year to progress. This will depend on your university's way of calculating the degree or what is called the **algorithm**.

In England, Wales and Northern Ireland, there are nine qualification levels of education (including entry level). The first year of a degree is referred to as Level 4, second year as Level 5, and the final year as Level 6. Postgraduate study (master's) is Level 7, and PhD/doctoral Level 8. Degrees are mapped to benchmark statements against these levels. To ensure credits are recognised across Europe, the European Credit Transfer and Accumulation System (ECTS) is used to work out equivalences. To ensure some consistency, Europe has the Convention on the Recognition of Qualifications concerning Higher Education in the European Region in 1997 and the Bologna Declaration (1999), which sought to ensure consistency across higher education systems in Europe. In simple terms, a degree is conferred upon completion of all the requirements of an award. Students can pursue associate's, bachelor's, master's, and doctoral degrees. The most common bachelor's degrees are a Bachelor of Arts (BA) or a Bachelor of Science (BSc). Many former British colonies have adopted the British approach (e.g. Sri Lanka, Bangladesh, India and Pakistan).

In terms of a bachelor's degree, honours are usually categorised into four classifications: first class honours (1st) (usually given for a final grade over 70%); second class honours, divided into upper second (2:1) with 60–70% average marks and lower second (2:2) with 50–60%; and third class honours (3rd), which is usually 40–50%. Students may be admitted without honours to the 'ordinary' bachelor's degree if they have met the required standard for this lesser qualification (also referred to as a 'pass degree').

In the US, a Grade Point Average system is used (GPA). This is a number calculated from the grades you achieve and is on a scale from 0.0 to 4.0, with 4.0 being the highest GPA. Grade-point average is the cumulative average of the grades in all the classes, and it is very important because students often have to retain a certain level of GPA to continue studying in the university.

A DIFFERENT WORLD WITH A DIFFERENT LANGUAGE

You will find that universities seem to have a language of their own, and no university seems to use the same acronyms or language as another. This book will also explain terminology as you read. You might also want to start writing your own glossary of terms to help you understand this new language of universities.

THE TRANSITION INTO UNIVERSITY LIFE

Universities are very different to schools and colleges. Don't underestimate the transition into the university experience. In 2002, the former Vice Chancellor of the University of Brighton, Sir David Watson, wrote about some of the challenges facing universities, including the internet being more important than TV, multitasking as a way of life, doing rather than knowing, and typing rather than handwriting (Watson, 2002). He cited Jason Frand, who put together a highly persuasive account of the 'Information Age Mind-set', which suggested students are now studying in very different ways:

Most students entering our colleges and universities today are younger than the microcomputer, are more comfortable working on a keyboard than writing in a spiral notebook, and are happier reading from a computer screen than from paper in hand. For them, constant connectivity – being in touch with friends and family at any time and from any place – is of utmost importance.

ADAPTING TO A NEW CULTURE: THE UNIVERSITY SETTING

You may experience what is called '**culture shock**' when you attend university. It is unlikely to be anything like a place you have lived in or visited before and you may go through a number of feelings (see Figure 1.1), from an initial excitement or a 'honeymoon' phase, to concern and feeling out of place with anxiety and stress (especially if you are away from your home country) – sometimes called a 'distress' phase – to 'adjustment' and 'adaption', and finally 'comfort and acceptance' (Gale and Parker, 2014). There will inevitably be a need to adapt your values, personality and behaviour to the host culture. International students in particular experience a lot of conflicting emotions.

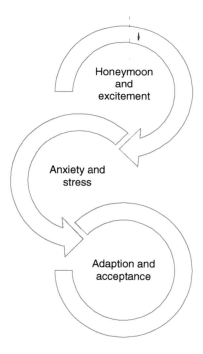

Figure 1.1   Stages of culture shock

Culture shock is real. The origins of the concept came from anthropologist Kalervo Oberg (1960) who first used the term 'culture shock' in 1958. Berger (1963) reports that anthropologists then started to use it to describe the impact of a totally new culture on newcomers and linked it to the excitement of any first journey abroad. Social scientists adopted the term to describe a new setting and this can explain the experience of a person moving from their home to an unfamiliar place. One of the key things is to become familiar with the place you are now living, whether that is a new country or new city. Go prepared, taking things that will comfort you (such as photos of family and friends).

Another model of culture shock is called the 'W curve' (Figure 1.2). The phases are: 1. Honeymoon; 2. Disintegration; 3. Reintegration; 4. Autonomy and adjustment (differences and similarities are accepted); and 5. Independence.

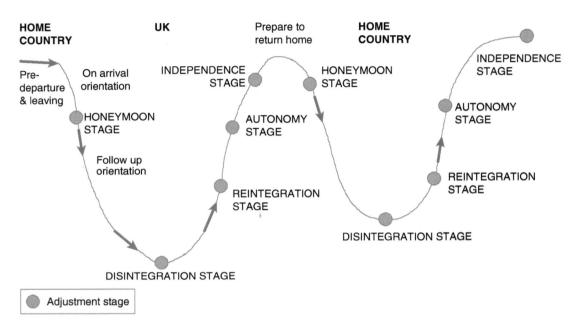

Figure 1.2   The W curve: Stages of adjustment experienced during orientation
Source: Reworded figure based on Barker, 1990

HOW MIGHT YOU ADDRESS CULTURE SHOCK?

Research suggests that mastering the cognitive processing of negative emotional experiences plays a leading role in the psychological adaptation of students (Rozhdestvenskaya, 2017). The key is not to spend too much time with your own community and friends from home (although it is important to keep in touch with fellow students from your own culture and it can be comforting to talk in your mother tongue). Research indicates that those who are more flexible, tolerant and with good social skills are better in dealing with these challenges (Holdsworth et al., 2018). This ability to cope and bounce back has also been linked to studies of resilience, i.e. the capacity to cope and adapt despite difficult or challenging circumstances (Howard and Johnson, 2000).

It might be that the prospect of meeting other people fills you with fear. This is quite normal and known as '**social phobia**'. Some ways to help you overcome this are offered by Smale and Fowlie (2015) and include putting yourself in busy places like a common room; asking open questions; looking for other people on their own; seeking meaningful conversations; and not avoiding social situations. The key thing to remember is that many students feel this way and there are ways to help overcome this feeling (Ayala and Manzano, 2018; Picton et al., 2018). Try to join societies at university, for example, so that you can develop a network of people with similar interests.

━━━━━ STUDENT INSIGHT ━━━━━

Overcoming culture shock – an international student's perspective

Xiaohua joined the BA Event Management course from Malaysia. Reflecting on her experience her advice to new international students is as follows:

'The key thing is to be proactive and start conversations with people. I missed home, but some of the things people told me to try which worked are:

- Not to isolate yourself – meet others even if you feel like you don't want to.
- Keep in touch with family at home but it's about a balance as too much contact can actually make the process of settling in more difficult.
- Ensure you have familiar things around you such as photographs. I had a couple of small toys that my friends had given me.
- Find a shop that sells your favourite food – I found a little Chinese shop that sold noodles and rice.
- Some of my friends joined a church and they found this a great source of support.
- Eat well as it's important to have a healthy and balanced diet.
- Take regular exercise. Join classes run by the university.
- Make friends with other international students. I joined games evenings and food events, speak to others that understand your experience.
- Try and find activities and clubs to join – I learnt to dance!
- Take advantage of all the support at university – there will be advisors, personal tutors, heath service, and student union help.'

━━━━━ THINK POINT ━━━━━

Do you recall experiencing culture shock in your life? How did this feel? How did you overcome and deal with it?

ENGAGEMENT AND BELONGING

One of the most daunting things when starting university is the first week (Induction, Welcome or Freshers' week). It is important that you talk to people and this is where friendships and your key networks will develop. Some suggestions to help you with the transition include:

- Talk to friends and family who have been to university.
- Check if your university has social media and social networking sites. Many universities have developed these for new students as well as their Facebook, Twitter, Instagram and Snapchat accounts. Some universities will also have their own app for you to download.
- Look through all the documentation that the university has sent you and familiarise yourself with their website.

- Some of the most important information is often sent to your university email account. You can often get this re-directed to your own personal account, but this is the main method of communication at many universities and where very important information is sent to you, so you should make sure you know how to access it and check it regularly.
- Universities often use an online learning platform (often called Learning Management Systems or Virtual Learning Environments). This will also be used to communicate with you about your course and modules/units but may also be used to develop student work groups and announce events. Again, make sure you know how to access it and check it regularly.
- Get involved. The key contacts to help you do this are often the Student Union and your course/module leaders. Many universities have a team to provide student experiences and they will be keen to ensure you feel welcome.

Smale and Fowlie (2015) talk about 'information overload' and encourage you to write down how you feel on your first day and at the end of the week. This is a good exercise if you feel overwhelmed by the amount of information you are given in the first few days, and indeed the large number of people you will have talking 'at' you! Don't worry about taking everything in as people will support and remind you of important things.

SELF-EFFICACY AND CONFIDENCE

The psychological theory of **self-efficacy** was developed by Albert Bandura. Self-efficacy influences how you behave when you encounter stress and challenges. It also determines how much effort will be expended to reach one's goals and for how long those goals will be pursued (Bandura, 1997). Importantly for university, self-efficacy is shown to influence academic motivation, learning and achievement, and students with high self-efficacy also tend to be more optimistic. If you have high levels of self-efficacy then research indicates you will enjoy better academic performance and more effective personal adjustment, as you will be coping with stress more effectively, leading to better health and greater commitment (Bozick, 2007; Chemers et al., 2001).

It might be easy to confuse terms, but self-efficacy is not the same as self-image, self-worth, or any other similar construct. Self-efficacy is the belief we have in our own abilities, specifically our ability to meet the challenges ahead of us and complete a task successfully (Akhtar, 2008). It is about our overall belief in our ability to succeed in what we set out to achieve. While self-efficacy and motivation are deeply entwined, they are separate constructs. Self-efficacy is based on an individual's belief in their own capacity to achieve, while motivation is based on the individual's desire to achieve.

 ━━━ THINK POINT ━━━━━━━━━━

There are numerous transitions to consider when you start at university: academic transitions (e.g. lectures, deadlines, reading, critical thinking) and social transitions (e.g. new friends, culture shock, first in family, financial, health). How might you get yourself ready for these?

========= REFLECTION EXERCISE =========

A simple self-efficacy test

The questions below are taken from a questionnaire by Gaumer Erickson and Noonan (2018). Answer each one on a scale of 1 (not very like me) up to 5 (very like me).

Belief in personal ability

1. I can learn what is being taught in class this year.
2. I can figure out anything if I try hard enough.
3. If I practised every day, I could develop just about any skill.
4. Once I've decided to accomplish something that's important to me, I keep trying to accomplish it, even if it is harder than I thought.
5. I am confident that I will achieve the goals that I set for myself.
6. When I'm struggling to accomplish something difficult, I focus on my progress instead of feeling discouraged.
7. I will succeed in whatever career path I choose.
8. I will succeed in whatever college major I choose.

Belief that ability grows with effort

9. I believe hard work pays off.
10. My ability grows with effort.
11. I believe that the brain can be developed like a muscle.
12. I think that no matter who you are, you can significantly change your level of talent.
13. I can change my basic level of ability considerably.

If you score 40–65, it is likely you have a strong sense of self-efficacy; if you scored less than 40, you may wish to try and improve your self-efficacy by setting yourself (achievable) goals and trying new things, looking beyond short term setbacks, and reframing obstacles you are facing. Try listing three things you did in the past week and reflect on how they made you feel. Think about how you want to feel when you tackle three new things in your first few weeks at university.

Your lecturers should also help you to improve your self-efficacy by building an inclusive learning environment and by providing you with helpful and constructive feedback.

Source: Erickson and Noonan, 2018

When an individual develops or maintains self-efficacy through the experience of success (however small), they will often get a boost in their motivation to continue (Mayer, 2010). This relationship can create a sort of success cycle: when an individual is highly motivated to learn and succeed, they are more likely to achieve their goals, giving them an experience that contributes to their overall self-efficacy. Think about how this knowledge might affect the way you approach university. Bandura notes,

> Confidence is a non-descript term that refers to strength of belief but does not necessarily specify what the certainty is about … [whereas] Perceived self-efficacy refers to belief in one's agentive capabilities, that one can produce given levels of attainment. (1997: 382)

UNIVERSITIES ARE CULTURES OF DIVERSITY

Universities are some of the most diverse organisations in the world, attracting people from all countries regardless of gender, sexual orientation, ethnicity, age or background. In the last few years, the experience and success of students from minority groups has become a top priority.

First-generation students

Are you the first in your family to go to university? Research finds that first-generation students have different needs to continuing generation students, coming from different backgrounds with different academic abilities (Choy, 2001). Work by authors such as Padgett et al. (2012) and Abdelmotaleb and Saha (2013) suggest policy ideas for institutions to support them.

 STUDENT INSIGHT

A first-generation tourism student – Karla

Although my parents were very supportive of me going to university, neither had gone themselves. My dad had left school at the age of 15, and my mum went straight into training as a nurse in the days when you didn't need a degree. My school were also very supportive, but I had no idea what to expect. I loved the idea of travel and wanted to know more about how to get a job which allowed me to travel but I think my parents just thought a tourism degree was needed to sell airline tickets! To be honest, I guess I didn't even know what I was going to do with it, but I was excited about learning more about the industry and hopefully working abroad.

The first week was stressful. I felt anxious and lonely. When I went to the registration day, it seemed everyone knew each other. I knew I had to go up to others and talk to them but it was just easier to avoid them as I felt awkward. Thankfully, there was a student experience team who organised a social event which was team-building. I thought I would hate it but I knew I had to go and try and get involved and I am so glad I went. I met a few other students who were the first in their family to go to university and they are in my classes now and I consider them good friends. We hope to go on a work placement to the same country, Canada, in a couple of years' time.

Research shows that first-generation students are more likely to drop out of college than their continuing generation counterparts (Mehta et al., 2011), so extra support is often available to ensure these students build a strong sense of community and belonging.

Students from ethnic minority backgrounds

In the last few years, the university sector has begun to focus on the experiences and achievements of minority background students. In particular, there has been concern that student with disabilities and from Black, Asian and Minority Ethnic groups (BAME) are particularly disadvantaged in terms of curriculum content, teaching staff not representing their identity and a lack of relevant and meaningful support. In the US, universities such as Harvard and Boston have been accused of not recruiting enough ethnic minority students and this is also the case in the UK at Oxbridge.

A relevant report was published by Universities UK and their #ClosingtheGap campaign. More students from minority backgrounds are accessing higher education and recent research (Office for Students, 2009) has found that black and Asian students are more than twice as likely to go to university than their white counterparts. However, statistics still show that disparities persist in terms of student outcomes, with nearly 79.6% of white students being awarded a first class or 2:1 degree, compared with 66% of BAME students. Although the gap of 13% (2017) was smaller than the 15% seen in 2016, 11.2% of black students leave HE without a qualification – significantly higher than 6.9% for white students (Advance HE, 2018). However, the situation is changing and many universities have invested a lot of time and resources in working with students from BAME backgrounds to address inequality across the student life cycle.

Universities are expected to offer diverse and inclusive environments that ensure all students have a sense of belonging at their university. You should never feel isolated and there is always support in the form of your academic lecturers, student societies, personal tutors, counsellors, welfare officers, student advisors, course leaders, student mentors and ambassadors, and your fellow peers.

STUDENT INSIGHT

Soloman, a student from a minority ethnic background

I am from Nigeria and came to study events management. I was really concerned about coming to study here, so far from home. In the end, it was an unforgettable experience. As a positive, I found that studying abroad, meeting people from all over the world, and learning about different cultures was an incredibly rewarding experience and it was useful to work with others on projects like putting on a real-life event.

I guess if I was to offer a downside, I would say I was never taught by anyone who wasn't white! I think universities need to try and get more black professors as we need role models. It was great when we had one event during Black History Month with music, food and dancing. Also, the student ambassadors are very friendly and helped us feel welcome here.

Non-traditional study patterns and different modes of learning

Studying is not always full-time and on campus. Many students choose to study part-time, online or in a blended form of delivery (a mixture of face-to-face and online). Although data from the UK (HESA, 2019) suggests that part-time student numbers have been declining since tuition fees rose for full-time undergraduates (a decline of 51% in England between 2010 and 2015), technology is making it a more attractive option for many (especially mature students) and there is a larger proportion of female part-time students.

The part-time mode is a very different experience to that of the traditional face-to-face, on-campus student. Increasingly many students are also commuting long distances and universities are having to change their approaches and practices to ensure these students have the same access to learning and resources as on-site students. If you are thinking of studying part-time, ensure your university has support in place for this mode of learning. Part-time study requires good time management, focus and independence (see Chapter 11). Ensure the university you choose offers a truly flexible learning delivery mode, flexible assessment, online support (library, resources and teaching), clear communication about how your studies can fit around you and some form of mentorship and peer support.

THE VALUE OF A TOURISM, HOSPITALITY, OR EVENTS DEGREE

Tourism and hospitality form two of the largest sectors in the world. According to the UNWTO (2020b), international tourism generated US$1.7 trillion in export earnings (approximately £1.3 trillion). This is a result of international tourist arrivals growing by 7% in 2017 and later increases of between 4% and 5% every year to reach 1.5 billion by 2019. By 2030, UNWTO forecasts international tourist arrivals to reach 1.8 billion (UNWTO Tourism Towards 2030), with around 1 in 10 jobs in the tourism and hospitality industry. This is an industry that offers many career opportunities (see Chapter 21), because:

- Many countries have highlighted a lack of skilled staff. With increasing professionalisation there is a need for people with knowledge of the industry, particularly how to manage people and projects.
- This kind of degree is highly international and there are opportunities to work around the world.
- It is a highly creative industry covering festivals, conferences and events ranging from weddings to the Olympic Games.
- It is a varied career that draws on business skills ranging from human resources, strategy, project management, marketing, finance and operations.
- You are likely to gain a wealth of industry-specific skills such as food hygiene and nutrition, as well as getting hands-on experience in the kitchen, hotel reception and more management-based roles dealing with contracts, other businesses and policy.
- Most programmes/courses offer a chance to travel, with many universities offering a year studying or working abroad.
- Many courses in tourism, hospitality, events or leisure particularly those with a specific focus on management, will include many transferable skills.

 ACTIVITY

Getting involved with student societies and groups

Research a couple of university Student Union websites. They often list hundreds of societies and clubs that students can join. From this research, think about how you can get involved with university life. What societies and groups might you like to join? What experience and skills might you gain from this involvement?

CONCLUSION

In this chapter we have covered:

- The development and history of universities and looked at the different types of university that you might want to consider.
- Looking at what a degree is and how they are calculated.
- Adapting to the culture of the university and thinking about how you might prepare for and deal with culture shock.
- How you might try to engage to develop a sense of belonging, which is the most important factor in feeling comfortable at a university and is linked to success.

- The development of self-efficacy and thinking about how you might build motivation and self-confidence.
- Provided case studies to highlight the university as a diverse population and the work universities are doing to support students from minority and ethnic backgrounds to ensure their success.
- Considered the value of a tourism, hospitality and events degree and the kinds of career you might want to consider.

FURTHER READING

Abdelmotaleb, M. and Saha, S. (2013) 'Academic self-efficacy and student vacademic performance', *Journal of Education and Learning*, 2(3). doi:10.5539/jel.v2n3p117

Bozick, R. (2007) 'Making it through the first year of college: The role of students' economic resources, employment, and living arrangements', *Sociology of Education*, 80(3): 261–285. doi:10.1177/003804070 708000304

Rozhdestvenskaya, N.A. (2017) 'The activity approach to the psychological support of the 1st year university students', *National Psychological Journal*, 3: 113–120.

Smale, B. and Fowlie, J. (2015) *How to Succeed at University*. London: Sage.

Universities UK (2019) *Black, Asian and Minority Ethnic Student Attainment at UK Universities*. Available at: www.universitiesuk.ac.uk/policy-and-analysis/reports/Pages/bame-student-attainment-uk-universities-closing-the-gap.aspx (accessed 17 June 2020).

Useful resources

Some useful guides for supporting transition to university:

Student Minds: Transitions into University – www.studentminds.org.uk/transitionintouniversity.html

Student Transition in Higher Education. Concepts, Theories and Practices. Report from the Higher Education Authority with the University of West Scotland. Available at: www.heacademy.ac.uk/knowledge-hub/student-transition-higher-education-university-west-scotland-uws. This report presents a project carried out at the University of the West of Scotland to explore contemporary theory and research in student transitions in higher education. The report includes a review of the literature on higher education transition, along with data collected about current practice in transition initiatives from a variety of higher education institutions.

2 TYPICAL TEACHING METHODS AND APPROACHES

CHAPTER LEARNING OBJECTIVES

By the end of this chapter you should be able to:

- Identify ways in which you will be taught at university.
- Feel prepared for lectures, seminars, workshops and tutorials.
- Describe what is meant by the term 'pedagogy' and explain the importance of it in your university experience.
- Identify when you have experienced the main principles of teaching and evaluate how successful each of these are in relation to your learning.

GLOSSARY

- **Active learning:** an approach to teaching that places students at the centre of their own learning.
- **Flipped learning:** an approach that provides the subject material and content before class. Class time is used to apply the knowledge and engage with your peers and tutor.
- **Pedagogy:** the art or science of teaching in terms of the theory and practice of learning.
- **Virtual Learning Environment (VLE):** online site hosted by your university or college where tutors will post materials but also use interactivity to support your learning. Sometimes called a Learning Management System (LMS) or Online Learning Environment (OLE).

INTRODUCTION

This chapter covers the typical teaching methods and approaches you will encounter at university. It starts with the overarching philosophical approach to teaching, known as **pedagogy**. The main principles of pedagogy are explored, followed by how these underpin different teaching methodologies. Finally, the mechanisms by which teaching and learning take place, such as lectures, seminars and tutorials, are discussed. This chapter aims to help you understand why you are being taught in a certain way to help you get the most out of your various learning experiences.

WHAT IS PEDAGOGY?

At its simplest, pedagogy is the art or science of teaching (Bhowmik et al., 2013; Entz, 2007). The term *pedagogy* originates from the ancient Greek language, in which the term *paidagogos* was a title given to slaves who accompanied boys to and from school and provided behavioural and academic support outside school (Entz, 2007). In time, the word evolved to become *pedagogue,* meaning teacher. The term was also used in Latin, *paedagogia,* and in medieval French, *pédagogie,* and is now understood to refer to the practice of teaching (TES, 2020).

Pedagogy does not just mean *to teach* but encompasses a teacher's philosophical approach to teaching and the methods they employ to facilitate learning. The term is currently understood in the context of higher education to encompass learning, teaching, and assessment and feedback (Flint, 2018). It is now widely accepted that learning is not simply knowledge-based, but also includes personal and professional growth (Riahi and Riahi, 2018). Pedagogy is applied at all levels and types of education and is no more complex in universities than at other teaching institutions (Kaynardağ, 2019), although universities tend to make this aspect of the educational experience more explicit to their students than teachers in schools and colleges.

WHY IS PEDAGOGY IMPORTANT?

Pedagogy is an important concept in education because there is no one way of teaching all students effectively (Bhowmik et al., 2013). University students are a diverse group of people in many ways, including factors such as age, gender, dis/ability, cultural background, ethnicity, nationality and religious background. In addition to this, students will have had very different previous educational experiences depending on the country they were educated in, the subjects they studied and the qualifications they took. This diversity means that teachers need to apply different approaches to help each student get the most out of the session and to meet the learning outcomes (Aubrey and Riley, 2019; Bhowmik et al., 2013; Entz, 2007).

THE MAIN PRINCIPLES OF PEDAGOGY

There are several pedagogical approaches applied to teaching. Some argue there are five: constructivism, collaborative, inquiry-based, integrative and the reflective approach. However, in this chapter we argue there are four main approaches to pedagogy: behaviourism, constructivism, social constructivism and liberationism. It is likely that you will have experienced one or more of these already.

REFLECTION EXERCISE

Self and peer reflective exercise

Part 1: Self-reflection

Answer the following questions on your own and ask one of your peers to do the same:

- How old am I?
- Where did I grow up and go to school?
- What sort of cultural background do I have?
- What qualifications did I gain before coming to university?
- What subjects did I study before coming to university?
- How was I taught in school or college?
- Did the way I was taught vary between teachers and subjects?
- Which teachers and methods did I relate to best?

Part 2: Peer discussion

Discuss your answers with a friend or fellow student. Consider the following things:

- Similarities between you and your experiences.
- Differences between you and your experiences.
- How you think your background and experiences shape how you learn in the classroom environment.
- What different needs you think you have from your peers to be able to learn effectively.
- How you could support each other to learn more effectively.
- Where you can get support in your university to help you learn effectively.

AN ADVANCED LOOK AT THE MAIN PRINCIPLES OF PEDAGOGY

If you have previously studied social sciences, you may already know some of the terms and key points in Table 2.1. Although the terms sound complicated, it is useful to understand why you are being taught in particular ways and how you might best learn in the classroom or online when your tutors adopt these approaches.

REFLECTION EXERCISE

Experience of different pedagogical approaches

Take each approach listed below in turn and answer these questions for each one:

- When have you experienced this type of approach?
- What subject was it in?
- Was it appropriate for the subject and context?
- How successful was your learning when this approach was used?

Table 2.1   Overview of some approaches to pedagogy

Approach	Key features	Where to find out more
Behaviourism	• Teacher-focused, teacher leads the lesson • The lesson will usually be a lecture • The teacher is the knowledge-holder • The lecture is about absorbing and accepting existing information	The University of California Berkeley Graduate Student Instructor Teaching and Resource Centre: https://gsi. berkeley.edu/gsi-guide-contents/ learning-theory-research/behaviorism/
Constructivism	• Rejects behaviourism • Student-focused • Asserts that you learn by having experiences and reflecting on them • Embedded in Active Learning practices • Focuses on learning through enquiry and problem-solving	The University of California Berkeley Graduate Student Instructor Teaching and Resource Centre: https://gsi.berkeley.edu/gsi-guide-contents/learning-theory-research/ cognitive-constructivism/
Social constructivism	• Combination of teacher- and student-focused learning • Asserts that learning takes place socially and individually and is then developed collaboratively in class • Knowledge is co-created between teachers and students • Students are active participants in lessons • Students develop questions and test theories in class • Problem-solving based learning	The University of California Berkeley Graduate Student Instructor Teaching and Resource Centre: https://gsi.berkeley.edu/gsi-guide-contents/learning-theory-research/ social-constructivism/
Liberationism	• Based on the philosophy of Paulo Freire • Effective teaching and learning can only take place once poverty and hunger are removed • The student voice is at the centre of the educational experience • The classroom is a democratic space where teachers and students learn together at the same time	Av Sigrun Haugdal Hitland, 'What does education for liberation really mean?': https://saih.no/artikkel/2016/2/what-does-education-for-liberation-really-mean

Behaviourism

This theory of learning has a history stretching back to the early twentieth century and the discipline of psychology (Sullivan, 2009) and follows the philosophy that the teacher is the only authority in the classroom, whose role it is to lead the lesson via instruction, usually in the form of a lecture. This approach is teacher-focused and assumes that the teacher is the gatekeeper of the knowledge in their area of the curriculum. Challenges to what is being taught are not expected in behaviourism and therefore learning will be by rote and there will be repetition to encourage the memorisation of *facts* and behaviours.

This very traditional, passive approach to education can work in subjects where a correct, standardised, answer is needed and where the content of a session is easy to memorise and is an exercise in stimulus and response. As this theory is around behaviours, memorising and repeating material constitutes positive reinforcement in the form of incentives and marks for correct answers. Behaviourists also tend to use assessments like exams, because exam performance clearly measures behaviours (Berkeley Graduate Division, 2020a; TES, 2020).

Constructivism

Constructivism rejects behaviourism (Berkeley Graduate Division, 2020b). It asserts that people learn from having real experiences and reflecting on them. This idea is student-centred, and assumes that students arrive in the classroom ready to learn, with existing knowledge built from previous experience, and that a teacher's role is to consolidate that knowledge, facilitate new learning in relation to it, and to allow students to make their own individual meanings (Berkeley Graduate Division, 2020b; TES, 2020). Teachers are expected to provide resources for students to explore and interpret as they draw together existing and new knowledge in relation to their existing knowledge, the stage of their learning journey, and cultural and personal background, and that each learner will actively construct their own meanings that reflect all of these things.

Constructivism advocates that students learn through an **active learning** process and involves the teacher setting students projects, encouraging them to engage with enquiry-based learning by looking at real-world scenarios and solving problems (McLeod, 2019). As constructivism attempts to build on existing knowledge, it is important that teachers understand where their students are on their learning journey, so they might incorporate diagnostic mechanisms such as tests, discussions, interim papers and presentations (Berkeley Graduate Division, 2020b).

Social constructivism

Social constructivism is a combination of both teacher-led and student-centred teaching and is founded on the principle that the process of learning is collaborative. It asserts that learning takes place socially before individually and that knowledge is co-created by teachers and students. To achieve the goal of collaborative learning, the teacher sets out the topics that will be explored by the students and asks them to work in pairs or small groups, testing the learning through questioning and peer exercises. Social constructivism also works on the principle that human interaction is an opportunity for people to acquire new knowledge and to interpret it within their own social context. Because of this, language is an important element of how learning takes place (Berkeley Graduate Division, 2020a; Lynch, 2016). This belief results in teachers encouraging students to actively participate in sessions; to come up with questions and theories they have developed themselves; and to test them for validity and reliability. Students are asked to investigate problems and to develop solutions that can be practically applied in contexts such as industry, and to engage in reflective practice as part of the learning experience (Lynch, 2016).

Liberationism

This approach is regarded as a critical pedagogy and is based on the teaching philosophy of Paulo Freire, who was a Brazilian educationalist. Freire believed that the key to effective teaching and learning was to remove two major barriers, namely poverty and hunger. He advocated putting the student voice at the centre of the educational experience, democracy in the classroom, and teachers and students learning together. An important element of this philosophy is that students develop a 'critical conscience, whereby individuals come to understand and overcome both personal and societal oppression' (Sullivan, 2009: 292).

CURRENT TRENDS IN PEDAGOGY

Just as the term *pedagogy* has changed over time, so have its philosophies. This evolution results in trends and changes in approaches to teaching. One of the biggest disruptors to pedagogy in recent years has been technological innovation. In 2019 the Open University published a report called *Innovating Pedagogy* and developed a list of trends for that year and the near future (Open University, 2019). The trends relevant to university teaching and learning are:

- Playful learning
- Learning with robots
- Decolonising learning
- Drone-based learning
- Learning through wonder
- Action learning
- Virtual studios
- Place-based learning
- Making thinking visible

These methods embed technology, creativity, curiosity, globalisation, authenticity and contextualised teaching and learning. They are designed to place students at the centre of the learning experience and to ignite a love of learning in new ways.

 ACTIVITY

Definitions and mapping

Part 1: Definitions

Use the internet to find a definition for each of these types of learning outlined by the Open University and write a short definition in your own words. Answers at the back of the book in Chapter 36, the Conclusion (page 545).

- Playful learning
- Learning with robots
- Decolonising learning

(Continued)

- Drone-based learning
- Learning through wonder
- Action learning
- Virtual studios
- Place-based learning
- Making thinking visible

Part 2: Mapping exercise

Map which attributes each has against technology, creativity, curiosity, globalisation, authenticity, and contextualised teaching and learning. See Table 2.2.

Table 2.2   Mapping of skills and trends in pedagogic practice

	Technology	Creativity	Curiosity	Globalisation	Authenticity	Contextualised learning
Playful learning						
Learning with robots						
Decolonising learning						
Drone-based learning						
Learning through wonder						
Action learning						
Virtual studios						
Place-based learning						
Making thinking visible						

APPROACHES TO TEACHING: STUDENTS AS PARTNERS, PRODUCERS AND CO-CREATORS

The student as partner/producer/co-creator concept is a relatively recent global movement in university education and is based on the core principles of social constructivism and liberationism. Ideas about students and teachers working together surfaced early in Europe in the early nineteenth century, with the idea that collaboration could result in the creation of new knowledge. These ideas became more radical as elitism and hierarchy in research were challenged by students (Neary, 2010). As the name suggests, it is about students and staff taking shared responsibility for, and working together to enhance, the learning experience in universities (some good examples of this work can be found in the *International Journal for Students as Partners* (*IJSaP*) (2020). This approach directly challenges behaviourism and draws on the ideas in social constructivism and liberationism, as it is based on the principles of partnership, the student voice being central to university activities and staff and students 'active collaborators in teaching and learning' (Healey et al., 2014; Mercer-Mapstone et al., 2017: 1). On a philosophical level it is about university staff (both academic and professional services) engaging as one community in activities that are mutually beneficial and aim to meet shared educational aims (Mercer-Mapstone et al., 2017). On a practical level adopting this ethos ensures that you are at the centre of the decision-making process in your university. It focuses on making sure you have a voice in the development of your own curricula, university initiatives, how your learning is delivered and assessed, the production of research, and many more activities.

Student as Producer

Healey and colleagues developed and published a useful model in 2014 that illustrates where students should be involved as partners within a university (see Figure 2.1).

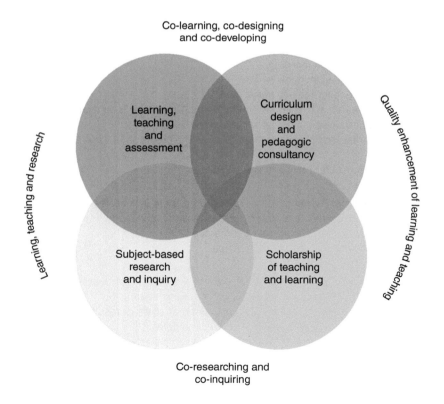

Figure 2.1 **Healey et al.'s model (2014) shows how students can be engaged as partners in higher education**

Source: Healey et al., 2014. Reprinted with permission

STUDENT INSIGHT

Student as producer, consultancy and the Lincoln Magna Carta – Miles Hedison

This project derives from a Lincoln International Business School consultancy module, led by Nick Taylor. Students work alongside organisations on a marketing issue, producing an actionable report. Depending on the number of companies available, work can be done in groups, in partnerships or individually. In the case of the relatively new Magna Carta exhibition at Lincoln Castle, one student, Miles Hedison, worked on behalf of Lincoln castle management. His role was to assess visitor perceptions of the exhibition of this famous document and to suggest improvements. After submitting a proposal in response to a brief from the castle, Miles created research objectives, prepared research questions, carried out the fieldwork and analysis and then made his recommendations, in the form of a written report and an oral presentation. In conducting his project, Miles had regular access to two supervisors who delivered the module in the context of student as producer. On completion, Miles said that 'thanks should be given to my supervisors Nick Taylor and Barry Ardley, who have both provided me with continuous support throughout the project.' Tailored student support is vital to the student as producer perspective.

Traditionally, students are seen to be passive recipients of the research work of academics. The student of producer perspective alters this dynamic, where students become part of the academic project of the university, being directly involved in generating research. The student as producer approach can be distilled into eight operating principles:

1.   The student as discoverer of knowledge.
2.   Making full use of technology in learning.
3.   Using space for teaching in an imaginative way.
4.   Using assessments that encourage active learning.
5.   Making certain that research activity is central to learning and there is an evaluation of this.
6.   Ensuring the student has a voice in the learning process.
7.   Providing support for research-based teaching through the provision of expert engagement with information resources.
8.   Creating a future for the student through employability.

Miles developed his independent learning skills and executed them in a professional way, based on a real brief. In recent comments to tutors, Miles pointed out this 'was the best module I did while at university and I could see through the module, how theory relates to practice'.

The project showed Miles utilising the above principles:

(1)   Discovery was demonstrated when Miles did a background literature review on Magna Carta and when he also discovered the views of visitors to the exhibition.
(2)   Technology was utilised when Miles undertook an analysis of results using software programs and where he took advantage of other web technologies.
(3)   The imaginative use of space was revealed when Miles engaged with castle visitors, with research being conducted in a variety of places, i.e., the castle grounds and the offices of castle management.
(4 and 5)   Using assessments that encourage active learning was demonstrated when Miles was provided with the opportunity to problem solve, by choosing and using different research techniques and evaluating findings.
(6)   In terms of student voice, Barry and Nick as supervisors encouraged Miles to talk about the problems he encountered in the work, and as tutors, made genuine attempts to help him deal with any contrary issues, like managing his time.

(7) Ensuring there is support for research-based teaching. Here, Miles showed that the module engaged with the university library, integrating skills and information resources in obtaining and synthesising facts and knowledge relating to the Magna Carta.

(8) Creating a future for the student through employability is a key feature of the module, where Miles worked on and developed a range of useful skills. These included project management, networking, communicating and working with others, understanding and using theory in a creative way and developing solutions to problems.

Since the recent project Magna Carta has been completed, three outputs have resulted. A book chapter is in progress, a conference paper was presented at the Academy of Marketing conference and a journal paper is currently under review. All provide evidence of the sound pedagogy that underpins the student as producer approach. Miles concludes, 'This module has improved my self-confidence a lot and helped me develop my business skills, things like oral presentations, I was nervous about them before, but not so now, and I am much better at things like analysis and communicating.'

Thanks to Barry Ardley, Nick Taylor, Miles Hedison.

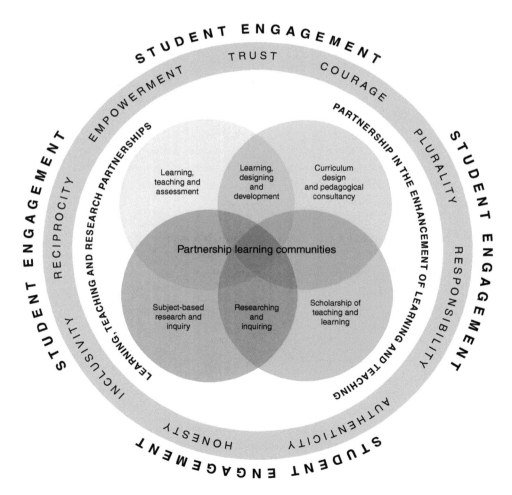

Figure 2.2   An adapted version of the Healey et al. 2014 model representing developments in engaging students as partners in universities – the addition of management processes

The Healey et al. model (2014) has since been extended by universities to include students working in partnership with staff in relation to core management processes such as the recruitment of new academic staff and students, and contributing to important management committees within their own department, faculty and across the university. This impacts positively on all dimensions identified in the 2014 model as students can shape all of these areas by being a core component of the university's management structure.

A management activity that students are taking part in more widely is as members of recruitment panels for new academic staff. This allows students to influence the development of the curriculum, the potential quality of teaching and learning, and to facilitate the potential for collaborative research projects, informing the university's overall learning, teaching and research activities.

APPROACHES TO TEACHING: ACTIVE LEARNING

Another approach that places the student at the centre of their own learning is active learning, a term used to describe a range of teaching methods (Prince, 2004). It is closely aligned to constructivism and social constructivism because it is founded on the principle that for learners to make sense of new information and ideas, they need to make links with existing knowledge, so that they can process and then understand new material (Cambridge Assessment, 2020). This student-centred approach has been adopted by many universities across the world because it allows students to be actively engaged with what is going on in the classroom, which has more positive results than if students are passive (University College London, 2019). It also closely aligns with the concept of students as partners, as

[e]ngaging students in partnership means seeing students as active participants in their own learning, and although not all active learning involves partnership it does mean engaging students in forms of participation and helps prepare them for the roles they may play in full partnership. (Healey et al., 2014: 8)

The types of activities adopted in an active learning approach include:

* Students conducting their own inquiry-led research projects
* Group discussions and debates
* Student presentations
* Problem-solving
* Analysing case studies
* Taking part in roleplay or simulation exercises
* Experiments
* Tests or quizzes

This type of teaching promotes learning at a deep rather than surface level (Cambridge Assessment, 2020) and helps develop a range of 'higher thinking order skills' such as being able to apply your knowledge to a given scenario, and being able to analyse and synthesis information (Queen's University, 2020). This sits well within Kolb's theoretical framework known as the Cycle of Experiential Learning, which built on earlier pedagogies and places practical experience at the centre of the learning experience. Kolb's cycle has four stages (see Figure 2.3), although you can enter the cycle at any stage, and the cycle is infinite as learning takes place over and over again, constantly building on what you have learned (Kolb and Kolb, 2009). The first stage is the concrete (or actual) learning experience; in the second stage you observe and reflect on the experience to make sense of it; the third is a cognitive process in which abstract concepts are formed (like a theory or a link to another idea) linked to the experience; and finally the fourth stage involves planning and testing your learning in a new environment, leading back to the first stage (Kolb, 1984). It is useful to be aware of Kolb's Cycle of Experiential Learning not only within the context of active learning, but within your academic work and life experiences generally. The process is not something that all of us do naturally, but it is an excellent way of thinking about your experiences and what you learned from them, how this links to the theoretical ideas or other practices you have encountered, working out different ways you could approach the same problem or situation again, becoming confident in trying out new ideas or ways of working, and engaging in on-going learning. Kolb also suggested that individuals have different learning styles that will play a part in particular stages of the cycle, but ideas around learning styles are now considered outdated and problematic. However, the learning style notion has been adapted to align it with more recent thinking (see Figure 2.3). For example, the term diverging has been introduced, meaning the thought process you go through as you make sense of the experience you've had and reflect; Assimilating, meaning the process linking your reflective observations to theories; Converging, meaning the process by which you use the experience and abstract ideas to plan ways of adapting your approach; and Accommodating, meaning the process by which you have the new experience.

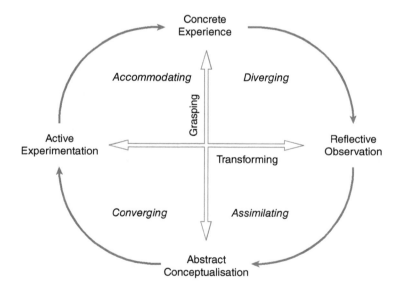

Figure 2.3   Kolb's Cycle of Experiential Learning

During your university life, you might also come across a model of teaching called '**flipped learning**', a teaching technique in which you are given all the materials needed to learn about a topic before a session takes place. Your classroom time is then spent exploring the topic in detail, with the aim of gaining a deeper understanding of it by engaging in tasks such as discussions and problem-solving activities (Advance HE, 2020; Cottrell, 2019). This method has faced criticism in recent research carried out by American universities such as the Massachusetts Institute of Technology (2019) for not improving student performance, and Brigham Young University (2017) for their being no difference between the performance of students learning in the traditional way and those using flipped learning. However, other university studies, such as one by the University of Utrecht (van Alten et al., 2019), have revealed that flipped learning does have a positive impact on students' learning outcomes and the University of Florida (Cheng et al., 2019) have found that the flipped classroom can have a significant impact on students' learning outcomes, particularly for subjects with a significant practical element like engineering (McKie, 2019).

One of the most widely used flipped learning methods is Team-Based Learning (TBL), in which you will be given preparation time to complete reading before class, and then take an Individual Readiness Assurance Test (IRAT), followed by a Team Readiness Assurance Test (TRAT). These low-stake tests are marked immediately and allow the teacher to assess the learning that has already taken place and any gaps in knowledge that need to be covered by a mini-lecture. The rest of the session is then used to complete a problem-based learning exercise that allows you to discuss the content you've learned and apply it in a team-working environment (Team Based Learning Collaborative, 2020).

TBL is strongly rooted in social constructivism as it assumes the knowledge of the team is greater than that of the individual and allows you to develop existing knowledge through collective working. Similar approaches include 'SCALE-UP', which is used extensively across Nottingham Trent University, and has replaced lectures with problem-solving and enquiry-based activities in groups (Nottingham Trent University, 2020). Instead of learning in traditional lecture theatres, students work on group tables, and they not only have flipped learning, but engage in peer teaching and take different group roles. This approach was adopted at North Carolina State University, just one of 100 universities in the US using SCALE-UP in 2011, and has been praised for allowing teachers and students to build a dynamic relationship rather than one based on one-way knowledge transmission, because research has shown the relationship between teachers and students is an important aspect of student success (Ryals, 2011).

The University of Hertfordshire has used the flipped classroom approach since 2010, providing video preparatory materials and a critical thinking skills-based lecture (see Chapter 8) for students who then complete the taught learning with a workshop (Berger and Wilde, 2016). A similar model that utilised technology for preparatory exercises was developed between 2012 and 2017 by the Australian Government called the 'Flipped Classroom Project', led by the University of Queensland (University of Queensland, 2017). Chinese universities have embraced mobile technology to enhance the learning experience as part of the flipped classroom. Teachers encourage students to use their mobile phones to share images of useful texts, interview their peers, and collect notes, all of which they can bring to class to aid in group learning (Hwang et al., 2015).

Another technique that encourages students to own their own learning and pace of learning is 'blended learning'. This approach harnesses technology alongside face-to-face contact to create an active learning environment that integrates the offline and online. This technique allows you to work at a pace that suits you and allows the teachers to concentrate on what learning is taking place, rather than how content can be learned. A blended learning approach allows much more personalised learning to take place and focuses on deep learning rather than recall. This approach is becoming much more common in universities as they invest more in technology and in particular their **Virtual Learning Environments (VLEs)**.

Krechowiecka (2003) wrote an article in 2003 in *The Guardian* newspaper entitled 'Welcome to the World of VLEs' to demystify these platforms to those working in education, as they were a relatively new concept. They now form a central part of education at all levels and are used as 'a means to structure, manage and deliver learning activities and content; recognised as having strengths in student tracking and managing online assessments' (JISC, 2016). In some ways VLEs act as a virtual repository for key information about your module or course on which teachers will often place everything you need for a module, including your module guide, assessment details, key learning materials and video-captured lectures if available. However, VLEs are much more than a repository and have become a key part of active and blended learning activities because of their collaborative potential and inclusivity. Features such as discussion boards and Wikis are frequently activated on VLE sites to allow students and teachers to have a dialogue outside of the classroom and co-create content throughout the module. The format allows you to engage in interactive feedback with your peers and teachers, and you can adapt it as you progress through the module (Proctor, 2019). Content can be placed on a VLE in different formats, allowing you to submit your assignment and access your marks and feedback (written or recorded) online, making them accessible for students with different learning needs, social situations, and working commitments (JISC, 2016).

VLEs do not necessarily connect with external social media platforms because they are only accessible to students and staff in your institution, but they are safe online spaces that are professional and well-moderated. Many universities are now focused on the development of online learning opportunities, so if you decide to do an online degree, your learning will be via a VLE. Over the next few years universities will integrate their VLE systems with their other systems to include real-time updates for important information, events and security notifications, which also protects resources and provides better analytical data for teachers that can be used to enhance the learning experience (Proctor, 2019).

=== THINK POINT ===

Teaching is underpinned by philosophical approaches, just like each subject you will look at in your degree. Can you recognise where you have encountered the learning and teaching theories covered here? Can you see the link between the overarching theories and teaching practice?

TYPICAL TEACHING METHODS

If you are studying on campus you are likely to have lectures, seminars, workshops and tutorials of various length, size and frequency.

Lectures

Lectures stem from behaviourist approaches to teaching and learning and remain a core part of university education. Lectures can be delivered to groups of several hundred students, and it is not unusual to find that your university has a lecture theatre that can sit 100, 250 or 500 students (some can hold up to 1,000-students). For example, Bristol University has an 800-seater, the University of Manchester a 1,000-seater lecture theatre and the University of Reading has 400- and 252-seater lecture theatres. As Figure 2.4 shows, lecture theatres can feel intimidating and impersonal so sit somewhere you feel comfortable and get used to the space. Often students sit at the back, but you will feel more engaged and hear more if you sit near the front and centre.

Figure 2.4   Inside a typical lecture theatre – the Isaac in the University of Lincoln, UK which holds 500 students

Lectures are generally used to introduce you to the main topics and concepts in the module, providing a framework on which you can build further knowledge, skills and attributes through seminars, workshops, tutorials and self-directed workshops. Lectures are usually supported by a presentation, which is often uploaded to your university's VLE before the lecture to allow you to read through it before the session. You might also be provided with a list of specific reading that you can do before or after the lecture. Lectures usually don't involve much direct interaction with the person presenting (Knowles, 2019) because they are often sessions with hundreds of students, although you can talk to the teacher before or after the session and you might find they ask questions or ask you to do tasks in small groups or pairs to check your learning. You will be expected to take notes, but you should do this in a way that suits you. Many students take their laptops into lectures and type into the notes section of the presentation or make handwritten notes. Some will audio record the sessions, although you will find that many universities now have a lecture capture system that allows you to watch an uploaded version of the lecture after it has taken place, as many times as you need to. If you want to make your own sound recording using your own device you should ask the lecturer's permission.

Top tips for getting the most out of lectures

- Make sure you know where your lecture is taking place. Check your timetable a few days before in case the location has changed, particularly if there is bad weather, building work or industrial action.
- Don't assume that everything you need to know is contained in the presentation.
- Make sure you attend lectures, even if they are described as optional.
- Read the supporting presentation before the session.
- Read recommended literature before and/or after the session.

- Find a place that suits you to sit – do you need to be near the front, in the centre, or towards the back to get the most out of the session?
- Bring your laptop and/or pens and paper.
- Make a set of notes, including areas you still don't understand so that you can discuss with your lecturer or peers, or in the supporting sessions for that module.
- Don't try to write your notes verbatim (word for word) as you will struggle to keep up with the session. Develop your own form of shorthand note-taking.
- Behave respectfully and considerately in lectures. Check your university's guidelines for behavioural expectations in lectures.

Seminars

Seminars often accompany lectures and tend to be interactive, smaller and more informal (Knowles, 2019). They are designed to build on the content of the lecture and to allow you to explore topics in more detail, discuss their complexities and apply what you've learnt to different scenarios. You are expected not only to attend the lecture, but to prepare for the seminars, and will be provided with information or reading material in advance. Seminars involve student contributions as a minimum requirement but can be student-led and you may be asked to present in them. Some universities assess activities and you should be clear what activities are formative and summative (see Chapter 6 for an explanation of these terms).

Workshops

Workshops are used to build practical skills related to the module and are highly interactive. They often involve the teacher introducing key concepts, followed by students undertaking computer-based work, simulations or projects that lead to the creation of something tangible, either in a group or as an individual. These types of sessions are common in practical subjects and would be used in hospitality, for example in a sommelier session or cooking demonstration.

Tutorials

Tutorials are similar to seminars but are often made up of smaller groups or can be individual. They often focus on discussing the ideas presented in a module and linking them to assessment. Like seminars, these are interactive sessions and require you to prepare and participate, but they might be more student-centred than a seminar because tutorials are designed to give you the opportunity to ask questions, raise issues and determine which ideas you want to explore further. You may be asked to look at case studies related to the topic you are studying, present your ideas to start a discussion, or answer questions set by the teacher.

Top tips for getting the most out of seminars, workshops and tutorials

- Follow the guidance on getting the most out of lectures.
- Prepare for the seminar: this might involve reading, preparing to talk about a subject, or completing an exercise.

- Join in discussions and activities.
- Add to your original lecture notes to extend your knowledge and skills.
- Ask about things you are still not sure about or don't understand.
- Try to make a link between the lecture, seminar and your assignment for that module.

 THINK POINT

Did you expect to be taught like this at college or university? How are you going to prepare for the different types of learning that will take place at university?

CONCLUSION

In this chapter we have covered:

- The nature and importance of pedagogy and how pedagogic theories underpin all teaching.
- The main theories that are applied in modern university pedagogy.
- How staff and students work in partnership and why it is increasingly important to do so.
- What Active Learning is and explored some of the more popular Active Learning methods.
- The kind of classroom formats that you might face at university and how you might best prepare yourself for them.

FURTHER READING

Aubrey, K. and Riley, A. (2019) *Understanding and Using Educational Theories*. London: Sage Publications.

Cottrell, S. (2019) *The Study Skills Handbook* (Macmillan Study Skills). London: Macmillan.

Knowles, E. (2019) *Getting the Most out of Lectures and Seminars*. Available at: www.prospects.ac.uk/apply ing-for-university/university-life/getting-the-most-out-of-lectures-and-seminars (accessed 18 June 2020).

Kolb, D. (1984) *Experiential Learning: Experience as the Source of Learning and Development*. New Jersey: Prentice Hall.

Sullivan, L.E. (ed.) (2009) *The SAGE Glossary of the Social and Behavioral Sciences*. London: Sage Publications.

3

RESEARCHING TOURISM, HOSPITALITY AND EVENTS

CHAPTER LEARNING OBJECTIVES

By the end of this chapter you should be able to:

- Explain why research is important in tourism, hospitality and events.
- Locate appropriate and useful sources of information for your studies.
- Feel confident in using databases and online sources for locating tourism, hospitality and events information.
- Determine scholarly sources, leading authors and seminal concepts in tourism, hospitality and events.
- Describe how to use evidence from primary, secondary and tertiary sources of information.

GLOSSARY

- **Big Data:** extremely large sets of computational data sets that reveal patterns, trends and associations relating to human behaviour and human interaction.
- **Cutting edge:** this refers to recent developments in scientific research that offer the most recent and innovative ideas. Also sometimes referred to as 'state of the art'.
- **Peer review:** a process wherein publications are reviewed by other academics before publication. A robust system for checking quality adopted by academic journals.
- **Seminal:** this masculine term originates from 'semen' and is used to denote work that influences later developments.

INTRODUCTION

This chapter explains why research is important and what it is used for. Research is fundamental to university life, whether you are studying at undergraduate or postgraduate level, or even working in an academic role. Research requires many key skills in its approach, including personal skills, study skills and academic skills. This chapter explores the different ways that you can find appropriate and useful sources of information relevant to tourism, hospitality and events. It presents databases and online sources that will support you throughout your university studies. It also introduces the different types of scholarly sources that you can draw upon, such as journal databases (e.g. JSTOR, Science Direct and EBSCO). It further identifies the leading key authors in tourism, hospitality and events and **seminal** concepts that are used within this field, such as Butler's notable Tourism Area Life Cycle (TALC) and Boorstin and MacCannell's work on authenticity.

Finally, this chapter presents the different types of evidence that you can use, from primary, secondary and tertiary sources. It offers examples of these different types of sources of data that include interviews, surveys, reports, government documents, indexes, encyclopaedias, as well as many others.

WHAT IS RESEARCH?

Researching or 'finding out' about something is a common task for people who want to know more about things. In 'finding out' about something of interest, we adopt methods that can vary depending on the set of circumstances that surround us and the topic in hand. This is the same principle for academic research (Cottrell, 2013).

Research is a systematic process of inquiry that involves the collection or generation of data, a critical documentation of the information, and analysis of that data/information through suitable methodological procedures relevant to the specific tourism, hospitality and events fields and academic disciplines.

Research is central to academic and business activities but it is difficult to define because research can mean very different things to different people. Despite this, the general characteristics that definitions of research share are summed up by Collis and Hussey (2014: 2), who defined research as 'a systematic and methodical process of inquiry and investigation with a view of increasing knowledge'. Collis and Hussey (2014) suggest that research can be categorised by its purpose (why it was conducted), process (the way in which data were generated/collected and analysed), logic (whether the research logic moves from general to specific and vice versa) and outcome (whether the outcome is a solution to a specific issue or problem or a general contribution to knowledge).

At undergraduate level, you will be required to research your assignments to gather relevant, useful and reputable information. In your final year, you may be asked to undertake a major project (dissertation) based on primary and/or secondary data. Therefore, it is important to learn to research effectively.

WHY IS RESEARCH IMPORTANT?

Research is important for understanding current trends, issues and innovations within tourism, hospitality and events. Understanding the benefits and impacts on host destinations is crucial for understanding how to leverage or reduce such effects. It is important not just for academia, but also government bodies and organisations making informed decisions. An example of this might be a

Destination Management Organisation (DMO), e.g. VisitBritain or I Amsterdam, who are responsible for promoting and marketing a destination's tourism product and services. DMOs research many aspects of the tourism industry to analyse and develop tourism to meet the needs of consumers, visitors, businesses, as well as other aspects associated with tourism, hospitality and events. A list of DMOs across the UK can be found on the VisitBritain/VisitEngland website.

INDUSTRY INSIGHT: VISIT KENT/CULTURE KENT RESEARCH PROGRAMME (UK)

This three-year project was led by the Tourism and Events Hub, Canterbury Christ Church University (CCCU) and Visit Kent, funded by the Arts Council England (www.artscouncil.org.uk/projectgrants) and VisitEngland (www.visitengland.com) as part of the Cultural Destinations Programme. The aim of the two-year project was to 'showcase Kent's cultural assets; extend reach by attracting new audiences; create new strategic relationships and develop the information and knowledge core required to strengthen the Kent cultural tourism offer' (CCCU, 2019).

The Project Director of Culture Kent Sarah Dance explained how the research project was significant for cultural tourism in the county of Kent, UK:

> The Culture Kent Project gave us important new insight into cultural tourism to the county. This new research allows us to understand our audiences better, meaning we are now able to deliver a real step-change in the visitor economy. We know that in order to become a really successful 'cultural destination' we need to be a networked area, delivering a total experience to visitors that helps them understand a location and its people, through history and contemporary culture. (CCCU, 2019)

For a full summary of the Culture Kent Research Programme and other resources, see CCCU Tourism and Events Hub here: www.canterbury.ac.uk.

Research is also important for tourism, hospitality and events businesses to market their products and services, foster public and critical reactions to their impacts on the environment and local communities as well as create innovation (Ferreira, 2019). This information is often generated from large data sets known as **'Big Data'**. If you think about the amount of people who travel both domestically and internationally through airports, this is a huge amount of data to collect and it is fast-moving. These data are useful for understanding how many people travel each year, where they come from and where they travel to. It can be used by airports for managing the large numbers of passengers that they transport every year, and useful for countries to understand relevant travel and tourist trends. An example of this may be to identify where people come from to effectively target a new group of visitors.

USING 'BIG DATA'

Big Data emerges from three different sources: direct, automated and volunteered. A direct source of big data may include contacting tourists for market research purposes such as monitoring travel behaviours to identify the different reasons for why people travel. Automated sources may include an indirect tally (e.g. flights sold) of the number of passengers who visit the airport on a yearly basis. However,

Volunteered Geographic Information (VGI) is when consumers give permission to share their location with online applications such as Google Maps to access GPS data (Ferreira, 2019). The content is gathered from these sources by businesses such as Yelp, TripAdvisor and Zomato. However, Big Data has brought many challenges to tourism, hospitality and events businesses as they require new capabilities to be able to process, analyse and manage large data sets. Sharing information between tourism, hospitality and events providers and key stakeholders, e.g. consumers, online communities, suppliers and advertisers, is termed the 'new digital economy', 'platform economy', or 'platform capitalism' (Ferreira, 2019: 76).

This new 'sharing economy' is a current and critical issue as it is essentially re-shaping the industries. Online platforms such as TripAdvisor, Booking.com, Trivago, Airbnb, Uber and so on, combined with volunteered information, have challenged tourism, hospitality and events providers with user reviews and ratings, classifications and other narratives and evidence. The online social interaction that some of these review platforms provide allows people to exchange information that may influence their buying behaviour (Lee et al., 2018). This can be positive or negative for providers, based on the reviewers' experiences, meaning that providers must manage customer reviews, issues and complaints.

THINK POINT

What are the key benefits for hospitality providers in analysing Big Data? What are the key issues facing hospitality providers from Big Data?

NOVICE RESEARCHERS

Brotherton (2015) states that research can be a daunting experience for new and novice students and researchers. However, it is less complicated than it appears. Research projects could include researching your next summer holiday or organising a birthday party, as these all require some investigation and methodological processes to explore the available options.

ACTIVITY

A simple research task ...?

Visit Lonely Planet's website and investigate the available destinations that you could travel to for your next holiday and how to book via Lonely Planet – that's research.

ACTIVITY (GROUP)

Understanding the tourism, hospitality and events disciplines

Tourism

Tourism is closely associated with many other approaches such as psychology, anthropology, geography, management studies and other disciplines and is considered a multidisciplinary subject (Robinson et al., 2011).

Based on this, tourism receives much scrutiny of its integrity as an academic field. However, there are many extensive opportunities for tourism research as new fields of tourism emerge. Tourism has many varying forms and types, which opens the door for new and innovative research.

Since the emergence of pilgrimage (travelling for religious purposes), education (e.g. Grand Tour) and notably, mass tourism during the 1950s opening the world to long-haul destinations across the world, tourism has evolved in contemporary ways. Many different forms of contemporary tourism include sustainable and alternative forms; community tourism; rural tourism; slow tourism to include slow food and slow cities (*CittaSlow*); events, festivals and the arts; sport and adventure tourism; cultural and heritage tourism; film and literary tourism and so on. The industry has also seen an emerging interest in more niche forms of tourism usually associated with independent travel. These can include dark tourism, LGBT tourism, health and medical tourism, sex tourism and so forth. Moreover, access to online platforms has resulted in tourists, visitors and consumers of the THE industries to seek and book their own accommodation, activities and attractions at their favourite places.

Events management

The term 'events management' was first used in 1986 (Yeoman et al., 2004) and is now a growing phenomenon in society. There are many definitions of events, due to the diversity of things covered by this term (Getz, 2005; Jago and Shaw, 1998). Event research is very recent, due to the rapid growth in events since the early 2000s and has become increasingly popular with academic researchers. Despite this, it is still an under-researched area due to the diverse nature of events, with much focus on economic impacts, leaving socio-cultural perspectives less explored (Mair and Whitford, 2013).

Academic interest in events has increased in mega-event (Roche, 2000) research on how such transformational events, more specifically the Olympic Games, impact the host destination economically, socio-culturally and environmentally. The three pillars of sustainability attracted a great deal of academic interest in what the positive and negative outcomes may be for the countries that host them.

In groups, research a wide range of sources and create a 'Tourism, Hospitality and Events Timeline' from the earliest recognised forms of tourism to the present day. Use key dates and significant happenings that have helped to shape the industry.

Research at university is far more involved and challenging than just looking up something on a website, and ideally it requires you to identify something new. You will need to explore what is already known about the subject that you are investigating. Your inquiry must be thorough and balanced (e.g. you cannot just consider the things that are interesting to you). Thomas (2011) created a pocket study skills book entitled *Doing Research* and proposed five steps of research as a systematic process (see Figure 3.1).

LEARNING TO RESEARCH TOURISM, HOSPITALITY AND EVENTS EFFECTIVELY AT UNIVERSITY

Your research skills will develop during your time at university and require a practical approach to conducting valid, ethical and useable research. Many of your existing abilities can be tweaked throughout your time at university through practice, feedback and reflection (Cottrell, 2013), such as your skill at finding information, and reading and making notes (further discussed in Chapter 4).

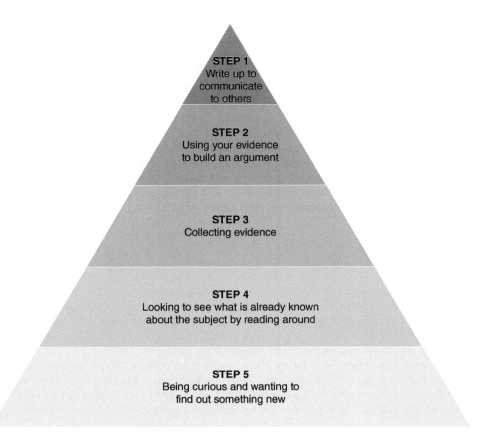

Figure 3.1   The 'five steps of research' (adapted from Thomas, 2011)

 ════════ ACTIVITY ════════════════════════════════

Research the United Nations Educational, Scientific and Cultural Organisation (UNESCO)

Refer to the UNESCO website and answer the following questions:

1. What is UNESCO's mission?
2. What are the key challenges facing the world today?
3. What are the key forces driving sustainable change?
4. What are the 17 Sustainable Development Goals (SDGs)?
5. How can these SDGs be achieved by 2030?

YouTube video: 'UNESCO: The lab of ideas, the lab for change' available at: www.youtube.com/watch?v=FF-cxNUR_0fo

PERSONAL QUALITIES THAT CAN ENHANCE YOUR RESEARCHING SKILLS

There are many personal qualities and skills that can help you in your studies. These may include the following:

- Self-awareness
- Determination
- Self-motivation
- Commitment
- Perseverance
- Positive thinking

Cottrell (2013) proposed four study skills: self-management, academic ability, dealing with people and managing tasks. Cottrell (2013) claimed that self-management is the precursor for developing the other three skills. Self-management skills can help you to develop your basic research skills. Self-management skills and basic research skills may include those presented in Table 3.1 below.

Table 3.1   Self-management skills and basic research skills

Self-management skills	Basic research skills
Independence	Finding information (Chapter 4)
Skills management (Chapters 12; 13 and 14)	Reading (Chapters 4 and 8)
Learning	Using multiple sources of information (Chapter 4)
Strategies (Chapter 18)	Making notes (Chapters 4 and 5)
Time management (Chapter 11)	Organisational skills (this chapter and Chapter 18)
Improving performance	
Metacognitive skills (Chapter 32)	

   Throughout your bachelor's degree you will develop your basic academic skills through attending lectures and seminars as well as through completing assessments, which may take various written forms, such as essays, reports, portfolios, dissertations, etc. and/or oral assessments such as individual and/or group presentations (see Chapters 6, 7 and 8). Your assessments will require research to explore the topic areas to complete them effectively.

DIFFERENT TYPES OF RESEARCH

Academic research comes in many different forms such as exploratory, descriptive and explanatory; pure and applied; theoretical, empirical, and primary and secondary research (Brotherton, 2015), as described in Table 3.2.

Table 3.2   Different types of research

Type of research	What is it?
Exploratory	Aims to explore and understand a new phenomenon to gain insights when few or no previous studies or knowledge exists. Most commonly associated with identifying patterns and ideas within the data rather than testing a hypothesis (Collis and Hussey, 2014).
Descriptive	Used to describe an existing phenomenon through identifying and obtaining information on the characteristics of a specific problem or issue (Collis and Hussey, 2014).
Explanatory/ Analytical	A continuation of descriptive research whereby the researcher analyses and explains why or how the phenomenon under investigation is happening (Collis and Hussey, 2014).
Pure (Basic) and Applied	Pure or basic research (Saunders et al., 2007; Wilson, 2010; Collis and Hussey, 2014) is a study that intends to contribute to general knowledge and theoretical understanding to form a theory rather than solving a specific issue or problem (Collis and Hussey, 2014). It can also support or refute existing theories and occasionally form new ways of thinking (Fox, Gouthro, Morakabati and Brackstone, 2014). Conversely, applied research has a practical basis in applying its findings to solve a specific, existing issue or problem (Collis and Hussey, 2014; Fox et al., 2014).
Theoretical	Mostly analyses existing theory and explanations for generating new ideas. This involves debating between existing theory and ideas rather than collecting/generating evidence in the form of data (Fox et al., 2014).
Empirical you	Evidenced-based research that is measured or observed and interpreted using existing theory – it can be inductive, deductive or abductive (Fox et al., 2014).
Primary	Primary research is something that is being investigated and analysed for the first-time and involves qualitative (written), quantitative (numerical) or mixed-methods (combined) approach (Fox et al., 2014).
Secondary	Secondary research is when information is retrieved and presented logically but without formal analysis (Fox et al., 2014).
Qualitative	Explores the meaning and understanding through individual experiences and perceptions. It is often descriptive in its nature and therefore is often argued to be biased, lacking validity and untrustworthy, as it is not objective, rather subjective, in nature. Qualitative methods for generating data commonly include interviews and focus groups and usually have a smaller sample size (Collis and Hussey, 2014).
Quantitative	The study and analysis of numerical data used to measure or assess social phenomena. Data collection is usually from a large sample size and analysis is often statistical. Quantitative methods for collecting data usually include surveys (Collis and Hussey, 2014).

Research should help you to understand tourism, hospitality and events better and gain a deeper understanding of how knowledge is constructed. You can investigate topics that are of interest, personally meaningful and/or relevant to you or your workplace (Cottrell, 2013).

 THINK POINT

Why do you think you should try and relate your assignments to something of interest to you?

HOW TO USE DATABASES AND ONLINE SOURCES

Your university library will provide you with online and physical access to many databases, journal articles, books, reports and numerous other sources that will support your studies. You will usually be given a key reading list alongside each module that you study. You should try to use the key textbook that your module/unit leader recommends, as this will usually run alongside your module delivery. Most universities will provide the e-book version so you can access it online, as there will not usually be enough physical copies for every student to borrow from the library, and academic textbooks are very expensive.

It is important that you are managing your searches for relevant and reputable information by defining the parameters or boundaries of information. It is not possible to research everything that is written about THE, so it is up to you to identify what is relevant. One way that you can do an effective search on your topic area and save time is to use keywords. It is a good idea to keep a record of your searches so as to avoid repeating them. An example of focusing your keywords from the general to the more specific is shown in Figure 3.2.

Figure 3.2   An example of a general to specific keyword search

You can use search engines such as Google Scholar, filtering by using keywords that are relevant to your topic area to identify the most appropriate material for your assignments (see Chapter 5 for academic writing and Chapter 6 and 7 for writing assessments).

USING YOUR UNIVERSITY LIBRARY

University libraries stock textbooks, journals and reports, and provide access to online sources and databases. The internet offers a huge array of different types of material that can be extremely useful for your assessments. However, the reliability of such information varies, as does its relevance. It is important you use work written by academics and peer-reviewed by other academics. You should consider the following elements of a book (or journal) when using the library to locate suitable sources of information:

- Title and author
- Index
- Contents page
- Introduction (or abstract for an article)
- Publisher's comments
- Reference list and bibliography
- Skim through the contents of a book to get a sense of what it covers

ACTIVITY

Searching for a suitable textbook

- Go to your university library (in person or online) and locate a book on hospitality management
- Note down the classification number as it is likely other books on the same theme will have this code (e.g. it might use the Dewey Decimal Classification method)
- Survey the book as per the list above
- Write down a brief summary
- Reflect on how useful the book is to your own specific study needs
- Store your notes somewhere sensible so that you can find them again easily.

STUDENT INSIGHT

The difficulty of locating reputable sources – an undergraduate Tourism Management international student perspective, Erick (1st year)

Familiarising and getting used to the environment whilst adjusting to a new educational system was already a challenge that I needed to face when I started university. Coping with the daily anxieties and expectations that I had created for myself has made it even more difficult yet motivated me to thrive and keep trying to give my very best. [The] UK's educational system, in general, is very different from what I have known and been used to throughout my life. This is especially true on how assessments are being made and provided, in which many cases are a form of research-based written essay, report or presentation.

Although I have done loads of writing and research in my previous education, the process of how it works and how it is conducted is completely different. However, with the given circumstances and challenges, I find myself continuously learning and determined to do everything in the correct way. Most assessments are a form of writing which consists of thousands of words; this, however, is only half of the battle and the other half of it is researching. Given that I had no clue on how to research properly and which materials to use and avoid, it was a struggle and confusing at first and it is still now. However, the eagerness to learn and the passion for the course made me put extra effort in to attend every single class and that helped my study habits a lot. Taking advantage of the free workshops that the university offers every week was a major advantage as well, from writing skills, organising workloads to locating reputable resources.

Also, using the key reading lists and putting in the hours and work at the library to read chapters whilst using Google constantly to search for unfamiliar words or phrases. This provides me with clarity on what I am reading and has since become my work ethic, so I can understand and gain a broader knowledge of certain topics. However, having the right materials or a credible source doesn't make it easier. Hours of reading and deliberating sometimes leads to tiredness and loss of interest in the subject and could sometimes also lead on to using off-topic materials. However, making it interactive and looking for different ways to make it more entertaining and fun, helped me a lot and made my learning so much easier. Rather than reading tons of information and looking through tons of materials, it is sometimes better to engage with alternative materials and sources such as watching YouTube videos, listening to podcasts, looking at current events through social media and exchanging opinions and ideas with colleagues. Also, by joining faculty societies I was able to interact with students further along in their degrees, who offered me extra tips and hints on what to do and expect through my modules and university experience.

JOURNAL ARTICLES

Journal articles offer high-quality academic information and are usually peer-reviewed, which means that they have been reviewed by experts in the tourism, hospitality and events fields before being published. It is expected that you will refer to a wide-range of sources and these must mostly come from academic journals to support and justify your claims. Your tutors will usually provide you with some relevant journal articles to support your studies and assignments. However, it is important that you familiarise yourself with how to use your library database and other online sources as presented in this chapter for yourself.

SCImago Journal and Country Rank Journal (SJR)

The SCImago Journal and Country Rank Journal (SJR) is a public portal that contains journals and indicators developed from information contained in the Scopus database.

Figure 3.3 show the indicators for the UK's and worldwide journal rankings based on the number of citations.

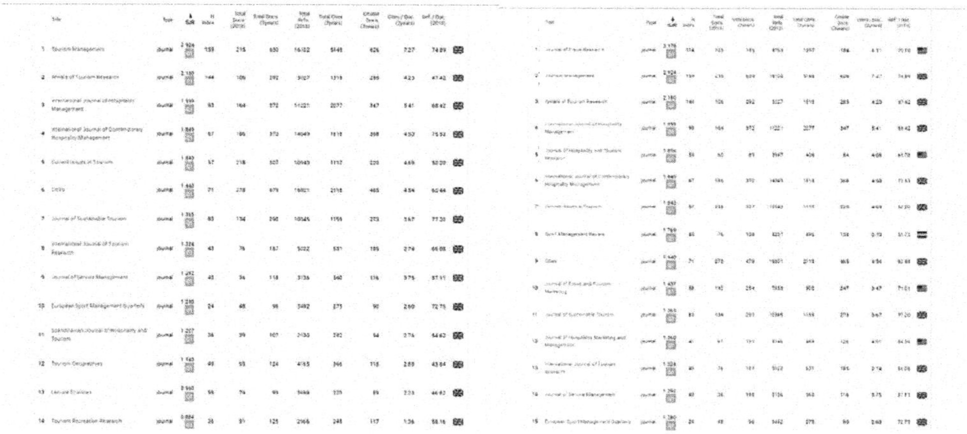

Figure 3.3   Tourism, leisure and hospitality management, UK and worldwide journal rankings

Source: SJR (2007-2020)

You can also assess the quality of journal articles through the Chartered Association of Business Schools (CABS) rankings. Using reputable journals will show your tutors that you have researched for your assignment well and broadened your knowledge, rather than just using the sources provided by your tutor.

The *Academic Journal Guide* (AJG) 2018 provides guidance on the quality and range of academic journals in which business and management scholars publish their research papers. It offers a useful way for new and existing academics to identify the best work of other scholars in their field as well as which journals to aim for when publishing work. The guide consists of publications that have been expertly judged by peer and editorial review. It is also informed by statistical information relating to the number of citations a paper receives (CABS, 2015).

The Academic Journal Guide (AJG) ratings

Below are the different ratings that journal publications are given ranked from 1 to 4*, 1 being the lowest rank and 4* being the highest.

4* Within the business and management field, including economics, there are a small number of grade 4 journals that are recognised worldwide as exemplars of excellence. As the world-leading journals in the field, they would be ranked among the highest in terms of impact factor. The initial paper selection and review process would be rigorous and demanding. Accepted papers would typically not only bring to bear large-scale data and/or rigour in theory, but also be extremely finely crafted and provide major advances to their field.

4 All journals rated 4, whether included in the Journal of Distinction category or not publish the most original and best-executed research. As top journals in their field, these journals typically have high submission and low acceptance rates. Papers are heavily refereed. These top journals generally have among the highest citation impact factors within their field.

3 These journals publish original and well-executed research papers and are highly regarded. These journals typically have good submission rates and are very selective in what they publish. Papers are heavily refereed. These highly regarded journals generally have good-to-excellent journal metrics relative to others in their field, although at present not all journals in this category carry a citation impact factor.

2 Journals in this category publish original research of an acceptable standard. For these well-regarded journals in their field, papers are fully refereed according to accepted standards and conventions. Citation impact factors are somewhat more modest in certain cases. Many excellent practitioner-oriented articles are published in 2-rated journals.

1 These journals in general publish research of a recognised, but more modest standard in their field. A 1 rating indicates the journal meets normal scholarly standards, including a general expectation of **peer review**. Papers are in many instances refereed relatively lightly according to accepted conventions. Few journals in this category carry a citation impact factor.

Source: CABS (2015)

Another way of identifying leading authors in the research fields of tourism, hospitality and events is to explore Scopus and Google Scholar (www.scholar.google.co.uk/citations). Accessing these databases offers you the opportunity to measure a scholar's work through identifying the number of citations an article or book receives for research quality.

═══════════ **RESEARCH INSIGHT 1** ═══════════

Authenticity in tourism

Notable authors who have offered a significant contribution to the sociological perspective of tourism are Boorstin (1962), Cohen (1988) and MacCannell (1999). Boorstin argued in his book *Lost Art of Travel* that tourists do not experience reality but thrive on 'pseudo-events'. He argued that the hyperreality of tourist experiences is enough to keep tourists satisfied. Cohen applied Boorstin's ideas in 1972 to his typology of conventional/institutionalised types of mass tourists (see Poon, 1993). Cohen (1988) later explored the motivation of tourists, arguing that travellers are active whereas tourists are passive. Cohen furthered his concept to include 'staged authenticity' whereby the host and visitor co-construct social reality. Later MacCannell (1999) argued that Boorstin's hyperreal approach claimed that tourists seek authentic experiences, like pilgrims, in another time and space. MacCannell mirrors Iso-Ahola's (1982) 'escapism' theory, arguing that people want to escape from their daily routine and search for authentic experiences in another time and space.

The argument of authentic versus inauthentic tourist experiences has been explored in many studies. The blurred line between authentic and inauthentic experiences is thought to have been shaped by globalisation, societal changes, technological advances, modernity and modern society creating homogeneity across tourism products and services. Rojek and Urry (1997) argued that the hyperreality of film, television and literary texts creates images and/or expectations in the mind that we then expect to see, terming this 'staged-authenticity'. The concept of seeking authentic experiences as seen in films is termed 'film-induced tourism' (Beeton, 2005). Therefore, tourists intend to seek the 'reality' created in the media, making it hard to distinguish between what is real and what is believed to be real (Baudrillard, 1994).

Furthermore, concepts exist to describe commercialised development of a society from westernised globalisation, and consumerist behaviours are used to explain the commodification of products and services. For example, 'Disneyfication' describes developments that resemble Walt Disney Parks and Resorts. The commodification of tourist products and services makes authenticity impossible, as one cannot distinguish between what is real and what is not (Baudrillard, 1994).

═══ RESEARCH INSIGHT II ═══

Butler's (1980) Tourism Area Life Cycle (TALC) model

Another seminal work is by Butler, who proposed that destinations follow a specific cycle of growth through six stages of tourism development. Although there are some criticisms of Butler's TALC model as being impractical and having significant flaws and limitations, it is still effective for identifying the components of the tourism system as well as providing useful insights for destinations to implement sustainable development (Ho and McKercher, 2015). These are identified below and in Figure 3.4.

Exploration – a small number of tourists visit the area; the area is unspoilt, and few tourist facilities exist and based on primary attractions with no secondary attractions; the economic or social value of tourism has no significance to the host community.

Involvement – local people start to become involved and provide some (secondary) facilities for tourists such as guest houses; a recognised tourist season may develop; increased pressure for government to provide improved transport infrastructure for tourists.

Development – the host country starts to develop and advertise the area as a tourist destination, creating a well-defined tourist market; the area becomes recognised as a tourist destination with tourists exceeding the local population during peak times; local communities may experience developments that they do not approve of and their involvement declines rapidly; new attractions will be developed and marketed, showcasing natural and cultural assets, with external organisations starting to provide secondary attractions.

Consolidation – the area continues to attract, and be marketed to, tourists, who still exceed the local population; the growth in tourist numbers may start to slow, but the economy is now heavily tied to the

(Continued)

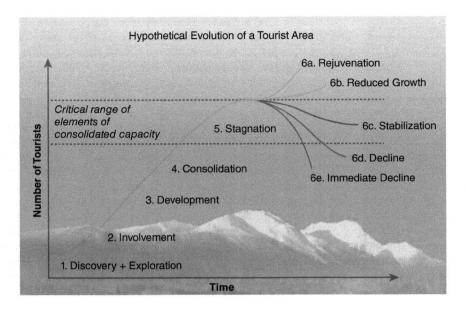

Figure 3.4   Butler's TALC model

Source: Butler, 1980 (reproduced with permission from Wiley)

tourism industry and some resorts may be dependent on this industry; many franchises and chains will dominate the area; some discontent and conflict between the host and the tourists may occur.

Stagnation – the 'carrying capacity' has been reached or exceeded and causes environmental, social and economic issues; original primary attractions are superseded by artificial tourist attractions and facilities for the tourists and may decline as they become old and run down; the resort's well-established image is less appealing and tourist numbers may decline.

Rejuvenation – investment and modernisation may occur, which leads to improvements and changes in tourist attractions and visitor numbers may increase again; some unexploited tourism resources may be found and developed.

Decline – if the resort is not rejuvenated or unable to compete with newer tourism attractions (stage 6), it will go into decline; tourist attractions may become non-tourism facilities and people will lose their jobs associated with tourism; the image of the area suffers becoming less appealing to tourists.

The final stage of Butler's TALC model offers alternative outcomes after stagnation, rejuvenation or decline. This final stage of Butler's model offers five scenarios between these two potential outcomes:

A: Successful redevelopment leads to renewed growth.

B: Minor modifications to capacity levels lead to modest growth in tourism.

C: Tourism is stabilised by cutting capacity levels.

D: Continued overuse of resources and lack of investment lead to decline.

E: War, disease or other catastrophes cause an immediate collapse in tourism.

━━━━ **RESEARCH INSIGHT III** ━━━━

Neil Leiper's Tourism System

A notable framework commonly adopted in THE studies is Neil Leiper's 1990 tourism system. Leiper was a leading Australian academic and his seminal paper was published in 1979 in *Annals of Tourism Research*: 'The framework of tourism: Towards a definition of tourism, tourist and the tourist industry'. This paper identified the key themes that marked Leiper's work on systems approaches, attractions, partial-industrialisation and their strategic development in tourism management (Hall and Page, 2010).

Leiper's tourism system comprises a tourist, a traveller-generating region, tourism destination regions, transit routes for tourist travelling between generating and destination areas, and the travel and tourism industry (e.g. accommodation, transportation, suppliers of products and services, e.g. travel agents, restaurants, leisure activities, etc.) (Page, 2013). Leiper's framework provides a useful insight into the overall process of tourist travel from both the supplier and the consumer perspectives, respectively known as the 'supply' and 'demand' chains. The tourism system also usefully identifies the organisations involved in influencing and regulating tourism in destinations (Page, 2013).

Figure 3.5   Leiper's tourism system
Source: Leiper, 1979

There is a wide range of accessible journals in tourism, hospitality and events and some of the better-known ones with a robust peer review system (as mentioned above) include:

- *Annals of Tourism Research*
- *Current Issues in Tourism*
- *European Journal of Tourism Research*
- *International Journal of Hospitality Management*
- *Journal of Convention and Event Tourism*
- *Journal of Tourism*
- *Tourism Management*

Some further useful online academic databases include:

- *IBISWorld*: Industry market research reports, statistics, analysis, data and trends for in-depth and concise world data on business information.

- *Passport/Euromonitor International*: provides worldwide strategic market research for Business to Consumer (B2C) and Business to Business (B2B) industries. Offers insightful key industry data and trends in consumer change, local and international business environments, etc.
- *Mintel*: Depending on your university's subscription, you can access Mintel (Market Intelligence) for a detailed analysis on reports and industry trends such as consumers, markets, new products, etc.
- *Hospitality and Tourism Complete (EBSCO)*: a database that covers all areas of tourism and hospitality including market trends, food and beverage management and hotel management. Offers hundreds of full-text journals as well as magazines, company and country reports, books and newspapers.

These databases may be provided for free through your university library.

Other useful scholarly sites include:

- *Research Gate* (www.researchgate.net/about): this is a useful network for scientists and researchers to share, discover and discuss research. It was founded in 2008 by physicians Dr Ijad Madisch and Dr Sören Hofmayer and now has over 15 million members.
- *Academia* (www.academia.edu/): a useful platform for academics to share research papers, monitor the analytics of their research impacts and track the research of other academics.
- *The Conversation* (www.theconversation.com/uk): an independent source of news and views sourced from the academic and research community for the wider public to provide open access and the free-flow of information.

 THINK POINT

Think of sources of information that you should not be using for academic writing and research. Examples include:

Wikipedia – not a reputable source of information and therefore unreliable. As seen earlier, peer-reviewed journals are robustly reviewed and ranked for their contribution to knowledge. Websites like Wikipedia can be written by everyone and anyone who may not be reliable for making such claims.

Some newspapers – think about which ones might adopt a certain perspective and why this might be.

Some websites – ensure that the sites you use are reputable and recognised by your university as such.

EXTERNAL PUBLIC SOURCES

There are many useful external organisations that conduct research and provide open access market intelligence about topics relevant to tourism, hospitality and events. Some organisations manage surveys that offer tourism data intelligence focusing on people's engagement with varying themes including the environment, transportation, leisure, sport, culture and heritage (Tourism Australia, Tourism New Zealand, Destination Canada, US Travel Association, VisitBritain). These sources include the Department of Digital, Culture, Media and Sport (DCMS), Sport England, Department for Transport,

Historic England, as well as many others. The Department for Digital, Culture, Media and Sport (DCMS) is an important UK governing body in tourism, hospitality and events and is responsible for driving growth, enriching lives and promoting Britain abroad (DCMS, 2019). This is another useful source of information where you can access information and statistics.

The Office for National Statistics (ONS) is a useful online source of information. They produce several publications through their Tourism Intelligence Unit including the 'Atlas of Tourism' which covers the supply side of tourism, employment in tourism, and measures of tourism locally. These can all be found on the ONS website under 'The Economic Value of Tourism' at www.ons.gov.uk. The UK Tourism Satellite Account (TSA) uses demand (consumer spend) and supply (business turnover) information to work out the value of tourism to the economy in terms of Gross Value Added (GVA) and is available via the ONS website.

Some further useful organisations and websites include:

- ABTA – www.abta.com/
- Association of Leading Visitor Attractions (ALVA) – www.alva.org.uk/
- Association of National Tourist Office Representatives – https://antor.com/
- The British Association of Leisure Parks and Attractions (BALPPA) – www.balppa.org/
- British Educational Travel Association (BETA) – www.betauk.com/
- Cruise Line International Association (CLIA) – https://cruising.org/
- Ecotourism Australia – www.ecotourism.org.au/
- Foreign Commonwealth Office (FCO) – www.gov.uk/government/organisations/foreign-commonwealth-office
- Institute of Travel and Tourism – www.itt.co.uk/
- International Ecotourism Society – https://ecotourism.org/
- Tourism Alliance – www.tourismalliance.com/
- Tourism Concern – www.tourismconcern.org.uk/*
- Tourism Management Institute (TMI) – www.tmi.org.uk/
- Tourism Research Australia – www.tra.gov.au/International/International-tourism-results/overview
- The Tourism Society – www.tourismsociety.org/
- UK Hospitality (UKH) – www.ukhospitality.org.uk/
- United Nations Educational, Scientific and Cultural Organisation (UNESCO) – https://en.unesco.org/
- United Nations World Tourism Organisation (UNWTO) – www2.unwto.org/
- World Tourism Organisation (WTO) – www.wto.org/
- World Trade Travel Council (WTTC) – www.wttc.org/

*Please note this website is now closed but you can still access some of the content uploaded prior to September 2018.

REFLECTION EXERCISE

Skills and strengths in researching THE

1. How could you apply your current skills and strengths in researching THE?

(Continued)

2. In what ways could researching tourism, hospitality and events support your development and skills for the future? How will you apply them?
3. On a scale of 1–10 (1 being not very confident to 10 being very confident), how confident do you feel now in researching for your assignments?

USING EVIDENCE FROM DIFFERENT SOURCES OF INFORMATION

It is generally agreed that there are three different types or categories of information: primary, secondary and tertiary. Primary data is new information that is generated (qualitative) or collected (quantitative) in the real world. It is new, original and empirical in its nature (Brotherton, 2015). There are many ways to obtain the information and these include questionnaires, surveys, interviews and/or observations. When you are identifying primary research, try to locate:

*   A methodology or method that describes the process involved in conducting the research study
*   The research sample and how they were recruited to the study
*   The methods used for data generation/collection, e.g. were the participants surveyed and/or interviewed?
*   The analysis procedure and key findings/results.

Source: adapted from Anglia Ruskin University Library, 2020

These themes are further explored in Chapter 4 which looks at how to read in an academic way by adopting various reading techniques.

Secondary sources of information are data that already exist and have been collected or generated by someone else, either individually (e.g. by a research student for their PhD) or as an organisation (e.g. ONS and airline passenger numbers). They are not often used as evidence on their own, but this form of information is usually presented as an analysis, presentation or discussion of existing evidence. Secondary sources of information include reports (e.g. by DMOs), government documents (e.g. Olympic Games bid books), books (Sage, Routledge, Taylor & Francis), journals (peer reviewed such as *Annals of Tourism Research*, *Leisure Studies*, etc.), magazines, websites (e.g. UNWTO), databases (e.g. ONS), Box of Broadcasts (BOB) and newspapers (*Financial Times*, *The Guardian*, *The Independent*). These sources are usually available in the public domain, but other secondary sources can also be unpublished dissertations or theses held in libraries (e.g. British Library), publications produced by government bodies (e.g. Olympic and Paralympic Games reports), conference proceedings and company reports, as well as many others.

The United Nations World Tourism Organisation (UNWTO) is an international organisation and United Nations agency that is responsible for the promotion of responsible, sustainable and accessible tourism, and is a useful resource for a secondary source of information. The UNWTO promotes tourism as a driver of economic growth, inclusive development and environmental sustainability and as an instrument in achieving the Sustainable Development Goals (SDGs) that are geared towards reducing poverty and fostering worldwide sustainable development (UNWTO, 2019). You can access tourism annual reports, international and domestic tourism statistics, executive summaries, various publications on tourism highlights, policies and advanced knowledge, as well as many others.

Secondary research is sometimes referred to as 'desk-based' research as it involves just that – finding information from your desk! This form of research evaluates and synthesises existing primary research. Examples include literature reviews, systematic reviews and meta-analyses.

Tertiary sources of information are essentially processed and summarised secondary information that has been condensed into abstracts, indexes, catalogues, bibliographies, databases, encyclopaedias and other formats (Brotherton, 2015). Tertiary information can be a useful way to search for information using keywords or phrases to help speed up the searching process and a useful way to identify the myriad of literature that exists in the tourism, hospitality and events fields.

=== **REFLECTION EXERCISE** ===

Research and using sources

1. What are the key skills required to research effectively?
2. What are the differences between reputable and irreputable sources of information?
3. How do I know if the sources I am using are reputable?
4. Why is research important for THE?

CONCLUSION

In this chapter we have covered:

- What is meant by the term 'research' in academia and why it is important when studying tourism, hospitality and events.
- The different ways in which research is conducted and illustrated this with several different case studies.
- Ways you can locate appropriate and useful sources of information for your studies.
- Assurance on how you can identify scholarly articles and online sources and databases for locating appropriate information related to tourism, hospitality and events and your studies.
- The differences between primary, secondary and tertiary sources of information and how to use them effectively in your studies.

FURTHER READING

Cohen, E. (1972) 'Toward a sociology of international tourism', *Social Research*, 39(1): 164–189.

Collis, J. and Hussey, R. (2014) *Business Research: A Practical Guide for Undergraduate and Postgraduate Students*. Hampshire: Palgrave Macmillan.

Mair, J. and Whitford, M. (2013) 'An exploration of events research: Event topics, themes and emerging trends', *International Journal of Event and Festival Management*, 4(1): 6–30. doi:10.1108/175829513 11307485

Robinson, P., Heitmann, S. and Dieke, P.U.C. (eds) (2011) *Research Themes for Tourism*. Wallingford, Oxfordshire: CABI.

Saunders, M.N.K., Lewis, P. and Thornhill, A. (2019) *Research Methods for Business Students* (8th edn). Harlow: Pearson.

The International Olympic Committee (IOC) (2019) *The International Olympic Committee*. Available at: www. olympic.org/the-ioc (accessed 18 June 2020).

Useful web resources

United Nations World Tourism Organisation (UNWTO) – www2.unwto.org/

World Travel and Tourism Council (WTTC) – www.wttc.org/

4

ACADEMIC READING, NOTE-TAKING AND ORGANISING MATERIAL

CHAPTER LEARNING OBJECTIVES

By the end of this chapter you should be able to:

- Understand what academic reading is and how to find relevant sources.
- Recognise different ways you can read, using various reading techniques.
- Take notes effectively.
- Organise your note-taking material.

GLOSSARY

- **Anthropologist:** someone who studies human beings and their ancestors through time and space and in relation to physical character, environmental and social relations, and culture.
- **Psychologist:** someone who studies the human mind and its functions, particularly those affecting behaviour.
- **Sociologist:** someone who has expertise in the development of structure and/or functioning of human society, and studies how social influences affect people and their lives.
- **SQ3R:** Search, Question, Read, Recite and Review technique for reading critically and effectively.

INTRODUCTION

As covered in Chapter 3, there are many different databases and sources that you will need to consult and use to complete your assessments and studies at university. However, it can be challenging to read scholarly articles as they are often written and presented in a more complicated and seemingly inaccessible format than other books or articles you may be used to. Therefore, the first section of this chapter covers what academic reading is and provides an insight into how this style of reading is different to everyday reading you might do for leisure.

Organising your study workload can be difficult. Some of the weaknesses students may have in their approach to work often include poor note-taking, not organising thoughts and ideas logically, learning in an unsystematic way (e.g. one idea at a time rather than integrating common ideas) and employing redundant strategies (e.g. rereading and rewriting notes). Some study skills books lack empirical support and therefore, lead students astray with a list of plausible study tips, but no systematic study plan (or in some cases, ineffective study plans) (Jairam and Kiewra, 2009). Therefore, this chapter outlines different ways that you can approach your academic reading. It gives you some useful reading techniques that you may choose to adopt such as the **SQ3R** method and offers examples of the different types of material that you may need to read during your studies, as well as in the tourism, hospitality and events workplace. By also presenting different ways of taking and making notes (for example summarised notes and diagrammatic plans in the form of Mind Maps), it suggests how you can effectively organise and store the notes whilst reading.

WHAT IS ACADEMIC READING?

Reading around a subject helps you build a framework of legitimacy for what you are writing about (du Boulay, 2011). It aids the development of your thoughts and views, and provides you with ideas on how to describe the world and society. Reading will help you to understand the subject areas you are studying, as well as being an invaluable asset in your future employment (Payne and Whittaker, 2006). The principle objective of reading is to gather ideas and information, interpret and synthesise it, and then use this to develop your own ideas and reflections, and express concepts in your own words. It is only through careful reading and critique of what you are reading that you can begin to understand key issues and concepts in tourism, hospitality and events. You must approach your reading in an intelligent and systematic way and ensure you put effort and thought into it, which will pay off in your assessments and class discussions.

Reading will be one of the most demanding activities that you do during your studies as this is how you develop and construct your own knowledge of the world. You will be expected to undertake a lot of reading for all your assessments to gather different views and ideas about a particular topic (Payne and Whittaker, 2006). Within each discipline, many theorists have examined subjects from various viewpoints. In the subject areas of tourism, hospitality and events, the subject has been informed by the work of numerous scholars including **sociologists**, historians, **psychologists**, cultural theorists, geographers, philosophers and others. They identify the key themes and issues that inform their discipline area and the assumptions made within them. You should make the effort to read the original concepts and theorists, such as Sigmund Freud, Emile Durkheim, Jean Baudrillard and Karl Marx, to learn about the fundamental, basic assumptions and how the arguments are observed, approached and constructed. Depending on what you are reading, these theorists might approach particular phenomena in different ways. For example, the impact of events on host communities may be described and interpreted differently by a sociologist, a psychologist or an **anthropologist**.

It is important that you first develop a suitable reading strategy. You may be daunted by the amount of books and journals that are available to you via your university library, both physical and online. However, you should also be excited by the amount of resources available to you and the opportunity you have to engage with an extensive range of texts, research and insights. Of course, you cannot read everything – it would not be practical to do so and your tutors do not expect this of you. Instead, a reading strategy will help you to filter out the most appropriate and relevant sources of information.

HOW TO FIND RELEVANT RESOURCES AND READING

The types of material you select will be dependent upon your purpose. For example, you may be tasked with writing a tourism marketing report on a visitor attraction in the UK that requires industry data for analysis. You would normally search for industry data in databases that store both qualitative (words) and quantitative (numerical) data such as Mintel, Office of National Statistics (ONS), The Tourism Alliance, local and national tourism boards and agencies (e.g. VisitBritain or Australia Tourism), Euromonitor International and so forth. Other types of reading in the tourism, hospitality and events disciplines include reports by different organisations and businesses as well as academic reports. Some of the more common resources include:

- The World Travel and Tourism Council (WTTC) reports, containing resource such as country data and the economic impact of travel and tourism on destinations
- International Olympic Committee (IOC) news and reports on the Olympic Games and Olympic Legacy
- United Nations World Tourism Organisation (UNWTO) reports on issues such as the sustainable development of tourism
- Tourism, hospitality and event organisers' annual reports
- Non-Governmental Organisations (NGOs) such as The Tourism Society
- Local and National governments, e.g. Australian Trade and Investment Commission.

These organisations provide material that will be structured and organised in varying ways. Academic reports may require deeper reading to understand the underlying assumptions and theories that the author is using to frame their argument and findings, while industry, government and NGO reports will be focused on statistical data covering areas such as tourism arrivals, tourist expenditure, length of stays, accommodation and issues of sustainability. Therefore, it is important that you think about what you should read, why you are reading and what methods you will adopt to use the material effectively.

 ═══════════════ ACTIVITY ═══════════════

Bookmarking sources

You can use bookmarks or store favourites on the internet domain that you prefer to use, e.g. Google, Internet Explorer, Firefox, etc. This is a useful way to manage your sources of information that you have

(Continued)

either selected to read or have read. Use the address bar at the top of the browser window and on the site/ source you want, click the bookmark icon. Create some bookmarks with titles to manage different sources of online information by arranging them into categorised folders. Your university library will also have an e-shelf where you can store your favourites.

Many of your modules will provide you with recommended reading lists that will contain textbooks and journal articles that are usually available via your university library. These can include items such as:

- Subject textbooks such as *Events Management* by Bowdin et al. (2011)
- Academic journals such as *Tourism Management* or *Annals of Tourism Research*
- Specific research-informed articles published in journals.

You might find that the core reading for a module is a key textbook and a tutor may use it to structure the module's content. However, it is not sufficient to use only one key text for an assignment. It is up to you to locate suitable, relevant material to complete your assessments. You can search for information via the internet (as long as the sites you are using are reputable), using sources such as company websites (e.g. travel agents, hotels, etc.), government sites (e.g. VisitEngland, VisitPortugal, and Ministry of Tourism sites) and NGO/Not for Profit (e.g. The International Ecotourism Society) webpages, news articles in national or local newspapers (e.g. *The Guardian*, *New York Times*, *China Daily*), online academic (e.g. *The Conversation*) and travel blogs (e.g. Lonely Planet, BeMyTravelMuse), review sites (e.g. TripAdvisor), as well as many others. However, you should be mainly using your university's library for academic reading (introduced in Chapter 3).

DIFFERENT TYPES OF READING

When you read for university studies, it is important that you are retaining the information, and this can be improved through different reading techniques. You will spend much of your time at university reading, compared to the amount of time you might spend on other tasks such as writing (Cameron, 2010). Therefore, it is important that you are reading material that is relevant, developing your reading skills to get the most out of your chosen texts. Reading is one of the most sophisticated skills that we possess, but we should always continue to practice.

When you are reading, it is important that you understand the meaning communicated by the author. You must think about why you are reading and the need for a variety of different approaches. Payne and Whittaker (2006: 71) claim that there are two different approaches to reading – the 'surface' and the 'deep' approach. Both approaches will be useful throughout your degree and beyond.

The 'surface' approach identifies highlights and key points without considering the significance of what has been read, while the 'deep' approach attempts to understand the key underlying principles, the relationships between them and their underlying assumptions (Payne and Whittaker, 2006). The approach you should take will depend on why and what you are reading. For example, if you are writing a detailed essay that requires understanding of the underlying principles and associated assumptions of tourist motivations, then you would adopt the 'deep' approach in your reading. However, if you needed to demonstrate a basic understanding of the key issues that surround host/visitor conflict in tourist destinations, then it is more important to pick up the key points.

Many students who explore their reading material in a more detailed and critical way will be invested in their work and will usually study for longer, as they have a keen interest in their subject. Students who adopt a 'deep' approach to reading tend to do better in their assessments as they can communicate the key points as well as having a better grasp of the subject. In other words, it is not enough to simply read the text; you must also interpret it (Cameron, 2010). Your interpretation of material is dependent on other things that you have read that have increased your knowledge and explicit judgement of its worthiness and relevance.

It is important to read academic work thoughtfully and actively to understand the underlying key meanings and assumptions made by authors and these provide the foundations for the next stage of your reading. Payne and Whittaker (2006) state that once you have grasped the fundamentals of a specific approach, an author's ideas can be evaluated, compared and analysed in terms of whether the argument is clear and explicit. In turn, this helps you to develop your own intellectual stance on the viewpoints of others, increasing your knowledge and understanding of your subject area. According to Payne and Whittaker (2006) there are four different ways of reading that will be useful to you. These are presented in Table 4.1.

Table 4.1   Four different ways of reading (adapted from Payne and Whittaker, 2006)

Type of reading	How it is useful
Background reading	Allows you to gain an overview of the topic area and is the foundation of further reading that develops your knowledge and understanding.
Skim reading	Involves you skimming through text very quickly to get a general idea of what the material is about. You will not always know what you are looking for and you would only use this approach when you need to know the surface level knowledge of what is being argued.
Scan reading	This is like skim reading, but you are looking for more detailed specifics. Usually you will read the introduction and the conclusion in detail and then speed-read the rest of the chapter or article. Pay attention to graphs and figures as these are useful for summarising the key points being made in the text.
Critical reading	This is important for analysing, comparing and evaluating the material. This is explained in more detail below and is covered more fully in Chapter 8.

Critical reading helps you to think differently and can deepen your learning and critical skills. Reading critically rests on the idea that you question the material you are reading. Critical reading can help you to read efficiently by reducing the time you spend reading a given text, improving your understanding and aiding the retention of information (Cameron, 2010). We discuss critical reading in more detail in Chapter 8.

═══ ACTIVITY ═══

Reading and evaluating the argument

Select a peer-reviewed journal article from the event management literature. Read the article and identify the primary and secondary arguments being made, and whether a theory, framework or model is being used. Make notes on what these may be and where appropriate, address the following questions:

(Continued)

- Are there any new concepts being defined?
- Ask yourself 'so what?' at regular intervals (why is it important?)
- If the claims being made are 'true', what does this imply?
- What evidence and/or arguments are being used to support the claims being made, and are they appropriate?
- What are the logical links used?
- Is the conclusion the only one that can be reached, or can it be generalised?
- Are there any hidden assumptions? What are they? Are they valid?

By understanding the context in which material has been written, you can better understand the sorts of claims being made (e.g. what an author believes or states to be true). There are numerous terms that are used when constructing arguments, some of which are shown in Table 4.2 (note that these terms may be used in different ways by different authors from different disciplines).

Table 4.2   Different terms for understanding arguments and theories (adapted from Cameron, 2010)

Term	Meaning	Examples in tourism, hospitality and events
Concept	Abstract idea that makes you aware of an aspect or situation and helps you to understand it.	Dark tourism Slow tourism Performativity Authenticity
Model	Simplified representation of something	Butler's Life Cycle Model Leiper's Tourism System
Metaphor	A creative and useful way to highlight key features of a situation by applying a familiar term to describe something less familiar, e.g. by understanding the familiar term, it will help you to understand the less familiar term.	The 'Research Onion' to describe the states of research (Saunders et al. 2007) 'Back stage/front stage' to describe authenticity (Goffman)
Framework	Indicate more organised abstraction. Common in management theories that can be used as checklists for analysing a situation.	SWOT analysis – Strengths and Opportunities (internal factors), Weaknesses and Threats (external factors); SMART objectives – Specific, Measurable, Achievable, Realistic and Timely; STEEPLE – Sociological, Technological, Environmental (physical), Economic, Political, Legal and Ethical factors of an organisation.

What is the SQ3R technique?

The SQ3R technique is covered in more detail in Chapter 8. It is the most popular and well-researched study strategy, believed to provide students with a structured approach to study (Huber, 2004; Jairam and Kiewra, 2009). It was introduced by Robinson (1941, 1946) and the acronym stands for 'Survey, Question, Read, Recall, Review'. This is summarised in Figure 4.1. More detail on how to use it is in Chapter 8.

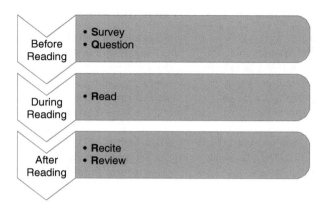

Figure 4.1   The SQ3R method

Speed reading

Speed reading was introduced in the 1950s by American educator Evelyn Wood. Wood established learning institutions for students to develop the ability to read hundreds of words per minute, reading lengthy papers quickly while also grasping the content (McMillan and Weyers, 2012). Speed readers use their peripheral vision (the furthest extremes to the left and right while looking straight ahead, tested regularly by your optician) to absorb clusters of words in one 'flash' or 'fixation' (McMillan and Weyers, 2012: 145).

Another way you can speed read is to use 'finger tracing', placing your finger underneath the line of text being read (McMillan and Weyers, 2012). This is thought to increase your eye speed and keep your mind focused. However, while speed-reading techniques can be useful in some situations, they are usually not thorough enough to allow you to fully assimilate the information.

=========== ACTIVITY ===========

Improving your reading efficiency

For a detailed insight into how you might use your eyes when reading see Cameron, 2010: 80.

As presented earlier in the chapter (and later in Chapter 8), critical reading is an efficient way to read. Students often find they are pushed for time, particularly when several assignments are due at the end of the same term (see Chapter 11 on Time Management).

Active reading can involve annotating text, making notes in the margins, underlying or highlighting key points. By developing an active reading approach, you will stay focused. Taking useful notes while reading is important not only for your studies but also in a range of work contexts.

INDUSTRY INSIGHT

From alternative forms of tourism to sustainable tourism

Alternative tourism emerged from the ideology that unregulated tourism development may negatively impact the economic, environmental and socio-cultural aspects of a destination and can be regarded as an early form of sustainability within the tourism industry (Robinson et al., 2011). The rapid development of mass tourism and its associated conventional tourism development resulted in destinations developing with more caution. This recognition and adoption of alternative forms of tourism can include adventure tourism, agrotourism (also agritourism), volunteer tourism, nature/wildlife tourism, fair-trade tourism and pro-poor tourism.

Sustainability within tourism has become an important field of research in tourism planning and development (Robinson et al., 2011). The realisation that tourism brings many impacts to a destination emphasised the need for research and new, sustainable ways to approach tourism development, such as visitor management to control visitor flows (e.g. limiting numbers and restricting opening days and times), adaptation of resources (e.g. protecting resources from wear and tear), and the modification of visitor behaviour (e.g. codes of conduct such as those adopted by English Heritage www.english-heritage.org.uk/). These three management approaches are conceptualised as 'carrying capacity', 'limit of acceptable change' and the 'recreation spectrum'.

Carrying capacity is defined as:

> the maximum number of people that may visit a tourist destination at the same time, without causing destruction of the physical, economic and sociocultural environment and an unacceptable decrease in the quality of visitors' satisfaction. (UNWTO et al., 2018: 3)

The concept of sustainability in tourism is researched in many ways and includes visitor experiences and management, conservation and resource management, collaboration and community participation, transportation planning and development, and policy development and assessment. Research can assess the effects of tourism on destinations and the development of effective visitor management tools (Robinson et al., 2011). More recently, we have seen terms such as 'overtourism' and 'tourismphobia' that reflect the challenges that face tourism management of tourist flows into urban destinations and the impact of tourists on the destination and host population (UNWTO et al., 2018).

Tourism will only be sustainable if developed and managed when considering visitors and local communities. The UNWTO state that 'tourism can and must play a significant role in delivering sustainable solutions for people, the planet, prosperity and peace' (UNWTO, 2019). Tourism is a significant economic powerhouse that has the potential to contribute to all the SDGs, directly or indirectly. Therefore, tourism has specifically been included in the SDGs relating to 'inclusive and sustainable economic growth, sustainable consumption and production (SCP) and the sustainable use of oceans and marine resources, respectively' (UNWTO, 2019).

ACTIVITY

Academic reading and taking notes

Read the Industry Insight above on alternative forms of tourism and make notes on the key points being discussed. Answer the following questions:

1.   What are the key issues being discussed?
2.   What is meant by the term 'over-tourism'?
3.   In what ways do you think that destinations can prevent or find alternative ways for overcoming the issue of over-tourism?

NOTE-TAKING

Note-taking refers to taking notes on someone else's thoughts and ideas, e.g. books, lectures, journals, etc., while note-making refers to the organisation of your own thoughts. Taking notes is key in your studies as well as the workplace and should go further than just jogging your memory. Notes are a key component for active learning, especially if you learn best from writing. This section will help you to adopt effective note-taking strategies so that your notes will be organised.

Why do you need to make notes?

Note-taking can involve a two-stage process: recording notes and reviewing notes. Most of you will record your notes from lectures and seminars either by hand or computer. The process of note-taking through recording notes (versus listening only) and reviewing your notes (versus no review) raises fact and relationship learning (Luo et al., 2016). Taking notes during your lectures increases your attention as well as achievement level. Students who take high-quality notes are more likely to achieve high-quality outcomes (Watkins et al., 2015). Note-taking is also important when reading online material. As you will take many notes during your course, it is important that you have an organised system for recording your notes. Cameron (2010: 92) states that you can take notes to aid your concentration, understanding, retention of information, and that they can be used later for reference and revision.

When you make notes, you should be organising your material as part of the process of organising your thoughts. By noting the key points and themes from what you are hearing, reading and/or observing in a way that makes sense to you, you are interacting with the material and/or situation. This interaction enables you to engage your mind and maintains your attention. The organised notes that you create will be more likely to be useful to you in your assessments and revision than original material such as lecture slides. Finally, a more active process allows for a deeper understanding and effective recollection of the information than what you will achieve from just reading passively.

━━━━━━━━━━ STUDENT INSIGHT ━━━━━━━━━━

One of the author's own experiences: Nicola Cade

When starting as an undergraduate student I thought I was well organised and ready to begin researching for my assignments. However, as a lot of information is required it quickly becomes difficult to manage your notes. You find that you have notes taken during lectures and seminars as well as notes from reading the appropriate material. Many times, I had referred to my written notes and realised that I had no idea of where they had come from. I mistakenly just wrote down notes during sessions either from the slides or my tutors and then failed to make note of the source of the information. Big fail!

(Continued)

So, the key point here is, when making notes from your lectures and seminars ensure that you are making note of the date of the session and whether the note you have made refers to what a tutor said or whether it was on a slide. When making notes from reading, I realised that I had lots of information and ideas generated from reading but no clue where it had come from! Oops! This is not good academic practice, as if I chose to use it, I could not reference the original source and risked plagiarising someone else's work. I quickly learned that I must make a note of the author(s), title of the source, and where I located it, e.g. journal/website/book, etc. Also, when making notes this way if I was to directly quote anything from the source, I would ensure that I made a note of the page number as this saved time later by not having to refer to the original document/source.

Sometimes I would use a word processor to make notes. However, I found this harder when in class as I cannot type that quickly! Nonetheless, this is probably a more efficient way of making notes as you can rearrange your notes more easily through editing, highlighting and reviewing them. You can also add many different notes from different sources and find a way to identify the different authors (e.g. colour coding) more easily. When making written notes, it is recommended that you leave wide margins for extra information and general thoughts and ideas to be added. My study life would have been so much easier had I adopted these useful techniques!

Good notes can also be more useful than the original material as they will be easier for you to understand, since they are your own interpretation of what was said. You will have organised them in a way that makes sense to you and can help you draw from other sources of information and material that you can cross-reference. Your notes must be clear as to what sources you have referred to; you need to ensure that you do not copy and paste information directly without referencing it correctly (see Chapter 5). It is not a good idea to take chunks of information either directly from the internet or from papers without supporting notes as this will mean you have not fully engaged or interacted with the material. Without actively absorbing, condensing and restructuring the information you will miss out on the many advantages of note-taking as discussed in this section. Some different ways to write your notes are outlined below.

Sequential notes

Sequential notes involve the process of reading or listening and then recording the information in your own words, in the same sequence as the original material was presented, as a summary or an outline (Payne and Whittaker, 2006):

- *Summary* – a shorter version of the original material with key points and ideas in note form. As they are written in your own words, they will be easier for you to understand and can be used directly in your essays or reports.
- *Outline* – only the keywords and phrases, either sequentially numbered or presented as headings and sub-headings.

Cameron (2010) proposes the following methods of effective note-taking:

- *Annotation* – highlighting key points and/or concepts and making brief marginal notes or comments, allowing you space to think while you read and making it easier to refer to the highlighted key points later.

- *Précis/summary* – a point-by-point organised summary.
- *Diagrammatic notes* – Diagrams are useful for representing relationships between the information and/or other material, such as in the form of Mind Maps (presented later) or sketch diagrams.
- *Lecture notes* – some lecturers may provide you with handouts that you can make notes on against the relevant lecture slides. Most students find that making notes during lectures has the same benefits as reading notes in terms of concentration and engaging with the key points and the relationships between them. As mentioned in Chapter 2, some universities have a 'lecture capture' or recording system and this is a useful way for you to re-listen to the lecture and write notes in your own time, as you can pause, rewind and stop the recordings.

REFLECTION EXERCISE

Are you an effective note-taker?

Think about how well and often you do these things when taking notes:

- Use words and diagrams to make notes when you read
- Organise the content by leaving spaces in your notes for anything you may have missed or for any areas that need expanding for more clarity
- Improve your notes by indicating areas that are insufficient in your notes to make good within 24 hours of taking them (otherwise you may forget)
- File your written and typed notes systematically.

Diagrammatic notes: Mind Maps

Mind Maps (see Figure 4.2) were first created by Tony Buzan and have become a hugely popular thinking tool for students, teachers, academics and businesses alike (Buzan and Buzan, 2003). In the late 1960s, Roger Sperry suggested that there are two sides of the cerebral cortex ('outer shell') that divide the major intellectual functions of the brain. Sperry's findings identified that the right hemisphere was dominant in intellectual areas of rhythm, spatial awareness, gestalt, imagination, daydreaming, colour and dimension (Buzan and Buzan, 2010). The left hemisphere was equally powerful in a range of mental skills such as word, logic, numbers, sequence, linearity, analysis and lists (Buzan and Buzan, 2010). Sperry discovered that although the two hemispheres are dominant in certain activities, they display basic skills in all areas and the mental skills identified in the left-side of the brain were distributed throughout the cortex (Buzan and Buzan, 2010). You may have heard that we either think with our 'left-side' or 'right-side' of our brains and one dominates the other. However, this is contested by neuropsychologist Michael Bloch, who concluded that if we acknowledge ourselves as either 'left-sided' or right-sided' we limit our abilities in creating new strategies (Buzan and Buzan, 2010: 8).

THINK POINT

What side of the brain do you think you dominantly use? Why do you think this?

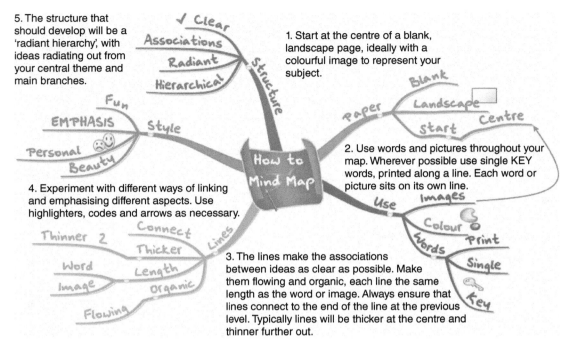

5. The structure that should develop will be a 'radiant hierarchy', with ideas radiating out from your central theme and main branches.

1. Start at the centre of a blank, landscape page, ideally with a colourful image to represent your subject.

2. Use words and pictures throughout your map. Wherever possible use single KEY words, printed along a line. Each word or picture sits on its own line.

4. Experiment with different ways of linking and emphasising different aspects. Use highlighters, codes and arrows as necessary.

3. The lines make the associations between ideas as clear as possible. Make them flowing and organic, each line the same length as the word or image. Always ensure that lines connect to the end of the line at the previous level. Typically lines will be thicker at the centre and thinner further out.

Figure 4.2   How to 'Mind Map'

Source: Illumine, 2019

 ━━━━━━ ACTIVITY ━━━━━━

Create a basic Mind Map

Organise your thoughts and ideas and create a mind Map on Airbnb and the sharing economy. Follow the process below:

1. Take a blank piece of paper (landscape orientation) – larger than A4
2. Start in the centre of the paper and write a central idea that represents the essay question above
3. Start adding the main themes of the question around the central idea using lines to connect them directly to the central image – think of these as the key headings you will use in your essay
4. From these Basic Ordering Ideas (BOI) start focusing the Mind Map by adding a second level of ideas connecting with lines – these lines should be thinner than the main lines connected to the central idea as they are the broader issues
5. If necessary, add third and fourth levels of ideas as the thoughts come to you
6. You can add boxes of information that add depth to your key thoughts and ideas
7. You can colour code, create images and be as imaginative and creative as you like!

Mind Maps attract your eyes and brain, helping to remember your ideas more easily.

Source: adapted from Illumine (2019)

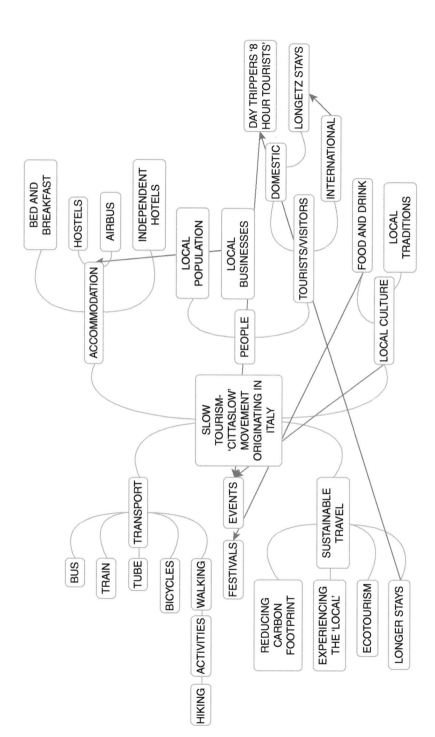

Figure 4.3 An example of a Mind Map of the concept of slow tourism

REFLECTION EXERCISE

Note-taking

On a scale of 1 – 10 (1 being not confident at all, 10 being very confident), how confident do you feel about taking notes that will be useful in your studies? Are you able to take notes effectively? How will you organise your notes?

There is no correct method for taking notes – it is a matter of individual preference and it may take some of us longer than others to read and write. It is important that you consider why you are taking notes and how they will support your studies.

ORGANISING YOUR MATERIAL EFFECTIVELY

Well-organised notes are invaluable. It is not effective or efficient to have piles of scrap paper with notes scrawled on them or files saved within your 'My Documents' folder that are not labelled or sorted (Cameron, 2010). You should have a good index system that tells you what notes you have on certain topics or lectures. You can do this easily on the computer by creating folders and giving them relevant titles and creating subfolders within them – see Figure 4.4.

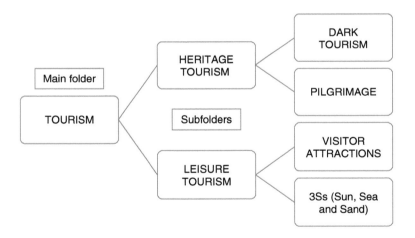

Figure 4.4   **Example of computer folders for organising material**

It is advisable to have back-up files or online storage rather than on a laptop or PC. If your laptop or PC fails or is lost or stolen, you will lose all your hard work, some of which you can never get back. Use USB memory sticks and online storage systems such as One Drive, iCloud, Google Docs or Dropbox to back up your files. Keep these backed-up files separate and safe. Chapter 9 covers the importance of back-ups and file storage in more detail.

If you are storing written notes in notebooks or loose-leaf files, then be sure to have an index system and clearly labelled sections so that you can easily identify what the notes are about and where to find them. A page numbering system is also useful for hard copy notes in case you drop them and they become muddled. It is best practice to keep a record of where you have found information. This is about being disciplined in your work and not copying or plagiarising others' work (discussed later in Chapter 5) and will save you from trying to locate a source of information later. There are various reference management systems that will allow you to store the full reference for you (see Chapter 5). If your notes are well-organised and disciplined, they may be a useful resource for your dissertation or project, or even a task at work.

=== **REFLECTION EXERCISE** ===

Reading

On a scale of 1–10 (1 being less confident, 10 being very confident), how confident do you feel about reading effectively and efficiently, and making notes effectively for your studies? Based on this chapter, what types of reading techniques do you think you will adopt in your studies? What note-making techniques will be the most appropriate for your studies?

CONCLUSION

In this chapter we have covered:

- What academic reading is and how you can find relevant sources.
- The different ways that you can read academically by adopting various techniques.
- The different ways that notes can be taken and made.
- Different ways that you can organise and manage your notes effectively.

FURTHER READING

Buzan, T. and Buzan, B. (2003) *The Mind Map Book*. Harlow, Essex: Educational Publishers LLP/BBC Active.
Buzan, T. and Buzan, B. (2010) *The Mind Map Book: Unlock your Creativity, Boost your Memory, Change your Life*. Harlow, Essex: BBC Active.
Fairbairn, G. and Winch, C. (2011) *Reading, Writing and Reasoning: A Guide for Students*, 3rd edn. Maidenhead, UK: Open University Press.

Useful web resources

Buzan, T. (2019) *Buzan* – www.tonybuzan.com/
City University of London (2020) *Journals, Articles and Research for Business: Journals, Articles and Peer-Reviewed Research* – https://libguides.city.ac.uk/c.php?g=662398&p=4682248
Godfrey, J. (2018) *How to Use Your Reading in Your Essays* [E-Book]. Red Globe Press – www.dawsonera.com/abstract/9781352002980
Illumine Ltd (2019) *How to Make a Mind Map* – www.illumine.co.uk/resources/mind-mapping/how-to-make-a-mind-map
Royal Literary Fund (2020) *Reading and Researching. How to Read: SQ3R* – www.rlf.org.uk/resources/how-to-read-sq3r/

5 ACADEMIC WRITING AND REFERENCING

 CHAPTER LEARNING OBJECTIVES

By the end of this chapter you should be able to:

- Identify different styles of writing, types of audience and methods of organising and structuring material.
- Appreciate the importance of the right setting and place for writing.
- Demonstrate where arguments and evidence have come from.
- Use different referencing formats, including Harvard referencing.
- Feel confident in how and when to reference correctly.
- Understand what plagiarism is and how to avoid it.
- Recognise the most appropriate reference management systems.

 GLOSSARY

- **Plagiarism:** using someone else's words, ideas, work as your own without acknowledging them.
- **Paraphrasing:** using others' ideas to create your own ideas expressed in your own words.

INTRODUCTION

This chapter covers the different styles of academic writing and referencing procedures that you will be expected to follow at university. The first section explains the different styles of academic writing that will be expected from you. Academic writing requires more critical and analytical thought than other styles of writing such as letters, emails or college assignments and coursework. The chapter explores the different writing approaches you might use based on the task or question set. It offers classic and novel ideas for finding the right setting and place to develop your thoughts. This section also looks at different ways to brainstorm your ideas for critical and analytical thinking.

The second section explores how you can show where the arguments and evidence has come from in your work via various referencing techniques (specifically Harvard referencing). By knowing how, why, what and when to reference correctly you can show academic rigour in your assignments and avoid offences such as **plagiarism**. Finally, this section introduces some of the reference management software systems.

REFLECTION EXERCISE

How confident do you feel about referencing your work?

Before you read this section on referencing, rate yourself on a scale of 1 (not confident at all) to 10 (extremely confident), on how confident you feel about referencing your work. Think about why you have given yourself this rating.

WHAT IS ACADEMIC WRITING?

Academic writing is a vital skill that you will need to develop during your time at university, although it is inevitable that individual writing skills will vary between you and your peers. As outlined in the next chapter on written assessments, some people prefer to plan and structure their writing first, while others people prefer to get their ideas flowing first and then create a structure later. The key principle of academic writing is that it is 'objective', using language that is impersonal (although do note that there are some exceptions to this), succinct vocabulary, and avoids personal or idiomatic tones (McMillan and Weyers, 2012).

There is no rule for how you approach your writing; do whatever best suits you and your learning. However, it is important to have a framework or focus to keep you on track. It is important that your personal opinions do not cloud your judgements when writing and this is avoided by using objective views and adopting an active or passive tone as appropriate.

ADOPTING ACTIVE OR PASSIVE VOICE IN ACADEMIC WRITING

Use of the active or passive voice is dependent on what it is you are writing and its focus or emphasis. An active voice in a sentence has a subject that acts upon its verb. For example, 'tourists seek adventure', or 'hotel managers develop budgets'. A passive voice means that a subject is a recipient of a verb's action, e.g. 'budgets are developed by managers'.

Some issues with using a passive voice are:

- It is commonly associated with more grammatical errors
- Overuse of passive voice can make heavy reading for the audience
- Cumbersome passive expressions can make it hard for the reader to grasp what your argument actually is.

If you are presenting a fact or action, then you will use the passive voice, e.g. 'The Tourist Gaze was a concept developed by John Urry.' If you want to emphasise the 'doer', then you would adopt an active voice, e.g. 'John Urry developed the concept "The Tourist Gaze".'

For your assessed written (and oral) work, it is recommended that you carefully plan your work and approach it in a focused and organised manner (see Chapters 6, 7 and 11).

AUDIENCES IN ACADEMIC WRITING

Academic writing is usually impersonal and must be evidence-based. While the writer's viewpoint might be stated, arguments are developed with evidence from external and approved sources. Before you begin to write, it is important to identify the audience you are writing for, i.e. the 'who?' If you were to write a letter to your tutor you would use a different tone and style than if you were writing a letter to an elderly aunt. Therefore, when writing an academic essay, bear in mind that you are writing for an academic: someone who is intelligent, informed, interested and authoritative. Consequently, your research for different projects needs to reflect different needs and audiences. Therefore, it is important to critically analyse information before you include it in your written work, making sure that what you have is appropriate and accurate.

WRITING ACADEMICALLY FOR YOUR ASSESSMENTS

As outlined in Chapter 6, the purpose of writing during your studies is to demonstrate your knowledge and understanding of a topic; your ability to research a specific aspect of that topic; that you can organise supporting information correctly; and that you can structure a piece of academic writing (McMillan and Weyers, 2012). In general, you will adopt three main styles of writing: descriptive, argumentative and evaluative. Some writing tasks may involve a combination of these with the application of critical and analytical skills (usually at levels 5 and 6). In tourism, hospitality and events, there is much criticism that scholars should be more reflective (personal) in their writing. However, it depends upon the task at hand whether you should write in the first person pronoun of I/we (e.g. 'I aim to explore…') or third person of he/she/it/they/this (e.g. 'This report analyses…'). The three styles of descriptive, argumentative and evaluative writing are now addressed.

Descriptive writing

This will usually require you to outline a sequence of events or summarise the main points of a theory or article. For example, if you were asked to identify the key themes for discussion in a task that asked you to discuss the macro-effects of mega-events (e.g. FIFA World Cup and Olympic Games) on the host community, you would investigate the key macro-factors such as urban regeneration, that affect the local communities living and working in the cities that host mega-events. This requires you to be clear, precise and accurate.

You would also need to present your discussion in a logical and coherent manner, e.g. you would start with the more general ideas and move to the specific ideas such as urban regeneration and displacement. You must try and keep to the point (e.g. do not wander off into an irrelevant discussion of drug-taking among Olympic athletes).

Argumentative writing

Present an argument to state your case or point of view, intended to be persuasive. You must clearly and concisely state your position and your reasoning, supported by reliable, relevant and valid evidence and examples. This style of writing is common at level 6 and above, especially for undergraduate dissertations.

Evaluative writing

This form of writing compares, contrasts and evaluates. Similar to argumentative styles of writing, evaluative writing will involve making judgements based on what you think is the most significant evidence, again justifying your views via data, and again, this should be objective for an equal balance of the information and evidence.

As you will see in Figure 5.1 there are levels of intellectual behaviour proposed by Benjamin Bloom (1956). The stages relate to the first, middle and final stages of your university degree and how you may progress from one form of writing to the next. Figure 5.1 connects these intellect levels with the different styles of writing described above.

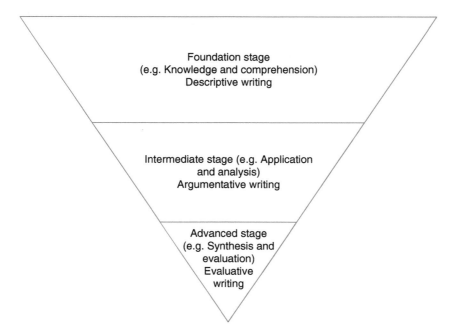

Figure 5.1 Levels of intellectual skills

Source: Authors' own image inspired by Bloom (1956)

When analysing information, it is important to know how you will use it. Your first piece of analysis for an assignment should be the words in the question you are answering. Table 5.1 provides some examples of words you may come across in a question and how you need to respond to them (see also Chapter 6 on assessments).

Table 5.1 Common key words that will inform your writing

Key word	Expectations in your writing
Analyse	Break it into sections and examine it in detail
Compare	Look for similarities between the things you are being asked to compare, present the relevance or consequences of the similarities and conclude with the most significant
Critically evaluate	Weigh up the arguments for and against, assessing the strengths of the evidence on all sides
Describe	Provide the main characteristics or features of the topic or outline the main events without judgement
Discuss/discursive	Investigate or examine through argument and debate, give reasons for and against, and examine the implications
Evaluate	Assess the topic and give your judgement on the merit, importance or usefulness and support your claims with evidence
Explain	Clearly present why something happens or why it is the way it is, and interpret and account for the reasons
Justify	Provide evidence that supports an argument or idea and why decisions and/or conclusions were made
Reflect	To turn or throw back a problem that has been identified. You need to think deeply about a topic through active engagement before a conclusion can be reached. See Chapter 10 for more on reflection

Source: adapted from advice provided to students from Anglia Ruskin University (ARU, 2019)

GENERAL POINTS TO CONSIDER WHEN DRAFTING WRITTEN WORK

- *Step 1: Clarify the purpose of the writing task*

  - What is the task?
  - What is the topic?
  - Why are you writing it?
  - What do you hope to achieve from it?
  - Who is your target audience to read it?
  - How will it be used and/or disseminated?

- *Step 2: Collect and identify the most appropriate material*

  - Brainstorm your relevant ideas in note form (introduced later in chapter)
  - Use techniques such as Mind Maps (see Chapter 4) to develop and extend your ideas
  - Create a structured action plan
  - Gather a wide range of information to support the assessment (see Chapter 3)
  - Note down information and sources as you progress (introduced later in chapter)

○ Keep a record of what you read (see Chapter 4)

○ Scrutinise the information for its relevance and importance (see Chapter 8)

- *Step 3: Organise the material (discussed further later in chapter)*

  ○ Follow the recommended structure for your subject area, e.g. an essay or report (see Chapter 6)

  ○ Organise the material by creating sections and subsections

  ○ Plan a logical order that is appropriate for the subject – see Figure 5.2

  ○ Keep sections focused on one topic/issue

  ○ Do not include too much information within each section

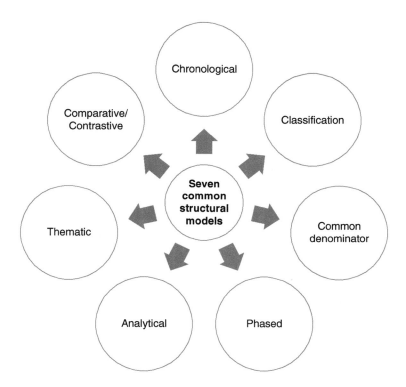

Figure 5.2   Written assignments: Seven common classic structural models

Source: adapted from McMillan and Meyers, 2012: 211

- *Step 4: Draft and edit/redraft*

  ○ Present the key facts accurately, clearly and concisely; evaluate key facts in the conclusion and provide recommendations where appropriate; write in a simplified and objective way; use conjunctions and linking phrases to show the connections between ideas.

- *Step 5: Presentation of final draft*

  ○ Check your grammar, punctuation and spelling. Use clear headings and sub-headings to inform the reader; use clear numbering for sections, subsections and paragraphs; use appendices for detailed findings; use images, tables and graphs where appropriate; ask someone to proofread your work.

Brainstorming and organising your ideas to start writing

Think about the question or task you have been given and brainstorm some ideas using a 'spider' plan. This is sometimes known as 'Mind Mapping' (originating from the work of Tony Buzan), which is a more advanced form of brainstorming (see Chapter 4). Other brainstorming methods include:

- Index cards with colour coding for different points
- Post-it notes with key points on a wall or on paper

For large-scale projects such as research projects and dissertations:

- Storyboards provide a mental map of the subject that you are investigating or intend to study (Thomas, 2011). This is the same as a Mind Map (see Chapter 4) but instead you draw images and pictures without text. Both these techniques enable you to think about some of the issues relating to your topic.

McMillan and Weyers (2012) recommend that after brainstorming, you should revisit the assessment criteria and see how your initial ideas respond to the required task. These initial ideas will be your own interpretations of the topic that have not yet been influenced by reading any material. Therefore, you are starting to apply your critical thinking skills (see Chapter 8) by analysing the most important issues that you think are important to your topic.

WHAT IS THE DIFFERENCE BETWEEN AN ANALYTICAL AND A CRITICAL WRITER?

It should be clear by now that you have almost certainly been using analytical thinking without even realising it. You have probably been considering if you are receiving any benefit from these chapters (hopefully the answer is a resounding yes!). You may have looked at the contents page and decided that you only need to read two or three chapters. This is an example of analytical thinking. An *analytical* thinker will scrutinise information from a variety of perspectives and these can include:

- Checking the information is correct and factual
- Searching for errors
- Checking to see if the information is 'leading' you to agree with its assumptions
- Using substantive argument to say why one set of information is better than another

On the other hand, a *critical* thinker is:

- Careful to consider information carefully and more than once
- Evaluating what you have and identifying the evidence in support of your view
- Checking that the evidence is based on reason (and if not, reconsidering your view)

Critical thinking is discussed further in Chapter 8, but you should be aware that your writing needs to reflect this kind of thinking.

—————— THINK POINT ——————

Not all academic writing has to be qualitatively presented (i.e. words). Graphs, charts, tables and diagrams are also useful ways for presenting information visually. Why do you think that using these kinds of diagrams and figures in your assessments is useful?

SOME FURTHER TIPS FOR ACADEMIC WRITING

Some general approaches should be applied to all your writing, including the following:

- Expression of ideas: remember the acronym *KISS* = keep it simple, stupid!
- Avoid over-long sentences by identifying the main idea as a separate sentence
- Place action in *verbs* (describing an action, state or occurrence), not *nouns* (person, place or thing)
- Grammatical precision
- Use plain, simple, clear and precise language
- Avoid abstract words and phrases
- Avoid over-using imprecise words such as 'practically', 'relatively', etc.
- Avoid filler phrases such as: 'In spite of the fact that …'; 'In the majority of instances …'
- Read, read, read!

LOCATING A SUITABLE PLACE TO WRITE

The more comfortable you are when writing, the more effective you will be. Some people prefer working and writing in quiet spaces, whereas others prefer noisier, busy locations. Whatever suits you personally will help with your concentration. You might consider the following places:

1. At home
2. A friend's or family member's house
3. University library
4. Local university campuses
5. Writing retreats
6. Coffee shops/shopping centres
7. Public park areas/botanical gardens
8. Co-working spaces – national and international
9. Museums
10. Aquariums/zoos
11. On public transport systems such as bus, boat, ferry or train and/or their stations
12. A 'she-shed' or 'man-cave'!
13. An equipped camper van!
14. A castle!

And last but not least…

15. Anywhere that has Wi-Fi connection!

Adapted from Pope (2019)

As you can see from the list above, there are some formal and informal areas that you can use to write. Some are very quirky and are perhaps places that you have not yet considered, but note that working in creative places can sometimes result in more creative writing.

THINK POINT

Based on the list above, what would be the most appropriate/comfortable writing space for you? Or is there a place/space not listed that you would prefer? Think about the differences between quiet and noisy places and spaces for writing. What are their advantages and disadvantages?

ACADEMIC REFERENCING AND SUBSTANTIATING YOUR WRITING

It is important to understand the information you have obtained and look at it objectively. Opinions can easily be clouded by personal beliefs (political, religious, cultural or moral). It is important to step away from your own beliefs and prejudices and analyse the information you have. By removing your own baggage from the equation, you can analyse the information you are presented with more thoroughly. For the purposes of academic work, your opinions cannot be simply intuitive or instinctive, but must be informed and supported with evidence.

REFLECTION EXERCISE

The importance of referencing

1. Why is referencing important in higher education?
2. How can referencing help to develop your ideas and expand your knowledge?
3. What is the difference between a reference list and a bibliography?
4. What is plagiarism?

ACADEMIC REFERENCING

Referencing is a key skill that students require to show good academic practice. All universities will have their own style of academic referencing. However, there is guidance on what, when, how and why you should reference regardless of the referencing style that your university adopts. Neville (2010) offers the following framework:

- *WHAT* (what sources to choose and what to reference)
- *WHEN* (when to reference)

- *HOW* (different styles of referencing and different sources)
- *WHY* (the academic rationale and the principles)

Referencing in higher education is underpinned by three key assumptions:

1. Facilitating the development and transmission of knowledge.
2. Practically manifesting critical ideas and theories adopted and the application of and engagement with knowledge.
3. Presenting the meaning of codes and formulae in a communicative manner that allows those who have learned the practice to recognise and understand them (Neville, 2010).

Neville (2010) outlines six specific and knowledge-related aspects of the importance of referencing:

1. Facilitates the tracing of the origin of ideas
2. Helps you to build a web of ideas
3. Supports your own voice in academic writing
4. Validates arguments
5. Helps to spread knowledge
6. Acknowledges the work of others.

Understanding *when* to reference is important because the ideas, theories, models and practices you are writing about will have originated from somewhere and someone. The original author or thinker needs to be credited for their work. Referencing also plays an important role in locating ideas and arguments in their historical, social, cultural and geographical contexts.

Sometimes it is very difficult or impossible to work back to the origin of an idea, especially if it is 'common knowledge'. The concept of 'common knowledge' is an area that divides opinion between tutors in higher education. Some argue it does not need referencing as everyone (or nearly everyone) has knowledge of it, but what one perceives as common knowledge may not be perceived in the same way by another, even in the same subject area. Knowing when to reference your work is just as important as understanding how to reference correctly for your credibility. From your perspective as a student, there are three key reasons for referencing:

1. Informs your reading and influences your work
2. Marking criteria (tutors will credit you for using academic sources properly)
3. Avoiding plagiarism.

What is plagiarism?

King's College London (KCL, 2019) defines plagiarism as 'The act of taking and using another person's thoughts, words, judgements or ideas as your own, without any indication that they are those of another person.' It is an academic offence to copy the work of others and present it as your own without referencing it correctly. If you are found to be plagiarising others or your own work (e.g. from a piece of work you have already submitted), it can result in severe disciplinary action and you are likely to either fail your assessment or be removed from your course. The student handbook or regulations from your university will outline the penalties given for academic offences, so be sure to familiarise yourself with them.

Plagiarism can and should be avoided. It is assumed that most students do not plagiarise deliberately and it is often an oversight because you can easily plagiarise work unintentionally (McMillan and Weyers, 2012). Some key things to consider when writing regarding 'unintentional plagiarism' based on KCL's definition are as follows:

*   'Words' can also include ideas, judgements, inventions, and images
*   The act of 'taking' and 'using' another person's work does not just mean 'word for word' but also 'in substance' (e.g. **paraphrasing**) (McMillan and Meyers, 2012: 229)
*   'Using' others' work is (of course) acceptable if you acknowledge the source correctly.

You should adopt the following three strategies to avoid plagiarism: quoting, summarising and paraphrasing. You should also make sure you can tell them apart, and that you have indicated which strategy you are using to your reader.

Remember, do *not* 'copy and paste' directly from sources without citation – this is plagiarism. This is common when using electronic sources of information. Universities have online systems that can check student's work and help identify where this has occurred in the document. Make sure you are familiar with the system used at your university. Sometimes universities allow students to submit draft work and check 'similarity', so make sure you try this with a draft assessment if you have this facility.

It is also an academic offence to copy another student's work, either past or present. You will usually fail the assessment if you are identified as cheating. If you allow another student to copy all or part of your work and allow them to pass it off as their own, this is known as collusion and you will both be punished.

It is also an academic offence to ask or pay someone else to write your work for you (e.g. using essay mills or online ghost writers). This is called contract cheating. Some UK universities hold plagiarism hearings and students who are found to plagiarise others' work are immediately expelled from the course. It is important that you follow your university's Examination Regulations on the procedures for dealing with cases of plagiarism. Never submit anything you did not write yourself, however tempting. If you are struggling with your workload and/or your health, you should seek immediate help from university staff and student support services, rather than being tempted to cheat. Always write your assessments yourself, with the support of reputable information that you can reference correctly.

Different forms of referencing
In-text citation

These citations reference a source that you have either paraphrased, drawn from or otherwise used in your work. There are many ways that you can use in-text citations depending on how you are referring to others' work. For example, if you wish to refer to an author's work *generally*, you should give the author(s) name followed by the year of the relevant publication (e.g. Urry, 2002). It is important to note that if you are using someone else's ideas to construct your own, you must still refer to this by mentioning the author(s) name and year of publication in brackets (e.g. *The Tourist Gaze* (Urry, 2002)). This citation should then appear in your reference list (e.g. Urry, J. (2002). *The Tourist Gaze*, 2nd ed., London: Sage Publications).

If you use an excerpt of another's work *directly*, you must include quotation marks and a page number (p.) or range (pp.). For example:

Ritchie (1984: 2) refers to large-scale global events as 'Hallmark' events, broadly defining them as: 'Major one-time or recurring events of limited duration, developed primarily to enhance the awareness, appeal and profitability of a tourism destination in the short and/or long term.'

This would appear in your reference list as: Ritchie, J.R.B. (1984). Assessing the impact of Hallmark Events: Conceptual and Research Issues. *Journal of Travel Research,* 22(1), pp. 2–11. Notice that in the main text you direct the reader to the specific page you are quoting from, whereas in the reference list you need to direct your reader to the whole paper by giving the complete page range.

All sources can be used directly or indirectly, depending on how you wish to apply them to your work. For example,

'According to Everett (2010) …'

Or:

'Writing "oneself" into tourism research (Everett, 2010) requires a reflective personal account from the researcher.'

It would appear in your reference list as:

Everett, S. (2010). Lessons from the field: Reflecting on a tourism research journey around the 'Celtic' periphery. *Current Issues in Tourism*, 13(2), pp. 161–175.

As you can see from the examples given, there are differences in how we cite a book and a journal article. Other common examples of references you may have in your list include:

- E-journals

Li, S. and McCabe, S. (2013). Measuring the socio-economic legacies of mega-events: Concepts, propositions and indicators. *International Journal of Tourism Research*, 15(4), pp. 388–402. Available at: Anglia Ruskin University Library website, http://libweb.anglia.ac.uk [accessed 20 June 2016].

- E-books

Doppelt, B. (2016). *Transformational Resilience: How Building Human Resilience to Climate Disruption can Safeguard Society and Increase Wellbeing* [E-book]. Sheffield: Greenleaf Publishing Limited. Available at: Anglia Ruskin University website, https://libweb.anglia.ac.uk [accessed 2 June 2018].

If your source has been located through your library database systems, then reference this link or use its DOI (Digital Object Identifier) number rather than URL (Uniform Resource Locator – an address identifying the location of a file on the internet). You should add the date when you last accessed the source and ensure this is noted at the end of the reference, as shown above, i.e. '[accessed 2 June 2018]'.

- Websites

International Olympic Committee (IOC) (2012). *Sustainability Through Sport. Implementing the Olympic Movements Agenda 21 – 2012* [Online]. IOC Commission for Sport and Environment. Available at:

https://stillmed.olympic.org/media/Document%20Library/OlympicOrg/Documents/Olympism-in-Action/Environment/Sustainability-through-Sport.pdf [accessed 2 April 2018]].

It is good practice to get into the habit of taking a screen shot or print-out of the first page of any web pages that you use. This will identify the necessary elements required for the reference list if you forget to include it at the point of accessing the source. Electronic information cannot always be trusted to be accurate: remember anybody can publish information on the World Wide Web and very little of it is edited or verified.

- Online reports

Rio Olympic Organising Committee (ROOC) (2014). *Embracing Change Rio 2016 Sustainability Report September 2014*. Edited by Organising Committee for the Olympic and Paralympic Games in Rio in 2016. Rio - 2014-2017. *Olympic World Library*, 2018. [Online]. Available at: https://library.olympic.org/Default/doc/SYRACUSE/73418/embracing-change-rio-2016-sustainability-report-organising-committee-for-the-olympic-and-paralympic-?_lg=en-GB [accessed 29 June 2016].

Some sources that you use may have more than one author. You must include all authors in the first time you provide the in-text citation then thereafter, use 'et al.' for all future citations for the same text:

Cade, Everett and Duignan (2019) or (Cade, Everett and Duignan, 2019)

In the reference list:

Cade, N., Everett, S., and Duignan, M.B. (2019). Leveraging digital and physical spaces to 'de-risk' and access Rio's favela communities. *Tourism Geographies*, pp. 1–26.

If you use Google Scholar, another useful tool when searching for academic journals and books (see Chapter 3) is the [″] icon under the results. If you hover over the icon it will read 'cite'. This automatically creates the citation for the reference list. You can choose the style of referencing from the list and copy it to your clipboard or directly into your work.

  STUDENT INSIGHT

Difficulties with referencing correctly – Cristina, undergraduate

Learning how to reference correctly is important as a student in university. My arguments had to be supported by previous research in order to be considered valid. In the beginning it was difficult for me to understand why my opinion was not enough. Researching must be objective, not biased as is the case with personal views. Therefore, my work must present a holistic view of the subject.

There are many ways to reference and each institution chooses a different one, so it is vital that the students are flexible and adapt to the method their university uses. Coming from another country, with a different approach to academic research, in the beginning it was confusing.

Thankfully, the university provides many ways to learn how to reference. The handiest form for me was the university guide. The library offers an online guide for referencing everything that research might contain from websites to pictures and audio material. The guide is available free to all students and it offers examples for typical situations: from research with multiple authors to more particular cases such as 'no author' or 'date missing'. Another resource that I used during my studies was the teachers' feedback on my assignments. They pointed out that I needed to improve my referencing skills as I tended to mix situations and forget to mention the date that I accessed online material. This could have had implications for plagiarism. Therefore, as I continued to research, I paid more attention to references found at the end of the material to understand better what academic references look like.

The university also provides a programme called 'Study Skills Plus' whose aim is to help students that need extra help adjusting to academic life. The programme includes workshops and one-to-one appointments for referencing to explain in more depth how referencing works and why it is important to do it correctly.

What are the differences between a reference list and a bibliography?

Reference lists and bibliographies are commonly used synonymously, but there is a difference in meaning (Neville, 2010): a reference list is an alphabetical list of sources used throughout your work that you have paraphrased or quoted, whereas a bibliography is a list that includes all the works you have consulted, whether or not you have actually quoted from them directly.

The *reference list* should include all the studies you have used in your work. It is listed in alphabetical order by first author surname with all the associated material about that reference in one sequence (see Figure 5.3). Citations in the main text and the list of references at the end need to match.

Alves, M. H. M., and Evanson, P. (2011). *Living in the crossfire: Favela residents, drug dealers, and police violence in Rio de Janeiro*. Philadelphia: Temple University Press.

Ateljevic, I., Pritchard, A., & Morgan, N. (2007) (eds.). *The critical turn in tourism studies: Innovative research methodologies*. Oxford: Elsevier.

Browne, K. (2005). Snowball sampling: using social networks to research non-heterosexual women. *International Journal of Social Research Methodology*, 8 (1), 47–60.

Cataldo, F. (2008). New forms of citizenship and socio-political inclusion: accessing antiretroviral therapy in a Rio de Janeiro favela. *Sociology of health & illness*, 30 (6), 900–912.

Clark, T. (2011). Gaining and maintaining access. *Qualitative Social Work*, 10 (4), 485–502.

Côté, I. (2013). Fieldwork in the era of social media: opportunities and challenges. *PS: Political Science and Politics*, 46 (3), 615–619.

Crowhurst, I. (2013). The fallacy of the instrumental gate? Contextualising the process of gaining access through gatekeepers. *International Journal of Social Research Methodology*, 16 (6), 463–475.

Davies, C.A. (2007). *Reflexive ethnography: a guide to researching selves and others* (2nd ed). London: Routledge.

Decroup, A. (2004). Trustworthiness in qualitative tourism research. In: L. Goodson, & J. Phillimore (eds), *Qualitative research in tourism: ontologies, epistemologies and methodologies*. London: Routledge.

Denzin, N. K., and Lincoln, Y. S. (2005). *Handbook of qualitative research* (3rd ed). London: Sage.

DiCicco-Bloom, B., and Crabtree, B. F. (2006). Making sense of qualitative research. The qualitative research interview. *Medical Education*, 40 (1), 314–321.

Figure 5.3 **An example of a reference list for a tourism paper**

Source: adapted from Cade et al. (2019)

A *bibliography* is a list of material that you have used to help you prepare and research your work, but you may not have quoted from all of them in your text. For example, you may have done some background reading on your chosen topic area that has enriched your thinking but does not need to appear in the essay; or you may have done some initial research with the idea of making a particular argument, but subsequently changed your mind and taken the essay in another direction.

Always familiarise yourself with the brief and relevant regulations when writing assignments to ensure that you know what you are being asked to do. Some institutions may require you to present both a reference list and bibliography. Occasionally, you may be asked to produce an *annotated bibliography,* which is a full reference list of sources used within your written work with added notes that summarise and evaluate the listed sources. An annotated bibliography can be of variable length depending on whether it is being used to assess an independent project or part of a larger research project (Anglia Ruskin University, 2019).

Important note: Universities will vary in what referencing techniques they adopt, so it is important that you use the recommended referencing style as per your university guidelines. For example, some universities have their own Harvard referencing style that does not include the use of footnotes or endnotes, nor do they recommend the use of Latin phrases when referencing such as 'ibid.'.

Other styles of referencing

OSCOLA: Oxford University designed the OSCOLA (The Oxford University Standard for Citation of Legal Authorities) referencing system specifically for legal materials. OSCOLA is now used throughout law schools in the UK and overseas, and legal journals and publishers alike (University of Oxford, 2019). This is a footnote style that links the small number in-text to the description at the bottom of the page in the footnote. You still require a reference list and/or bibliography at the end of the document.

Chicago: this uses footnote numbering as citations with an alphabetical reference and/or bibliography list. A sample list of this style of referencing can be found at the Chicago of Manual Style Online – www.chicagomanualofstyle.org/tools_citationguide/citation-guide-1.html. The Modern Humanities Research Association (MHRA) also use this style of referencing.

Vancouver: This is common in medicine and the life sciences and uses bracketed numbers in the text (e.g. (1), (2), and so on). These numbers correspond with the numbered references in the list at the end of the document. This can be tricky for the reader, as they have to flip back and forth to identify the sources.

Modern Languages Association (MLA): This style of referencing differs from Harvard by providing the author of the material and the page number that detail has come from in the in-text citation. MLA does not include the year of the publication. It is presented alphabetically in the reference list.

Further referencing advice

Here are some other styles of referencing that you need to consider:

- Usually if there are more than four authors, after the first mention of all the authors, you can use the term *'et alia'*, which is the Latin term for *'and others'* and this term should be shown as an abbreviation 'et al.' (with a full stop)
- If you are citing two works by the same author(s) from the same year, they should be differentiated using a lower-case letter next to the year of publication. This must be in sequence

throughout your work (e.g. first publication '2019a', second '2019b', third '2019c' and so on). It is important that you apply this consistently in your final reference list, too.

- You may find that some authors have more than one publication relating to the same point published in different years. These references should be cited chronologically (e.g. earliest publication first).
- If there is no author that you can identify for any written work that you use, you must use *'Anon'* as the author name. Also, if there is no date, use *'n.d.'*.

Secondary referencing

Wherever possible, you should refer to the primary source. For example, there may be occasions where you come across a summary of another author's work in the source you are reading that you find interesting and would like to refer to, and you should attempt to locate that original work. It is preferable to locate the original source because the author of the source that you are reading may have interpreted the original source differently, made errors in the quotation or perhaps altered/skewed the original meaning. However, if you are unable to locate the original source (e.g. your institution does have access to it, it has gone out of print or is not available in a language you can read), then you can cite it where you find it via secondary referencing. The place that you found this information is included in your reference list at the end of your work, not the original source.

=== THINK POINT ===

Why do you think referencing is important?

REFERENCING SOFTWARE

The most commonly used software packages for referencing include Mendeley, EndNote, RefWorks and Zotero. These systems will help you to manage and store references and do most of the formatting for your citations and reference lists and/or bibliographies. Using these reference management systems will help reduce the amount of time that you spend on sorting, arranging and presenting your references, but you must identify the most suitable referencing software for you early in your studies as an effective way of managing your work throughout your time at university. It is important to note that these systems are not fool-proof and you should still check your referencing carefully.

=== REFLECTION EXERCISE ===

Re-rate yourself on how confident you feel about referencing

Now that you have read this chapter, re-rate yourself on a scale of 1 (not confident at all) to 10 (extremely confident), on how confident you now feel about referencing your work after reading this chapter. Has this rating changed from your first one? Why do you think this? What will you do to ensure that you reference correctly?

CONCLUSION

In this chapter, we have covered:

- Exploring different styles of writing for your assessments, different types of audience and methods of organising and structuring your material.
- Finding suitable places to write.
- Referencing where arguments and evidence has come from.
- Referencing formats including Harvard referencing.
- How and when to reference correctly.
- Ways to avoid plagiarism.
- Appropriate reference management systems for you to use.

FURTHER READING

Bloom, B. (1956). *Taxonomy of Educational Objectives*. New York: David McKay Ltd.

Cameron, S. (2010). *The Business Student's Handbook: Skills for Study and Employment*, 5th edn. Harlow: Pearson Education Limited.

McMillan, K. and Weyers, J. (2012). *The Study Skills Book*, 3rd edn. Harlow: Pearson Education Limited.

Payne, E. and Whittaker, L. (2006). *Developing Essential Study Skills*, 2nd edn. Harlow: Pearson Education Limited.

6 ASSESSMENTS: WRITTEN COURSEWORK AND EXAMS

CHAPTER LEARNING OBJECTIVES

By the end of this chapter you should be able to:

- Confidently approach different types of written assessments and exams and be aware of what tutors might be looking for in these assignments.
- Understand how to break down written assessment tasks and know what is required of you to complete them successfully, i.e. understand the 'rules of the game'.
- Confidently approach exams and understand what is being asked of you.
- Demonstrate understanding on how to use feedback from your assignments (formative and summative feedback) for your learning.
- Evaluate and reflect on your academic writing, construction of arguments and approach to assessments and be aware of how you might improve your own practice.
- Reflect on assessment writing skills and identify where you might need to seek further help and guidance.

GLOSSARY

- **Assessment literacy:** being able to make sense of key terms such as criteria and weightings, and understand why you are being assessed, what is expected of you and how you will learn from it.
- **External examiner:** academics from a different institution appointed as impartial reviewers of the assessment process. They are appointed to ensure that standards are kept the same across universities and play a fundamental role in assuring academic standards by providing an external perspective on academic standards, student achievement and the conduct of the assessment process.

(Continued)

- **Formative assessment:** primarily concerned with feedback that aids your improvement. It is often continuous and usually involves words not marks. If an indicative mark is given, it does not contribute to the final mark for the module or degree classification. It checks your learning.
- **Learning outcome:** what learning you should have achieved and can demonstrate at the end of a module/unit and overall course. Assessment is built on what you should know and be able to do by the end of your studies on the module/unit or course/programme.
- **Peer assessment:** students evaluate each other's performance on a task. You may be asked to assess the work of your peers against the assessment and marking criteria for the assignment and then provide feedback to your fellow students. Often used to assess individual effort but also group work – it can be open but also anonymous depending on the purpose of its use.
- **Self-assessment:** this is a way for you to reflect on your own work and judge how well you have done in relation to the assessment criteria. Self-assessment is not generally used for you to generate your own grades, but helps you evaluate your work. Methods include diaries, logs or questionnaires. It is important that you can assess your own work and recognise where you may need further improvement.
- **Summative assessment:** this is used to make evaluative judgements and is an assessment with a mark that contributes to the final grade of the module (or degree outcome if the module counts in the calculation of this). Some modules may use summative assessments mid-way through a module and will certainly have them at the end.

INTRODUCTION

The word 'assessment' comes from the Latin word '*assidere*' which means to 'sit beside' and is essentially about observed learning. Assessment can be the most rewarding part of your learning experience, but also can be the most anxiety-inducing part of university life. Being assessed and tested on anything is stressful and is often the one aspect of university study that students struggle with the most. To ease your anxiety and help you deal with this part of your studies, this chapter introduces you to the most common forms of written assignment used for tourism, events and hospitality modules and courses/programmes, and explains why they are used and how they are usually designed and organised.

This chapter offers advice on making the most of assessment to aid your learning. It offers tips to help you tackle the most frequently used assessments, including planning essays or reports, and offers practical help on how to break down and understand assignments including longer projects, reflective portfolios, assessed online discussion boards, as well as writing strategic reports and evaluations, and exams. The chapter offers you subject specific examples (e.g. a tourism topic Mind Map and an outline contents of a portfolio for a live event) to help contextualise your learning.

The language of assessment can be confusing, so we look at the differences between different formats of written work, e.g. essay and reports; the nature of tutor and **peer assessment**; group and individual assessment; structuring arguments; and using persuasive and academic language. Although the way you should research for assessments is addressed in Chapters 3 and 4, this chapter helps you unpick and make sense of marking criteria and uses different types of feedback which should help you gain a confident level of **assessment literacy**. This chapter should be read in conjunction with Chapter 7 which addresses individual and non-written (verbal) group assessments such as presentations, vivas and debates. The best assessments also evidence skills such as reflective thinking (Chapter 10), good time management (Chapter 11), project management, and project-solving skills as outlined in the later chapters in Section B.

===== REFLECTION EXERCISE =====

How confident do you feel about tackling assessments?

Before you read this chapter on assessment, rate yourself on a scale of 1 (not confident at all) to 10 (extremely confident), about how confident you feel about tackling assessments. Think about why you have rated yourself like this.

WHAT IS ASSESSMENT AND WHY DO YOU WE NEED IT?

Assessment is probably the most important aspect of a student's learning. At its most basic, assessment is a way of finding out whether you have learnt what is required on your module/course and is an evaluation of what you are able to show and do. Phil Race and others comment that, 'Nothing we do to, or for our students is more important than our assessment of their work and the feedback we give them on it. The results of our assessment influence students for the rest of their lives' (Race et al., 2005). According to Sambell et al. (2012), assessment should be meaningful to you and should be fully embedded within the learning process. The act of being assessed should help you make sense of your learning and be informative, developmental and remediable to provide a framework for activity.

According to Brown (2014), assessment should not just come at the end of learning but should be part of the learning process. Increasingly, there is awareness that students should be involved in **self-assessment** and reflect on their learning to help judge their own performance, rather than it be something that is 'done' to you. At its best, assessment should encourage metacognition (i.e. thinking about one's thinking) and help you think about the learning process and not just passing the module, or strategically doing enough to pass the **learning outcomes** (Bloxham and Boyd, 2007). Often the way this is done is by setting **formative assessments** that do not lead to a grade or mark (as opposed to **summative assessment**). Formative assessment will usually be provided in class as it will be a 'practice' for a final assessment and the feedback should be used to help develop your learning and lessen your anxiety. Examples of formative assessment include online or in-class quizzes; seminar tasks; class and peer activities; practice exams; and submission of draft work or structure of planned work.

Table 6.1 Formative and summative assessment

Formative assessment	Summative assessment
Used to evaluate and assess your own learning	Contributes to your overall performance in the module/unit
Identify your strengths and weaknesses in a way that does not induce anxiety	Shows whether you have met the learning outcomes of that module/unit
To help you target your learning and think about where you need to invest more time	Linked to a mark and grade
Builds knowledge before you are summatively assessed on it	Is usually included in a university's regulations on assessment, e.g. you might only be able to retake or resit these once

PLANNING YOUR APPROACH TO WRITING AN ASSIGNMENT

Before you start to research and plan for an assignment, think about what it is you are being asked. There is no point in reading a book that is 30 years old if the information it contains is out of date and has been superseded with other information. You will be given a reading list of the most relevant sources relating to the topic you are covering in a module in the first couple of weeks of a course. Make sure you look at that and use the sources from the reading list to help inform your thinking. Your tutor would not have provided a reading list if they didn't believe the information provided within was credible and worthy of consideration.

To prevent wasting time (refer to Chapter 11), before you start any reading, try and make a list of the sort of information you are looking for and brainstorm the subject to help you decide the approach you will be taking for the assignment. For example, if you are talking about whether all-inclusive hotels damage local businesses and the local economy, then you need to be looking for case studies in specific areas which both support and refute this argument. Therefore, you can create an informed discussion of your own. Knowing this will prevent you spending lots of time looking through texts that are irrelevant. When you go to the library, search for relevant information you want by using the library catalogue. Libraries run useful courses on how to use their service efficiently, helping you find the information you need. Refer back to Chapters 3 and 4 on how to locate relevant information. A top tip is to put into quotation marks any notes you make from the book and write the title, author/date and page number down when you find it. This will save you time having to look up this information for your bibliography and prevent you using someone else's words as your own by mistake (plagiarism), as discussed in Chapter 5.

HOW ARE ASSESSMENT TASKS SET AND CHECKED?

The task of setting a summative assignment is a complex one and it is worth knowing how the process works. Your tutors will tend to follow a process of what John Biggs called 'constructive alignment' (2003) where there is a matching of learning outcomes to assessment criteria to grades. Writing and setting assessments is a complex task as there needs to be an assurance of learning at the end of the module/unit or course. There will be a process at your university to ensure the assessment is appropriate in terms of level and subject, and this is then usually checked by an internal moderator and sometimes an external moderator (at another university). An external moderator is usually involved if the assessment contributes a large percentage of the overall assessment for the module – often this is over 20%. After you submit your assessment, your work will usually be marked, moderated, checked by the external moderator and then sent to an award board for confirmation. Processes vary from institution to institution and from country to country, but you need to ensure you find out how it works at your university. You can usually find this information in your handbook. A standard process is outlined below which has been adapted from Bloxham and Boyd (2007). This is a typical process in the UK, but do note that **external examiners** are not generally used in the US system.

WHEN WILL I BE ASSESSED?

You are likely to have a mixture of *formative* and *summative* assessments during your course of study (see glossary of terms). The summative assessments will each have a weighting towards your overall mark. The number of assessments you will have to undertake usually depends on the size of the module (how many credits the modules are worth – see Chapter 1). Most modules (also called units) are equivalent to about 100–300 hours of learning, and most will have two or three elements of summative assessment.

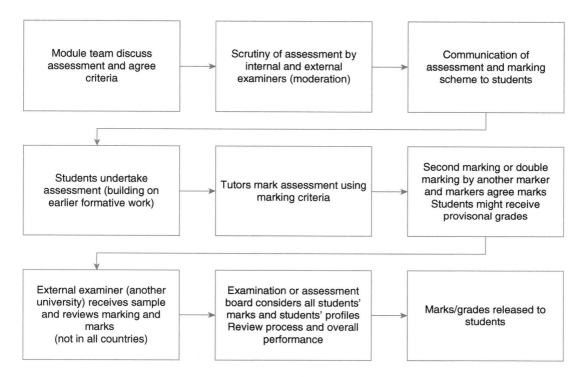

Figure 6.1   Flowchart of the process of setting and marking an assessment

An example module assessment summary could look the one shown in Table 6.2 (the format will differ for your institution). This is one for a 'Current Issues in Tourism' module for second year undergraduate students. This is a very standard approach to assessment using reports and essays, and mixes group and individual assessment.

Table 6.2   Example module assessment for a 'Current Issues in Tourism' module

Assessment number	Type of assessment	Word or time limit	% of total mark	Submission method	Final submission date
1	Group report (individually marked including peer assessment)	1000 words by each person	40%	Online submission	Week x
2	Individual essay on a contemporary issue in tourism	2500 words	60%	Online submission	Week y

Table 6.3 shows a more original example from an events module.

Table 6.3   Example of an assessment breakdown for an events module

Assessment number	Type of assessment	Word or time limit	% of total mark	Submission method	Final submission date
1	Concept (Mind Map) of ideas	Diagram with text (c. 500 words)	20	Online	Week x
2	Event tabletop simulation with reflection – planning the final event	15 minutes and 1000 words	80	In class followed by written reflection	Week y

STRUCTURING ARGUMENTS

Regardless of the type of assessment you will be asked to complete, they will all have a few things in common (see Chapters 5 and 8). In addition to demonstrating knowledge and understanding, undertaking data analysis, critical thinking and synthesis of information, you will need to demonstrate that you can structure an argument and use persuasive language.

In social science and business subjects like tourism and hospitality, there are usually no right or wrong answers (unless you have a multiple-choice exam or test!). It is about the argument and the quality of the debate. A useful overview of the expected criterion in different methods of written assessment is outlined in Table 6.4 (adopted from Morgan, 2017).

Table 6.4   Assessments and different requirements

Criterion	Essays	Reports	Exams
Critical thinking skills	Yes	Yes	Yes
Relevance	Yes	Yes	Yes
Use of examples	Yes	Yes	Yes
Support claims with references, citations and literature	Yes	Yes	Yes, if you can recall a few relevant citations to support key points
Grammar and spelling	Yes	Yes	Yes, but tutors recognise that writing at speed can introduce some errors
Structure	Yes	Yes	Yes
Academic style of writing	Yes	Depends, as you might be asked to write as a business – read the guidance!	Yes
Good memory	No	No	Yes
Avoid plagiarism (copying the work of others without acknowledging source)	Yes	Yes	Yes, although not usually an issue as you will not usually have access to sources in an unseen exam

USING PERSUASIVE ACADEMIC LANGUAGE: WRITING IN AN ACADEMIC STYLE

As noted in Table 6.4 and in Chapter 5, it is important that you use an 'academic style of writing' in your assessments. But what is academic language and style? In brief, you need to write in a style and manner that mirrors the work you are reading in textbooks and journal articles. Different subject disciplines have different writing conventions and vocabulary. As you read more work in tourism, hospitality and events, you will quickly become familiar with the writing style they tend to adopt. In general, your writing should follow a few simple rules:

- Ensure your writing is clear, concise and focused. You need to ensure the reader understands what you are saying so try to avoid ambiguous pronouns.
- Avoid grammatical errors. You need to demonstrate you check your writing and can communicate without error.
- If you are making an argument, then always support your claims with evidence (from research and academic literature). Citations show where your evidence can be found.
- Ensure your tenses and plurals all agree; for example, your writing is all in the past or present tense. Avoid inconsistencies here.
- Generally, essays, reports and exams will require a formal tone and style.
- Write in paragraphs. A paragraph should be around three to five sentences long. Any shorter than this and you need to question the decision to start a new paragraph; any longer and it is hard to follow and you may not have a focused point.
- Avoid long, complex sentences and vocabulary.
- Try to avoid definitive statements of truth, such as 'there are no sources on ...', or 'destination marketing organisations never ...'. Adding 'usually' or 'may' is a more balanced argument.
- Keep your writing simple but not colloquial. Avoid using the kind of informal language you might use to talk to your friends, and do avoid 'text talk' such as 'okay' or 'u' (use 'you') and abbreviations such as LOL, BRB, etc., or worse still, emoticons! You should also avoid contractions, for example 'it's' for 'it is'.
- In general, it is expected that you write in the third person and use the passive voice – i.e. 'this was done' rather than 'I did this'. However, in recent years, many scholars have argued that it is valuable to use the first person. Academics tend to have strong personal preferences here, so you should consult your tutors.
- Try to avoid repetition of verbs and nouns in one sentence, for example avoid 'although they had to consider which plan would be appropriate, they planned to develop ...' It would be better to replace 'plan' with 'option', 'project' or 'action'.

TYPES OF WRITTEN ASSESSMENT COMMON TO TOURISM, HOSPITALITY AND EVENTS PROGRAMMES

Did you know that at least 80% of higher education assessment uses three main forms: unseen time constrained exams, essays and reports? In more recent years, universities have begun to diversify the types of assessment they use to better reflect the workplace and to ensure students who struggle with one form of assessment are not disadvantaged. Employers value students who can quickly engage in real-life tasks immediately upon employment, having practised and developed relevant skills and competences through their assignments. Assessment forms are therefore evolving to reflect these real-world demands. Wiggins (1990) says assessment must involve students being able to cope with potentially ill-structured challenges and roles, with incomplete information, that help them rehearse for the complex ambiguities of adult and professional life. The more authentic an assessment means you should be able to complete it and then use the experience to answer questions in job interviews (Sambell et al., 2017).

Some of the types of assessment you may come across are shown in Table 6.5. Regardless of the type, when they are set you should be provided with marking criteria clearly showing you how and where you will be awarded marks and informing you what is expected in your assignment.

Table 6.5 Types of assessment mapped against skills

Type of assessment	Skills being assessed
In-tray exercises	Making judgements, undertaking calculations, time management
Assessed placements	Numerous transferable skills, including problem solving, reflection and practical skills
Fieldwork notebooks	Written communication, subject understanding, subject knowledge, practical skills, reflection, problem solving and research skills
Short-answer questions	Subject understanding, subject knowledge and problem solving
Reflective diaries/log	Critical thinking, written communication, subject understanding, subject knowledge, reflection and research skills
Online content (e.g. blogs, wiki, websites)	Critical thinking, written communication, subject understanding, subject knowledge, construct arguments, creativity, practical skills and presentation skills
Viva voce exams (live oral tests)	Critical thinking, oral communication, subject understanding, subject knowledge and construct arguments
Storyboards, Mind Maps and design	Critical thinking, written communication, subject understanding, subject knowledge, construct arguments, creativity, practical skills and presentation skills
Team based learning (individual and group elements)	Critical thinking, written communication, subject understanding, subject knowledge, construct arguments, creativity, team work, practical skills and presentation skills
Presentations (individual or group)	Critical thinking, oral communication, subject understanding, subject knowledge, construct arguments, creativity, practical skills and presentation skills
Posters	Written communication, subject understanding, subject knowledge, creativity, practical skills and presentation skills
Simulations	Oral communication, practical skills, problem solving, creativity and self-reflection
Multiple choice questions in class	Subject understanding, subject knowledge and problem solving
Oral report (individual or group)	Critical thinking, oral communication, subject understanding, subject knowledge and construct arguments
Business/elevator pitches	Critical thinking, oral communication, subject understanding, subject knowledge, construct arguments, presentation skills and self-reflection

Type of assessment	Skills being assessed
Case studies	Critical thinking, written communication, subject understanding, subject knowledge, construct arguments, problem solving
Annotated bibliographies	Critical thinking, written communication, subject understanding, subject knowledge, research skills
Artefacts (images and drawings)	Subject understanding, subject knowledge, creativity and practical skills
Student-led and managed conferences	Oral communication, team work, creativity, problem solving, practical skills and presentation skills
Reports	Written communication, subject understanding, subject knowledge, reflection, problem solving and research skills
Portfolios	Written communication, subject understanding, subject knowledge, practical skills, reflection, problem solving and research skills
Live projects	Oral communication, team work, creativity, problem solving, practical skills and presentation skills

 ACTIVITY

The differences between a report and an essay

Some of the key differences between a report and an essay are outlined below. Try to think of two more characteristics for each type.

Report	Essay
Has a formal structure	Structures around an introduction
Has a specific purpose	More open to your interpretation
Has sections with headings	Written in paragraphs

For the purposes of this chapter, some of the more common forms of written assessment are discussed and presented, i.e. reports, essays, portfolios, case studies, online discussion boards and exams. The following sections look at what they are, the common concerns, and how to understand and break the tasks down, including top tips for approaching the assessment and an example in the tourism, hospitality and events industry. The chapter then covers a few more innovative types near the end.

WRITING ESSAYS AND REPORTS IN TOURISM, HOSPITALITY AND EVENTS

Reports and essays are very different types of assessment. Writing a report is a very different skill than writing an essay. Reports have a formalised structure that can differ depending on the person or people that you are writing the report for.

Written reports

These are several reasons why you may be asked to write a report. The assignment may require that you read a case study and then produce a report to make a proposal or recommendation for change. Alternatively, you may be asked to analyse and solve a problem and report on your findings, or it could be as simple as reporting on the progress of a project. Before you start writing your report it is important to plan it first. There are many ways to plan a report – the most common are Mind Maps (see Chapter 5). The standard structure for a report is usually as follows:

1. *Title page*

   The title page provides the reader with the details they need to know about, who the report is from, who it is for, the date the report was created and the title of the report.

2. *Contents page*

   The contents page is used to identify the page numbers in relation to the separate headings and sub-headings for the reader.

3. *Summary*

   This is sometimes called the Executive Summary. It provides the reader with an overview of what to expect in the report.

4. *Introduction*

   The introduction gives the reader an outline of how to read the report, what has been included, why it has been included and how you have used this information in your findings.

5. *Main body of the report*

   The main body contains everything that you want to inform people of. This section is divided into headings and sub-headings relating to each of the areas you are presenting.

6. *Conclusions*

   It may be that you are asked to produce your conclusions and recommendations in one section. This is why it is important to check on how the report needs to be structured. However, a conclusion should provide the reader with clear information on what you have found in the overall report.

7. *Recommendations*

   These follow the conclusions. For example, you have been asked to read a case study on the productivity of the kitchen staff in a hotel. From your conclusion you have identified that the kitchen has too many staff in the afternoons, with staff not having enough work to do. However, in the evenings the kitchen staff are finding it difficult to cope with the volume of customer orders, which results in customer complaints. Your recommendations would be to change the shift patterns of staff to ensure there are a suitable number of trained staff in the evenings and less staff in the day.

8. *References*

   You must reference all the literature you have used to provide supporting evidence in your report.

9. *Appendices*

This is where you add information that is not necessarily part of the report but could be background reading. For example, you could provide the reader with a detailed spreadsheet on the number of food covers provided daily both in the afternoon and in the evening for a period of six months to show where you obtained your findings from.

Remember, a report is about providing formalised information, where you can make proposals or recommendations for change. Present the findings of an investigation or project, or just report progress. Report writing is an important skill to master, as you will be frequently asked to provide a report to managers, committees or working groups in the workplace.

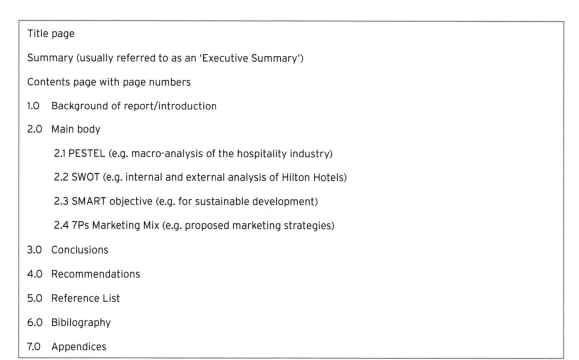

Title page

Summary (usually referred to as an 'Executive Summary')

Contents page with page numbers

1.0   Background of report/introduction

2.0   Main body

    2.1 PESTEL (e.g. macro-analysis of the hospitality industry)

    2.2 SWOT (e.g. internal and external analysis of Hilton Hotels)

    2.3 SMART objective (e.g. for sustainable development)

    2.4 7Ps Marketing Mix (e.g. proposed marketing strategies)

3.0   Conclusions

4.0   Recommendations

5.0   Reference List

6.0   Bibilography

7.0   Appendices

Figure 6.2   Example of a marketing report structure for Hilton Hotels

Writing an essay

The other form of longer written assessments are, of course, essays. These are particularly popular in social science-based subjects like tourism. An essay is very different to a report, although they share some similar principles. Sometimes the assessment might even just be the essay plan. This planning stage is a popular 'mid-term' assessment for many modules used by tutors to ensure students are planning their work.

Essays do not have sub-headings. They are structured but free-flowing narratives with an argument woven throughout. You may think it counter-intuitive but you might find it helpful to write your introduction last! First, start drafting your essay from the main body by separating each main topic/idea and write a paragraph about it. Let the ideas flow rather than being concerned with your spelling, punctuation and grammar – this can be checked in the final draft. Leave some space for editing, i.e. adding or removing text.

Ensure paragraphs have an opening sentence that situates your topic/idea, making it clear to the reader what the paragraph is about. The rest of the paragraph should include information that is relevant to that topic and that supports your argument. After you have constructed a main body, then write the conclusion. A conclusion is a summary of the key points/areas discussed within the main body of the essay and should relate back to the title and/or overarching question.

Finally, write the introduction. Why? It is easier to introduce what the essay says after you have written it. Introductions should 'set the scene' for the reader to inform them of what will be discussed within the essay.

The basic structure of an essay is along these lines:

1. *Introduction paragraph*

    First sentence – make it a strong and clear one.

    State your argument and position – this is your thesis statement.

2. *Body paragraphs*

    These paragraphs should explain, describe or present an argument related to your topic. You will need several of these covering different points, but each must include: an overall narrative on the theme of this paragraph in relation to your overall argument and evidence to support your idea in this section (your thesis). This might include some data and statistics; information and research on the subject with supporting references to literature and material; and perhaps potential counter/ opposing arguments but provide a convincing reason why your argument is more plausible.

3. *Conclusion and summary*

    Restate your main argument.

    Support the argument with a brief recap of the evidence.

What does a tutor look for in an academic essay?

There is some basic advice that Creme and Lea (1997) offered which remains true: 1. answer the question; 2. answer the question; 3. answer the question! In brief, the most important aspects in writing an essay are:

*   Ensuring your answer adheres closely to the title and question set.
*   Having a clear and relevant structure that will help you show the development of your argument.
*   Using critical writing, with descriptive writing being used where necessary, but kept to a minimum.

If you wish to find out a little more about how to write essays and structure them, there are many study guides available, including Greetham (2018), Godwin (2019) and Weyers and McMillan (2011). Hounsell (1984) has also written on essay writing and how essays should be marked. His research has shown that areas that cause students the most difficulty are planning and selecting material, so you need to invest time in these areas.

PORTFOLIOS AND PATCHWORK ASSIGNMENTS

A portfolio or patchwork assignment is a format which brings together different elements (patches) over time into a consolidated assessment. In THE subject areas, this could be several documents relating to a work placement, a field trip or a real-life business case. For this kind of assessment your tutor will be expecting you to present diverse kinds of learning and/or content. You can express knowledge and learning in a variety of different ways. This form of assignment is a collation of materials which make up a series of patches which are brought together via integrative writing and a narrative that stitches parts together.

You will need to provide a reflective and unifying commentary where you produce a personal synthesis that draws together research, reflection and references. It pulls together learning throughout the module, rather than a single assessment at the end. To make it manageable for marking, you might find that your fellow students will peer assess elements of your portfolio and then the tutor will mark the overarching narrative.

Sometimes the tutor will review an early 'patch' as formative assessment. The top tip is to build it up over the course of the module and not leave it until the last moment.

Increasingly, portfolios are submitted and compiled electronically. Common portfolio software systems are Mahara (Moodle based platform), Pebblepad or MyPortfolio. These technological approaches often allow small sections to be built up over time and can be made available for review and comment by your tutor as you build it up. An online approach can also facilitate a group portfolio where different members of a team can contribute different elements with each person contributing a single patch and then there is some 'stitching' to bring it all together.

ACTIVITY

Portfolio assessment for a live event exercise

A common way to assess a live event assessment that you might be asked to plan and deliver (usually as a group assessment) is with a portfolio. The portfolio must demonstrate understanding of the research, design, planning, coordination and evaluation processes involved in putting on an event. Evidence needs to include marketing, administration and a risk assessment. It should be presented clearly, creatively and structured in a way that is accessible and professional. Below are the kinds of documents you should consider including, but can you think of any other documents that might be useful to include?

- Table of contents
- Executive summary
- Introduction
- List of the event goal and objectives – what was it aiming to achieve and why?
- Research into other similar events and into all key aspects such as choices of food and drink, décor and location
- Marketing plan and strategy
- Potentially include a SWOT analysis (strengths, weaknesses, opportunities and threats for holding the event)
- Budget
- Organisational chart of how the group worked and roles taken
- Floor or site plan with stalls/key elements shown

(Continued)

- Risk assessment
- Timeline and production schedule
- Example of how feedback on the event was collated, e.g. survey
- Evaluation and reflection of the event (including how it could have been improved)
- Images of the event and key moments
- Examples of printed material (publicity, e.g. leaflets, social media, press release, sample invitations)
- References and resource list

CASE STUDIES AS AN ASSESSMENT

Case studies are real life examples of tourism, events and hospitality in action and can link between theory and practice. If being used for a time-constrained assessment, they tend to be provided in advance. Usually you will be asked to work through a case study to identify the problem(s), reflect on it and offer potential solutions. Ensure that you draw out the important information and key points in the case and write it up in a similar way to a report.

Deloitte has an interactive tool where you can practise answering case study scenarios. It demonstrates what makes a good answer and can be found at: www2.deloitte.com/us/en/pages/careers/articles/join-deloitte-case-interview-preptool.html.

In addressing a case study, some top tips are:

- Be clear about what you're being asked to do. Understand what the problem is and read the questions carefully.
- Read the case study carefully and assess which parts of the information are relevant.
- Try to list key points to be considered and perhaps some arguments for/against the various strategies or issues raised.
- Manage your time to ensure you complete the exercise.
- Ensure your response is relevant, clear and concise.

ONLINE DISCUSSION BOARDS

Increasingly online discussion boards are being used as an assessment method. Graded discussion assessments are increasingly used for online distance learning courses, but they are also used to deliver a blended learning offering (mixture of face-to-face teaching and online material and exercises) and you should know how to engage with these kinds of assessed discussions. Hoag and Baldwin (2000) found that students actually learn more in an online collaborative forum than in face-to-face teaching and, through this assessment method, you also gain experience of team work, time management, technology and communication as well as being able to defend ideas, explain concepts and integrate different views. Its reflective nature means that they are regarded as more equitable ways to assess because it gives voice to all students (Swan et al., 2006).

You will usually be expected to contribute both ideas and thoughts, but also evidence your response to posts by your peers. Most assessments will focus on engagement and participation, academic discourse and intellectual contribution, supporting evidence and structure. Here is an example of a typical assessment rubric for an online discussion showing the criteria for a fail, pass and high grade. Weighted marks are purely illustrative of this kind of assessment.

Table 6.6   Example marking criteria for an online discussion

Assessment criteria (example)	Fail	Pass	High pass/distinction level
Frequency and timing of contributions 15%	Postings are minimal and made on a random basis without adding any substantive content or contribution to the discussion. Does not respond to most postings from peers; rarely participates freely; makes initial discussion posts last day of module/week.	Several contributions, although not well placed within the discussion. Responds to most postings several days after initial discussion; limited initiative; initiates discussion late in the module/week.	A very good balance of posting frequency has been achieved. Posts are well considered in terms of their frequency and drive the discussion forward. Consistently responds to postings made by peers and/or faculty in less than 24 hours; demonstrates good self-initiative.
Interaction and engagement with group 15%	Does not make effort to participate in learning community as it develops; seems indifferent to others. May convey antagonistic attitude towards views of others.	Occasionally makes meaningful reflection on group's efforts; marginal effort to become involved with group. Simply acknowledges views of others.	Displays a high level of sensitivity towards the needs of community; consistently attempts to motivate the group discussion; presents creative approaches to topic.
Content of contribution 40%	Posts do not relate to discussion topic(s); no relevancy; makes short remarks with little substance.	Frequently posts items that are related to the discussion content; posts prompt further discussion of topic(s). Contributions demonstrate the ability to critically evaluate ideas.	Without fail posts topics related to the discussion; incorporates and cites highly appropriate additional references related to topic(s). High level analysis and critique shown of the discussion topic.
Supporting evidence 20%	No supporting evidence or theoretical underpinning evident within the contributions.	Some evidence of wider reading and research to inform contributions and provide evidence for argument. Very descriptive in nature.	Extensive evidence of wider reading and research to inform contributions and evidence argument. High level of critical evaluation of theoretical underpinning.
Clarity and structure of contribution 10%	Most posts have poor spelling and grammar and appear as though they were rushed.	Some spelling and grammatical errors in posts. Unclear connection to topic(s) as evidenced in minimal expression of opinions or ideas.	Consistent use of correct grammar and spelling. Expresses opinions and ideas in a clear and concise manner with obvious connection to the discussion topic(s).

EXAMINATIONS

Exams are the assessment type that seem to cause the most anxiety, but examinations are increasingly rare in the subject of tourism, hospitality and events, as many argue they don't assess the kinds of skills required for these subjects. However, in many undergraduate courses, you may well need to complete modules in business subjects useful for a career in these subjects, such as accounting, strategic management and project management. Often these subjects are assessed with an exam because they are based on undertaking calculations and adopt multiple choice questions.

Exams are not an authentic assessment, so why are they used?

Exams are often considered to be non-authentic methods of assessment because they do not require you to demonstrate skills that are used in the workplace. What sort of job would ask you to complete an exam as part of a project? You will be asked to write a report, provide a plan or present at a meeting, but you are not going to be asked to take an exam, so why are they used in some universities? They are often used if there are large numbers of students taking a particular subject as it is quicker for staff to be able to mark large numbers of exams rather than larger numbers of essays and reports.

Additionally, they can show how well you can work and produce information in a pressurised situation that is timed. They can also be used to test and provide feedback earlier in the teaching period so that lecturers can evaluate how well students are understanding the subject area. If this is the case, then the exam is often an in-class test and the lecturer is able to identify what needs to be covered again or any additional support they need to provide to students. Additionally, exams can be used to give you the experience of having to explain your knowledge under time pressure conditions. This is often the case with oral presentations. Whatever the reason for the exam being set, the purpose of the exam is to test your knowledge, understanding and ability to apply that knowledge and understanding to answer set questions.

Types of exams

There are many different forms of exams that you could be asked to complete. The most common ones used in universities are:

- Multiple choice

  This type of exam can vary in length. Sometimes you will be given a lot of questions to answer and in others there could only be a short number of questions. For each of the questions set you are required to choose an answer or answers to that question from a list of answers provided, by either putting a cross, blocking out a box or putting a tick in a box next to your choice of answer/answers. Never leave an answer blank; it is far better to have an educated guess than have no answer at all.

- Short answer exams

  This form of exam can contain several questions that you will have to provide a short answer to. They often require you to write one or two paragraphs when answering the set questions. Write your answers using full sentences (unless you are asked to provide bullet pointed answers) and use appropriate language and terminology for your subject area.

- Exams that require an essay

  These are a common form of exam. You are often presented with several questions and asked to choose which to write your answer on. You will be expected to write a short essay, engaging with theories and supporting evidence in your answer. You will be expected to write in full sentences and follow the structure of an essay: introduction, main body and conclusion. Sometimes the marks can vary for each of the questions so allocate your time and approximate word count accordingly.

- Open exam or open book exam

  This is where you are given the questions in advance of the exam to allow you to prepare an answer. You are often allowed to take a set amount of notes in with you and a textbook. However, the expectations of this exam are higher than if you had not been given time to prepare. Therefore, it is important that you organise your notes well and ensure you have everything you need prior to entering the exam.

- Vivas (oral exam)

  A viva (oral exam) is designed to test your knowledge and your ability to voice that knowledge and the key concepts and theories related to the subject you have been studying. More often than not you will be able to take notes with you. If you are asked a question you do not understand you can ask to have it repeated or re-phrased. These are covered more in the next chapter.

- Online exams

  These are becoming more and more common and can be set as any of the above. You will be expected to log into a particular area and follow the instructions for the exam.

However, with all these different forms of exam above, none of them should come as a surprise. You will be notified in advance what type of assessment you will be expected to undertake and informed how that will take place.

Preparing for exams

Table 6.7   Top tips for success when taking exams

Read the paper carefully	Too often students don't read what is expected of them and waste time answering too many questions or not enough. You only need to answer what you are asked to answer. Always make sure you know exactly what it is you are expected to do. The instructions should always be with the exam paper. Knowing what you need to do can help alleviate the stress of the actual exam.
Manage your time	Check that you have identified how many questions you are going to answer in the time allotted. Write a brief plan on how much time you are going to take for each question and brief notes on what you are going to say. If you stick to your plan, then you will be able to provide a suitable answer to all the questions. Remember the examiner will know how much time you have had and will not expect an answer that would have taken you three days to write.
Read the selected question/s	Read each question a couple of times before you decide on the most appropriate for you to answer. Then make notes on what you want to say in your answer and how you are going to structure the answer.

(Continued)

Table 6.7   (Continued)

Plan your answer	You should follow a similar method to that used when writing any other essay. Less evidence and fewer examples than for coursework. You can write less about each point. You do not need to give a bibliography or detailed references.
Don't panic	Panicking causes more panic and anxiety.
	Use a relaxation technique; slowing down your breathing can help. Note down any words that you feel are relevant on a separate sheet of paper and you will be surprised at how quickly you can break through that block and start writing. Ask yourself questions about what it is you think the marker will look for in an answer. Write those questions down if it helps you stay on track. It is better to make these notes to kick-start your writing than to sit there doing nothing.
Common pitfalls	Not turning up on time or arriving at the wrong room. Check that you have the correct details for your exams in advance.
	Fill in the correct details on the exam form. Make sure you have your student card with you with your ID number.
	Give the appropriate amount of time to the questions you are going to answer. There is no point in a three-hour exam giving two hours to the answer of a question that only holds ten marks and one hour to a question that has 90 marks. Do not spend most of your time on one answer and only leave a few minutes for another.
	Don't just give a list of the information you know about an answer. Show that you have engaged with the question and that you can make sense of the question through your answer. Develop an argument, a line of reasoning, evaluate opposing viewpoints and give supporting evidence. It is important that you keep to an academic written structure. Make sure you have an introduction and conclusion.

 REFLECTION EXERCISE

How you feel about exams

The exercise below is a reflective task (see Chapter 10 for more information on personal reflection). This task is designed to help you as an individual to identify what it is about an exam that you struggle with. Take some time to complete the sections. There are two areas. The first asks you to identify what areas you struggle with when leading up to an exam. In this area list down all the issues you have experienced in the past (you have been given a couple of examples to get you started), then reflect on these problem areas you have identified. Through your own personal reflection, identify what you can do to turn this around and prevent it being an issue for you.

The second section is similar to the first. However, here you are asked to identify issues and struggles that you may face in the actual exam (again there are two examples to start you off). Make sure that you are as honest as you can be with yourself when reflecting, as this honesty will be what allows you to reflect and make changes to your approach to exams. Remember no one is going to see this except you.

Most universities will have some form of study support or counselling available for people who struggle with taking exams. If you identify through your reflection below that you would benefit from some professional support in overcoming your exam struggles, then find out what is available and use the service. Asking for help demonstrates maturity and professionalism. We have all at some time or other struggled with some aspect of academia and have had to ask for help or guidance.

Table 6.8 Personal reflection on taking exams

Identify the areas that you struggle with leading up to an exam	What can you do to change this?
Poor revision and preparation	I can prepare in advance for the revision and preparation, making sure I make notes on the subject area so that I can use them to revise. I can also make sure that I have read through some previous exam papers to see how to give a model answer and identify the types of answers I need to provide.
Lack of time management to allow for revision	I need to ensure that I do not leave my revision to the last minute. I will do this by ensuring I manage my time in advance of the exam to revise and prepare.
Identify the areas you struggle with during the exam	**What can you do to change this?**
I struggle with recalling information	I can undertake some old papers to train myself in answering the questions and recalling information. I can make notes and plan my answer in the exam. I can note down everything I know about the subject area that the question relates to. In the exam I can ensure that I use the most relevant points from my notes, ticking them off as I go.
I panic during an exam and end up running out of time to complete all the questions	I can produce a brief plan and time schedule and stick to those times to ensure I answer all the questions and have time to read through my answers at the end. I can learn some relaxation techniques and apply them during the exam to avoid panicking.

Revision timetable, notes and guides

It is important that you manage your time and give yourself enough time to revise effectively for an exam (see Chapter 11 for further information). The following table will guide you on the areas that you might want to consider implementing before you start to revise so that the process of revision is as organised and stress-free as possible.

Table 6.9 Planning an exam revision schedule

Start early	Don't leave your revision to the last minute, as this is not an effective way of learning information.
Make a plan, decide what you are going to cover and stick to it	You should know what will be covered in the exam, as it will follow the teaching of the module you have covered. This makes life easier for you. You should make a note of all the areas that you have covered and schedule time to revise them all. The plan can be set up the same way as you have set up your time management plan. Allocate the amount of time you want to spend on each area and book it into your time management plan.
Make notes you can refer to	Find a method that works for you in note taking. Make sure you keep your notes tidy and organised. Keep all the topics separate and ensure that you know exactly what your notes are relating to and why. There are many different methods for example (as covered in Chapter 4): • Use note cards with headers telling you the topic and area covered • Make notes on your lesson notes (if these notes are organised well) with sticky notes, colour-coded if that helps

(Continued)

Table 6.9   (Continued)

	• Use files on a computer. Give each file a subject title and topic area. You can put all the files relating to one subject in a master file with the module/subject title. Notes will help you retain the information you are trying to learn and allow you to clarify the relationships between the materials you are trying to remember. Additionally, if you make notes it helps you to remember and return several times to test yourself on the knowledge that you need to know.
Give suitable time to each subject	Think of revision as a job that must be completed. You need to give suitable time to revision. Only revising one hour per day is not going to give you the same results as spending five hours per day. Don't spend all your time on one subject or area. If you have more than one exam for a range of modules or subjects, then it is important to ensure that you have suitable time for all the areas.
Take regular short breaks	You will need to make sure you have regular breaks while you are revising to ensure that you stay as fresh as possible to learn the materials. Try to have 10 minutes break for every 45 minutes of revision.

FEEDBACK AND FEED-FORWARD

So, you have completed an assessment, and you want to know how you have done! This will happen through a process of receiving feedback and feed-forward. Carless (2015: 192) defined feedback as 'a dialogic process in which learners make sense of information from varied sources and use it to enhance the quality of their work or learning strategies'. Hattie (1999) presents feedback as 'the most powerful single moderator that enhances achievement'.

As a student you will be expected to demonstrate 'feedback literacy' (Carless and Boud, 2018) where you are encouraged to develop an understanding of what feedback is and how it can be managed effectively for your learning. It is important that you recognise when you are receiving feedback and learn how to use your feedback to aid your learning. Using feedback from an assessment to help you in the future is known as 'feeding forward' as it will help in future assessments.

 REFLECTION EXERCISE

Using feedback

Think about a time when you were given a piece of feedback. Who gave you the feedback and what was it about? Write down how you could use that feedback to help you feed forward to a different assessment or situation?

1.   What were the main points in this feedback?
2.   What were the positive aspects in the feedback?
3.   What were the negative aspects in the feedback?
4.   What will you do differently in a future assessment?

Forms of feedback

There are numerous ways you receive feedback on your work; it is not just a mark at the end of a final assessment (summative assessment). Rather, the most valuable feedback is often during the class and is formative. The key thing is that you receive a range of feedback types and these will be from your tutor but also from your fellow students, and you are also advised to self-reflect and provide feedback to yourself (Sackstein, 2015).

Table 6.10   Types of feedback

Type of feedback	Nature of feedback
Informal feedback	Can occur at any time as it is usually spontaneous such as comments in class, or during an online session. The trick is identifying when you are receiving this kind of feedback and working with it to improve your work.
Formal feedback	Usually planned and scheduled into the assessment process (via office hours or tutorials). Usually linked to assessment tasks and draws on the marking criteria set in the module/unit.
Formative feedback	This type of feedback aims to help improve your learning and understanding. It should be provided early in the module/unit and seeks to help you identify mistakes and where you can improve without affecting your final mark/grade. It should be provided at regular intervals during your course/module.
Summative feedback	Usually planned and scheduled into the assessment process. This should explicitly link your work to learning outcomes and marking criteria. You will usually get written feedback (increasingly online for written assessments) on your work accompanied with a grade.
Student peer feedback	Your fellow peers can often provide the most useful and insightful feedback. This can be informal during the course of your classes and learning but can be more structured in terms of exercises in class such as reviewing each other's work. Providing feedback to other students will also help you develop skills such as writing constructive feedback and reflection. Often your peers will be much harsher markers than your tutors!
Self feedback	It is important you can assess and judge your own work so you become more independent (Sackstein, 2015). You should be given model answers and marking criteria. Use these to identify your own strengths and weaknesses. This approach is the ultimate way to develop your own feedback literacy. To support and develop a greater depth of learning and assessment literacy, it is important to be able to accurately self-assess your own work. The kinds of questions that you should be asking yourself in each assessment are: 1. Where do I see the strengths of my assignment with regards to the marking criteria? 2. Where do I think my assignment needs improvement with regards to the marking criteria? 3. How could I improve these weaknesses with regards to the marking criteria?

Once you have received your feedback, try to identify the main points and think about what it actually means. You might find that it is useful to write it down in your own feedback log and that will help you look back and learn from earlier mistakes. If you know which areas you need to improve on, you can plan how you will address these areas in future assessments.

Using a feedback log

When you read Chapter 10 on Reflective Thinking, you may want to think about how you reflect and use your feedback. One way is to develop a feedback log which you return to every time you complete an assessment. This way you should learn from your mistakes and start to identify where you need to improve your writing. An example that you might like to follow as a template is shown in Table 6.11.

Table 6.11   An example of a feedback log

Date	Assessment type	Areas done well (positive feedback)	Areas for improvement	What I need to do for future assessments? Personal reflection
Example entry 6/7/20	Essay	Good structure and well presented Clear argument throughout the essay	Include more evidence to support claims – use more academic references and evidence by using citations Ensure you include a conclusion paragraph to summarise key arguments	Read more academic sources and ensure these are cited where appropriate Include a clear summary paragraph at the end Ensure I re-emphasise my argument

Start to build up a feedback log for yourself. It is also a useful document to have when you start applying for jobs as you may have examples of some lovely comments that colleagues or peers have written or said about you.

 ━━━ THINK POINT ━━━━━━━━━━━━━━━━━━━━━━━━━━━━━

Now that you have read this chapter on assessment, re-rate yourself on a scale of 1 (not confident at all) to 10 (extremely confident) about how confident you feel about tackling assessments. What was most helpful? What will you do to improve this self-rating?

CONCLUSION

In this chapter we have covered:

* Key words and terms used in the assessment process.
* Outlining the value and purpose of assessment.
* The different types of written assessment most commonly used in tourism, events and hospitality degree programmes.
* How to approach, plan and structure your written assessments.
* The skills you will need to demonstrate in different forms of assessment such as using persuasive language and forming arguments.
* Advice on how to prepare for different types of exams and how you reflect on your approach to them.
* What are the different forms of feedback and how to use feedback to improve your work and enhance your learning.

FURTHER READING

Creme, P. and Lea, M.R. (1997) *Writing at University: A Guide for Students*. Buckingham: Open University Press.

Godwin, J. (2019) *Planning Your* Essay, 3rd edn. Pocket Study Skills. London: Macmillan/Red Globe Press.

Greetham, B. (2018) *How to Write Better Essays*. Macmillan Study Skills. London: Macmillan.

McMillan, K. and Weyers, J. (2011) *How to Succeed in Examinations and Assessments*. Harlow: Pearson.

Sackstein, S. (2015) *Teaching Students to Self-Assess: How do I Help Students Reflect and Grow as Learners?* Danvers, MA: ASCD Arias.

Weyers, J. and McMillan, K. (2011) *How to Write Essays and Assignments*. Smarter Study Skills. London: Prentice Hall.

Useful web resource

An excellent student-written guide on using feedback has been written by Sheffield Hallam University (2010) and is available via the Advance HE website – www.advance-he.ac.uk/knowledge-hub/feedback-student-guide-using-feedback

7

ASSESSMENTS: PRESENTATIONS (GROUP AND INDIVIDUAL)

 CHAPTER LEARNING OBJECTIVES

By the end of this chapter you should be able to:

- Describe what a presentation is.
- Explain the purpose of presentations.
- Differentiate between informative and persuasive presentation tasks.
- Describe the different types of presentation that exist and what is involved.
- Be prepared to work individually or in a group to research, deliver and evaluate a presentation.

 GLOSSARY

- **Pecha Kutcha ('chit-chat' in Japanese):** a 20 x 20 presentation format where 20 slides run automatically for 20 seconds each, giving you just a few minutes in which to tell your story.
- **Presentation:** a process of presenting and communicating a topic or idea to an audience (physically or online).

INTRODUCTION

This chapter covers an important type of assessment you will encounter at university: the **presentation**. A presentation is an oral assessment that can be stand-alone or supported with visual aids, props and handouts. This chapter outlines what presentations are, their purpose, the types of presentations you might be asked to give, and the skills you need to prepare, practise and perform effectively in both group and individual presentation tasks.

You will be assessed in a variety of ways at university or college. Your tutors need to assess your learning but they will also want you to develop the skills required in the workplace and for further academic study. Presentations are a key component of any university's assessment strategy, and you will find that as you progress through your course you will be expected to give longer, more complex presentations. They are used as an assessment method within tourism, hospitality and event courses in particular given their customer-facing nature, the importance of working as a team in most roles, and the requirement of many jobs in the sector to engage an audience effectively and professionally.

Giving presentations can be nerve-racking and the key is to prepare, practise and perform (Gallagher, 2013). You should receive tutor and peer feedback on each of these elements and, as outlined in Chapter 6, you should be able to reflect on what you did well and your areas for development, which will help you build a set of actions to implement when you give your next presentation.

WHAT IS A PRESENTATION?

Presentations as part of your university studies will normally take the form of timed oral assessment and are designed to test your verbal communication skills, as well as your ability to research, select and structure information effectively. They also assess your knowledge of a topic and your ability to answer questions from the audience and/or your tutor (Dryden et al., 2003; London School of Economics, 2020). Anderson (2013) suggests that presentations are much more than this: they are a story and you are the narrator – the expert in the room – whose job it is to take the audience on a journey of discovery about your topic. It has also been argued that presentations should be considered a form of performance that draws on theatre techniques such as delivering monologues to engage audiences (Curren-Everett, 2019; Salit, 2017). Much like an actor on the stage you need to use your voice and body to keep people interested in what you are saying and elicit positive responses from your audience. For example, you should avoid being monotone in your presentation, make eye contact with your audience members and avoid standing behind the lectern or computer station as you are presenting (see Chapter 14 on how you can use your body language in a positive and engaging way).

THE PURPOSE OF PRESENTATIONS

Presentations tend to have one of two objectives: informative or persuasive. As the names suggest, the purpose of an informative presentation is to convey key information about a topic to your audience, while a persuasive presentation is an attempt to influence your audience's attitudes, beliefs, behaviour or opinions. It is important that you read the assessment task carefully to determine which type of presentation you are being asked to deliver and structure your presentation around this objective (Chivers and Shoolbred, 2007; University of Leicester, 2020b).

ACTIVITY

Informative and persuasive presentations

Read the presentation tasks shown in Table 7.1 and decide if you are being asked to give an informative or a persuasive presentation.

Table 7.1   Informative and persuasive presentation tasks

Task	Informative or persuasive?	Why?
Select one of England's Destination Management Organisations (DMOs) and describe its key features.		
Why are Destination Management Organisations (DMOs) a crucial part of tourism infrastructure in England?		
How might a destination rebrand itself after a crisis to reassure and attract tourists? Use examples from recent crises		

Presentations may also have other purposes. Firstly, they give you an opportunity to practise and hone skills that you will need in the workplace in a safe space as you will have to conduct research on a given topic and communicate about it either informatively or persuasively to different sorts of audiences, using visual aids (Dryden et al., 2003). Secondly, presentations may help you to become a more confident communicator in other scenarios or formats, which is a valuable skill in the workplace (University of Birmingham, 2020).

STUDENT INSIGHT

Clara Rowe, student on International Tourism Management, The University of Lincoln (2017–2020)

Throughout my first degree, presentations were an integral part of my learning. Having no experience of presenting prior to university, I quickly had to learn the relevant skills. During the first semester of University I was faced with the daunting prospect of recorded and assessed presentations alongside regular informal presentations during seminars. During my first presentation I felt very anxious, but still achieved a high grade due to the content of the presentation. Through regular exposure to presentations I slowly became more comfortable presenting in front of peers and tutors and learnt to manage my nerves. Having the ability to present effectively has also developed my spoken communication, body language and confidence.

I have learnt that it is essential to fully understand your topic in preparation for questions that you may receive regarding the presentation and to rehearse the presentation so that you can speak with confidence and avoid the unprofessional practice of reading from the screen. I highly recommended putting the time and effort into developing presentation skills, as they are essential for both academic assessments and employability.

TYPES OF PRESENTATIONS

Presentations can be prepared and delivered individually or as a group (Van Emden, 2010). The most common types of presentations you will be asked to do as a student are:

- Oral presentation with or without visual aids
- Poster presentation
- Workshop presentation
- Role play exercise
- Video presentation
- Online presentation

The most common type of presentation is a timed oral presentation in front of a live audience. You might be asked to use a visual aid via a software package, a digital or hard-copy infographic diagram, or a whiteboard. You will probably be asked to present formally, followed by a question and answer session with the audience.

For the last 30 years or so PowerPoint has been the most common visual aid for students and staff at universities (Beyer, 2011). It has many benefits, such as the ability to seamlessly link to multi-media sources, the flexibility to allow the presenter to create slides with textual, visual, and audio cues on them, and the potential for ensuring the materials meet the needs of students with specific learning needs, However, PowerPoint has also been criticised for creating a culture in which students may feel they must use visual aids when in fact they are redundant in many situations; speak to or read from a screen rather than engaging with their audience; and spend their preparation time playing around with fancy visuals rather than making sure the structure and content of the presentation is sound (Morgan-Thomas, 2015). This has led to teachers trying to encourage students to use different presentation techniques such as **Pecha Kutcha** (Pecha Kutcha, 2020).

Poster presentations are becoming more common and are a way of presenting your work visually and verbally at the same time as your peers (Bracher, 1998; Hollander, 2002). Poster presentations usually take place in an open area and are less formal than oral presentations. You will usually be asked to produce a large poster critically explaining the key elements of your research and you will be expected to be able to stand close to your poster so that you can discuss the content. There are various tools to help you prepare your poster, including PowerPoint for Posters, which allows you to prepare your poster on your PC and have it enlarged to A1 or A0 size at a printers.

THINK POINT

What technical or ICT skills might you need to develop? Are you comfortable with all the key elements of PowerPoint?

If you complete a live events module as part of your degree, you may be required to deliver a workshop presentation to your peers, teachers, industry professionals and members of the public. A workshop presentation usually involves an informative or persuasive presentation alongside a practical element that allows people to learn a new skill. These types of presentations allow you to develop your training and demonstration skills.

Another type of assessment that uses some of the same skills as giving a presentation is a role play activity. Role play exercises explore a specific scenario in which you may be asked to take on particular characteristics or behaviours, allowing you to prepare for and practise real situations. They also help you and your audience critically analyse issues from different perspectives, which can help develop your problem-solving skills and emotional intelligence (Bethal, 2014; Morgan-Thomas, 2015).

STUDENT INSIGHT

A live assessment in the Tourism and Events Business Management Module (Level 4), Anglia Ruskin University, UK

Small groups of three or four students participated in a role-play practical exercise in which they were interchangeably clients and travel consultants/tour guides (leisure, business or niche).

The first stage was, as clients, to discuss their needs, wants and expectations, the type of trip/tour that they would like to participate in, and their reasons for travelling (e.g. leisure, business). The travel consultants were then expected to present their ideas based on their first meeting with the 'client'. If it failed to meet the brief, tour guides revisited their initial objectives and presented a revised proposal.

The roles were then reversed so that each person in a group played both roles. This assessment enabled the students to work as part of a team, manage their own activities and keep a reflective log of the overall process.

Technology now allows us to prepare, create and upload video presentations via a mobile phone or digital camera and can be uploaded to a Virtual Learning Environment site (VLE). This will assess whether you can deliver a presentation without visual aids, develop your technological skills, and to prepare you for using video conferencing technology in the workplace. This same technology and software may also mean that you will be asked to produce an online presentation, which can stretch you creatively.

ACTIVITY

Practice a presentation

Select a tourism topic you feel passionate about. Write down the key points of the topic in bullet form. Set your timer on your mobile phone for two minutes. Video yourself talking about the topic for the allocated time. Watch the video back and critically reflect on your performance:

- What are you good at? For example, do you speak clearly and confidently? Did you manage to get all the key points across?
- What areas for development might you have? For example, are there any habits that you have when speaking that you weren't aware of, but that could be distracting for your audience?
- How are you going to address your areas for development before your next presentation?
- How are you going to incorporate the things you are good at into your next presentation?

PREPARING YOUR PRESENTATION

Preparing a presentation individually or as part of a group requires you to:

- Read the task carefully to ensure you understand what the assessment requires and what type of presentation you are being asked to give.
- Plan your time carefully to allow you to identify the aims and objectives of your presentation, complete the research, collate the research material, write the content, create supporting materials, practise, evaluate and edit the presentation.
- Familiarise yourself with the venue (e.g. classroom size, IT equipment).

In additon to this, a group presentation requires you to:

- Identify the different roles and tasks and distribute them fairly across the group members.
- Manage yourself and your peers effectively.
- Communicate effectively with everyone in the group. Listen to everyone in the group, even if you do not agree with their ideas. Join in discussions, conveying your own opinions to the rest of the group in a professional and respectful way.
- Use an online shared storage system that allows you all to contribute to one live document.

Group work can be challenging and frustrating at times, but it is highly likely that you will have to work as part of a team in your chosen career. In the workplace you rarely get an opporunity to choose who you work with, so group work allows you to learn about how you like to work, how you develop positive group dynamics, and how you might approach project management (see Chapter 18).

WORKING AND PRESENTING AS A GROUP

Some students dislike group work because of the problem of 'free loaders' who don't contribute or engage and yet expect to benefit from the hard work of others. There may be policies and processes to prevent this at your university (also see Chaper 15). You might care to establish group guidelines (perhaps in the form of a learning contract that everyone signs) and you should get to know the members in your group so that work can be divided between you sensibly. Ensure decisions are recorded and that every group member takes responsibility for their tasks.

How to structure a presentation

Whichever type and form of presentation you are asked to give, the basic structure of any effective presentation is similar, and should include:

- A clear introduction that 'sets the scene' (and introduces group members).
- The aims and objectives.
- A main body focused on your topic which is well organised, concise and logical with progression from general points to more specific ones.
- Slides with the key message (two or three key points) that the audience will take away (also called the 'take-home' message).

- A good conclusion that summarises the key points presented.
- A slide of references.
- Time to engage the audience in a question and answer session.

Effective supporting materials

If you are required to provide supporting information, you should ensure that:

- Your materials are accessible and inclusive. For example, they should be formatted appropriately to make sure that your audience can read and engage with them easily (a sans serif font of a large size) and that they are relevent to the members of your audience (e.g. you should take account of anyone in the audience with visual needs who might appreciate a large-print copy, for example).
- You use a good range of supporting visual information (e.g. graphs, images, data and illustrations).
- You do not put too much information on individual slides.
- You use a professional template and font.

 **THINK POINT**

This is a tip from Guy Kawasaki of Apple. He suggests that slideshows should:

- Contain no more than 10 slides
- Last no more than 20 minutes
- Use a font size of no less than 30 point.

DELIVERING THE PRESENTATION

To be an effective speaker, you should:

- Use a microphone wherever there is one available, rather than shouting.
- Make sure you have some water with you, placed where you are in no danger of knocking it over as you speak.
- Check that everyone can hear you in the room.
- Speak clearly and slowly.
- Face your audience and make eye contact with them as you speak.
- Speak in different tones to keep your audience interested.
- Try not to read from a script. Cue cards can be very helpful, but if you have practised your presentation you may not need any aide memoir. This will make your presentation feel a lot more natural.
- Give your audience the opportunity to engage with you.

Think about what aspects of giving a presentation worry you. How might you deal with these issues? What mechanisms have worked in the past to help you overcome similar concerns?

DEALING WITH NERVES

It is natural to be nervous before you give a presentation, but there are lots of things you can do to manage this. The first is to make sure that you are well prepared and rehearsed (Su, 2016; University of Birmingham, 2020), so that you can feel genuinely confident and in command of your material. You may practice mindfulness befroehand to raise your awareness of how you feel, to connect with your emotions and body, and to calm yourself (Grieve 2019; NHS, 2020; Su, 2016). Padesky and Greenberger (1995) found that thinking in a positive way can help improve your mood, so ensure you are well-rested, have eaten at your usual times and not let your nerves cause you to become obsessive. Continue to do things you enjoy in the lead up to an assessment (Gallagher, 2013).

If you have any physical, mental or emotional issues that mean giving a presentation is over-whelming for you, you should speak to staff in your Student Wellbeing Centre as they can include presentations in a Learning Support Plan, and ensure that reasonable adjustments are made for you. It is worth knowing that no matter how confident your peers appear, they are probably feeling nerv-ous as well, as highlighted by Rebecca below.

STUDENT INSIGHT

Rebecca Cardell, International Tourism Management Student at the University of Lincoln (2017–2020)

Presentations have always been an aspect of learning that challenged me during my time within education. The nerves of speaking within a large crowd of people without the aid of a script and losing my train of thought was always something that made me feel anxious and thus I avoided delivering presentations wher-ever I could.

During my time at university, presentations were inevitable, and my first presentation in my first year of university brought about nerves. However, due to the extensive research I did on the subject matter, I gained confidence and positive feedback. The skills needed for presentations are clear communication, confident delivery and leadership of your target audience. Due to extensive practice, especially within my study abroad period, I have developed confident delivery and adaptability, able to bring the presentation back to topic if necessary.

I recommended students delivering presentations to keep the presentation simple, keep eye contact and interact with the audience; this enables the audience to remain focused and make you sound more confident than you may be feeling.

Giving a presentation in your second or third language can be frightening, and you may be particu-larly concerned about your spoken language skills, technical language, pronunciation and grammar.

Again, do practise your presentation in advance and calm yourself using mindfulness techniques. Another tip is to just do the presentation in front of some friends who are native English speakers who can help you check your pronunciation and grammar. You should also access support in your university's language centre and library: nearly all universities offer international students support sessions via an English Language Centre and the university library. These centres have specialist staff who can help you develop your spoken language skills alongside your degree course.

 THINK POINT

Where can you get help at your university to help you develop your presentation skills? How are you going to develop the skills and attributes needed to work effectively in a group presentation task?

CONCLUSION

In this chapter we have covered:

- What a presentation is and what it is for.
- The difference between informative and persuasive presentation tasks.
- What types of presentations exist, what they involve, and why they are useful.
- How to plan, prepare and deliver an effective presentation as an individual and in a group.
- How to manage your nerves and deal with anxiety about giving a presentation.

FURTHER READING

Bethal, E. (2014) *Posters and Presentations*. Pocket Skills Guide. Basingstoke: Palgrave Macmillan.
Chivers, B. and Shoolbred, M. (2007) *A Student's Guide to Presentations*. London: Sage Publications.
Grieve, R. (2019) *Stand Up and Be Heard: Taking the Fear Out of Public Speaking at University*. London: Sage Publications.
Van Emden, J. (2010) *Presentation Skills for Students*. Basingstoke: Palgrave Macmillan.

8 CRITICAL THINKING AND QUESTIONING WHAT YOU ARE READING

CHAPTER LEARNING OBJECTIVES

By the end of this chapter you should be able to:

- Define the term 'critical thinking'.
- Identify the core principles of critical thinking.
- Read critically.
- Evaluate arguments effectively.
- Audit yourself to see if you have applied critical thinking and critical thinking skills to your work.

GLOSSARY

- **'Armchair observations':** commonly held notions that may be instinctively or intuitively appealing ('that feels right'), but that may not be borne out by the evidence.
- **Critical reading:** careful consideration of texts, assessing reliability, veracity, bias and relevance to your work.
- **Critical thinking:** the ability to evaluate the logical and evidence base for an idea, theory or opinion, objectively and considering the quality and provenance of the data available.
- **Fourth Industrial Revolution:** the introduction and widespread use of artificial intelligence (see also Chapter 35).
- **Greek Sceptics:** (*skeptis*, meaning investigation in Greek) some ancient philosophers called themselves sceptics meaning 'investigators'.

INTRODUCTION

This chapter begins with an examination of what we mean by the term **'critical thinking'** and explores some of the key tenets of critical thinking in Western and Eastern traditions. The chapter also briefly explains why critical thinking is important, both at university and in the workplace, particularly in the context of the **Fourth Industrial Revolution**, which is now well underway. It then goes on to explore the three key stages of critical thinking (**critical reading**, evaluating arguments and critical writing) and the skills you will need to be able to do these effectively. Finally, it provides you with a critical thinking checklist to help you draw together the content of the chapter and apply critical thinking and critical thinking skills to your university work.

WHAT IS CRITICAL THINKING?

Critical thinking is a complex notion (Tümkaya et al., 2009); it is much more than being able to gather information, present other peoples' ideas in a logical format, or to recall 'facts' (Hitchcock, 2017). It is the ability to think rationally and clearly, recognising 'good arguments even when we disagree with them, and poor arguments even when these support our own point of view' (Cottrell, 2015: 47). It is also the type of thinking adopted when looking at data, questioning reading, and communicating your ideas in a well-structured and reasoned manner that persuades the reader your arguments are justified and valid (University of Sussex, 2020). Critical thinking also involves the ability to engage in reflective thought and to challenge assumptions (Tümkaya et al., 2009).

All university graduates are expected to be able to engage in critical thinking; it is a core graduate attribute that we use to measure the standard of your work by (Hitchcock, 2018). To meet the threshold of a critical thinker you need an evaluative approach to all the sources you engage with, be able to make judgements on the extent to which the academic ideas, arguments and research findings that you come across in your studies are supported by valid, reliable information (University of Sussex, 2020). Critical thinking is also a key part of being creative, solving problems and coming up with new, original ideas. Without being able to think critically, in particular being able to see 'both sides of an issue, being open to new evidence that disconfirms your ideas, reasoning dispassionately, demanding that claims be backed by evidence, deducing and inferring conclusions from available facts' (Willingham, 2008: 21), you can't challenge existing wisdom to create new knowledge (Brookfield, 2015).

 ━━━━━━ STUDENT INSIGHT ━━━━━━━━━━━━━━━━━━━━━

Reflections on Critical Thinking, Michael Cartwright, University of Lincoln, BA (Hons) Business and Marketing

Critical thinking is one of the most important principles to apply at university to get the most out of your experience. To me, it's the process of looking at a piece of literature or research, and really understanding what it's saying. It's not enough to read a study and move on; to think critically means to dig into the heart of it. What does it say? Why does the author think this? What other topics does the article not explore? I find it particularly useful to get a holistic view of all these factors in my mind, so I can determine the overall usefulness and relevance of the article to my work. It's not enough in an academic setting to just accept the conclusions presented - you have to make up your own mind about them, and to do that you need to eval-uate everything, from the methodology to the author's perspective to other literature on the topic.

Critical thinking is crucial to develop strong and reasoned arguments in writing. Being able to apply this criticality to others' writings will not only make your own writing stronger, but also makes you think more deeply about the subjects you study. I find that thinking critically about every article I read makes me think about topics below the surface and has really helped to develop my understanding about the things I have studied. I personally have found it to be one of the most important factors of academic writing, improving my essays and reports, and enhancing my studies immeasurably.

CRITICAL THINKING: IDEAS FROM DIFFERENT TIMES, CULTURES AND GEOGRAPHIES

You will find that most textbooks will provide you with a linear timeline showing the development of Western critical thinking through Ancient Greece, Medieval and Renaissance Europe, Britain and Western Europe during the Enlightenment, and finally modern critical thinking across the Western world. However, it is important to understand that critical thinking is not solely a Western idea, but rather one with roots in many different cultures. This section explores some key tenets of critical thinking from two different perspectives to help you understand what critical thinking is and how you can use it.

Western critical thinking can be traced back to Ancient Greece, around 2500 years ago, and the teach-ings of Socrates. Socrates's ideas were documented by Plato and influenced his work and that of the **Greek Sceptics**, who were concerned with not accepting things at face value and the ability to see things for what they really are (Dalhousie University, n.d.; The Foundation for Critical Thinking, 2019).

Socrates and critical thinking

The key features of Soctratic thinking are:

- Asking people probing questions can reveal that, whilst they may sound confident and knowledgeable, they are not able to justify their claims in a rational way. It is important to ask probing questions before we accept what people tell us, and they should be used to seek clarity and consistency in the argument presented.
- An argument might appear sound at first, but underneath could be confused, self-contradictory, or poorly substantiated. It is therefore important that we look closely for evidence that supports an argument, examining a person's reasoning in their arguments and challenging assumptions, thinking about the practical and theoretical implications of things presented to us.
- We cannot depend on people in positions of power to have sound knowledge and insight at all times. These people can be confused and irrational just like anyone else.
- We should be reflective in our approach to accepted wisdom and question common beliefs and explanations held within society, with the aim of being able to tell the difference between those that are logical and supported by evidence, and those that are not.

The Buddha, Buddhism and critical thinking

Buddhism was founded over 2500 years ago in India by Siddhartha Gautama, who is known as The Buddha. Buddhism is widely practised across Southern, Eastern and South Eastern Asia, but has gained popularity in the West and currently has around 470 million followers worldwide (Watson, 2015). Some of the core ideas of Buddhism centre around critical thinking and can be found in the Kalama Sutra of the Anguttara Nikaya, which is sometimes referred to as the Buddha's Charter of Free Enquiry (Bloom, n.d.; Jayatunge, 2018).

- Buddhism is based on rationality and encourages its followers not to simply accept beliefs, revelations or traditions (oral and written). People can question hearsay, legends and even scriptures.
- Critical thinking involves being open-minded.
- Freedom of thought and enquiry are important.
- We should reflect internally and consider the value of what is being presented to us rather than simply believing it. We should also critically reflect on, and challenge, new ideas, and rethink our own ideas in light of new knowledge.
- We should not accept what someone says just because they are in a position of authority.
- We should look for evidence to support claims and engage in scientific investigation to find new knowledge.

 **ACTIVITY**

Compare and contrast the two examples above of Western (Socrates) and Eastern (Buddhism) ideas around critical thinking. Where are they similar and where do they differ?

WHY IS CRITICAL THINKING IMPORTANT?

Over recent years, education at all levels across the globe has started to embed critical thinking and the ability to solve problems as core attributes of a successful graduate. You need to apply critical thinking skills to be able to effectively manage or react to change, demonstrate flexible intellectual skills and analyse data from a range of sources to solve problems (Battelle for Kids, 2019; Hong Kong University, 2020). Critical thinking can help you carefully consider all your options and the possible consequences of your decision-making (Hitchcock, 2018). Critical thinking can therefore help us in the way that we develop, present and express ideas in the workplace (Hong Kong University, 2020).

We are now in what is termed 'The Forth Industrial Revolution' (see Chapter 35), and it is anticipated that artificial intelligence and robotics will replace humans in the workplace to do tasks that don't require critical thinking. This means that it is becoming more important to be able to think critically as this is a skill employers will place an ever-growing emphasis on since it sets humans apart from robots, machinery and artificial intelligence (Hong Kong University, 2020). In addition to the Fourth Industrial Revolution, our world is driven by technology and media, which has resulted in a huge amount of information becoming available to us at the click of a button. Technology and media have also changed very quickly, meaning we are constantly having to adapt and learn new ways of working, communicating and living. Tech also allows collaboration between people across time zones, geographical regions and fields of expertise. All of these things mean that to be successful in the workplace, you need to demonstrate a range of practical and critical thinking skills when navigating the digital world (Battelle for Kids, 2019).

CRITICAL THINKING SKILLS AND THE STAGES OF CRITICAL THINKING

There is a core set of critical thinking skills that you will need to develop and demonstrate. Figure 8.1 identifies each skill, how to apply it, and how to demonstrate that you have applied it.

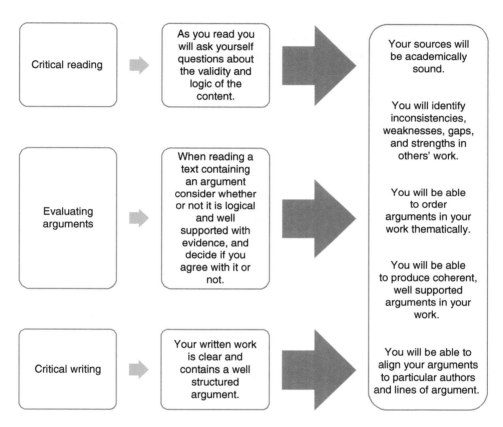

Figure 8.1 **An overview of critical thinking skills**

Source: adapted from University of Sussex, 2020

Critical reading

The first skill you will need to develop is critical reading. Critical reading is different from simply reading and absorbing the information provided. The initial stage of critical reading is one of thinking carefully about the sources you select to read. When you are looking for sources, you may ask yourself a series of questions, such as: When was this published? If it is old, is it accepted as a classic text or is it now considered out-of-date? Is the author credible? What is the scope of this work and how is it relevant to what I am doing? Who is the intended audience for this work?

When you start reading you will need to develop an active reading technique. It is important that you are critical in your approach to reading because it is the first stage of the research process. The term 'critical reading' does not mean that you disapprove of the work that you engage with.

Rather, being critical means engaging with the literature at a 'deep' level to ensure that you understand the claims being made and the arguments and evidence that support these claims. You will be required to understand how such claims relate to claims made by other authors, as well as understanding the context in which these arguments are situated. In some cases, certain cultural, discipline-based or other assumptions that underpin the claims made may not be explicit ('hidden' assumptions). Reading critically requires you to be alert to such assumptions and prepared to question them (Cameron, 2010: 88). Hidden assumptions can be difficult to identify, but they may be central to an argument. If a reason is offered, it is always worth exploring whether it is justified to support the claim. There are several things you need to do in order to read critically, as shown in Figure 8.2.

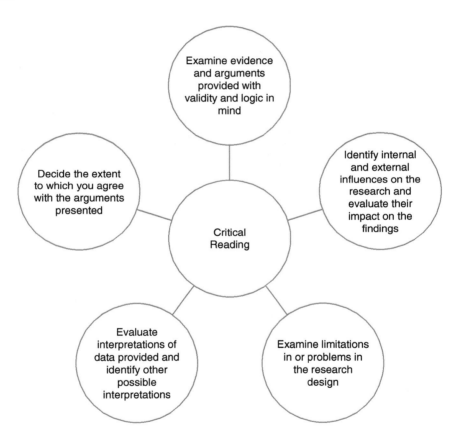

Figure 8.2   Actions for critical reading

Source: adapted from University of Leicester, 2020a

However, there are also some more specific, practical, things that will help with your critical reading. One approach you can apply is the SQ3R method which was introduced in Chapter 4. This method has three key stages before, during, and after the reading process and can help you to engage with what you are reading, as well as preparing effectively for assessments (NHTI, 2014; Open University, 2020).

Survey

- Survey the text you are about to read including identifying the text structure, subject headings and previewing illustrations.
- In books you can scan the chapters for their content and organisation.
- Read first paragraphs (or introductions) and last paragraphs (or conclusions) and major headings for a general overview of the material.
- Take note of graphs, diagrams, charts, glossaries, summaries, appendices, etc. as they will usually contain important and relevant information.

Question

- Based on your pre-reading, you should then ask questions such as:
- What is the material about?
- What are the main ideas being discussed?
- What is the viewpoint of the author?
- Is the material presented as fact or opinion?
- How are the main perspectives presented?
- Are the conclusions supported by the main material?

The 3Rs

- **Read** - read actively and search for the questions previously identified. Read quickly and fluently, underlying key text but not entire paragraphs. Do not make notes at this stage. Once you have read the whole thing through, go back and re-read smaller sections more carefully and thoroughly.
- **Recite** - reflect your reading through interacting with the text and answering your self-generated questions.
- **Review** - summarise the reading through taking notes and recording the information that you have judged to be the most important and/or relevant.

Figure 8.3 The SQ3R model expanded

Source: adapted from Huber, 2004; Payne and Whittaker, 2006

The first stage takes place before you read the text and is to *survey* the text you are looking at. This means skimming through the text to pick up on the titles, subtitles, images, figures in the text and note them down. You then turn these headings and sub-headings into *questions,* using how, what, where, why, when and who. This helps you read critically because it sets up an active approach to detailed reading. The second stage takes place whilst you are reading and involves a *close reading* of each section with the aim of answering the questions mentioned above. This helps you to focus on the information you need, stops you copying down information verbatim and encourages you to challenge the content you are looking at. The third stage takes place after you have read the material. Firstly, *recite* in your own words your answer to each question you have asked and then write them down. This helps you make sense of what you've read and again stops you from copying down other people's work directly. Finally, *review* your answers without using your notes. This last part is most useful if you are preparing for an exam or a presentation, encouraging you to rethink your ideas and reshape your argument.

━━━━━━ ACTIVITY ━━━━━━

Using the SQ3R method

Read the following online chapter and adopt the SQ3R reading method: Zhang, T., Bufquin, D., Lu, C. (2019) 'A qualitative investigation of microentrepreneurship in the sharing economy', *International Journal of Hospitality Management*, 79: 148–157. doi.org/10.1016/j.ijhm.2019.01.010.

Now select a short book chapter or article of your choice that you would like, or need, to read. Follow the SQ3R steps again and then reflect on the method.

Answer these questions:

1. Did you find the method easy to follow?
2. Did you answer the questions you set out?

(Continued)

3. Do you have more questions now?
4. Have you been able to put your reading into your own words?
5. Does your summary simply describe what the author has written or:

   i. Are you able to agree or disagree with their ideas?
   ii. Have you spotted any strengths and weaknesses in their argument?
   iii. Do you think they have interpreted their data correctly or could other meanings come from it?
   iv. Is there adequate evidence to support their argument?
   v. Are their claims reasonable in light of the evidence?

Other reading techniques: SOAR

There are other different approaches to reading that you might wish to try. Another popular one is the SOAR method. Introduced by Kiewra in 2005, SOAR is an integrated study plan that stands for four steps: Selection, Organisation, Association and Regulation (Daher and Keiwra, 2016; Jairam and Kiewra, 2009). SOAR was introduced as an alternative to SQ3R to overcome some of the ineffective study strategies that students adopt, such as poor note-taking (Jairam and Kiewra, 2009).

 ━━━ THINK POINT ━━━

Are you clear on what we mean by the term critical thinking? Can you appreciate that critical thinking is not just western in nature? Can you list why critical thinking is an important skill and why you need it at university and in the workplace?

Evaluating arguments

The second core critical thinking skill is the ability to evaluate arguments effectively, both in terms of other authors' work and your own. As you progress through your degree you will have to deal with increasingly complex concepts and will be expected to present your own ideas in relation to existing ideas. Many authors make claims and assumptions that they consider to be justified, true and/or useful, supporting their arguments with evidence such as other theories, research data or **'armchair observations'**. You will need to identify the primary key claim that the author is making as well as any secondary ones. You can scrutinise the argument(s) using the SQ3R method or graphically in a form similar to a Mind Map, depending on how you like to work (see Chapter 19 for various methods). You can start with the central claim/argument and then draw lines (branches) off this that represent the pieces of evidence that may or may not support the central idea. Some arguments can be extremely complex, making it difficult for you to establish what may be accurate and/or justified. This is dependent upon the strength and consistency of the evidence itself and the strength of the links between the evidence and claims being made (Cameron, 2010). No matter how complex the argument is you need to consider whether or not it is logical and supported, and decide if you agree with it or not. To do this, you first need to recognise the core components of any argument.

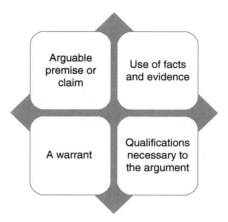

Figure 8.4   The core elements of an argument
Source: adapted from Open University, 2020

The premise or claim is the argument that the author wants to make to the reader. To be able to evaluate this you firstly need to identify if the argument is relevant to what you are trying to achieve (Open University, 2020). This is crucial because you may come across lots of interesting ideas as you read, which might not always be relevant to the questions that you have. You also need to ascertain if the argument constitutes a significant contribution to the subject you are investigating.

The evidence is the material that is used to support the argument. Every academic argument is an exploration of an idea or concept and should be supported with a range of evidence. This can come from other authors (secondary data), case studies (secondary data), or data collected as part of the research (primary data). This evidence should be valid, justified, and should support the argument being made in a clear, logical, way. To evaluate this, you should look closely at the claims being made by the author and how the evidence is presented to support the claims. You should also look for weaknesses and gaps in the evidence (Open University, 2020). There are some good examples in advertising of issues with claims and the evidence to support them. For example, the cosmetics industry has been criticised in recent years for the claims they make about their products. One example was Maybelline's 2013 claim that its Volum' Express, the Rocket mascara, made eyelashes eight times bigger than they are naturally. However, they used a model wearing false eyelashes in the print campaign as evidence of the effect of the product (Newham, 2013). The small print on cosmetic advertising is also interesting, as products will often claim that a large percentage of people that use the product agree it has the intended effect, but the small print often shows a very small sample in comparison to the possible population of interest. In 2015, academic research showed that claims made in cosmetics advertising could be classed as deceptive because the evidence used to back up claims made was vague and important information omitted (Fowler et al., 2015).

The warrant is an explicit or implied link between the claim made and the evidence used to support the claim (Purdue University, 2020). It is the logical reasoning an author makes based on the evidence that supports their claim (Open University, 2020). What you are looking for in this case is that the author has used evidence accurately and logically to support the claim they are making in their work. Finally, there are the qualifications in an argument. These are the limitations or parameters within which a claim can be made. You will often find a limitations of research section in the methodology or conclusion of an academic article, when the author makes the limitations of their research explicit. Qualifications often relate to sample sizes, bias, internal and external factors that influenced the research, and may include time and funding constraints. You will also find that authors often include a future research section, where they explain how the limitations of their study can be addressed, which you can use to help you evaluate the extent to which their argument is valid and justified.

The components of an argument provide you with a framework within which to apply the criteria for evaluating an argument. The key criteria are as follows:

- Is there a clear premise or argument presented?
- Is the argument supported by adequate, relevant, and sound evidence?
- Is the argument deductive? Do the conclusions drawn from the evidence logically link to the premise or argument?

Critical writing

The final critical thinking skill is the ability to write critically. At its very basic level, this means making sure the arguments you present in your work are clear and logically structured. To be able to achieve this you need to go through the practical steps we have outlined in Chapter 5. The most important thing is that once you have written your work you go back and critically read it to see if you have structured it and communicated your points effectively. Critical reflection is an important part of the critical reading and writing process, and you should always build in time to critically reflect and make improvements to your work.

 THINK POINT

Do you know what the stages of critical thinking are? Do you know what critical thinking skills you need? How are you going to apply these skills to your practice?

A CRITICAL THINKING CHECKLIST

A critical thinking checklist can help you audit yourself at each stage of the critical thinking process. We have provided you with a full checklist in Figure 8.5, but as you develop areas of strength you may wish to adapt it to focus on your areas of weakness.

Critical reading

Task	Tick if completed
Selected appropriate academic and professional sources	
Considered publishing date	
Considered if the source is a classic text or out of date	
Evaluated author credibility	

Task	Tick if completed
Evaluated scope of the work	
Identified the relevance of the work to what I am doing	
Identified appropriateness of the intended audience	
Surveyed the text	
Prepared the questions I want to answer	
Read the text closely	
Recited the content of the text	
Written the contents of the text into my own words	
Reviewed my summary and ideas in light of new knowledge	

Evaluating arguments

Identified a clear premise or claim	
Critically analysed and evaluated the evidence provided to support the claim	
Identified a logical warrant	
Assessed the qualifications given for the limitations of the research	

Critical writing

Deconstructed the question or task to ensure you understand it	
Made a clear premise or claim	
Provided a balanced argument	
Supported claim and statements with a range of evidence	
Made judgements on the evidence reviewed	
Have a logical warrant	
Explicitly stated any qualifications	
Stated the significance of your argument	
Critically reflected on content against task and intended outcomes	

Figure 8.5 Critical thinking checklist

CONCLUSION

In this chapter we have covered:

• What critical thinking is and why it is important in the university and workplace.

- The core ideas within critical thinking from different historical and geographical perspectives, to further and deepen your understanding.
- The main stages of critical thinking – critical reading, evaluating arguments and critical writing – and the skills you will need to employ to be a critical thinker at university.

FURTHER READING

Chafee, J. (2014) *Thinking Critically*. Stamford, USA: Cengage Learning.

Cottrell, S. (2017) *Critical Thinking Skills: Effective Analysis, Argument and Reflection*. London: Palgrave Macmillan.

Moon, J. (2007) *Critical Thinking: An Exploration of Theory and Practice*. London: Routledge.

Swatridge, C. (2014) *Oxford Guide to Effective Argument and Critical Thinking*. Oxford: Oxford University Press.

Williams, K. (2014) *Getting Critical*. London: Palgrave Macmillan.

Useful web resource

A free online course in Critical Thinking at University by Future Learn – www.futurelearn.com/courses/critical-thinking-at-university.

9 DIGITAL LITERACY AND THE APPLICATION OF ICT

ALESSANDRO PESARO

CHAPTER LEARNING OBJECTIVES

By the end of this chapter you should be able to:

- Understand how digital literacy and ICT will impact your university life.
- Feel confident in how you might create, manage and archive your digital documents for efficient retrieval.
- Understand advantages and disadvantages of different solutions and decide which suits your needs.
- Have a robust strategy in place to prevent failure and irrecoverable data.
- Optimise workload, increase productivity and reduce lead time.
- Avoid common pitfalls and manage risks correctly, working safely online.

GLOSSARY

- **Operating system (OS):** The low-level software that supports a computer's basic functions and determines the applications supported.
- **Application:** a program primarily intended for end users. Examples include word processors, spreadsheets, databases, web browsers, email clients, media players, photo editors, etc.
- **End user:** the person who ultimately uses a product, especially when contrasted with those who produce or market it.

INTRODUCTION

Information and communications technology (ICT) is a broad umbrella term describing the integration of telecommunications and computers in order to create, store, transmit and manipulate information. A computer connected to a network, a mobile phone using wi-fi or mobile data, smart-blackboards, virtual learning environments and real-time video conferencing tools are examples of ICT devices currently used within the higher education industry.

This complex ecology of hardware, software and policies has some prominent characteristics. Firstly, it is market-driven and evolves rapidly, with solutions becoming obsolete at an increasing rate. **Operating systems**, software and hardware are discontinued, phased out, or no longer supported by the vendor. Secondly, students are expected to use hardware and software provided (and sometimes *prescribed* by their university) while at the same time relying on their own devices for a range of tasks, such as independent study and research. While there is some convergence, universities may offer a unique mix of commercial solutions, internally developed products, or components produced under specification. Conversely, the consumer market has been traditionally split between Mac and Windows operating systems, with their mostly mutually incompatible hardware and software. While alternatives do exist, such as Linux platforms, they are unlikely to be used by the majority of undergraduates. The advent of smartphones in the mid-2000s has further confused this landscape. The possible combinations of all the above are so numerous that even a sketchy overview of features and options is probably pointless, and this is further complicated by significant variations in terms of personal preferences and national differences.

Finally, what a student studying tourism, hospitality or events may be expected to produce digitally as part of their studies varies enormously because of the vast array of modules, seminars and programmes currently offered. From case studies of destinations and services, to a massive portfolio of high-resolution photographs (e.g. a marketing brochure); from a minor data set to complex architectural rendering, apps, multi-track recordings and geodesic data. While a small, text-only dissertation is likely to be only a few kilobytes in size, high-resolution digital footage is normally gauged in terms of terabytes. Changing the nature of the assignment may increase the necessary storage space by many orders of magnitude.

This chapter follows some guiding principles, which include a focus on general concepts and ICT skills that are applicable across multiple subject domains and that are platform-independent and therefore less likely to become obsolete as technology progresses. Mastering these principles will give you a significant advantage and strengthen your employability. Tourism is, by its nature, international and multi-cultural and it has been convincingly argued that a knowledgeable workforce who can use business applications and have digital skills are able to overcome cultural differences (Mössenlechner, 2017).

Furthermore, this chapter suggests approaches that can be easily customised according to specific needs, rather than advocating solutions depending on a specific technology. We also avoid describing specific software, unless it is so widespread as to be a de-facto standard.

PREREQUISITES

This chapter takes for granted basic ICT skills that are normally taught at secondary school, combined with a reasonable proficiency of office productivity software: creating, opening and saving documents, renaming files, creating folders, etc. We expect that you are familiar with devices such as computers, tablets or mobile phones, and conversant with tasks such as sending emails, browsing the internet, uploading content on social media, using a search engine, filtering search hits and so forth. If you are not confident in these, please see further reading and useful web resources at the end of this chapter.

THINKING STRATEGICALLY

You are frantically looking for an ingredient, a book, a tool, a train ticket, that pair of shoes you would like to wear ... if only you knew where to look. Frustration mounts quickly, priceless time is wasted, and after long, anxious moments the missing item is found, only to discover that it is not fit for purpose: broken, dirty, unserviceable or has passed its best-by date. In the end, you go to the shop to buy another. Does this sound familiar?

There is little difference between being without a certain item and knowing that you own one but cannot find it. However, while most objects can be easily replaced (if I cannot find my pizza cutter I can improvise with a knife or buy a new one), personal digital assets are normally unique, having been created by a specific person for a specific purpose, requiring a substantial amount of time, dedication, skill and effort.

Wasting time searching for a misplaced file or data can derail tight schedules. Further, re-doing work is not always feasible, especially close to a deadline. Extenuating circumstances are not normally granted on the grounds of software and hardware failure. To paraphrase Arthur C. Clarke's dictum that 'any sufficiently advanced technology is indistinguishable from magic' (Clark, 1973), it is fair to assume that any highly disorganised mass of information is indistinguishable from an ineffectual mess. Poorly organised, unstructured information is useless.

This chapter will help you see the information you create or use as a personal strategic asset: the time and effort needed to keep it accessible, organised and usable should be regarded as an investment. Managing digital assets enables other, more far-reaching efforts.

MANAGING YOUR DOCUMENTS AND WORK

The file

A computer file is a resource for recording data on a storage device. Files can be opened, read, changed, saved and closed an arbitrary number of times by **applications**; they can be stored on different devices and transferred through the Internet. A computer file (from now on simply a file) may be designed to store a wide variety of data, such as still or moving images, a written message, a computer program, geographic information, etc.

Computer files consist of a name and an extension, separated by a fullstop (e.g. Certificate.docx). The latter specifies how the file content must be interpreted. For instance, the sequence of bytes of plain text file (.txt in a Microsoft operating system) is associated with characters of a specific alphabet; .jpeg or .jpg indicates that the content is an image.

During your university life you will use a vast number of files: handouts, presentations, papers, lecture notes, forms, templates, etc. How you organise and name these is likely to have a big impact on your ability to retrieve those files when you need them, as well as to understand what they contain. Organising files with consistent and descriptive file names is one of the easiest solutions to implement

(Braid, 2017). There are, of course, other ways of organising content but they tend to be either plat-form-specific (the colour-coding of files in Mac systems) or format-specific. Some images and audio files, for instance, allocate bytes for metadata, which allows a file to carry some basic information about itself: date of creation, author, size, etc. Furthermore, do not forget that your documents may be viewed, shared and edited by multiple users who are likely to use a wide variety of OSs and devices (desktop PCs, mobile devices, tablets, etc.). This is relevant to your university life (tutors, supervisors, admins, fellow students) and will become more and more important in your future career: think of colleagues, customers, stakeholders, etc. Never assume that what works for you will automatically work for anyone else.

A good metaphor for a file naming system is shorthand, which is both concise and effective. Note how the following names could easily lead to confusion: New document (2).docx; New document.docx; Copy of New spreadsheet.xls; Blank project.pub. The first two are especially bad: it is unclear what they might contain, which one is the most recent and how they relate to each other. In the same vein, resist the temptation to use creative, or humorous file names: The most stupid tourism seminar ever.docx; Bring to lecture.mp3 and so forth. It may be amusing at a first glance, but if these files are accidentally shared someone is likely to be offended. When in employment, this can even be framed as a case of professional misconduct in the workplace. Remember that dealing properly with digital information shapes your professional image.

It is impossible to condense here all possible requirements for an adequate file name although the following points may provide guidance. This applies to all data, regardless of subject matter and context.

a)   Keep filenames under 30 characters; the shorter the name, the easier the management of the archive and the wider the compatibility. Long file names may create issues when stored in nested folders, especially when folder names are long as well.

b)   The most relevant bit of information, normally providing context, must be at the beginning (a personal name, a project code, a unique identifier, the name of an organisation, etc). When alphabetically sorted, all files about the same activity or project will thus be grouped together, making them easy to retrieve; a file search will easily retrieve all relevant items regardless of format and content.

c)   Multi-part content (episodes, parts, chapters, etc.) or multiple instances of the same content (successive takes of the same performance, repetitions of the same experiment) are differentiated by using an index at the end of the file name.

d)   Never use Roman numerals.

e)   Do not use punctuation marks, symbols and special characters. They are reserved for system use or explicitly forbidden.

f)   Use hyphens or underscores rather than spaces (or avoid spaces altogether).

Be aware that the sorting of numbers is problematic. For instance, the sequence 1, 2, 3, 4, 5, 6, 7, 8, 9, 10, 11 might be sorted as 1, 10, 11, 2, 3, 4, 5, 6, 7, 8, 9. This can be avoided by using padding or leading zeros (e.g. 001, 002 …. 099, 100). The following examples are fine, although many individual variations are possible. There is no universally accepted naming principle. If it has an internal logic, is used con-sistently and makes sense to the author(s), then it fulfils its purpose.

ACME2019Sales.xls

ACME2019BoardMeeating.xls

TOU2005submission.doc

TOU2005classnotes.doc

TOU2005tutorial.doc

SwanLakeROH2109-12-14_take01.mov

SwanLakeROH2109-12-14_take02.mov

JoeBlogg-interview2020-01-04.mp3

TourismPodcast_ep001.docx

TourismPodcast_ep002.docx

An important decision is whether to incorporate information in full, or to capture it as initials, codes or acronyms. In the example above, Royal Opera House is abbreviated to ROH. When information is spelled out in full, file names become self-evident, but users rapidly run out of characters – conversely, capturing information in highly condensed form may lead to file names whose meaning may be obscure.

Some academic work may entail collating and organising a vast number of individual files. Examples include repeated scientific observations, multiple photographs of the same object, interviews with a vast array of informants, a series of discrete archival documents such as letters, receipts, bills, laws, etc., multiple takes of the same performance, or consecutive iterations of the same experiment. Information likely to be incorporated into a file name includes:

- Project or experiment name or acronym
- Place/coordinates/administrative division
- Module code
- Name/initials
- Date
- Type of data
- Conditions
- Revision number
- Item sequence

CASE STUDY: THE IBCC DIGITAL ARCHIVE AT THE UNIVERSITY OF LINCOLN

When work started at the IBCC Digital Archive, staff faced a difficult situation. There were already a significant number of files in the repository, but the file management system intended to retrieve content was not in place (and would not have been for another year).

Thankfully, our colleague Robin Evans had devised a robust file naming system based on author, format and document type (see Figure 9.1).

This made it possible to retrieve content until a proper system was in place. The system is so well designed that it is still used after years and has survived multiple software and OS upgrades. Lesson learned: simple solutions may be surprisingly efficient, long-lived and reliable.

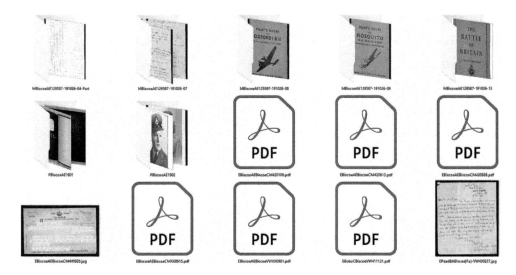

Figure 9.1 A system of codes and indices gives information on content and shows how different documents relate to each other

'The best is the enemy of the good.' Look for adequate, usable solutions that may be readily available and easily implemented. Do not wait for the 'perfect' approach that may never materialise and be difficult to adopt, especially when needs have changed. Never assume that the latest fad is automatically better. Always research and compare different options.

DATES

It is frequently necessary to incorporate dates into file and folder names. Academic life is organised around progression through successive years, which are convenient time markers as some work involves repeated observations through an extended period of time (e.g. most fieldwork). Other files must be organised chronologically, for instance successive revisions. The latter is also a matter of personal preferences: while some are comfortable with having all the revisions in one place, others point out the potential for errors and confusions. Ask your instructor/tutor for advice.

Dates have to be captured consistently. The main hindrance is the variety of conventions for writing them, all mutually incompatible: different styles prescribe various combinations of numbers or words, with either Arabic or Roman numerals; the names of the months are language-dependent, while the sequence used depends on national usages (e.g. the American preference for month/day/year, while other countries tend to use day/month/year). This has the potential to create misinterpretation and confusion, hinder information retrieval, and increase the likelihood of mistakes. It is recommended that you use ISO 8601, a standard for representing dates and times issued by the International Organisation for Standardisation (ISO) in 1988. Dates are expressed as yyyy-mm-dd (e.g. 2020-02-08).

- Dates are arranged from largest to smallest unit.
- Each date has a fixed number of digits, using leading zeros as needed.
- Values may be dropped from the least to the most significant. For instance, 2016-05-02, 2016-05 or 2016 are all ISO 8601 compliant, while allowing for different accuracy levels.

This format has many advantages. Firstly, ISO 8601 is completely culture-neutral; secondly, it eliminates the ambiguities between different systems, especially American and European usage; finally, most-to-least-significant structure means that ordering coincides with chronological order. This allows dates to be immediately sorted by file systems – this is especially useful while dealing with a vast number of files and folders.

MANAGING REVISIONS

Most academic work is produced through an iterative process consisting of multiple revisions and editing, especially if you are undertaking a group project (see Chapter 7). Managing multiple revisions can be a frustrating and time-consuming experience, since minor mistakes can lead to confusion and delay. When starting to work on a new revision, the first step must be making a new copy of your file and naming it accordingly to the scheme you have chosen. If something goes wrong, there will be a previous state to go back to. Alternatively, you could just back up your files at frequent intervals. Just make sure that your backups do not overwrite old data – different backup copies must be kept carefully separated. There are features that allow users to revert documents to a previous state (undo functions or 'wayback machines'). The main issue with these solutions has more to do with a widespread fallacy: most users tend to see them as cast-iron guarantees, insurance policies or fail-safe safety nets, rather than technical solutions that are necessarily subject to malfunctions. Over-reliance on a system that can fail is ill-advised.

━━━━━━━━━━━━━━━━━━ THINK POINT ━━━━━━━━━━

One of our tourism students had the habit of producing reports in stages. Firstly, he copied and pasted sources into the assignment template, then paraphrased some and kept others as quotes. Different versions of the assignment were saved in the same folder, so he mistakenly submitted an early draft instead of the final version. His submission was immediately flagged for poor scholarship and he failed. There is nothing wrong with this workflow, but care must be taken when different versions are kept together. This is a preventable failure: if he had a reliable file naming and version control system in place, he would have avoided a lot of trouble.

Status descriptors may be incorporated into your naming system: draft, revision [number or revisor], proof, final, submitted, etc. Other steps may be added when needed. The software versioning method uses a decimal index. This system is flexible since it allows room for interim revision numbers. Revision 5.0 may be followed by 5.1, 5.2 or go straight to 6. Unit revisions are normally major, while decimal revision numbers indicate minor adjustments e.g. MarketingandTechnology-revAP-2020-01.docx or PeopleManagement-revAP-v6.3.docx.

Most of the editing process entails streamlining, taking out and condensing, rather than adding information and expanding. This applies to written documents, and to a lesser extent other files. It is not advisable to completely delete unused parts. It is rather sensible to park them in a specific file or folder, where they can be reused at a later stage. This can happen either in the same project, as consequence of an afterthought, or for other purposes.

SINGLE-PART FILES

It is possible to work on each part of a work as a separate document file, for instance different paragraphs or chapters. There are advantages to this, in that the system is inherently compartmentalised since a fatal mistake or a total loss in one of the files leave the others unaffected; furthermore, it allows a great deal of flexibility as different parts can be edited independently, for instance by working on one part while another is under revision by a supervisor. The system can be usually supplemented by revision or version control markers, such as StudySkills-Introduction-3.1; StudySkills-chapt01-2.2; StudySkills-chapt02-1.0; StudySkills-literature-1.1 and so on. Care must be taken at the end of the process when all parts are reassembled into a single file, with a uniform document style.

RENAMING FILES IN BULK

Bulk rename utilities can automate, to a larger extent, substantial batches of files. This is normally the case with digital photography, scans and data generated by automatic data recording systems. For instance, a digital camera is likely to name image files according to the following pattern: DSCN_00001, DSCN_00002, DSCN_00003, DSCN_00004 and so on. These may be better renamed as below, revealing the content at a glance and showing how individual parts form a sequence:

> 1999-01-25-SwanLake-0001,   1999-01-25-SwanLake-0002,   1999-01-25-SwanLake-0003, 1999-01-25-SwanLake-0004 and so on.

This renaming will work for a limited number of images but becomes unmanageable when hundreds or thousands of items must be processed manually. A possible alternative is to use batch renaming utilities, a broad category of software intended to add, remove, or replace parts of the filename according to a preset rule. They can save a substantial amount of time but should be used with caution: the user interface can be intimidating, and a mistake can propagate unwanted edits across thousands of files in multiple folders. Make sure that preview and undo functions are working before processing large batches. Some devices may be set up to name files according to a user-defined pattern (date, batch, creator, device, etc.), but this is not always possible or practical.

USING FOLDERS TO STORE FILES

A folder provides a logical, named space in which to keep items with something in common: purpose, origin, content, date, revision status, etc. Folders can be nested within each other, thus creating hierarchical structures starting from broad, general concepts and ideas and then branching off into finer subdivisions. A well-designed folder structure, also known as a taxonomy, can be invaluable for organising information in a logical way.

The order of the elements in a folder is normally crucial. They should be added according to the way the file will be retrieved. For instance, if files will be primarily retrieved according to module name or code, this should appear first. If chronological order is crucial, date must appear first (see Figure 9.2).

- Avoid folders named things like 'Misc', 'various' or 'unclassifiable'. If too many items are placed in such a folder, this should indicate to you that your system is badly designed.

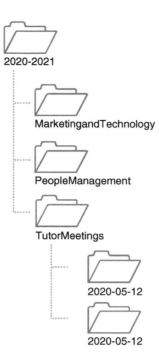

Figure 9.2 A possible folder structure which can be adapted to personal preferences and individual circumstances

- Five or six levels should be enough for most practical purposes. Deeper structures become difficult to navigate and **end users** become confused.
- Short names are even more important for folders. Some interfaces, especially web-based ones, truncate long folder names thus rendering the system unusable. See also recommendations regarding file length.

━━━━━━━ ACTIVITY ━━━━━━━

Thinking forward

When in employment, you'll be managing a substantial number of files: minutes of meetings, reports, blog post drafts, press releases, business proposals, contracts, etc. A mistake can easily lead to embarrassment, bad feedback, or loss—think of the time needed to redo a piece of work saved in a deleted or corrupted file. In a business environment, time is money. A properly organised system also supports efficient collaboration, especially when colleagues work shifts. Nowadays, most major firms have sophisticated in-house systems for sharing information, collaboration tools and other services. Evidence that you can keep files logically organised for retrieval will increase your employability. Consider a common job interview question: 'Can you provide an example of your ability to work in a systematic and organised way?' Answer: 'When I was a student, I organised all my files logically and put appropriate measures in place to make sure I didn't lose anything. Because of that, I never missed a deadline or had to re-sit exams due to data loss.' This is good evidence of being prudent and able to plan.

PLANNING A PERSONAL REPOSITORY

There is an important distinction between the current archive (in which documents about current matters are created, edited and discarded on a regular basis) and a repository or data warehouse. The latter is normally understood as a destination for data that does not serve an immediate purpose but retains enough value to justify preservation. Retention of documents no longer needed may appear counterintuitive, but in fact it is underpinned by a sound logic. Firstly, it charts your progression through university and provides evidence of your development through successive milestones; secondly, it allows remixing and building upon existing content. A report, for instance, can be expanded into a project or condensed as a poster. Finally, the smaller the current archive, the easier its maintenance and data retrieval.

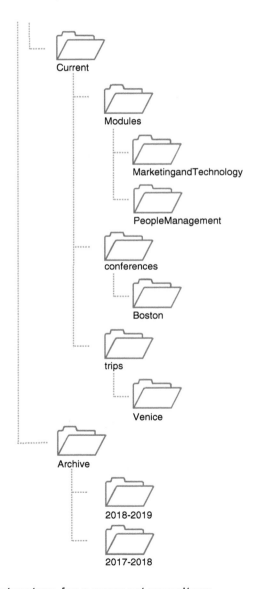

Figure 9.3   A possible structure for a personal repository

At periodical intervals, content is assessed for permanent retention. What is moved to the repository largely depends on personal preferences. Some may wish to keep only what was submitted (e.g. report, portfolio, etc.), while others may want to preserve a wider range of materials including classroom notes, annotated literature, early drafts, notes, Mind Maps, etc. Organisations normally have their own retention policies, but at this stage the choice is largely yours (see Figure 9.3).

Paraphrasing a legal maxim, it is sensible to assume that every piece of information has value unless proven otherwise, particularly when we consider the amount of time and dedication needed to create it. As cost of storage has declined over time, space is not usually an issue; on the other hand, the higher the file count and more complex the structure, the more difficult information retrieval becomes.

══ INDUSTRY INSIGHT ══

Making your contents sharable with Adobe Portable Document Format

Adobe Portable Document Format, better known as PDF format, is a multi-platform file format developed by Adobe Inc in the 1990s to display documents in a way that is totally independent from software and hardware. While originally marketed as commercial software, it was later standardised as ISO 32000 (2008). Consequently, a wide range of applications are currently available to read, create and edit it. Examples include scholarly literature, complex documents that include tables, annotated images, charts (especially when the layout is essential to the correct understanding of the information), and also examples of graphic design where the correct arrangement of the items on the pages and reliable reproduction are as important as the content itself.

There are several circumstances in which producing a PDF document may be advantageous. Firstly, content exported as PDF can be viewed by anyone, even if they don't have the software needed to create it in the first place. The advantages of this become evident when considering licence requirements or cost: it is not uncommon for some software to cost more than the machine to which it is uploaded. This strategy is advantageous for documents consisting mainly of text, graphics and images, but less and less practical in case of dynamic, interactive files when the display changes according to user's queries and inputs. Secondly, PDF documents preserve the content and layout. A report, for instance, may combine text, images and complex tables according to a specific layout that is essential for the key message to get across. Using PDF allows the user to see the document exactly as it was intended to appear.

Furthermore, images can be compressed to a lesser or greater extent. This means that the same documents can be exported according to different quality standards: low quality and small file size, suited for internet distribution, or best quality and large file size (the setting of choice for high quality commercial printing). For instance, the draft of a conference poster can be circulated online for feedback as low-quality copy, while the high-quality version is generated only immediately before printing. Since PDF has been standardised worldwide, it can be used as a form of insurance policy against obsolescence: the software house may withdraw support or discontinue new releases such that hardware is no longer manufactured or supported. The most extreme scenario is abandonware: a product is ignored by its owner/manufacturer, and no form of support is available. This happens because software houses cease to trade, or customer support is deemed unprofitable and stopped. Exporting the content as PDF may preserve some of the content in a usable form. It remains an eminently sensible option for relatively static documents that are submitted in total or partial fulfilment of academic requirements and may need to be accessed over an extended period of time.

STORAGE OF FILES

Files can be stored either locally, normally on your own device, or remotely, as in a cloud system. The latter is a set of computer system resources (especially data storage and computing power) that can be accessed through a network. Cloud systems are normally provided by your university, although you may want to invest in a cloud you have private access to.

Table 9.1   Different storage systems

Cloud storage	Local storage
Data stored on the cloud is readily accessed by any device that has an internet connection. Content on multiple devices can be automatically synced real-time; recovery of deleted files is normally available as a standard feature.	Local storage may be the only possible solution when network connectivity is unreliable, expensive or simply non-extant. Fieldwork on remote locations is a common example.
If a device is lost, stolen or broken, content can be easily retrieved.	Local storage tends to outperform cloud in terms of speed - storing data on internal or external hard drives is faster than uploading/downloading.
While cloud services are normally offered free of charge by the university, space is normally limited and may not suffice for some critical applications. Furthermore, an ICT department may turn down a request for more space. A university cloud is normally enough for text document but may be totally inadequate for high quality video footage.	Substantial batches of massive files naturally call for local storage.

Another thing to consider is that, with local data storage, it is possible to have full and complete control of your data: security is based on the physical control of a material object. The obvious drawback is that devices are vulnerable to theft and carelessness, and external hard drives are frequently lost or forgotten in public places. In this case the loss is not the cost of the hardware, but rather the cost of re-doing work which may have taken a substantial amount of time to be produced. In some instances, the loss can never be recovered. If you opt for local storage, some sensible strategies can be easily implemented (Wiggins, 2016):

- Make sure you have both redundancy and differentiation in place. Vital content must be saved on multiple devices (redundancy) of different kinds (differentiation). Examples are an external hard drive *and* a laptop; a memory stick *and* a PC. If one method of storage fails, the other will still provide access. Furthermore, the same adverse event is less likely to impact different devices working according to different principles: crushing a memory stick under an office chair is a relatively common incident, while accidentally trampling a desktop PC is less likely.
- Be aware that multiple copies should be kept at different locations. A common mistake is to store all the copies in the same room, but remember that a thief who takes your laptop will also steal an external drive hooked up to it; a catastrophic event such as a fire will likely destroy all devices in the same building. Content must also be regularly synchronised and checked for integrity.
- Choose an encrypted external hard drive: content is password-protected, and this will reduce the likelihood of data breach.
- Clearly label external hard drives, memory sticks and anything that can be lost, misplaced or accidentally dropped, just as address tags are attached to items of luggage.

- Invest in a sturdy, well-padded case. If the storage device has moving parts, as happens in some external hard drives, a mishandling can be fatal.

MANAGING RISKS

Risks can be controlled and managed but never eliminated. By the same token, you should never regard ICT as a fail-safe, 100% reliable safety net, but rather a complex technical system which may not always behave as planned. For instance, you may drastically edit whole parts of a document by deleting swathes of text from a report you're not entirely happy with, and then replacing them with a new structure. You duly save it at intervals (or have an autosave feature enabled) so as not to lose your work. As editing progresses, the new version is automatically uploaded in the cloud with changes being immediately propagated across all devices synchronised. Then you have an afterthought, but the version you started with at the beginning of the process may no longer be available. A possible countermeasure is saving multiple copies at different stages of editing but be aware that this strategy will increase the risk of mis-managing different files with similar names. 'I'll improvise a solution if trouble arises' is normally a bad idea – when the incident has happened, it is normally too late to implement countermeasures (National Cyber Security Centre, 2018).

THINK POINT

Big Data aims to extract usable information from data sets that are at the same time very large *and* highly complex. Think of a booking portal handling millions of customer transactions. Not only are numbers massive, but the mass of data is impervious to analysis: travellers can choose among a potentially unlimited number of destinations and itineraries, select different options, being receptive to one marketing strategy or another, etc. This, in turn, is influenced by an enormous number of other variables: gender, age, spending power, online behaviour, device used, time of the year, date of travel, etc. Furthermore, everything is shifting in real time.

Big Data is connected to predictive analytics, the systematic process of converting 'raw' data into useful information such as business intelligence and future strategies. Massive data sets grow rapidly because of the pervasive spread of data recording devices (plate number recognition, smart card access control systems, biometric passports and so on) and the capacity of most internet applications to automatically and inconspicuously gather users' behaviour data. Human editing or inspection at the big data scale is impossible: analysis involves automated tools such as artificial intelligence and machine learning (Holmes, 2017). The sheer amount of personal information has raised issues with privacy, trust and invasive surveillance.

INTERNET SECURITY

Students must become aware of the possible implications of a learning environment in which a substantial amount of interactions and information exchange takes place online: examples include sending and receiving emails, using library services, submitting pieces of work via plagiarism detection services (see Chapter 5), taking part in online courses, lectures and seminars, and using a VLE or self-access services. This is part of a broader landscape of online interaction in which people shop for goods and services, entertain or are entertained, send or receive money, share information and form communities.

Many negative consequences may easily arise when the above is not managed correctly. They include threats to a person's security and financial health; privacy breaches (when confidential information is disclosed unlawfully) altering, destroying, suppressing or stealing data; bank fraud; identity theft; and extortion and blackmail, among many others.

A common objection is that most of what the average student does while at the university does not warrant such a level of care. You might wonder, 'who might be interested in my lecture notes?' This is a common fallacy:

- It is important to consider the implications of apparently innocent online services. Your own online order history may reveal an incredible amount of information regarding political persuasion, tastes, sexual orientation, ongoing medical issues and so forth.
- When in employment, you will deal with highly sensitive, business-critical information, either your own or at company level. The quicker you reach an adequate level of awareness the better – a prospective employer will look for evidence of sound data security practices.
- You may be a relatively unimportant person now, but this will hopefully change in the future.

 THINK POINT

Think about the most serious adverse events that can realistically take place and what you could have in place as a realistic action plan. What happens if my flat is burgled, my laptop broken beyond repair, my password lost? Do you have a countermeasure in place?

The first line of defence is a robust password.

- A strong password is difficult to guess, cannot be easily cracked by a sequential run through lists of existing words, or using a brute-force approach trying all possible combinations of characters.
- It should have as many characters as possible. Requirements vary, but a minimum of eight characters is normal. The more characters are used, the more difficult to guess it will be.
- Do not use correctly spelled words, especially if commonly used. This includes place names, personal name, title of creative works, etc.
- Mix special characters, upper and lowercase, and numbers.
- Never use your birthday, national insurance number, place of birth, student number, ID number or any other personal information. This information may be readily available.

Do not share your password with anyone. The person you share your password with may be loyal and trustworthy, but that is of no relevance here. Under normal circumstances, do not use the same password for multiple purposes and never reuse a password. It is certainly easier to re-use a password, but a security breach will immediately propagate across multiple systems. In a cascading effect, an easier-to-access password for a low security website may give a thief access to a high security platform, such as an online bank account. A possible variant is to devise a very strong password and then append a shorter, unique sequence which may be easier to remember.

The embarrassed presenter

The trouble with highly complex passwords is that they may be fiendishly difficult to commit to memory, especially when used infrequently or when you have got used to the 'remember me on this computer' options. This can backfire spectacularly.

A student was attending a student research hospitality conference and all students were asked to deliver short presentations supported by visual aids. Her turn came and she tried to access her cloud files but ran into all sorts of difficulties. She anxiously fiddled with the PC for a couple of minutes, before becoming nervous and eventually giving up. Her presentation was weak and uninspiring – for a start, the incident had spoiled her concentration and weakened her drive; secondly, a key element was missing. An important opportunity was wasted because of the optimism bias, the notorious it-won't-happen-to-me mindset. Hope for the best but prepare for the worst.

- Always have a plan B in place, for instance a copy on an USB memory stick. Some critical events may even call for multiple copies on different devices.
- In really critical circumstances, have a last-resort option ready, for instance a PDF version of a presentation. Some features may be lost, but the content will still be usable.
- Make sure you are not locked out from your own account by having alternative means of authentications in place: many online services allow you to input a secondary email address or a mobile number.

It may be tempting to write passwords down somewhere, but this merely shifts the problem. A possible solution is using a password vault service or password manager, to store all your passwords and other essential information in protected online space. Again, the problem is critical interdependence as one single breach may jeopardise multiple online assets at once. Passwords must be changed on a regular basis and make sure you always log out, especially when using a shared device, such as a PC in a university library. Familiarise yourself with two-factor authentication. It works by combining what users know (e.g. a username/password) and what they have, for instance a mobile phone that can receive one-off access codes.

Wolves in sheep's clothing

Passwords can also be obtained by using 'social engineering' methods, normally by a fraudster posing as a trustworthy person, or through messages that have been deliberately crafted to look genuine, using an official logo/crest or apparently signed by someone with an official-sounding job title. This is normally a fraudulent attempt to get sensitive information (usernames, passwords and credit card details). No reputable organisation will ask for a password on the phone or via email.

TYPES OF TOURISM INFORMATION

Roughly speaking, there a four main types of tourism information available online.

Blog

A blog (short for 'weblog') is a discussion consisting of informal diary-style entries, normally displayed in reverse chronological order. Blogs can be authored by a single person (a tourist, for instance) or associated with media outlets, universities and higher education establishments, think tanks, advocacy groups, etc. The purpose of a blog post is to inform in a direct, unmediated and engaging way. Blog posts may sometimes be biased: they can be produced in furtherance of a specific agenda or point of view, for example voicing the frustration of unhappy customers. Twitter is an example of 'microblogging', when the priority is sharing information almost real-time.

Public websites

Public websites represent the official voice of an organisation, for instance a government, a local authority or a tourist board. Although examples may vary, their tone is normally formal or even official; there may also be emphasis on credibility and authority. They are also a good source of regulations, standards and codes of practices governing the industry.

Company websites

Company websites are normally geared toward engagement. Their purpose is to promote, but the approach is more aggressive and dynamic. The intent is to attract customers, and content is normally market-driven and tailored to a specific user base.

Social media

Social media refers to a broad range of interactive online technologies that facilitate the creation or sharing of ideas, interests and information by fostering social communities and interactions. They consist mainly of user-generated content (text posts and comments, plus digital photos or videos) and are based on users' profiles and identities. Users share, discuss and modify content in a direct, timely and unmediated way. Information on social media must be approached with caution: the wide user base means that news circulates almost real-time, but the lack of factual control also means spread of unsubstantiated rumours or even deliberate misinformation.

Their boundaries are not always clean-cut and hybrid models are becoming increasingly common: a public organisation can have social media presence or a company website may include a blog section, etc. An important skill is assessing information for credibility and relevance. Claiming that an event was a success may be backed up by a post shared by an anonymous blogger; cancelling a trip on the grounds of potential civil unrest must be substantiated by multiple, independent official sources. As Carl Sagan said, 'Extraordinary claims require extraordinary evidence' (Sagan, 1980).

 REFLECTION EXERCISE

Assessing online information

The International Federation of Library Associations and Institutions (IFLA) has produced a concise eight-point guide:

1.   Consider the source. Click away from the story to investigate the site, its mission and its contact info.
2.   Read beyond. Headlines can be outrageous in an effort to get clicks. What's the whole story?
3.   Check the author. Do a quick search. Are they credible? Are they real?
4.   Supporting sources? Click on those links. Determine if the info given actually supports the story.
5.   Check the date. Reposting old news stories doesn't mean they're relevant to current events.
6.   Is it a joke? If it is too outlandish, it might be satire. Research the site and author to be sure.
7.   Check your biases. Consider if your own beliefs could affect your judgement.
8.   Ask the experts. (IFLA, 2020).

===== REFLECTION EXERCISE =====

Assessing your own file naming system

Descriptive: Is it clear? Will it still make sense in a few years?

Brief: A name that is too long will likely be truncated, which undermines the whole exercise.

Consistent: Once you have found a method that works, stick to it. Back-rolling changes over a vast archive may be painful.

CONCLUSION

This chapter has covered:

- The types of file naming systems you could use.
- How risks can be controlled and managed but never eliminated.
- The cost of a loss/failure is not only the cost of the hardware, but also the cost of re-doing work. In some cases, a loss can never be recovered.
- Ways of storing files. Your documents will be viewed, shared and edited by multiple users who are likely to use a wide variety of OSs and devices (desktop PCs, mobile devices, tablets, etc.).
- Staying safe online.

FURTHER READING

Braid, K. (ed.) (2017) *Functional Skills ICT, Study and Text Practice*. Broughton-in-Furness: Coordination Group Publications Ltd (CGP).

Holmes, D.E. (2017).. *Big Data, A Very Short Introduction*. Oxford: Oxford University Press.

National Cyber Security Centre (2018) *Top Tips for Staying Secure*. Available at: www.ncsc.gov.uk/collection/top-tips-for-staying-secure-online (accessed 20 February 2020).

Wiggins, B. (2016) *Effective Document and Data Management. Unlocking Corporate Content*. London and New York: Routledge.

Useful web resources

Most universities offer tutorials, online courses and one-to-one ICT sessions. This should be your first port of call, as platforms and online services tend to be university-specific. Some universities may also offer access to online platforms with video courses delivered by industry experts (e.g. LinkedIn Learning and others).

10

REFLECTIVE THINKING AND BECOMING A REFLECTIVE PRACTITIONER

CHAPTER LEARNING OBJECTIVES

By the end of this chapter you should be able to:

- Understand the terms 'reflective practice' and 'reflective thinking'.
- Identify models and methods to develop and use these skills.
- Think and write reflectively and with confidence.
- Understand how reflective thinking is an important employability skill.
- Complete a personal reflection audit.

GLOSSARY

- **Lifelong learning:** learning for continuous growth, development and happiness.
- **Personal development:** activities and methods to improve yourself.
- **Reflection:** consciously examining and thinking about your feelings, responses and actions. Processing thoughts, feelings and considerations about a situation.
- **Reflective practice:** reflecting on your actions and responses as part of a process of continuous learning.

INTRODUCTION

This chapter explores **reflective practice**, identifying what it means to reflect on events and situations. It covers what reflective practice is, why it is important to reflect, and how you can do this. As you read, you may realise that you already have several of the skills needed to be a reflective thinker. So, alongside developing those skills further, this chapter should help give you the confidence to demonstrate reflective thinking and practice verbally, as well as in your writing.

You will no doubt hear and read a lot about reflective practice and reflective thinking during your time at university. These terms are used frequently, and you may struggle at first to fully understand or apply these ideas to their work, but reflective thinking is not difficult, and you will no doubt have used reflective thinking in your daily life for many years. Reflective practice and thinking are about stepping back and looking at your actions, behaviour or approach to a situation and deciding what went well, and what did not. You then take the information and reflect on it to identify where/what you need to develop and change and why, so that you can engage in continuous, **lifelong learning**.

WHAT IS REFLECTIVE PRACTICE?

Reflective practice is one of the most important ways in which we learn. It enables you to be able to make the connections needed between theory and practice (Jasper, 2013; Nguyen-Truong et al., 2018). Reflective practice helps you to develop critical reasoning skills, and therefore aids your learning and academic development. As a young child if we misbehave, or have a tantrum in a public place because we are not allowed to have the bar of chocolate that we so desperately want and we are punished by our parents for that behaviour, we understand that this approach is not going to be rewarded. Children learn through understanding a situation and applying that understanding in the future. In this example, the child will reflect on the outcome of the behaviour, coming to the conclusion that this approach did not lead to the desired outcome. As children we think about the consequences of our behaviour and negative outcomes, learning from this and perhaps behaving differently in the hope of avoiding punishment and gaining the desired reward. This is a very simple example of reflective thinking and practice: we have done something that hasn't worked, thought about it, identified what went wrong, created a new approach, put it into practice and achieved a different outcome.

 THINK POINT

Reflective practice skills are no different to any other skill: the more you practise, the better you will become and the more natural it will be to reflect on situations. How well do you think you reflect on what you do? Can you recall a recent incident or situation upon which you reflected, and would act differently if faced with the same situation again?

Reflective thinking and practice is not only about just taking the negative experiences and seeing how we can make changes. It is important to reflect on all experiences both positive and negative, as we may not be sure why something has worked well. As Boud et al. (1985: 19) suggest,

> Reflection is an important human activity in which people recapture their experience, think about it, mull over and evaluate it. It is this working with experience that is important in learning.

━━━━━━━━━ STUDENT INSIGHT ━━━━━━━━━

Ying talks about how reflection has helped her to think about problem-solving

When I started university, it was a bit of a shock to me. I had always been taught using the repeat-and-memorise facts method and then recite them. Coming here [to the UK] that was not expected of me. I was expected to provide critical thinking and provide possible solutions to questions and problems set. I found this really hard to start with. I went to the Study Support at the university and said I didn't understand how to reflect. They spent some time with me showing me how I could take a question, or problem and then break it down into parts. I looked at a situation in my life that I was not happy with. I then wrote down what I was not happy about, why I was not happy, how it made me feel, how I would like to have changed the outcome and what the actual outcome was. I then went through these all again and wrote down how I could have changed my approach, what I could do differently in the future to prevent it happening again. A few months after I did this, the same situation came up again. Rather than losing my temper and getting frustrated as I had before, I thought about what I had written down and practised the reflective advice I had given myself. This really helped and the outcome was much better and was exactly what I was looking for. If I hadn't of taken the time to reflect, I would not have had a positive outcome.

I am much more reflective as a person now and find myself questioning and reflecting on most things that I do, in my personal life, work life and academic life. I think this has made me a much more rounded person, who is less likely to react before reflecting. Learning these skills has also allowed me to be far less descriptive in my academic work. I am now more critical and reflective, allowing me to make the connections between theory and practice. This has resulted in me being awarded higher marks and learning far more. I am sure these skills will be a great help to me in the future.

HOW CAN I BECOME MORE REFLECTIVE?

Before you can begin to reflect, it is important to identify why you are reflecting on an experience or situation and what it is that you hope to achieve. **Reflection** is about being more aware of yourself, your beliefs, actions, feelings and responses (Taylor, 2015). Reflection is a method of self-development and learning that can help you to become a lifelong learner.

- Reflective practice is a skill which will help you with your continued professional and **personal development**.
- Understanding and practising reflection will allow you to appreciate the significance of both sides of a situation, seeing things from your perspective and the perspective of others.
- Reflective practice will enable you to develop the leadership and employability skills that employers are looking for.

━━━━━━━━━ REFLECTION EXERCISE ━━━━━━━━━

Handling situations

Think about the student insight above and the lessons that Ying learned. Write down a situation where you have not given enough thought about a situation and have reacted in a way that you were not happy with. Now think about how you could have handled that situation differently:

(Continued)

- Could you have seen things from another's point of view?
- Were you reacting because of an emotional reason?
- How could you have handled the situation differently?

Keep these notes available for an activity later in this chapter.

Reflection can help you identify an action, or outcome that you weren't happy with and explore what you could do differently if the situation arose again. These skills can also be applied to academic writing, as reflective practice is a method of critically analysing a problem, case study or assignment question. You are seeking to provide a clear balance between your personal perspective based on your research; asking yourself questions and reading; and ensuring that you adhere to good academic practices and expectations (Williams et al., 2012a). This will require you to link together your experiences/practices and supporting evidence from research and reading to provide a rounded and reflective answer.

When undertaking any reflection, it is important to step back from what you are reflecting on. A method that can help you reflect is to think about how other people you respect would deal with a similar situation. What did they do to ensure a positive outcome? What knowledge do they have that you don't have? How can you gain that knowledge? Look at the information as objectively and honestly as you can, endeavouring to set aside your own beliefs and prejudices (Jasper, 2013; Nguyen-Truong et al., 2018). By removing your own baggage from the equation you can reflect more deeply, thoroughly and honestly on the information you are presented with.

 THINK POINT

Reflecting on an experience is a great way to learn and continue to learn. We don't always get things right on the first or even the second attempt.

It is not sufficient to have an experience in order to learn. Without reflecting on this experience it may quickly be forgotten, or its learning potential lost. (Gibbs, 1988: 9)

A reflective thinker is careful and thoughtful, considering information carefully and thoroughly to ensure that it is based on evidence and reason. Often the words 'reflective' or 'reflection' will be incorporated into a question you have been set for a module and it is important to reflect on any information you are provided with to develop your reflective skills, as well as filtering out information and approaches that are weak, incorrect or don't provide the results you are looking for.

THE VALUE OF BECOMING REFLECTIVE THINKERS AND PRACTITIONERS

There are several benefits to being able to reflect on what we do and how we do it:

- To enable us to learn from our experiences
- Promote the development of autonomous learning for self-directed professionals

- To help to close the gap between theory and practice
- To understand your actions and approach to career and personal life.

Below is a case study from Bryn (not his real name), a student who was advised by their personal tutor to reflect on their attitude to their academic work. Bryn was more than happy to share his experience if it helped other students avoid the same mistakes. This student's understanding of what went wrong shows that through reflection we can learn from our experiences, promote autonomous learning and learn to understand our actions and identify how to change.

═══════ STUDENT INSIGHT ═══════

Bryn talks about the importance of being honest in his reflective practice

I hadn't really thought about reflective practice until after my first year of being at university. I had been really excited about going as I was the first person from my family to go to university and as a result I felt a lot of pressure on me to achieve high marks. I also wanted to achieve high marks as I had done well at school without having to put too much effort in, it came naturally to me. I was really surprised when I got my marks for my first year and I had only just passed. I spoke with my personal tutor about my marks and what I could do. She advised me that I needed to put more effort in and reflect on what more I could have done and how I could achieve the marks I was hoping for. I took this advice to heart and decided to see what I could do to improve for next year. I was very honest with myself and wrote down what had gone wrong. I then put the reasons why it had gone wrong. For example, I believed that as I had done well at school that I didn't need to work hard to do well at university. I realised that I had only attended about half of the lectures and seminars and had never done the reading or work needed in preparation for the classes. I made a column of actions that I needed to take to prevent this in the future (see Table 10.1).

Table 10.1 Table of actions needed

What went wrong	Why it went wrong	What I need to do to improve
Scoring low marks with my assignments and only just passing	Because I didn't attend the classes or prepare for the classes that I did attend I was under a false impression that I already knew this information	I need to attend all the classes and make sure that I have given myself time to ensure I have prepared as I don't already know all the information
That I had provided mostly opinion in my assignments rather than having supporting evidence	I had not done enough reading and just filled up my assignments with my own ideas and opinions that were not supported	Make sure I have the key texts in advance of the semester starting and read them. Also read the recommended reading and read around the subject. This way I will be informed and not just going from my own opinion
That I had not fully understood the question and answered the question set	I had not bothered to find out what I needed to do in the areas that I didn't fully understand as I had missed the class where the assignment was discussed	Make sure I understand the question. Show the lecturer a plan of the assignment so that I am confident that I have it right

(Continued)

Table 10.1   (Continued)

What went wrong	Why it went wrong	What I need to do to improve
That I had rushed the assignments and not given myself time to proofread them, resulting in lots of typos and sentences that didn't really make sense	I hadn't given myself time to work on the assignments and to meet the deadline I had to just knock them out quickly, with the belief I would be fine	Ensure that I manage my time correctly and plan ahead to give myself time. Start a diary and schedule my study time and stick to it
That I had waffled or put a lot of unnecessary filler into the assignments to make up the word count	Because of the above I added a lot of stuff that wasn't relevant	Avoid not engaging with the information that I have provided and avoid waffle in the assignments. If it does not add anything to the answer, don't use it.
I had cut and paste a lot of information from websites that caused me to be investigated for poor academic practice, which then resulted in a resit being capped at a pass	Because I was short of time, I tried to use information that was not mine to fill up the assignment	Never try and pass others work off as mine. Cut and paste is a no-no. I will get kicked out if I do this again. Ensure that if I use other people's words that I reference them correctly

I went back to the table constantly during my second year to remind myself what I needed to do. I also reflected on how well I was doing and kept a record of that in another column. Taking the time out for reflection really had a big impact on me. I was very honest with myself and I learnt that I could make changes that would allow me to improve in the future. These skills are something that I use regularly now if there is a problem or a situation that I need to improve or change. I learnt a lot from this and I know that these skills will enable me to continue to develop my learning and awareness of myself going forward. As a result of reflecting in my first year I was able to complete my degree with first-class honours. If I hadn't taken these steps and learnt from my mistakes, I don't think I would have completed my degree at all.

 **ACTIVITY**

Improving your marks

Write down an example where you have been disappointed with a mark that you have received (could be at school or at university) and think about what it is that you could have done to improve that mark. Copy the grid shown in Table 10.2 onto paper and complete the columns. Complete 'What went wrong' first then complete the other two columns. Add more boxes if needed.

Table 10.2   Marks and actions to improve them

What went wrong	Why it went wrong	What I need to do to improve
Example: Scored low marks with assignments in XX subject and only just passed with 40%		

KEEPING A REFLECTIVE JOURNAL

Writing an experience down to be able to reflect upon and learn from can be both rewarding and practical in developing your reflective practice, whether you use a simple diary or a complicated in-depth journal. There are several models you can use, but there is no 'right' model: you need to use whichever model best fits you, your requirements and/or your needs at the time.

═══════════ ACTIVITY ═══════════

Recording reflections

There are several methods of recording and reflecting and it is important for you to find the method that works best for you. Use an internet search engine to find out what other methods (in addition to those below) are available, and choose one to try.

When reflecting, you do not just identify and observe more; you are providing yourself with deeper information and greater understanding in relation to the challenges, perception and theories that help you make sense of the knowledge and information that you want to see differently. When you start keeping a log or journal, remember to include:

- A clear description of the situation
- An honest account of the situation identifying what did or did not go well
- An analysis of your feelings at the time (angry, sad, annoyed, frustrated, etc). Understanding our feelings can help us understand our reaction to a situation. For example, if you know you are angry, you may reflect that this is not the time to talk to somebody about something that is bothering you, but rather wait until you have calmed down.
- An evaluation of the experience. Were there things that you could have avoided or done differently?
- An analysis of the experience. Think about what you have learned about yourself and your approach to the situation. Did the outcome surprise you? Was it what you hoped for? How do you feel about the reaction of others involved? How are you making sense of the situation?
- A conclusion and examination once you have taken time to reflect and come to a solution to move forward. Write a brief conclusion to allow you to summarise the situation. What would you do in the future?

In 1988, American sociologist and psychologist Graham Gibbs published his Reflective Cycle model in his book *Learning by Doing*. This is a useful framework to use as a starting point when you need to reflect on something. It is circular, so the more you reflect on something the more of the process you can go through until you have achieved the desired level, outcome, or approach. Look at a version of the Gibbs model in Figure 10.1 and then complete the task to start your reflection. If you are not comfortable with this template then use the one above in the activity or devise one of your own (remember it's about what works for you).

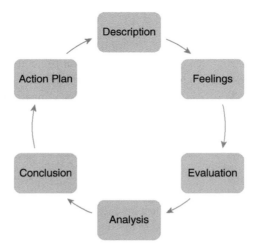

Figure 10.1   Reflective Cycle model. Based on work by Graham Gibbs (1988)

OVERARCHING SKILLS AUDIT TO TRACK YOUR REFLECTIVE SKILLS

REFLECTION EXERCISE

Using Gibbs's Reflective Cycle model

Identify a situation that you want to reflect on or develop the situation you used in the first activity in this chapter. Look at each of the headings in Table 10.3, draw up a similar table and fill it in to align to your chosen situation. This can be an argument, a problem, a difficult decision or anything that you feel you need to give more thought to so you can learn from the experience. Be as honest as you can with yourself (no-one else will see this). Review as often as you feel is necessary.

Table 10.3   Tracking my reflective skills

Describe what happened	What were you thinking and feeling at the time?	What was good and bad about the experience?	What sense can you make of the situation?	What else could you have done?	If it happened again, what would you do differently?

A reliable method of auditing your reflective practice and thinking skills is to be honest with yourself; to think about what it is you need to change; and later, when you are feeling more confident about your reflective skills, come back to this audit (see Table 10.4 below) and complete it again to see how much you have developed in these areas. There are no limits to the amount of times you can do this exercise.

Table 10.4   Audit of my reflective skills

Question	Answer	Is this always helpful?	Do you need to do anything to change this? (and if so, what?)
Do you make decisions without thinking?	Yes/No		
Do you consider events before making a decision?	Yes/No		
Do you research or investigate a situation before trying to solve a problem?	Yes/No		
Do you think you are always right and that others are wrong?	Yes/No		
Do you always give your opinion without having the evidence to support it?	Yes/No		
Do you look for other people's views and try to understand things from their perspective?	Yes/No		
Do you question your own beliefs and biases?	Yes/No		
Do you consciously reflect on situations or approaches?	Yes/No		
Do you consider how you can overcome barriers or problems?	Yes/No		

THINK POINT

By using reflection, you can become a more rounded person who can demonstrate a thoughtful approach to your life and work. Take the time to use reflection. Do not allow the pressure of a situation to prevent you from reflecting.

CONCLUSION

In this chapter we have covered:

• What is meant by reflection and becoming a reflective practitioner.
• The different models that are available when identifying and recording the need for reflection.

- How to complete a self-reflection personal development plan.
- The benefits to continued learning and personal development that becoming a reflective practitioner can have on us.

FURTHER READING

Boud, D., Keogh, R. and Walker, D. (1985) *Reflection: Turning Experience into Learning.* London: Kogan Page.

Jasper, M. (2013) *Beginning Reflective Practice.* Andover: Cengage Learning.

Open University (2020) *Strategic Study Skills: Be Aware of your Habits* [online]. Available at: https://help.open.ac.uk/be-aware-of-your-habits (accessed 23 June 2020).

Plymouth University, Learning Development (2010) *Reflective Writing* [online]. Available at: https://www.plymouth.ac.uk/uploads/production/document/path/1/1717/Reflective_Writing.pdf

Taylor, S.S. (2015) *You're a Genius: Using Reflective Practice to Master the Craft of Leadership.* New York: Business Expert Press.

Williams, K., Woolliams, M. and Spiro, J. (2012) *Reflective Writing.* Basingstoke: Palgrave Macmillan.

11

TIME MANAGEMENT

CHAPTER LEARNING OBJECTIVES

By the end of this chapter you should be able to:

- Demonstrate understanding of what time management means.
- Identify the skills required to manage your time effectively.
- Locate resources on time management.
- Apply knowledge to prepare a time management plan.
- Put into practice a method of time management.

GLOSSARY

- **Procrastinate:** to delay, postpone or put something off.
- **Productivity:** the state of being productive: how much you are producing as a result of your efforts.

INTRODUCTION

How often have you said to yourself, 'I don't have the time to do this' yet spent a considerable amount of time playing video games, socialising, on social media or watching television? How many times have you said to yourself, 'I'll just watch one more episode/play one more game/stay in bed another ten minutes', rather than start working on something that you know you need to finish, like an assignment? This is procrastinating. It is easier to **procrastinate** and then complain that you have no time than it is to make a start.

During the process of writing this book, the authors often realised we were procrastinating rather than getting on with it. At those points we stopped and reflected (see Chapter 10) that if we kept doing this, the publishers will be concerned that the book will be unfinished. We did not want to work long and late days and nights to finish the book. We did not want to be in the situation of leaving everything to the last minute, as most people do not produce their best work under those conditions. Additionally, in your mind you can then blow out of all proportion how big and how difficult the task may be. This can also become a real barrier to getting on with something.

 ━━━━━ STUDENT INSIGHT ━━━━━

Nanthi talks about how he procrastinates

I love writing and thinking, so it is not a chore for me. I am just a natural procrastinator. I also live with a procrastinator. If it was an Olympic sport, we would have gold and silver medals! I have to really take the time and plan my schedule to ensure that I have set times for set tasks. I also set alarms in my phone to help remind me. It has taken a lot of willpower for me to stick to the schedule, but I am so glad I do. It has made a tremendous difference to me, my peace of mind and to the quality of my work. In fact, I now don't find that I procrastinate half as much as I used to. I am far more motivated as I have seen the results. The best bit of advice I could give a student who doesn't manage their time well is to have a go. If I can do it so can they.

Figure 11.1   Procrastinating is easy!

As authors, we have learnt the skills we need to manage time effectively and we share these methods with you in this chapter. Although our advice is not rocket science, there are simple, yet effective methods that you can use to be able to achieve your goals, without (no pun intended) taking up too much of your time. Sometimes time management for a project is just about allocating yourself a set amount of time to complete something within a deadline. That is how we approached the chapters for this book. We knew what we had to achieve and by when, so allocated a set amount of time to work on the chapters. We will be looking at how we managed this later on in this chapter, alongside other methods of time management.

═══ STUDENT INSIGHT ═══

Kavita reflects on her first year at university undertaking her tourism and marketing degree and how she had to start to be more organised

Where do I begin? This was my first time living on my own and away from my mum and dad. I didn't realise how unorganised I was until I had to manage my own time. I also didn't realise just how much my parents did for me that I took for granted. As soon as I got to university I went and found myself a part-time job in a hotel. I loved the job and it gave me a real insight into the area of hospitality and tourism that I would like to work in when I have completed my degree. I worked on the reception greeting guests and checking them in and helping them settle up their accounts at the end of their stay. I worked shifts, so some late nights and some early mornings. In addition to this, I met and made a lot of new friends who were real party people. I enjoyed the socialising and the going out on my own; I hadn't been one for going out when I lived with my parents as they were there to remind me that I had homework to do.

I never missed classes, but I was often tired when I went to class and I never really found the time to do any reading or pre-work. I thought I would be fine. That was until the week before all the essays were due to be handed in. I had three assignments to complete in seven days, which I had not started. I began to panic a bit about them and I could really feel my stress levels building up. It was at that point that I realised I had to use my time wisely. I looked at my calendar and put in when I had to work. The rest of the time available to me I scheduled for writing the essays. I didn't go out during this week other than to work and I did complete the essays. However, I only just scraped by with passing them, which I was really disappointed about as I had worked really hard that week, along with really late nights and early mornings. What has this experience taught me? I just can't leave things to the last minute. There were plenty of opportunities in the weeks leading up to the hand-in week that I could have found time to plan, read around and start work on these essays. I would have been far less stressed and would have written far better assignments. For me it is just about making sure I find the time. This is my future. If I can find the time to go out, work, go to the gym, and all the other things I do, then I can certainly find the time to study. In my second trimester I did just that. I made a time management plan and I stuck to it. I still had time to work, and go out, but I also had enough time to study. For me this really paid off. The following two assignments were much better than the previous trimester – I achieved a 70 and above for them all. I also engaged more in class as I had more knowledge to be able to contribute. I felt much less stressed and found the assignments much easier to write. I would recommend to all students that it is important to find the time to study every week, and every day if you can. It really makes a difference.

WHAT IS TIME MANAGEMENT?

Time management is how you organise and spend your time. There are 168 hours in a week – what are you using those hours for and how productive are you during those hours? Lee-Davies (2007: 170) describes time as 'perishable, so once it is spent it is natural to justify to ourselves that we have spent it wisely and we may go to great pains to do this'. However, often we are not spending that time wisely, we are procrastinating, not getting on with what we need to achieve. As a result we have 'spent' our available time and have none left to complete what we need to complete effectively.

Mackenzie and Nickerson (2009) talk about 'Time Traps' which are distractions that can eat into your time and prevent you from using the time you have to complete the things you want to complete as they are a 'drain on your time'. They believe that to see if you have managed your time effectively, at the end of your day you need to ask yourself, how many minutes or hours was I able to concentrate on a task without being distracted? It would make sense that before you are able to manage your time effectively you need to be able to remove as many of those distractions as possible. Firstly, this can be achieved through knowing how you use your time. Secondly, by identifying time within a day or week that you have available to you. Thirdly, by ensuring that the time you have available to you is used effectively, by setting it aside to complete the tasks you need to complete.

Remember, time management skills are not something that we are born with; we learn these skills throughout our life and from experiences, which we then use and put in practice to allow us to be productive (Williams, 2011).

- Plan your time to prevent distractions
- Find a method of allowing yourself to plan and complete your goals with the minimum amount of stress
- Organise your time to allow tasks to be worked on and completed

TIME MANAGEMENT METHODS AND SKILLS

You will be able to find a range of apps that can be downloaded for free on your phone or tablet to help you manage your time. In addition, there are several different methods or project management programmes available. These can be extremely useful methods for managing large projects where you have a lot of other people involved that you need to manage and communicate with. However, as a student, you do not need to make time management complicated or spend as much time on managing your time as you do on the actual task you are looking to manage. For many students to effectively manage their time, all they need to do is:

- Write a to-do list (this is a basic method)
- Schedule appointments with yourself to create time blocks for work that has priority.

Keep a diary/calendar and keep it up-to-date (electronic diaries/calendars are easy to use and are with us most of the time). Ideally, have your electronic calendar linked up to your mobile phone, so you have it with you all the time and can also update it on the go.

- Plan to spend 50% of your time working on activities that produce results
- Set goals before starting a task, so you can measure your success

By setting yourself goals and achieving those goals, you will be surprised how much you can get done and the sense of achievement you will feel. This will also become a habit for you over time and you will find you become naturally productive.

- Block out other distractions: emails, mobile phones, Twitter, YouTube, Instagram and Facebook; it is easy to be drawn into these and lose valuable time
- It is impossible to get everything done in one session; make notes on the things you need to focus on next time so you don't forget

It is surprising how much we can be distracted by things around us and how much time we can waste on those distractions. Before you start to work, turn off those possible distractions so you can concentrate on what you are scheduled to achieve in that session. Additionally, make sure that you are being realistic in what you are hoping to achieve in the session. Give yourself a list of what you want to achieve and tick each thing off as you complete it.

- Review on a weekly basis how well you are using your time
- Identify the relevant resources you need prior to starting

Know the stages you need to cover

Think about what you need to consider and do to help with your own time management:

- A simple to-do list that you can mark tasks off as they are completed
- A weekly planner detailing what you have to complete and what you would like to complete on top
- Check off each completed task (gives a sense of achievement)
- Have a long-term planner so you know deadlines you are working to
- Only you can do it

Using a weekly planner: One way to manage your time

Some students find that using an online calendar is a useful way of managing their time. Some of the key stages in this are:

- Identify at the beginning of each month what has to be completed and by when – divide that into weeks
- Identify anything that has not been completed from the previous month
- Identify how much time is needed to complete the tasks
- Identify what time you have available in that month and when
- If not enough time available, then prioritise tasks

When prioritising a task, think about when that task has to be completed, how important is the task, and what are the outcomes of completing the task. Hospitals prioritise ('triage') all the time. For example, if two people turn up at Accident and Emergency at the same time, one has a sprained ankle and the other has severe pains in their chest and numbness down the arm. The hospital staff will prioritise the latter patient over the sprained ankle. This is because a person is very unlikely to die from a sprained ankle. However, the person with the pains in their chest could be having a heart attack and this could be life threatening. While this is an extreme example of prioritising, think about the consequences of not adopting this approach.

You have an assignment due at the end of the week and you want to proofread it and make a couple of changes and at that same allocated time you want to watch a television programme. Which one is your priority? Not watching the television programme is not likely to affect your future. However, not handing in the assignment with the best work you can do could affect your future. Therefore, the assignment should take priority. Prioritising work is an important employability skill, one that will allow you to be productive and avoid distractions (Mackenzie, 1990). Additionally, being able to prioritise is often a task that can be part of an assessment centre exercise, where you will be given a full in-tray and you will have to prioritise the work in it (see the exercises in Chapters 32 and 33). It is useful to be able to allocate each task with the date and time that you need to be able to complete the task.

Example of a typical student's day

Table 11.1   Daily planner

Daily planner

Time	Monday 1st	Notes	Date to be completed
9.00	Leave home to get to university by 10am		
10.00	Seminar: Tourism and the Future; room 536	Take notes for group activity	
11.00			
12.00	Lunch		
13.00	Library: work on planning the assignment for the module Tourism and the Future. Need the key text, laptop and the notes from seminars		Hand in on 31st this month
14.00			
15.00	Lecture: Eco Tourism; room 242		
16.00	Meet Group: finish rehearsing the presentation for Eco Tourism. Find empty classroom	Meeting group in the canteen	Friday 5th this month
17.00			
18.00	Evening meal		
19.00	Attend the film society	My turn to take snacks	
20.00			
21.00	Spare time		

Daily planner

Time	Monday 1st	Notes	Date to be completed
22.00	Spare time		
23.00	Bed		
	Notes		
Remember that tomorrow you need to be up early for rowing club and have a personal tutor meeting at 11am.			

From this example you can see the student has:

- Identified what has to be completed by when
- Allocated suitable time for each task
- Given themselves enough time
- Highlighted where they have space for unexpected tasks
- Understood and is realistic about what they can achieve in a day or a week
- Understood that if they stick to the plan, they will not be unprepared or late for anything

============== ACTIVITY ==============

Your calendar for next week

Using the approach above (either on paper or use an online calendar such as Outlook or your phone), plan out your week in full.

FACTORS THAT CAN NEGATIVELY INFLUENCE YOUR STUDIES AND HAVE AN IMPACT ON YOUR PLANS TO MANAGE YOUR TIME

Everyone's life is different and everyone has to deal with competing priorities. However, there are usually a few common factors that can affect a student's ability to manage their time:

============== REFLECTION EXERCISE ==============

Factors that negatively influence your own studies and time

Before you read the following page, write down five factors that have tended to negatively influence your own studies and have an impact on your plans to manage your time.

Poor study environment

It is important to have somewhere that you are comfortable working and that is conducive to being able to work without too many disruptions. This will be different for everyone, so know where you need to be in order to be productive. For some people, it is sitting on the sofa with a laptop. For others it may be sitting at a desk or using the library quiet areas. Plan your time to be in a suitable area when studying.

Lack of sleep

If you are tired, then it is difficult to concentrate on your studies and easy to avoid your plan. Try to ensure that you are able to get some good quality sleep prior to a busy day. A good night's sleep will help you to stay on plan. Sometimes when we have a lot on our mind or we are worrying about completing a task then it is difficult to get to sleep. Avoid caffeine for five hours prior to wanting to go to sleep as this will help. Additionally, there are many mindfulness and relaxation apps that can help you drift off to sleep; a quick app search will turn up lots of these, for example Mindbody, 10% Happier, Sleep Cycle and Calm. There are many more apps available and it is about finding the one that best suits you.

Peer pressure to socialise

This may very well be your first time living away from home. You will have made a lot of new friends and it is very tempting to forget everything else you need to complete and go out. Therefore, it is important when you are scheduling your time management plan to ensure that you allocate yourself time for fun. That way you will have the best of both worlds. Keep in mind that the reason you have decided to go to college or university is to provide yourself with the foundations you need to gain employment in your chosen area. Don't allow others to put pressure on you which might distract you from your longer-term goals.

Not understanding the task

If you do not understand a task, worrying ineffectually is not a good use of your time. Make a few notes on what it is you are confused about or don't understand and arrange to meet with the appropriate person, normally a member of teaching staff. Take your notes with you and ensure you have some clarity. Do not leave this until the last minute. Additionally, your peer group can be a good source of information and support. Talk to them about the task, ask how they are getting on with it, or if there are any areas they are not sure about. Do it as soon as you can. This will give you the confidence to move forward and to keep on track with your set tasks.

Not asking for help and advice

Always ask for help and advice as soon as you need it. Often teaching staff will have office hours and also leave time after class. They also have email addresses or communication portals available on their virtual learning environment. Make use of these as soon as possible. Clarity is important and will give you the reassurance that what you are doing is in the right area.

Not reading the assignment question carefully

It is a regular occurrence that students come to tutors and say they don't understand what they should be doing for the assignment. By asking them a few questions, it soon becomes clear that they haven't read the assignment, looked at the marking scheme/rubric or even looked at the additional materials provided on the virtual learning environment. Before talking to your lecturer or planning your assignment, make sure you have read it and all the additional information available on the assignment. Then if you still don't understand what is required, talk to the lecturer. Then you are ready to plan the research, reading and any other tasks.

Not allowing yourself time

Again, this is one of the issues that can cause students to fail or receive a low mark for an assignment. If you leave it to the last minute, you are not going to be able to produce the quality of work you are capable of. Additionally, a rushed assignment often lacks clarity, structure and supporting evidence. If you plan your reading and make appropriate notes on the reading, then you will be prepared ahead of time. Giving yourself the time to work on your assignment allows you to provide the best assignment you can.

You cannot usually write an assignment just from your own head and personal knowledge. You need to plan it, read around the subject and support your statements and findings. Without this you are just filling a page with opinion that is unfounded and you do not demonstrate to the reader that you are providing a rounded assignment.

Going out and partying, watching TV, playing games, social media

This speaks for itself. While these things can be useful distractions and can allow you time to clear your mind and feel relaxed, they should not come at the cost of your studies or achieving your set task. If you have planned time to socialise or do something other than study, then you will not miss out. However, make sure you stick to the times you have allocated for study as well as play. Remember, you are paying a lot of money for your education, don't waste the money, make the most of it and manage your time wisely. Think about your studies as a job: it has to be done and done to the best of your abilities.

There are bound to be many other things that you might be tempted to put in front of your studies and academic work. However, if you have a clear plan that you know is manageable then you will be able to finish the day feeling confident that you are on top of things. Kavita showed in her student insight how she overcame the issue of finding time to study.

======================== ACTIVITY ========================

Reflecting on Kavita's story

Reflect on Kavita's story from earlier in this chapter. Write a list of the issues that she had that you can relate to. Then add any further issues you had to that list. What are the similarities to you when it comes to struggling with managing your time? Keep the list until you have completed reading this chapter. Once you have finished the chapter, return to this list and write down how you will use the knowledge gained from this chapter to overcome the issues you have identified.

BENEFITS OF GOOD TIME MANAGEMENT

─── REFLECTION EXERCISE ═══════════════════

Good time management

Write down a few notes on how you would benefit from adopting good time management and the advantages you would gain from managing your time more effectively.

Good time management will help you organise and manage your studies to ensure that you cover and understand the work you are required to undertake as part of your course. Those students who achieve a top-class degree (e.g. in the UK this would be a First with honours) do so because they plan to do so. They ensure that they have completed all the work and reading set for their course and manage their time effectively to meet deadlines. They are surprisingly the least stressed students, as they have planned in advance what they need to complete and have stuck to that plan. Therefore, they have reduced their stress levels and increased their **productivity** (Williams, 2011). Knowing what you need to complete and by when is really important. The organised student will access their virtual learning environment before the teaching period starts. They will identify what tasks need completing by when, what reading needs to be completed and know the dates of assignments, exams, presentations, etc. They will also meet with or talk to their lecturers several times during the teaching period to ensure they are on track and working in the correct areas.

All the tasks listed above can be scheduled using an online calendar to spread out the work and tasks over the amount of teaching weeks. It is also a good idea to print out the weekly schedule and have this above your work area so that you can constantly remind yourself what is coming up. Additionally, setting alerts for the scheduled study time on your phone or tablet, so you receive a reminder, can be useful. Breaking down a task into manageable steps will help you to manage a large project. That is why you need to plan in advance.

Managing your time takes practice and commitment. However, the more you do it the more it will become second nature. You will also enjoy the feeling of knowing that you can achieve and complete tasks and projects on time and without too much stress and anxiety (see the time management skills audit at the end of this chapter). Remember, good time management saves you time, energy and sleepless nights, and proves to future employers what you are capable of (Williams, 2011). Time management is a skill that is highly valued by employers and what you learn about managing your time at university is directly transferable into the workplace (Adebisi, 2013; Institute of Leadership and Mana, 2007; Knox, 2012). Employers are specifically looking for people who can be productive, who know how to prioritise their work and who can deliver projects and tasks on time. Often in an interview you will be asked about a project that you have had to deliver and how you managed that project (see Chapter 31).

Identifying time available to you

Before you start to try and manage your time, it is important to know what your current commitments are, for example, part-time work, lectures, seminars/workshops, caring responsibilities, travel, planned holiday, leisure time, etc. Once you know your commitments then you can identify what time you have available to you. Think of time as a commodity: you only have a finite amount available to you in a week, month or year. If you waste that time, it is gone forever and cannot be retrieved. No amount of money can buy back one second of time. Once you have completed this list, then be honest with yourself about what the distractions are that cause you to use your time up without being productive. For many students, it can be their mobile phone, the news, sport, YouTube and Netflix.

STUDENT INSIGHT

Jake talks about how he manages his time

When I realised that I had too much information to keep in my head (after I missed an important appointment) I decided I needed everything written down. I didn't want to keep a written diary that I had to carry around all the time. If I lost it, I would lose everything. I decided to use an online calendar system, Outlook, which syncs with all my electronic devices, my phone, laptop and tablet. I have notifications turned on and reminders so that I don't forget to look at what I have scheduled. Mapping this all out in a weekly calendar really helped me to visualise how I use my time. What it also did for me was to show me that I had a lot of time available to me to use. I don't know how I filled that time in the past, I just seemed to waste it doing nothing. Below is an example of one week that I have mapped out. From this I can easily see the whole week's activities and if something else comes up I can easily see where I can fit this in. I always have a lunch break scheduled every day. Normally every 60 minutes I take a 5–10 minute break. Having a break away from what I am doing helps me to stay fresh and focussed.

Figure 11.2   Example of online time management schedule

Additionally, you can add more detail for each of the time allocated tasks. For example, if you double-click on Tuesday 28 April you can write more detailed notes.

Figure 11.3   Example of adding notes to an online time management schedule

In this area you can paste information, drag and drop information that you may need or just make notes. This function allows you to have information you may need at your fingertips. If you are going to a meeting always drag and drop the agenda and minutes from the previous meeting here. The same if you are going to class: drop in the questions that you may have on what is going to be covered. It will also help you to add hyperlinks to information that you may need to access when you are in class, especially if you are working in groups and you had to have some pre-work or reading prepared ready for the class and group activity. This helps you to manage your information and time, preventing you having to go looking for information when in a meeting or in a class which can prevent you from engaging with what is happening. It also provides you with confidence and reduces your potential stress levels as you are prepared and have the information at your fingertips.

Table 11.2   Overarching skills audit to track your development

Activity

Complete this checklist. Where you have a cross, take time to consider how you can make changes to turn that into a tick. Revisit this audit after a week and undertake it again to see if anything has changed. If you have made changes and have turned a cross into a tick, reward yourself with something.			
Checklist	**✓ or X**	**If you have a X in the box, consider the following**	**Reflect here: how can you change the situation?**
Do you leave everything to the last minute?		How can you plan ahead?	
Do you turn up to class without undertaking the pre-class preparation?		Allocate yourself time to prepare for class a week ahead and make notes to take to class	
Do you sit in front of your computer and not know what you should be doing?		Ensure that you plan what you are going to work on and have the reading or proprietary work/notes and your assignment plan available and complete before you start to write an assignment	

Activity

When facing a task, does it feel like it is far too big to manage?	Break the task down into small manageable sections. Work on those sections one at a time and then bring together to create a whole. Mind Mapping can help here (see Chapter 4)	
Do you suffer from anxiety and stress when thinking about completing an assignment?	Plan your work carefully, spreading it out over several weeks so that you are prepared for the writing up of an assignment	
Are there times when you don't understand what it is you should be doing?	Talk to your lecturer or your personal tutor	
Do you receive feedback telling you that you have missed the point of the assignment or that you have not met all the requirements of the assignment?	Give yourself time, through your time management, to create an assignment plan. Take this plan to your lecturer	
Are you confident on what it is you need to complete on a daily or weekly basis?	Create a to-do list and cross off tasks as you complete them. This can give you a real sense of achievement and satisfaction	
Are you always running late, or missing things that you need to attend or complete?	Think about how you are managing your time and map out a clear calendar of events, times, dates and locations	
Are you easily distracted by other things when you sit down to work?	Turn off the distractions, so that the time you have allocated for study is uninterrupted	
Do you procrastinate (not get on with things)?	Set an alarm to sound when you are scheduled to study. Whatever you are doing at that point stop. Open your books or computer and just start.	

If you have any crosses in the boxes then you are probably not managing your time effectively and you need to think about how you are going to use the examples in this chapter to take control of your time, give yourself the support you need to achieve your goal and ensure that you are being the best student that you can be. In the box on the right, write down what you will do to make these changes and to be able to meet your deadlines. Commit to yourself, have confidence in your abilities to manage your time and make the most of the time you have available.

REFLECTION EXERCISE

What is stopping you?

Think about what it is that has caused you stress about studying in the past. Make a list of all the things that have prevented you from studying (be as honest as you can here). Then make a list of when you have achieved a high mark or received positive rewarding feedback on your work. What are the differences between the two? What can you identify from these lists? How can you make changes to your time management to ensure you have suitable time to complete tasks?

Figure 11.4   The benefits of good time management

THINK POINT

Remember, only you can make this happen. No one can do this for you. Think about what it is you want to achieve and plan to succeed rather than procrastinate and fail. Manage your time effectively, rather than letting time get away from you and leaving everything to the last minute.

ACTIVITY

Planning your time with an electronic calendar or diary

This activity can be completed using an electronic calendar or using a diary that you write in. Open up next week's calendar and start to plan your week. Firstly, fill in everything that you want to complete that is not study related. Place everything you can into the calendar that will take you away from study. Most of us have commitments that we just cannot get out of, such as lectures, seminars, workshops, work, caring, travel, social events, etc. Once these are entered into your calendar then identify what time you have left for study. If you have no time left for study, then you will have to look again at what you have entered in the calendar and prioritise differently to allow time for study. Try to aim for 50% of your available time dedicated to study.

Secondly, enter where and when you are going to study into the calendar. Stick to this for a week. At the end of the week go through the calendar again and check off the time slots you were able to allocate to study. Then reflect on how this has made you feel. If you have met all the time slots, do you feel a sense of achievement? Has it made you more productive? Are you able to engage more in class and contribute more to the sessions? Do you feel less stressed or anxious about attending class? Understanding how you feel about being more organised can help you train your brain to expect this in the future and stick to your plan.

Understanding how to manage your time will allow you to reduce the stress and anxiety that many students face in attending classes and completing assignments on time and to a high standard. By developing the skills of effective time management, you can allocate time to your studies in addition to fitting in all the other commitments you have as a student.

CONCLUSION

In this chapter we have covered:

* The benefits of good time management and planning.
* How to avoid procrastination.
* Why it is important to plan ahead to meet a deadline or complete a project.
* How to create a simple time management plan.
* How effective time management can increase your productivity and reduce anxiety and stress.
* Identifying the skills you will need to help you manage your time and how to reflect on what has not worked for you in the past to make changes to your approach to your studies.
* Identifying the areas where you need to make changes and how these changes can ensure you meet your commitments, deadlines and personal goals.

FURTHER READING

Mackenzie, A. (1990) *The Time Trap*. New York: AMACOM.
Institute of Leadership and Management (2007) *Achieving Objectives Through Time Management Super Series*. Burlington: Taylor & Francis.
Tracy, B. (2014) *Time Management*. New York: AMACOM.
Williams, K. (2011) *Time Management*. Basingstoke: Palgrave Macmillan.

SECTION B

PERSONAL DEVELOPMENT AND EMPLOYABILITY SKILLS

Level: 5

12

DEVELOPING SKILLS FOR WORK AND LIFE

CO-WRITTEN WITH ROSY JONES

CHAPTER LEARNING OBJECTIVES

By the end of this chapter you should be able to:

- Understand the skills and competencies that contribute to your employability.
- Analyse which of those skills you have developed and which you could work on.
- Develop a plan for building and developing your skills.
- Action the plan and review what your next steps should be.

GLOSSARY

- **Employability:** 'a set of achievements – skills, understandings and personal attributes – that makes graduates more likely to gain employment and be successful in their chosen occupations' (Yorke, 2006: 8).
- **Human capital:** the experience and skills an individual or population has and their value or cost to an organisation or country.
- **Psychological capital:** personal attributes that define a person's attitude to risk, resilience, confidence and goal-setting.
- **Social capital:** the networks and social ties between people, which 'create a bridge between graduates' educational, social and labour market experience' (Tomlinson and Holmes, 2017: 18) and helps broker access to job opportunities.

INTRODUCTION

This section outlines some of the skills that you will need to acquire in order to prepare for the world of work. The skills described in this chapter and those that follow will help you to develop skills that employers might find attractive in their staff and to research, seek out and define the kind of jobs that you would like to work in. The phrase **'employability** skills' has become a shorthand for a collection of personal skills, competencies, knowledge and connections that employers and researchers have worked together to define over the last 40 years of so (Whistance and Campbell, 2019). For a long time, employers have asked universities to produce graduates who are knowledgeable in the subject that they are studying, capable of the technical skills that are required by the industry (for example, event management knowledge and experience) and who have less 'concrete' attributes such as self-confidence and resilience. This chapter will give you an overview of those that are the most sought after by employers and students.

Employability skills are not something that you will learn overnight, and indeed some are innate for some and difficult to acquire for others. These are skills that you will develop and hone over the whole of your lifetime. This section includes several chapters that highlight the most important key skills and attributes for your industry.

WHAT ARE THE EMPLOYABILITY SKILLS YOU NEED?

Employability skills fall into three inter-related groups: human, psychological and social capital, all of which are underpinned by the experience of work.

Human capital includes the personal skills and knowledge that you might consider to be the core of the university degree that you are studying:

- Personal skills and capabilities (including the development of digital capabilities)
- Interpersonal and communications skills
- Work-related skills (including workplace etiquette, essential processes and procedures, and health and safety knowledge where applicable)
- Industry-specific knowledge
- Career skills (including job opportunity identification, skills for applications, and interviews and job readiness).

Psychological capital includes key personality traits that employers ask for:

- Self-efficacy ('I can'/'I believe I will be able to')
- Resilience ('I am able to recover quickly from a difficult situation')
- Goal-setting ('I may not be able to do that now, but I can see a way to learn how to/plan to do it and I will put that in place')
- Confidence ('I trust that my skills and capabilities are good enough').

Social capital refers to the connections, networks and people that you have relationships with, and who would be able to support your search for work through introductions, potential offers of placements or internships, or supporting the development of your industry knowledge and skills. In the literature, social capital is divided into two areas:

- Forming connections (the 'bridge' into a community or knowledge group, often called 'bridging capital')
- Embedding (the 'bond' with a community, such as becoming part of a team or taking part in the organisation of a wider group, often called 'bonding capital').

Key to all these skills and attributes is work experience itself (see Chapter 21). Experience of work will help you to develop each of these; and if you find yourself in a place where you would like to further your career, then the social capital you will develop as part of work experience will be invaluable. We can formulate these skills into a handy diagram, shown in Figure 12.1.

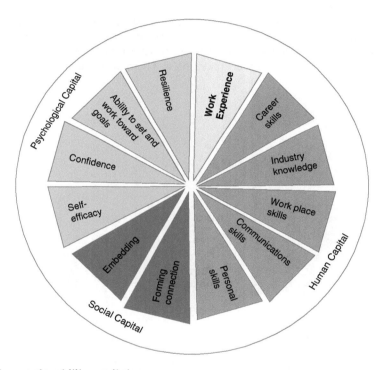

Figure 12.1   The employability capital compass

Source: developed from Jones and Sant (2013) and updated for this chapter, March 2020. Permissions given.

ACTIVITY

Using the employability capital compass

Using the employability capital compass above, do the following:

- Analyse which skills you have developed and which you could work on.
- Develop a plan for building and developing your skills.
- Action the plan and review what your next steps should be.

REFLECTION EXERCISE

Analysing your skills

Reflect on your own personal skills. Which of these do you feel you already have, or are currently developing as part of your course, work or leisure activities? Which do you think that you are unlikely to build at the moment?

1. Write a list of the skills that you have.
2. Grade them: which are well-developed? Which are not?
3. Identifying the skills that you are *most* confident with, consider how you can use these to best develop your employability and job skills. What plan could you put in place to make the best of these skills?
4. Thinking about the skills that you are least confident about, which is the highest priority?
5. Map all the skills that you want to work on, taking note of both their importance and your current level of skill.

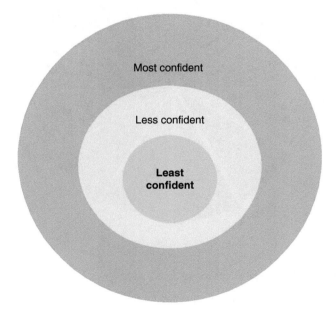

Figure 12.2   Skills target

DEVELOPING YOUR SKILLS: TAKING STEPS

For each of the skills that you want to develop, you should practise the skill of goal-setting. Depending on your outlook and the method you are most comfortable with, you can start either with the kite (if you like thinking about the landscape and context first and actions later) or the string (if you tend to develop ideas from a small start and grow them).

Flying high exercise

From the perspective of the kite, how would you describe being fully competent in the skill that you have identified? Can you say what it would feel like, or look like to someone else? What would you be able to do? Now think of what would make you *almost* that confident or capable. What would be the one task or exercise that you could undertake to master the skill? What would the last polish entail? Now work down the string of the kite, thinking of each of those levels being just a little less skilful than the one before. For each of those levels of competence, what would you do to work up to the next step?

If you are someone who likes to develop your thoughts step by step, think about your current capability. Considering a small step towards full mastery of the skill, what would be the first thing you could do that would take you up the string of the kite? Don't try and rush all the way up to the kite itself – just feel your way along the string in stages. Plan to do that first task alone, and then review how confident you feel once you've done it. In this way, you can set goals to gradually improve your skills.

===== ACTIVITY =====

List the five key competencies that you want to develop this term

1.
2.
3.
4.
5.

DEVELOPING PSYCHOLOGICAL AND SOCIAL CAPITAL

While human capital traits are generally simple to develop alongside your course and other activities, developing social and psychological capital may be more daunting. Your approach to risk is a very personal one and impacts on your confidence and self-efficacy in different situations. Most of the human capital traits included here are covered in sections A and B of this book, and social capital (generally developed through the workplace, networking and work-based skills) is covered in sections C and D. Psychological capital is generally developed through practice and self-reflection. For example, if you consider the skill of resilience in the context of giving a presentation, it allows you to control your nerves when presenting to others and allows you to learn from a presentation that doesn't go well. Other techniques can be brought over from research in high-risk and extreme sports. For example, mental tasks that have been developed by gymnasts to challenge themselves to perform exercises they consider risky can be used to further your resilience and confidence (Chase et al., 2005). Their tips are as follows:

1. *'Just go for it'*. Once you've got to the point of no return (e.g. lingering by the entrance to a networking event), just do it. It may feel tough the first time, but the second time will be easier.

2. *Seek trust, advice and support from a mentor or friend.* Bounce your ideas (and fears) off a mentor or a friend, or take up some of the support that your college or university might have available. Speaking about your fears to someone who is less emotionally involved might help you to get perspective.

3. *Imagery.* Imagine yourself doing whatever it is that you need to do. This is a technique that top sportspeople use to help them to imagine success.

4. *Positive self-talk.* Counter any negativity or doubt with positive thoughts and self-talk. It takes practice, but it's effective.

5. *Selective focus and attention.* Otherwise known as 'fake it till you make it'! Imagine that you've done it three times and that therefore this time will be a success too.

6. *Relaxation.* Practise some self-relaxation techniques, such as breathing slowly, mindfulness exercises or concentrating on something complex and physical, such as juggling. This should reduce your anxiety level and clear your mind.

OTHER ACTIVITIES THAT DEVELOP EMPLOYABILITY SKILLS

- Join a team, group activity, club or performing group and take some responsibility for the organisation of the club or some of its activities.
- Take a holiday on your own or with a friend. Don't go for a package holiday; instead, book your accommodation yourself and organise your own transport.
- Find some work experience, or internship in a place that is out of your current experience. For example, you might contact your dream employer and ask for a couple of days shadowing a current or recent graduate trainee.
- Go to a networking event and come away with five business cards or contact details of people who could help you find work experience or a job.

 EMPLOYER INSIGHT

Carnival UK

If you're looking to find out more about employability skills and which ones are considered important in the hospitality industry, then the best place to look is the employers themselves, starting with their recruitment websites. Carnival UK is one of the largest holiday companies in the UK, running both the Cunard Line of transatlantic liners and P&O Cruises. Its head office is based in Southampton, across the road from the dockside. Carnival employs more than 2500 people in roles from shipbuilding to children's entertainment.

A recent job advert (see below) outlines the skills and capabilities that Carnival UK is looking for in its graduate employees. Job adverts can tell you a lot about the culture of the organisation. In this case, the Health, Environment, Safety and Security section of the job description underlines Carnival UK's commitment to these areas throughout their company and businesses. Look at the language used by the recruiter. There are knowledge-based skills (human capital) that they expect their applicants to demonstrate, such as the ability to manage surveys or use internal systems, and there are terms that suggest a psychological approach (or capital), such as 'proactively champion' and 'drive guest satisfaction'.

P&O Cruises Job Description – Assistant, Guest Insight & Research, Carnival UK

Role Description: To drive guest satisfaction by providing understanding of guest needs, motivations and experiences.

Accountabilities

- Manage surveys
- Support development of research
- Support internal teams
- Use internal systems

Scope

- Problem-solving: Apply a range of techniques, apply analytical expertise
- Impact: Seek and suggest ways of improving guest experience
- Leadership: Proactively champion our guests

Demonstrable behaviours

- Analytical
- Good at communication
- Conscientious
- Shows initiative

Knowledge, experience and qualifications

- Manage data
- Interpret and analyse data
- Understanding of market research

Health Environment Safety and Security (HESS) Responsibilities

- Promote safe working
- Lead by example
- Adhere to GDPR

General responsibilities

- Adhere to codes of conduct and Corporate Policies and Procedures

(*Source*: CarnivalUKcareers.co.uk, 2020)

WORK EXPERIENCE – THE ALL-ROUND SKILL DEVELOPER

Employability skills may not all be included in your coursework, but you will develop them in the workplace. There's nothing like a job that you *don't* want to do to help focus your mind and identify what you *do* want to do. Never pass up on the opportunity to spend some time in the industry, via a part-time job, work placement or internship.

Work experience will also help you to develop your confidence, resilience and psychological skills. Working with other people (perhaps in your field, or perhaps not) will help you to focus on what you might want to do and set goals. You can build resilience with tough customers or long shifts, learning about yourself as well as about the industry. Moreover, work placements will help you to develop your networks and connections. Many employers think of internships as an opportunity to 'interview' potential graduate trainees for a few weeks or months; research by the Institute for Student Employers showed that 34% of graduates recruited had previously interned for the same company (Cullinane and Montacute, 2018) and that those who had interned were generally paid higher on graduation than those who had not. Even if you choose not to work with the company that you have spent time with (or, as may be the case with smaller businesses, opportunities may not arise), you will have developed key contacts and an insider's understanding of the industry. Work experience works.

 ━━━ THINK POINT ━━━━━━━━━━━

Think of employability skills as dynamic life skills that require on-going development to ensure that your career is future-proofed. Employability is linked to a graduate's ability to demonstrate technical know-how, soft skills and behavioural attributes. These three facets form the basis of most careers in tourism, hospitality and events sector.

CONCLUSION

In this chapter we have covered:

* The wide range of skills and capabilities that contribute to employability.
* The different types of capabilities that make up a holistic, employable skill set, and considered the differences between human, social and psychological capital.
* Some of these skills and competencies will be learnt during your studies, but others will be the result of experience gained in the workplace.
* The importance of work experience whenever you can as this will develop your confidence, resilience, industry knowledge and your network and connections.

FURTHER READING

Deegan, J. and Martin, N. (2018) *Merging Work and Learning to Develop the Human Skills that Matter* [online]. Available at: www.echs-nm.com/wp-content/uploads/2019/10/DDE_Pearson_Report_3.pdf (accessed 2 March 2020).

Tomlinson, M. and Holmes, L. (eds) (2017) *Graduate Employability in Context. Theory, Research and Debate.* London: Palgrave McMillan.

Yorke, M. (2006) *Employability in Higher Education: What It Is — What It Is Not* [online]. Available at: www.advance-he.ac.uk/knowledge-hub/employability-higher-education-what-it-what-it-not (accessed 2 March 2020).

Useful web resources

Carnival UK is the largest cruise company operating out of the UK, with nine ships and another in development. They own the historic Cunard brand and P&O Cruises. They employ over 2500 staff across the globe and are based in Southampton, UK – www.carnivalukcareers.co.uk/

Creative Attributes Framework, University of the Arts, London (2016). A useful resource for developing employability skills, focused particularly on those in artistic career paths but useful for all – www.arts.ac.uk/about-ual/teaching-and-learning-exchange/careers-and-employability/creative-attributes-framework#

LifeSkills from Barclays has been set up to help young people to access the jobs market. Although focused on those aged 16–19, there are some interesting skill development sections – https://barclayslifeskills.com/educators/tags/age-groups/16-19

Rome2Rio: discover how to get anywhere – www.rome2rio.com/

13 COMMUNICATION AND INTERPERSONAL SKILL DEVELOPMENT

CHAPTER LEARNING OBJECTIVES

By the end of this chapter you should be able to:

- Understand the process of communication and recognise the link between interpersonal skills and communication.
- Feel confident in handling difficult conversations.
- Explain the importance of interpersonal skills.
- Develop strategies for managing your own emotions.
- Deliver and learn from constructive feedback.

GLOSSARY

- **Generalisation:** when knowledge about a specific case (person, situation, group) is inferred to apply to wider populations
- **Interpersonal skills:** social competencies relating to relationships between people.
- **Self-awareness:** being aware of your strengths, weaknesses, thoughts and beliefs. Understanding how others may perceive you.
- **Stereotype:** a fixed and often over-simplified idea or belief about what something or someone is like.

INTRODUCTION

The tourism, hospitality and events sectors are centred around people. To host or to be hospitable means to welcome, to be friendly, to offer generosity and warmth towards others. Central to hospitality and therefore to tourism, events and leisure is the ability to interact with others, to have good people skills, more commonly known as interpersonal and communication skills. The global nature of today's markets and the importance of networking across global supply chains, partners and customers emphasises the importance of interpersonal and communication skills across all industries (Oxford Economics, 2012). The global reach of the THE sectors means organisations often have global workforces and therefore require employees who can interact with a variety of people from a range of demographics, backgrounds and cultures with varying needs and demands. Communication and **interpersonal skills** are in high demand by employers.

THE IMPORTANCE OF PEOPLE SKILLS IN TOURISM, HOSPITALITY AND EVENTS

People skills comprise subjective and soft skills relating to the way we engage and interact with others. Service industries are being increasingly surpassed by 'experiences' involving the engagement of customers, 'connecting them in a personal, memorable way' (Pine and Gilmore, 2011: 5). The ability to create personal connections is a soft skill, along with being able to communicate effectively, demonstrate emotional intelligence, problem-solve and work as part of a team. Technological advances have been able to simulate many technical or hard skills previously delivered by people. Soft skills, however, are more difficult for computers to replicate and therefore increasingly valued by employers (Davidson, 2016). '[T]he rise of AI is only making soft skills increasingly important, as they are precisely the type of skills robots can't automate' (Petrone, 2019). Training for soft skills is the number one priority for executives, managers and talent developers (LinkedIn, 2018) with 57% of senior leaders believing soft skills are more important than hard skills (Petrone, 2019).

REFLECTION EXERCISE

The role of people in the restaurant encounter

Think about your last restaurant visit.

- How many people did you encounter?
- What role(s) did these people play?
- What were your interactions like with these people? Why? Were you welcomed? Were you made to feel special? Were staff attentive but not intrusive?
- What was your overall experience like? What could have improved the experience?
- How important were people to your experience?

Within customer-facing (front of house) roles, the lines between hard and soft skills are often blurred; you can rarely separate delivery and consumption in consumer-facing roles. Tasks are often bound within the experience and therefore hard and soft skills need to be implemented simultaneously. Soft skills are often crucial to the implementation of hard skills, enabling you to think on your feet in difficult situations and respond to uncertainty.

COMMUNICATION SKILLS

Tourism, hospitality and events industries are not alone in citing communication skills among the top skills required by employers globally. Think how empty your world would be if you could not communicate – verbally, physiologically or even virtually. Human beings have developed signs, symbols and sounds with common understandings through which we interact and make sense of the world around us.

A simple linear way of thinking about communication is as the transmission of information, instructions, thoughts, ideas, belief, attitudes and emotions from one entity to another (see Figure 13.1). Most communication is far more complicated than this, with several influences on the flow of communication.

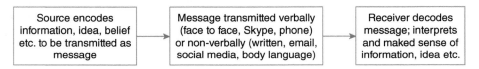

Figure 13.1 Simple communication process

Communication rarely (if ever) exists in a vacuum and so the impact of what we call 'noise' can be considerable. There are personal, psychological and social influences that impact encoding and decoding of messages by source and recipient; essentially, the way we interpret (source) and then re-interpret (recipient) message content. Feedback also needs to be included, i.e. the feedback loop from receiver to source (as shown in Figure 13.2). Whilst this is a simplified version of the communication process, it highlights the complexities involved in communication. Ignoring these influences may result in miscommunication.

Be clear

The first step to encoding your idea or information is to know what you want to say. This is vital in professional situations such as dealing with customers or potential employers, as a lack of clarity is often synonymous with a lack of knowledge. Make sure your core idea is clear and consider supporting this with further information. Use assertive language ('I will complete this by …' or 'There will be a solution to …') rather than passive ('I wonder if you would mind …' or 'Perhaps I could approach …'). These are vague, non-committal openers that do not provide clarity of intent. Active language offers clarity, commitment and detail, reassuring others that you are to be believed and trusted.

With verbal messages, delivering with confidence includes limiting the use of fillers (um, er, ah, like and so on). Often these add-ins become habitual, but customers and employers may mistake fillers for lack of confidence or knowledge.

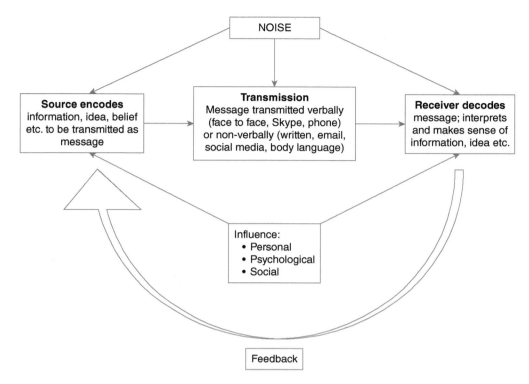

Figure 13.2 Influences on the communication process

Source: adapted from Fil and Turnbull, 2016

REFLECTION EXERCISE

Using fillers

The next time you hold a conversation with a friend, take a mental note of the number of times you use fillers. It is useful to be aware of any bad habits so that you can work on reducing your reliance on such non-words.

Consider your audience

Ideas, information and emotions at work should be structured and communicated in a professional manner. It is also important that you think about your audience in terms of their understanding of the message. A good way to think about this is to imagine telling a small child what hospitality means. How would you describe it? Now think about a friend or family member. What would you tell them? Finally, imagine you are in an interview and are asked what hospitality means to you. How would you answer? The concept in all three examples is the same, but the message would be framed or encoded differently to suit each audience. This is a difficult skill that requires practice and experience to master (see activity below).

When your audience are customers, it is important that you can pitch your information accurately and appropriately, remembering that they may not understand technical jargon and are not necessarily familiar with your company policy.

ACTIVITY

Going jargon-free!

The next time you finish an assessment, set yourself a 'three-minute jargon-free challenge'. Discuss your work without jargon for three minutes.

- What are the main concepts of the assessment?
- What were your main arguments?
- What were the principle findings or conclusions?

Verbal messages

The spoken word is crucial to many interactions within tourism, hospitality and events, with customers, suppliers, colleagues and managers. Industries built on relationships need employees with the confidence to speak up, understand professional vocabulary, mitigate difficult situations and build relationships.

Face-to-face, telephone or video link communications

- Think about someone that talks to you in a monotone voice (where the voice stays at the same pitch). You need to add life to your voice, with rise and fall.
- Think about how loud your voice is. Is your tone suitable for the audience?
- Speed of delivery is crucial. If we feel we are delivering a difficult message, the temptation can be to talk more swiftly, but this can confuse or alienate your audience.

ACTIVITY

Message delivery

The daily news on TV offers great examples of message delivery. Watch a news programme and consider the following:

- What do you notice about the newsreaders' voices when they are delivering different types of message?
- What speed do they speak at?
- Is it obvious what they are talking about?

The next time you must deliver a message or convey important information, consider the newsreaders you watched. You might use a similar format:

- Announce the headline, i.e. deliver the main point of the message in a clear, concise single sentence
- Use additional information and evidence to support the message and tell the story behind the headline.

A positive attitude in a conversation is most likely to lead to a positive outcome. Try to let go of negativity and avoid snap judgements. Body language can also be used to convey a positive attitude (see Chapter 14), although this falls under non-verbal communication. Build awareness of how you come across when you speak – a conversation in front of a mirror is a good starting place. As outlined in Chapter 14, eye contact should not be underestimated. In Western cultures a lack of eye contact suggests a lack of confidence, disengagement and disinterest. This can be troublesome during video link calls where the webcam may be located higher than your usual eye-line, making it difficult to maintain eye contact whilst looking at the participant(s) for non-verbal cues. Making eye contact shows that you are listening and committed to the conversation, showing your employer or customer that they are valued, respected and heard.

Telephone conversations

Perhaps our over-reliance on email or text has overtaken the telephone. Telephone skills remain important nonetheless; employers still conduct telephone interviews and customers use the phone to seek advice, for example. The problem many students have with phone conversations is that there are no non-verbal cues, and for those working in their second or third language, being solely reliant on sound can be daunting.

When you are the caller:

- Be prepared; know what you want to say and do any research you might need to respond to additional queries. Long pauses may be misconstrued as you having hung up, so try to avoid this.
- Introduce yourself and the reason for the call: 'Good afternoon, this is …, from…. I'm calling to speak to … about …. Is this a convenient time to speak?'
- Speak clearly, remembering there is no lip reading, body language or facial expression to support the message. You must speak with clarity and at reasonable pace so that the person on the other end of the phone can process what you are saying.

When you receive a call:

- Do not simply say 'yes' but rather something that reassures the caller that they have come through to the right person. For example, you might wish the caller a good morning/afternoon, tell them who they are speaking to and/or the name of your organisation/division and perhaps finish with 'How can I help you?'
- If you are receiving a customer call in the workplace and are not the intended recipient, try to find out who they need to speak to instead. Either help put them through or take a message, rather than asking them to dial another number.
- At the end of the conversation, check for understanding and summarise the key points ('so, just to confirm …'). You could finish with 'Have I missed anything?'

Before you end a call, make sure you both understand what will happen next. For example: 'So to confirm, I will contact the supplier and will get back to you tomorrow afternoon before 4pm.' The close of call is as important as the opener; for example, thank them for their time if you have made the call.

Written communication

Email is a core business tool for most organisations. The immediacy and speed of emails is particularly important to global organisations who have multiple locations, suppliers and consumers spread across the globe. Our familiarity with emails presents certain challenges, not least that we often fail to differentiate between professional emails and those sent to friends or family. Even when we remember to maintain a professional tone, in a 2013 survey, 64% of respondents reported having sent or received an email that unintentionally resulted in anger or confusion (Sendmail, 2013). Poor grammar, delayed responses or the sheer number of emails being sent suggests that email is not always being used correctly.

A key piece of advice when sending an email is to think first – do not just type and send. Remember emails have longevity, i.e. they can be traced, saved and re-read. The following activity should allow you to think about your own email etiquette.

 ACTIVITY

Email etiquette

Find the last email you sent to a lecturer at university or manager at work.

1. How long is the email? You should keep emails to one paragraph wherever possible, and no more than three.
2. Did you open with a greeting and the name of the person you are writing to? If in doubt, use 'Dear …'
3. How does your email sound? Have you conveyed your point in a constructive manner? Have you used appropriate language? Do not use text-speak (such as 'LOL' or 'cn I hv an appt wiv u').
4. Was there any sensitive or unprofessional content? Imagine if you had accidentally cc'd in your boss, head of department or the entire student body. Could anything you said be misconstrued? Remember that under the Freedom of Information Act a person has the right to read anything with their name in it.
5. Did you sign off in an appropriate manner? Emails should be signed off professionally: 'kind regards' is usually appropriate for colleagues, managers and lecturers, or if you are writing to someone you don't know or have not yet met in person, use a standard letter sign-off such as 'yours faithfully' (if you do not know their name, e.g. if you are writing to a shared mailbox) or 'yours sincerely' (if you do).
6. Could you have had the conversation in person? Often colleagues will email each other while in the same room, but where possible you should meet face-to-face or talk on the telephone as sometimes emails can be more easily misinterpreted and it can be regarded as unfriendly. It is sometimes useful to have a paper trail that emails provide, e.g. to prove you sent something, but otherwise limit emails within the same team.

Receiving a message

 THINK POINT

How often do you find yourself making assumptions when people are speaking, thinking you know what they are going to say or jumping to conclusions before they have finished? Why do you do this?

Your main role as a recipient of a message is to listen actively. This means concentrating on the speaker, taking note of expressions, body language, tone, enunciation and feelings associated with what is being said, why it is being said and what is not being said. Active listening enables you to build stronger relationships based on understanding and respect and is both integral to effective communication and a sought-after interpersonal skill by employers.

At the heart of active listening is the desire to understand, recognise and appreciate the sentiment behind conversations. It is therefore important that you limit the temptations to judge and rather empathise with their situation. When you engage in the conversation and allow others to fully express what they are feeling, they are more likely to feel understood and willing to listen to you in return.

REFLECTION EXERCISE

Dealing with complaints

Consider a time when you have had to deal with (or observed someone else dealing with) a disgruntled customer. Did the person dealing with the complaint demonstrate active listening skills? What was the outcome? How might active listening help to diffuse this type of situation?

Below are a few tips in building listening skills to establish strong and positive relationships through effective communication.

- *Minimise distractions.* Do not watch TV, scan emails, read text messages or engage with social media while someone is talking. It is not possible to actively listen unless you are concentrating and present in the moment.
- *Try to avoid judgement.* You do not always have to agree with what is being said, but rather take on board other people's perspectives.
- *Show you are listening.* Make eye contact and/or gestures to show that you are engaged (e.g. such as nodding). If there is an opportunity to ask questions, this is another point at which you can demonstrate that you have absorbed what you have heard and engaged with it.
- *Let people finish.* When you feel threatened or challenged by what someone is saying, the temptation is to cut them off mid-conversation, to defend yourself before they have finished making their point. Allowing people to voice their opinion in full and show you can listen to this with patience is more likely to gain respect from them, as well as their own patience as they listen to you.
- *Use check backs.* Paraphrase or rephrase parts of the conversation back to check that you have understood (e.g. 'If I understand you correctly …', 'So what you're saying is that …' 'Are you saying that…' 'What I'm hearing you say is …').

Interpreting the message

The recipient of any message goes through a decoding process in which they interpret what they believe is being communicated. We all perceive information differently, have different outlooks and values. It makes sense, then, that our interpretations will be based upon our own personality, attitudes and experiences. This is why sending a clear message in the first place is so crucial, to reduce the subjectivity of interpretation.

Think about a message you or a friend have sent that was misinterpreted. A student recently told a story of sending a text she thought may have been misread by her employer. Reading the text back aloud, she had clear intonation and expression in her voice that gave the message meaning, but of course a text message may not carry the meaning you have in your own mind when writing it. Even emojis are subject to interpretation: a kissing face may be sent to a friend, intending to be a friendly sign-off, but this could easily be mistaken for flirtation. Think about someone you dislike or are annoyed with. How do you interpret their messages?

Interpretation can be subject to several influences, from **stereotypes** and attitude to cultural awareness. We are often guilty of making stereotypical or generalised judgements on a category of person such as gender, nationality, religion or the hobbies and activities we or they engage in.

 THINK POINT

The next time you are in class or in a group of people, think about the assumptions you made when you first met them. Did these turn out to be true? Did anyone surprise you? What are the dangers of using stereotypes and making snap assumptions when you first encounter someone?

Stereotyping, **generalisations** and limited understanding of cultural differences act as barriers to communication, inhibiting the openness required to empathise, understand diverse perspectives and build trust. Communicating across cultures requires patience, respect and time.

Within tourism, hospitality and events, English is often the common spoken language, but this often leads to a false assumption that everyone speaks, reads and can understand English at the same level. It is important to respect those communicating outside their mother tongue and have patience, without patronising them or shouting! Communicating in a foreign language requires both translation and then interpretation (see Chapter 14 on non-verbal differences in communication and Chapter 16 on languages, cultural sensitivity and the diversity in attitudes and behaviour across cultures).

Noise

Communication rarely occurs in a stress-free, noise-free place. Think about a mother trying to chat to her friend when her child is constantly talking to her. 'Noise' can also include junk mail crowding out other messages that are important. In a customer-facing role, dealing with problems may occur in a busy or crowded area. Perhaps they are being hassled by others or perhaps you can see your queue of other guests growing. Maybe the space itself is loud, with music playing or people talking. These interruptions and annoyances all create noise that can impact interpretation and decoding of the original message.

 ACTIVITY

The whisper game

Sit in a circle with a group of friends. Space yourselves out so there is enough room between you that you will not overhear one another. Give the first player a message (ideally, a single sentence, but with at least one important detail). This player whispers the message to the person on their right, and then this player does the same to the person on their right and so on. The message can only be said once to each person. The final person to hear the sentence then says out loud what they think the message was, so that everyone can hear it. Was the message the same for the last person as the first?

Once you have accepted the distracting nature of noise, you can work on blocking out unwanted disturbance and being present in the moment via mindfulness and learning to tune out background noise when you need to focus. Mindfulness is often associated with yoga and spiritual activities such as meditating but should not be restricted to this type of activity. Any of us can practise mindfulness by allowing ourselves the space and time to be present in the moment, blocking out external noise and ceasing to think about the past and the future. By concentrating on the present, you can build self-awareness, reduce stress and generate a sense of calm.

═══════ ACTIVITY ═══════

Practising mindfulness

Choose one of the following activities and try to remain present in the moment throughout.

- Take a walk and really take notice of the environment around you – nature, architecture, people.
- Buy a coffee, sit in a café or on a park bench and notice the people around you. What are they doing? How are they behaving?
- Watch a favourite movie or TV show and actively listen for jokes, nuances or words that you might have missed before.
- Sit on your own and listen to music. Really listen to the words, if it has lyrics. What is the song about? How do you think the artist felt when they were writing it?

CONSTRUCTIVE FEEDBACK

Many of us take criticism personally, becoming defensive and argumentative. However, feedback should be considered a useful tool in developing and improving performance. Success and uptake of feedback is often dependent on how it is delivered: a criticism-based approach pointing out failures and apportioning blame will likely incur a negative response. Instead, constructive feedback should be used to highlight areas for improvement and personal development. Remember that feedback can also be used to reinforce positive behaviour. Here are some tips:

1. *Know why you are giving feedback.* Have you been asked for feedback? In a managerial or leadership role at work you may be required to give uninvited feedback, but this would usually take place as part of a review or following a task/project exercise. Are you genuinely giving feedback to enable improvement or is there an ulterior motive?
2. *Be specific.* It is important to be specific, focusing on the exercise, task or situation at hand. Similarly, avoid generalisations such as 'always', 'usually', 'never' and 'generally'. For example, rather than saying 'You are always so rude to her', you might say, 'I noticed at lunch yesterday you ignored Sue, even when she asked you a question.'
3. *Present the consequences.* Give examples of reactions and consequences to the person's behaviour/ attitude. It is important in feedback to explain why change is needed.

4. *Remember it is a two-way conversation.* Feedback should not be one-sided. The recipient must be allowed time to reflect and respond. Ask a probing question such as 'What do you think?', 'How do you feel about this?' or 'What are your thoughts?' Be prepared to explain any areas they do not understand or agree with.

5. *Make suggestions.* If the purpose of feedback is improvement, then suggest how this could be done. If the feedback is to reinforce positive behaviour, then suggest ways this could continue or be expanded.

6. *End on a positive note.* Show that the feedback comes from a well-intentioned place. If you are able, offer future training or development opportunities. If feedback is to a colleague or friend, offer your personal support if needed.

7. *Consider message delivery.* Your tone and body language will also be an important part of the feedback communication process. Avoid a confrontational stance, make eye contact without staring the person out and speak quietly but firmly.

 REFLECTION EXERCISE

Using feedback

Think about feedback you have received from a tutor on an assessment. Did you read it fully? How did you use it? Did you receive similar feedback in subsequent assessments? Do you think you used it as an effective tool to improve? The next time you receive feedback, make notes on the areas in which you have done well as well as where you need to improve. Use this as a part of your personal development plan. What objectives could you give yourself to improve in the future?

INTERPERSONAL SKILLS

In THE, employees are a fundamental component of the overall experience. Engaging encounters with tourists, guests or attendees are central to creating memorable experiences. The nature of these encounters is also fundamental to determining service quality and customer satisfaction. It is no longer about meeting customer needs, but anticipating and then exceeding them: delighting, exciting, wowing, amazing and thrilling. Experience delivery is therefore linked to the ability of employees to engage with, relate to, interact with and understand others.

Emotional intelligence

Emotional intelligence is the foundation of effective communication and other related skills: leadership, teamwork (see Chapter 15), problem-solving (see Chapter 19) and handling difficult situations (Dacre Pool and Qualter, 2018). Interacting and communicating with others requires emotional intelligence (EI): the ability to read your audience, empathising with and respecting their feelings. Emotional intelligence is the ability to recognise emotions in yourself and others, and understand the effect these may have in various situations.

REFLECTION EXERCISE

Recognising emotions in yourself and others

- Are you able to empathise and interact with others easily?
- Would you consider yourself self-aware and able to recognise your own emotions?
- Can you control your emotions in the presence of others?
- Are you able to refrain from getting angry or upset in stressful situations?
- Are you able to calmly consider a problem and find possible solutions?
- Do you respond positively in the face of adversity?

If you answered 'yes' to these questions, you are likely to have a higher level of emotional intelligence.

Emotional intelligence includes empathy, being motivated, self-aware, self-regulated and self-controlled (Goleman, 2006), as shown in Table 13.1.

Table 13.1   Components of emotional intelligence

Component of EI	Explanation	Example
Ability to **perceive** one's own emotions and those of others	Ability to identify display of emotions in faces, voices, body language, including own emotions	You ask your friend if they are OK. They say they are, but you can tell from their voice and body language that this is not the case. You have an argument with a friend and leave feeling uncomfortable; you are able to recognise that this feeling is hurt/anger/sadness.
Ability to **use** emotions to enable thought	Draw upon emotions as a means of making motivational and practical contributions	You feel happy and positive and are able to use this to find solutions to problems. If you feel hurt you are able to think about the experiences that contributed to this and consider what could have been avoided or done differently. When you feel happy, sad, angry, hurt, you are able to use these emotions to reflect and think about the last time you felt like this: what happened, why did it happen and what triggers this emotion in you?
Ability to **understand** emotions and their meaning	Understand the impact of emotions on behaviour	You have an encounter with a rude driver first thing in the morning, but you do not let this put you in a bad mood all day or make you rude to others. You see a child run out into the road and their mother scream at them and then tell them off severely; you recognise this as their being terrified that the child could have been run over rather than their being angry at the child.
Ability to **manage** emotions in yourself and in others	Beyond identifying emotions, you understand how to deal with emotions; both in yourself and in others	You are in a meeting at work when you feel a colleague is speaking out of turn and showing up other teammates. You can maintain your composure rather than shouting them down and have a reasonable discussion voicing your concerns after the meeting. You are dealing with a customer complaint and they keep saying 'you' when they mean the company. It makes you cross, but you can extract yourself as an individual from the conversation and recognise that their anger is not personal.

Source: Mayer and Salovey, 1997; Mayer et al., 2016

Workplaces are often emotionally charged spaces. Whilst emotions were once considered something you did not bring to work, there has been a shift in thinking towards emotions as being integral to relationship-building and sound decision-making (Dacre Pool and Qualter, 2018). Organisations are increasingly interested in recruiting emotionally intelligent people: compassionate, reliable individuals able to lead teams and work under a variety of conditions with a diversity of people.

Empathy is crucial to managing relationships and therefore people. When dealing with customer complaints, it is important that employees can control their own emotions and rationalise the emotions of others to understand why the customer might be feeling angry in that moment. Think about how quickly situations can escalate when we become defensive and respond emotionally rather than rationally. However fair or unfair the complaints, the costs of dissatisfied customers can be extensive: negative feedback, damaged reputation and poor customer retention. Empathy can be difficult to develop and some may need to work on this (see Table 13.2).

Table 13.2 Activities to strengthen empathy

Activity	Example
Push yourself outside your comfort zone	Try a new activity. When you challenge yourself or do something you have not done before, you will likely feel uncomfortable and a sense of humility. Being humble is fundamental to building empathy.
Ask for feedback	Ask your friends and family how you come across. Do they see you as empathetic? Are you able to identify with their emotions, offering advice and comfort when necessary?
Use parallel thinking	When faced with a problem, try to take a multi-perspective point of view. Your own reactions will be immediate, but stop and think: why might others feel differently? Are they justified in feeling so?
Ask questions	If you want to be able to deal with the complexity of human relations, you need to understand behaviour. Why do people respond the way they do? Do not be afraid to talk to others. Ask why they are feeling the way they do. This will help reinforce your own understanding and ability to recognise and deal with a variety of emotions.

 INDUSTRY INSIGHT

The emotional intelligence of cabin crew

Emotional intelligence is key for flight attendants. Cabin crew must be prepared to deal with highly emotional situations, from abusive customers and dealing with on-flight incidents to maintaining calm in an emergency. Remember that cabin crew perform most of their duties in front of an audience, whether a person falls ill mid-flight, unexpectedly passes away or is intoxicated, the cabin crew must maintain a 'business as usual' attitude for other passengers. They must try to maintain professionalism or risk reputational damage if individual incidents are misinterpreted, particularly if other passengers only witness or hear part of the story.

Cabin crew training is notoriously rigorous and involves candidates being pushed outside their comfort zone to see how they react to stressful situations. It is important that simulated activities replicate the realities they may face in the air. Once they are in the air, there is little room for emotional instability. A difficult customer cannot be removed mid-flight and the emergency services cannot attend a critically ill passenger after take-off. Imagine being mid-flight and being informed the plane must make an emergency landing. Think of the panic you would feel. As stress builds in the cabin, how is order maintained? How can chaos be minimised? It comes down to the cabin crew, who may be scared but are also trained to continue fulfilling their role throughout the incident.

A less hazardous yet more frequent incident comes in dealing with difficult (often alcohol-fuelled) individuals. This type of customer will likely push emotional buttons and test the crew's ability to control their own feelings. This is also a test of the ability of the cabin crew to empathise with customers. People want to enjoy their holiday and perhaps over-indulge in alcohol as a means of enjoying the perks of upper-class travel. The crew must empathise with the notion of having fun, but balance this against safety and the experience of other passengers. The emotional intelligence of cabin crew, then, is paramount to the overall passenger experience.

We have discussed building **self-awareness** through mindfulness above and self-motivation will often be a natural consequence of self-awareness and reflective thinking (see Chapter 10). Self-regulation is your ability to manage your own emotions, taking time to reflect and respond rather than react. Allowing time to understand your emotions is a powerful tool in self-control.

==== ACTIVITY ====

Facing your emotions

Recognising our stressors is an important step in developing the ability to self-regulate. Think about the last time you faced a stressful situation.

1. What was the situation? Be honest and state the facts.
2. Who was involved?
3. What triggered the event/conflict?
4. How did you feel?
5. What specifically made you feel this way?
6. How did you react?
7. What were the consequences?
8. Did your feelings change over the next day/week?

Now that the situation has passed, do you feel you overreacted? Do you wish you had behaved differently? How would you handle it differently now?

Understanding and recognising emotions and cues is associated with emotional intelligence. However, we are increasingly expected to relate to global populations, including those with cultures, backgrounds and experiences different from our own. Cultural intelligence is the ability to recognise and respond to behaviours and emotional displays across different cultures: a fundamental skill in cross-cultural service encounters (Alshaibani and Bakir, 2017). Building cultural intelligence begins with being open to those with diverse cultures; understanding cultural differences and taking the time to interact with diverse groups of people. Emotional intelligence does not necessarily translate to dealing with people from other cultures.

Handling conflict

The ability to handle conflict is perhaps at the epitome of the combination of interpersonal skills and communication (see Figure 13.3). Uncomfortable situations may cause us to feel defensive, aggressive or indiscreet. It is important to draw upon all the interpersonal skills discussed and developed throughout this chapter, but the guidelines below give you a framework for dealing with conflict.

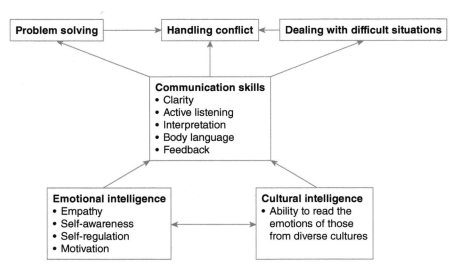

Figure 13.3   The skills required for handling conflict

1. *Stay calm.* Manage your emotions and remember you are probably not being attacked personally.
2. *Be patient and listen actively.* Difficult situations are exacerbated by misunderstanding. Allow the other person the space to vent and tell their story whilst you give signals to show you are actively listening (see above).

   Something you might want to try is each time someone is rude to you, use that as a prompt to become more and more polite to them. This makes you feel better, stops you sinking to their level, reminds them that you are doing your job and models the behaviour you want to see in them.
3. *Acknowledge the issue.* It is important to let the person know you hear them. Do not try to deflect or dismiss their problem. If there has been a misunderstanding, then explain it: 'I can see why you might have thought …' 'I understand this must have been frustrating for you.' You are not necessarily agreeing with what they are saying, but still acknowledging their upset. Rather than disputing the issue, if you or the organisation are at fault, then admit it and apologise.
4. *Consider the main issue.* What is the person upset about? They may have a list of several issues, but there is usually a specific trigger for the complaint or conflict. For example, a customer that had to wait a long time for their food to arrive only to find it was cold may then turn their attention to other smaller issues, such as missing cutlery, not being welcomed on arrival, a lack of toilet paper in the bathrooms and so on. They would perhaps not have complained about any one of these things individually, but the final thing that has upset them has had a cumulative effect, making them think about all the other issues they encountered. It is important to acknowledge all the issues but identify and address the main problem.
5. *Explore solutions.* Find out what the customer wants: 'How can we resolve this?' 'What can we do to address this issue?' 'How can we move forward from here?' and so on. It is important you do

not overpromise and then underdeliver. Be honest and make sure your offer is in line with company guidelines, as well as that it is deliverable.

6. *Take ownership.* In order to regain trust, follow up with the solution. Tell them your name and assure them that you will take responsibility for this being sorted out. If you know you will not be around to provide a solution, pass them to a trusted colleague.

CONCLUSION

In this chapter we have covered:

- The process of communication.
- How to perform active listening and how to interpret messages.
- Cutting out noise in communication.
- Emotional intelligence and handling conflict.

FURTHER READING

Alshaibani, E. and Bakir, A. (2017) 'A reading in cross-cultural service encounter: Exploring the relationship between cultural intelligence, employee performance and service quality', *Tourism and Hospitality Research*, 17(3): 249–263.

Bharwani, S. and Jauhari, V. (2012) 'An exploratory study of competencies required to co-create memorable customer experiences in the hospitality industry', *International Journal of Contemporary Hospitality Management*, 25(6): 823–843.

Dacre Pool, L. and Qualter, P. (2018) *An Introduction to Emotional Intelligence.* West Sussex: Wiley & Sons.

Fil, C. and Turnbull, S. (2016) *Marketing Communications: Discovery, Creations and Conversations*, 7th edn. Harlow: Pearson Education.

Goleman, D. (2006) 'The socially intelligent', *Educational Leadership*, 64(1): 76–81.

Mayer, J.D., Caruso, D.R. and Salovey, P. (2016) 'The ability model of emotional intelligence: Principles and updates', *Emotion Review*, 8(4): 290–300.

14 BODY TALKS: BODY LANGUAGE AND NON-VERBAL COMMUNICATION

CHAPTER LEARNING OBJECTIVES

By the end of this chapter you should be able to:

- Discuss how the study of body language has evolved.
- Categorise key gestures and non-verbal communication methods.
- Identify what different movements of different body parts mean and how they are interpreted by others (i.e. your head, face, eyes, physical gestures, arm movements and body position).
- Demonstrate the kind of body language that is appropriate in different work contexts and how your body language can make a positive impression on potential employers.
- Understand key cultural differences when it comes to non-verbal communication and how you can be sensitive when communicating with people from different cultural contexts and countries.

GLOSSARY

- **Haptics:** interaction involving touching, whether this be how people and animals communicate or recognising objects via touching. The word '*haptic*' means anything relating to the sense of touch and it is derived from the Greek word for touch.
- **Kinesics:** this is a study of how body movements and gestures provide non-verbal communication. It is the interpretation of body motion communication such as facial expressions and gestures.

- **Oculesics:** this is a sub-category of kinesics and is the study of how the eyes move. It focuses on gaze and eye-related non-verbal communication.
- **Proxemics:** the study of the human use of space. Edward Hall, a cultural anthropologist developed the term and defined it as 'the interrelated observations and theories of humans' use of space as a specialized elaboration of culture' (Hall, 1963).
- **Rapport:** originating from the French word 'rapporter' meaning to bring back or to return. It is about building a positive connection between yourself and others.

INTRODUCTION

This chapter draws on the theories of non-verbal communication (**kinesics**) and concepts such as **haptics** (touching and how it is used in communication, e.g. effective use of handshakes) and **proxemics** (space and spatial relationships) to explain the role of body language. It particularly looks at the role of body language in terms of fostering effective communication and how it reveals attitudes and feelings.

This chapter outlines how to read body language, how to be aware of your own body language and reveal what it is saying about you and your thoughts. Non-verbal behaviour is crucial to understand, especially as you think about securing employment, working with others and presenting yourself most effectively. In breaking down different elements to look at, such as facial expression, gestures, physical positioning and **oculesics** (eye movements, eye behaviour, gaze and eye-related non-verbal communication), this chapter helps you think about how others are perceiving you and how to improve your silent communication, but also helps you read signs from other people which is particularly useful in the service industries like tourism, hospitality and events.

A HISTORY OF BODY LANGUAGE

How many times have you heard the phrase, 'actions speak louder than words'? It is true in many ways because our body language conveys a lot more than the spoken word and arguably, it is certainly more truthful. Our bodies play a key role in conveying our feelings, our views, emotions and messages. The way we use non-verbal physical action has a much longer history than spoken communication. Indeed, human beings were using different physical movements to express emotion and attitudes hundreds of years before spoken words. Physical gestures provide key signs and signals. Albert Mehrabian found that 55% of the messages we convey in face to face communication are relayed through body language so it is certainly worth spending time to understand how it works (Mehrabian, 1971).

The first known study of body language was in 1644 by John Bulwer, *Chirologia: Or the Natural Language of the Hand*. In the nineteenth century, actors were perfecting the art of conveying emotion through action and in 1872 Charles Darwin explored how expressions are shared with apes and monkeys. If we skip forward to the 1970s, Paul Ekman and Wallace V. Friesen developed the 'Facial Action Coding System' (FACS) to decipher and understand facial expressions. The FACS is a sophisticated research tool that measures the entire spectrum of human facial expressions and provides a taxonomy of human facial expressions.

ACTIVITY

Positive or negative messages?

Are these gestures conveying positive or negative messages?

- A smile from a customer
- A fist being raised towards you
- A hug from a friend
- Shaking of the head from side to side
- A frown from a tutor
- A hand placed over your heart
- A manager waving her finger at a member of staff
- A colleague holding their head in their hands
- A thumbs up from your line manager during your presentation

Sometimes it is hard to know unless you have the context, so it is important to read such movements as part of a wider interaction with someone.

THINK POINT

Do you have a physical movement or gesture that you do regularly that has become part of your brand (see Chapter 28)? For example, more obvious ones include sticking your tongue out or winking. Usain Bolt's victory 'lightning bolt' move with his arms has become his signature gesture.

The power of gestures

You only have to look at a silent movie to see the power of gestures. When actors are unable to use words, the way the body works to communicate can be extremely powerful and effective. Non-verbal signals can convey volumes of information; it has been suggested that body language may account for between 60 and 65% of all communication (Foley and Gentile, 2010).

Ray Birdwhistell (1970, first edition 1952) developed the concept of kinesics where non-verbal behaviour was studied in terms of emblems, illustrators, effective displays, regulators and adaptors. Some of the categories shown in Table 14.1 are taken from Kuhnke (2015).

Try to ensure your gestures reinforce the impression you want to convey to others. Think about ensuring gestures suit the setting. For example, when you attend an interview for the first time, you need to ensure your actions are contained and formal and as you get to know people, then you might start to relax your movements. There are generally four types of gesture: descriptive gestures which clarify or enhance a verbal message; emphatic gestures which underscore what is being said and indicate earnestness and conviction; suggestive gestures which present ideas and emotions (to help create a certain mood or thought); and prompting gestures which can help evoke a desired response from the audience (e.g. asking people to raise hands by doing it yourself first). The different kinds of gesture can also be categorised as shown in Table 14.2.

Table 14.1   Gesture categorisation

The categories of gestures	Examples
Emblems – clear symbols which are universally recognised	The V sign (with two fingers) – depends which way the fingers are facing as can mean Victory or is offensive
	Closed fist (generally showing anger or frustration but can also show solidarity)
	Finger waving
	'Ok' sign with your hand – be careful as in some countries this implies 'you are nothing' and in some South American countries, the symbol is actually a vulgar gesture.
	Thumbs up or down – again, be careful with this one as it can have different meanings around the world and are not universal (see below)
Illustrators – a visual image to reinforce speech	Pointing in a direction when giving instructions
	Using hands to show the shape of an object
Affective displays	Movements which present emotional meaning such as crossing arms to show worry or concern, or a broad grin to show pleasure. They are often automated signals and are less conscious than illustrators.
Regulators	Body movements that can control and manage a conversation such as head nodding or moving forward into a conversation, or holding up a hand to stop someone speaking (not advised!)
Adaptors	Changes in body posture with a low level of self-awareness such as twitching or touching

Table 14.2   Types of gesture

Type of gesture	Examples
Universal gestures	Blushing
	Smiling
	Crying
	Struggling
Fake gestures	Smiling
	Frowning
	Sighing
	Crying
Micro-gestures	Mouth movements
	Eyes
	Nostril movements
Displacement gestures	Playing with your hair
	Stroking your chin
	Fiddling with an object such as a pen

— ACTIVITY —

Watching the news in silence

Try this. Watch your national news on television but turn the volume off. Can you tell from the non-verbal communication of the news broadcaster what kinds of stories are being presented? Note down all the various gestures they use.

You might also want to try this exercise with a comedy and see how messages are conveyed in a more exaggerated style.

Movements of the head

In general, people will see your head and face first, and during a conversation its movements will be the most pronounced. How many times have you heard the phrase, 'don't hang your head'? You will know this is a sign of feeling down or low, perhaps rejected and unhappy. On the flip side, if you hold your head up it projects a sense of confidence, pride and even authority. However, be aware that if someone's head is tilted back and the chin is forward then it can often suggest arrogance and you certainly don't want to come across like this during interviews or assessment processes. Some of the more common head movements are outlined in Table 14.3 with the general message they are giving. Be aware, however, that in different cultural contexts the meaning of movements can be very different (see below).

Table 14.3   The meanings of movements

Movement of the head	General meaning
Head up and looking straight ahead	This conveys neutrality towards the conversation
Shaking the head from side to side	Disagreement
Nodding the head up and down	Depending on the speed this could indicate agreement or more slowly can indicate understanding Demonstrates active listening Beware that in some cultures a nod can mean 'no' (see cultural differences section below)
Throwing head back	Often regarded as a sign of defiance
Using it to show direction – pointing it in a direction	Unless in a situation where talking is inappropriate or where you are among friends, this should be avoided as it suggests a lack of willingness to verbally communicate or not being bothered to show someone properly
Cocking your head	May come across as submissive but also seeking sympathy and reassurance
Bowing of the head	Shows respect and deference
Clasping the head	Often seen on the sports field when people narrowly miss a goal or to score a point. Portrays disbelief. A protective position and response to disaster
Resting head on hands, in hands	Generally indicates boredom. Never do this during an assessment centre or when talking to a prospective employer or tutor!
Touching the head, e.g. chin strokes	Thinking or trying to reflect on something

Try to think of some more head movements that convey messages. Are there any you tend to use more regularly than perhaps you should? Which ones might you try more to help build **rapport** in a conversation?

Facial expressions and lip reading

Your facial movements and expressions reflect your feelings and emotions, far more than words can. This is why it is important to be aware of what your facial expressions might be saying when you communicate with others, as saying you are happy with a plan or strategy when you are frowning is going to make people suspicious or confused of what you really think about them and their ideas. It is useful to think how you might put your point across without saying a word, whether this be a positive endorsement or a disapproving look. One study found that the most trustworthy facial expression involved a slight raise of the eyebrows and a slight smile (Todorov et al., 2008).

If you want to appear open and interested in others (which is of course what we need in an interview, assessment centre or with customers) then tilting your head a little, ensuring your eyes are engaged and facial muscles are relaxed will help. On the other hand, if you do not wish to engage in conversation then a furrowed brow and pursed lips would probably be effective! Table 14.4 shows some examples of more commonly used facial movements.

Table 14.4 Common facial movements and their meaning

Facial movement	General meaning
Smiling	Generally thought to reflect happiness but this can of course be fake or genuine and often the eyes will give away a fake smile
Gritted teeth	Conveying anger or trying not to say something
Pursed lips	Indicator or disapproval or distrust
Lower lip bite	Suggests care and concern about what you are hearing and seeing
Chewing lower lip	Indicates worry or insecurity
Frown	Unhappiness or disapproval
Covering the mouth	Person is either hiding a yawn or hiding an emotional reaction
Protruding eyes	Indicates anger or annoyance
Eyebrows lifting up	Surprise but also sometimes fear, often accompanies exposure of the whites of eyes

Oculesics: The 'eyes' have it

The eyes are frequently referred to as the 'windows to the soul' and this is with good reason. The eyes are one of the most powerful vehicles of non-verbal communication (see Table 14.5). Oculesics cover eye movements, eye behaviour, gaze, and eye-related non-verbal communication.

Table 14.5 Eye movements and their general meaning

Eye movement	General meaning
Blinking	Rapid blinking can indicate distress or discomfort, but it can also be used intentionally to flirt
Eye gaze	Paying attention and interested. Prolonged eye contact can feel threatening but if you avert your eyes too quickly then you might look like you are hiding something
Pupil size	This is complex as the pupil will change with light levels, but dilated eyes can suggest the person is interested or aroused
Widening your eyes	Lowering eyebrows is a sign of dominance and can be perceived as the person being aggressive whilst raising them is a sign of submission. Widening eyes is often used to instigate feelings of protection for the person
Sideways glance	When combined with either raised eyebrows or a smile, this can show interest. However, alone this may indicate hostility or a suspicious attitude
Squinting	Similar to animals before they make a move on their prey, a narrowing of the eyes may be used to assert authority or to intimidate others. However, it could just be that the person has visual difficulty and is trying to read/see something in clearer focus
Looking someone up and down	This will make someone feel very uncomfortable and it is never appropriate in a work setting!
Looking back and forth	Looking for an escape. If a person feels insecure, they will naturally scope for exit routes. However, this can also be true of those feeling bored or 'trapped' by an individual in a conversation and therefore can be read as lacking interest
Brief look down and to the right	Suggests a person is trying to recall a feeling or emotion
Brief look upwards	Suggests a person is trying to remember something they saw

PHYSICAL CONTACT

Physical contact draws on the concept of haptics (touching and how it is used in communication, e.g. effective use of handshakes). This section looks at physical movement with focus on arms and body position.

Table 14.6 Physical movements and their general meaning

Physical movement	General meaning
The handshake	Keep your palm straight and return the same pressure you receive; a limp handshake can be seen a sign of weakness, but gripping too hard can suggest aggression
Standing head on	Standing directly in front of someone to deliver a message is confrontational and aggressive
Open positions	When each person stands at a 45 degree angle to the other person. A message delivered from a speaker that stands side on to the other person is more likely to come across as confident but non-aggressive. This stance is recommended when dealing with customer complaints for example
Mirroring	It is said that people in rapport with each other mirror each other's physical movements. If you mirror others it suggests you understand their perspective. Avoid mimicry where you try too hard to copy and match behaviour
Standing tall	Even if you are not tall physically, standing tall and creating an image of height can command respect and show confidence

Physical movement	General meaning
Excluding others	When two people stand in a closed position, straight on with feet facing into each other they are excluding others from joining their conversation
Including others	When two people are in an open conversation with their bodies at 45 degrees to one another, they are welcoming others to join in, forming a triangular position
Direction of foot	The direction to which people's feet point suggests the direction of their interest. In a situation where all feet point in the direction of a single person, they are likely commanding the conversation

Arms and body

Your arms can be a significant giveaway to your emotions; from using them as a barrier to protect yourself when feeling threatened or uncomfortable in a situation, to using them to make yourself appear larger, signalling dominance or power (see Table 14.7). We are often unsure of what to do with our arms in situations such as an interview – where to place them and when to use them to gesture. Get it right and it can complement your verbal communication, but get it wrong and it may contradict the verbal messages of the conversation.

Table 14.7 Arm movements and their meaning

Arm movement	General meaning
Crossed arms	This is a defensive position and suggests self-protection and being closed off
Hands on hips	This could be a sign of aggression or you are in control
Opening arms widely to the side	Either someone wants to hug you or they are wanting to seem larger
Arms and hands behind back	Can reflect someone feeling frustrated, bored or impatient
Arms raised with hands clamped behind head	Suggests arrogance, confidence, over-complacency or intimidation. This stance should not be used during an interview situation as it suggests over-confidence and superiority
Keeping elbows out	When sitting in a chair, try and keep your elbows slightly out or on the chair arms. Keeping your elbows in suggests a lack of confidence as timid people use this to protect themselves
Arms slightly raised (below hip height) with palms open	This is an open, non-aggressive pose; open palms suggest submission and that the person has nothing to hide
One hand crossed across the body with the other touching its wrist	This acts as a barrier and shows a lack of confidence and being unsure. Try to keep arms from being crossed across the body
Hands in pockets	This shows an unwillingness to participate or disinterest in the conversation. Avoid having your hands in pockets when in professional situations

Stance and body position

Posture is incredibly important in your working career and securing roles (see Table 14.8). An open posture where your body is open will indicate you are open, friendly and willing. On the other hand, a closed posture where you hide your body with arms or legs may indicate anxiety or unfriendliness. In general, the three main types of posture are standing, sitting or reclining (lying down).

Table 14.8   Body position (posture) and general meaning

Stance and body position	General meaning
Balanced weight on both feet	Comfortable and confident position, but do consider some movement to avoid coming across as rigid
Crossed legs	Crossing legs away from someone can be interpreted as disliking that individual or someone in need of privacy
Shrug	Used to convey a lack of understanding, but can also be interpreted as not being bothered; a lack of care
Leaning forward	Showing interest in what the other person has to say. A very positive and engaged response
Rocking and swaying	This will make your audience feel uneasy as you will come across as nervous
Pacing	This will make you look nervous and anxious
A Figure Four position with the leg bent and one ankle rested upon the other knee; both hands clamped on the shin.	This is a competitive stance that signals dominance. However, in parts of the Middle East and Asia this would be seen as an insult as the sole of the shoe is showing: the part of the shoe that walks in dirt is considered a sign of disrespect
Feet withdrawn under the chair	When you take your feet out of the conversation it signals you are not fully engaged. To show interest and involvement in a conversation your feet should remain just in front of your knees.

Proxemics and space

Space is incredibly important and much of the work on space and spatial relationships has been the subject of research, such as the book, *The Hidden Dimension* by the anthropologist Edward Hall (1966). Hall looked at the distance between people when they interacted and coined the term 'proxemics' to describe the distance between people. You have probably experienced someone in your 'personal space'. How did this space invasion make you feel? Views on space varies between cultures. We encourage you to speak with your friends from other cultures about personal space and see what you can discover from doing so.

Hall claimed there are five zones of physical distance between people:

- *Close intimate* (0–6 inches/0–15 centimetres): close family, friends and partners; shows a high degree of familiarity
- *Intimate* (6–18 inches/15–45 centimetres): providing comfort and often involves touching and physical contact but it is a comfortable space if you know the person well
- *Personal* (18 inches–4 feet/45 centimetres–1.2 metres): about the right distance for personal conversations (in Western countries)
- *Social* (4–12 feet/1.2–3.6 metres): a comfortable distance for business engagements and acquaintants. A slightly larger distance is appropriate for people such as in a shop. If you leave more distance you can appear rude, but much closer and people might feel uncomfortable
- *Public* (12 feet+/3.6 metres+): speaking to an audience in a formal setting such as giving presentations. Creates connection but avoids feeling intruded

═══════ ACTIVITY ═══════

Observing the non-verbal clues of others and yourself

In the next face-to-face conversation you have with someone, just take note of the various non-verbal gestures they use and the body language they employ to convey their messages. Don't stare at them and make them feel uncomfortable, but you might be surprised by just how many of the movements presented above they use.

Likewise, take time to think about your own conversation with someone. You may become very self-conscious but this is a useful skill to have – reflect on how you come across to others. Mentally note what you do over a few conversations. Is there anything you do regularly? Did you use a non-verbal action that did not reflect what you said? Why?

Increasingly, companies are having meetings where participants remain standing. Rather than being fixed in position to a chair and table, the ability to move around is said to facilitate more creative thinking.

BODY LANGUAGE DURING AN INTERVIEW

As you think about securing employment, you need to think about what does all this mean for you and your chances of success at an interview and in the workplace. Being self-aware in how you come across to a potential employer or team will mean the difference between a potential offer and a rejection. You need to ensure that you make a positive impression from the second you meet a potential employer to the very last moment of the interaction. Likewise, you need to read their movements and think about whether they reflect the kind of team you want to join.

You never get a second chance to make a first impression'. This is incredibly important to remember when it comes to a job interview. You are on show and you need to think about what your body and expressions are saying about you. Your body can be an effective tool for adding emphasis, bringing attention to key points and clarity to your words.

Some advice on improving your non-verbal communication for your professional and personal life, and particularly during business and employer interactions are:

- Use good eye contact when you talk to people – you can come across as interested, engaged and people will not want to see you looking away or seemingly evasive
- Occupy the space and walk with confidence, but be polite and not overly arrogant (i.e. don't dominate the space)
- The 'power position' if you are standing and waiting is to keep your hands in front of you at waist height, usually one resting one on the other
- Smile when you meet people as you will come across as approachable but ensure this is not a fake smile – people will notice!
- Pay attention to the non-verbal clues and gestures of other people (as the activity above covers) so you know how to respond and read situations
- Watch out in case someone's words do not match their actions and behaviours – noticing this incongruence can be useful to be aware of

- Use non-verbal communication to convey your message more powerfully than just words. In an interview or presentation, use confident poses and keep your head up
- Ensure you read gestures as part of a whole and try not to take one gesture out of context as sometimes the action might not mean anything
- Consider the situation and context. For example, think about your body language with friends and what is more appropriate in the workplace
- Your handshake says a lot about you – ensure it is firm but not aggressive. A weak and limp handshake can be a sign of weakness (although it might be a result of ill health too so be aware)

 EMPLOYER INSIGHT

Visitor Services Manager, Leisure industry

Candidates often underestimate the power of body language during the interview process. Of course, it is expected that there will be nerves on the day, but showing you are able to control these can have a significant impact on your likelihood for getting the job. Perhaps worse than candidates that are introspective and lack confidence are those that demonstrate arrogance and over-confidence in their non-verbal communication. I have had candidates march into the room, grab my hand to shake it and then sit down open-legged before being asked to. There is confidence and then there is arrogance; being over assertive is likely to turn an interviewer off.

During the interview I would always say to be honest and truthful because your body language will likely tell the truth anyway. I once had a candidate attend an interview for a managerial position. Their CV gave a number of examples of previous experience within management roles, the most recent being at a rather famous luxury retail department store in London. Throughout the interview, the candidate displayed a closed position: arms and legs crossed with limited use of hand movements and gestures. Whenever I asked questions relating to this experience, they became visibly uncomfortable, rubbing their eyes and constantly touching their nose. I sensed either a lack of confidence, or, worse a lack of truth to what they were saying. We ended up not offering them the job largely based on what we saw rather than what we heard. I happen to have a friend who worked in their previous establishment and it turned out that they had not actually been in a managerial position and had in fact left after a few weeks.

My advice would be to:

- Be genuine; if you are trying to be someone you are not, what happens if you get the job?
- Consider the fundamental rules such as not crossing your arms, having a firm handshake, not slouching and making eye contact
- Be responsive; it is not just about your own body language but the ability to read and respond to the interviewer's body language
- Don't overthink it; if you spend the interview concentrating on your non-verbal communication, your verbal communication will likely suffer!

Power posing for confidence

Research has shown a link between body language and self-confidence (Cuddy et al., 2015) – that our non-verbal behaviour can affect how we feel about ourselves.

ACTIVITY

Body language and feelings

To see what effect your body language can have on your feelings, think about how you feel when you smile; over an entire day, make an effort to smile at everyone you make eye contact with and note down how you feel at the end of the day. Even without a responsive smile, the act of smiling more than usual over a day may improve your mood.

Adopting a so-called 'power pose' prior to your interview has been shown to boost confidence, performance and increase the likelihood of being hired (see Figure 14.1). Holding a power pose produces physiological changes in our bodies through fluctuations in hormones. Even if you lack confidence and are nervous, adopting a power pose for just two minutes before an interview can increase confidence levels whilst decreasing stress levels. To compound findings, those found to adopt non-power poses where you make yourself look smaller (crossing arms, stooping or sat cross-legged whilst holding your neck) have the reverse affect (see Figure 14.2). Performance is likely to be worse and stress levels increase. Psychologist Amy Cuddy presents these findings in a fascinating Ted Talk (see www.youtube.com/watch?v=Ks-_Mh1QhMc) which is well worth watching.

Figure 14.1   Adopting a power pose

Figure 14.2   A non-power pose (avoid this!)

CULTURAL DIFFERENCES

By their nature, the businesses involved in tourism, hospitality and events are international in their reach and impact. As future employees you should be aware of how different actions, behaviours and verbal cues that might mean something to you can potentially mean something completely different in another country or context. Knowing and researching some of the differences will potentially help you avoid any embarrassing situations, or worse, ensure you avoid coming across as rude and offensive. If in doubt, watch and learn from others.

Gestures are a common cause of misunderstanding and misinterpretation between cultures. Think about the 'V' sign (see Figure 14.3); how would you interpret this? To Britons, Australians and New Zealanders it is likely to cause offence meaning 'Up yours', but to most Germans it would mean victory and for many French, it means peace (Pease and Pease, 2004). The sign for 'OK' in Europe and North America means zero or being worthless in Tunisia, Belgium, France and the Mediterranean, and in parts of South America it is a symbol linked to sexual insult (see Figure 14.4): one hand gesture yet several entirely different meanings. In fact, in Japan, this same symbol means money; making this gesture to a Japanese business-person may be misconstrued as asking for a bribe!

Some countries are known for their openness, exuberance and public warmth, whereas some other cultures are generally known for being more private and contained. India, the Middle East, France and Italy are among those countries considered high-touch cultures; where bodily contact such as hugging, touching arms or shoulders is readily displayed throughout conversations. In the UK, USA, Canada and Australia, touching is usually only seen on the sports field. Think about greetings: in France greetings and farewells are made with kisses on the cheek; in the UK a handshake usually suffices unless it is family and then perhaps a single kiss on the cheek is given. In Japan, bodily contact is considered ill-mannered. Instead, bowing is considered the more courteous way of greeting, with the person with the highest status bowing the least.

Figure 14.3   The V sign

Figure 14.4   One hand gesture with many different meanings

Gestures mid-conversation can also be confusing; in many western cultures, nodding in conversation signals agreement. In Japan however, a combination of smiles and nods throughout conversation are made to keep the person talking, not necessarily to signal agreement. In India, headshakes need to be interpreted with finer detail: a head nod from side to side (left shoulder to right) or up and down means yes, whilst shaking or twisting the head left to right means no. This can be confusing to western cultures where head movements from left to right in any direction generally mean no!

A good way to begin understanding foreign cultures is to watch a foreign film, preferably with the subtitles off and try to work out what is going on. Play the film again with subtitles on to see how well you interpreted the body language.

 STUDENT INSIGHT

Jeff, Tourism and Hospitality student

I came to the UK from China to study as I had to take a placement year as part of my degree. I was nervous as I had not worked before and had never had a proper interview. I applied for many positions and eventually got an interview with a hotel as part of their front of house team.

The week before the interview, I made an appointment with my university careers department who really helped me to practise. I had done a lot of research on the company and had developed lots of mock answers to questions as recommended by my tutors, but I had not thought about how I would come across in an interview situation. I am not very confident with public speaking and find it awkward meeting new people as I know my English is not perfect.

During the mock interview, the careers representative said I kept touching my nose which might be seen as a lack of confidence or perhaps even lying. I was shocked because in China we often touch our noses when we are talking about ourselves! She also said that I did not seem that interested in the conversation. This really worried me because I was concentrating very hard. She felt that because I sat still and did not

(Continued)

use my hands much, that I was bored. This was not true. I think that Chinese people are not used to making big gestures with their arms or hands; we are more restrained with our movements!

I realised that body language was an important factor in how I would come across in an interview. Fortunately having this mock interview allowed me to prepare and find out about how I should sit and react in a conversation to make it known that I was prepared, interested and wanted the position! Thankfully it worked; well I got the job anyway!

Exposure to American and Western television, film and the proliferation of social media has diffused some intercultural miscommunication, particularly among younger generations. This is often one sided towards an understanding of Western culture rather than developing mutual understanding. While there are signs and symbols you can learn and adopt, these are generic and often stereotypical; they do not necessarily reflect individual's experiences, backgrounds or nuances, and diversity across generations, locations or religions. For example, do you have the same understanding and beliefs as your parents? Probably not, so why would we expect a graduate in Japan to display the same cultural behaviour as their parents? This does not mean you should ignore general cultural norms; these should be respected to avoid cultural conflict and appearing rude. However, the point is that there is really no substitute for learning by mixing with a diverse group of people; those from other cultures, backgrounds, religions and nationalities from our own. It is through these interactions that we most likely develop mutual understanding and respect for one another's behaviour including non-verbal communication.

CONCLUSION

In this chapter we have covered:

- The evolution of body language and non-verbal communication.
- The types of non-verbal communication and how to spot them.
- How you might use and interpret non-verbal communication in an interview setting.
- The meanings different cultures assign to non-verbal communication.

FURTHER READING

Birdwhistell, R.L. (1970) *Kinesics and Context: Essays on Body Motion Communication*. Philadelphia: University of Pennsylvania Press.

Cuddy, A., Wilmuth, C.A., Yap, A. and Carney, D.A. (2015) 'Preparatory power posing affects nonverbal presence and job interview performance', *Journal of Applied Psychology*, 100(4): 1285–1295.

Foley, G.N. and Gentile, J.P. (2010) 'Non-verbal communication in psychotherapy', *Psychiatry*, 7(6): 38–44.

Hall, E.T. (1963) 'A system for the notation of proxemic behavior 1', *American Anthropologist*, 65(5): 1003–1026.

Pease, A. and Pease, B. (2004) *The Definitive Book of Body Language*. London: Orion.

Todorov, A., Baron, S.G. and Oosterhof, N.N. (2008) 'Evaluating face trustworthiness: A model based approach', *Social Cognitive and Affective Neuroscience*, 3(2): 119–127.

15 TEAM-WORKING AND LEADING OTHERS

WRITTEN WITH DR LYN COLLIER-GREAVES AND MARYVONNE LUMLEY

CHAPTER LEARNING OBJECTIVES

By the end of this chapter you should be able to:

- Understand the different types of teams in Tourism, Hospitality and Events (THE) industries.
- Explain the key stages in team formation and maintenance and how these can be facilitated.
- Identify key team roles and understand how culture and diversity affect team functioning and effective team working.
- Understand the key elements for successfully leading others and identify your own preferred leadership tendency.
- Understand the role of effective communication, effective leadership and successful team-working.

GLOSSARY

- **Cross-functional team:** people drawn from different operational functions coming together to work towards a common strategic goal.
- **Functional teams:** teams linked to a particular operational function.
- **Hofstede's uncertainty:** the degree of personal and or group tolerance for uncertainty or instability.
- **Hofstede's power-distance:** attitudes to authority between individuals and groups from different cultures.
- **Matrix teams:** characterised by 'two-boss' systems in which an individual works across functions, reporting to a different manager depending on the task.
- **Teamwork:** a group of individuals working together to achieve a goal.

INTRODUCTION

This chapter will help you work effectively with others, regardless of whether or not they have the same geographical location, culture or background as you. It will help you to be aware of how differences between different cultures may cause inadvertent communication problems. You will also be guided through the important differences between being a team leader and a co-operative team member. The different roles people can play in teams will be discussed and the importance of covering these roles effectively will be examined. You will be encouraged to understand your own preferred leadership approach and to identify whether this is appropriate for the circumstances you are in.

Teams do not just form themselves and they do not always work smoothly so it is important to appreciate the stages of team formation and how they can be facilitated. Case studies are used to help you put the theoretical elements into practical contexts. On completion of this chapter, you should have a better idea of how the dynamics of **teamwork** effect the performance and outcome of a task, and how you can play a valuable role in ensuring that outcome is successful.

WHAT IS TEAM-WORKING?

Team-working is well established in both education and industry and plays a vital role in supporting individual and collective success. However, when people talk about being part of a team, they often describe situations which sound almost the opposite of 'working together'. The following comments, from first- and second-year undergraduates interviewed about their experience of teamwork, are typical:

> I tried really hard, but half the group didn't turn up to meetings or do the work on time – we could have done so much better if they had.

> Our self-appointed leader just wanted us to do all the work while they took all the credit and got cross if it wasn't done the way they thought it should be done. I just didn't bother in the end. It was all too horrible.

Working together as a group to achieve something is often more complicated than it appears. Here, we look at how teams are made up and try to understand some of the things that can help a group of people work successfully together.

 REFLECTION EXERCISE

Working as a team

Think of a time when you have had to work in a team to complete an assessment or task. Did you experience the same kinds of problems as these students? How did you overcome them? What would have been helpful?

TYPES AND CHARACTERISTICS OF TEAMS

Whilst teams may vary in many ways, three important things to consider are size, purpose and length of formation.

Size

There is no right or wrong size for a team. In smaller teams, it is easier to share individual thoughts and contributions and to make decisions about which ideas will be used. However, teams can also be much larger with many organisations often viewing themselves as one large team. Belbin (2010) has done a lot of work to help us understand teams, arguing that sometimes very large teams can cause problems such as role overlap and a tendency towards team members passively conforming. This shows the importance of being clear about the purpose of the team's function.

Purpose

A **functional** team is related to a particular operational function. For example, in the THE industry there are various **functional teams** such as facility maintenance, accommodation, restaurant, events, sales, etc. The team purpose within each group is to ensure the smooth running of their particular function, providing optimal customer satisfaction.

A **cross-functional team** consists of people drawn from different operational functions coming together to work towards a common strategic goal. The members of this team could be experts from different operational functions (for example, one person from maintenance, another from housekeeping, events, sales, etc.). Together they work on a project that crosses all their operational areas. For example, planning a large event should include people from those areas at the very start of the project.

A **matrix team** is often characterised by a 'two-boss' system, in which an individual works across functions, and reports to a different manager as appropriate to the task (see Figure 15.1). This usually means an individual can have more than one reporting line. For example, consider a matrix team brought together by an events co-ordinator to service a wedding. There might be waiters serving food reporting to a kitchen team manager and waiters serving drinks who report to the bar team manager. Both have operational responsibility for product delivery but there is clearly a need for the two services to complement each other. Thus, all waiting staff would report to their operational manager but also to the events co-ordinator to ensure an efficient service.

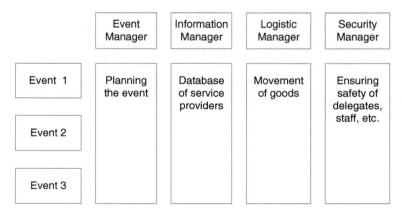

Figure 15.1   Matrix management system across three events

Whilst many teams can come together physically, a virtual team is not located in a shared physical space. Members may be in different time zones, from different cultures and possibly working in different languages, yet still working towards a common goal using technology to support their team experience.

One final type of team is the kind that forms itself. You may find while you are working with a couple of other people that you gradually work out a way to do your jobs better by co-operating and complementing each other's work. This kind of informal but 'proactive' team can go unnoticed by higher management but is often very effective.

Duration

Teams may be set up for a particular purpose or function, such as a group working regularly together for purposes such as a housekeeping or restaurant service, and this may be time-limited, e.g. for a particular event or organisational activity. Whatever the reason team members are selected, they may not have worked together before. It is therefore important to come together quickly as a team to maximise performance. In THE industries this is particularly important due to the customer-facing nature of the work. A positive customer experience is the best public relations an organisation can have, while equally missing deadlines can mean losing contracts. These pressures mean that individuals must learn quickly to work together in order to ensure successful operational performance. Understanding your role, the roles of others and how they all connect helps facilitate this coming together of teams.

TEAM FORMATION AND MAINTENANCE

Getting groups of people to work together effectively is not always easy. How teams form and work together is naturally a matter of much study (Honey, 1994; Tuckman, 1965) since the sooner teams start functioning well, the better able they are to complete their tasks successfully. According to Tuckman (1965) in his work on group formation, teams go through four stages in order to form a fully functioning team:

Forming: regardless of the task to be completed, teams need to be introduced to one another to discuss the purpose of the group. Roles might be allocated, and a leader identified. At this stage group members may wish to establish their position within the group and may, depending on their personality, wish to make an individual impression.

Storming: groups generally go through a period of conflict where individual 'understandings' of original purpose, roles and leadership are challenged. At this stage it may become clear that some group members have a personal agenda, and personality conflicts may emerge. However, careful management of this stage can lead to more clearly formulated aims and objectives and a consensus can be reached on how the group will share work and achieve its goals.

Norming: the group establishes the rules and norms which will govern it. The amount of commitment required and appropriate behaviour expected of members is established.

When the above stages have been successfully negotiated, the team should start successfully *performing* the task it was set up to achieve.

Other researchers provide different descriptions of the stages of team formation. For example, Honey (1994) considers that there are three main stages:

- The *chaotic* stage in which there are no real procedures, there is no 'leader', the team has no systems in place and people are generally getting a feel for the project.
- In the *formal* stage a strong leader is elected (if one hasn't been allocated) and people identify their roles. Time is spent determining procedures and rules.
- After a time of following the procedures, the team reaches a *skillful* stage where members become more comfortable with one another and the task, and more flexibility can be introduced into the system. People become more willing to share responsibility.

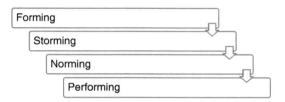

Figure 15.2   Four stages of a fully functioning team according to Tuckman (1965)

Teams are dynamic and however well they function, it is important to regularly monitor performance to ensure optimal outcomes. Also, some teams are brought together to carry out a particular project and it is important that, once a project is complete, team members celebrate their successes and learn from their mistakes.

TEAM MEMBERS AND ROLES

INDUSTRY INSIGHT

A team in a silver service restaurant

A restaurant manager in an established silver service restaurant became aware of tension between runners (staff who bring plates for service from the kitchen to the waiters, who then serve the food to customers) and a member of waiting staff. The team had previously worked well together, but this new member of staff appeared not to be accepted as part of the team. When the manager asked the new waiter what he thought the problem might be, he indicated that, as many of the runners and other waiters were Italian, they excluded him from after-work gatherings. The waiter was popular with the customers and the manager was keen to find out if the team could accept the new waiter.

The manager spoke with one of the longstanding runners and asked him to suggest a way to make the new waiter feel more included. The runner explained that, contrary to the explanation having to do with nationality or language barriers, all the waiters pooled their tips and shared them with all other restaurant staff, but this new waiter had refused and kept tips for himself, which the rest of the team felt was unfair. Through exploring the tensions with different parties, the restaurant manager gained a fuller picture and was able to explain to the new waiter the existing custom in place in the restaurant. Explaining to the rest of the team of Spanish, Portuguese and Italian waiters and runners that the new waiter had misunderstood and would now share with everyone helped address the team problems. He also emphasised the importance of speaking English whilst at work.

━━━ ACTIVITY ━━━

Managing and alleviating tension

Think about ways the restaurant manager in the industry insight above could have avoided tensions arising in the first place. Could things have been managed differently or was this the best solution?

Team dynamics continues to be a well-researched area. For example, in the last century Fiedler (1967) identified those with 'people skills' and those that are 'task-oriented' as valuable in a team: people skills can help mediate possible conflict and misunderstandings, whilst task-orientated people help keep the team on track and meet deadlines. Later research by Belbin identified nine categories or roles that help to ensure good team performance (see www.belbin.com/about/belbin-team-roles). Depending on the type of project, the relative importance of each role differs; Belbin suggested that covering each of the identified roles would help a team function well.

Honey (1994) (see Figure 15.3) simplified the categories or roles that Belbin identified and proposed that teams need the following people:

- Co-ordinator: to make sure that objectives are clear and that everyone is involved and committed
- Challenger: to question ineffectiveness and take the lead in pressing for improvements/results
- Doer: to urge the team to get on with the task in hand
- Thinker: to produce carefully considered ideas, weighing up and improving ideas from other people
- Supporter: to ease tensions and maintain harmonious working relationships.

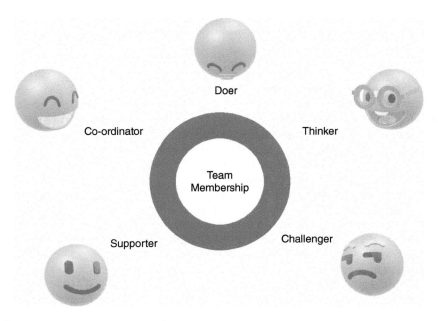

Figure 15.3 Honey's five categories of people

When working in a team, what is your preferred role and why?

HOW CULTURE AND DIVERSITY AFFECT TEAM FUNCTIONING

The cultural differences between countries are particularly relevant to the THE industries. The mental 'programming' that takes place as we develop our culture has a strong effect on how we behave and how we expect others to behave. One key researcher in this area describes our cultural up-bringing as a kind of 'software of the mind' (Hofstede, 1994: 4). For this chapter, it is useful to focus attention on the four areas that could affect teamwork within multi-cultural teams.

Uncertainty

Hofstede's studies (based on International Business Machine (IBM) employees) suggest that the ability to deal with **uncertainty** varies from culture to culture. The need to avoid uncertainty can cause some people from a culture with a strong need to avoid uncertainty (e.g. Poland, with an Uncertainty Avoidance Index (UAI) of 93) to crave rigid rules and guidelines. This can clash with someone who prefers to be more flexible, perhaps from a culture with a lower UAI (e.g. the UK, which scores 35).

Power

Hofstede also identified differences in the way cultures accept power. There are cultures in which individuals are expected to accept their place in society unquestioningly, as well as the authority of bosses, teachers and other leaders, behaving deferentially towards them. There is a **power distance** between the authority figure and those that lead. In other cultures, people are encouraged to question and think independently. At a simple level, this could manifest itself in one person using courtesy titles such as Sir, Ms, etc. while another might be more familiar and use given names. It is easy to see how a leader from a high-power distance culture could choose a very authoritarian style of leadership, which could be difficult for team members from a low-power distance culture to accept.

Relationships

a) *Individualism or collectivism.* The individualism (IDV) score for Great Britain is very high (89) compared to China (20) and this can affect teams in terms of whether someone is task- or relationship-focused (see team roles). Someone from a collectivist culture may feel the need to ensure that relationships between members are good so that people work well together, whereas someone from an individualist culture may focus more on the task. Having both these cultures can be good for a team, provided everyone is aware of what is going on.

b) *Harmony and face*. In collective cultures the need for harmony is high, so people take care in what they say and how they act in order to avoid offending someone or causing them to 'lose face'. This can lead to indirect communication. It is possible that those from a more individualistic culture can find this 'time-wasting' difficult to fathom.

Time

Hall (1976: 17) identifies two types of time: *Monochromic Time* (M-Time) in which tasks are approached sequentially; and *Polychronic Time* (P-Time) in which several tasks may be carried out at once (what we might call multi-tasking). These different ways of working can be related to the 'task versus relationship' dimension. For cultures mainly concerned with an individual schedule and completing tasks, things are done in M-time and allow for no distractions. However, if relationships and communication with people (by whatever means) are more important than sticking to a rigid timetable, they are more likely to respond to someone's call for help or information rather than carrying on with the task (P-Time). Some tasks in THE require people to work on various tasks at once, so the ability to work in P-Time might be very useful.

 ═══ ACTIVITY ═══════════════════════════

Understanding culture through meals

There are many team-building exercises that can support a team to form and develop trust, but when drawing a cross-cultural team together it is particularly important to help folk understand the different approaches in communication. The key to a successful cross-cultural understanding is to support each team member in being able to 'stand in someone else's shoes'. A simple exercise around the last festive family meal shared together will illuminate culinary and cultural differences and enable team members to relate to others' shared experience. Next time you are in a group, ask everyone to share how they prepared the meal and what the food represents.

Identify the key elements of effective team-working

To achieve high service innovation performance, organisations first need to develop knowledge-sharing behaviours and a good team culture. Good teamwork means finding a way of working with each person, with everyone committed to a shared goal. Through working with many teams, Kazemek (1991: 15) observed ten criteria which he deemed critical when building effective teams:

1. *Goals and objectives*. Successful teams understand and agree on these.
2. *Trust and conflict*. In effective teams, conflict is not absent but rather dealt with openly and constructively.
3. *Leadership*. Effective teams share leadership roles among members, so that all members are engaged and have ownership of leadership activities from the start. Ineffective teams often have one person dominating, which can affect the level of engagement and participation of team members.

4. *Use of resources.* Team members' resources (such as skills and existing knowledge) are recognised and used effectively. Under-use of some members can be a great source of frustration. For some people, not being used to their full potential is worse than being overworked.

5. *Interpersonal communication.* Effective teams pride themselves on open, participatory communication among members. Ineffective teams often are marked by defensive communication.

6. *Control and procedures.* Effective teams have procedures to guide team functioning and the members support these procedures and self-regulate.

7. *Problem-solving and decision-making.* Effective teams have well-established procedures.

8. *Experimentation and creativity.* Well-functioning teams often experiment with different ways of doing things and encourage creativity, while ineffective teams may be bureaucratic and rigid.

9. *Self-evaluation.* Effective teams regularly evaluate their functions and processes. A regular retreat dedicated to team development issues and processes is a popular tactic used by strong teams.

10. *Roles, responsibility and authority.* An effective team's members clearly understand their roles, responsibilities and degree of authority.

REFLECTION EXERCISE

Using the key elements of effective team-working

The above list could be made into a checklist. Next time you work in a team you could suggest to your fellow team members that you check regularly to see whether you are doing the above. Use this as a reflection exercise to see how well your team did against the above criteria.

Effective teamwork seeks to maximise the individual strengths of team members, bringing out the best of everyone whilst striving to achieve the shared goals. A project is a dynamic activity with ever-changing circumstances, so building teamwork skills needs to be worked at constantly. Being open to differences and not allowing them to develop into full-blown disputes involves appreciating and listening to the various viewpoints involved in conflict to find resolution, and are key skills for all team members to develop. Ignoring or complaining about the conflict is not effective in supporting a positive and healthy constructive difference of opinion. Being direct and clarifying the issues helps avoid negative and destructive conflict that disrupts the team's progress.

BUILDING AN EFFECTIVE TEAM

Elements crucial to building a productive team include communication, support, delegation, efficiency, creativity and reflection.

Communication. Communicating effectively is the most important part of teamwork and involves systematically updating each person – never assume that everyone has the same information. Being a good communicator means sharing and listening to other team members in a respectful way, not bombarding your fellow students or colleagues with information and questions.

Support. Building bonds of trust is fundamental for a strong team. This is particularly important in the THE industry where a group may face a sudden change of team member whilst being required to maintain customer-facing efficiency. A strong team environment acts as a support for staff, enabling the team to develop.

Delegation. Teams that work well together understand each other's strengths and weaknesses. Strong teams are adept at regularly identifying all aspects of a project and ensuring tasks are undertaken by the most appropriate team members.

Efficiency. An effective team has embedded systems that allow efficient collaboration to ensure tasks are completed in the designated timeframes. Colleagues remain aware of their own competence and the abilities of the group in general and can adjust accordingly.

Creativity. When a team works well together and creates a respectful and trusting team environment, the members will feel comfortable offering creative suggestions and ideas. This environment in turn leads to a productive and collaborative atmosphere.

Reflection. Finally, team members should look back on their project and reflect on the progress made. Even in a successful project there will be areas that could be improved on, and in an unsuccessful one there will still be things to celebrate. The team should take time to acknowledge each other's contribution, and to thank all those involved.

SUCCESSFUL TEAM LEADERSHIP

It is not easy to define what makes a good leader and indeed it may be that in different circumstances, different types of leadership will be more appropriate than others. It is usual to identify the difference between a manager and a leader.

 ACTIVITY

The difference between a manager and a leader

Discuss the difference between a manager and a leader. Share your experience of people you have worked under if you have had a part-time or full-time job. Was it just their job title that made the difference, or did you observe differences in behaviour? Identify the traits you admired in the person your worked under. Discuss ways in which they influenced your behaviour.

Management has a more strategic role, and is an integral part of an organisation's structure. The position of leader, on the other hand, could be quite informal and may even be appointed by the team themselves. To do their job well, leaders should be able to motivate others to achieve the objectives the team has been set. It is easy to identify powerful historical leaders, or to assume that people are 'born' leaders. However, it is less easy to quantify the qualities that make a good leader, as they are so numerous and interdependent. Some or all of the following are likely to be needed.

- A strong belief in one's ability to guide the team successfully towards its goals.
- Good 'people skills' demonstrated by the ability to empathise with others and persuade others to give their full support.

- Competence and experience in the relevant area, to set an example to others and coach where necessary.
- Openness to new ideas that can generate novel solutions.
- The ability to give constructive feedback in a way that is acceptable to the team.

=========== THINK POINT ===========

Think of leaders from around the world and using the list above, think about how they have demonstrated these skills, and how the skills worked effectively together.

Probably the word most often used in relation to good leaders is charisma – the ability to inspire admiration and willingness to follow in others and indeed to change people's beliefs. For example, Nelson Mandela was a charismatic leader who used that quality to tackle institutionalised racism, encourage racial reconciliation and lead the transition of South Africa from apartheid to a multiracial democracy.

Leadership styles

According to Newstrom and Davis (1993), a leadership style is the manner and approach that individuals use to provide direction, implement plans and motivate people. It includes both explicit and implicit actions. It is important to accept that no one style is right for every situation. The effectiveness of a style may depend on the number of people in the team, the timescale in which objectives need to be achieved and the cultural make-up of the team itself. Some of the earliest research into leadership styles was by Lewin and colleagues (1939), who identified three styles:

- *Autocratic*: the leader assumes total authority and responsibility and makes decisions without consulting the team. This is a top-down approach and often results in limited communication with the team members.
- *Democratic*: in which the leader consults the team and delegates work, but still maintains overall responsibility.
- *Laissez-faire*: a hands-off approach in which teams are allowed to get on with tasks in the way they think best. Obviously, this requires a good deal of competence on the part of team members.

An alternative categorisation was proposed by Bass (1990) who considered the 'transformational' and 'transactional' nature of leadership and how these two styles impact on overall team performance:

- *Transformational*: a motivational approach in which acknowledging and addressing the expectations of the team should result in high performance.
- *Transactional*: aims to maintain the status quo and keep things running according to existing rules.

Table 15.1 summarises the difference between the two styles.

Table 15.1   Transformational and transactional leadership

TRANSFORMATIONAL LEADER	TRANSACTIONAL LEADER
Is charismatic Provides vision and a sense of mission, instils pride, gains respect and trust	Uses rewards to produce results Contracts exchange of rewards for effort, promises rewards for good performance, recognises accomplishments
Inspires workers Communicates high expectations, uses symbols to focus efforts, and expresses important purposes in simple ways	Management by exception (active) Watches for deviations from rules and standards, and then takes corrective action
Stimulates the intelligence of workers Promotes intelligence, rationality, and careful problem-solving	Management by exception (passive) Intervenes only if standards are not met
Treats workers as individuals Gives personal attention, treats each employee individually, coaches, advises	Laissez-faire Abdicates responsibility and avoids making decisions

Source: based on Bass (1990) and adapted from Lumley and Wilkinson (2013: 85)

Key leadership theories

Given the diverse nature of teams and the activities they can be involved in, it is not surprising there are many theories on the influence and impact of different leadership styles on team-working. In the following section we consider Adair's (1973) action centred leadership model and Blake et al.'s (1964) concern for people.

Adair's seminal leadership theory (1973) fits well with the cultural theories of tasks and relationships discussed elsewhere in this chapter. His model focuses on task, team and individual (see Figure 15.4). To successfully accomplish the task, a leader:

*   needs clear strategic objectives and must set achievable, timely goals
*   must be able to delegate
*   should share in success BUT is responsible for failure.

To ensure the *team* works together to accomplish the task, a leader:

*   must set up and maintain formal group structures
*   should encourage/shape informal structures towards objectives
*   should maximise motivation by example/charisma and appropriate recognition and rewards
*   should persuade individuals to sacrifice own goals
*   must administer discipline if necessary

To get the best out of each *individual* team member, a leader needs:

- skills in satisfying individual needs
- sensitivity to and understanding of what motivates individuals
- the ability to administer appropriate rewards (and penalties)

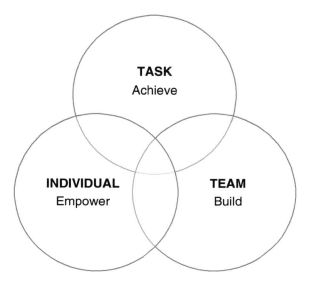

Figure 15.4 Adair's leadership model

Fiedler (1967) formulated a theory of leadership effectiveness, seeking to identify the leadership factors likely to achieve maximum performance in teams. He identified two key types:

- *Relationship motivated people* who get job satisfaction from relating to people
- *Task-motivated people* who get job satisfaction from successful completion of a task.

Neither of these types is 'better': either could be appropriate depending on the circumstances.

THINK POINT

How effective is your leadership style? Is there another, non-leadership team role that you prefer to play? How can you expand the number of team roles in which you feel comfortable?

Blake et al. (1964) designed a grid that demonstrated the features and tendencies of some leaders. They identified five key management patterns: Impoverished, Country Club, Pendulum, Task and Good Team. These are outlined in Figure 15.5 below.

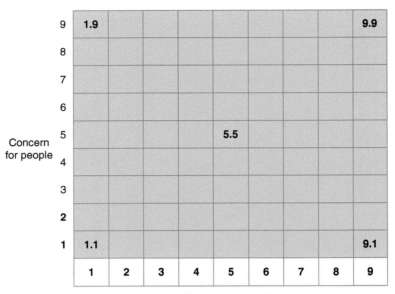

Grid ref.	Management pattern
1.1	*Impoverished Management* – where the leader avoids both responsibility for tasks and confrontation wherever possible
1.9	*Country Club Management* – where the leader engenders a sense of cosy 'togetherness' with tasks being secondary
5.5	*Pendulum Management* – extremes are avoided, and adequacy is the main goal
9.1	*Task Management* – authoritarian leadership that focuses on the task and treats people simply as tools
9.9	*Good Team Management* – high concern for people AND production. Human needs satisfied in a team motivated by achieving excellence in the task. Considered the most efficient management style.

Figure 15.5   Concern for people vs task management patterns

The model suggests that, when concern for both people and results are high, employee engagement and productivity is likely to be strong. The ideal place to be in terms of team management style is the top right-hand corner at 9.9, but context also must be considered. For example, if an organisation was undergoing a period of significant change, more emphasis would need to be placed on people to support the process and retain staff.

━━━ ACTIVITY ━━━

Some key team-working questions

* How will you deal with cultural differences in your team?
* How can you improve your communication with team members?
* Can you identify your own leadership tendency?
* Where do you think you fit on the Blake et al.'s (1964) Grid?
* What work would you need to do to be nearer 9.9?

One chapter cannot cover everything about team-working and leadership and we recommend further research (see below). Whatever style of leader you tend (or are required) to be, good leaders are always learning by listening to others, asking people with good skills to mentor them and reading up-to-date material. They also acknowledge their weaknesses and look for ways to improve.

CONCLUSION

In this chapter we have covered:

* The relationship between effective leadership and successful team-working.
* How culture and diversity affect team functioning.
* The role of effective communication to facilitate successful team-working.
* The key stages in team formation and maintenance and how these can be facilitated.
* The different types of teams in THE and key team roles.
* The key elements of effective team-working and successful leadership.

FURTHER READING

Belbin, R.M. (2010) *Management Teams: Why They Succeed or Fail*. London: Routledge.
Belbin, R.M. (1993) *Team Roles at Work*. London: Butterworth-Heinemann.
Fiedler, F.E. (1967) *A Theory of Leadership Effectiveness*. New York: McGraw-Hill.
Hall, E. (1976) *Beyond Culture*. New York: Anchor Books/Random House Inc.
Honey, P. (1994) *Teams and Leaders: Trainer's Guide*. London: Melrose Film Productions.
Kazemek, E. (1991) 'Ten criteria for effective team building', *Healthcare Financial Management*, 45(9): 15.
Lumley, M. and Wilkinson, J. (2014) *Developing Employability for Business*. Oxford: Oxford University Press.

16 LANGUAGE AND CULTURAL SENSITIVITY

CHAPTER LEARNING OBJECTIVES

By the end of this chapter you should be able to:

- Describe what is meant by the term 'culture'.
- Explain the role that culture shock has in business.
- Understand the role of intercultural skills in the working practices of THE industries.
- Demonstrate cultural sensitivity and fluency.

GLOSSARY

- **Culture:** the knowledge, beliefs, art, morals, law, customs, and any other capabilities and habits acquired by a member of a society (Tylor, 1871).
- **Cultural advantage:** promoting cultural differences as positive and repositioning the legitimacy of different cultural heritages (Malia Kana'iaupuni et al., 2017: 316).
- **Culture shock:** the impact of moving from a familiar culture to one which is unfamiliar (Marx, 1999).
- **Tourism translation:** making the cultural values of a given destination accessible to an audience that is not familiar with them (Agorni, 2018).

INTRODUCTION

Earley and Mosakowski (2016: 1) consider **culture** to be so powerful that it influences our perceptions on the world around us, stating that

> the human interactions, gestures, and speech patterns a person encounters in a foreign business setting [are] subject to a wide range of interpretations, including ones which can make misunderstandings likely, and cooperation impossible.

Being able to work across cultures is critical for THE professionals, given that this industry is based around the experience of difference, whether this is at a hotel, a holiday or indeed an event: all involve moving from one culture to another to a greater or lesser extent. According to Hofstede (1997: 215), the most 'superficial form of cultural encounter' is that between a tourist and the place they are visiting, with the risk of miscommunication and misunderstandings being high because of limited cultural awareness, which can result in both customer and supplier dissatisfaction.

The positioning of THE employees as cultural brokers and mediators that act as a bridge between guest and host (Salazar, 2014; Smith, 2001) has strengthened over recent years and resulted in a demand for employability skills that reflect cultural fluency (Sucher and Cheung, 2015). These include foreign language proficiency, cultural empathy and an appreciation of values; these are factors that can affect customer and client service relationships. Given that the reputation and indirect selling of a THE product or service can be by word of mouth or from interpersonal influence, any enhancement of the visitor experience is likely to have positive results. For example, work by Chen and Hsu (2000) revealed that clients were more likely to book a holiday if someone in customer services spoke their language, and that customer satisfaction can have a positive influence on spending behaviour and contribute to economic sustainability (Disegna, 2016). Being able to greet clients in their own language (Leslie and Russell, 2006) and communicate effectively irrespective of the cultural context aids the transition from a local to a foreign environment.

CULTURE

Before you start a career in the THE sector, you need to understand what is meant by the term 'culture'. We might define culture as a particular way of life, made up of or heavily influenced by the customs and beliefs of particular groups of people. This might be expressed through art objects and performances or religious practices, or perhaps more subtly in unspoken assumptions and beliefs. For example, the Easter Service at the Vatican in which the Pope celebrates mass is a large, public ritual that anyone can attend, as well as an expression of both Catholic and Italian culture. We might also consider something more nuanced such as the fact that, while haggling and overcharging are culturally acceptable in China, it is considered bad form to tip in a restaurant (something many visitors first discover when their exact change is returned to them).

Culture is a complex expression of human values, present in our everyday lives in many forms:

- *Artefacts and attitudes*, including architecture, rituals, dress-codes, eating, and language
- *Beliefs and norms*, including cultural rules, values and behaviours
- *Assumptions* that may produce particular behaviours that do not immediately make sense to an outsider.

Given the complex nature of culture, it is easy to understand why the link between culture and nation-hood is strong. This includes groups with a disputed home territory such as the Palestinian or Tibetan peoples; groups without any legally recognised home territory, such as the Bedouin, whom the Israeli government (incorrectly) regard as nomads with no meaningful understanding of 'home' as a physical place; and groups obliged to 'share' their nation with others, such as Canadian First Nations people, who live alongside the descendants of European invaders. Further, a sense of nationhood and culture may still be powerful, regardless of whether the 'nation' in question is recognised as a state. For example, the Kurdish people have a distinct cultural identity even though the territory known as Kurdistan is spread across several countries and is not recognised as a state in its own right. The majority of Kurdish people live in Iraq, Iran, Syria and Turkey, for example, but many still consider themselves Kurds rather than Iraqis, Iranians, Syrians or Turks, and preserve Kurdish culture in their behaviours and traditions. The ability to work seamlessly across cultures without causing offence, compromising work-ing relationships or undermining the visitor experience, requires cultural sensitivity in THE practices. This includes a willingness and ability to use cultural knowledge, which 'involves understanding and respecting values, beliefs and attitudes' (Ulrey and Amason, 2001: 450).

 THINK POINT

When you started university, what cultural differences did you notice amongst your fellow students and your lecturers? How easy did you find adapting to the university culture? How confident were you meeting and working with students from different cultures?

IMPORTANCE OF INTERCULTURAL SKILLS IN THE INDUSTRIES

The world of work comprises cultures within cultures, with negotiations taking place on a daily basis. Tourism is by definition an international business, about experiences among different cultures and meet-ing people from all over the global village (Vanneste et al., 2009: 25). It requires employees to be culturally sensitive. In many respects the role of the THE professional is that of a translator, because of the impor-tance of being able to work across boundaries and handle situations that arise between customers from diverse cultures, religions and ethnicities (Cuocci, 2015). The growing recognition of the role that inter-cultural skills play in business is partly in response to the acceleration of boundary- and border-less working, resulting from the Fourth Industrial Revolution (see Chapter 35). This is resulting in a growth in automation and artificial intelligence, and increasing emphasis on the individual to provide the 'human' soft skills for translation purposes. Globalisation in the twenty-first century means that:

1. We are required to communicate across national, cultural and linguistic borders. For THE graduates working in the visitor economy, there is an expectation that you will be able to bridge the foreign/local gap and have appropriate intercultural communication and **tourism translation** skills. The former is the ability to work across cultures and ethnicities, whereas the latter is the ability to 'make the cultural values of a given destination accessible to an audience that is not familiar with them' (Agorni, 2018: 253).

2. We are more likely to oversee diverse, geographically dispersed teams. As the world begins to respond to the climate change crisis and the United Nations' Sustainable Development Goals, the process of how we work together will change. We have already witnessed a seismic shift in the adoption of remote working as a result of the 2019/20 COVID-19 pandemic at the time of writing, which is likely to have a long-term effect on our working practices for the future. Many THE industries have experience of geographically distributed teams. For example, a travel agent's place of work is often just a screen and an earpiece through which the tourist experience is shaped. The travel agent helps the tourist by sourcing the holiday, undertakes the flight and accommodation negotiations, and liaises with the local representatives to identify and promote excursions or cultural experiences. Many of these activities are undertaken virtually and between teams based in different countries, with being able to understand verbal and non-verbal cues being critical for these roles.

3. There is increasing interest in ethical business practices and corporate social responsibility. In THE industries, the emergence of Tourism 4.0 is requiring a responsible management approach to the tourism ecosystem that takes into consideration reducing the carbon footprint, using smart technologies to protect the environment (which includes historical and heritage sites), and increased collaboration between all stakeholders in the exploitation of **cultural advantage**s through considered practices (see Chapter 35).

Without appropriate intercultural training, diversity can be a source of conflict with cultural differences potentially being perceived as a nuisance at best and a disaster at worst. Lack of cultural awareness can compromise businesses, and for THE employees, not preparing their clients adequately can result in reputational damage for the company and the country. You only have to read the headline from *The Guardian* newspaper (Khaleeli, 2017) 'From Barcelona to Malia: How Brits on holiday have made themselves unwelcome' to see how cultural ignorance, lack of effort or lack of respect for another culture can result in causing offence, and (as in this case) causing problems for all tourists from a particular country. For example, those who work and study in the ancient university towns of Cambridge and Oxford may find the huge numbers of Chinese tourists visiting the colleges difficult or frustrating to deal with, particularly at road crossings or where pavements are narrow. The lack of cultural understanding here is twofold: the Asian visitors are not used to narrow streets or fast-moving vehicles, while the British natives lack knowledge of the wide streets, slow cars and countdown streetlights that are common in the East.

Intercultural skills form the basis of cultural competence and enable you to work across cultures seamlessly. The core skills that are required for you to be culturally competent are listed in Table 16.1.

Table 16.1   Core skills for cultural competence

Skill	Focus
Soft skills	• Being able to read verbal and non-verbal signs, including facial expressions and body language • Being aware of and able to attune to difference • Empathy • Communication skills (spoken, written) • Relationship management (building, strengthening)
Attitude	• Openness, intellectual curiosity and a willingness to interact with different cultures • Uncertainty tolerance (being comfortable in the face of ambiguity) • Emotional intelligence, resilience and adaptability

(Continued)

Table 16.1 (Continued)

Skill	Focus
Knowledge	• Cultural awareness – demonstrating knowledge of different cultures • Self-awareness – recognise your own conscious and unconscious bias (prejudices, stereotyping and misconceptions about individuals, races, genders, countries or cultures)
Technical skills	• Languages and being able to meet and greet people • Understanding cultural socio-behavioural expectations • Understanding how to navigate the physical environment

Language is part of cultural identity, and there is little doubt that knowledge of language is a key employability skill in tourism. English language proficiency is almost taken for granted in some countries (Tomić and Čolić, 2019), with the real employability competitive advantage being linked to proficiency in multiple foreign languages (Sindik and Božinović, 2013) and being credible when working in an international context. A solid grasp of several languages and broad cultural knowledge can benefit you in terms of 'what experiences, opportunities, rewards, recognition, and personal satisfaction come to people as a result of their foreign language proficiency and cultural understanding' (Uber Grosse, 2004: 353). It is interesting to note that the motivation to learn languages increases if students have studied abroad and/or had some international work experience (Luka, 2015). Customers' perceptions of authentic tourism are influenced by language and the appearance of staff, for example expecting to be served by Thai staff at a Thai hotel. The notion that language learning broadens the mind and shrinks the world is particularly true for tourism because it can enable more effective and efficient communication and increase the potential for foreign visits and related direct and indirect THE expenditure.

 STUDENT INSIGHT

Xi Li

Xi Li came from Suzhou, PR China to the UK to study for a bachelor's degree in tourism. When she joined the university in 2001, she had just enough English to be able to cope with her studies. After six weeks, she realised that she was not proficient enough to fully participate in the programme, so she decided to improve her language competence taking advantage of links with local organisations. Through her volunteering and immersion in the local community she was able to strengthen her language proficiency and gain considerable insight into the local culture. This greatly enhanced her employability prospects when she completed her studies.

 EMPLOYER INSIGHT

Hapag Lloyd Cruises

Terminal host/hostess

The language of the passengers is German. Therefore, excellent knowledge of German language is compulsory, as well as fluent business English.

- Greeting and saying goodbye to the cruise guests at the port terminals and train stations in Kiel and Hamburg Airport
- Care of guests at information counters
- High level of service and customer orientation
- Motivation
- Stress resistance
- Very good knowledge of foreign languages, primarily English

Source: www.leisurejobs.com/job/2679833/terminalhost-terminalhostess-international/

CULTURE SHOCK

We introduced the concept of **culture shock** in Chapter 1 in terms of starting your university studies. Here, we build on this and argue that even if you have undergone some form of intercultural training, you may still experience culture shock during your studies or work.

As outlined earlier, culture shock describes the impact of moving from a familiar culture to one that is unfamiliar, perhaps to work or study. It refers to unpleasant experiences that can make a person feel lost, lonely or baffled when immersed in a new culture (Marx, 1999). This is a normal reaction to being confronted by the strange and the unknown. For example, social roles and behaviours may confuse, surprise or offend you, or you may find constantly listening to and attempting to speak a foreign language tiring, and that you miss your own language, familiar foods and smells, and your home surroundings. As future THE employees, it is important to be able to recognise culture shock and identify ways to manage it effectively. You might care to revise the five stages of culture shock in Figure 1.2.

Consider the processes outlined in Table 16.2, which are loosely based on Maslow's hierarchy of need. Can you map yourself across the various phases of cultural transition? Are there any actions that you could have taken to better prepare yourself for transitioning across different educational cultures? If so, what were these?

Table 16.2 Students' cultural transition challenges

	Maslow's Hierarchy of Need	Transition themes and key actions
Self-actualisation	- Achieving one's full potential	Cultural fluency - Social mobility and employment prosperity - Protean and boundaryless career plans
Esteem	- Confidence - Self-esteem - Achievement - Recognition - Respect by others	- Cultural adaptation and adjustment - Development of coping strategies to address personal and family pressures to succeed - Negotiation of the differences within and across different education systems
Love/belonging	- Friendships - Family - Sense of connection	- Cultural connectivity - Re-negotiation of existing (and the creation of new) relationships - Cultural acquisition resulting from new experiences and understandings

(Continued)

Table 16.2 (Continued)

	Maslow's Hierarchy of Need	Transition themes and key actions
Safety	• Personal security • Health (physical and mental) • Accommodation • Travel	• Cultural disorientation • Discord and confusion as familiar social structures are replaced by unfamiliar ones
Psychological	• Air, water, food, shelter sleep, clothing	• Cultural awakening • 'Coming of age' and taking responsibility for addressing own basic needs outside the family, community and cultural unit

According to Cronen and Shuter (1983), there are six levels of complexity in cross-cultural interaction between a tourist and a host that can result in conflict and misunderstanding:

1. *Verbal and non-verbal behaviour*: how clearly people understand one another's speech, gestures, posture or signals (see Chapter 14 on body language). This might also have a relationship to the law of the country. For example, in China, where homosexuality is illegal, a visitor from a Western country may find the way teenage boys touch one another to be very different from how boys of the same age might interact at home and might misinterpret these interactions.

2. *Speech acts*: the way meaning is attached to forms of address, such as status or level of formality. For example, students from non-UK countries may address British lecturers very formally as 'Sir' or 'Ma'am' because this is how such individuals are addressed in their home countries. Meanwhile, British lecturers may have a wide range of preferences in terms of how they like their students to address them, from 'Professor' right down to first-name terms, depending on their own backgrounds, the culture of their own university and the nature of the teaching that is taking place.

3. *Episodes*: sequences of behaviour, rituals, arrangements for eating, sightseeing and tipping. For example, an exchange of gifts ceremony in China between visiting and host academics may seem odd to Western visitors as there is no real equivalent in their own culture. Similarly, a large and apparently familiar event such as a wedding may look very different from nation to nation, including what is considered appropriate as a gift, how long the event lasts, traditional foods, what those involved choose to wear, and how legal status is conferred.

4. *Relationships*: the nature of social relationships, rights and expectations, the formation of friendships and other relationships. For example, a Western woman visiting China might find other women extremely tactile very early on in their acquaintance, and yet not be invited into the homes of their friends for many months (or indeed at all). It can be difficult to know what the etiquette of making friends can be, particularly when physical or social cues differ across cultures (e.g. walking arm-in-arm is very common for female friends in many Asian countries, but far less so in Western nations). Remember also that you may come from a country or cultural background where the legal recognition of relationships (such as who can get married, or what marriage looks like) may differ wildly from the culture you are

visiting. For example, as mentioned above, homosexual acts are illegal in China, whereas in the UK it is legal for same-sex couples to enter into a state-sanctioned marriage that has exactly the same legal status as that of a heterosexual couple. Your own relationship might appear strange to those you are meeting, perhaps in terms of a visible age gap, the point in your lives at which you chose to get married and whether or not you have children. Moreover, you may find that such matters (which might be considered private or inappropriate subjects for general chit-chat in your home culture) are considered perfectly acceptable topics of conversation in another culture.

5. *Life script*: the way people perceive themselves in their behaviour, their relationship to others and the physical environment. This might include broad ideas such as which areas of the outside environment are considered 'dirty' or safe, as well as finely grained notions and attitudes, such as which insects can be handled or which species are regarded as food, wild animals or pets.

6. *Cultural pattern*: the way the larger community is defined, what is perceived as honesty, justice, reality, truth or equity within a society (Reisinger and Turner, 2011: 58). In a professional context, this might include matters such as timekeeping, what is considered professional dress, how likely someone is to actually undertake a task they have said they will carry out, and how promptly such a task might be done.

Becoming culturally fluent takes place over time and involves progressive skills development. Tourists visiting a foreign country for a short time undergo a period of transient adaption and compromise as a result of experiencing a new culture, albeit on a temporary basis. Acculturation (the adoption of some, but not all, aspects of a host country's culture) can be seen in the British expat community in France, where it is usual to buy a property and then develop strong links with the British community living in the area, rather than integrating into French society. Such people might also make frequent trips 'home' to the UK even though they no longer live there, perhaps to purchase particular foods or products (rather than seeking out a local substitute), as well as to visit relatives and friends. THE agents selling foreign properties to this type of client are potentially selling a 'new' culture, but with the reassurance of retaining links to something much more familiar. The same could be said of international students, who study abroad, engage with and adopt elements of the host's culture as part of the learning process. In acculturation, the individual has some choice in terms of how far she or he is prepared to change, and the more an individual knows about the host society and culture, the more likely they are to become acculturated. For THE companies that establish themselves in host countries, it may be necessary to be fully assimilated into the host society because this ensures the smooth running of the business.

FLIPPING ME

One of the most important aspects of working across cultures is to gain an understanding of the differences that exist before you are faced with them and develop a plan of how to deal with them in advance. The Flipping Me exercise (see Table 16.3) provides you with an opportunity to reflect on how much you know about a particular culture before you experience it. For example, if you are going to China to run an event, how can you prepare yourself for the East–West difference?

Table 16.3 Flipping Me

Before I interact with people from a different culture, I need to understand the different approaches to the following:	Yes	No
Business interaction: Is there anything I need to be careful about?		
Formality: What is the correct term of address?		
Communication: Should I anticipate different communication styles?		
Time: What are the expectations? Fashionably late, or absolutely on time?		
Gestures: Should I avoid particular gestures?		
Local traditions: Is there anything specific I should be aware of?		
Food: Are there restrictions, bans or combinations I should be aware of?		

To be truly culturally competent, you should first understand yourself and your own cultural inheritance. As the THE sector becomes more diverse, tourism employers and employees need to ensure that they can work across boundaries seamlessly.

CONCLUSION

In this chapter we have covered:

- What is meant by the term 'culture' and how it can affect our working practices.
- The various skills required to be culturally competent.
- How being sensitive to cultural differences (whether these be gender-, ethnic- or community-based) can result in positive visitor experiences.
- Digital literacy and automation and how the role of the THE professional providing the 'human' side in translating tourism opportunities to clients and stakeholders is a key part of a professional's role.

FURTHER READING

Baker, M.A. and Kim, K. (2018) 'The role of language, appearance, and smile on the perceptions of authenticity versus rapport', *International Journal of Hospitality Management*, 74: 171–179.

Bury, J. and Oka, T. (2017) 'Undergraduate students' perceptions of the importance of English in the tourism and hospitality industry', *Journal of Teaching in Travel & Tourism*, 17(3): 173–188.

Guirdham, M. (2005) *Communicating Across Cultures at Work*, 2nd edn. Basingstoke, UK: Palgrave Macmillan.

Hofstede, G. (1997) *Cultures and Organizations: Software of the Mind*. London: McGraw-Hill.

Leslie, D. and Russell, H. (2006) 'The importance of foreign language skills in the tourism sector: A comparative study of student perceptions in the UK and continental Europe', *Tourism Management*, 27: 1397–1407.

Marx, E. (1999) *Breaking Through Culture Shock*. London: Nicholas Brealey.

Reisinger, Y. and Turner, L.W. (2011) *Cross-Cultural Behaviour in Tourism: Concepts and Analysis*. London and New York: Routledge.

Useful web resources

UN Sustainable Development Goals – www.un.org/sustainabledevelopment/sustainable-development-goals/

Tourism Jobs Abroad – https://jobs.goabroad.com/search/tourism/jobs-abroad-1

17 SOCIAL RESPONSIBILITY AND SUSTAINABILITY AWARENESS

CHAPTER LEARNING OBJECTIVES

By the end of this chapter you should be able to:

- Demonstrate understanding of the significance of sustainability and social responsibility in today's world.
- Discuss the role of sustainability in tourism, hospitality and events.
- Recognise the role of responsible tourism in meeting sustainability goals.
- Deliberate the future of tourism and sustainability.

GLOSSARY

- **Common pool resources:** Shared goods which are usually finite and where the exploitation and overuse by one party reduces the resource availability for another. Examples include air and the atmosphere, ecosystems, forests, oceans, water and wildlife (Alipour and Arefipour, 2020).
- **Overtourism:** Where carrying capacity has been exceeded and 'residents or guests, locals or tourists feel that the character of the experience of the place and the place itself has been degraded by too many tourists' (Goodwin, 2019: 112).
- **Sustainable Development Goals (SDGs):** The UN 2030 Agenda for Sustainable Development maps out 17 goals across 169 targets to address global challenges including poverty, inequality, climate change and environmental degradation.

INTRODUCTION

> Fostering emerging talent found in universities, government and industry can help build the foundations for the public private platforms required to channel substantial investment in greener, more efficient destinations of the future (Epler Wood et al., 2019: 45).

It is hard to imagine that as little as ten years ago this chapter would probably not have been included in an employability book. Such has been the momentous shift over the last decade towards raised awareness of sustainability and responsible practice that it is now firmly on the agenda – locally, nationally and globally. In 2018 travel and tourism outperformed growth in the global economy contributing 10.4% to global GDP and accounting for 1 in 10 jobs (WTTC, 2019a); for many countries it is a major source of income and development. Unfortunately, years of exploiting and over-using resources, behaving unethically and pursuing growth under economical terms have contributed considerable pressure on the planet, its ecosystems and human societies that function within it.

The gravity of our global situation in relation to unsustainability and consequential action demands that future workforces are not only aware of sustainability issues but demonstrate their ability to take responsibility and contribute towards addressing such challenges. The Higher Education Authority in the UK (2008) reported that 50% of employers will look to recruit socially and environmentally responsible graduates in the future. The reasons for this are, firstly, because it suggests something about who you are. Your ethics and values are reflected in your behaviour and therefore your actions as an employee. Secondly, there is increasing demand for businesses to behave in a more ethical manner; to take responsibility for their impact and action to minimise negative effects. Businesses are made up of individuals so hiring on the basis of these traits is crucial to steering future organisational change towards more responsible behaviour. So, the question is are you prepared? Do you have a good understanding of sustainability? What does sustainability look like in tourism? How can tourism be made more responsible? This chapter explores these questions and ensures that sustainability and responsibility feature on your radar to enhance your graduate employability opportunities.

SUSTAINABILITY

Sustainability has become a global buzzword in recent years; from the fashion world to tourism, it is firmly on the agenda. Spurred on by the UN **Sustainable Development Goals (SDGs)** and more recently the Agenda 2030, sustainability addresses the balance of three key areas: people, planet and prosperity (UN, 2019). At its heart, sustainability provides a more equitable means of development, addressing current population needs, but also in consideration of the future and meeting the needs of generations to come. It is an ethically bound principle that recognises that what we do now in the present has an impact and that these should not be to the detriment of those in the future. The focus is longevity and long-term viability – financially, socio-culturally and environmentally. This is often discussed as three pillars (economic, social and environmental), the idea being that if one of the pillars is removed, the balance is offset and the foundation collapses. Therein lies the sustainability nexus – economic gains must be balanced against environmental and social costs.

═══════════ THINK POINT ═══════════

What criticisms might the term sustainability face?

Sustainability represents a shift from how much of the world has lived (and in many cases continues to live), that is, in an individualistic bubble where decisions are made based on self-enhancement values relating to individuals and their close family or friends rather than on self-transcendent values that consider the collective (see Table 17.1). It has often become the common norm to make decisions based on the good for ourselves and those close to us rather than considering the consequences to others. Certainly, this is not the case for all populations, but as examples, the USA, Australia, Western Europe, UK and New Zealand are considered individualistic cultures (Hofstede Insights, n.d.). The issue with this type of behaviour is that, despite beliefs and actions to the contrary, individualistic action has both cumulative and collective consequences.

Table 17.1 Self-enhancement versus self-transcendent values

VALUES			
Self-enhancement values (centred on the self)		**Self-transcendent values (beyond the self)**	
Egoistic values	Hedonic values	Altruistic values	Universal and benevolent values
Cost and benefits affecting individual's resources (usually in relation to power and money)	Enjoyment and pleasure Reducing effort	Concern for welfare of others (others determined as human beings)	Concern, tolerance and care for others as well as nature and animals

Source: based on De Groot and Steg (2008); Schwartz et al. (2012); Steg et al. (2014a, 2014b)

What we do as individuals also has an impact on others, environmentally, socially and culturally. The irony is that while we may not see the direct immediate impact of our own personal behaviour, the cumulative impact of such behaviour is now evident, i.e. through climate change, the effects of which will undoubtedly be felt by us all if not now, then in the future. We can no longer afford to make self-ish decisions based on individual progress, gain and fulfilment; doing so to the detriment of other people and the planet threatens the very means by which we all survive.

Sustainability and tourism

Tourism, hospitality and events represent unique sectors as they rely on high quality natural, cultural and social environments for success. For destinations and all the enterprises within them, to remain competitive and attractive there is a need to encourage sustainability and protect natural and cultural assets; failure to do so may risk the very basis on which the destination is built (Weedon, 2014). Despite this, tourism, hospitality and events are often criticised for their considerable footprint and their negative economic, socio-cultural and environmental impact (as shown in Table 17.2).

Table 17.2   An overview of the socio-cultural and environmental costs of tourism

Dimension	Aspect	Negative impact or cost
Economic	Local economy	Economic leakages occur due to foreign owned enterprises or events
	Infrastructure costs	The economic income from tourism does not necessarily represent the amount of spending required or indeed available on supporting infrastructure, conservation and cultural maintenance
	Over-inflated employment opportunities	The creation of jobs is often cited as a positive impact of tourism, yet many of these are low-skilled and lower paid opportunities. Many management and higher positions are outsourced to foreign (often western) candidates. There are also examples of limited opportunity for progression
Socio-cultural	Host community	Local displacement; to make space for tourism, hospitality or event development
		Gentrification of local area; property prices rise and become unobtainable for local populations
		Local amenities and shops disappear in favour of those for tourists, i.e. gift shops
		Increased social issues: sex tourism, prostitution, gambling and alcohol/drugs. If social carrying capacity is exceeded, then locals may be irritated by tourists
		Physical carrying capacity exceeded; increased pedestrian traffic, local access to public transport, amenities and resources restricted
	Culture	Tourists may not respect local culture or religion and cause offence; need to observe rituals and beliefs
		Commodification of culture; traditions and festivals packaged as tourism products for sale questioning their authenticity
		Acculturation: local culture may be changed over time via exposure of different foods, lifestyle, fashion through tourism
	Tourists	Overcrowding may be detrimental to experience
		May desire an authentic experience, but fed a commodified, staged experience instead
		Antagonism and friction between guests and hosts may generate negativity and a feeling of not being welcome
Environmental	Water	Water consumption in tourism is high: pools, golf courses, showers, garden maintenance, laundry usage. This puts significant strain on local resources with tourism use often far outweighing that of locals
		Effects on marine life through diving and snorkelling. Anchoring boats creates disturbance to coral reefs and further stress on marine life
	Waste	Insufficient infrastructure for refuse collection sees a build-up of solid waste from tourism, particularly in lower income states. Waste is often dumped in oceans, accumulates untreated in under-developed landfill sites or is disposed of outside the view of tourists
		There is evidence that waste water treatment facilities are underdeveloped or completely lacking in many parts of the world. Hotels and cruise ships in particular need to increase investment in water waste management. Currently much sewage still ends up being dumped in oceans, rivers and seas contaminating water and harming ecosystems

Dimension	Aspect	Negative impact or cost
	Land	Land may be illegally gained, privatised or taken from local populations to be used for tourism purposes
		Physical impact on land from increased tourist numbers; erosion of pathways, littering, trampling
		Tourism infrastructure and development can have its own environmental consequences; aesthetic pollution, noise pollution, air pollution
		The erosion of beaches from creating the typically desired sea view as mangroves are often pulled up and palm trees removed
	Wildlife	Commodification of nature and wildlife; when the environment is valued for its economic means, it effectively becomes a commodity to be packaged and sold, i.e. zoos, elephant sanctuaries, safaris with ethical questions over habitat and conditions, and rights of animals
		Changes in breeding patterns where wild animals come into contact with humans (i.e. on safari)

Sources: Cole (2014); Edgell (2016); Epler Wood et al. (2019); Holden (2016)

Tourism, hospitality and events should also be held accountable for their role in exacerbating global issues including climate change. As an example, tourism is estimated to contribute 8% towards global greenhouse gas (GHG) emissions (Lenzen et al., 2018). This is a paradox given that the industry is extremely vulnerable and susceptible to the damaging effects of climate change. Think about levels of snow on mountains, extreme temperatures, forest fires, bush fires, flooding; none of these are conducive to tourism development. A deterioration of such environments therefore rocks the very foundations on which the sectors are built; damage to nature, culture and society equates to damage of the industries. Without greater sustainability awareness and action, 'tourism will die its own death' (Singh, 2018: 415).

The industries often identify with an individual's pursuit for hedonism or enjoyment, enabling an escape from everyday rules and rituals. Consequently, certain hedonistic or egoistic behaviours may be actioned, accepted or potentially packaged as part of these experiences. Lovelock and Lovelock (2013) provide the example of flying: air travel makes considerable contribution to climate change and GHG emissions and is considered an 'unnecessary luxury consumption' (Lovelock and Lovelock, 2013: 140). Morally then, the decision should be an individual choosing to reduce flights taken in favour of mitigating global climate change. Despite the environmental consequences of flying, with international air passengers projected to double by 2037 reaching 8.2 billion air travellers (IATA, 2018), it seems that this impact on the environment does not necessarily result in the choice not to fly.

 THINK POINT

Should individuals be shamed for taking unnecessary flights?

Socio-cultural and natural environments are comprised of **common pool resources**, goods which should be shared by all with equal access yet are in finite supply. The tourism, hospitality and events industries often ignore this 'common' aspect, selling what is not theirs to sell and exploiting these resources based on the needs of tourists without considering the needs of local populations; all in aid of maximising profits.

Unfortunately, these egoistic tendencies in tourism, hospitality and events industries are often demonstrated through 'exploitative, entitled' behaviours that put profit and tourist needs before the needs of society, the environment and future generations (Canavan, 2017: 1322).

The focus of much of the industries remains firmly on economic gain as being a marker for success: growth in tourism numbers and economic contribution. This means that many of the costs associated with such growth are ill-considered or ignored. Global mega-events are one such example where a focus on the economic gains often overshadows social and environmental costs.

 **INDUSTRY INSIGHT**

UCI Road World Championships, 2019

In 2019 Harrogate in North Yorkshire (UK) hosted the UCI Road World Championships. With the slogan 'Harrogate Welcomes the World', the focus was on driving tourism growth and showcasing Yorkshire as a world-renowned destination. Televised around the world and with 69,000 visitors, the event was reported to have generated £17.8 million to Harrogate's economy (EY, 2019).

Despite the promise of a boost to the local economy and increased visitors generating additional business, many local companies felt that this failed to materialise. Local residents were also angered by the number of road closures throughout the two-week period and the subsequent effect this had to local commutes.

The main infrastructure for the event was constructed on public parkland known as 'the Stray'; meaning that during the event period the public had limited access. The marquees set up to house various activities have taken their toll on the land; grass has all but been destroyed and flooding still remains (see Figure 17.1).

The financial success of the Championships was heralded in the post-event economic impact report. Unfortunately, consumer welfare, social benefits and environmental costs were not accounted for as they could not be 'fully captured' (EY, 2019: 3). This is an example of providing a skewed perspective of the success of an event, highlighting the (supposed) benefits to the economy but omitting the wider socio-cultural impacts.

Figure 17.1   The environmental damage to the Stray, Harrogate

A lack of acknowledgement of the costs of tourism, hospitality and events contributes to **over-tourism**, where the limits of growth are not considered and a lack of responsibility over the consumption of common pool resources leads to their deterioration and decline.

━━━━━━━━━━━━━━━ INDUSTRY INSIGHT ━━━━━━━━━━━━━━━

Overtourism

Overtourism is the result of destinations becoming victims of their own success; attracting a growth in visitor numbers has been a success but has reached the point of being detrimental to the local area. Essentially carrying capacity has been exceeded; there are too many tourists than the destination can cope with. Tourism has not been managed sufficiently and the negative impact or costs of increasing visitor numbers are not forecasted, mitigated or assessed.

The symptoms or signs of overtourism include:

- overcrowding and disruption in the destination, in streets, at key attractions
- strain on existing infrastructure and natural resources (i.e. water)
- increases in costs for local housing and food
- lack of respect and understanding of local culture and cultural norms
- deterioration of local culture to accommodate tourists' tastes and needs
- local amenities usurped or closed down in favour of tourist-driven trade
- environmental damage and aesthetic pollution
- rapid change to everyday life in and around the destination
- local populations disgruntled and protesting against tourism development.

Destinations including Amsterdam, Barcelona, Goa, Kerala and Venice have suffered the effects of overtourism. Many such destinations are urban areas that are more equipped to deal with tourism numbers than fragile rural areas where overtourism can be an issue. In Thailand, Maya Bay on the island of Phi Phi Leh was made famous by the Hollywood film *The Beach* and its subsequent popularity saw visitors arrive in their thousands. As a result, the area suffered environmental damage, including to coral reefs, and has consequently been closed to the public until 2021 to allow it to recover.

Questions

1. Why do you think some forms of tourism have become destructive?
2. What might the consequences of overtourism be?
3. What examples can you find of places suffering from overtourism?
4. How have certain places reacted to overtourism?
5. How could destinations manage the effects of overtourism?

Sustainability awareness

Sustainability awareness means you are able to:

- Identify ethical dilemmas and situations that warrant ethical decisions
- Consider the wider socio-cultural and environmental impact that decisions and actions have
- Recognise the impact of global challenges such as poverty and climate change are likely to have on society (including business)

Sustainability awareness is akin with both ethics and citizenship; your ability to deliberate ethical decisions considering your role and place as a member of society. Are you able to deliberate and make decisions based on the collective good? Are you able to demonstrate an ability to distinguish that actions have a greater impact than just to you as an individual? Are you able to consider that the way you behave, that the things you consume and the ways you interact, directly or indirectly, have an impact on other factors – the economy, wider society, culture and the environment? It is clear that human activity is responsible for many challenges facing global communities, but what impact will these challenges have on you, industry, society? Are you aware of the influence external factors have on the ability for society to function?

 ACTIVITY

The impacts of climate change on tourism, hospitality and events

Brainstorm the possible impact and consequences of climate change on tourism, hospitality and events industries.

- Which of these are already evident?
- Which are likely to happen in the near future?
- How concerned do you think these industries should be?

The importance of graduates understanding socio-environmental impacts and concerns is compounded in the knowledge that half of employers reportedly use social and environmental responsibility in their graduate selection process (HEA, 2008). Importantly, sustainability awareness is also the first stage in taking responsibility and actioning ethical behaviour; if there is no awareness that an issue exists or that the issue relates to an ethical dilemma, then appropriate action is unlikely to be taken.

 STUDENT INSIGHT

The value of training in sustainable tourism to promote responsible tourism behaviours among final year undergraduates

Authors: Faye Taylor, Rachel Welton and Ian Gregson, Nottingham Business School

A unique feature of the International Tourism: Sustainability, Development and Impact module at Nottingham Business School is that students gain an additional Certificate in Sustainable Tourism [CST], awarded by Nottingham Trent University. This mandatory, self-study certification aims to deepen students' knowledge of the practical application of responsible leadership and sustainability principles to the tourism industry. It encourages reflection upon the student's own consumption habits in the context of tourism, aligned with The Oath Project that they also participate in within their final year as an undergraduate student. The Oath Project flows from the United Nations' Global Compact initiative based around the development of an effective learning culture through emergent reflective skills. Participating universities make a commitment to develop students as responsible leaders of the future.

The BA (Hons) International Business Oath Project (Smith and Welton, 2016)

The Certificate in Sustainable Tourism is delivered online via the university's virtual learning environment. Learning material is structured into four sessions, comprising of rich multimedia content, text and discussion-based research activity. After completing the four sessions, students complete a multiple-choice quiz to demonstrate their knowledge gained and furthermore assess their own responsible tourism practice, and intended future practice, in light of what they have learned.

The course team were interested to understand the impact of this additional sustainability certification on both students' knowledge and skills. Specifically, does the CST complement and enhance International Business students' study of responsible tourism and enhance their employability skills? The most employable graduates are those who not only possess such 'soft' skills but are able to reflect and articulate how they have developed their skills and why they are important. Nye (2005) refers to soft power: the ability to attract and co-opt, rather than coerce or give force. A mixed methods approach was utilised that included module evaluation, a survey and focus group with module participants.

Key findings indicate that CST students:

- have a deeper insight into the principles and practice of sustainability within tourism
- develop a broader awareness of the influence of sustainability upon the external business environment and complexities of systems thinking
- gain from additional Continuous Professional Development opportunities to enhance their CV
- have evidence of attaining NTU Graduate Attributes in Global Citizenship and Sustainability

In practice, students taking this certificate have been found to display a greater awareness and understanding of the practical application of sustainability principles and practice of sustainability within the tourism industry. They appear to have the ability to draw upon relevant examples of projects and initiatives which display best practice in balancing the three pillars of sustainability. Their knowledge of systems thinking and critical evaluation skills of sustainable tourism projects have been greatly improved and anecdotally employers recognise these as students transfer into the workplace. Students appreciate the opportunity for the 'value added' learning opportunity and that engagement in the certificate helps to develop a reflexive approach to learning.

In summary, the evaluation of this initiative shows how the students' knowledge and skills altered and what were the triggers. Reflective learning can be transformational and provide a relevant platform to change and inform the learner's knowledge, attitudes, values and future actions.

In the face of global discussions, news stories and political campaigns, there is little excuse for not being aware of sustainability issues. Notable public activists including Greta Thunberg and David Attenborough have publicly shown support for the critical challenges the world faces and have inspired increasing calls for action, particularly among younger generations who have taken to the streets in their millions to campaign for action in face of the ecological crisis. Coldplay singer Chris Martin recently pulled plans to tour their new album until he felt tours can be made more sustainable, 'environmentally beneficial' and even carbon neutral (*BBC News*, 2019). Despite awareness, this alone is unfortunately not enough; we need to accept social responsibility and understand the means by which we can become more socially responsible.

SOCIAL RESPONSIBILITY

The consequences of global challenges and unsustainability have increased pressure on industries to respond and adopt socially and environmentally responsible policies and practice. In 2020 we entered a pivotal decade of action, a period during which we are committed to deliver on two fundamental global issues: climate change and meeting sustainable development goals. With a commitment by all United Nation member states to meet targets by 2030, the next decade is crucial to delivering these goals. Similarly, a sense of urgency in addressing climate change is now critical; global awareness of the burgeoning effects of our changing climate have risen. In order to meet the 2030 deadline for limiting global warming to 1.5 degrees, we would collectively need to halve GHG emissions, meaning a reduction of GHG emissions by 7.6% per year over the next decade (Brown, 2020). This is a difficult target given that current GHG emissions are still on the rise (UN, 2019). It is widely accepted that human activity is the most significant influence on climate change and the environment; that we are therefore responsible for the deterioration of nature and therefore all have a duty, a responsibility, to rethink behaviour and mitigate effects.

These currently unprecedented times of climate change and the threat of rising temperatures, poverty, inequality and population growth all highlight the need to change the way we currently function including the way we do business. For many years the pursuit of profit has come at the detriment and cost of the environment and the societies it supports. Exploitation and over-use of resources became commonplace but now the consequences of such behaviour are being felt. Businesses that previously felt accountable only to their shareholders now face pressure to address the needs and demands of all stakeholders, including local and often global communities. Globally, businesses are being held accountable for their actions by stakeholders, i.e. governments, consumers, shareholders, local and global communities. The pressure to evidence ethical behaviour and a sense of doing the right thing is rising. In a recent Higher Education report, students themselves were reportedly keen to work for a more responsible employer; 75% suggested they would be willing to earn £1,000 less to work in a company with a positive social and environmental record (NUS, 2019).

 THINK POINT

Who do you think is responsible for the impact of tourism? Who do you think has a greater responsibility to act: industry or tourists?

Consumers are also now questioning the ethical practice of business and demanding more responsible behaviour. In a 2017 report, 86% of US consumers expected businesses to address social and environmental issues as well as making a profit (Cone Communications, 2017). Within tourism, research by TUI (2017a) found that 66% of tourists felt brands were more responsible than themselves for making sustainable decisions. In more recent global research by Booking.com (2019), 72% of travellers believe we need to act now to make more sustainable travel choices to safeguard the planet. With this, consumers are also demanding more sustainable products meaning there is market value in sustainable practice; 70% of travellers would be more likely to book accommodation if they knew it was eco-friendly and 71% said they think companies should offer more sustainable travel options.

This increase in consumer demand for sustainable products provides a competitive incentive to organisations questioning the benefits of socially responsible action with enhanced reputation, consumer loyalty and potential for market share growth. As an example, 92% of US consumers said they have a more favourable image of companies that support social and environmental issues and 88% said this would make them more likely to stay loyal to the brand (Cone Communication, 2017). TUI's research (2017a) found that 52% of tourists are more positive about brands that invest in sustainability.

At a very basic level, the 'responsibility to respect human rights is a global standard of expected conduct for all business enterprises wherever they operate' (UN, 2011: 13). In human rights we include the right to life, to a standard of living adequate for health and wellbeing, to work and favourable working conditions, to be free of slavery and to equality (UN, 1948). There is a need for businesses to accept social responsibility and perform due diligence; to be proactive in preventing human rights' abuse as 'doing no harm is no longer a defence' (Cole, 2014: 100).

INDUSTRY INSIGHT

Shiva Foundation and modern slavery in hospitality

It is estimated that there are around 45.8 million people currently held in modern slavery, 24.9 million of which are in forced labour (ILO and Walk Free Foundation, 2017). Employing 10% of the global workforce, the hospitality industry is considered a high-risk area for forced labour. The Shiva Foundation is a UK corporation set up to tackle human trafficking and modern slavery. In recognition of the need for collaborative action, in 2016 the foundation worked with some of the top companies in the UK hotel industry to see how they could address the pressing issue of modern slavery in hotel supply chains. With a collective turnover of £14 billion the group known as 'the Network' comprised some of the key industry players in the UK. The result was the production of the 'Framework for Working with Suppliers', a tool offering practical guidance for action within the industry.

As future industry employees, leaders and managers of the future, these guidelines provide practical advice on acting against modern slavery:

1. Define the organisation's policies: ask the questions of your employer. Do not be afraid to ask about their ethical practice and stance on tackling modern slavery; remember that someone who cares about this topic is likely to care about other things. It shows they have strong values.
2. Identify the risks: factors such as the country, human rights governance and corruption levels will have an impact risk of forced labour.
3. Map the risks: the risks identified above need to be mapped across the supply chain for each supplier ensuring a note is made about how critical each supplier is.
4. Engage with your suppliers: work with suppliers and not against them. Support and train suppliers on the risks and challenges in the meaning of and identifying forced labour.
5. Ongoing management: make sure there are policies and practices for monitoring supply chains, including spot checks.
6. Reporting incidents: any concerns or suspicions of forced labour should be reported and investigated. In the UK the Modern Slavery helpline (08000 121 700) are specialists in dealing with such cases.

Sources: ILO and Walk Free Foundation (2017); Shiva Foundation (2018); Stop Slavery Hotel Industry Network (2017)

Within tourism and hospitality, specific interest has been paid to the pressure the consumptive needs place on fundamental water resources, access to which is considered necessary for life and therefore a basic human right (Cole, 2014). The impact on such finite resources is particularly pertinent in desert areas and island states such as Bali where such resources already face critical depletion

(Cole, 2014). The significant demands for water in tourism compete against the right of access to water for locals as well as other industries such as agriculture (Cole, 2014).

 THINK POINT

Why do you think tourism places such pressure on water resources?

Beyond human rights, the role of all organisations to positively contribute to sustainability is also evident within the SDGs – the call for 'all businesses to apply their creativity and innovation to solving sustainable development challenges' (UN, 2015: 25). The expectations are for businesses to contribute to all goals, but tourism is explicitly cited as having the capacity to contribute to three such goals: decent work and economic growth (SDG 8), sustainable consumption and production (SDG 12) and life below water (SDG 14).

Table 17.3   The opportunities for tourism to meet the designated SDGs

Sustainable Development Goal	Opportunities for fulfilment through tourism	Example
8: Decent work and economic growth	Contribution to GDP and local economies	France considers tourism as a priority area of growth for the country. Tourism can also present as a viable alternative to other industries.
	Employment and job creation	Small Island Developing (SID) states such as the Maldives are reliant on tourism's contribution to employment levels – in the Maldives, 20% of employment falls within tourism
12: Sustainable consumption and production	Policies and plans for sustainable consumption in tourism	Cyprus is one of many countries citing tourism as part of their National Action Plan for a Green Economy; ensuring more sustainable growth, considerate resource use and responsible consumption
	Campaigns for ecological certification and auditing	Promotion of certification instruments for the hospitality industry include: Ecolabel, European Union (EU) Ecomanagement and Audit Scheme (EMAS) and Green Key.
14: Life below water	Development of the Blue economy	New opportunities for development through coastal and marine tourism; ecotourism is recognised by Bangladesh and Norway. This comes with significant demands for policy and regulation in this area to protect resources for a more sustainable form of tourism development

Source: UNWTO, 2017

So, in the face of criticism concerning exploitative behaviour, overuse of resources and unequivocal demands on socio-cultural and natural environments, how can the tourism, hospitality and events sectors rise to this sustainability challenge?

RESPONSIBLE TOURISM, HOSPITALITY AND EVENTS

The antithesis to overtourism and unsustainable behaviour is responsible tourism (Singh, 2018). When performed responsibly tourism, hospitality and events have the great potential to be a force for good – to contribute to global sustainability and achieve sustainable development goals. Responsible tourism is about making better places to live and to visit; by developing better places to live, they are more likely to be better places to visit.

 ACTIVITY

The Cape Town Declaration

The Cape Town Declaration (2002) recognised that responsible tourism takes a variety of forms but is characterised by travel and tourism which:

1. Minimises negative economic, environmental and social impacts
2. Generates greater economic benefits for local people and enhances the wellbeing of host communities, improves working conditions and access to the industry
3. Involves local people in decisions that affect their lives and life changes
4. Makes positive contributions to the conservation of natural and cultural heritage, to the maintenance of the world's diversity
5. Provides more enjoyable experiences for tourists through more meaningful connections with local people, and a greater understanding of local cultural, social and environmental issues
6. Provide access for people with disabilities and the disadvantaged
7. Is culturally sensitive, engenders respect between tourists and hosts, and builds local pride and confidence

Choose a tourism or hospitality organisation or an event and draw out a grid like the one in Table 17.4 and populate it with examples of activities they engage in that meet each characteristic of responsible tourism.

Table 17.4   Examples of responsible tourism activities

Characteristic	Examples
1	
2	
3	
4	

The aim is to maximise the potential for positive impacts of the industries (see Table 17.5), while minimising and managing the occurrence of negative impacts with the evaluation and assessment of socio-cultural, economic and environmental 'costs' (see Table 17.2).

Table 17.5 Examples of the positive impacts of tourism, hospitality and events

Dimension	Aspect	Positive impact
Economic	Boost local economy	The opportunity for economic linkages between local enterprises, i.e. a hotel uses local suppliers (food, laundry), recommends locally owned activities and restaurants and local transport options
		Tourism multiplier effect (TME) – the money earned from working in the industries is then re-spent in the local economy
		Tourism offers opportunities for a diversified income, a viable alternative to other industries that may incur greater negative impacts such as agriculture or logging
	Employment	There may be opportunities for women to work particularly as some jobs in the industry do not demand women be taken away from family responsibilities
		As service industries they are reliant on a human workforce, potentially providing more jobs than other sectors
		Opportunities for training and development to upskill the workforce
	Regional development	Opportunities for local regeneration of urban or rural areas
		Can maintain viability of other businesses in the area as income earned from tourism allows for improved living standards and creates demands for goods and services
		Tourism expenditure contributes to increases in GDP and therefore money available to be spent on public services such as schools, health and social welfare
Socio-cultural	Host populations	Opportunity to be exposed to and interact with different cultures
		Responsibly developed tourism and events where local populations have a participative role, can increase social cohesion and civic pride in local area
	Tourists	Opportunities to see diverse ways of life and conditions – voluntourism and ecotourism may educate or change individual's perspectives
		Opportunities for education about diverse cultures and societies
	Culture	Can protect local culture and heritage by giving an economic value to historical sites and artefacts
		Tourism cannot be blamed as the only vehicle for changes in culture and society as mass media has a significant effect
		Traditions and festivals may be maintained through tourism with opportunities to share and tell stories
Environment	Conservation	Tourism gives the land an economic value and thus increases the likelihood of preservation. Consider safari tourism where elephants are a significant draw. The economic value tourism brings generates greater need to protect elephants in order to protect tourism
		Opportunity to educate tourists on fragility of land and disseminate environmental education, e.g. on climate change
	Land use	Tourism may have less impact than other more damaging industries, for example, many crops can be damaging to the environment as they require large expanses of space and deforestation occurs through logging trade
	Zoning	As in the Great Barrier Reef, areas are zoned for use: tourists have access to a designated areas while other areas are left for scientific research or kept free from human touch

Sources: Edgell (2016); Holden (2016); Holden and Fennell (2017); Sharpley and Telfer (2014)

INDUSTRY INSIGHT

Responsible action at TUI

With a recognition of the scope the tourism industry has for positive impact and in a commitment to responsible tourism, TUI is an example of a large corporation making a responsible contribution to society through tourism.

TUI Care Foundation

The foundation supports and initiates partnerships and projects for tourism to contribute to the sustainability of destinations now and in the future. With a mantra of 'work global and act local' they aim to have a meaningful impact on the people and places in which they operate (TUI, 2017b: 4). With transparent governance and a commitment to spending 100% of donations in destination programmes, the company is dedicated to making a positive difference.

Project 'Taste Crete'

Traditional farmers in Crete face increasing pressure to access markets and make a sustained living; as a consequence, many face closure. TUI Care Foundation is supporting such farmers and therefore the local economy by linking them with the tourism industry and promoting their local products:

- Hotels are encouraged to use locally produced olive oil and wine in their dishes
- Restaurants serve locally produced wine
- Shops sell the local products
- Tourists are encouraged to go on excursions that showcase such products

For further information on these projects, see: www.tuicarefoundation.com/en/projects

---

The concepts of responsible tourism are equally applicable to the events industry, for example, considering the opportunities for leave no trace events such as Burning Man in Nevada, USA. A topic discussed at Confex (2019) was that of regenerative events: how events might go beyond mitigating negative impacts towards improving the natural environment.

INDUSTRY INSIGHT

Examples of responsible tourism

Feynan Ecolodge, Jordan

Winner of the Gold award for reducing carbon at the World Responsible Tourism Awards 2019, Feynan Ecolodge is committed to low emissions. The lodge is off-grid and generates all its electricity from solar panels. Locally produced candles light the lodge and a waste water management system converts leftover food and waste into biogas used for cooking. Food deliveries are kept to a minimum to avoid carbon footprint and laundry is air-dried to avoid the impact of tumble drying.

(Continued)

Green People and Bakri Chhap for the Goat Village, India

Winner of the Gold award for benefitting local communities at the World Responsible Tourism Awards 2019, Green People and Bakri Chhap joined forces in 2013 to create goat villages in Himalaya. Severe flooding in high altitude areas in 2013 saw many locals leave farms for urban opportunities. To provide greater prosperity for the area, Green People helped develop community-run homestays and provide free computer education for village children. Meanwhile, Bakri Chhap helped rejuvenate local goat-based farming, vaccinating goats and working with over 500 famers to promote local produce now for sale in many luxury hotels and superstores and available for guests staying in the goat villages.

For further information see: responsibletourismpartnership.org/world-responsible-tourism-awards-2019/

Understanding the positive impacts of tourism, hospitality and events is the first move towards responsible tourism, but there is also a need for action to make sure that these impacts are felt. Suggested strategies for managing tourists and minimising the potential for overtourism include:

- *Interpretation and guiding*: encouraging social inclusion by treating tourists as temporary local residents and educating them on cultural differences and expected behaviour
- *Marketing*: diversifying attention and avoiding concentrating marketing on already popular areas. Using marketing to spread the load of tourism, e.g. across seasons
- *Local linkages*: Businesses should actively seek to network and develop economic linkages between complementary organisations
- *Zoning*: having residents-only zones, pedestrianised zones. Essentially this provides the opportunity to adjust the flow and arrival of tourists in certain areas
- *Charging*: tourism tax, entrance to national parks or sensitive areas can help limit numbers, provide data on visitor numbers and boost funds for spending on local infrastructure
- *Visas*: can help prevent mass tourism and provide an additional revenue stream. Can help to limit numbers and again feed into financial resources for increased infrastructure and management plans for tourism development
- *Limit visitor numbers*: destinations such as Bhutan and individual attractions such as Macchu Picchu in Peru have recognised the dangers of exceeding carrying capacity and as a consequence are limiting the number of tourists able to visit

A good understanding of both the opportunities and costs associated with tourism, hospitality and events is crucial to developing a career in the industries. Social responsibility and sustainability awareness are likely to increase in significance with companies demanding graduates demonstrate the skills to contribute towards progressing tourism, hospitality and events towards a more sustainable future.

CONCLUSION

In this chapter we have covered:

- Global challenges and the significance of sustainability.
- The relationship between tourism and sustainability.
- Social responsibility for business.
- Developing responsible tourism.

FURTHER READING

Epler Wood, M., Milstein, M. and Ahamed-Broadhurst, K. (2019) *Destinations at Risk: The Invisible Burden of Tourism*, The Travel Foundation. Available at: www.thetravelfoundation.org.uk/invisible-burden/ (accessed 25 June 2020).

Goodwin, H. (2016) *Responsible Tourism: Using Tourism for Sustainable Development*, 2nd edn. Oxford: Goodfellow Publishers.

Holden, A. and Fennell, D.A. (2017) *The Routledge Handbook of Tourism and the Environment.* Oxfordshire: Routledge.

UN (2019) *Global Sustainable Development Report 2019: The Future is Now – Science for Achieving Sustainable Development.* Available at: https://sustainabledevelopment.un.org/content/documents/24797GSDR_report_2019.pdf (accessed 25 June 2020).

18 PROJECT MANAGEMENT

 CHAPTER LEARNING OBJECTIVES

By the end of this chapter you should be able to:

- Understand what is meant by the term 'project management'.
- Identify the skills required for successful project management and how you might adopt these in your learning as well as future career.
- Evaluate and identify the most appropriate methods and tools for managing a project.
- Design a comprehensive project master plan and an effective delivery strategy.

 GLOSSARY

- **Project manager:** the person responsible for the planning and execution of a project.
- **Project management:** the application of knowledge, tools and techniques to ensure a project is delivered to a set specification, on time and to budget.
- **Project management skills:** the ability to schedule work, organise individuals (or teams), monitor progress against targets, and manage risk.

INTRODUCTION

With the rapidly changing context of modern business, the process of introducing new technologies, products, processes or systems has become vital to ensure competitive advantage. It has also become more challenging due to often conflicting stakeholder expectations, operating constraints and associated risks. Any business change has to be project-managed if it is going to be successful and ensure that an organisation remains flexible, responsive to customer demands, and retains and develops its market share at a time of economic uncertainty. Regardless of the underlying business imperative, and given the nature of the sector, THE managers increasingly require a **project management** style that cuts across traditional functional roles and delivers on-going service enhancements and improvements.

Before thinking about project management, it is important to understand what is meant by the term 'project'. According to the Project Management Institute (PMI, 2013a: 3), a project can be defined as a 'temporary endeavour with a beginning and an end ... used to create a unique project, service or result'. It is temporary because, once the project's objectives have been achieved (or even if they cannot be achieved), it will end and will no longer be classified as a project. Projects can be cross-functional and/or cross-organisational. For example, the development of an online customer relationship management database which needs to track consumer activities requires expertise from IT, sales and finance departments to work together to ensure that individual department functional needs are taken into account, and that the end product is fit for purpose. Likewise, the project management of a festival may require a company to convene a cross-organisational project management team with representatives from logistics, sound engineering, marketing, catering, environmental management (site 'scouts', waste-control site managers) as well as health and safety. For example, if you look at the LinchPin Event Solutions website (linchpineventsolutions.com), you will notice that it promotes a one-stop shop approach to event installation and clearance drawing upon expertise from different areas within the company, delivered through cross-organisational project management.

A project is unique because it is not routine work but instead has a set of actions aimed at delivering a goal within a set period of time after which the product, service or process becomes 'business as normal'. For example, the upgrade of a hotel room booking system is a project which may require the installation and implementation of the new version of software, after which it becomes part of routine vacancy management operations. Thus, project management is the application of knowledge, tools and techniques to ensure a project is delivered to a set specification, on time and to budget. Put simply, it is the management of time, people and quality to accomplish agreed goals. While the ability to schedule work, organise individuals (or teams), monitor progress against targets and manage risk are essential **project management skills**, interpersonal skills are by far the most important. According to the *Pulse of the Profession Report*, poor communications account for more than half of the money at risk in any given project, and that for every $1 billion spent on a project, $135 million is at risk, and 56% of that risk is due to ineffective communication (PMI, 2013b: 2).

A SHORT HISTORY OF PROJECT MANAGEMENT

Projects and the legacy of project management activities are everywhere, in every town, city and country. Some projects are instantly recognisable, such as the Eiffel Tower in Paris which was built between 1887 and 1889 for the Exposition Universelle by Alexandre Gustave Eiffel, and the London Eye which was built to celebrate the Millennium. Others are not so readily apparent but actually take place on a regular basis, such as wedding events, festivals and all manner of social and corporate events. The person responsible for ensuring these projects are delivered on time and to budget is the **project manager**.

Although the history of the project management profession can be traced back to the 1950s (Carayannis et al., 2005), it is through the pioneering work of Henry Gantt that the importance of planning and controlling workflow was officially recognised. Gantt produced many different types of charts that could be used to provide detailed summaries of:

a.   what an individual or a team should be working on at any given time
b.   when a task should be completed
c.   the time it should take to complete it.

Current approaches to project management that exist today incorporate some element of Gantt's management tools (see Table 18.1).

Table 18.1   A simple Gantt chart

		TASK					
	LEAD	**Wk1**	**Wk2**	**Wk3**	**Wk4**	**Wk5**	**Wk6**
Activity 1	Asia	X	X				
Activity 2	Bob		X	X			
Activity 3	Christine		X	X	X	X	
Activity 4	David				X	X	X

The professionalisation of project management began in the late 1950s and early 1960s following such projects as the Sydney Opera House (Australia), the Apollo Space programme (USA) and the national housing programme (UK). This is not to say that projects were not managed or indeed that no one was in charge until then, but that the approach was not standard and the risk of failure was high. The US Project Management Institute (PMI) led the way to professionalisation by creating a set of standards and guidelines – the *Project Management Body of Knowledge* (PMBOK®) (PMI, 2013a) – which could be used to support both the individual and companies alike. The UK version of the PMI, the Association for Project Management (APM) was subsequently set up in the early 1970s and this too adopted a similar approach to developing knowledge and skills amongst practitioners. The project management profession is now well established with many associations reporting year on year growth. In 2017, the PMI claimed to represent 3,234 project management professionals who they support through a global network of 300 branches (called *Chapters*) (2017a: 2). The Association for Project Management claimed to have 30,000 individual members and more than 500 organisations participating in their Corporate Partnership programme (Association for Project Management, 2019) and in the 2019 Annual Report, the Australian Institute of Project Management (AIPM, 2019: 8) stated that its membership now includes 7,800 individual and 40 organisational members.

These associations all uphold common features: to champion professional project management, promote best practice and reduce the risks associated with failure. Most, if not all, have student membership opportunities which are ideal ways to broaden your knowledge and engage with the PM community in general.

Working in the THE sector, you are likely to be involved in different types of projects throughout the course of your career. These include:

- Basic project management of a single standalone initiative like a wedding event
- Programme management consisting of several parallel or sequential projects that share a common goal and resource(s) such as the development of a new hotel complex

Irrespective of the type of THE project you are managing, they all have the same key components. These have been summarised in the SPECTRE project management (see Table 18.2).

Table 18.2   SPECTRE project management grid

Phase	Activity	Focus
1	**S**tart-up	This includes the project brief, which provides an overview of the project, the business case and any limitations
2	**P**lanning	Plans are developed and approved
3	**E**xecution	Work-packages (tasks, outputs and deliverables) are developed. Where appropriate critical pathway analysis and interdependencies are used to ensure seamless alignment across deliverables
4	**C**ontrolling	The project team will have regular meetings at which progress against targets will be reviewed, the risk register updated and any emerging issues addressed
5	**T**ermination and closure	The project is officially closed, when the new service, product or system has been implemented and become part of routine operations, or when the project has been terminated due to unforeseen circumstances
6	**R**eview	Once the project is completed, review how it went, and any lessons learnt that could be used to improve future individual, team and organisational project management capabilities
7	**E**valuation	Once the service, system or product is in use, it is important to evaluate the end-product/final outcome

Looking at the SPECTRE grid, consider each phase and see if you can recognise where Gantt's approaches to the project management process might appear.

━━━━━━━━━━━━━━ THINK POINT ━━━━━━━━━━━━━━

When do you need to capture who is doing what, how much time they need to complete a task, and when a task should be completed?

Do you think data capturing and monitoring are one-off activities or something you would need to review regularly?

SETTING UP A PROJECT

To set up a project the first thing you need to do is be incredibly organised. Find out about any pre-existing documentation about the project. This is especially important if you have not been involved with any discussions with the client or project sponsor. You can then use this information as the baseline for any work going forward. If you cannot find anything, then organise a start-up meeting with key stakeholders and representatives from the project team and agree the Terms of Reference (ToR) for the project. The ToR will include a project brief which is essentially the business case for the project along with the expected outcome. Locking this down early will mitigate the risk of *project creep*, which is when a project has started and new elements keep being added (piggy-backed) to the project, quite often without additional resources being made available.

Once you have this basic information to hand, then you need to translate the project brief into a realistic plan. This is how project managers allocate work, oversee the effective deployment of resources, and monitor the progress of all related activities to ensure that projects are delivered on time. Planning is not a one-off activity but is something that you will do throughout the project's life cycle as you review, revise and re-align actions as the status of activities change. Key areas that you need to consider when starting up and planning project activities include:

- *Financial planning*: Forecasting and allocation of funding between activities
- *Resource planning*: In addition to finances, what other resources do you need? For example, software, hardware, staff skills
- *Work-package (or task/action) planning*: The allocation of work requires clarity about who is doing what, where and by when along with the identification of dependencies. For example, setting up foot-lighting for a stage is likely to require the stage to be built first which means the lighting engineers may depend on the stage builders to complete their jobs before they can install the lighting. The progression of one is dependent on the completion of another
- *Monitoring and control procedures and systems*: The project manager must ensure that those involved with a project are clear about how the project will be monitored: whether this is progress against targets, compliance with health and safety legislation or regulatory bodies. The lack of control and failure to monitor adherence to quality guidelines can have a devastating effect on a project. The collapse of the hotel on the Oba-Ile Housing Estate (Akure, Nigeria) was linked to poor quality and an insufficient quantity of the cement used in the main building causing structural collapse (Taiwo and Afolami, 2011). Arguably, the integrity of the project management had been compromised

 THINK POINT

How would you ensure the quality of catering for a large-scale function? Would there be a difference if the catering was in-house or outsourced?

- *Communication plan*: Remember that communication plans are primarily about transparency, clarity and consistent messages. As a project manager you need to consider how you are going to keep everyone informed of the progress and any changes that might take place along with the impact that these changes might have on those inside and outside of the immediate project team. For example, automating a manual theatre booking system has implications for the staff currently doing the job: will they be offered retraining and/or redeployment to a new role? These staff may not be part of the project team but are likely to be affected by the outcomes of the project

- *Risk register and risk management plan*: All projects have an element of risk so it is important to identify them early, agree actions (interventions) that can either prevent the risk or reduce the impact that a risk might have. Consider a rollercoaster which has a launch speed of 110mph; without a safety harness there would be strong risk of customer injuries. The introduction of safety harnesses cannot remove all risks associated with rollercoasters, but they do reduce them. Risk registers need to be maintained and updated regularly to ensure all project stakeholders are fully informed of any risks as they emerge
- *Governance plan*: Governance is first and foremost about responsibility and accountability. It covers elements such as who owns the project, the various reporting lines, how often the project team meet to report on progress, and the approvals as well as sign-off protocols.

Execution of work packages is at the heart of any project. This is when the development of processes, systems or a product takes place as individuals and teams focus on delivering their specific tasks.

 THINK POINT

Look at the project life cycle diagram in Figure 18.1. Notice the spread activities and consider how the project manager and team might respond to the different phases.

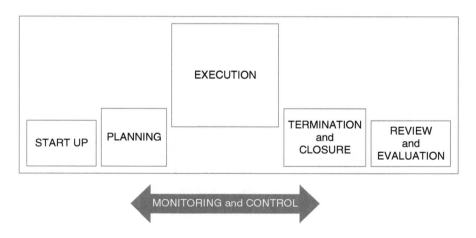

Figure 18.1   **Project life cycle**

RUNNING A PROJECT

In the previous section we considered some of the key plans required to ensure the successful delivery of a project. Once these plans are in place, it is the role of the project manager to ensure that they are acted on, and that the outputs are delivered on time. In this respect, the project manager can be compared to a conductor of an orchestra whose role it is to interpret the music (the project brief), ensure that the various sections understand what is expected of them (allocation of project work packages), and ensure all of the elements come together in the final performance. Given the breadth and diversity of projects, there are a number of standard tools that can be used to ensure the effective delivery and implementation of a project, such as MS Projects, MS Excel and a RACI Matrix which identifies who is Responsible, who is Accountable, who should be Consulted and who should be Informed before actions are agreed, and what should happen on their completion. An example of a RACI Matrix is shown in the Activity and Table 18.3 below.

 ━━━━━ ACTIVITY ━━━━━━━━━━━━━━━━━━━━━━━━━━━

DAEDALUS and the RACI assignment matrix

DAEDALUS is an events management company based in Bristol with a growing reputation for overseeing art exhibition installations. The company is now seeking to open new premises. A new building has been identified which is owned by Lavender Green Ltd, who had a lease with a coffee shop until recently. Before DAEDALUS can move into the premises, planning permission will be needed for a change of use after which DAEDULUS can sign the lease, refurbish the building and move in. The aim of the project is to publicise the new premises with a launch event: an exhibition.

   Key actions include:

1.   Drafting and submitting a change of use request by DAEDULUS to the local planning authority
2.   Refurbishment of the new premises
3.   Agreement on the contents and theme of the launch exhibition
4.   Installation of the launch exhibition once the premises have been refurbished

Use the RACI grid below to identify who is **R**esponsible, who is **A**ccountable, who needs to be **C**onsulted and who needs to be kept **I**nformed.

Table 18.3   The RACI assignment matrix

Critical Points	Project Manager	Builders	CEO DAEDULUS	CEO Lavender Ltd	Exhibition Logistics Manager	Caterer	Artist
Planning application drafted and submitted	I	I	R /A	I	C	N/A	N/A
Approval gained							
Refurbishment plans drafted and approved							
Refurbishment completed							
Launch date confirmed							
Exhibition items identified							
Transportation arrangements agreed							C/I

R = Responsible; A= Accountable; C = Consulted; I = Informed; N/A = Not Applicable

While the SPECTRE approach provides one way of managing a project there are others, such as PMBOK, PRINCE2 (**Pr**ojects **IN** **C**ontrolled **E**nvironments) and Agile (an iterative and life cycle process which results in the end-product being delivered in increments). The most common project management technique is the waterfall method (Balaji and Sundararajan Murgugaiyan, 2012) which prescribes definition, analysis, design and testing in a strict *pre-planned sequence*. Progress under a waterfall approach is measured in terms of deliverables at each step, such as design documents, test plans, test results and completed products. The drawbacks of waterfall project management include: inflexibility, and commitments made early on which makes it difficult to react to unexpected changes in requirements. Because of the pre-set nature of project activities, iterations and unexpected changes are expensive to incorporate into any plan, and if a project is cancelled at any point before the end, there is little or nothing to show for it. Agile, on the other hand, is based on flexibility and the ability to respond to changes at short notice (Dayal Chauhan et al., 2017). Agile is ideal for:

- early delivery of business value (beta-version)
- bottom-up idea flow
- greater face-to-face interaction and constant feedback
- simplicity (maximise the work *not done*)
- individual empowerment, self-organised teamwork, accountability
- customer collaboration over just-contract negotiation
- changes are welcome!

Although all project management techniques and methodologies have their own strengths and weaknesses, they all advocate the same approach to project management in that running a project requires:

- A consistent approach to project management with clear approval and refusal procedures
- Effective team management (see Chapter 15)
- Regular meetings between project team members and other key stakeholders to review progress against targets, the effectiveness of risk interventions and resource deployment. These meetings are unlikely to be one single group but multiple groups with differing remits. Using the example of the introduction of a new hotel management system, the following project-related meetings might be held (see Table 18.4).

Table 18.4   Project meetings to implement a new hotel management system

Group (or Committee)	Remit
Strategic Oversight Group (SOG)	• Overall responsibility for the project – likely to include the person who has commissioned the project, as well as a member from the hotel senior management
Project Operations Group (POG)	• Accountable to SOG • Responsible for delivering the project to the specifications and timelines approved by SOG
Customer Services Sub-Group (CSSG) ICT Sub-Group (ISG)	• Accountable to POG • Responsible for work package outputs

- A coherent approach to knowledge management which includes a post-implementation review and assessment of lessons learnt
- A robust control system for documents so that each decision and the rationale for each decision is clear and based on evidence
- The ability to respond to change and emerging situations
- Clear lines of communication

 THINK POINT

If you were a member of a project team, what would you expect from your project manager? How would you like to be managed? As a project manager, how would you deal with an under-performing team that is not hitting its deliverables on time?

CLOSING A PROJECT

As mentioned earlier, projects are one-off temporary initiatives which result in a change that then becomes part of normal operations. This means closing a project is not a case of switching something off overnight but involves a series of actions to ensure the service, process or production is implemented (or rolled out) through a controlled exit. Closing a project starts when the last deliverable has been completed at which point the client or project sponsor will confirm that the project outputs have been delivered to the correct specification, that any testing has been done, and a date for implementation has been agreed. For example, closing a software upgrade project for a hotel booking system will require evidence that the new version is available, that it is fit for purpose and that it has been tested on 'live' data, after which a completion date for the implementation will be agreed along with a formal 'handover' to the users of the new system and a switch-off date for the old system agreed. This stage also includes the closing down of project teams and, in some cases, agreeing plans for the redeployment of staff.

 THINK POINT

What do you think are the pros and cons of direct and parallel implementation approaches (see Figure 18.2)?

Now that we have considered some of the practicalities around project management, we should reflect on what makes a successful and unsuccessful project.

HOW DO PROJECTS SUCCEED?

There are many successful projects, and they all have the same features:

1. *A realistic goal.* In other words, there is strategic fit, goal congruence, an understanding about what is expected from the project, and where the project team and end-user capabilities are acknowledged and taken into consideration throughout the project life cycle.

2. *Client and stakeholder satisfaction.* These are dependent upon consistent project leadership, effective relationship and expectation management, and goal congruence amongst key stakeholders.
3. *Delivered on time, to budget.*
4. *Perceived value.* If a project is undertaken without stakeholder buy-in, and it is not considered as adding value by the end-users, the end-product may be compromised due to a lack of input during the key stages of development.

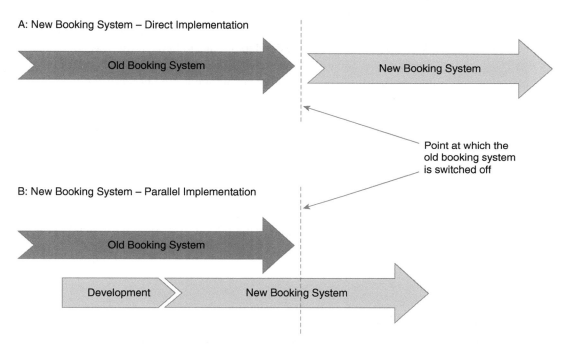

Figure 18.2   Direct and parallel implementation strategies

WHY DO PROJECTS FAIL?

According to Discenza and Forman (2007), there are seven causes of project failure and these can be categorised under people, process and communication.

People

1. *Ineffective performance management.* Recruiting, retaining and motivating project teams can be a complex exercise and requires a set of skills that may be difficult to find. It is not unusual for project teams to work across functions which means that the project manager needs to understand how an organisation works, and the relationship between the various functions, departments and teams, and expertise (and any skills gaps) that exists within the team.

2. *Restricted access to appropriate project management tools and techniques.* Projects can require both generic and specialist tools if they are going to be successful. If these are denied or limited, then elements of a project could be compromised.

Process

3. *Unclear accountability* with no one being responsible for specific actions or decision-making. This can range from the wrong person being appointed as the project manager or a lack of buy-in and commitment from the senior management team. This is where the RACI grid can help because it provides a logical approach to clarifying who is responsible for what. For example, the Harmon Hotel project in Las Vegas cost $170 million to develop but due to flaws in the steel structure it was unable to be completed after significant investment. According to Way (2011), a lack of quality control around engineering standards and poor communication between teams contributed to the project's closure and it being dismantled without ever opening. This project failure cost approximately $1 billion to rectify.

4. *Ineffective monitoring and ambiguous control mechanisms* can be a major contributor to both cost and schedule overrunning, as is project creep (Kendrick, 2015).

5. *Inconsistent project management.* According to Egeland (2018), project teams find it hard to follow inconsistent project management. He suggests that everyone is looking for consistency in decision-making and failure to provide this leaves teams and employees uneasy and uncertain about what direction to take. From the perspective of the client and senior management, if the project team is unsure about its leadership, then they too may lose faith in the project manager's ability.

Communication

6. *Focus on the business value, not technical detail* can result in a lack of understanding about organisational expertise, capacity and resources available to deliver a successful project.

7. *Goal incongruence* between the end-users (the client/customers/senior management) and the project team. Research by Sperry and Jetter (2019) identified that projects that make effective use of project stakeholder management run smoothly because there is agreement on the project outcomes.

 THINK POINT

If you are the project manager, what strategies will you use to ensure and maintain buy-in from the project team and other key stakeholders?

There are many different approaches and techniques for project management, and below is a list of the main ones that you may well come across in your working life. As a student, you may have an opportunity to work with a company on a specific project. Below is an example of a student consultancy project.

━━━━━ STUDENT INSIGHT ━━━━━

THE Student Consultancy Project

Company: Lincoln Golf Club

Student Project Managers: Lincoln International Business School

Phase One – The project brief

1. To develop a strategic plan to increase the membership of the Golf Club with particular attention to increasing the number of female members.
2. To develop a facilities management plan along with an options appraisal for 50 acres of spare land owned by the golf club.

Phase Two – Scoping and planning the project

The students are divided into small teams who are responsible for certain elements of the consultancy project. Students develop project plans with key milestones and deliverables which are then presented to the LGC senior management for approval.

Phase Three – Running the project

Each team member is allocated specific tasks as part of reviewing the club's position using secondary data, analysing current membership, identifying gaps and undertaking market research. All student teams participate in project progress reviews with LGC management during which feedback on the development of the plans is provided.

Phase Four – Presenting the outcomes

The final reports are reviewed and two are selected to be presented to the Golf Club for consideration.

Phase Five – Closing the project

Once the client has selected the 'best' report and confirmed that the outputs for the project brief have been met, the student teams are disbanded and each student submits an individual report for assessment purposes.

EXAMPLES OF THE-RELATED IMPLICIT AND EXPLICIT PROJECT MANAGEMENT JOBS

There are many types of projects, which also means that job titles in the tourism, hospitality and events sectors may not necessarily include the term 'project manager' in the recruitment documentation. For example, a production manager role is likely to include elements of project management, but unless you read the job description and person specification details carefully, you might miss it.

EMPLOYER INSIGHT

Implicit and explicit tourism, hospitality and events sector roles in project management

Private Coordinator (Events)

The Role (A)

- Account management: retaining and developing existing clients while also growing the database
- Venue management: building relationships with the operations team and promoting good venue partnerships
- Ensure high-quality service is delivered across every event, with every client and every venue, ensuring repeat business
- Attend familiarisation trips, site visits and client entertainment as required
- Proactive market research: wedding trends showcases, tradeshows

The Skills

- Must have previous weddings sales experience for a caterer or venue
- Knowledge of the market, including suppliers and agencies who work

Production Manager (Live Events)

The Role (B)

- Manage delivery of all production on large-scale production heavy projects
- Identify new partners and review existing suppliers
- Undertake project debriefs, share insights with production teams
- Attend client workshops representing production, operational and H&S
- Support development of new client relationships
- Financial management
- Collaborate closely with the creative team
- Take initiative in moving projects forward
- Provide leadership to freelance and junior team members

The Skills

- Exhibition and live event delivery, including greenfield ideally
- Strong understanding of health and safety
- Strong leaderships skills
- Finance specifically in the sector
- Have a passion for sales with strong negotiation skills and driven to exceed expectations both personally and commercially
- Strong admin and organisational skills
- A natural people person and team player
- Creative, motivated and positive
- Excellent attention to detail
- Excellent interpersonal and communication skills
- Have a genuine interest in the weddings and private events market

- Must be willing to work evenings and weekends as required due to the nature of the wedding industry; flexibility and lieu days/good holidays offered in return
- Excellent client-facing and supplier liaison skills
- Team-orientated, good leadership skills
- Flexible, calm under pressure, highly organised
- Strong interpersonal and negotiation skills
- Proactive, enthusiastic, confident
- Proficient in Google Drive, Microsoft Office, PowerPoint and CAD

Source: Reed.co.uk

In terms of what tourism, hospitality and events employers are looking for when they are recruiting staff, the following example provides an indication of the type of skills that are being sought. You will notice that like job titles, the advert does not necessarily explicitly state that a candidate must have project management skills but will ask for many of the core skills associated with project management, such as organisational and communication skills.

EMPLOYER INSIGHT

Pronovias Group, Senior Event Coordinator, Italy

We at PRONOVIAS GROUP, global leader in the bridal industry, are currently looking for a talented and outstanding Senior Event Coordinator to join our Marketing Team in our HQ in Centallo (Cuneo, Italy). PRONOVIAS GROUP seeks people who are passionate about fashion; love to be part of a growing and challenging international environment; inspiring and empowering people and are not afraid to make the difference. Our mission is bringing HAPPINESS into the world by dressing with style our customers' dreams, being the best partner to our clients and building together an exciting place to work.

Responsibilities

- Support in event management
- Coordination of a team during the preparation of an event
- Search and design of visuals in events
- Coordination of trunk shows
- Graphic and creative support in event management
- Support in creative development and coordination of the shootings
- Search for suppliers
- Search for locations for events and shooting
- Visual search and coordination within the stores

Requirements

- Studies in Fashion or Events Management
- Accuracy, sense of responsibility and punctuality in delivery in respect of deadlines
- Passion for Graphics and Fashion, sensitivity, elegance and good taste
- Able to work in a team
- Able to work on multiple projects simultaneously

(Continued)

- Ability to organise work efficiently
- Creativity and ability to interpret the brand identity in an original way
- Excellent knowledge of English (knowledge of Spanish would be a plus)
- Excellent knowledge of Adobe Creative Suite
- Availability to travel (20%)

Source: www.glassdoor.co.uk

Once you have read the job descriptions and considered the skills requirements, use the SPECTRE Skills Audit activity below to assess your current skills (see below).

 ═══ ACTIVITY ═══════════════════════════

SPECTRE Skills Audit

Go to page 575 in the Appendix which gives a list of some basic skills required to deliver a wide range of generic projects. This is not intended to be an exhaustive list, but an overview of some of the key skills that employers are looking for.

Complete the Personal Improvement Plan column to list the actions you plan to take to improve them and/or address any gaps that you might have.

Table 18.5   SPECTRE personal improvement plan

SKILL	Personal improvement Plan
Specialist: Management Skills	
Participatory: Team Working Skills	
Environmental: Technical Skills	
Communication: Interpersonal Skills	
Time: Organisational Skills	
Resource: People Management	
Entrepreneurialism: Soft Skills	

CONCLUSION

In this chapter we have:

- Discussed how projects are managed from inception to delivery.
- Considered some of the key project management techniques that project managers can use.
- Reflected on the skills and knowledges required for successful project management.

FURTHER READING

Carayannis, E.G., Kwak, Y-H, and Anbari, F.T. (2005) *The Story of Managing Projects: An Interdisciplinary Approach*. Westport, CT: Praeger Publishers.

Discenza, R. and Forman, J.B. (2007) *Seven Causes of Project Failure: How to Recognise Them and How to Initiate Project Recovery*. Atlanta, GA: Project Management Institute.

Egeland, B. (2018) *Lessons Learned from the Inconsistent Project Manager*. APM, 18 May. Available at: www.apm.org.uk/blog/lessons-learned-from-the-inconsistent-project-manager/ (accessed 26 June 2020).

PMI (2013) *A Guide to Project Management Body of Knowledge*. Newton Square, PA: Project Management Institute.

Useful resources

Association for Project Management is the charter body for the project profession. Student membership is available to any full-time or part-time student ages 16 yrs or over – www.apm.org.uk

Institute for Apprenticeships (IFS) offers project manager and associate project manager apprenticeship frameworks – www.instituteforapprenticeships.org

International Project Management Association (IPMA) – www.ipma.world

Project Management Institute (PMI) offers student membership – www.apm.org.uk

19 PROBLEM-SOLVING AND CREATIVITY

 CHAPTER LEARNING OBJECTIVES

By the end of this chapter you should be able to:

- Apply creative thinking to develop solutions to challenges and problems you may face in the tourism, hospitality and events sectors.
- Appreciate the value and benefits of taking (calculated) risks when approaching problems and try something new that has not necessarily been tried and tested before.
- Identify when it is appropriate to adopt creative approaches to problem-solving in the tourism, hospitality and events sectors.
- Articulate what design thinking and lateral thinking are and how such approaches can help in a more creative approach to problem-solving.

 GLOSSARY

- **Brainstorming:** a technique where a group tries to find a solution to a problem or issue by spontaneously generating ideas together.
- **Blue sky thinking:** Thinking differently. It's brainstorming with no limits and concerns about what is possible, or 'right'. It is designed to allow the freedom you need to be creative without any inhibited areas.
- **Design thinking:** A process of creative problem-solving which uses innovative ways such as sketching and prototyping to test out new concepts and ideas. It is a process with a human-centred core. It is a solution-based approach to solving problems.
- **Lateral thinking:** Solving problems by viewing the problem in a new and unusual light and using indirect and creative approaches. This challenges traditional step-by-step logic.

INTRODUCTION

This chapter encourages you to think about how you might develop ideas and solutions which sit 'outside' the box. By drawing on examples of individuals and businesses in the tourism, hospitality and events sectors who have done this, we hope to provide you with the confidence to try a new approach to a problem and for you to embrace your creative side to provide an alternative approach to a challenge or issue. Being able to solve problems (independently and with others) is a key skill that employers say they want in their graduates, so it is important you develop this skill and approach.

As part of building your toolkit to solve problems effectively, we provide guidance on how to analyse facts, data and statistics, and in turn, demonstrate how these methods can be applied to situations. This chapter will outline some of the practical techniques people use in the service sectors to effectively foster creative thinking and look at problems differently, namely the practice of **lateral thinking** and adoption of some decision-making techniques and approaches. In addition to these skills being highly valued in the workplace, problem-solving and how to use analytical thinking will be useful to help you complete your coursework. It also presents some techniques that should be useful in your own personal problem-solving.

WHAT ARE PROBLEM-SOLVING AND CREATIVITY?

Problem-solving is a skill that we can all learn and develop, combining many of the skills you have read about in other chapters in this book, but by bringing some of these together should help you develop more insightful and more effective problem-solving skills. We are constantly faced with problems that need solving throughout our daily lives. These can range from small problems that are easy to solve, for example thinking and deciding what to wear in the morning, to more significant problems about how are you going to balance an academic workload with your professional and social engagements (see Chapter 11).

═══ REFLECTION EXERCISE ═══

A creative approach to a problem

Think of a recent problem in your life. Reflect on it (refer back to Chapter 10). What possible methods of resolving it did you consider? Why? What was the determining factor? Keep a list of these for now as you might want to add a few new approaches after reading this chapter. Once you have read this chapter, go back to this list and see how you could have used creativity to help you resolve the problem and if there is anything that you would have done differently.

By entering the tourism, hospitality and events field, you will be taking on jobs that require management expertise and problem-solving skills. Confidence is said to be the backbone of problem-solving, and you will only develop this confidence through practice, and trial and error. In tourism, problem-solving challenges might include how you will re-accommodate 500 people who have to vacate their hotel (perhaps due to a natural disaster or risk to life), and in events, this might mean coming up with a plan at short notice if a venue suddenly becomes unavailable, or a key speaker is unable to make the launch event. So, in this chapter we will be looking at the skills (and attitude) you will need to be able to solve an academic problem but also how you can transfer those skills into your future workplace.

Creativity is closely linked to problem-solving. Often a set issue or problem will require a creative solution to solve it. You may hear a lot of students say that they struggle with creativity or have no creativity. We are all capable of being creative; it's about us not recognising when we are being creative, or perhaps not feeling brave enough to follow our instincts. This chapter should encourage you to be reassured that with practice you can develop a creative approach to your work and incorporate this into your problem-solving and other areas of your life.

Creativity doesn't just mean that you are good at drawing, painting, other arts and crafts or even dance and music. Creativity is also about being able to look at a situation and think around that situation to improve it, change it or develop it further. We will be looking at how to think creatively, through examples, case studies and completing some set tasks.

DEFINING THE PROBLEM

This might sound obvious, but the first step in being able to solve a problem is being able to define exactly what the problem is. Without clearly understanding the problem, the issues a problem presents or the complexities of the problem, then you are not going to be able to find a suitable solution (Clegg, 2007; Gregory, 2010). It may be a simple problem that can be solved with a simple solution. For example: the power has gone out in a restaurant. You investigate and find that the main electrical fuse has blown; you replace the fuse and then power is restored.

However, the problem may be more complex. A more involved problem might be that you own a restaurant and you are not getting the number of customers that you had planned for. This is a complex problem that you will need to address and solve if you are able to continue to be in business. This problem may need a creative, innovative or inventive solution to solve. It may be a problem that needs a team approach to be able to solve (Cottrell, 2015; Gregory, 2010).

- Brainstorm the issue to identify what is causing the problem with the lack of customers. This can be done in a few ways: creating a Mind Map, listing the issues, or compiling a table of the issues and undertaking some research about competitors and perhaps what societal or economic changes have taken place in the area. Then, with these data, you are ready to think about possible solutions to the problem.
- Using a question and answer technique, where you ask yourself or team a question and try to provide an answer. It's as simple as asking why this has happened and then answering. You write down the answer and then ask why to that answer until you identify the problem and a solution.
- A systematic approach (Probst, 2014) requires you to create an action plan, which allows you to set priorities and identify the resources you may need (for example data, team members, and complaint forms from guests or clients). Once you have the information you need you can then set the priorities and implementation of the solutions.

WAYS TO SOLVE A PROBLEM

There are different ways to identify and approach a problem (Clegg, 2007). For example, we have a wealth of information at our fingertips with search engines and the internet. It is unlikely that we will come across a problem where something similar hasn't happened to someone else. Undertaking a simple internet search through sites such as Google or YouTube can provide us with a range of answers to choose from.

Blue sky thinking

This has become a rather over-used phrase in business. But, what does it mean if you scratch under the rhetoric? It is about thinking differently, and it's about **brainstorming** with no limits and concerns about what is possible, or 'right'. What happens if you are given a problem and you are told that there are absolutely no limits, no judgements and no consequences, where could your imagination take you? What ideas have you got if money was no object? This approach can give you the freedom to be creative, without any boundaries or consequences. **Blue sky thinking** is designed to allow the freedom you need to be creative, without any inhibited areas (Fisher, 2018).

THINK POINT

When we are young children, our imagination knows no bounds. However, when we become adults we tend to hold back and try the 'sensible' approach. But why? Think about what stifles your creativity. This might be self-consciousness, or previous examples where something didn't work, or fear.

Using blue sky thinking requires you to open up new areas of thinking in a completely open-minded way. There is nothing that can't be considered. It is very much centred around conversation that does not necessarily revolve around knowledge or experience, but more on curiosity and the desire to find out. If you are involved in blue sky thinking you need to be prepared to be surprised and to put aside your normal ways of thinking and look at information that would not have occurred to you previously and may take you out of your normal comfort zone.

A useful resource on blue sky thinking is https://letstalk.voiceprint.global/facilitate-blue-sky-thinking.

ACTIVITY

A practical problem

Imagine you have a problem in your house that you have not previously encountered: a blocked sink. You don't want to call a plumber as you know this will be expensive, so you type into a search engine, 'how to unblock a kitchen sink'. What did you find? Were there tutorials, videos and lists of examples on how to unblock sinks, in addition to a list of plumbers to call?

From the activity above you will see how easy it is to find help with a simple problem such as unblocking a sink. This is still considered to be a creative solution: you have used your creativity to identify the problem, look for help, find a solution and then hopefully use that information to achieve your goal of unblocking the sink.

Now let's take this a stage further by exploring a more complex problem. The activity below is a starting point for problem-solving. As the owner of the restaurant you have identified the areas and main causes of lack of customers and repeat business. Before you act on these, it is advisable, as for any problem, to discuss these areas with other stakeholders in the restaurant – the customers, suppliers and staff. This will allow you to have a fully informed understanding of the problems and the opinions of others that you may not have considered.

 **ACTIVITY**

Finding solutions to problems

In Table 19.1 you will see that some sections have been completed. Think about these solutions and complete the areas where there is no solution provided. Additionally, if you disagree with the solutions provided and feel you have a better solution to the problem then provide this in the spaces under the given solutions. This activity encourages you to brainstorm and think creatively to find a solution to a problem. At the bottom of the table there are some spaces for you to provide other reasons as to why the restaurant has very few customers. Complete these and think of solutions in the grey boxes.

Table 19.1   Different solution approaches to problems

The problem	Simple solution	Creative solution	Innovative solution	Inventive solution
The restaurant is cold. Customers are unhappy and not staying	Fix the heating	Add ambiance to the restaurant through adding an open fireplace and fire	Install underfloor heating and heat lamps	Having seating booths that can be individually heated through an app on a phone that allows the customers to determine their own ambient temperature of the areas they are sitting in
Food is taking too long to get to customers and they are waiting far too long in-between courses		Change the restaurant to a buffet style that allows people to help themselves from a selection of pre-prepared dishes	Provide entertainment in the restaurant for the customers to enjoy while waiting for their food. Create a whole evening experience (themed restaurant).	Have an app that customers can use to pre-order their food prior to attending their booking to allow for preparation to be made and avoid delays
There is no alcohol on offer, despite having an alcohol licence	Offer a corkage fee, where customers can bring in their own wine. Start selling alcohol		Offer a wine, beer, spirit of the month club, where customers can enjoy trying something new on a monthly basis and they are rewarded through regular attendance	Start a microbrewery and produce your own specialised beers

The problem	Simple solution	Creative solution	Innovative solution	Inventive solution
The quality of the food is not consistent and there is a large range of dishes available at all times	Hire better chefs	Reduce the number of dishes available and concentrate on fewer dishes and ensuring they are of a top quality		Change your specials on a regular basis and always ensure that they are of excellent quality. Offer an experience with these specials that is unique to your restaurant
Customers are not aware of the restaurant as there has been no marketing	Put an advert in the local newspaper or put flyers in the local paper telling people about the restaurant			
You have had complaints about the staff being unhelpful and rude to the customers.				
You have had complaints about staff not knowing about the specials or the contents of the restaurant				

PROBLEM-SOLVING AT UNIVERSITY

Rothstein and colleagues stated that,

> throughout nearly 300 years of policymaking in the United States, educators have promoted eight broad goals of schooling: basic academic skills, critical thinking and problem-solving, social skills and work ethic, citizenship, physical health, emotional health, the arts and literature, and preparation for skilled employment (2007: 8).

Problem-solving is central to an academic education and yet it has also been argued that university students seldom use critical thinking skills to solve complex, real-world problems (Bartlett, 2002) – for more, see Chapter 8.

=== STUDENT INSIGHT ===

Stephen, looking back on dealing with problems

As a student I worried about the problems I was faced with, whether that was a personal problem or an assignment problem. It wasn't that I couldn't think of solutions or ways to avoid a problem, it was that

(Continued)

I lacked the confidence in my ability to apply the solution I had thought of or found. This was holding me back and made it look like I was ignoring the problem rather than dealing with it. This changed when I was set an assignment around a set problem that needed a solution. This was a group assignment and there were six of us in the team. We got together and looked at the set problem, making sure that we first understood what exactly the question was asking us to do, as well as how we should approach the problem set.

The group worked on a flat level structure with no one taking the leadership of the group. We also worked as a democracy, allowing everyone in the group to have a voice. After breaking down the problem through Mind Mapping and asking questions around the problem, we came to a clear understanding of what needed to be solved and why. We then went off as individuals, arranging to meet up again a couple of hours later, to undertake some research and present a solution.

The first place I looked was in academic textbooks that dealt with the area I was looking at. This gave me some notes on what else I needed to find out. I researched the issue and there were hundreds of videos and text examples of how to overcome the problem I was responsible for dealing with. I watched two or three videos, making notes, then read a few articles on the solutions. From these notes I then collated a suitable solution that I felt would contribute to the whole problem we were looking at. Unfortunately, I still felt very uncomfortable in presenting my findings in case someone said that it was a stupid solution and would not work.

We met up as a group and I listened to the others present their findings and solutions with confidence. Some of them were excellent, others were not well thought through and, in my opinion, would not work. I plucked up the courage to explain what I had found as a solution. The group were unanimous in saying that it was a brilliant solution and one that they, as a group, should adopt. We did go on to talk it through and apply my solution to the problem. We received an excellent mark for this assessment.

On reflection, I have learnt that talking things through with others is a great way to deal with a problem, as you can see it from many different angles. I have also learnt that it is important if you have thought something through and have a rational solution then you need to have confidence in that solution. If not, it just looks like you don't care or are ignoring the problem. Now I am very different: I look for problems before they become one and put solutions in place before they are needed. It is much easier to deal with something before it happens than having to deal with the fall-out of a problem. Be confident in your creativity and ability to find solutions.

There are many situations that you might face as a student which you may have to deal with that aren't necessarily to do with your academic work. How would you react if the following problems presented themselves to you?

 REFLECTION ACTIVITY

Problem-solving

- How would you solve the problem of being evicted from your accommodation?
- If you were lonely, what would you do to counteract this?
- How will you juggle having to work part-time and also study full-time (see Chapter 11)?
- How would you resolve an argument with a friend?
- You were working on your laptop, saved your assignment to the hard drive which then broke and your assignment was gone forever – what would you do?

These are just some of the situations you could find yourself in while at university. Some of them you can prepare for and avoid (for example, ensuring that you back up on an external device everything you are working on so that you don't lose it if your computer breaks). Others could happen at short notice that you may need to find a solution quickly. Having the skills to solve problems and the confidence to act on your solution will stand you in good stead.

There are also the academic problems that you will be faced with in answering questions. It is important to ensure that when you are faced with an assignment question that you break it down into solvable, manageable sections and that you plan the answer using all your creativity and problem-solving skills. Chapters 4, 6, 8, 10 and 15 have all been written to help you develop the critical skills needed to become creative thinkers and problem-solvers.

As students, we are often taught using different teaching styles and education strategies, but they are all working towards the same goals. These goals are to develop knowledge and understanding, develop skills, promote autonomous learning, develop problem-solving and independent thinking (Bender, 2012; Brown, 2002; Sonntag, 2010). Therefore, it is important to ensure you engage and immerse yourself fully with these different teaching methods to develop the range of skills you will need. These can include short presentations, critical arguments, active learning and many more.

ANALYSING FACTS, DATA AND STATISTICS

Tourism, hospitality and events businesses are no different to any other business in regard to the importance of data and how it can help you understand areas of the business. Data is important and can provide you with informed information (Albright, 2015). For example, there is no point changing the whole menu in a hotel restaurant because one guest complains about it. However, if you are experiencing a dramatic downturn in the number of guests visiting the restaurant and you have numerous complaints from guests about the menu during checkout, then this would be valuable data that you would need to look into and consider a change.

When using data, you need to ensure that the data is the data you need and that it is accurate. If not, then you may waste any financial investment in the data collection and ultimately not have dealt with the presenting issue. The information you use should be specifically to inform any decisions you make. There are more factors beyond the data, as discussed in this chapter, that should also be considered. If you are specifically setting out to collect data, whether from a questionnaire or interviewing guests at checkout, it is important to ensure your data collection methods are not biased or asked in a manner to give you the results that you want to obtain.

Your data can be a useful tool to contribute to your decision-making process. It can support your decisions, along with informing you early on if there is a problem.

━━━━━━━━━━━━━━━ STUDENT INSIGHT ━━━━━━━━━━━━━━━

Martha, my family business

I commenced a course in hospitality as I had been working at my parent's hotel since I was a teenager. I loved working in the hotel and wanted to learn more about the industry. It is a medium-sized hotel in a popular tourist spot. My parents had always promised me that one day the hotel would be mine when they retire.

(Continued)

After the first year of my course, my parents told me that the hotel was struggling to attract customers and they were not sure why. I had learnt from a module I was taking about the importance of data collection and how this could help inform businesses to understand what was going on with a business. I spoke to my parents and decided to put together a questionnaire to give to customers to find out why we were not getting repeat business and why we were not attracting new guests. The questionnaire was sent to all of our guests on our mailing list, which didn't return very many results: about 1% returned, which was very disappointing. I convinced my parents to provide the questionnaire in the rooms the day before the guests checked out. They just had to fill it in and leave it in the room when departing. These were popular with the guests and we had a 75% return rate. It seemed the customers wanted to have a voice. We ran this for a month and then I collated the results: the results were quite shocking for my parents. While everyone commented that the service was excellent, helpful and friendly, they also didn't pull any punches on what was wrong. The biggest issue was that everything was outdated, looked tired and didn't look fresh and clean. The televisions in the rooms didn't work well and the internet was non-existent. Additionally, the tea and coffee facilities were not re-stocked, nor the toiletries. The bathrooms were tired and lacked a shower.

My parents took this hard and were trying to find excuses for this and saying the guests weren't looking at the positive aspects but only the negative. It took a while before they calmed down and decided to do something about the issues. Within a year, they had had the whole place re-decorated and modernised, had showers put in some of the rooms as well as introducing some themed rooms. They had flat screens put in all the rooms alongside installing broadband in all the rooms.

The hotel looks amazing now and has a real boutique spa feel about it. I ran the questionnaire again after the first year and the feedback from that was amazing, with the vast majority of people loving the look and feel of the hotel. There were one or two who didn't like the changes, but you can't please all the people all the time. What my parents experienced proved to them that the original data we received was correct. The hotel is now mostly fully booked well in advance, with a lot of the guests providing repeat business. Collecting the right data for the hotel was absolutely fundamental in informing my parents what they needed to do to improve the business. It has certainly paid off for them and me. They bought me a car for helping them turn the hotel around!

DESIGN THINKING

This is a powerful and increasingly popular process which helps people redefine problems. **Design thinking** has proved useful in tackling problems that are complex, unknown and multi-faceted. By re-framing a problem and experimenting with solutions with testing, prototypes and creative redefining of problems, alternative strategies and solutions that might not be instantly apparent at first, can be identified (Chung and Chung, 2018). At its core, there are three main pillars of design thinking, which are:

* *Empathy*: think about and understand people involved in the problem or need (stakeholders)
* *Ideation*: this is where you generate ideas. Brainstorming is one technique as shown in Mind Maps (see Chapter 4)
* *Experimentation*: test ideas out with prototypes.

This kind of human-centric process aims to provide a solution-based approach to solving problems. It is a way of thinking and working as well as a collection of hands-on methods. It provides a road map to help move you towards a solution which is creative and developed in an interactive way.

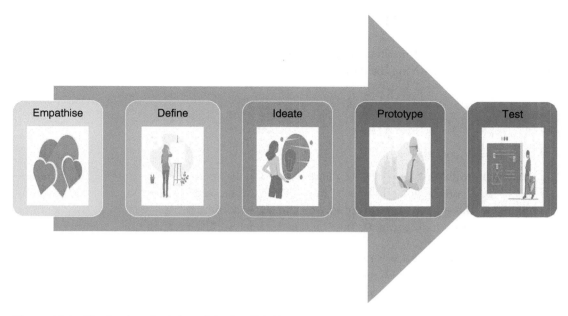

Figure 19.1   The basic principles of design thinking

Design thinking has been successfully applied to the hospitality industry to identify the needs of guests (Chung and Chung, 2018). The process can help you clarify exactly what you are trying to achieve and help you gain a smarter understanding of what exactly your guests' opinions and needs are of your services and facilities.

By putting the needs and behaviours of your customers and/or guests first when designing your business strategy, you will be able to determine the investment that needs to be put in place and be confident that this investment is being used wisely. The attractive part of using design thinking is that you do not have to be a designer to use it. You just need to cover the areas described above and apply them to understand what it is your customer/guest wants.

NURTURING LATERAL THINKING

Lateral thinking is a problem-solving approach that looks beyond obvious options, developed by Edward de Bono. It first appeared in De Bono's *Six Thinking Hats* (2009). De Bono suggests that leaving traditional modes of thought behind encourages people to discard preconceptions. Lateral thinking is a thought process that steps outside of the constraints with which a problem is expressed. You might know this process as 'thinking outside the box'. This phrase is helpful, as you are trying to think about solutions that are beyond the obvious and those that are evident. Some of the most successful entrepreneurs in tourism, hospitality and events use lateral thinking to think differently to disrupt and break or bend the rules.

It is important with lateral thinking to be thinking outside of the proverbial box. If you are seeing everyone around you pushing one form of tourism then it is important to look for another way to break away from the crowd and offer a unique selling point, experience or service (see Chapter 34). Tarlow (2020) suggests that if there is already a surplus of one form of tourism then you need to find a different angle. For example, if all the hotels in your area are offering beach holidays, there is no reason why you can't specialise in cultural holidays, offering a whole new experience in addition to the sun and beach. This is thinking laterally: you are thinking outside of the box and identifying new and untapped areas to increase the desire for people to stay at your hotel over others available.

SOME DECISION-MAKING TECHNIQUES AND APPROACHES

You might want to think about a few techniques known to help problem-solving. For example, try the mnemonic IDEALS (Facione and Facione, 2007). There are six steps to effective thinking and problem-solving. As the student problem-solver, you should work through a problem or activity by using the IDEALS which are to: **I**dentify, **D**efine, **E**numerate, **A**nalyse, **L**ist, and **S**elf-Correct.

- **I**dentify the problem: What is the real question we are facing?
- **D**efine the context: What are the facts that frame this problem?
- **E**numerate the choices: What are plausible options?
- **A**nalyse options: What is the best course of action?
- **L**ist reasons explicitly: Why is this the best course of action?
- **S**elf-Correct: Look at it again … What did we miss?

Additionally, you can try the six thinking hats method developed by de Bono in the 1950s. This is a group thinking activity and allows the people in the group to discuss an issue from the perspective of the particular hat they are wearing at the time. The hats need changing frequently between the participants to allow for lots of different perspectives and ideas to be explored. The theory behind this method is that, as humans, we are capable of thinking in a variety of ways that can be challenged, thus encouraging new approaches to thinking about a problem. De Bono (2009) uses coloured hats that represent different approaches or perspectives, for example:

- Blue – gut feelings
- White – information
- Red – emotions and ego
- Black – evaluation
- Yellow – judgement
- Green – concept challenge

Everyone in the group is presented with the problem that needs to be discussed and solved and then they all literally or metaphorically put on one of the hats and answer the problem from the perspective of that hat. Then, when everyone has exhausted their perspective, the hats are changed.

This method can encourage an honest open approach to lateral thinking and problem-solving and you will be surprised at the freedom this approach can give to the participants engaging with the exercise. This freedom results in a deeper brainstorming session which can challenge previous ideas that may have been presented on the problem prior to the exercise starting.

STUDENT INSIGHT

Imogen, dealing with a problem at work

Being a student can be financially difficult. I made the decision that I would not ask my parents for money when I started at university. One of the first things I did was to get a job that I could start as soon as I arrived on campus. Without the job, I was concerned I would not be able to socialise, engage in social activities, or eat very well. I was offered a part-time job for an airline, working at an airport near to the university. It was a part-time job with flexible hours, so I would still have time to study and attend all my classes. The person who interviewed me was clear that they would accommodate my needs. They had a flexible working policy in place for staff. The person I was interviewed by was the manager of the section I would be working in. However, below her were supervisors who didn't seem to have the same caring and flexible approach to their staff.

I had been working there for two months when, without notice, my shifts were changed. I spoke to my supervisor and told her that these shifts would not fit in with my other commitments. She told me I had two choices: (1) do the shifts and stop moaning, or (2) go and work somewhere else. I decided that I would try and work with the new shifts as the job was well paid. I would also struggle to find another job that gave the same benefits as I had here. I missed my classes and went into work. I think the supervisor was surprised to see me and that whole day was rude and negative towards me. It was when I took a break and met up with another colleague that I found out why she was behaving like this towards me. She wanted her sister to have my job and was trying to force me out so her sister could apply.

This concerned me a great deal. I was being bullied and treated badly for something that was no fault of my own. I went home that evening and thought about how I could deal with the problem. I was worried about speaking to the manager as I knew she was friends with my supervisor. I looked at the problem and listed down the things I could do to improve the situation. My first approach was to be as nice and friendly to the supervisor as possible in the hope that this would change her mind about me. This didn't work; she was equally as rude towards me. I then checked the staff handbook, which gave advice on how to deal with these sorts of issues. It suggested talking to the person, which I did, only to be told by the supervisor that I was useless and had to put up with it. I looked on the internet for help and found a chat room where I discussed my issues. I kept my name and the name of the company anonymous, but I got some great advice. Before getting the advice, I was thinking of leaving, but I couldn't see how this would benefit me or others if they were put in the same position by this supervisor. I realised I had nothing to lose by speaking to the manager. The next time I was in, I spoke to the manager and explained that the new shifts were hurting my academic work. I offered to be more flexible in my working pattern and that with adequate notice of shift changes I could possibly cover more shifts. I also suggested that there was a clash of personalities and would it be possible to be managed by a different supervisor. The manager was really understanding and was already aware that there was a problem as the supervisor had spoken to her. She thanked me for talking to her and providing an alternative perspective of the situation and offering solutions. The manager told me that I had dealt with this situation professionally and suggested that I would make a good manager with the airline when I had finished university, suggesting I apply for their graduate scheme. The supervisor was put on a warning for not complying with the company's processes and protocols and I was removed from her management, and my shifts were changed back to the original times. I got to keep a job I enjoy and carry on earning a good wage. I still face problems at work, but I know I have the support to deal with them and I also know I am capable of finding solutions.

My advice for dealing with any problem would be to think it through first. Don't react in a negative way or jump to a solution that may harm your chances of satisfactorily solving your problem.

The insight above should encourage you to ensure you have the facts, examples and rules that you need to be able to implement a possible solution. Stick to the facts you have and talk to people, take advice and see what others have done. Create a plan of action and then implement the changes that you have the power to implement. Don't ignore or walk away from a problem.

CONCLUSION

In this chapter we have covered:

- The importance of being able to define a problem to be able to solve it.
- How to use creativity to solve a problem.
- How developing problem-solving skills will enable you to develop autonomous thinking.
- Methods that can be used to help you solve problems such as design thinking and lateral thinking.

FURTHER READING

Clegg, B. (2007) *Instant Creativity: Simple Techniques to Ignite Innovation & Problem Solving.* London: Kogan Page.
Cottrell, S. (2015) *Skills for Success: Personal Development and Employability.* Basingstoke: Palgrave Macmillan.
De Bono, E. (2009) *Six Thinking Hats.* London: Penguin.
Frisendal, T. (2012) *Design Thinking Business Analysis: Business Concept Mapping Applied.* Dordrecht: Springer.
Probst, G. (2014) *Tackling Complexity: A Systematic Approach for Decision Makers.* Sheffield, UK: Greenleaf Publishing.

Useful resource

Skills you Need (2020) *Problem-solving Skills You Need* – www.skillsyouneed.com/ips/problem-solving.html

SECTION C
GAINING WORK EXPERIENCE

Level: 5

20 GRADUATE EMPLOYMENT IN TOURISM, HOSPITALITY AND EVENTS

CHAPTER LEARNING OBJECTIVES

By the end of this chapter you should be able to:

- Outline the size, scale and character of the graduate employment market in the tourism, hospitality and events sector.
- Articulate the different types of careers, roles and opportunities available and be able to reflect on the areas of work you might wish to pursue and why.
- Describe the kinds of challenges the industry is facing and the impact these events and challenges have on the graduate employment market.

GLOSSARY

- **Brexit:** the withdrawal of the United Kingdom from the European Union.
- **COVID-19 (also called coronavirus):** an infectious disease caused by the severe acute respiratory syndrome coronavirus 2 (SARS-CoV-2). It led to a global pandemic, which began in China in 2019 and quickly spread across the globe, leading to significant disruption to the global economy and people's lives.
- **Industrial action:** where employees of a company strike or work to rule as a protest (usually for better wages or conditions).

INTRODUCTION

This chapter provides an overview of employment trends in the tourism, events and hospitality sector, graduate opportunities and the issues that affect gaining employment in this sector. It looks at the size and scale of relevant markets and offers an analysis of potential graduate employment. This chapter reviews the possibilities of graduate employment across the industry, from airlines to accommodation, and from food and drink establishments to travel agencies and events management. It will delve into the types of career and work you might want to consider by using examples of what you might need to demonstrate to secure a role and career in the sector. By looking at examples, the chapter highlights the opportunities in areas including customer service and client facing roles, marketing, sales, product development, IT and administration. This chapter should give you a good understanding of the potential opportunities ahead of you.

Tourism, events and hospitality are one of the largest areas of global employment, but the sector is often plagued by low wages, seasonality and low status when compared to some other career options. This chapter will also tackle and explore the sector in terms of unpredictability and fluidity due to unexpected events, i.e. economic recession, terrorism, natural catastrophe and **industrial action**. Some examples of events that affect employment in the tourism, hospitality and events sector will be presented in this chapter so you are fully aware of the challenges facing the industry, and as a consequence their impact on your employment opportunities.

TRAVEL AND TOURISM EMPLOYMENT

According to the World Tourism and Travel Council (WTTC, 2019a), the travel and tourism industry generated 122,891,000 direct jobs in 2018 (3.8% of total employment) and this grew by 2.2% in 2019 to 125,595,000 (3.9% of total employment). In 2016, the number of people employed in the EU tourism industry was over 13 million. The total contribution to employment (including wider effects from investment, the supply chain and induced income) was 318,811,000 jobs in 2018 (10.0% of total employment) and was set to rise by 2.9% in 2019 to 328,208,000 jobs (10.1% of total employment). By 2029, travel and tourism are forecast to support 420,659,000 jobs (11.7% of total employment), an increase of 2.5% per year.

In their 2015 report on global talent trends, the WTTC (2015: 7) reported that:

> At a global level, the research shows that the industry is facing a shortfall of 14 million jobs – that is equivalent to the population of Cambodia – and stands to reduce its contribution to global GDP by US$ 610 billion over the next ten years, 5.8% less than our baseline forecasts … Travel & Tourism's Human Capital challenges are significantly higher than those faced in other sectors, with 37 out of 46 countries showing a talent 'deficit' or 'shortage' in Travel & Tourism over the next ten years, compared with only 6 out of 46 for the economy as a whole.

The sector is growing quickly with an extremely broad and wide-ranging collection of industries, businesses and opportunities. Shortfalls in labour means the whole world opens to those who choose in work in it.

THE GRADUATE EMPLOYMENT MARKET IN TOURISM, EVENTS AND HOSPITALITY

Many companies will have specific graduate schemes and purposely employ recent graduates, but many others will not have specific schemes and employ graduates as the need and relevant positions arise. Many graduate schemes are rotational, allowing employees to experience working in different departments and with several functions of the same business. Many of the brands and large companies in the hotel industry offer graduate level career options, including Whitbread, Marriot, Carlson Rezidor Hotel Group and Jurys Inn. In the wider travel industry, companies with similar schemes include TUI Group, Thomas Cook, P&O Cruises and Expedia. The events management sector offers graduate opportunities in companies such as Clarion Events, Zibrant, and Sodexo. An example is outlined below. However, do look beyond these big players as often SMEs recruit graduates.

━━━━━━━━━━━━━ EMPLOYER INSIGHT ━━━━━━━━━━━━━

TUI Global Graduate Programme

The TUI Group offers three different graduate schemes for the TUI Group International Graduate Programme, with specialisation in the fields of Commercial, Aviation or Digital & IT. Each programme lasts 20 months and is open to talented and passionate individuals from around the world. The objective is to develop future leaders and experts for roles in TUI Group, to develop your soft, business and management skills and provide experience in several aspects of our business.

TUI claim, that 'On our International Graduate Leadership Programme, you can expect real business exposure, key relationships with senior people, and world-class training with one of the world's leading travel groups. That's everything you need to kickstart your career as one of TUI Group's international leaders'. TUI group is a leading tourism business with over 70,000 employees across the world. United under one roof, the group includes an unique hotel portfolio, cruise ships, aircraft, tour operators and travel agencies.

International graduate programme

Two entry dates per year: March and September

Five assignments

- Three assignments cover commercial disciplines
- One assignment in a predefined finance discipline
- One assignment in a hotel destination

What you will be doing

- Choose your own assignments in different TUI Group locations (mostly in Europe)
- Experience day-to-day business and project work in different fields of IT (e.g. IT Architecture, Blockchain, Big Data, Cloud Solutions, IT Security, AI)
- Take responsibility for a team as project lead during your 8-week leadership assignment
- Develop your skills through tailored personal development with workshops, coaching, mentoring and feedback sessions

(Continued)

- Gain experience in all aspects of the organisation
- Collaborate with engaged employees and senior managers from their global businesses
- Work on a common business project as a virtual graduate team

What TUI look for

- Minimum of 2:1 degree (or equivalent) from a university or business school
- Language talent, with English language skills to business standard. Additional European languages are preferable
- Minimum of 3 months international experience
- Minimum of 6 months IT/HR/finance related work experience
- Excellent customer focus with strong analytical and communication skills as well as strong management potential
- Innovative and adaptable approach suitable for working in a fast-paced environment
- Flexibility to be internationally mobile

Details sourced from: http://tuitravelgraduates.com/

According to the UK *Guardian*'s top 300 employers publication (2019), the employers in this field rated most highly by students are: British Airways, Hilton, Marriott International, Thomas Cook, InterContinental, Hotels Group, TUI Travels, Camp America, Merlin Entertainment, Centre Parcs, P&O, and Fitness First. However, the sector is vast. A useful resource to explore the graduate level marker is TargetJobs (2019a). In addition to the numerous skills for the service sector (covered below), you will need to demonstrate higher level skills to secure a graduate level job. In an interview conducted by TargetJobs with Fabienne Rolladin, executive director of external relations at the Swiss Hospitality Management School, they claimed the key competencies include customer service, languages, specialist knowledge (with specific focus on sustainability, and health and safety), financial management, industry understanding (work experience), marketing, IT, professionalism, flexibility, and managerial potential.

These skills are also found in work by the Statista Research Department (2020), which found that 88% of employers (UK survey) said customer service skills were key for the future, and 69% stated this about management and leadership skills. Sustainability skills were sought by 58% of respondents. Additional important skills mentioned included social media and e-marketing, computer literacy and languages. Although a degree in the field is not essential for many jobs, skills are. However, you may also wish to consider a postgraduate degree in tourism, travel, events or hospitality to demonstrate your interest and commitment to this industry. You are also likely to be asked to undertake additional qualifications relevant to your role.

The World Travel and Tourism Council (2015) found a lack of information about what a graduate career in the tourism and leisure sector involves. The graduate market is competitive, and you will often be competing with non-graduates for many high-level opportunities. On the flip side, many other industries will be trying to secure you. The Standing Committee for Economic and Commercial Cooperation of the Organisation of Islamic Cooperation (COMCEC) (2014) identified the problem of 'losing' talent to other sectors and employers' failure to attract qualified personnel into the sector. Interestingly, in a WTTC (2013) research report of undergraduate students, they found that in China, 87% of respondents say they would consider a career in tourism but only 61% in the USA and 49% in the UK would consider this (WTTC, 2013: 1). The picture is that graduate level jobs (and pay) are increasingly hard to find, but there is work in this sector as it's a growing sector. Some of the types of careers available are outlined below.

===== REFLECTION EXERCISE =====

Do I have the skills required?

Although you have reflected on your skills in earlier chapters, take a few minutes to update your thinking on skills and consider how you might evidence the specific skills identified by Fabienne Rolladin, executive director of external relations at the Swiss Hospitality Management School. If you don't have them, how can you gain them?

Table 20.1 Developing skills

Skill	Where have I gained this (previous work or study)?	How might I gain this skill?
Customer service		
Languages		
Sustainability knowledge		
Health and safety		
Financial management		
Industry understanding		
Marketing		
IT		
Professionalism		
Flexibility		

DIFFERENT CAREERS, ROLES AND OPPORTUNITIES

Unfortunately, jobs in hospitality, tourism and travel sometimes have a poor reputation despite offering clear opportunities to progress up the ladder (TravelWeekly, 2019). The industry is regarded as low paid in some areas and the industry is working hard to ensure it attracts government support and backing.

===== REFLECTION EXERCISE =====

What do I find appealing?

Reflect on the jobs you might wish to pursue and why. There are numerous types of jobs and there are some examples in this chapter. Think of two reasons you might wish to pursue a career in them (attractive to you),

(Continued)

and two reasons that might put you off (not attractive). Draw and complete a table like Table 20.2. What do your statements in each column suggest you should be looking for, and what should you be avoiding?

Table 20.2   What to look for and what to avoid

Career/job	Attractive	Unattractive

EXAMPLE GRADUATE CAREERS AND JOB DESCRIPTIONS

There are numerous roles that you might not have considered, including customer service and client-facing roles, marketing and sales, product development (e.g. tourist attractions), travel and aircraft (see http://careersthatmove.co.uk/) and specialist areas within companies such as IT and administration. In this section, we provide a few examples of graduate level jobs in tourism, events, hospitality and leisure. These are not comprehensive lists but should give you a flavour of the kinds of opportunities that you might like to consider and review against your own personal interests (in conjunction with completing the reflective activities in this chapter).

Travel agency

A travel agent arranges and sells holidays. Employers of travel agents tend to be tour operators, package holiday operators, cruise lines and other independent travel agents. You will need to be knowledgeable in terms of different destinations and providers so that you can confidently give advice on where to go and what to do within that location (you will learn much of this on the job). Often, it is about pulling together packages of experiences within a budget. Graduates tend to join the profession as junior counter staff (travel agency clerk/consultant), moving into managerial positions after a few years. In terms of your degree, any subject is usually acceptable, although one in travel, tourism, languages, leisure, business studies or management can be an advantage. Further travel training company qualification or sales work experience can also be helpful.

Tasks will include the promotion of the business, customer service, offering advice, training staff, managing budgets, working with statistics, planning and organisation, selling holidays and insurance, and sorting out promotional materials. The Employer Insight below provides an example of an advert for this kind of graduate-level role. You will need to be commercially aware, have good interpersonal skills, be confident with numbers, and ideally have command of a foreign language. If you are particularly adventurous, there are specialist roles such as adventure travel agents. Some are advertised here: https://careers.adventuretravel.biz. How do your skills and experience match up the job description for the Graduate Travel Consultant role below?

====== EMPLOYER INSIGHT ======

Adventure Travel – Graduate Travel Consultant

In July 2019, Adventure Travel advertised for a Graduate Travel Consultant (London). It offers a good example of the kind of work a graduate travel agent might undertake. The following advert appeared via Travel Job Search with a starting salary of up to £23,000 plus commission.

Role: A Graduate Travel Consultant is required by an award-winning luxury adventure travel company who provide unique and cutting-edge travel experiences to travel junkies just like you! You will be creating travel experiences for clients who want to explore and experience the world's most exotic destinations and have a true cultural exchange. The ideal Graduate Travel Consultant will have a passion for travel, with recent personal travel experiences of places such as South America, Asia, North America, Africa and Europe. This role would suit a well-travelled recent graduate, a tour leader, or someone with previous sales experience looking to develop a career in the travel industry.

Tasks

- Creating and selling group travel and tailor-made travel experiences
- Dealing with client enquiries by telephone, email and website
- Understand customer needs through effective rapport-building
- Ensure all client data is captured correctly
- Respond to travel requests promptly and efficiently
- Check final tailor-made itineraries are correct, before they are sent to clients
- Update client history records on a daily basis

Skills

- Excellent knowledge of travel geography
- Ability to set and work to deadlines
- Attention to detail, ability to plan ahead
- Able to work on own initiative
- Ability to deal with clients and agents face-to-face
- Understanding of what the adventure/cultural traveller wants to experience

Cabin crew

This career is a great way to see the world. Most international airlines require you to have at least 4 GCSEs at grade C or above (or equivalent), or a degree, or significant levels of customer service experience. Airlines tend to employ people who have taken the time to research and study the role and often request that candidates take a specialist course. A range of cabin crew jobs are advertised here: http://cabincrew.careerintravel.co.uk/latest-cabin-crew-jobs/. Generally, salaries start at around £17–20,000 and can increase with experience. A recent Virgin Airways role with no previous flying experience advertised a salary of £14,178 plus excellent benefits – it is modest compared to other roles, but might be a way to see the world for a few years. The Employer insight below provides a typical job description.

 **EMPLOYER INSIGHT**

British Airways cabin crew, Gatwick, UK

BA regularly advertise for cabin crew. A typical advert is as follows:

As a British Airways cabin crew Gatwick Fleet member, you will be enthusiastic and passionate about our products and services and focus on putting the customer at the heart of everything you do. You'll have the opportunity to develop new skills and take control of your career path and be recognised and rewarded for your outstanding contribution.

Reward: As Gatwick Fleet Cabin Crew you will have the potential to earn between £20,000 and £21,500 per annum, potentially increasing to £23,000 per annum in conjunction with corporate pay initiatives. This comprises a starting salary of £12,638 per annum, an hourly payment of £2.95 when you are flying, performance related annual increments and commission for Inflight Retail sales. Annual leave starts at 28 days per year rising to 34 days per year.

Principal Accountabilities

- To ensure operational safety, security and health and safety responsibilities are performed to the highest standards and are compliant with EASA, British Airways requirements and all other relevant legislation
- Maintain safety compliance at all times with Safety & Equipment Procedures training
- Deliver world-class service excellence in line with our service standards and behaviours
- To ensure compliance with all corporate policies and procedures in accordance with relevant legislation
- To act as a British Airways role model to crew, colleagues and customers
- To build effective working relationships with colleagues and service partners

The Individual

- Always focused on safety
- Customer-centric and passionate about delivering service excellence
- Confident in dealing with all our highly valued customers
- Physically and mentally resilient
- Strong team player, able to communicate effectively
- Proactive and able to use initiative when problem-solving
- Shares best practice with colleagues and communicates customer feedback
- Remains calm and resilient when dealing with challenging situations
- Sets high personal standards of achievement and is goal-orientated
- Demonstrates pride and knowledge of the British Airways brand and understanding of the business strategy

BA like candidates to complete their Cabin Crew Diploma course (online) and sometimes it forms part of a tourism course.

Source: https://careers.ba.com/gatwick-cabin-crew

Hotel and hospitality manager

Hotel managers in larger organisations may be mostly office-based, whereas managers of smaller establishments often have frequent contact with both customers and employees. Opportunities include hotel chains, residential clubs, resorts, inns and leisure groups. The typical responsibilities of a graduate role include recruiting and training staff, managing budgets and finances, planning maintenance events and room bookings, overseeing maintenance work, handling customer complaints and queries, promoting and marketing the business, and ensuring compliance with health and safety legislation and licensing laws. Increasingly, research has found leadership skills are a priority for graduates (Cheung et al., 2010).

If you are committed and work hard, then it is possible to enjoy fast career progression into higher managerial roles. For example, see Laura's story later in this chapter – she progressed quickly in this sector to become a regional operations manager of a hotel chain. If you are willing to be flexible in terms of location, specialise in one area such as marketing, sales or human resources, or to move into related areas of employment, then the opportunities are extensive.

In terms of qualifications, a hospitality qualification is advantageous, but graduates with other degrees could obtain a postgraduate diploma in hotel management or build up an extensive amount of experience. A management, languages, leisure, business studies, travel or tourism degree may also be helpful. Relevant work experience is essential and can include hotel, catering, retailing, waitressing or bar work. Key skills required include reliability and stamina, and excellent numerical, verbal and written communication skills. Numeracy is particularly important for finance-related and office-based roles, while good interpersonal skills and customer service are vital for roles involving contact with clients. Knowledge of foreign languages can be an advantage.

=== EMPLOYER INSIGHT ===

Laura Hinson Yates, Regional Operations Manager, Premier Inn

Holidays are always the best days. When I was a child the absolute highlight of any summer would be our family trips, camping in France.

Even now, as a mum of two, I live for that precious family time together and, looking at my career, I think the seeds of how powerful great hospitality can be were sown on those early holidays. My lasting memories were made by superb service by people who really cared that we had an amazing time.

I grew up near Skegness, a seaside town, so tourism was all around and I took advantage of the opportunities for seasonal work as a teenager. From an early age, my parents instilled such a work ethic in me that I got into the world of work as soon as I could, helping out washing dishes in the kitchen of a restaurant. My favourite part of the role was the end of the shift – though not because it had finished, and not because of the free food! No, I was happy because we all came together with a sense of pride at the end of a busy shift and the chance to reflect. We'd all gather on a table and talk and eat – long after my shift had actually finished.

Alongside my studies I became a waitress and must have made every mistake possible – including leaving the bananas out of every banana split I served one night! But even so, I learnt that genuine mistakes can be forgiven with the right attitude, and in hospitality you are surrounded by people who want you to succeed.

French and Tourism was the ideal degree for me, with a return to the country of all those holidays for six months too as part of the course. I've always enjoyed travel, broadening my mind and seeing different cultures.

(Continued)

The French were so authentic at what they did in their bistros, cafes and restaurants. There was a focus on coming together – for mealtimes as well as events – and always with family and friends.

Throughout university, I'd carried on with my part-time job and the business offered a graduate programme. I saw a forward-looking business living up to their promises to roll out amazing guest experiences, with values similar to mine. As a young Trainee Hotel Manager, with my first assignment in Glasgow there were challenges and moments I wondered if it would work out. It was a 105-room site and a new team, a long way from home and my husband had moved with me as a head chef, so we were both in it together.

The ten months up there were the making of me though and Hotel Management has since taken me to Leeds, Leicester, Coventry, Milton Keynes, Essex, North London and Birmingham. Different towns, different cities – but always with incredible people who have hospitality at their heart.

I've been fortunate to build my career quickly and I'm now a Regional Operations Manager with 23 hotels, 350 people, responsible for £25 million revenue. I'm still managing people and still guest-focused, but not necessarily always guest-facing.

My role is to inspire the next generation of leaders and a huge part of this includes motivating my teams to go the extra mile for our guests and create those priceless moments. Simply put, if you can go home every day knowing you have made somebody else's day, you've done a great job. What other job can you do this in?

Figure 20.1   Laura Hinson Yates, Regional Operations Manager, Premier Inn

Events officer

Many visitor attractions hold events to raise their profile and provide additional revenue streams (Connell et al., 2015). McCabe (2008) finds that, as with careers in tourism and hospitality, event career paths are often not well-defined, and it is difficult to outline a clear path as leaving a position is generally a prerequisite for a promotional opportunity. There remains a view that events as a field of study, and indeed as a career, is 'quite young and immature' (Getz, 2002: 12). The sector is worth around £40 billion, and currently employs over 500,000 people. If you are organised, punctual and meticulous, this might be the perfect career move for you.

Careers in events bring great variety. You might be planning a festival one day and a large corporate event the next, and events range from a few people to large complex corporate galas to festivals. Many people no longer have time to plan their own events, so hiring someone to do all the hard work for them makes sense. This kind of work is flexible, with some companies employing their own team of events planners who work on a year-long calendar of events, or they might hire an events planning agency who will employ people to join them. If you are studying events management, you will already have a good idea about what this sector involves. The kinds of duties you would need to undertake include:

- Creating event proposals within deadline for clients including all details such as venue, seating, menu and guest list
- Delegating event planning tasks
- Taking clients on tours of potential venues
- Organising entertainment, including music, performers, and guest speakers
- Ensuring the event stays to budget and produce financial reports
- Managing the actual event and welcoming guests, overseeing the set-up (including venue staff)
- Designing and developing marketing materials
- Anticipating and planning for different scenarios
- Identifying and creating sales opportunities
- Multi-tasking to organise several events at the same time

A recent job advertisement for an Events Graduate is given in the Employer insight below.

EMPLOYER INSIGHT

Events Graduate (or equivalent)

This example advert specifically seeks to attract event graduates (from July 2019)

Company: An international distribution company

Hours: Monday–Friday 9am–5pm. However, you will need to be extremely flexible as it will involve international travel

Benefits: 20 days annual leave + bank holidays, international travel

Reasons to work for this company: You will gain a great insight into the Events industry; the role is varied; you can manage your own projects; the training is brilliant with a 6-month induction; you'll be working with high-end corporate clients and you will have the opportunity to stay in the countries after the event too (using your annual leave). We're teaming up with the Operations Manager to recruit an Events Assistant.

Responsibilities

- Supporting the Events Coordinator and Events Managers in organising events with 150 to up to 5,000 attendees
- Research venues, food suppliers, take client briefs, quotes, update timetables and project deadlines
- Communicate with attendees and answer any queries
- Using MS Excel on a daily basis to calculate costs, percentages etc.

Museum or gallery exhibition officer

A museum officer will be involved in the planning of special and permanent exhibitions, which involves the acquisition of items for loan or purchase, creating schedules for the exhibition, managing events such as the openings and previews, overseeing the marketing including design and wording of catalogues and displays, managing staff and budgets, generating income via fundraising activities, writing plans and reports, liaising with numerous organisations such as schools and charities, and managing visitors to the site (including activities, access and interpretation).

Some museums and galleries are national institutions that employ large teams of staff and are funded by central government, whereas others are smaller and rely largely on volunteers. Although not all roles need a degree, most jobs are secured by people with a minimum of a 2.1 undergraduate degree in subjects such as archaeology, history, fine art, history of art and cultural studies. If you have a tourism or events degree with modules in visitor attraction, this would also be considered but you would need relevant work experience.

Fixed-term contracts of varying lengths are increasingly common in this area so you may have to move to different places as opportunities for permanent, direct employment become fewer. Museum and gallery officers are increasingly providing their services on a freelance or consultancy basis. Jobs are advertised in local authority vacancy lists, newspapers and specialist publications including *Museums Journal* and the *Times Educational Supplement*. You can also find vacancies on the website of the Museums Association, on Museum Jobs, and on the websites of heritage organisations such as the National Trust and English Heritage. Starting salaries for museum/gallery exhibition officers typically range from £19,000 to £25,000, and as you become more senior and gain experience, salaries can rise to between £27,000 and £40,000 (Graduate Prospects, 2020f).

FUTURE JOBS IN TOURISM, EVENTS AND HOSPITALITY

The world is changing and therefore the way that jobs support how people experience the world changes too. Niche areas of tourism, events and hospitality are emerging (see Chapter 35). For example, the latest UNWTO report on Gastronomy Tourism (UNWTO, 2017) stated that food tourism should be placed 'as a horizontal layer of … destination marketing and product development strategies instead of a vertical one'. Also, according to the report, this tourism segment 'offers enormous potential in stimulating local, regional and national economies and enhancing sustainability and inclusion'.

 ═══ INDUSTRY INSIGHT ═══════════════════════

Gastronomic tourism as a future employment opportunity

Food tourism is one of the most popular emerging areas for interesting career choices. The World Travel Association has found that food tourism generates over $150 billion pa. In delivering the unique and exclusive, destinations will need to capitalise on their distinctive character, culture, traditions and landscapes to give them competitive advantage. We are seeing the emergence of digital marketing roles with the growth of new social media channels promoting food; celebrity chefs building gastronomic empires; destinations using food to promote places; technological advances in the interpretation and experience of food (culinary game simulations, virtual kitchens, interactive streaming to smart devices of food being prepared, and live streaming of cooking); molecular food development; and more ethical and sustainable food sources alongside a move to slower food (see Slow Food Movement).

As Everett (2016) finds, people are increasingly willing to travel long distances to try different types of cuisine and beverages, and this requires people to plan, design and deliver such experiences. People are also increasingly willing to pay more, try more and eat more. Food tourism offers destinations an attractive vehicle of new streams of revenue and is being added to the destination marketing portfolio of numerous regions to provide unique selling points and places of specific interest.

For more ideas, see the 'Working in food tourism' sections in Everett, 2016.

Source: https://nexttourismgeneration.eu/future-skills-in-tourism-and-the-importance-of-gastronomy-tourism/

SALARY AND PAY IN THE TOURISM, HOSPITALITY AND EVENTS SECTOR

Graduate salaries vary significantly across the sector. However, some graduate management starting salaries are in the region of £20,000 although this can be higher in specific functions within companies (e.g. finance or HR departments). For example, a trainee manager for Nando's will earn around £20,000–26,000 (TargetJobs, 2019a), and a hotel graduate programme such as the InterContinental Hotel Group starts around £21,000. In the events sector, starting salaries are similar, although companies offering large specialist events can see graduate salaries rise to around £30,000. Obviously as you progress, you can start to attract higher salaries alongside roles that may come with bonuses and commission.

More detailed reports on salary and pay can be found via the Statista reports. A report on the average Travel and Tourism Graduate Salary can be found here: www.grb.uk.com/industries/travel-tourism-graduate-career. The other issue that challenges the sector is the high number of part-time workers in the hotel and restaurant industry, with many part-time staff earning an average of £8.07/hour compared to £10.72 for full-time workers. The sector also suffers from a high turnover of staff and trying to maintain its competitiveness is difficult as similar roles in competitor industries are challenging the travel and tourism market (WTTC, 2015). An example of a company shifting the way it attracts graduates is the cruise company Royal Caribbean.

EMPLOYER INSIGHT

Royal Caribbean plans shift in recruitment

Royal Caribbean Cruises is changing its approach to recruitment in order to attract more talent and grow its graduate pool. It is now offering a six-week internship as part of a university partnership that creates mentoring opportunities and real-life learning projects. It is hoped that these internships in partnership with universities, will help students gain experience and offer new ideas for development of the company. For example, student interns came up with the idea of a fish and chip stall on the ships, so they now offer this. They have also offer 10-week paid internship programmes and look for students who:

(Continued)

- Are currently enrolled in a 4-year Bachelor or Graduate degree programme
- Have a minimum cumulative 3.2 GPA on a 4.0 scale
- Must have authorisation to work in the US on a permanent and ongoing basis
- Have strong analytical skills
- Are self-driven and motivated
- Have exceptional communication skills (both oral and written)
- Emulate pride, passion and commitment for their job and convey excitement and enthusiasm for RCL
- Value teamwork and collaboration
- Have proven leadership ability, either in a student organisation, project, and/or outside the classroom
- Demonstrate a passion for service and commitment to dedicated and continuous improvement

Details from: https://jobs.rclcareers.com/page/internships-college-graduates#intern-intro

In addition, it has introduced flexible working and is looking at ways to change how it engages with its workforce to try and attract new talent and retain people as hours can be long. According to their 'onboarding' (induction) information,

> You can expect to work approximately 70 hours per week, seven days per week [*], or as stated in your Employment Agreement. Occasionally, you may be required to work more than 70 hours per week, or overtime. Overtime pay is provided to eligible employees who work more than 303 hours in a month.

They are always looking for new talent, and their website is: www.royalcareersatsea.com/jobs/search. Also, see employee testimonials: www.royalcareersatsea.com/pages/employee_testimonials.

Note: it is worth nothing that this number of hours would violate the law in several countries if national laws applied to cruise ships (they don't). You should think about annual salaries in relation to how many hours you are expected to work, and how much annual leave you get and other rights.

The deficit talent trend in the sector is a worry. WTTC (2015) suggested that the most acute deficits (demand growth more than 1% point faster than supply growth) will be in the countries of Thailand, Poland, Taiwan, Russia, Peru, Costa Rica, Argentina, Sweden, Singapore, Italy, Turkey and Greece. For many the source of the talent deficit is a result of strong talent demand growth (down to a strong forecast for tourism direct employment) and weak talent supply growth (linked to weak demographics). WTTC suggest that, 'over the long-run to 2024, Travel & Tourism's talent balance projections are considerably more challenging compared to the wider economy' (WTTC, 2015: 29). The industry also is subject to numerous unpredictable challenges, outlined in the final part of this chapter.

THE CHALLENGES FACING THE INDUSTRY AND HOW THEY AFFECT EMPLOYMENT

It is essential that you understand how the industry and sector is affected by unpredictable events and global events such as economic recession, the **COVID-19** global pandemic, Brexit, terrorism, natural disaster and industrial action.

Economic recession

Economic downturns can have a paradoxical impact on employment. For example, during the UK recession, the number of 'staycations' increased as people stopped travelling overseas. In 2013, total tourism revenue went up 12.6% to £40 billion between 2007–2011 against a general economic upturn of 8%, and 120,000 new jobs were created in 2011. Likewise, currency depreciation also makes inbound tourism cheaper, which leads to job creation. For example, in the US, in response to the recession, President Obama launched a new national tourism strategy in 2012, focused on creating jobs and economic growth.

The global financial crisis, according to Puschra and Burke (2012), saw more than 50 million jobs lost, together with a massive loss of wealth and depressed consumer confidence. However, Jucan and Jucan (2013) argue that tourism should be part of a solution to stimulate economic growth. This is supported by Taleb Rifai, the UNWTO Secretary, who argued that, despite economic volatility around the globe, international tourism managed to stay on course: 'Tourism is thus one of the pillars that should be supported by governments around the world as part of the solution to stimulating economic growth.' Of course, recessions hit different markets and different sectors. For example, the business travel industry will be hit when companies spend less. We have seen some major airlines go bankrupt as markets change. However, in response, people will increasingly take more domestic trips and seek more local forms of entertainment.

Turning to events, research tends to suggest that a downturn in the economy can stimulate creativity and innovation and can be a boost for the events industry. In a study of a youth event, Devine and Devine (2012) found economic recession led to some shrinking of public and private sector budgets, so 'outside the box' thinking is needed to turn challenges into opportunities. As an events graduate, if you can devise novel ideas, and consult and collaborate with event stakeholders, this may prove invaluable when the industry is under pressure. In the context of graduate employment in THE, it seems that if you are prepared to travel, there will always be opportunities.

COVID-19 (Coronavirus disease 2019)

One of the most devastating impacts on the economy and THE industries in recent years came in the form of the global pandemic, COVID-19 (Coronavirus 2019). During the final stages of writing this book, we saw countries across the globe implementing restrictive measures in all areas linked to travel, hospitality and events. Many countries (especially in Europe and Asia) locked down cities and placed strict restrictions on bars, hotels and restaurants. Cruise ships were anchored offshore with passengers on board (in quarantine); borders were closed; visas were restricted; aircraft were grounded; and large public events and gatherings were cancelled or postponed, including some of global 'mega' events such as Euro 2020, the London Marathon and the Tokyo 2020 Olympics. UNWTO (2020c) predicted COVID-19 would bring about an economic decline of at least 3%, leading to a loss of US$30–50 billion in spending by international visitors. The greatest impact was on small and medium-sized enterprises, which make up around 80% of the tourism sector. They had to respond quickly and pro-activity to survive. Many THE businesses struggled to pay bills, made staff redundant and some went into liquidation. This pandemic was a once-in-a-generation crisis and it hit the THE industry hard. You may find yourself involved in work that helps the world and the sector to recover. Despite the panic and disruption, there were some enterprising people who diversified and adapted their business, using it as an opportunity to problem solve (see Chapter 19) and engage in entrepreneurial activity (see Chapter 34). Some started delivering food from their restaurants; others launched online cookery lessons; many sold items such as toilet rolls and masks.

 ———— REFLECTION EXERCISE ════════════

Responding to a global pandemic

Research and find examples of positive ways the tourism, hospitality and events industry was able to respond to the COVID-19 global pandemic. What role could you play in the evolving global rebuild of businesses and livelihoods? What else do you think THE businesses could have done to survive and thrive in this kind of unprecedented crisis?

Brexit

When the UK voted to leave the European Union in 2016, it had an immediate impact on the tourism industry. The pound fell against the Euro, which meant the UK became a popular and cheaper place to visit; however, people raised concerns about the impact it would have on mobility and the ease of travel for UK citizens to Europe. Ongoing delays further exacerbated the sense of uncertainty, and thus willingness to invest in new projects, infrastructure and human resources.

An ABTA report reports that UK residents made 37 million holiday and business trips to the EU in 2015, and EU residents made over 16 million similar trips to the UK. **Brexit** will affect employment across the sector. For example, many airline routes are secured through EU negotiated agreements so it is critical to retain or replace these agreements. Fewer routes would negatively impact visitors to the UK and the entire sector. EU residents alone spend £6.4bn in the UK on holidays. ABTA estimated that up to 3,500 workers are posted across the EU working for UK-based travel companies. Around 24% of the tourism and hospitality workforce are EU nationals and many tour operators rely on seasonal workers, so protecting the reciprocal employment rights for EU and UK nationals was a key concern following Brexit.

Based on an International Monetary Fund (IMF) analysis, a no-deal Brexit was predicted to lose more than 700,000 jobs, as there would be a 7.7% decline in economic activity if the UK left with no deal. The World Travel and Tourism Council (WTTC) further suggested that 308,000 UK-based jobs and 399,000 roles in the EU would be at risk. According to a KPMG report based on a survey of British Hospitality Association members, EU citizens make up as much as a quarter of the 3 million workers in hospitality. You might think this could offer jobs for non-EU citizens, but it could also spell economic disaster for the whole industry and the knock-on effect may well disrupt tourism and the creative industries.

Figure 20.2   EU Passports – another queue now for the British?

Terrorism and civil unrest

There is no doubt that terrorism directly impacts tourism. The impact of the September 11 attacks in the USA highlighted the value of tourism to the global economy as tourist numbers fell across the globe. Collier et al. (2003) contend that terrorist incidents have economic consequences as they destroy infrastructure, redirect funding to security, limit trade and reduce consumer confidence. Terrorism also raises the costs of doing business in terms of insurance premiums, costs for security precautions, and larger salaries to employees at risk. Terror can be a major disruption to the travel industry, and the 1980s and early 1990s witnessed mass cancellations and a loss of jobs in the sector. For example, around half of holiday reservations from North America to Europe in 1986 were cancelled following America's bombing of Libya, with travellers fearing reprisal attacks.

More recently, the 2019 bombings in Sri Lanka that killed over 253 people hit an island reliant on tourism. The Sri Lanka Tourism Development Authority says that tourism is the country's third-largest and fastest-growing source of foreign currency in 2018, worth almost $4.4 billion (€3.9 billion), accounting for almost 5% of the country's annual GDP. More than 800,000 jobs (around 10% of total employment in the country) depend on the sector, both directly and indirectly. Similarly, terrorist attacks in Tunisia (2015) and Egypt (2013) led to sharp declines in the numbers of European tourists visiting those countries in the short term. International tourists arriving in Tunisia dropped from 6 million to just over 5.4 million following the attack, but this figure recovered to 5.7 million in 2016 and 6.7 million in 2017. Turkey attracted more than 40 million visitors a year in 2014 before it fell below 25 million in 2017 after a spate of terror attacks and a perpetual state of emergency.

In Kenya, between 2011 and 2017, there were around 60 attacks each year and tourist numbers fell. Kenya's vision 2030 aimed to increase tourism arrivals from 1.7 million in 2012 to 3 million visitors by

2017, but only reached 1.45 million in 2017. Tourism provides huge employment and foreign exchange earnings, about 9.7% of the country's GDP and 9% of total employment in the same year (WTTC). In 2010, over 14 million people visited Egypt, but that number has dropped significantly in recent years. However, despite terror attacks in London, 2017 saw 30.2 million overseas visitors in the first nine months, up 7% compared to 2016. In Bali after the bombing in 2002, the Indonesian minister of culture and tourism asked people to visit Bali, saying 'it makes no sense to isolate them [i.e. the people of Bali]'. There is evidence that tourism decreases in the short term, but soon bounces back, as was seen after terrorist attacks in France and Tunisia.

Statista (2018) found that terrorist attacks put off around 5% of holiday makers in the EU, and some countries, such as Egypt and Turkey were particularly avoided. Following political unrest, Egypt saw an average annual decline in UK visitor numbers of 18.5% from 2010 to 2014, according to the Office for National Statistics.

During the Hong Kong protests in 2019, the occupation of the main airport (one of the world's busiest aviation hubs) severely disrupted tourism. Concerns rose across Southeast Asian countries as the airport is key to their economies and employment: over 75 million passengers used it in 2018.

Industrial action

The irony of industrial action is that it is usually trying to save jobs, and usually improve pay and conditions. However, disruption to the travel market can see companies collapse. For example, when British Airways pilots threatened to strike in August 2019, it would have hit holiday-makers hard and the share-price. Likewise, in France, frequent industrial action has meant the tourism industry has become unpredictable. In 2016, Japanese tourists dropped 56%, Italians 24%, and Russians 35%. Chinese visitors decreased 13.9%, versus a 49% increase in 2015. Inevitably, tourism and hospitality were impacted. Frédéric Valletoux, the CRT's president, said that the sector employs 500,000 people in the Paris region and strikes put jobs at risk.

A 2016 PWC report on air traffic management (ATM) services found about 15,000 air traffic control officers across the EU. In 2015, the Airports Council International estimated the economic impact of aviation-related activities at €338 billion across the EU. The aviation sector supports 5.5 million jobs and yet ATM is reliant on a relatively small group of highly skilled peoples. Between 2010 and 2015, there were 95 ATC strikes across ten EU countries (equating to 176 days of strike activity). Such industrial action inevitably has a disruptive impact on air traffic and travel, particularly during longer strikes that may prevent travellers reaching their destinations as scheduled and leaves planes in the wrong countries.

Natural disasters

Natural disasters tend to hit hardest the poorest countries and those most reliant on tourism. The WTTC (2015) has found that destinations can recover from terrorist attacks quicker than they would an environmental disaster. Following disasters, there is always a push to encourage people to keep visiting, although such disasters will often lead to infrastructural damage and it can take time to rebuild to attract tourists and events. For example, Thailand launched a campaign after the 2004 Boxing Day tsunami, encouraging tourists to 'stop fearing ghosts'. However, it is a sensitive market and local people found it difficult when the tourism infrastructure was not in place quickly to restore the previously thriving tourism industry and the income it generated (see Figure 20.3).

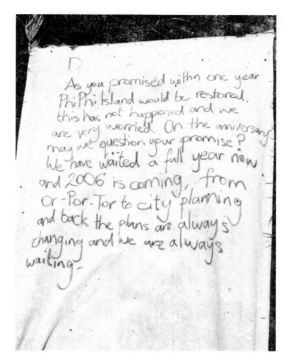

Figure 20.3   Local concern expressed on Phi Phi Island, Thailand. Photo courtesy of Faye Taylor

Similarly, the 2001 earthquake in Fukushima, Japan triggered a nuclear disaster, followed by tourists not returning for several years. In 2018 in Hong Kong and China, typhoon Mangkhut disrupted aviation, tourism, and transportation which led to almost 1,000 flights being cancelled or delayed. In 2009, natural disasters cost insurers about USD 110 billion, while in 2010, the cost was doubled at USD 218 billion. Some negative employment impacts include losses in sales and profits, inability to operate due to infrastructure failure, breaks in forward-linked or backward-linked production to businesses caused by changes in demand. There will inevitably be income losses if companies close and 'employees of the firms experiencing reduced production and sales suffer income losses and subsequently curtail their own expenditures, initiating a new round of firm cutbacks' (National Research Council, 1999: 37). However, employment can also lead to flows outside the damaged area with gains to be made where there are commodities inflated in price by disaster-induced shortages. The National Research Council (1999: 38) claims that 'Positive economic stimuli of jobs and production [is] generated from cleaning up and rebuilding and the multiplier effect of those increases'.

CONCLUSION

In this chapter we have covered:

- The competitive nature of the graduate market and that you will often be competing with non-graduates for many high-level opportunities so ensure you get the skills you need. Many companies will have graduate schemes but be open to finding employers that do not have specific schemes as some only employ graduates as the need and relevant positions arise – this might require speculative applications.

- The variety of graduate roles, from tour operator to cabin crew, events officer, hotel manager and visitor attraction officer and you should research them carefully.
- How the sector is significantly affected by global issues such as economic recession, civil unrest, terrorism, natural disaster and industrial action. As a graduate, you also need to think about how post-disaster communities and the tourism industry can work with each other.

FURTHER READING

Cheung, C., Law, R. and He, K. (2010) 'Essential hotel managerial competencies for graduate students', *Journal of Hospitality & Tourism Education*, 22(4): 25–32.

Devine, A. and Devine, F. (2012) 'The challenge and opportunities for an event organiser during an economic recession', *International Journal of Event and Festival Management*, 3(2): 122–136.

Useful web resources

British Institute of Innkeeping – www.bii.org

Graduate Recruitment Bureau (2019) – www.grb.uk.com/industries/travel-tourism-graduate-career

Institute of Hospitality – www.instituteofhospitality.org

Institute of Travel and Tourism – www.itt.co.uk

WTTC (2019) *Economic Impact Reports* – https://wttc.org/Research/Economic-Impact

21 WORK PLACEMENTS AND INTERNSHIPS

CHAPTER LEARNING OBJECTIVES

By the end of this chapter you should be able to:

- Understand the value and benefits of internships.
- Identify and apply for internship opportunities.
- Know how to select the right internship for you.
- Seek advice from previous interns.

GLOSSARY

- **Internship**: short-term practical work experience as part of your degree, with a focus on gaining experience through training and development.
- **Small and medium-sized enterprises (SMEs):** businesses that employ a small number of employees (usually fewer than 50). They are often non-subsidiary, independent firms.

INTRODUCTION

As growing global industries, the tourism, hospitality and events sectors need highly trained individuals to fill a breadth of new positions. These sectors are reliant on those with soft skills such as communication, problem-solving and negotiation. Unfortunately, it has been noted that a fifth of graduates are leaving university unready for the workplace as they lack these critical skills (Baska, 2019). How you can build these skills to become more employable and fill one of these positions in the future? The answer may lie in a work placement or internship. This chapter will help you think about how you might research and secure this kind of work experience, and how you can make the most of it.

Work placements and internships represent a bridge between academic learning and professional work. As opportunities for experiential learning, they enable you to apply academic knowledge and understanding in a real-world professional setting. Universities are increasingly embedding work placements into their courses, recognising their contribution to graduate employability as well as academic achievement and personal development. It is recognised that the longer the placement the better, so whilst summer internships no doubt add value, a year in industry as part of your degree will likely foster greater opportunities and career prospects overall (Smith, 2019b).

WORK PLACEMENT OR INTERNSHIP: WHAT'S THE DIFFERENCE?

Globally, the terms 'work placement' and 'internship' are used interchangeably to denote 'short-term practical work experience in which students receive training and gain experience in a specific field or career area of their interest' (Zopiatis, 2007: 65). In the UK the terms are different but relate to similar practices: work placements take place as part of your university degree, also commonly known as a sandwich year, year in industry or professional practice year, lasting between 30 and 52 weeks dependent on the HE provider. Internships are short-term work experiences that take place outside your university course, usually over the summer or post-graduation, typically lasting between a week and a year.

The main difference here is the level of university involvement. As part of a degree, an internship is a three-way relationship between university, employer and student (Seyitoglu and Yirik, 2015; Yiu and Law, 2012). If you choose to take an internship outside your degree, university resources may be helpful but there would be no direct responsibility for the university to advise or support you. Table 21.1 lists the fundamental differences between internships as part of your degree programme and those taken outside of term time. Given the global audience of this book and that most research adopts a holistic view of internship, this chapter will use the term **internships** rather than placements, distinguishing where necessary between internships taking place in or outside a degree.

Table 21.1   The differences between internships in and outside your degree

Internship within degree	Internship outside your degree
Taken during your third year as part of a four year sandwich course; during term-time if not a sandwich course	Usually over summer or in the year post-graduation
Typically lasts between 30 and 52 weeks	Opportunities available that last between a week and a year
University guidance, support before, during and after internship	May use university resources to find placement but university not responsible for internship

Internship within degree	Internship outside your degree
Student assigned a tutor by university	No tutor support provided
May be assessed and awarded academic credit for the placement	No academic credit awarded
Placements can be paid or unpaid (apply for paid internships where possible, although these can be more competitive)	In the UK most interns are classed as workers and therefore entitled to receive the minimum wage. Unpaid and paid internships are available globally so it is important to check local payment practice and apply for paid internships only (volunteering is different and dealt with in Chapter 24)
Three-pronged stakeholder relationship: university, employer and student	Self-managed relationship between you and employer

THE VALUE OF INTERNSHIPS

Recruiters often find that graduates struggle with the disparity between university and the workplace. Gordon (2018) found a skills gap in graduates, particularly in soft skills such as the ability to work with a boss, dealing with conflict, negotiation, commercial awareness and resilience. With the number of internships on the rise (High Fliers, 2019), organisations have begun to address these short-comings in their internship programmes. The same survey found just 5% of graduates possessed the skill of 'managing up' and knew how to work with a boss (Gordon, 2018). These types of soft skills are difficult to teach in a classroom and are more likely to be learned in the workplace. Recent research has noted that graduates with internship experience are more likely to have the skills required by recruiters (ISE, 2018). Whether you undertake an internship as part of your course or on your own initiative, the benefits are wide-reaching (see Table 21.2).

Table 21.2   The benefits of an internship

- Practise and acquire skills required in the workplace; particularly soft skills and administrative concepts difficult to teach in a classroom setting
- Provides valuable work experience often desired by employers, making you more employable
- Adds to your CV and helps you stand out (see Chapter 26 Personal branding)
- Allows you to acclimatise to and experience 'real work' in a 'test setting'
- Gives you experience of workplace culture: how people are managed, the rules, regulations and workplace norms within which employees must function
- Space to identify your career options and hone your career trajectory
- Allows you to create a personal development plan
- Builds a network of contacts
- Provides future career opportunities: many interns are kept on as permanent employees
- Increased maturity and confidence
- Minimises the culture shock between university and workplace

Sources: Baska, 2019; Mei, 2019; Neugebauer and Evans-Brain, 2009; Ngia and Duyen, 2018; Smith, 2019a; Seyitoglu and Yirik, 2015; Zopiatis and Constanti, 2012

Student benefits

Students are not only able to apply theory learned in the classroom and enhance technical skills but also learn to work with multitudes of people, personality types, and deal with issues on the 'human' side of the business (Jack et al., 2017: 18)

Firstly, and perhaps most crucially, you should view an internship as an investment in your future. Some of the rewards may not be immediate (for example, you will graduate later than some of your peers). Internships offer valuable opportunities for learning skills that cannot be learnt in the classroom (Mei, 2019). You will be able to practise current skills as well as acquire new ones. You will be able to develop an evidence base crucial for STAR examples (see Chapter 31) and put your theoretical knowledge into practice. It will give you first-hand knowledge of the industry and what it takes to run an organisation day-to-day. Organisations hosting internship programmes often offer additional training and workshops to develop soft skills. There may be opportunities for you to travel and attend events and you will often be interacting with senior management. These types of opportunities are rarely matched in a permanent job role.

Internships are also a test environment; a 'safe' space for you to try out a role without committing to it as a permanent career move. It allows you to acclimatise to a work setting in a more structured programme with a mentor, rather than being left to fend for yourself. A placement allows you time to reflect on career aspirations and learn about organisational culture. You will gain experience of managing potentially difficult relationships, negotiating office politics and working as part of a team. As workplaces celebrate diversity, you will often function as part of a multi-cultural team and therefore gain experience in managing diverse cultural sensitivities and communication. Finally, internships demonstrate your commitment to the industry and your chosen sector, which will be valuable in future applications and interviews.

Significant value lies in self-development. Students that undertake an internship often become more self-confident and generate a sense of self-awareness. This is crucial to personal development.

 STUDENT INSIGHT

Why I chose to do an internship

Here are some reflections from a few students on their choice to undertake an internship:

> … because I wanted to experience my field of study in a professional environment, so that I would have a better idea what is coming once I am finished with my degree. I also wanted to meet new people in the industry that might offer me new opportunities. (Vilius, UK student)

> I wanted to do something more than learning theoretical concepts at university. I wanted to be able to put them into practice. I hoped it would give me valuable work experience for my future career as well as improve my understanding of the industry. (Millie, USA student)

> Even though it meant delaying graduation by a placement year, I do not regret it at all. You are 'thrown' into a company, where you learn to develop yourself, your skills and put all your academic knowledge into practice. It helped to demystify some concepts I learned throughout university and provide a whole new real world perspective to my understanding. (Daniela, UK student)

> … to enhance experience after my graduation. Since university started, I worked many part-time jobs but that wasn't enough for me. I wanted to feel the experience to work a full-time job and focus mainly on the tasks given without thinking of university or assessments or exams. In addition, I knew I was going to write a dissertation so I hoped that the placement year would help me find a topic. (Iona, UK student)

Employer benefits of an internship

The main purpose of an internship is to provide a graduate with experience in the workplace. It should reduce the gap between academic learning and practical real-world, professional experience. Internships develop tacit knowledge that is difficult to teach in a classroom, better achieved through experience and reflecting theoretical knowledge in real-world settings (Phelan et al., 2013). Essentially, the aim is to generate more employable graduates; to demonstrate they have both the ability and skills to thrive in a work-based setting. It is therefore an opportunity for employers to embrace and foster new talent, imparting work-related skills and knowledge to graduates so that industry is better prepared to grow in the future.

Interns can contribute to workplace diversity and change the dynamics of existing teams. They may bring new ideas and innovative solutions to the organisation. There will be opportunities to interact and develop a strategic alliance with students on an internship as part of their degree (Busby and Gibson, 2010), giving employers a gateway to future talent and the availability of a skilled workforce (Zopiatis and Constanti, 2012).

Higher Education provider benefits

The role of a university is not only to support and teach students to achieve a degree – it is to develop employable graduates, equipped and confident to move into the workplace. Within the THE sectors, there is global recognition of a skills gap in university graduates: they are not equipped with the necessary skills to embark on a career in these dynamic industries (Baska, 2019; Bello et al., 2019; Jack et al., 2017; Mei, 2019; Mohanty and Mohanty, 2019). In response, many THE courses now build internship opportunities into their structure to ensure students gain exposure to the workplace in a more structured and nurturing environment and to build skills that are easier to acquire and hone outside the classroom.

For UK-based students, several universities offer such internships. For example, Bournemouth University have made a placement year a compulsory element of their degree. Similarly, at Ulster University, students must either choose to complete an internship or a year abroad as part of their degree. Numerous other UK universities support and encourage students in opting to undertake a placement or internship year at the time of writing: Leeds Beckett University, Manchester Metropolitan University, University of Central Lancashire (UCLAN), University of Greenwich, University of Lincoln, University of Northampton, University of Plymouth and University of Sunderland. Internationally, courses at Vietnam National University, Taylors University in Malaysia and Michigan State University USA are a small proportion of those offered with internship opportunities.

CHOOSING THE RIGHT INTERNSHIP FOR YOU

There are several considerations when deciding on which organisations and roles to apply for. Try not to be too narrow in your thinking, as places are competitive. Make sure you are realistic about your expectations, particularly relating to salary: remember this is an investment! Make sure you undertake significant research as all applications will require you to show what makes you suitable for the role and apply early (see Chapter 30). You should be looking to apply for positions 14–18 months before your internship starts. For internships outside a degree course, applications should still be around 9–12 months of when you want to undertake the role.

Practicalities

Type of organisation

It is important that you consider the type of organisation you want to work for. Are you going to choose a large organisation or a **small or medium-sized enterprise (SME)**? A large organisation may have 'headline' opportunities with greater scope for trying out varied roles and with vast amounts of previous experience. However, there is often significant competition for these roles and perhaps less opportunity to make a difference when within the role. In an SME, you may form part of a small team that may give you greater responsibility and opportunity for autonomous projects. Remember that SMEs make up the majority of the tourism, hospitality and events sectors but may not always advertise opportunities widely. Refer to Chapter 30 for advice on making speculative applications.

Type of work

In conjunction with reflecting on the type of organisation you will apply to, you should think about the roles you would like to do. Chapter 20 offers suggestions of some of the roles available in tourism, hospitality and events sectors which you could use as a starting point.

Location

Where are you looking for internships? There are international opportunities that offer placements abroad: a great chance to experience a diverse culture, live in a different country and meet new people. The USA, for example, offers a J-1 Visa scheme under the Exchange Visitor Programme for students undertaking an internship on US soil. To apply for a visa you must register and be sponsored by an approved organisation (access the Exchange Visitor Program website at https://travel.state.gov/content/travel/en/us-visas/study/exchange.html for the complete list).

You may also find that larger organisations such as IHG (InterContinental Hotels Group) offer international opportunities. They also have Frontier Programmes – opportunities for students in China to take part in a cross-regional internship programme in hotels across Asia Pacific. GoAbroad.com offers a few intern programmes from as short as a week and this is a great place to start searching but remember these intermediaries may charge fees. It is important to look at what is included in the fee and where the fee is going! Most of these programmes offer additional support and training/development opportunities as well as organising the placement, but it is important that you know what you are paying for.

If you are considering an internship abroad, it is important that you are realistic; opportunities may sound fancy, but you need to be honest with yourself and the practicalities involved. It is important to consider pay in the country, which may differ from what you are used to elsewhere. The cost of visas and travel to and from the destinations would need to be covered and some international organisations charge a 'finders' fee or a package fee to cover certain costs of organisation. Safety and security are also relevant, so make sure you are aware of any country-specific risks and check national advice for travellers to these regions.

 THINK POINT

Many large organisations offer internships in city locations which may require you to move. How realistic is this for you? Are you able to leave your current accommodation? Do you have dependents that might make this impossible? What are the things that you need to consider?

Finance

Make sure you are aware of how much your internship will pay. Remember you will need to pay for your accommodation, food, bills and living costs out of this. You will need to budget for clothing suitable for the role and travel costs. You will often still be liable for university fees (albeit at a discounted rate) and may only be entitled to a reduced proportion of your student loan.

Your income will be subject to tax and social security in whichever country you are working in. British students working abroad must contact HMRC with organisation information in order to be eligible for any tax reimbursements. Overseas interns should also consider the cost of healthcare as this may not be covered by your country of origin or your usual healthcare provider.

Where to find opportunities

There are many resources you can draw upon to find the right internship for you. You must remember that places are highly competitive, and you will most likely need to make a few applications before you are successful. Of course, you need to be happy with the decision you make, but being too fussy may put you at a disadvantage.

University resources

Your first port of call for any internship, but particularly course-related internships, should be your university's careers department. They will have a host of connections and a wealth of experience in how, when and where to apply for these types of opportunities. They may also be able to provide advice and support to navigate the numerous online opportunities and separate those that look too good to be true from those that might actually be! Your tutors and particularly your placement year tutor or module leader will also be able to speak from experience and give you advice. Take advantage of any careers fairs your university holds to build contacts and ask about internship opportunities: often smaller, local companies will attend these fairs so it can be a great way of finding out about opportunities that may not be widely advertised. It is important that your university approves or at least sees the terms of your internship to make sure the placement falls in line with legalities and standards.

Websites

There are many intermediary websites that offer various placement opportunities. It is important to do your research when using certain sites, particularly those requesting a fee. Of course, you can also go to organisations directly. Accor, Fairmont Hotels, Four Seasons, Hilton Hotels, IHG and TUI are just a few of the many large organisations to offer internship programmes.

Table 21.3   A selection of intermediary websites listing internship vacancies

Places to find an internship vacancy
Prospects also have a list of websites for internships abroad: www.prospects.ac.uk/jobs-and-work-experience/work-experience-and-internships/internships.
BSG Hospitality Interns: http://bsginterns.com/
Caterer: www.caterer.com/jobs/internship

(Continued)

Table 21.3 (Continued)

Places to find an internship vacancy

e4s (employment 4 students): www.e4s.co.uk/
Glassdoor: www.glassdoor.co.uk/Job/event-planning-intern-jobs-SRCH_KO0,21.htm
Global Experiences: www.globalexperiences.com/students/internships-abroad/event-planning-internships
Go Overseas: www.gooverseas.com/
Hosco: www.hosco.com
Prospects: www.prospects.ac.uk/jobs-and-work-experience/work-experience-and-internships/work-placements
Rate My Placement: www.ratemyplacement.co.uk/hospitality-leisure-travel-tourism
Targetjobs: https://targetjobs.co.uk/internships

Networks and contacts

Chapter 27 discusses networking in detail and your networks and current contacts are a good place to start when considering an internship. Hopefully you will have built up your LinkedIn network and begun following some organisations. Remember that opportunities are often posted online particularly on social media (see Chapter 25). Even if you do not have a personal contact, you can use networks and social media to follow particular organisations: use Chapter 30 to develop and send speculative applications to those you have an interest in working for.

Beyond virtual contacts, you may also have contacts from previous/current work experience. Previous interns themselves are also a rich source of information: they will already have experience of the application process as well as their own placement.

 STUDENT INSIGHT

How I found my placement

I was introduced to this placement through a representative of BSG Interns who came to my university and offered opportunities for internships. The whole enrolment process was fast and easy, I had a couple of Skype interviews, followed by the guided documentation processes. (Vilius, British student interning in the USA)

I found my placement through the website HOSCO who have a global network of employers through which to apply for placements. (Manpreet, Indian student interning in the USA)

I found out about my placement from the career manager at my university. They advised me to send out my CV and a cover letter to country club HR team. I was then invited for a Skype interview; after 2 hours they sent me the job offer! (Aleksandra, British UK student interning in the USA)

I found my placement at an award-winning event management- and venue-sourcing agency through my own research. I made a speculative application via email and ended up getting an interview. Prior to this application I had made numerous others which were unsuccessful. Fortunately, this did not deter me as this placement was fantastic and ended up being the best decision I have made. (Daniela, British student interning in the UK)

I walked into the hotel with my CV and gave it to the receptionist. Two weeks later the assistant manager called me to arrange an interview. Two days later I was sitting on a chair face-to-face with my future job.

One of the questions was the most common one: 'Why do you want to work for this company?' I told her information about the company that she didn't even know. It's good to be prepared with basic and beyond information about the company you want to work for. Then, she gave me time to complete 4–5 handwritten pages about myself and my future; the next day she offered me the job. (Iona, British student interning in the UK).

Internship positions

Positions are wide-ranging and often extend beyond front-of-house opportunities, but for any position it is crucial to do your research to demonstrate your passion (see Chapter 30), map your skills (Chapters in Section B) and show an understanding of what is required for roles (Chapters 20 and 30). The application and interview process will most likely be similar to that for a graduate position; be prepared with your current CV (see Chapter 29), write an engaging and tailored cover letter (see Chapter 30), practise your interview skills (see Chapter 31) and assessment centre techniques (see Chapter 33). The good news with such a rigorous process at this stage is that you have had valuable experience of work-based interviews, and your organisation is in a strong position to be able to hire you post-internship should they choose to do so.

A few employer insights are provided below. Details are taken from their websites (correct at the time of writing). These four examples demonstrate the kind of internships that are available to students interested in tourism, hospitality and events. Think about which ones that you might like to do, and why.

━━━━━━━━━━━ **EMPLOYER INSIGHT** ━━━━━━━━━━━

Four Seasons, Internship, USA

Areas of internship	**Operations** – Food and Beverage, Rooms **Non-operations** – Human Resources, Finance, Catering, Sales and Marketing **Specialised** – Culinary, Spa, Golf
Preferred qualifications	Major in Business or Hospitality (preferred) GPA of 3.0 (or equivalent) or higher Second-year university student or higher (Sophomore)
How to apply	Internship opportunities vary by hotel/property and so applicants should contact the specific hotel/property of interest directly. Contact information can be found on the website. Initial contact should be made via telephone for most up-to-date information on current openings.
Duration	3, 6 or 12 months
Timeline	Internships are available at various times throughout the year, depending on the location. Contact should be made direct to the property of interest.
Eligibility	Applicants must possess work authorisation for location(s) applied to. A strong proficiency in spoken and written English is essential.

Source: http://jobs.fourseasons.com/home/students/internships/

EMPLOYER INSIGHT

Hilton Hotels, Restaurant Development Placement, UK

With a salary of £18,000–£19,999 Hilton Hotels recently advertised the following placement (10 months+) for those looking to gain experience in a globally renowned hospitality company.

A bit about the team

The Restaurant Development team are responsible for driving the development of high-quality food & beverage concepts for Hilton's Luxury, Lifestyle, Full Service and Focus Service Brands. This includes every-thing from the look and feel of the restaurant, the identity of the restaurant, to the food that ends up on the plates. As an intern, you will support on a variety of projects and will gain great exposure and insight to a career within Food and Beverage Concept Development and Branding on an international scale.

A bit about the job

As an intern, you will be an integral part of the team and will play an active role in our continued success. Some of the more specific responsibilities you will be taking on are detailed as follows:

- Carrying out extensive desktop market research on food and beverage trends, analysing and reporting your findings and sharing these with the wider team
- Supporting the development of concept briefs, presentations and prototypes
- Tracking pipeline for future projects and statuses of existing projects
- You will be instrumental in the day-to-day organising of the team which will include providing general administrative support, attending meetings and communicating with a range of internal stakeholders, both in the UK and internationally.

What are we looking for?

As with any job, we do have certain criteria that you will need to meet in order to be considered for this amazing opportunity. These are detailed as follows:

- Must be in your second or final year of undergraduate study at the point of application
- Must be able to start in June 2020 and available for the full 12 months.
- Must be eligible to work in the UK. If you are a non-EU national then you will need to be studying at a UK university in order to be eligible to undertake a placement here.
- The ideal candidate will have a passion for food and dining out and will be able to input sugges-tions that will help us to deliver exceptional dining culture internationally.
- Some hospitality industry experience is preferred although not essential. Knowledge of restaurant concepts, restaurant design, food and beverage trends and menu planning would also be great.

Source: www.ratemyplacement.co.uk/jobs/18984/hilton/restaurant-development-placement

EMPLOYER INSIGHT

TUI, Digital Sales and Merchandising Placement, UK

With a salary of £16,000–£17,999, TUI recently advertised the following opportunity: a minimum 10-month placement for those seeking experience in a leading tourism business.

What you'll be doing

During your Digital Sales and Merchandising placement, you'll be creating, implementing and managing a range of on-site merchandising campaigns, working alongside the rest of the team to maintain website promotions and special offers to drive conversion through to the TUI UK & Ireland websites. You'll also be liaising with our Commercial, Tourist Board and Design teams to ensure effective on-site marketing support for Tourist Boards. You'll work with a wide range of teams across the whole business, giving you a broad and in-depth understanding of the whole company. You'll build a close relationship with the Design team to produce innovative and engaging content which balances the needs of the business with that of the customer, and you'll be responsible for aligning customer communications across multiple channels, coordinating messaging and promotions alongside teams such as Social Media, Online Marketing, CRM and User Experience.

A key part of your placement will also be balancing customer needs with the broader TUI UK & Ireland goals. You'll be monitoring and reviewing online sales performance, as well as identifying merchandising opportunities to hit targets. Understanding customer needs and wants will also give you the opportunity to suggest changes to the customer journey and experience, while contributing to the execution of the Digital Marketing Strategy. You'll also carry out regular competitor analysis to track activity within the rest of the industry.

What we're looking for

Our placements are suitable for those who are on a sandwich degree course, looking for a 12-month placement to commence in August 2020, and due to graduate by September 2022, as you'll complete the industrial placement in your penultimate year of university. You'll be on track for a 2:1 or above in any subject and have a minimum of 120 UCAS points under the 2017 tariff system (extenuating circumstances will be considered on a case-by-case basis).

We're looking for agile-minded, innovative thinkers, who are keen to learn and take on new challenges. Those who have a flair for collaborating with others, a natural drive for results, and are able to think strategically about the business. Adaptable individuals with a talent for thinking analytically, and a focus on providing unrivalled service to our customers. You'll also have a passion for digital, marketing and merchandising, as well an interest in the travel industry.

Source: https://www.ratemyplacement.co.uk/jobs/18896/tui-uk/digital-sales-and-merchandising-placement

---

==================== EMPLOYER INSIGHT ====================

Porsche, Motorsports Events Placement, UK

With a salary of £16,000–£17,999, Porsche recently advertised the following placement. An opportunity for a student to be responsible for elements of the Porsche Carrera Cup GB (PCCGB) Hospitality Programme delivery within the Porsche Motorsport Department, working with internal teams to assist in the management and delivery of Motorsport events.

Core Specific Responsibilities

- To implement and deliver the Porsche Centre Motorsport Hospitality Programme
- Collate hospitality package in conjunction with PCMS – tickets, info packs, guest lanyards
- Ensure Porsche Centre Hospitality bookings are invoiced correctly

(Continued)

- Arrange payment links for the hospitality packages via internal invoicing structures
- Co-ordinate hospitality allocation to relevant Porsche Centres around the UK and ensure all guests are assigned a BP number
- Deliver the event and host guests at the Circuit
- Collate 'Goody Bags' for all Motorsport events
- Event interdepartmental liaison
- Manage all hotel bookings for Porsche Carrera Cup GB staff and create a 'Rooming List' for each event
- Deliver a 'Paddock Tour' to groups of Centre Guests at each event
- Create and arrange production of timetables for Centre Guests at each event
- Oversee the allocation, distribution, return and disposal of PCCGB 'Team Kit'
- Ensure the Motorsport stock room is well organised and stock levels are recorded
- Assisting in production of working documents for each event, distribution throughout the team ensuring accuracy and understanding from each party
- Key point of contact for clients prior, during and post the events
- Liaison with external suppliers with joint event responsibility
- Resource planning
- Input to PCGB systems, manage all Motorsport finances (raising Invoices, purchase orders, etc.)
- Liaison with PCGB departments

Requirements for the Job and Person Specification: Due to the nature of the role, candidates must be 21 years old+ on start date and a full clean driving license held for a minimum of 2 years is essential.

Required Qualifications: Events Management or Motorsport related degree is desirable.

Required IT-skills: Microsoft Word, Excel and PowerPoint.

Required specialised knowledge: Customer Service experience, attention to detail and organisation skills are essential.

Required language knowledge: Highly competent in spoken and written English.

Other requirements: An interest in Motorsport or Sporting Competition is desirable.

Source: www.ratemyplacement.co.uk/jobs/19391/porsche/motorsport-events-placement

---

Making the most of your internship

After such a lengthy process and wait for your internship, it is crucial that you make the most of the opportunity. Skills and personal development will not happen by accident or via osmosis! According to Zopiatis and Constanti (2012), to make the most of experiential learning opportunities you should undertake the following processes:

- Engage
- Reflect and review
- Assimilate
- Plan and develop

Engaging with your internship

Engaging with the process means you are present: that you are taking ownership of your own learning, embracing opportunities when they are offered and making sure you use your own initiative where possible. Perhaps the most crucial part of engagement is attitude: positivity and friendliness in the workplace. You are more likely to be offered additional responsibility, opportunities and mentoring if you maintain a can-do attitude, which is also fundamental to networking. If you are feeling despondent, you need to learn how to discuss this maturely rather than develop a negative attitude. It is important to remember you are representing your university, your tutor and ultimately yourself: you are your personal brand (see Chapter 26).

Your behaviour is crucial to the success of your internship and creating a lasting impression. It is also important that you understand company policy: wearing the right attire, adhering to the correct start and finish times, making sure you know when your breaks are and how long you are entitled to take. Make sure you follow company policy: this includes use of IT and social media at work and personal mobile use. Everyone in the workplace has the right to fair treatment regardless of gender, age, sexual orientation, disability, ethnicity or religion. In the UK, discrimination on the basis of any of these things is against the law under the UK Equality Act (2010). If you are working internationally, consider workplace regulations before you apply.

Engagement also means taking advantage of all opportunities, regardless of the task. Make notes where possible (you can use voice notes if this is easier), listen actively in meetings and take time to absorb the organisational culture.

REFLECTION EXERCISE

Making notes in meetings

Meetings are a valuable asset to an intern's learning process. They represent opportunities to learn about the organisation, the workplace culture, employee relations and communication. When you are in a meeting, you may wish to reflect upon the following:

- How do people communicate?
- Is there evidence of an employee hierarchy?
- How long was the meeting and what was the subject?
- What types of points were made in the meeting?
- Did you feel the meeting was effective – why/why not?
- What was the outcome of the meeting?

Reflection on the internship process

Reflection is a significant part of the internship process (you can use Chapter 10 to guide this process). It is a great idea to keep a reflective diary throughout the placement (see below), as you can then draw on this data for future assessments and job interviews (also, if you are taking an internship as part of your course you may be asked to produce a reflective piece of work). You may also have the opportunity to shadow another employee, which is another great way to observe diverse job roles.

ACTIVITY

Keeping a reflective diary

Your diary can be handwritten, digital or online. As well as a general overview each day, try also to complete the table below, adapting the format to suit your own needs.

(Continued)

Table 21.4 Task and skills audit

Day	Task/project	Time spent on task	Experience of task – whom did you work with, how did you feel, what was the outcome?	Skills used/developed during task

Note down any other important information or thoughts, particularly relating to potential career options, dissertation topics or the industry as a whole. Think about using this data a year later, when you are unlikely to remember all the details.

The art of reflection should culminate in a review, making observations about your reflections and how you might develop, improve or adapt in the future. It is important to make full use of feedback; to listen to what colleagues say about you; find out how your managers view your performance; and where they feel you could develop. It is your responsibility to find out who your line manager is (if you are not told) and find out how your performance will be assessed. Interns are usually reviewed in line with usual company policy, three, six and nine months after joining a company. Taking ownership of your own learning means developing your own personal goals and using these as objectives for future improvements. Reviews are a useful means of gaining employer feedback and setting out a development plan for your own career goals based on their experience and knowledge. Figure 21.1 gives you some points to consider for an internship-based assessment.

You may be expected to deliver a reflective piece or a task-based assessment depending on your course. Many institutions require interns to produce a reflective report or presentation based on their experience: what they have learned, how they feel they have developed and how they have planned for the future. Points to consider include:

- Why did you choose this placement?
- What were your expectations of your placement?
- How did the reality of the placement meet or fall short of your expectations?
- What have you learned about the industry?
- What would you consider to be your main success?
- Did you have any major challenges? How did you overcome these?
- How did you feel on your first day compared to your last day?
- What skills did you use throughout your internship?
- What skills do you think you developed? What evidence do you have of this?
- How do you feel your course prepared you for your placement?

Remember a reflective report should address the 'why' and 'how' of your thoughts and feelings; do not fall into the trap of being overly descriptive (see Chapter 10 for advice on reflective thinking).

Figure 21.1 Assessment as an outcome of an internship taken as part of a degree

Assimilate the theoretical with the practical

The process of assimilation includes the combination of your theoretical knowledge with your practical experience. Think about the lessons you have learnt as a student and try to apply them to real-life situations. Take stock of what you learn: make notes and take all opportunities as a learning experience. However menial the task, the outcomes could be a new skill or a great example to use in the future. Theories are not always apparent in any given situation so it is important you assimilate knowledge after events. You should be given introductory and mandatory training when you arrive on placement, which may include health and safety, fire safety, diversity and GDPR training. These courses represent an opportunity to demonstrate experience and knowledge of the industry and workplace requirements. Take all training seriously as it is as much about your own protection as the organisation itself.

Plan and develop

Your internship should help you to plan for your future and manage your self-development. Your reflections should include analysis of the skills you have used and those you have seen in others, but have yet to develop yourself. You should take the time to explore career options, to see what drives you and what you are passionate about. It may be that your internship role is not for you and you decide to move into another direction. How will you get there? If you have been assigned a workplace mentor, use them! Make sure you ask them pertinent questions, delve into the opportunities in your chosen field and where they have seen others succeed and fail.

━━━━━━━━━━ **REFLECTION EXERCISE** ━━━━━━━━━━

Reflect upon your work placement

Ask yourself the following questions to reflect upon your experience and make plans for your future career:

- What were you expecting work to be like in the industry?
- What were your expectations of the job role(s) you undertook?
- How did the job role and industry live up to these expectations?
- From your experiences, are there any new job roles you would consider?
- What did you like and dislike about the organisation itself and its culture?
- Did you feel your own values aligned with those of the organisation and fellow employees?
- What skills do you feel you need to develop?
- What else do you think you would benefit from doing in order to gain further employment?
- What contacts have you made and how do you envisage these being useful in the future?

Just as with your degree, the success of your internship is dependent on the effort, time, reflection and dedication you put into it. Students are often advised of extra-curricular, networking, volunteering and mentoring opportunities, yet the uptake often remains low. Your internship is no different; you can go through the motions and still fulfil the placement, but to what purpose? If a successful career is your measure of success, then you will need to take every opportunity offered to you as well as seeking your own. A recruitment officer for a leading global tour operator recently said that the interns that go on to be most successful are those with a positive attitude, that fulfil the tasks they are given with enthusiasm and reflect upon what else they could be doing. Once they have completed the expected task, they ask for more: they seek out opportunities and volunteer. The final section provides insights from current interns sharing their experiences so far.

STUDENT INSIGHT

Daniela Tome, Event Management student

The application process

I started by sending my CV with a cover letter to the company. A couple of months later, the company emailed me confirming that I had been shortlisted to the next stage of assessment for which I had to make a video, answering two simple questions: "Why the company?" and "Why Me?" I put my creativeness into practice and made an interesting and funny video. With this, I passed to the third and final phase, which was a one-to-one interview. The interview itself was great, and it took close to 30 minutes. The interviewer asked me questions about my work experience, academic life, expectations for the future and why should I be chosen to take the placement. Upon answering all the questions, the interviewer apologised for the following question, as she asked how old I was, as I looked to have so much experience at such young age. That made me feel comfortable and hopeful. I believed the interview went really well and was so pleased to receive a call the following day offering me the position.

The placement

For the first three months, I was placed in the venue-sourcing teams, finding meeting spaces in hotels or private rooms in restaurants. The clients were usually related to technology, education and consultancy.

After that, I moved to the events team where I became registration coordinator. There, I was responsible for everything related to the delegates and was the first point of contact. I was responsible for building the registration websites, gathering the information necessary of each delegate. Information included whether they required accommodation and when for, any dietary medical requirements, the need for travel arrangements or help with visas. Upon gathering all the information, I used to build reports for the event manager to then present to the client and make any necessary amendments. I was also responsible for creating on-site documentation such as name badges, welcome letters, dinner vouchers, dietary reports.

The different departments I worked on gave me a wider perspective of working within an agency for events. It gave me knowledge of different venues for various types of events, how to look for these venues with specific requirements and how to contact each venue appropriately. I also learned what are the essential resources that we need to hold any types of events from small meetings (20 people) to big conferences (500 people). It also gave me an insight into how agencies work, the different departments that are crucial for the success of an event and the size of the workforce.

Opportunities

I was fortunate to have the opportunity to attend some of the events that I was responsible for and had the chance to visit new destinations across Europe and South America. My favourite experience was being registration coordinator as I had direct contact with the delegates, with responsibility for ensuring that good relationships were created between the company, the client and the visitors. Positive feedback from clients and delegates really gave my confidence a boost. My placement gave me the chance to interact with different clients, network with the delegates all whilst travelling and encountering new destinations. It also gave me the opportunity of developing industry knowledge and experience and opened doors for future work positions. My team manager has since recommended me for freelance work with the company as he was impressed by my performance.

Skills developed

I have developed my communication skills, especially in a professional context. I learned how to dress formally and appropriately for corporate event settings: things I would never have learned in the classroom. I developed problem-solving skills; learning how to deal with unpredictable situations, complicated delegates, issues with catering and clients' last-minute requests. I had to be able to prioritise tasks and tackle these situations in an orderly manner, always meeting the clients' and delegates' expectations. I have also learned how to remain calm in difficult situations, learning there is always a solution for everything. Above everything, I have learned how to control my emotions, including managing my anxiety.

STUDENT INSIGHT

Vilius Abaravicius: Food and Beverage, USA

Placement: The basics

I am a British student studying International Tourism Management and am currently on a work placement in the USA at one of the most prestigious country clubs in the world. It has recently been added to the list of 100 best country clubs in the world! My current role is as a waiter in the food and beverage department where I am working in a fine dining restaurant. When I first started, I was given a brief by the club that answered a lot of common questions, like where to find the nearest stores, accommodation rules and travel advice.

The first month of my placement mostly consistent of training and learning about the club and how it operates. The training itself was well organised and interactive making it more interesting and easier to remember. For instance, each day we were given different games to revise the topics that were discussed the previous day and the best performers were recognised and rewarded. On the other hand, there were some of the things that I have learned during the training which I still have not used during service, but I don't mind because it contributed to my general knowledge! A typical day on placement is really fun: every day you can expect something new to happen or hear certain work gossips. The job itself is not really demanding as long as you help your fellow co-workers and seek help yourself. Once done with the service, everyone leaves for home and we usually all meet up to chill out and enjoy each other's company.

Skills required

As front of the house staff we are expected to recognise and memorise members' last names as well as their preferences: what they like to drink, how they like their meals prepared. I would say good *interpersonal skills* play a vital role in order to avoid stress and get the job done faster. For example, there are a lot of different steps of service, so when it gets busy, I need to seek help from my co-workers so it has been important to build strong relationships with them. I would say that if someone starts their internship within a different country that has other cultural ideas and belief system it is really important to be able to *adapt to a new environment*. One of the easier ways to do so is to start bonding with your fellow co-workers, most of the people that I met made my time here a whole lot more fun and exciting. Being away from home you start feeling homesick and we have had people leave for this reason. Another main skill needed is *patience* and *knowing how not to take things personally* when dealing with complaints or negative attitudes. Some individuals can be rude (including other staff members!), and I believe because of the cultural distance it might seem that they address you in an unpleasant manner, thus it is important to process these interactions without any hard feelings.

Challenges

To remain competitive, the club has very high standards and expectations for all employees as many of the members are considered VIPs: many are multi-millionaires. Working with such clientele who are used to receiving outstanding customer service makes it a bit stressful for new team members especially for international staff. The majority of interns came to the USA for the first time and even though they received proper training during induction weeks, they still have to learn aspects of the new culture.

At the beginning I sometimes suffered from a lack of confidence when dealing with members' requests. However, the club believes that hiring diverse staff is also part of the whole member experience, as the members get to see people from all over the world and learn their stories. Also, as most of the members visit the club on a daily basis, interaction between members and staff is constant, which helps to form connections between us. Once I manged to familiarise myself with some of the members and learn their preferences it helped me to boost my confidence and service skills. Overall, I have found members to be friendly, warm and funny.

So far, I haven't experienced any communication issues with the members, though the majority of them are seniors and some of them struggle when talking so I often spend more time by the table just to make sure they get exactly what they want. Communication has been more of a problem for some students who have struggled more than I did mostly due to the language barriers. Luckily, the club decided to offer free English classes for those who felt the need to improve their language.

Most memorable moment

Perhaps the most memorable interaction that I can think of was when I was taking a 'to go' order over the phone for a member that was ill. The lady on the other end of the phone really appreciated questions that I asked her in order to get exactly what she wanted. In addition, as I have learned that she was sick I altered my tone to let her know that I care about her situation and wished her to get better soon, as all of the staff misses her. The conversation made her so happy that she forgot about her sickness and came to the restaurant just to give me a hug. Or maybe I cured her with kindness – who knows?

CONCLUSION

In this chapter we have covered:

- The value of undertaking internships to develop skills and provide real-life work experience
- The benefits of internships to you and your employer
- How to select the right internship for you
- Lessons learned from the experiences of previous interns

FURTHER READING

Baska, M. (2019). 'One in five graduates not 'workplace ready', research finds'. *People Management*, 17 December 2019. Available online at: https://www.peoplemanagement.co.uk/news/articles/graduates-not-workplace-ready

High Fliers (2019). 'The graduate market in 2019: Annual review of graduate vacancies & starting salaries at the UK's leading employers'. Available online at: https://www.highfliers.co.uk/download/2019/graduate_market/GMReport19.pdf

Jack, K., Stansbie, P. and Sciarini, M. (2017). 'An examination of the role played by internships in nurturing management competencies in Hospitality and Tourism Management (HTM) students', *Journal of Teaching in Travel and Tourism*, 17(1), pp.17–33.

Neugebauer, J. and Evans-Brain, J. (2009). *Making the Most of Your Placement*. London: Sage Publications.

Seyitoglu, F. and Yirik, S. (2015). 'Internship satisfaction of students of hospitality and impact of internship on the professional development and industrial perception', *Asia Pacific Journal of Tourism Research*, 20 (1), pp.1414–1429.

22 VOLUNTEER OPPORTUNITIES AND PART-TIME WORK

CHAPTER LEARNING OBJECTIVES

By the end of this chapter you should be able to:

- Understand the value of part-time work and volunteering
- Know where to look for part-time and volunteering opportunities
- Visualise how part-time work and volunteering can benefit your CV
- Reflect upon the transferable skills that part-time work and volunteering experiences may offer you
- Describe the concept of voluntourism and be able to debate the advantages and disadvantages of voluntourism

GLOSSARY

- **Altruistic behaviour:** An unselfish act that benefits the wellbeing of others
- **Gig economy:** A term to describe short-term or temporary contracts and freelance work rather than jobs with permanent contracts
- **TEFL:** Teaching English as a Foreign Language
- **Voluntourism:** The opportunity to combine travel overseas with participating in voluntary work; volunteering for all or part of the trip

INTRODUCTION

Your time at university is an excellent opportunity to enhance your CV and gain work experience through part-time or voluntary work. Recent research by Pearson Business School found that almost half of businesses said that having work experience was important when recruiting (Baska, 2019). In the UK, a third of recruiters warned that graduates without any previous work experience were less likely to be successful during the recruitment selection process (High Fliers, 2019). Employers seek candidates that are familiar with the workplace environment, that have the confidence and maturity to build strong professional relationships and that ultimately have the skills to thrive in an organisation. A student with no work experience may pose a higher risk to recruiters as they will not be able to demonstrate they can switch from a university and study-based setting to an organisational business environment with its own culture and behavioural expectations. Work experience does not necessarily have to relate to the industry in which you are applying; it is the transferable skills you build when working in any organisation, paid or unpaid, that contributes to your employability. It goes without saying that work experience of some sort is crucial to your employability status as a graduate.

CLOSING THE SKILLS GAPS

As outlined in Chapter 20, employers are finding that graduate students lack fundamental skills required in the workplace. While the measure of skill gaps varies according to country, there is a clear message that graduates are not necessarily leaving university as 'employable' citizens. So, what can *you* do to close this gap for yourself? Many skills sought by employers are soft skills (as covered in Chapter 12); those that are more difficult to teach in the classroom and benefit from real-world experience. Getting a part-time job or taking advantage of volunteering opportunities will enable you to develop several skills outside of your degree course. Ideally your part-time work or volunteering would be in the industry you are interested in developing a career in; however, the transferable skills are what are important, and these can be built up in a range of work settings and not necessarily those related specifically to tourism, hospitality and events.

PART-TIME WORK

Your studies will demand around 25–35 hours of your time per week dependent on your institution and the stage of your degree; a combination of lectures, seminars, tutorials, workshops, guided and independent learning. So, there is ample time for you to undertake a part-time or weekend job to fit around your degree schedule. A weekend job for example may provide a good balance between your university week and earning potential.

For several students, part-time work is not optional; it is a requirement in order to fund their degree. Even though work is crucial for some, this should not come at the cost of your degree. Remember why you decided to undertake a degree course, the reason why you felt university was the right choice for you. Work experience is important but should not take priority over your studies. Many students have taken on full-time positions throughout their studies for financial reasons; while this is understandable, it is not something to advocate as the work/study balance is tipped in favour of work. Not only will your studies likely suffer, but your student experience; university is not just a space for learning in the classroom, there are numerous other opportunities, such as working abroad, volunteering, taking part in projects, becoming student representatives, joining societies and being a student ambassador, that offer valuable learning experiences, skill development and contribute to your CV.

Advantages of part-time work

1. Earn money
2. Gain transferable skills to close the skills gap
3. Boost confidence
4. Develop interpersonal skills and communication
5. Learn time management and balance university, work and social life
6. Adds credibility to your CV through work experience
7. Allows you to consider future career decisions from what you see, hear and do
8. Network and build up valuable contacts
9. Make new friends and meet new people
10. Gives structure to your week; contact time at university may not be more than 12–15 hours per week so work gives another sense of purpose to your day

PERMANENT PART-TIME CONTRACTS

There is a difference between permanent part-time work and those on flexible contracts; permanent part-time positions mean that you are on a permanent contract, but for part-time hours (usually anything up to 25 hours a week). Flexible contracts include zero-hours contracts that are casual and where you have no formal hours but are offered work according to organisational demand. Zero-hours contracts have previously come under fire from employees who felt they were being forced into a state of uncertainty in employment; being overworked for any period, but then facing periods of time where minimal or no hours were being offered. This nature of contract makes it difficult to apply for other positions as work may be offered or cancelled with limited notice and no compensation (Butler, 2019). Work in the tourism, hospitality and events sectors is often criticised for long hours, shift work, working at weekends or during peak periods, such as Christmas and summer. As a student, this can be advantageous; greater flexibility to work around your study timetable. It is not, however, recommended for students to commit to any more than 10–15 hours per week of work.

Permanent part-time work means that you are bound by a contract to fulfil a certain number of hours per week; do not overpromise on the hours you have available. It is better to take a lower-hours contract and then increase shifts as and when required, rather than committing to hours that you continually feel you cannot satisfy. Contracted part-time work allows you the security of a minimum wage coming in each week or month as well as holiday pay, sick pay and other company benefits. It is important to remember that your contract will not stop for summer or Christmas; just because university term ends, the contract will continue. If you need to go home during this period, you must notify your employer as soon as you can and book holiday to cover the time off. While organisations may respect that you are a student, to them you are a paid employee and university is not their priority. Make sure you behave responsibly and professionally; you should be the one to balance your work and university commitments.

PART-TIME WORK IN TOURISM, HOSPITALITY AND EVENTS AND RETAIL

There are several roles you could take to develop transferable skills applicable to various careers and adding value to your CV. Hotels, bars, restaurants, event management companies, event venues, retail outlets and leisure attractions offer numerous part-time permanent roles. Jobs are usually entry level roles including bar staff, front of house roles such as receptionists, waiting staff and customer service advisors. There are often opportunities to progress to supervisory or team leader roles and come with the flexibility of shift work and the chance for increased hours outside of term-time (i.e. during the summer vacation). All these roles would offer an opportunity to build crucial skills with relevant examples in communication, teamwork and problem solving.

WHERE TO FIND OUT MORE

Along with several online recruitment agencies, university resources, network contacts and individual organisation websites, do not forget physical presence. Physically going into places allows you to sell yourself, to make a personable impression and for the potential employer to gain a sense of who you are and what you might offer. Applications are usually completed online, and it is rare that larger organisations and chain companies will accept physical CVs, but you should not underestimate the power of a personal introduction. This may be even more crucial to small- and medium-sized enterprises (SMEs) where they may be more inclined to recruit in an ad hoc fashion and still accept face to face introductions as the first step in the recruitment process.

Consider rural and coastal areas where tourism may be seasonal and a few small establishments, such as tea rooms, freehouse pubs and bars, exist potentially without a website. These types of businesses and communities often run on word of mouth recommendations and local networking to recruit. In these areas keep an eye out for in-house notices, noticeboards in shops and post offices and local social media pages for job advertisements.

Your university career centre or department will have multiple contacts and will display a variety of part-time job vacancies across several industries. They will also be able to offer advice on your CV, cover letters and the application process (see Section E for chapters on how you secure employment).

Furthermore, use online intermediaries to search for part-time vacancies. Caterer, Indeed, Monster, Prospects, Student Job, Reed and Targetjobs are just a handful of the online recruitment sites listing part-time vacancies in the service sectors.

Individual organisations

Most companies have a career or 'work for us' section on their website. If you have identified an organisation you would like to work for, then this is a good place to start. They will not only advertise current roles but may also provide job specifications and requirements so you can see if you meet the criteria for positions before you apply.

Do not be afraid to send in a speculative application to see if there are any impending roles you may be suitable for. As most students start university at a similar time, competition for roles around September/October is high. It is recommended that you get in early and start to look around May. Organisations will likely be losing staff that have completed their degrees and be looking to replace them around this time.

Networks and contacts

Part-time work positions may well be shared via word of mouth or through friends. Pay attention to social media pages and friends or university colleagues discussing opportunities. Refer to Chapter 25 on using your networks and social media for ideas on how you might find positions using your personal (online) contacts.

TEMPORARY JOBS AND FLEXIBLE CONTRACTS

The emergence of the so-called '**gig economy**' has all but replaced discussions of zero-hours contracts (Lehdonvirta, 2018). The gig economy suggests the power has shifted towards the employee; you are able to decide when, where and who you work for. Several websites have developed where you can sign up and then choose to take job opportunities and ad hoc work as and when you have the time to do so. If you feel you are unable to commit to a permanent position with weekly designated hours, this can be an opportunity to build work experience with numerous benefits:

- There are no obligations to commit prior to accepting a job so the work can fit around your schedule
- Most sites promise fair wages
- You are exposed to a variety of job roles and different employers so there is always something new to learn and reduces boredom and mundanity of jobs
- By experiencing work in a diverse range of organisations you can use this to make decisions on your future career options

However, whilst being somewhat disguised as a new and more flexible way of working, the same issues may arise:

- Shifts can be cancelled at the last minute without compensation
- There are no guarantee that shifts will be available when you need them
- Shifts may be highly competitive with several individuals applying for jobs
- Working for multiple employers means that working terms and conditions vary between organisations; breaks, food/drink entitlement and rules around managing and keeping tips may differ

SEASONAL WORK

Seasonal work is also synonymous with the tourism, hospitality and events industries; summer work in campsites, clubs and resorts, events and festivals, ski season work and Christmas temping staff. These would be performed outside of term-time and without long-term commitment. They can be a great way to fill your time over summer and are particularly popular before beginning a degree and in the year post graduation to gain valuable work experience. Many of these positions also include an element of travel often with the chance to extend your stay beyond the seasonal contract and travel within the destination. BUNAC, Campo America, e4s, Eurocamp and hotbox are a few examples of organisations and websites that offer temporary seasonal work.

STUDENT INSIGHT

Clodagh, campsite courier, leading European provider of camping holidays

The recruitment process for seasonal work on a campsite was simple. I filled out an online application form on the company website in early January, stating my availability and experience. The company recruits well into the season due to staff shortages and turnover. I was invited to an informal interview at their head office where I answered a few questions relating to my situational judgement and discussed the role; the overall experience was pleasant. A short while later they called me to say I had been selected for the role of a campsite representative for a 3-month contract; perfect for me as I was about to start university. I was given the opportunity to select my destination; I chose Spain as I had visited a few times and spoke basic Spanish. I was told I would be contacted nearer the time to arrange my flight to the destination as all flights were covered by the company. I was contacted in early June and asked to fly out to Barcelona literally days later. The destination is chosen based on the needs of the company as some sites are much busier than others, so I was lucky to get my first choice. The short notice was overwhelming and scary but being relatively young and inexperienced it made it exciting. I would probably prefer much more time to prepare now!

At the airport I was greeted by a company rep and then on arrival at my camp I was shown to my accommodation which was a static caravan, shared with another girl. The caravan was relatively small and had no aircon, so it came as quite a shock. I was expecting much nicer accommodation since it's a large, reputable company. It seemed unfair that I was cleaning much better accommodation than I was staying in!

I was trained for the role of campsite courier alongside other new staff. Mostly, this was how to properly clean the accommodation and deal with minor maintenance issues; it also covered basic health and safety procedures. I felt I needed more training on dealing with maintenance issues or for the contracted maintenance man to be more available. I thought the role would be like a holiday rep; making recommendations and checking in and chatting with customers, but most of my time was spent cleaning inside a caravan alone. I had to be willing to get my hands dirty and had to work hard in testing conditions with a smile on my face; it took great customer service skills.

A standard working day would be 9am–3pm then 6pm–8pm dependent on duties. Most days would begin at around 9am. We would start with a morning briefing from the site manager and team leader who assigned tasks for the day. After this we were given a list of three accommodations to clean and were sent on our way. We were provided with a trolley and cleaning products; the target was to clean each accommodation in under an hour. Accommodation varied in size and what additional extras would be needed, such as linen and cots. You were required to sort through any linen or items you had collected during the day and clean your cloths. My working day was dependent on how fast I could complete the assigned tasks.

One night a week I had reception duties which involved manning the desk for any queries or check-ins for around 3 hours. Other nights I was asked to visit customer accommodation to notify them of their departure date. Once a week I was left with the emergency phone which meant dealing with any incidents that occurred throughout the night. Luckily, I never got a call! Some members of staff were called out to deal with domestic arguments in the early hours of the morning; at the age of 18, I would have been terrified and unprepared to deal with this. After my shift I had free time to relax which usually involved visiting the beach or socialising with new friends. I got 1.5–2 days off per week depending how busy it was. The rate of pay allowed me to live and enjoy the experience but not to earn any savings as such.

I did really hate the level of dirt I had to deal with in such a short time-frame, but the experience gave me the most intense, interesting summer. I could not have prepared for how dirty people are willing to leave their accommodation and how much of the role was cleaning-based, but during my contract I had the opportunity to visit different cities, do new activities and meet people from all around the world. Sometimes I did feel like I was having the best time but had no one close enough to me to share it with as the season had already begun prior to my arrival so I felt most people on the site had already bonded, which left me feeling outcast for a while. I also missed my parents and friends given it was my first time away from home for longer than a week.

I gained practical experience of dealing with the challenges of international teams in a foreign country with a culture different from my own. Despite some of my misgivings about the role itself, it truly ignited my passion for travel and for the tourism industry. If I were to do this again, I would do a lot more research; I would look for a company that better suited me. In that sense it taught me what I want from a job; flexibility, sustainability, excellent training and fair management.

My advice to those looking for a seasonal job abroad is start applying early! Gather as much information as possible on different organisations before making your final decision so you have a good feel for the company. Consider the location of the job; you may say you want to be as far away from your parents as possible, but when you're feeling low a phone call doesn't really substitute a hug from your mum! Overall, I made no losses from my experience only gains so definitely recommend it!

WHERE TO FIND OUT MORE

There are several intermediary websites that bring together employers seeking flexible workers. Roles in tourism, hospitality, events and facilities management include:

- Bar staff
- Baristas
- Hostesses
- Waiting staff
- Receptionists
- Team leaders
- Festival staff
- Event security
- Bar back staff
- Cleaners

Always remember to check out the terms and conditions, wages and small print before you sign up. Some websites also charge a fee in order to match and locate jobs for you. To find out more, check out the following sites:

Table 22.1 Useful websites to search for part time work

Australia:
Indeed: https://au.indeed.com/Casual-Hospitality-jobs
Off to Work: https://www.offtowork.co.uk/
SEEK: https://www.seek.com.au/jobs-in-hospitality-tourism
Sidekicker: https://sidekicker.com/au/work/
Asia:
PartTimePost: https://parttimepost.com/

(Continued)

Table 22.1 (Continued)

UK:
Arc events staff specialists: https://www.archospitality.co.uk/
Coople: https://www.coople.com/uk/worker/
Gig: https://www.gigtogig.co.uk/seeker/
Rota: https://www.rota.com/member/
Syft: https://syftapp.com/looking-for-student-jobs/
USA:
Flexjobs: https://www.flexjobs.com/jobs
Shiftgig: https://www.shiftgig.com/im-a-worker/

VOLUNTEERING

A period of volunteering and giving your time to help others without pay can really enhance your CV. Although unpaid, volunteer opportunities can be taken alongside paid part-time work, or as an alternative way to build work experience through providing valuable insight into the world of work (Indeed, 2016). A real advantage of volunteering is that you can commit the time you have available; it can easily be fitted around your university schedule. The commitment could be on a weekly basis, as little as an hour or two per week, or it could be ad hoc or a one-off commitment, for example a festival or major event. The range of opportunities and roles are diverse so there really is something for everyone; even charities need help in marketing, finance and event organisation. With this in mind it is a good idea to be strategic; of course any act of helping others should be admired, but from the perspective of your CV, it is important that you search for opportunities in line with your passions and values. Consider the type of skills you hope to develop and might be set to gain.

Why volunteer?

'I knew from previous experience within charity work that volunteers were a valuable part of any event and that there were always so many opportunities. What I didn't realise then was that it would also give me a chance to build a client base and make contacts that would allow me to freelance and get paid for working on events during and after university.'

Student insight: Jessica Behenna, Graduate, Event Management

The benefits of volunteering have not gone unnoticed by employers; over 70% of recruiters in hospitality and leisure said it was important to include volunteering on your CV when applying for jobs (Indeed, 2016). Over 50% of employers said they would use volunteering experiences as a deciding factor when selecting between two candidates. In fact, the benefits are so far reaching that many companies have adopted employer supported volunteering; enabling employees to participate in volunteering roles as part of their personal development. So, apart from enabling readiness for the workplace, what are the other benefits?

Personal development

Like paid part-time work, volunteering is an opportunity to learn new skills and practise current skills. Several positions will demand a certain skill set; a recent position as a hospitality volunteer at a library, for example, required written and verbal communication skills, effective interpersonal skills as well as time and self-management skills. You can therefore expect that you would be using this on a regular basis and would be building up your confidence in these areas with relatable examples to use in future job applications and interviews. Dependent on the individual role, volunteering allows you to prepare for dealing with stressful situations as well as the opportunity to learn several new skills; team work, self-confidence, communication, self-motivation and interpersonal skills regarded as the top skills employers identify as being developed through volunteering (Indeed, 2018). Employee volunteers have attested to being more energised, sharper and stronger professionals from their volunteering experience (TedX Talks, 2014). Providing you set personal goals, you are likely to be able to demonstrate greater creativity, efficiency through having to balance resources, positivity and passion.

REFLECTION EXERCISE

Mapping skills for volunteering

For any volunteering role, it is important you map out your current skills and think about what you have to offer:

- What are your current strengths?
- What/where do you need to develop?
- What skills are you looking to be able to demonstrate for your future career?
- Where do you feel you lack confidence that could be boosted through a volunteering role?

This will also be an important exercise to complete post-volunteering; when using volunteering as an example of work experience on your CV. Make sure you are able to focus on the transferable skills you have gained rather than the specific tasks you were set. Your mapped skills should be matched to the job specification.

Volunteering gives you access to experiences you may otherwise not have had the opportunity to participate in. From working at large-scale events such as the Olympics to roles you may not yet be qualified to apply for, volunteering may allow access to these areas. If you are an event management student but have not had any work experience in the field, graduate level job opportunities may be limited. Through volunteering you can build up a portfolio of experience within events through a variety of roles and in a diverse set of organisations. You could volunteer at sports events, music festivals or even locally working on the events team for a charity or other non-profit organisation. These roles may help you eliminate or substantiate plans for your future career prospects. It may also lead to a paid role; you never know who you might meet either within the organisation or through the organisation and tasks you deliver.

Beyond future career plans, volunteering can also help ignite passion; make you realise what you are passionate about, what causes are close to your heart and develop a sense of your true self.

These opportunities can be a chance to work out what makes you happy; without the need to commit to a contractual, permanent role. The key to any opportunity is to reflect; keep a diary or keep your CV up to date with activities you have done, skills you have developed and an evidence trail to demonstrate your qualities.

Helping others

Volunteering and charity work are synonymous with helping others; giving your time to a cause you believe in and hopefully are passionate about. This is an example of **altruistic behaviour**. According to the UN (2018), the total global volunteering hours are equivalent to 109 million full-time employees. Without volunteers many charities and non-profit organisations would cease to exist. By volunteering you would be adding to the global movement of volunteerism and contributing to your community.

Many companies engage in corporate social responsibility and look for their employees present and future to display similar values to their own. Volunteering is an excellent means of demonstrating altruistic behaviour and ethical maturity; to show you understand the wider world and the impacts a collective community can have on global sustainable development agendas (see Chapter 17).

VOLUNTEERING OPPORTUNITIES

The following section will discuss the types of roles available when volunteering; of course, this will not be exhaustive, but provides insight into the opportunities available. The focus of these experiences is to build transferable skills; not all roles need to be in tourism, hospitality and events related organisations. There are several skills that can be practised and developed from a variety of positions and within several diverse organisations and charities.

Charities and non-profit organisations

There are thousands of examples of volunteering roles in charities including anything from working in a charity shop, participating in a befriender service for the elderly, volunteering at a homeless shelter or being a hospitality volunteer in a hospice, welcoming visitors and preparing teas and coffees. The possibilities are endless as organisations are often wholly reliant on volunteer hours for survival. If you are passionate about a cause, for example working with animals, education, supporting children, conservation or environmental action or mental health, then this is a good place to start. Once you have reflected upon what you have to offer you and what you hope to achieve from the role, then you can consider the types of roles that may suit or where you feel you could add value.

Charities often host events as a means of fundraising and so again can be a great opportunity for a volunteer role. The following account is from Jessica Behenna, a recent graduate in Event Management from Manchester Metropolitan University. Volunteering sparked Jessica's interest in events leading to her make the decision to study an event management degree. Through her years of volunteering she gained valuable skills and considerable network contacts, but it also led to paid employment in the industry.

━━━ STUDENT INSIGHT ━━━

Jessica Behenna, Starry Lunch – Gala Dinner (charity fundraiser)

I began volunteering on the Starry Lunch Christmas event when the charity (that I have volunteered for regularly over the last eight years) became a beneficiary of this event in December 2015. This was also my first year at Manchester Metropolitan University which meant that I was able to use this experience to reflect upon for some of my foundation year studies. The charity became a part of this event fairly last minute and therefore I was thrown in at the deep-end and told that I had to look after a group of approximately six other volunteers and coordinate them to welcome guests, sell raffle tickets, 'spot' during a live auction and collect any further charity donations throughout the day. I was also responsible for liaising between the event organiser and the charity.

This event taught me a lot of the skills I have mentioned before and really became a stepping stone for me as over the next four years I continued to manage this event and was then also paid for the extra responsibility I took on. This often involved helping in dressing the room and working alongside the audio-visual team to achieve our outcomes. I was also responsible for recruiting the volunteers for the event in 2016, 2017 and 2018. Now the event has a new charity beneficiary, Cash for Kids, who have their own volunteers.

I loved being a part of this event because I was able to build relationships with the venue staff, audio-visual team and even some of the event attendees; some I would see each year and was able to discuss the event with them and gain feedback on what worked well or what we could change the following year. Although this event was a huge responsibility, for four years it felt like my event; I knew it like the back of my hand. Starting as a volunteer led me to becoming a freelance event manager; the event organiser requested I be employed as they had asked me back each year based on my performance and the relationship we had built; this really brings home the importance of networking as a student! This was something that I was very proud of during my studies and still am to this day.

VOLUNTEERING IN TOURISM, HOSPITALITY AND EVENTS

Table 22.2   Volunteering in tourism, hospitality and events

Volunteering organisations
Australia Volunteering:
Go Volunteer: https://govolunteer.com.au/volunteering
UK volunteering:
Do It: https://do-it.org/
NCVO: https://www.ncvo.org.uk/
Time Bank: https://timebank.org.uk/
Vinspired: https://vinspired.com/

(Continued)

Table 22.2   (Continued)

Volunteer Now (N.I): https://www.volunteernow.co.uk/
Volunteer Scotland: https://www.volunteerscotland.net/
Volunteer Wales: https://volunteering-wales.net/vk/volunteers/index.htm
USA volunteering:
National and community service: https://www.nationalservice.gov/serve

While most tourism, hospitality and event organisations are for-profit, there are volunteer roles that can provide specific knowledge of the sectors and help you demonstrate experience of working within these industries. There are several roles within environmental or cultural heritage conservation protection trusts and organisations, for example, UNESCO (global), Australian Heritage Council (Australia), National Trust (UK), English Heritage (UK), National Trust for Historic Preservation (USA), Heritage New Zealand (NZ), Canadian Heritage (Canada) and National Parks (global). Roles could be in a local museum as a visitor guide or admissions officer, as a customer service advisor or events assistant; you could volunteer in the tea or gift shop or become a tour guide or information advisor.

Events, festivals and country shows offer considerable volunteering opportunities, giving you the chance to get valuable experience in both hospitality and event management. From mega events, such as the Olympics and FIFA World Cup, to annual music events like the Eurovision song contest, volunteers are integral to the success of these events. So, the Olympics may not be held in your country any time soon, but sporting events are a regular addition to many local places from marathons to triathlons and cycling. Keep an eye out for locally-held events as recruitment for volunteers is often started well advance of the event itself.

Your local tourism board is another avenue for volunteering roles; in the tourism office itself advising tourists and guests, or as part of the administrative and marketing team making decisions about the overall tourism strategy in the area. Not only will this give you an excellent insight into the industries but will allow you to build customer service and communication, understand how to manage and respond to difficult situations and problem-solving.

  EMPLOYER INSIGHTS ▬▬▬▬▬▬

Example volunteer roles

National Parks: Cuyahoga Valley, Ohio, USA

1. Park Promoters

Promote Cuyahoga Valley National Park and the Conservancy at on-site and off-site special events. Events include the Lyceum Series, park concerts, Pint Nights, and various other community events in Akron and Cleveland.

> **Responsibilities**: Greet guests; answer questions; engage them in conversations about the national park; promote ways for the guests to become more involved in the national park through the Conservancy operations, including membership, Extraordinary Spaces, Trail Mix and Park Place in Peninsula, volunteering, and Trails Forever. Duties include carrying and lifting

Commitment: A few shifts per year

Likely skills gained: Communication, interpersonal, customer service, confidence, self-management

2. Countryside

Volunteers needed to assist Countryside staff and vendors at the Farmers' Markets.

Responsibilities: setting-up/tearing-down, parking, produce inventory, cheese demonstrations, market ambassador, photographer, and zero-waste ambassador

Commitment: 1–2 shifts per month of 1–4 hours

Likely skills gained: Event management, communication, interpersonal

Find out more: https://www.nps.gov/cuva/getinvolved/seasonal-and-on-going-volunteer-opportunities.htm

Museums: British Museum, London, UK

1. Eye-opener tours

Eye-opener tours introduce visitors to the Museum's collection through a variety of guided talks that take place in different galleries across the Museum. There are 15 tours that run every day on a range of topics.

Likely skills gained: Communication, confidence, time management, cultural sensitivity, interpersonal

2. Touch tour volunteers

A volunteer-facilitated touch tour is available for blind and partially-sighted visitors in the Egyptian sculpture displays (Room 4). The tour features nine objects and lasts about an hour. Volunteers welcome the attendees, helping them navigate the physical space of the Museum and guide their exploration of the tour objects through touch and discussion.

Likely skills gained: communication, emotional intelligence (empathy), confidence, self-awareness and time management

Find out more: www.volunteers@britishmuseum.org

Volunteering as tourism

Volunteering in another country offers the ability to combine the opportunity to travel, to experience other cultures and destinations, alongside doing good. '**Voluntourism**', as it is more typically known, is a combination of the words volunteer and tourism and essentially means travelling to volunteer and give your time to a cause without pay; either as part of or for the entirety of a trip. The industry was born out of a drive towards more responsible travel and a desire to give back to society as well as enjoy a 'transformative learning for volunteers' (Wearing, Young and Everingham, 2017: 512). A form of niche tourism, voluntourism is recognised as a global industry with over 1.6 million people volunteering abroad annually and is reputed to be worth an estimated $2.6 billion per year (Save the Children, 2017). Destinations are usually within South and South-East Asia and Africa (ECPAT, 2016) with popular choices for volunteering often being humanitarian and environmental projects in areas such as sport, education, agriculture, animal welfare and conservation (Han et al., 2019).

Examples of voluntourist activities

Humanitarian:

- Teaching English as a foreign language (**TEFL**)
- Construction and renovation
- Sport coaching
- Hospital support
- Childcare
- Care for the elderly and those with disabilities

Environmental:

- Nature conservation
- Wildlife monitoring
- Wildlife protection and rehabilitation
- Action against climate change

One of the main differences between volunteering and voluntourism (besides the aspect of travel) is that these experiences come at a financial cost to you, the voluntourist. You will be expected to pay a fee often in excess of $2000 for a week to engage in these types of experience. These fees usually include training and orientation, accommodation, food/drink, support in the destination and any materials or equipment for the project itself. Fees will rarely include flights, transfers or spending money; depending on the destination, a budget of around $250 per week is recommended. Some organisations such as gvi (see: www.gvi.co.uk) offer scholarships and fundraising opportunities as well as discounts for certain trips. As with all organisations, you must make sure you research companies and their small print thoroughly before committing to a trip.

Benefits of voluntourism

For you the voluntourist:

- *Opportunity to give back and make a difference*: the intention of many voluntourists is altruistic and comes from a desire to some good
- *Personal development*: as with volunteering in your home nation, voluntourism experiences will no doubt offer the opportunity to develop new skills, as well as test your strength of character, ability to work in diverse settings and ability to communicate across cultures
- *Escapism*: the role of a voluntourist is often appealing as it allows the individual an escape from routine, from everyday life. An escape with purpose often gives volunteers the chance to find themselves and the freedom to reflect upon what is important to them
- *Education*: as well as learning new skills, voluntourism can generate new knowledge in areas you may not have dreamt possible – construction, for example, or conservation practice. It will

provide insight into other cultures and diverse ways of life and cultural norms beyond those of your own society

- *Psychological*: voluntourism experiences offer a chance for realising your own potential; for recognising your strengths and ability to complete tasks in often challenging conditions

For the destination:

- *Sustainability*: projects can contribute to the sustainable development of the area. Long-term impacts can be achieved with the right management; for example, projects teaching English could aim to teach local instructors rather than individual children
- *Cultural exchange*: just as the voluntourist can immerse themselves in a new culture, the host destination has the chance to interact with those from diverse cultures
- *Stimulate the local economy*: the development of tourism can bring economic benefits to an area as well as the opportunity for economic linkages. Local businesses may benefit from volunteer spending in shops, restaurants and activities
- *Philanthropic learning:* there is an opportunity for learning about global issues such as climate change, poverty, inequality and diversity. Projects may highlight these issues and related causes to those rarely exposed to impacts therefore raising awareness of the plight of those facing such issues on a daily basis

WHAT TO CONSIDER BEFORE APPLYING

You should make sure you do due diligence and research properly before applying for any roles. Make sure you consider the following points.

1. *Skills match*: What skills do you have that would benefit this role? It is important that you are offering your strengths and not just your passion.
2. *Suitability*: Do your research on the company; is the project suitable? Are the local community involved?
3. *Learning opportunities*: What skills are you likely to develop in this role? Are you open and willing to learn? Do you understand you are not going to solve the world's problems in a single trip?
4. *Costs*: How much are you willing to pay? How and where is the fee being spent? What extras are there to pay for? A higher fee does not necessarily equate to a better experience.
5. *Duration*: How long will you spend? Often the longer the trip, the more meaningful it is and the greater the benefits will be. This of course needs to balance against finance and time away from home.

Source: adapted from Save the Children, 2017

Criticisms of voluntourism

So far, this all sounds great; however, before you book your next trip there is a more challenging, not so attractive side to this industry. The industry has faced criticisms over ethics, particularly in work with children and vulnerable adults; where skills are not evident in voluntourists to cope or be of value in this type of work. A recent campaign against volunteering in orphanages, for example, has gained momentum with global charities such as Save the Children and UNICEF abdicating for a ban on practice. Many of these issues do not necessarily relate to voluntourism itself, but rather to the lack of governance and regulations maintaining standards within it (ECPAT, 2016). The following criticisms are not supposed to deter all voluntourism action, neither is it to condemn the industry as a whole; it is to raise awareness of malpractice and highlight responsibility of the industry, but also for you, the voluntourist, to make sure voluntourism is not taken lightly so that efforts are beneficial rather than a hindrance.

 INDUSTRY INSIGHT

Orphanage tourism

Legitimate orphanages exist for children with no parents or for vulnerable children where parental or familial care is not appropriate or deemed possible. There are a number of reasons children may be placed in such an institution – from poverty, conflict, neglect, illness, disability, discrimination or the threat of harm.

Orphanage tourism is a form of voluntourism where volunteers travel to spend time in an orphanage setting; teaching children English, playing sports, spending leisure time or providing manual labour, money or resources for institutions (Lyneham and Facchini, 2019). In many areas such as South-East Asia, orphanages have become reliant on the support and donations of voluntourists. Issues have arisen where illegitimate and often privately-owned institutions have developed into scam regimes where children become the victim of exploitative orphanage operators seeking to exploit the charitable essence of voluntourism to line their own pockets with voluntourist money.

According to Save the Children (2017) 'unscrupulous people are capitalising on the goodwill of visitors who want to donate money or volunteer by filling orphanages with children who are not, in fact, orphans. To meet the demand of foreigners wanting to support poor children, some orphanages have taken children from their parents, after convincing them their children would be better off in care.'

Children in these types of institution may have been trafficked or been illegitimately subjected to orphanage care based on a promise of money for families. It is estimated that as many as eight out of ten of these children have at least one living parent or family member that could indeed take care of them (ReThink Orphanages, 2018). The lack of policies, regulations and governance of such institutions has also made it possible for sexual predators and sex offenders to engage with children in orphanages via voluntourism opportunities.

While the pull of helping an orphan or a child in need may be strong, it is important to stop and think; global guidelines suggest that ethically and responsibly, you should find an alternative means of volunteering in consideration of the dire costs of orphanage related tourism.

Sources: Lyneham and Facchini, 2019; ReThink Orphanages, 2018; Save the Children, 2017

Commercialisation

As an overseas trip, the costs of travel and accommodation would most likely fall to you to cover, but there are varying levels of organisations from non-profit to those fully commercialised that leverage part of the fee to feed into profits. It is important to remember that while you are volunteering, your trip is part of an industry. The work you do may be charitable, but the organisation you book with may well be making a profit. This would seemingly juxtapose the very idea on which volunteering is based.

Your intentions as a voluntourist may well be good, but there are questions over who is really benefitting from the trip. For example, where is the fee going? Is the money you spend being distributed in the local destination or leaking out to foreign business owners?

THINK POINT

As a voluntourist you are buying your experience and many organisations offer these without vetting you first, taking time to understand your strengths or skills (Hernandez-Maskivker, Lapointe and Aquino, 2017). Do you think organisations have a responsibility to find out what skills you have? Do you think all roles should be open to all people regardless of skills and experience?

The spectrum of organisations ranges from those offering luxury voluntourism opportunities where volunteers stay in high-quality accommodation and give a few hours of their day across a range of geographical locations and communities to those not seeking profit where travel to volunteer and the project is the trip. In the former, the trip is heavily commercialised with volunteering almost becoming an activity, an added extra, rather than the purpose of the trip. In the latter, commercialisation may be less visible; accommodation is often basic or in homestays and the volunteer is there to work rather than play.

ACTIVITY

Criticisms of voluntourism

Consider the headings below.

- Increased pressure on the local area
- Duration of voluntourism projects
- Cultural changes
- Issues of power

Now brainstorm ideas to answer the following questions:

1. What impact(s) might each of these have?
2. How might each of these represent a criticism of voluntourism?

Where to find out more

Below is a list of voluntourism opportunities, but it is not exhaustive. Ensure you do your own due diligence and research into any organisation you may choose to use (including these). Some may charge a fee while others may not; it is not our place to suggest which you should use. However, the activity provides you with a checklist of research points to use when selecting or debating various organisations.

- British Council European Voluntary Service: https://www.erasmusplus.org.uk/
- Camps International: https://campsinternational.com/
- Go Abroad: https://www.goabroad.com/
- Global Vision International: https://www.gvi.co.uk/
- International Volunteer HQ: https://www.volunteerhq.org/
- gvi: https://www.gvi.co.uk/
- Love Volunteers: https://www.lovevolunteers.org/
- Podvolunteer: https://www.podvolunteer.org/
- Projects Abroad: https://www.projects-abroad.co.uk/
- Travel Philanthropy: http://www.travelphilanthropy.org.uk/giving/
- Tru Experience Travel: https://www.truexperiencetravel.co.uk/

 ━━━ ACTIVITY ━━━

Checklist for researching voluntourism organisations

Use the following list of checkpoints to inform your research on voluntourism organisations. The table is a suggestion of how you might collate and lay out your findings:

Checkpoint 1: Track record

- Is there evidence of their past achievements?
- Is there any evidence of research or how they monitor long-term impacts?

Checkpoint 2: Integrity

- What language do they use; is there overuse of the word ethical, for example?
- Do they offer orphanage placements?*
- Within animal welfare positions are there opportunities to ride elephants and have hands on contact with animals?*

*If you answer yes to the last two you should probably rule these out.

Checkpoint 3: Accountability

- Who owns the organisation?
- Who is running the project?
- Are they the same organisation? (Many projects are offered via a broker rather than those running projects)

Checkpoint 4: Selectivity

- Do you need to make an application?
- Are you vetted as part of this process?
- Are you asked about your skills or required to provide a reference?
- Do you have to attend an interview?

Checkpoint 5: Credibility

- Does the organisation oversimplify the cause for commercialisation?
- Are sweeping statements made such as 'end poverty' or 'help a child survive'? These suggest a more commercial enterprise commodifying serious causes for monetary gains

Table 22.3 Checkpoint-based research on voluntourism organisations

Organisation name	Checkpoint 1	Checkpoint 2	Checkpoint 3	Checkpoint 4	Checkpoint 5

Source: ReThink Orphanages, 2018; Save the Children, 2017

It is important to understand the criticisms and challenges facing voluntourism in order to establish greater responsibility and understanding when undertaking such roles. These types of experience can be significantly beneficial to both you and the destination; they can be all they are often perceived to be. However, you should also feel better prepared to take ownership of where you apply and possess the tools to make an informed decision about their ethical practice and whether the emphasis is on you as a tourist or on the project and you as a volunteer.

CONCLUSION

In this chapter we have covered:

• The benefits of volunteering and how to find opportunities
• The transferable skills you can build through volunteering
• The ethical debate associated with voluntourism

FURTHER READING

ECPAT (2016) *In Brief: Volun-tourism* (www.ecpat.org/wp-content/uploads/2016/10/Volun-tourism.pdf)

Indeed (2016) *Volunteering and the Workplace: Hands up for New Skills* (www.london.gov.uk/sites/default/files/indeed_report_-_final_version.pdf)

ReThink Orphanages (2018) *Responsible Volunteering Abroad: How To Be A Responsible Volunteer?* (rethinkorphanages.org/individual-orphanage-volunteering/responsible-volunteer-checklist)

Save the Children (2017) *The Truth about Voluntourism* (www.savethechildren.org.au/Our-Stories/The-truth-about-voluntourism)

Wearing, S., Young, T. and Everingham, P. (2017) 'Evaluating volunteer tourism: Has it made a difference?', *Tourism Recreation Research*, 42(4): 512–521.

SECTION D

CAREER PLANNING AND PREPARATION

Level 5 - 6

23 SUCCESSFUL TRANSITION INTO THE WORLD OF WORK

By the end of this chapter, you should be able to:

- Feel confident in the career planning process as you contemplate leaving university or college and embark on your first job
- Understand concepts about the transition into the world of work and how you might approach getting started on your career ladder
- Approach starting at a new organisation and work environment with confidence and awareness
- Make the most of the few first weeks and months of a new job
- Understand the value of purpose of an induction, a probation period, and a mentor to support you in your transition into work

GLOSSARY

- **Induction:** a formal introduction to your new organisation and workplace. A period of training, development and support to help you ease into the organisation. Usually comprises a few days in which you meet key people and receive key information and guidance
- **Mentoring:** a relationship where a more experienced or more knowledgeable person guides a less experienced or less knowledgeable person, although sometimes you might come across 'reverse mentoring' where a less experienced colleague mentors a more senior colleague for a range of reasons (e.g. an insight into the work 'on the shop floor')

(Continued)

- **Payroll:** a list of employees that an organisation must pay. An organisation will keep a record of payments given to employees, including salaries, wages, bonuses and deductions
- **Probation:** a safety net for employers after the recruitment stage (and for you too if you change your mind). The probation period is a period of time (typically anywhere between one and six months) in which you are expected to meet certain performance levels that might include specific targets. The probation period usually ends with a report and review. Failure to meet probation requirements could lead to an employer dismissing an employee without fear of unfair dismissal claims and employment tribunals

INTRODUCTION

This chapter introduces the concept of moving from university or college into a job within the tourism, events or hospitality sectors. The transition to the workplace can be extremely daunting, so this chapter provides advice, guidance and insights into how you can make this adjustment as smoothly as possible. It is our aim to reduce your uncertainly and trepidation as you embark upon your career and reassure you as you start applying for roles and take your first steps into the working environment after you graduate. By examining different perspectives on the transition to work, it looks at how you can engage in positive adjustment processes, as well as how you might approach socialisation into a new organisation.

In examining some of the possible challenges of starting your first job, we hope to build your confidence. In drawing upon models such as regulatory focus theory and models of transition success, we also look at 'fit' (see Chapter 24) and navigating the politics in a new workplace, whilst also discussing how you might develop and make the most of emerging networks and work relationships. Finally, we look at the importance of **mentoring** in the workplace.

SOCIALISATION INTO A NEW ORGANISATION

Joining a new workplace and organisation can be extremely daunting and aligns to what Jones (1983) has referred to as 'psychological orientation' in the workplace and the process of organisational socialisation (Ashforth, Saks and Lee, 1998). A well-established model of socialisation was offered by Van Maanen and Schein (1979) who categorised formal and informal tactics for workplace socialisation. They argue that organisations will generally seek to put newcomers through a common set of experiences (see **induction** below) whilst ensuring there are also unique experiences that allow individuals to differentiate themselves and forge their own workplace identity. It is suggested that successful socialisation seeks to foster some conformity (as opposed to innovation) amongst newcomers, which helps aid adjustment to their new work environment as well as alignment to the company or organisation's goals (Baker and Feldman, 1990). If you can effectively socialise, this has been linked to positive work attitudes and behaviours, which include your motivation to work, job involvement, organisational commitment, low turnover, innovative and cooperative behaviour (Feldman, 1981).

You may have gained work experience through internships or a part-time job (as covered in Chapters 21 and 22) but you may still feel under-prepared. To combat this, you might develop a quick elevator pitch about yourself. This brief introduction should include where you used to work, who you are, and what you hope to do in your new role. This will help prepare for you for the inevitable conversations you will have with multiple new colleagues when you start. People will be interested in you, what you can bring to their organisation and if they can work with you. Some more top tips about socialising yourself into the workplace are listed below (see also Chapter 27 on effective networking).

What should I wear?

This depends on the job. You might be issued with a uniform (e.g. if you are cabin crew for an airline), or their might be a formal dress code. You should ask well in advance of your first day and if in doubt it is better to be too smart – you can always dress down if you find that others are wearing more relaxed attire (see the Student insight from Emma below). Another useful tip is to discreetly ask a colleague if you're dressed appropriately, if you still have concerns. You may wish to wear a suit, particularly in an office environment. Certainly avoid ripped jeans, trainers, shorts and similar informal 'leisure' wear. A good rule of thumb is to wear something similar to what you wore for your interview (see Chapter 31).

Your first day at work

Your new colleagues will know it is your first day and should be around to tell you where key places are such as the toilets and coffee machine. Reduce any anxiety by planning your first day thoroughly, ensuring you have read everything your employer sends you before your start. It is always advisable to do a practice run into your workplace if you have to navigate traffic or public transport. Ensure you do this at the same time of day as your commute will be, as 'rush hour' might take you longer than travelling in later in the day.

Top tips for first day of work:

- Always double check the time they are expecting you. This will be in your appointment letter or email. Try to show up around 10–15 minutes earlier than your start time so that you don't feel stressed about being late. Enter the office on time or just before your official start time.
- Ensure you bring the documents you need (e.g. passport, national insurance details, driving licence, visa etc.) as well as some cash for parking, buying lunch or maybe a coffee for new colleagues.
- Bring a notepad and pen so you can make notes of passwords, people's names and key information
- Try to get to know at least one colleague and introduce yourself. The sooner you have someone that you can ask for help, the sooner you will feel comfortable and confident.
- Avoid using your phone (turn it on silent). If colleagues and employers see you on social media or texting friends on your first day it won't give a good first impression. You will be distracted and you may come across as disinterested. If you are worried about having your phone off, in an emergency, someone will call you on the work landline. Ensure your family have your work landline number because your mobile might also run out of battery or get lost. Remember to give your partner and family the name of your manager and a landline number where you can be contacted in an emergency if your mobile is off, out of battery, or left somewhere.
- Be positive. Ensure your body language projects someone who is enthusiastic and keen (see Chapter 14).
- Don't bring in lunch or snacks with a strong smell (e.g. egg salad or tuna sandwiches) until you know what the lunchtime arrangements are – you don't want to risk making a whole corridor smell of your lunch.

A typical first day will include:

- Final Human Resource checks – this might be photocopying your ID or certificates and qualifications. You might also need to complete a lot of forms which require details of your bank details and sign a contract. You will need to complete these final checks to set you on the **payroll**, i.e. to get paid.
- You are will be given company policies (email, online or as printed handbook) and although you should not feel obliged to read it on the first day, it is a good idea to familiarise yourself with them during the first few days
- Meet your line manager. This is likely to be a very short meeting as they will be aware you will be feeling nervous and need to get used to the workplace before thinking about specific tasks, projects and responsibilities.
- Being shown to your desk or office and being introduced to your key work colleagues. You might be concerned that people won't like you or won't talk to you. Be brave and approach a few people and introduce yourself. They will know you are new and will want to help you settle in.
- You may well be given a laptop or computer if it is relevant to your job and you will need to ensure you have key passwords, usernames and the applications you require for your work.
- You are likely to be given an office or building tour. You are not expected to remember where everything is and learn everyone's names, so don't be afraid to ask people their names again or ask them to remind you where key things are, like the stationary cupboard or printing room.
- You are likely to be invited to lunch. Ensure you join colleagues, to show you want to be social and become part of the team. Socialisation like this is key as it shapes the way employees view teamwork and encourages the sharing of information
- You will receive advice on what compulsory staff training you will need to undertake. Our advice is to complete this sooner rather than later (they are often mandatory online courses covering key legal obligations and health and safety issues).
- Check if you have a **probation** period. You should ensure that you understand what you need to do to pass your probation, including any targets that you need to meet.
- Don't be tempted to stay late on your first day. Keep your energy as it will be an exhausting time for you.

 THINK POINT

When you meet a lot of new people, you might find it difficult to remember their names. A top tip is to sketch a little map of your office on your first day and put people's names in where they sit and what they do.

Think about how you best remember names. This might be recalling where they come from, their role or something about their appearance. Find a way that works for you.

According to *Psychology Today* (2020), the ability to remember names worsens with age, as nearly 85% of middle-aged and older adults forget names. A tip to help other people to remember your name is to repeat your first name when introducing yourself, e.g. 'Hi, I'm Sally, Sally Everett.' Although it sounds a little like James Bond introducing himself, this method of repetition works. You can also use this at conferences and in large meetings. We also suggest if you have a long name that you introduce yourself with your full name and then give the name you actually use e.g. 'I'm Mary-Jayne Monk. Please call me MJ.' It has been noted by Foer (2012) amongst others that we no longer remember telephone numbers because our mobile phones do that for us, and likewise we don't remember addresses as we use computers to send emails. Put simply, he suggests that we are forgetting how to remember. This was also highlighted in a study where the use of more memory aids such as lists and our phones for navigation purposes was found to make us lose the ability to remember things (Gilbert et al., 2020). However, one area in which you need to find a way to remember a lot of names is in your new workplace, so Hedges (2013) offer five ways to remember names! Try these out in the activity below.

═══ ACTIVITY ═══

Remembering people's names

The next time you meet a group of new people, try out the five ways Hedges (2013) (writing for *Forbes* magazine) suggests:

- Meet and repeat − try to use their name again shortly after they introduce themselves, e.g. 'Hi Elena. It's nice to meet you, Elena.'
- Ask them to spell their name or quietly spell it yourself (unless it is very straightforward and easy to spell). This process helps create a visual memory. If they have a business card, take it so you have a visual prompt.
- Associate their name with something or a place, e.g. Ahmed is in advertising, or Bibi lives in Brighton.
- Make a connection with someone else you know or someone famous. For example, Michelle in finance is American, so you might remember her name by associating her with Michelle Obama.
- Decide to care − take the time and make a conscious decision to remember a name.

ENSURING YOU HAVE A SUCCESSFUL FIRST COUPLE OF WEEKS AND MONTHS

Be proactive in your approach with people (conversations, going to lunch, meeting after work if you are invited, etc.). If you are passive, your colleagues may assume that you do not wish to interact with them. Try to set the tone for the rest of your career in those first few days (see Chapter 27 for advice on networking and getting to know people). Talk to people about their own first days and what helped them succeed in your organisation. You might also think about more formal questions that you want to ask about the role and company. You will meet your managers in the first few weeks and this is your opportunity to ask those naïve questions about things you might be expected to know later on.

You might have heard the phrase 'office politics'. This refers to who has the power and authority in the organisation, and who reports to whom. Every organisation has a culture and it is useful to understand this and 'how things are done around here' so you can get along with people. Of course, down the line you might wish to challenge the orthodox ways of working, but it is advisable to get to know a place first. It may be wise to keep your own counsel to start and not be too trusting at first (Rook, 2013). Try to avoid becoming drawn into any gossip or politics before you understand the relationships and people involved. Learn from your own mistakes and ensure you continue to reflect on your behaviour, what others are saying around you, and what you say and do. You should also be able to accept constructive criticism and use this feedback in your own personal development. We have encouraged you to be reflective throughout this book (as well as more explicitly in Chapter 10) and it is a great skill to be able to learn from one's own errors and experiences.

Induction

ACAS (2020) offer employers some excellent advice on what an induction should include and you should expect at least some, of these components.

- A brief history of the organisation
- Future plans, strategies and developments for the organisation
- An organisational chart of who is who
- Training needs – ensure you write these down as you get to know the organisation
- Probationary requirements, your holiday allowance, when you will get paid, and how pensions work.
- You should become familiar with the organisation's rules on absence, sickness, discipline, complaints, and performance. It may also be helpful to obtain the policies on email and phone use, parental leave and periods of notice (although best not to ask about notice periods explicitly and this early!)
- Health and safety training (and if you are using a computer, this will include a display screen and working station check).

After a couple of months, you may wish to ask about future development needs and coaching. By then you should have been allocated a mentor, whom you are meeting with regularly. Ensure you also regularly meet with your line manager and agree on timescales and work targets. It would also be a good opportunity to reflect on your probation requirements (if you have them) and think about what you still need to do to ensure you pass your probation period.

 STUDENT INSIGHT

My first day in the office (Emma)

I had left myself plenty of time to arrive to my new office on my first day, but the postcode I was given was incorrect and took me to a completely different carpark! Consequently, I couldn't get in and then I had to phone my new manager, Richard, and say I did not know where I was. He had to provide directions by telephone to help me get in! Unfortunately, this meant I was late. This made me feel really stressed and I hadn't even got into the office!

I made the error of turning up in my jeans as they said the office was 'informal', but wearing a rock concert T-shirt and jeans was not what they had meant! I had not been to the office before and soon became embarrassed because it was an open plan office! This meant that everyone saw me as I arrived to 'informally' meet my team and so I couldn't hide the fact that I was completely underdressed! Thankfully people thought it was funny and I ended up working for them for six years! I would advise students to check the dress code properly when they start!

Once the embarrassment has passed, Aysha, my mentor, showed me around the office and helped me obtain my key card. I was encouraged to chat through my job role, what I was responsible for and how the different tasks were distributed across the team. Later that day, I was given time to set myself up at my desk and computer before I had to attend a few meetings with key people (still in my jeans and rock T-shirt!). I was excited to start as this was one of the travel companies I had longed to work for, but in hindsight I should have dressed a little more smartly!

Learning how to work

In a recent online article based on her doctoral research, Moynihan (2020) explored why some employers felt that some students were weak in their transition out of university, finding many students who thought they were prepared and experienced were often the most dissatisfied post-transition. She has developed her findings into the 'The Implicit Model of Transition Success', which highlights how many graduates are missing out on the essential planning and preparation needed to successfully transition into the working world. Moynihan's advice includes talking to alumni at your university and those already in work, so that you feel prepared. You should also be making an effort to manage your own career and personal development before you apply for your first job. You should then be thinking about how it might link into the rest of your career: what you might want to do next in terms of skills development; what other parts of the business might you care to explore; what projects would you like to get involved with.

There are theories on how people 'learn' to work, especially if they are just out of university or moving into an office workplace from a very different employment setting e.g. bar work, entrepreneurial roles, outdoor or location-independent working, or within a factory environment, for example. You will need to grasp the dynamics of an unfamiliar and complex environment quickly. Jacquelyn Smith, writing for *Forbes* (2013), argues that students and blue-collar workers can often find it challenging to understand office politics, to learn a more delicate etiquette structure, and to decipher unwritten rules and norms. Our advice is to cultivate positive relationships those around you and show you are a team player. The quicker you fit in, the sooner you will feel comfortable and confident.

Try to avoid making assumptions about what is expected of you and instead listen carefully to your manager. Be as flexible and pragmatic as you can. If you don't please your manager, it will be difficult to progress within the organisation. Furthermore, as a student you may have been able to skip the odd lecture, or hand in work a day late (usually with a penalty) but in the workplace you need to make a good impression from day one and that will include arriving on time, dressing appropriately, and respecting those around you. Above all, be patient as it will take time to get used to a new environment. Unlike at university, you won't have a team of welfare officers, student experience teams and academic lecturers to frame and support your first few days. Your first few months should be focused on learning exactly how you fit into the big picture of the organisation

THINK POINT

What learning strategy will you adopt when you start work? Think about your approach and draw on what has worked in the past.

Aligning your goals with your values and beliefs

As you develop goals for your career and life, you should fit with those around you (see Chapter 24). One of the common theories in this area of work is regulatory focus theory (Brockner and Higgins, 2001). Self-regulation explains the process by which people seek to align themselves (i.e. their behaviours and self-conceptions) with appropriate goals or standards. Ultimately, it is a goal-pursuit theory, which considers how people make decisions in line with goals. Regulatory fit theory suggests that a match between orientation to a goal and the means used to approach that goal produces a state of regulatory fit that ensures you will have a feeling of 'rightness' about the goal pursuit and the way you engage with tasks. One of the key foci the research posits is that this sense of alignment directly translates into job satisfaction. It is important that you pursue a goal that aligns with your own personal values and beliefs. What are the values of the organisation you are applying for? Are they aligned with your own?

As you think about moving into work, it is advisable to gain a fuller picture of what it might entail. Of course, internships and/or part-time work can help this process, but talking to people in the roles you wish to apply for is also invaluable.

 EMPLOYER INSIGHT

A Day-in-the-Life of an Events Officer. Jeannie at Event Planet, Australia reflects on her role

Event Planet is a full service event management agency. They design, manage and deliver bespoke events for clients in Australia and abroad. Jeannie reflects on what she was doing during an average day two months into her time as an events officer after graduating in event management.

- 6:00 AM: I'm up and ready to start my day. I have a half hour commute so will often take coffee with me as I leave the house.
- 6.50 AM: If there is an event that day, I try to arrive an hour before it starts.
- 7:15-7.45 AM: We need to prepare for the day so I need to check the venue, pack the delegate bags, check and arrange the chairs, check the food and ensure the security is in place. It is important that I have my phone as I need to check for last-minute emails and for any issues that might make people late, like traffic. I print the guest list.
- 8-9 AM: The event starts. I check the IT and presentations work. I introduce people and ensure front of house are ready with name tags and that the sales team are ready and prepared and that banners are displayed.
- 10:30 AM: The morning event finishes and we need to tidy up quickly to ensure we leave the venue on time. I thank the guests for attending and with the sales team we chat with clients about future events and ensure that their guests leave with the packs.
- 12:30 PM: I need to get back to the office and check emails for anything that I need to sort urgently. I then need to set up some meetings with the team and ensure we start planning for the next event.
- 1:30 PM: If I can squeeze it in, I try and grab lunch. This is, however, a good time to catch up with colleagues, and check what is happening in the news in case of traffic jams or adverse weather expected during future events. An hour for lunch is rare, as something will pull me back into the emails!
- 2:30 PM: I'm back at my desk, meeting the design team regarding marketing and how we are going to generate interest for future events.
- 3:30 PM: It is likely I am in meetings with my boss the events manager and the events team to plan for future events. We finalise the plans and schedules for those happening in the near future.

- 4:30 PM: I use social media to raise awareness about some events and update the website.
- 5:30-6 PM: I catch up on any emails that I didn't get to, and I write my to-do list for the next day.
- 6:00 PM: I try and leave the office by this time and head to the gym or go out with colleagues! It's a social place to work!

Event Planet. https://www.eventplanet.com.au/

MENTORING AND MAKING THE MOST OF YOUR MENTOR

Many travel companies are investing in formal mentoring schemes (Travel Weekly, 2006). Many organisations will assign new members of staff to a mentor. This will usually be someone more experienced and senior than you and you will have regular meetings during your first new months (probably once a month).

For you as the mentee, it is valuable to 'learn the ropes' from someone who understands the organisation and can provide guidance, advice and reassurance. Mentors will be chosen because they are trusted by the organisation and can positively influence new members of staff. They might be able to open doors for you, introduce you to key people and champion your ideas in meetings. There are also rewards for the mentor as they can learn from you and be positively challenged by your new approaches and ideas. Having a sounding board (usually conversations are confidential) can reduce anxiety and stress. You can test out ideas with your mentor or ask questions that you wouldn't feel comfortable asking in a large staff meeting. Mentoring should be part of your self-improvement and development plan, and in time, it will be important for you to 'give back' and mentor others.

Even if you don't have a formal mentor, you should consider shadowing those in the know. Find an ally or a nearby colleague who can show you the processes. Watching how they work should make you more confident that you can engage with your role and the organisation. Take time to observe people first and ensure you shadow people with a positive attitude and work ethic, as not everyone will be a good person to follow! Ask questions sparingly (too many may become annoying) and use the support around you.

According to Shine (2020) (an organisation that sets up mentoring schemes for travel and tourism companies), not enough travel companies are taking advantage of this relatively low-cost form of training and development. Do ask if there is a mentoring scheme when you join your organisation.

═══ INDUSTRY INSIGHT ═══

Mentoring female leaders in the hospitality industry

In 2018, Odgers Berndtson launched a 'Charter for Change' and with input from leaders in the hospitality industry, they developed mentoring and development initiatives that could support and launch more women into senior leadership roles.

Odgers Berndtson found that the hospitality industry 'represents a serious challenge for diversity and inclusion. There are plenty of women in entry-level and management-level roles but the numbers dwindle in the c-suite and the boardroom. Furthermore, the women who have been appointed to hospitality industry

(Continued)

board positions tend to be non-executive directors from other industries.' Given that only three FTSE 250 hospitality firms had female executives, mentoring was identified as an effective approach to ensure women are encouraged in their career progression.

Building on this, in October 2018, Odgers Berndtson launched the Plan B Leadership Mentoring Programme in collaboration with UKHospitality, Elliotts and BT Sport. This work was premised on the belief that mentoring is key within the workplace for new members of staff and for ongoing development. They noted that in addition to formal mentoring, informal mentoring relationships also develop organically. However, 'in the hospitality industry especially, women can feel very lonely at the top and there may not be many obvious role models' (Odgers Berndtson, 2018).

Source: https://www.odgersberndtson.com/en-gb/insights/launching-women-into-hospitality-senior-leadership

---

Although this chapter has looked at the transition to work, you should use all the chapters in this book to gain a full understanding of the career planning process, how you can best prepare for your first job and how you approach recruitment. The more you understand about the selection process and how you might 'fit' with an organisation (Chapter 25), your own personal brand (Chapter 26) and how you can make the most of networking and other people (Chapter 27), the less daunted your should feel by the workplace.

CONCLUSION

In this chapter we have covered:

* What to expect on your first day of work and how to get the most from it
* How to prepare yourself for the first months of work
* How to successful manage the transition to work from studies
* The importance of aligning your goals, values and beliefs with those of your organisation
* The importance of having a mentor at work and the value that both the mentee and mentor gain from this relationship

FURTHER READING

ACAS (2020) *Checklist for Inducting New Staff into a Business*. Available from https://www.acas.org.uk/checklist-for-induction-of-new-staff

Foer, J.(2012). *Moonwalking with Einstein: The Art and Science of Remembering Everything*. London: Penguin

Gilbert, S.J., Bird, A., Carpenter, J.M., Fleming, S.M., Sachdeva, C., & Tsai, P.C. (2020). 'Optimal use of reminders: Metacognition, effort, and cognitive offloading'. *Journal of Experimental Psychology: General*, 149 (3), 501–517.

Hedges, K. (2013). *The Five Best Tricks to Remember Names*. https://www.forbes.com/sites/work-in-progress/2013/08/21/the-best-five-tricks-to-remember-names/#7dd1d4f501f6

Smith, J (2013) '12 tips for transitioning to an office job'. Available from: https://www.forbes.com/sites/jacquelynsmith/2013/11/22/12-tips-for-transitioning-to-an-office-job/#6ece703b4dbe

Useful web resources

Shine (2020) 'Build your tourism marketing strategy and planning'. Available from: https://www.shinepeople andplaces.co.uk/

Travel Weekly (2006) 'Mentoring in the travel industry'. Available from: http://www.travelweekly.co.uk/ articles/22054/mentoring-in-the-travel-industry

24 UNDERSTANDING THE SELECTION PROCESS

CHAPTER LEARNING OBJECTIVES

By the end of this chapter you should be able to:

* Define recruitment and selection
* Understand the process of selection within tourism, hospitality and events organisations
* Appreciate the importance of job descriptions and person specifications
* Know what is meant by 'fit' and how you can judge it
* Understand what is meant by bias and how this can play out in the selection process

GLOSSARY

* **Recruitment:** the process a company undertakes to attract high quality, suitably qualified and experienced candidates to apply for jobs
* **Job description:** a description of the role and responsibilities of a job that is being advertised
* **Person specification:** a description of the range of knowledge, skills, experience, attitudes and behaviours that an organisation is looking for in an employee
* **Fit:** the compatibility between two things, in this case the compatibility between applicants and a job or an applicant and an organisation
* **Bias:** a positive or negative inclination towards a person, consciously or unconsciously, based on our own background, experiences and stereotypes

INTRODUCTION

Having read Chapter 23, you might now feel happier about the transition into the world of work and have some ideas about how you might approach your first days in a new job. However, you need to first secure this job! After you have spent time searching for a job, applying for a full-time job in the tourism, hospitality and event sectors can feel like a step into the unknown. Depending on your level of experience, you might have gone through the application process before or you might be doing it for the first time. In either case, you are possibly wondering what happens within an organisation when they are looking for new staff, and how you can get ahead with your application to improve your chances of being invited to interview and chosen ultimately as the ideal candidate. Understanding some of the processes behind the scenes before you engage with the actual application process covered in Chapters 31, 32 and 33 should help reassure you.

In this chapter, we attempt to de-mystify the process of selection, that is, the steps an employer might go through while considering your suitability for a job. We will look at **recruitment** and selection from an organisation's perspective initially so you can understand what the process is, the different stages involved, and what employers are looking for. Through case study examples and activities, you will gain experience of evaluating what employers are looking for and reflecting on the extent to which you might **fit** with the 'employer insight' example roles in this chapter. In doing this, you will hopefully develop an understanding of whether you are a good fit for a job, which will give you the confidence to apply for your dream job.

THE RECRUITMENT AND SELECTION PROCESS: AN ORGANISATIONAL PERSPECTIVE

The act of recruitment and selection is the process that an organisation undertakes when it is looking to hire new staff. The nature of the process varies from organisation to organisation and is informed by an organisation's strategies and employment policies, as well as national laws relating to employment and workers' rights (e.g. equality and diversity legislation). It might also vary depending on the position that is advertised. For instance, Nickson (2013) notes that a graduate hotel management recruitment scheme might use expensive and sophisticated methods, such as assessment centres, whereas a part-time seasonal employee might be recruited by word of mouth. While being mindful of these differences, this section of the chapter focuses on the more formal process of recruitment and selection of college/university graduates for management positions.

Figure 24.1 presents the typical recruitment and selection process, and the two sections that follow will explain the stages in more detail. However, it is important to note that the figure is highly simplified and suggests that the process is linear. However, in reality there could be many 'backward loops' from one stage to an earlier stage, for instance if the process results in no appointable candidate and the organisation has to advertise again for more applications. Despite this limitation, it can provide you with a broad understanding of the different phases involved in recruitment and selection within tourism, hospitality and event organisations.

Recruitment

Recruitment and selection are complementary activities, but they are not the same thing. Recruitment is the first part of the process, which aims to attract a high quality, suitably qualified and experienced

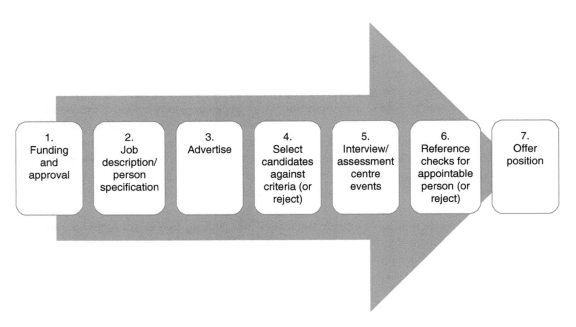

Figure 24.1   The phases of the recruitment and selection process

field of candidates for vacant posts that contribute to organisational goals. This is the point where the organisation is in contact with 'the outside world' and usually refers to stages 1–3 of Figure 24.1. The recruitment process typically begins with a hiring manager procuring approval and funding to advertise a position. This approval is usually given because the post, be it a new post or an existing vacancy, meets the strategic and/or operational needs of the business.

The hiring manager will work to develop a **job description** – which outlines the key roles and responsibilities of the job that is being advertised – and a **person specification**, which summarises the range of knowledge, skills and experience that they are seeking in the post-holder. The importance of accurate job descriptions and person specifications cannot be over-stated. Doing so should ensure that the pool of candidates is not too great to be processed by an organisation. When this does not happen, the impact can be problematic: Van der Wagen and White (2014, p.148) describe a local council that advertised for an event manager post and received 1,000 applications to review through because it had not been sufficiently specific during the recruitment process.

Next, the organisation will advertise the vacancy using their own website or social media platforms, local/national press, tourism, hospitality and event trade publications and professional associations, recruitment agencies or college/university careers services (see Chapters 20 and 21). You can see two examples in the 'Industry Insight' examples later in this chapter. The advert will often include information about the organisation, the job description, person specification, the nature of the position (permanent/fixed term, full-/part-time), a starting salary and the closing date for receiving applications. It will also tell you how to apply for the job (e.g., online, by post or in person) and what you need to submit in order to apply (e.g., application form, covering letter, CV etc.). You can find out more about how to write a strong CV, application form and covering letter in Chapters 29 and 30.

Restaurant Manager needed

This job was advertised in *The Caterer* (www.caterer.com), a source that is well worth looking at if you are searching for a job in the hospitality industry. Because it was advertised in *The Caterer* on behalf of a recruitment agency, you will see that the name of the employer is not mentioned, only the location. It should be noted that the layout of this advertisement is relatively informal and the typeface, including some typographic errors, are as presented in the original advert. The tone is also quite informal, describing the ideal candidate as a 'bubbly character' who is willing to be 'very hands on', while stressing quality at the heart of the inn's offer. The contract type, salary and benefits (tips and live-in accommodation) are outlined.

> Hard working, Restaurant Manager needed for very high-quality Inn £22,000 + Great Tips Leyburn area, North Yorkshire Live-in available on site

This is an excellent opportunity for an bubbly character that **has Restaurant, Pub or hotel supervisor/ managerial** experience within a high quality food and beverage outlet and would thrive in a quality local inn/ restaurant environment.

This small Inn has a popular Restaurant and Bar which also serves a vast array of quality ales and wines.

You will within a very small team and report to the GM. You will have a very small team with you therefore this **role is very hands on.**

This is a excellent opportunity for a candidate with some quality gastro /restaurant experience **looking for their first MANAGER role or an existing Supervisor /manager seeking a new challenge.**

As **Restaurant Manager** you are expected to be well presented, friendly, enthusiastic and willing to give 100% and be a very hands on.

As **Restaurant Manager** you will lead and work within a small team – therefore strong leadership and organisational skills are essential.

As **Restaurant Manager** duties will also include running duty manager shifts, doing rotas, staff training etc.

You are also required to promote and maintain the reputation of the establishment by ensuring and providing excellent customer care and service.

For this role the ideal Restaurant Manager will have supervisor/manager experience a quality environment.

This Restaurant Manager role is a full time, permanent role

This Hotel is near Leyburn and has live in available on site. You will ideally have your own accommodation due to the village location. The successful applicant for this Restaurant Manager role will receive a salary of up to £22,000 + good tips and live in.

Event Coordinator

This job was sourced from *The Guardian* Jobs website (https://jobs.theguardian.com/), which advertises a range of jobs across tourism, hospitality and events, as well as other sectors. *The Guardian* was advertising

(Continued)

the post on behalf of a recruitment agency and so the company name is not revealed, only the location. The layout of this advertisement is a relatively standard example of the presentation of job description (tasks and responsibilities) and person specification (the candidate). It also includes the type of contract and the salary (note: DOE means 'depends on experience').

Location	South East London
Salary	£22–27,000 – DOE
Job level	Experienced (non-manager)
Hours	Fulltime
Contract	Permanent
Education	Undergraduate degree (or equivalent)

Rapidly expanding B2B conference and events company with a great company culture are looking to bring on a Graduate Event Coordinator to join their team.

Do you see yourself running a conference, troubleshooting at a live event, organising everyone on the day and loving the atmosphere and challenge of a room full of people you are in charge of?

Do you love checklists, organising, communicating and the satisfaction of being the organisational centre of an event? Can you see yourself meticulously preparing conference materials, liaising with speakers, sponsors and delegates and making sure everything is just right?

This company prides itself in being a fun and exciting place to work where everyone counts, and everyone's say is important. They look for ambitious individuals who want to bring new ideas to the table and contribute a positive attitude.

This fun, friendly and warm team is expanding so if you're a bright, organised, well presented and a high-energy individual, they will be committed to help drive your career forward.

Key tasks and responsibilities

- Organising and running events from start to finish
- Onsite troubleshooting and innovations
- Liaising with key stakeholders (sponsors, exhibitors, speakers and venues)
- Liaising with customers and delegates
- Issuing invoices and chasing payments
- General administration

The candidate

- Minimum 1 year experience in conferences
- Bright graduate with a good academic background. Minimum 2:1 degree
- Computer literate and proficient in Excel, PowerPoint and Word
- A proactive, positive and 'can do' attitude
- A commercial mind and determination to succeed
- An exceptional eye for detail. Must have perfect written English – experience in proofreading is an advantage
- Ability to work under pressure and to tight deadline
- Problem solving, self-motivation and initiative

Reviewing job advertisements

Read the two advertisements for a Restaurant Manager and an Event Coordinator within the two Employer insight boxes above. Compare and contrast the format and tone of the advertisements.

1. What do you think are the strengths and weaknesses of these advertisements?
2. Do you have a preference for a particular advert style, and why?
3. What impressions do the adverts suggest to you about the companies and their cultures, and why?
4. How would you tailor your application to best fit the culture?

Selection

Selection refers to stages 4–7 of Figure 24.1. Selection takes place after applications have been received and hiring managers review the candidates to establish the best person to do the job (Hook, Jenkins and Foot, 2015). Stage 4 describes the first step in the selection process. This involves hiring managers and sometimes involves a wider recruitment panel reviewing written submissions, such as application forms, covering letters or CVs. At this point the criteria included in the job description and person specification, developed in Stage 2, will be used to evaluate applications and an initial judgement will be made about the goodness of fit between the candidate and the post's requirements. Candidates who score well, usually because they meet all the essential and all/some of the desirable criteria, will proceed to the next stage of the selection process. Those applicants who do not score highly will be rejected and notified. It is worth noting, however, that some organisations do not notify candidates that they have been unsuccessful; a survey by Clutch (2018) revealed that more than a third of unsuccessful job seekers in the US did not receive notification from the company.

Applicants who make it to stage 5 of the selection process will often be interviewed by the hiring manager. However, sometimes an interview panel will also be involved, possibly including a senior manager, a representative from the Human Resource or Personnel division, a line manager and/or a peer co-worker. It is important to note that composition of interview panels differ between organisations and countries. Equally, the style of the interview can vary depending on the role that is being advertised: sometimes applicants are interviewed individually and sometimes it is amongst a group of applicants.

Interviews are sometimes supplemented with other selection techniques as part of an assessment centre event, lasting anywhere between a few hours or a few days. The benefit of an assessment centre is that it allows large organisations to select candidates from a wide pool of applications using a variety of techniques, such as presentations, group tasks, psychometric tests, role plays and written tests (Prospects, 2019). It also benefits you as an applicant because it allows you to demonstrate the breadth of knowledge and skills that you have more effectively than you can on your paper application and CV. You can find out more about interviews, psychometric tests and assessment centres in Chapters 31, 32 and 33.

When successful candidates have been identified through interview or other selection techniques during an assessment centre, references and other background checks are performed. If these return satisfactory results, the employer then offers the successful candidate the job and they will talk to you about your start date and starting salary. Unsuccessful candidates will be rejected and usually informed although, as stated previously, this does not always happen.

THE IMPORTANCE OF 'FIT'

There are different ways of viewing fit. Mikkelsen (2015) explains that 'person-job fit' is an overarching measure of the compatibility between the applicant and the job, but that it has many sub-sets of fit because jobs and organisations are complex. Examples of these sub-sets include:

- Person-role: fit with the job requirements
- Person-group/team: fit with co-workers
- Person-organisation/company: fit with organisational attributes
- Person-person: fit with individuals

Fit, therefore, is a judgement of the closeness of match between you, as a candidate that is applying for a position, and the requirements of a job and an organisation, which are typically outlined in job descriptions and person specifications. Thus, Nickson explains that fit might be '"loose" – that is, applicants have the ability to do the job – or "tight", where the individual has to demonstrate not only technical competence but whether they have the specific personality profile to "fit" the organisational culture' (2013: 90).

Of all these fit types, Mikkelsen goes on to state that we usually talk about person-role fit when we speak about person-job fit. Getting the right 'person-job fit' can contribute to improved organisational performance (Dessler, 2016). It will ensure that the person that has been appointed is able to perform well in the job as quickly as possible after induction/orientation and any initial training that is required. It is also costly to recruit new staff, and a US study by Bloomberg (cited in Dessler, 2016: 203) reveals that 'bad hires' were found to cost organisations an average of US$50,000. In addition, improper selection processes, such as those that are perceived to be discriminatory or negligent, can have legal consequences for a company or tarnish its brand.

When it comes to making judgements about person-job (P-J) fit, Kristof-Brown (2000) found that knowledge, skills and attitudes were considered most often by employers. In contrast, personality traits – which 'may be inferred from nonverbal behavio[u]rs and appearance, as well as applicant responses' (Kristof-Brown, 2000: 663) – were considered most often when evaluating person-organisation (P-O) fit. However, it is important to note that, to varied extents, personality *and* knowledge, skills *and* attitudes were used in both P-J and P-O assessments.

Is the job a good fit for you?

We have just learned that it is important to get a good fit between the person applying for a job and the job and the organisation. However, when applying for jobs, you should also consider that the opposite is true. In other words, it is important that there is a good 'job-person fit' from your perspective as the applicant. That is to say that you feel a close (or tolerably distant) fit between your own knowledge, skills and values, and those required of the job and of the wider organisational culture. A good fit can lead to enhanced workplace motivation, satisfaction and performance, and help to contribute to your overall wellbeing in terms of work-life balance.

The importance of job-person fit is recognised by many employers, and some large organisations make reference to it in job advertisements. A good example of this is by British Airways. The airline featured a 'fit finder' on its careers webpages during its 2019 recruitment round (https://careers.ba.com/fit-finder). Using this interactive tool, before you begin to apply for a job, you can answer a short series of multiple-choice questions about your personality and preferences: such as, 'Which are you? Tried and tested, or Weird and wonderful'. When you have completed the quiz, you will discover whether you are what British Airways call an inspirer, a hero, an advocate or a challenger. When you have found out which of these roles you are, you can read a description of that role and understand where you can contribute to British Airways.

A perfect match?

As you might know from life experience in personal relationships, the idea of a perfect match is rare indeed and some might say impossible. The trick is to find a match that fits as closely as possible and to explore ways of overcoming differences.

In a professional context, whether it is you looking for a job or what might be going through the minds of the selection panel in front of which you are about to sit, the same principle applies: it is rare to find a perfect match. Instead, a more realistic and achievable view is usually taken and really what matters is closeness of fit. Where gaps exist, they might be too wide to be bridgeable or other candidates might have these skills and experiences already. In other situations, the gap might not be too much of a problem and development opportunities offered by the company can remedy gaps between experience and job requirements where they exist.

To help you learn how to judge the closeness of fit between you and your next job, try the perfect match activity as one way of quickly judging whether or not you have what it takes to apply for a job.

— ACTIVITY —

A perfect match?

By completing this activity, you will learn how to do a quick check of your fit with a company.

Job A: Trainee hotel manager (https://jobs.hilton.com)

To successfully fill this role, you should maintain the attitude, behaviours, skills and values that follow:

1. Must be regionally mobile
2. Graduates in any discipline or 3-year diploma education in hospitality and tourism or its equivalent
3. English fluency (communication skills) with good command in one local language
4. Commitment to delivering high levels of customer service
5. Excellent grooming standards
6. Flexibility to respond to a range of different work situations
7. Ability to work on your own or in teams

Job B: Retail travel advisor (https://tuijobsuk.co.uk)

There is more than one way to the perfect fit – here are some of the ideal things:

1. Excellent customer service skills

(Continued)

2. Strong commitment to achieve targets and overcome challenges
3. Team player who engages and collaborates at all times with customers and colleagues
4. An organised individual who takes pride in their work and responsibility for their own development
5. Ability to use initiative to proactively spot and resolve potential problems
6. Passion to work within tourism, although travel experience is not essential
7. Confidence to handle multiple currencies and administrative tasks whilst complying with procedures
8. Flexibility to work variable shift patterns each week which include evenings and weekends in line with customer demand. Shift patterns are normally shared four weeks in advance

Task

Read the two person specifications, above, and choose one that best fits your experience, knowledge, skills, attitudes and behaviours. Using the table below, list the criteria that that organisation is looking for and, in the other columns, write down the experience you have of each. Examples might come from your education, part-time work, volunteering, extra-curricular activities or hobbies. When it is complete you will be able to see how closely you fit the requirements of the job.

Table 24.1   Matching experience to a personal specification

List the person specification criteria.	What experience do you have of it?	Describe briefly an example when you demonstrated it.	How did you know it was successful (e.g., feedback from customers, managers, co-workers)?
1.			
2.			

Although this exercise is only a learning activity, using this technique can help when you find a job for which you do want to apply. The table will not only give an indication of whether you fit the job requirements, but it will also give you a head start in collecting evidence when you begin to put together your application.

 THINK POINT

Take time to read job adverts, particularly the job description and person specifications, carefully to check how closely they fit with your knowledge, skills, attitudes and behaviours

Do your research on the company to which you are applying to check that their missions and values fit with yours. You are more likely to be happy working for a company that has the same values as you

SELECTION BIAS

Although there are a range of tests that offer objectivity in the selection process (see, for example, Chapter 32) these are sometimes difficult and costly to administer. Other techniques, usually the inter-view, are somewhat easier and cheaper to run; however, the outcomes of these techniques rely on human judgement (Nickson, 2013). Even when these judgements are made against agreed criteria, within the human resource policies of the organisation and in compliance with employment and equal opportunity legislation, the fact that they are made by humans means subjective judgements can be made and with that comes the potential for **bias**.

Bias is a perception of a person, positively or negatively, based on assumptions or stereotypes in a way that is often unfair. Bias comes in many shapes and forms, but two types predominate (Equality Challenge Unit, 2013):

- Conscious bias: sometimes called explicit bias, and these assumptions are known to the person making the judgement although they might not always admit to them
- Unconscious bias: sometimes called implicit bias, is unknown to the person making the judgement and can be based on 'our background, cultural environment or personal experiences' (Equality Challenge Unit, 2013: 1).

Organisations often try to reduce the potential for bias by offering training for recruitment and selection panels. Such training might include the organisational procedures for recruitment and selection, but also give panel members an understanding of employment law, the potential for discrimination and bias. Although this is good practice, because much of the tourism, hospitality and events sector is made up of SMEs, not every organisation has the capability or capacity to provide this form of training to panels.

Does appearance matter?

Back in the 1971 an airline in the USA, National Airlines, ran an advertising campaign featuring an attractive female flight attendant/cabin crew and the slogan, 'I'm Cheryl. Fly me.' It was immediately criticised by women's groups for its sexual objectification of women, but the following year saw a 19% increase in revenue per passenger mile for the airline and led to several similar campaigns (Lavietes, 2003).

Although you might find this type of advert shocking and it is doubtful that this type of derogatory advertising would be used today, the effect of physical appearance in the workplace and during the selection process still has some influence.

Depending on the type of job you are looking for, employment within tourism, hospitality and events organisations might put you in a role that has direct face-to-face contact with customers. The nature of these interactions sometimes results in a particular type of person being selected for the jobs because of characteristics beyond their knowledge and skill set – the way they appear. Aesthetic labour is a term that has been coined to describe the recruitment of 'employees who have the 'right' look, the right sound, or the right attitude to appeal to customers' senses will provide competitive advantage' (Dashper, 2013: 137).

Research by Ruffle and Shtudiner (2014) looks at whether good looking people are more employable. They created an experiment to send out a pair of CVs to employers, one with a photograph and one without, to establish the rate to which they were invited to interview. The study was based in Israel, where the inclusion of photographs with CVs is optional. In total, six versions of the same CV were produced: four of which contained a photograph (attractive male, plain male, attractive female, plain female) and two did not. Their findings revealed that using a photograph on the CVs led to a slightly lower call-back rate than those with no photographs. What you might find surprising, however, is the differences in call-back rates depending on gender. CVs with attractive male photos received 50% more interview invites that those without photos, and twice as many as those with plain male photos. The difference between the CVs of females was less clear, although CVs with no picture received more interview calls that those with both plain and attractive photographs. Interestingly, female CVs without photos were more likely to receive responses than males without CVs.

Ruffle and Shtudiner (2014) conclude that there is evidence for beauty discrimination and recommend that, in cultures where including photographs in CVs is optional, attractive males would improve their selection chances by including a picture. In contrast, females and plain looking males would do better without a photograph. Although you might find these results surprising, you should not be overly concerned. Remember, not all countries and companies permit the inclusion of photographs on CVs. Some go further still to make selection a fair process, removing information that might create the potential for bias – like name, gender, ethnicity, age, disability, sexual orientation and other protected characteristics – from applications before they reach the selection panel (see Chapter 29).

That said, there is still the potential for judgements based on appearance, particularly when it comes to customer facing roles and aspects of appearance that represent personal identity. For example, with more people having tattoos, there is increased discussion about what is and what is not permissible in the workplace, as the next Industry insight on tattoos illustrates.

 INDUSTRY INSIGHT

Tattoos in the workplace

Do you have a tattoo? The chances that you might answer yes to this question is greater than it was in the past, but it might vary depending on the country you live in. Although the number of people who have tattoos, and visible tattoos particularly, is unknown, there is an overall growth trend. A recent article by Thomas (2019) suggested that the number of Americans with tattoos grew from 21% in 1999 to 40% in 2014. In 2015 in the UK, Perraudin (2018) reported that 20% of all adults had a tattoo but that proportion rose to 30% amongst 25–39 year olds.

If you have a tattoo, particularly a visible tattoo, you might be worried about how employers will react. Experimental research has shown that people with visible tattoos or piercings were perceived to be less likely to be hired than those without, and this was more pronounced if the role in question was a customer-facing role (Timming, Nickson, Re and Perrett, 2017). However, you should not be too discouraged if you have a visible tattoo. Writing about hotels, Mogelonsky (2016) suggests that although traditional hotels might be averse to visible tattoos on their employees, in other properties it might be entirely permissible.

Indeed, there is evidence that attitudes are changing towards applicants with tattoos. Even beyond tourism, hospitality and events sectors, employers are beginning to recognise that a ban on tattoos affects organisational talent. For instance, the UK's Metropolitan Police have relaxed a previous ban on tattoos because it was found to be affecting recruitment detrimentally, with 10% of applicants to the Metropolitan Police in 2017 rejected for having a tattoo (Thomas, 2019).

The change in attitudes is taking place slowly, too, in tourism, hospitality and events sectors. Many airlines have bans in place against visible tattoos on employees dealing directly with passengers. However, Air New Zealand recently reversed its ban on employees with tattoos 'amid criticism it was discriminatory against potential indigenous Maori employees' (TravelMole, 2019).

TravelMole reports that 'the airline wants to prove it is "embracing diversity and enabling employees to express individuality or cultural heritage"'. Therefore, in future, it will allow all forms of non-offensive tattoos and, if a tattoo is questionable, a review panel will decide whether it is permissible.

CONCLUSION

In this chapter we have covered:

- The recruitment and selection process and its different stages
- The meaning of 'fit' and how to judge whether you are a good fit for a job
- The meaning of bias and being aware of it in the selection process

FURTHER READING

Nickson, D. (2013) *Human Resource Management for the Hospitality and Tourism Industries*. London: Routledge.

Van Der Wagen, L., and White, L. (2014) *Human Resource Management for the Event Industry*. London: Routledge.

25

SOCIAL MEDIA AND YOUR JOB SEARCH

BARTOSZ BUCZKOWSKI AND STEVEN RHODEN

CHAPTER LEARNING OBJECTIVES

By the end of this chapter you should be able to:

- Demonstrate understanding of the evolution of social media
- Identify the main social media platforms that are used to recruit staff and appreciate how social media is used in this process
- Outline the advantages and disadvantages of social media during the job search
- Evaluate your own current social media presence

GLOSSARY

- **Social media:** networking sites that allow users to generate content and interact with the content of other users
- **Content:** the posts, pictures (photos, gifs, memes etc.) and videos contained on user profiles
- **Social media aggregators:** applications that allow users to collect content from multiple social media platforms/apps

INTRODUCTION

Do you have a mobile, cell or smart phone? If so, how long has it been since you last looked at **social media**? Perhaps you are looking at it *whilst* reading this chapter (which everyone likes to call multi-tasking, because it sounds better than procrastinating!). Which social media platform do you use most? How long do you spend on social media per day? And based on that, how long does that mean you spend on social media per week? Or per year?

The reason we ask you to think about these questions is because this chapter is about social media. In it, we are going to be asking you to reflect on your use of social media and, particularly, help you to consider how social media can be used to search for jobs within the tourism, hospitality and events industries.

The answers to these questions are likely to be different from person to person. Indeed, the use of social media varies depending on many things, like age, gender, socio-economic background, job/profession, culture, regional and national levels of internet connectivity, amongst a range of other determinants. For example, society can be segmented into attitudinal generations rather than age groups. Millennials (people born between 1981 and 1995) and Generation Z (people born after 1995) are more likely to use social media than their parents and grandparents who belong to Generation X (1965–1980) and Late Baby Boomers (1946–1964). No doubt, the large variety of portable smart devices – phones, tablets and laptops with a wide choice of social media applications (apps) that younger generations have been experiencing earlier on in their lives – is a contributing factor to those differences.

SOCIAL MEDIA AND EMPLOYABILITY

The popularity of social media and its widespread use allows for making connections between people of all ages placed around the globe. Through various platforms, websites and apps, we are now connected to the world almost in real-time, 24 hours a day, seven days a week; something that was unimaginable merely 24 years ago. Although that might seem like a long time, when set against the history of humanity, social media should be considered a comparatively new phenomenon in human communication. With the vastness of information readily available on social media, it should come as no surprise that social media can be of great help with regards to career planning and looking for employment.

The very nature of social media is that they consist of user-generated **content**. Therefore it follows that employers may use social media to contribute job adverts, and thus seek talent relevant to their organisation. Other users may seek employment, and may have talent to offer, and use social media profiles to present themselves to employers. Openness and accessibility of social media means that potential employers may be interested in looking through the profiles of users who apply for employment. Later in this chapter, we will explore the interplay between employers, jobseekers and social media, and the use of social media to improve employment prospects.

SOCIAL MEDIA: DEFINITION AND EVOLUTION

'Media' is the plural form of 'medium', a term referring to the agency to do something or to convey a message. Social media, or Social Networking Sites (SNS), allows the creation of profiles for users of the media to interact (Brown and Vaughn, 2011). Social media allows users to convey information either informally (personal use) or formally (professional use). Many research articles explore the nature of social media, and communications that take place on social media platforms, but arguably the most important defining characteristic of social media is that it allows users to contribute content (for example, profiles, posts and comments). In other words, it is users who decide what they post or share on social media. Thus, social media requires users to interact with the content, thus creating additional content or data.

The invention of the World Wide Web by Tim Berners-Lee in 1991 allowed the reimagining of how humans communicate. Once revolutionary inventions, the stationary telephone, the fax and telegraph have now become largely obsolete. Even though the invention of a digital computer is dated back to the 1940s, and the e-mail was invented in the 1960s, it was not until the 1990s when connecting with individuals located in different locations worldwide became a possibility. Nowadays, facilitated by the human need to connect, even across vast distances and through globally improving access to the Internet, SNS boast large numbers of users. For example, Facebook, launched in 2004, had 1.59 billion daily users worldwide in June 2019 (Facebook Inc., 2019b). Nearly 2.5 billion people use Facebook on a monthly basis (Facebook Inc., 2019b); that, astonishingly, is nearly a third of the world's population. It comes as no surprise, therefore, that for many, the use of social media has become the means of being connected to the world. Improved connectivity has benefited social relationships, business transactions, and links between businesses and individuals, be that as customers or as employees. Indeed, it is the last of these categories that we focus on in this chapter.

SNS are an incredibly useful tool for career-planning and creating a personal and professional profile that may add to your resumé/CV. You should be mindful of the fact that the great number of people and organisations that use social media results in a vast amount of information. It is important that you reflect on your information-searching skills, as around 50% of individuals seeking employment are active on social media daily, and only 11% of jobseekers do not use social media at all (Forbes, 2013). This means that any individual who uses SNS for job search should be organised and focused on a well-developed and well-maintained network of people in their profession in order to maximise the exposure that a social media presence can offer.

Remember that employability is the ability to present yourself and your skills, experience and attitude to set you apart from the remaining crowd of jobseekers. Social media truly offers a space where you can present your attributes directly to potential employers. Good social media networking is not about how many connections or followers you have. As is the case with family and close friends, it is the *quality* of connection that matters rather than the *quantity*. In the world of social media recruitment for jobs, the number of followers does not really count for much.

SOCIAL MEDIA AGGREGATORS

Many of us use multiple SNS, and as a result, we may find ourselves overwhelmed with information or spend a far greater than necessary amount of time looking for information that is of use to us. You must remember that time is the most valuable resource that anybody has. Several **social media aggregators** exist. They are applications or websites that allow users to collect (or aggregate) and analyse content and data from multiple social media sites or apps. Often, social media aggregators allow you to schedule posts in advance. It is good to have specific terms, key words or hashtags set up for which you want the content to be aggregated (collected). Examples of free social media aggregators are Hootsuite, TweetDeck and Juicer.

BUSINESSES' USE OF SOCIAL MEDIA

The vastness of information generates a paradoxical situation. Because there is so much content relating to jobs, job adverts and employment on social media, searching for a job has never been easier. On the other hand, the same volume of information might be making finding the right opportunity overwhelming. That is why you need to understand first how businesses use social media, and then evaluate the way in which you could be using broadly defined social media in your job search. As with personal use of social media that most people use, businesses (for-profit organisations) are more likely to use social media platforms as a recruitment tool. However, the likelihood of government (non-profit sector) organisations using social media for recruitment is lower than that of businesses (SHRM, 2015), but the increasing trend of utilising social media as a recruitment tool is continuing, as the communication technology continues to develop.

It might be difficult for you to imagine what life was like 30 years ago, before the advent of smart devices that allow constant connection to the Internet and social networks. We obtain updates on our networks' lives and local and global news stories in almost real time. Consider the impact that the development of smart phones, with virtually unlimited access to the Internet, has had on companies' recruitment practices. Finding a job has probably never been easier, but being able to demonstrate to future employers that you are the right person for the job can be slightly more complicated for the same reason – easy access to information about a vacancy creates a very competitive environment. That is why it is good to know why and how employers use social media, and how to present yourself in order to create the desired first impression (see Chapter 26).

While businesses use social media for a variety of reasons (building brand recognition or sales), an increasing number of companies and organisations are using social media to recruit new employees. An SHRM (2015) survey revealed that 81% of businesses use various social media as one of their recruitment tools, and for a minority (5%) of businesses, social media platforms were the only method of recruitment of new talent or skill base. It is also worth noting that according to the same survey findings, 43% of recruiting companies use social media to screen applicants. We will come back to this aspect of social media recruitment later in the chapter, when we discuss the dos and don'ts of presenting yourself on social media platforms when applying for a job.

There are several social media platforms that are used by employers in filling vacancies. Depending on the source of information, Facebook is one of the most popular platforms from employers' point of view, with 66% of recruiting companies using Facebook for this purpose (SHRM, 2015). Other platforms are also used by employers, but to a lesser extent. These are: Twitter (53%); Google+ (12%); YouTube (11%); and Instagram (7%). However, as the next industry insight shows, the most popular social networking site by far among employers looking to acquire talent is LinkedIn, with 98% of employers using it. It is worth pointing out that in October 2019, LinkedIn reported a record amount of job posts and level of engagement (Social Media Today, 2019; Verdonck, Clark and Storkey, 2019).

═══════ INDUSTRY INSIGHT ═══════

Social media in hiring process

A Robert Walters whitepaper found that LinkedIn is the most popular social media platform, used both for hiring (by 50.8% of hiring managers) and for job seeking (by 85% of jobseekers). Facebook took second

(Continued)

place according to the whitepaper, but there was an interesting difference in usage. Although 73.5% of jobseekers have a profile on Facebook, only 11% of employers have a company profile on Facebook. Indeed, most jobseekers and employers view Facebook and Twitter as social media platforms for personal, rather than professional, use. The use of other social media is less pronounced in hiring. Overall, the trend in using social media in the recruitment and hiring is increasing but job-seekers and recruiters often prefer more traditional methods like using the services of recruitment agencies/consultants, and posting job adverts on social media job boards. We suggest that this might be true, particularly, for small- to medium-sized employers within the tourism, hospitality and event sectors.

The Robert Walters whitepaper shows that job seekers use social media mainly to find more information about a company they want to apply to work for and about the company culture. Some 60% of employers admitted that they use social media to screen prospective employees but only 11% admitted to doing so routinely. Only about 39% of employers do not ever use profiles on social media.

Source: adapted from Robert Walters whitepaper, 'Using social media in the recruitment process' (No date).

There are various reasons why employers use social media to recruit new employees. These include:

- reaching out to potential employees who would not otherwise see the job advert or apply for the job
- targeting groups who may be under-represented in employment
- making the job advert posts visible to a wide audience, both nationally and internationally
- target potential employees with relevant skills, experience and attitude, who are more likely to buy in to the values of the organisation (for a review, see Koch et al., 2018).

That is why, when looking for a job, you should be mindful of the fact that while the business is looking for somebody with relevant skills, it is important that you take time to look at your potential employer's social media pages. This is so you can evaluate what you see in terms of company values and employee engagement in the creation of the company's social media content and presence, and decide whether your values align with that of the company whose job advert you are viewing.

SEARCHING FOR GRADUATE OPPORTUNITIES USING SOCIAL MEDIA

The best first step in finding the right employment opportunity on social media is ensuring that you are connected (i.e. follow) the employers and/or their employees. A lot of employers in the tourism, hospitality and event sectors globally have websites or profiles dedicated specifically to jobs and career opportunities.

 THINK POINT

How active are you on social media? How often do you interact with potential employers and their content, and keep your profile(s) updated? Try and be clever in how you connect to existing networks and identify opportunities based on knowledge of where previous graduates from your course went to build their careers.

Think about your networks. Universities and colleges are usually active in setting up alumni (past graduates) networks, often based within their careers services. If that is the case for your institution, we recommend you speak to your alumni/careers office on how to utilise this existing network.

An up-to-date CV is always a great resource to have at the ready because you never know when the perfect job opportunity will present itself to you (constructing a CV is explored in Chapter 29). A social media profile is a way in which you can enrich your job search based on your CV, because you should not use your profile as a complete replacement for the all-important CV. Bear in mind that although, in theory, it is possible to find a job on any social media platform, LinkedIn, Facebook and Twitter are used mainly by employers to acquire new talent. Sometimes LinkedIn and Facebook allow jobseekers to apply for a job directly from their website/app, although not every company will utilise this option. If this is not possible, you will usually be redirected to the company/recruitment agency's web page with details of how to apply. It is worth noting that direct application is not currently possible on Twitter.

LinkedIn

LinkedIn is the oldest and most popular professional social network dedicated specifically to careers. It offers you an opportunity to list your experience, education and skills. You can also have your skills endorsed by your connections, who can verify that you in fact have those skills and therefore allow you a full and honest presentation of who you are as a potential employee. Also, searching for a job on LinkedIn is quite easy because it has a 'jobs' tool, which allows you to adjust the geographical location and search terms applicable to your dream job. In using LinkedIn, there are many things that can make your profile attractive to employers, as the next insight box shows.

=== INDUSTRY INSIGHT ===

Using Linkedin

Based on conversations with experts at Linkedin and independent specialists, Katie Warren (2018) shares tips on how to get your Linkedin profile noticed by employers:

1. Get a referral from someone you know who works at the company where you're applying
2. Fill out every part of the 'Career Interests' section of your profile to let recruiters know you're looking
3. When reaching out directly to a potential employer, write a succinct, personalised message – don't just copy your cover letter
4. If you can't find a mutual connection with your potential employer, reach out to them through a common group
5. Turn on job alerts to be notified of new positions as soon as they're posted
6. If you're currently unemployed, create a 'current position' anyway so that you show up in search results
7. Follow the pages of specific companies that interest you to be the first to see hiring announcements
8. Emphasise your skills rather than your job titles
9. Like, comment and share items in your LinkedIn feed

Source: businessinsider.com

Twitter

The search tool on Twitter is also easy to use, and many companies with Twitter presence use specific accounts to post job opportunities. Although Twitter is not a professional networking website or application, it can be used with professional networking in mind. However, there is a limited amount of information that your Twitter profile can contain. According to Murray (2019), the most important aspects when using Twitter during your job search are professional appearance of the profile and well-developed network of professional contacts. Again, we recommend that you utilise existing networks, but also follow hashtags relevant to your job search.

Due to the large amount of information that Twitter contains, the use of a social media aggregator such as TweetDeck to collect Tweets relating to job postings, following specific hashtags and creating alerts for tweets from companies that are of interest to you can help you to search for your dream job on Twitter.

Facebook

There is also a jobs-dedicated section on Facebook, alongside the usual News Feed. Using this function, you can select the type of jobs you are looking for and specify location and industry. When searching for a job, you can check whether the company that you are interested in (if you have a specific employer in mind) has a Facebook profile and whether any jobs are posted there.

 ACTIVITY

Top tips for looking for a job using social media

- Take time now to ensure your social media profiles state that you are actively job seeking and the type of role you are interested in; make sure you use keywords so recruiters can find you
- Start to follow relevant companies and individuals in your industry or network
- Get involved in LinkedIn groups related to your industry and let them know the type of role you are looking for
- Start (or continue!) to initiate conversations with individuals and companies on any interesting topics related to your industry
- Keep your personal updates and professional updates on separate social media accounts

Source: The Guardian (2017)

SEARCHING FOR THE RIGHT CANDIDATE

It is worth knowing that there are other ways in which employers use social media to recruit. For many employers, especially in large companies, using a wide range of social media helps to promote their unique brand. Businesses may wish to develop and maintain their customer base, but the brand promotion and awareness is important in recruiting new candidates, or inspiring potential candidates to aspire to work for the business in future. Employers often use their existing employees' profiles to achieve that task, as the employees are often the face of the company. Of course, this is accompanied usually by employee guidelines with regards to the online presence of the organisation.

What should also be clear after reading this chapter is that there are many people like you (i.e. competitor candidates) on social media, and businesses can make use of it to make quick decisions who they recruit. Occasionally, it happens that a candidate with a specific profile of skills and experience might be needed in an organisation. Candidates with up-to-date online profiles detailing their experience, knowledge, skills and achievements might become a target of recruitment activities. This is especially so for jobseekers who do not realise that there is a vacancy suitable for them in a company with a profile similar to their existing employer.

Remember that employers may be using social media to simply create an interest in their job adverts by creating numerous posts on various social media. This way, employers can ensure that a large and diverse group of potential employees with a relevant skill set apply for the advertised position, that the recruitment process is competitive and that the candidate who is the best for the role gets the job. Remember, businesses, especially larger organisations, are likely to have coordinated and well-planned recruitment strategies.

When you consider applying for a job, you should ensure that you make time to look at the social media profile of your potential employer. This way you will be able to judge early on in the application process whether you are a good fit for the company (as covered in Chapter 24) but also whether the company values align with your own principles. The following activity can help you to make this judgement.

=== ACTIVITY ===

Self-evaluation of your social media presence

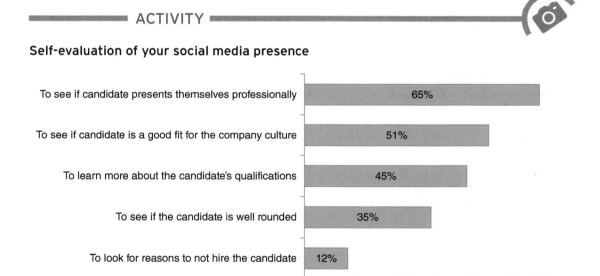

Figure 25.1   Reasons why employers review social media profiles of prospective employees

Source: CareerBuilder (2012)

Figure 25.1 from CareerBuilder (2012) shows the most common reasons why employers review social media profiles of prospective employees, whether rightly or wrongly. Remember that information available in the public domain allows anybody to view it. Imagine that you are applying for a role in the

(Continued)

tourism, hospitality and events sectors. The company you applied to work for has a strong culture based on the following principles:

- Customer trust
- Friendliness and helpfulness
- Professional customer service of highest standard
- Responsiveness to customer needs
- Pride in company values
- Utmost respect for customer confidentiality.

Review your social media profiles (LinkedIn, and if they are publicly available, Facebook and Twitter) and score them on a scale from 1 to 10 (with 1 meaning not at all and 10 meaning fully meets criterion) against the criteria: professional presentation, good fit, qualifications, skills and employability using the following table. Take a look at Section B for chapters covering how you evidence employability and skills relevant to employment.

Table 25.1   Your profile

Criterion	To what extent does your profile meet the criterion?	What evidence have you got for that score?	What can you do to improve the score of your profile?
Does your profile present you in a professional manner?			
Does your profile indicate that your values fit well with the company values?			
Does your profile contain information about your qualification?			
Does your profile show that you are well-rounded? Consider the variety of skills that you possess			
Does your profile indicate that you are employable?			

REJECTING INAPPROPRIATE CANDIDATES USING SOCIAL MEDIA

Imagine that you are going for an interview. Chances are that you would look in a mirror before you leave the house to check how you look. You do this because you appreciate that the way you look creates a first impression for the people who will be interviewing you. Although face-to-face first impressions count, employers can get a virtual first impression of you before you step into the room through your interactions with them on social media, and indeed your presence on social media more broadly. For this reason, thoughtful use of social media can contribute towards a good first impression.

If you are looking for your first job or applying for a graduate or managerial position, it is possible that your use of social media while you have been a student will have been largely, if not entirely, for personal use. Depending on how active you are on social media, how many platforms you are active on and the nature of your posts, you might undoubtedly have many and varied social connections: family, close friends, colleagues, acquaintances, celebrities, social media influencers, companies, lifestyle or political groups, and the list goes on. And while you might be comfortable sharing your personal life with these people and groups, there might be certain people with whom you are less comfortable seeing everything that you post on social media: your future boss, for example! News reports would indicate that you are right in being cautious, as the next industry insight shows.

INDUSTRY INSIGHT

What happens in Vegas...

Adapted from the successful 2003 marketing campaign for Las Vegas, USA, the phrase 'What happens in Vegas, stays in Vegas' is often quoted when people want to say and do things in one realm of their lives without it having consequences in another. While that might have been possible back in 2003, more people are using social media to share the highs and lows of their lives and the chance of something public happening without people knowing about it in the 2020s is rare.

Take the impact of personal social media on the workplace as an example. A quick internet search for 'fired for social media posts' will return a shocking set of results, and lots of them! When we were writing this book, that search returned 43 million results and, if you do the search when reading this book, that number might have risen further.

But what about employers' use of social media when you are applying for a job? The results, here, are less sensational but, for a tourism, hospitality or event graduate seeking their first job, it is still worth considering before sending your application.

An article published on bbc.co.uk explores whether social media posts can affect career prospects. Quoting Laura Holden from Reed, a UK recruitment agency, it reported that 43% of companies that are hiring staff check online profiles because 'it's a quick and easy way to learn more about the individual' (Marston, 2018).

In the USA, the picture is similar. Wood (2017), writing on Forbes.com, notes that 37% of companies use social media to review applicants. Whatever the actual figure, with the growing use of social media in both personal and professional life, it is possible that at some point in your future a hiring manager will look you up online during the recruitment and selection process.

This news might make you uncomfortable and you might wonder whether employers are within their rights to check profiles. The answer to this question, unhelpfully, is that it depends on how the information that is gathered is used. Marston notes that looking at prospective employees 'isn't snooping, it is perfectly legal for a prospective employer (or anyone) to look at whatever they like'. This view is supported by the Chartered Institute of Personnel and Development (CIPD):

'That's fine - and they can act on what they see - as long as it is not against the law'... [that is to say] they must not discriminate against people because of a 'protected characteristic', which can become clearer online, such as religion, age, ethnicity or disability. (David D'Souza (CIPD) cited in Marston 2018)

 **THINK POINT**

Social media screening is used by some companies as part of their recruitment and selection process. Whether this is permissible may vary from country to country depending on data protection laws, which are changing rapidly, and discrimination legislation to govern how data is used by employers

Your social media presence tells other people a lot about you, in terms of the content (text, pictures, videos etc.) that you post and the content that you share that other people have posted. Bear in mind, not everyone will have the same opinion of your content that you do

Would you be happy for a future hiring manager to read/show you your social posts in an interview? If not, you might want to review your online presence and your social media privacy settings before applying for jobs

AVOID CAREER-LIMITING POSTS

As the Think point encourages, you might want to pause to consider the potential impact of your current social media use on your employment prospects. Is there anything that you would not like your future employer to see? Do your posts present you in the best light? Sometimes people on social media add a small 'disclaimer' on social media that what they post represents only their views. As much as that may be the case, you should ensure that the contents of your profile(s) do not compromise your ability to secure a post or are career-limiting. For instance, a study conducted by Alexander et al. (2019) on the differences between the use of social media between recruiters and students looking for jobs showed that it is not possible to account for the impact of employers' assessments of jobseekers' online profiles on evaluation and job fit. It is difficult to predict what others deem as appropriate and what content others may find offensive. Therefore, think twice before you post anything potentially controversial or offensive and, if you are in doubt and especially if you are upset or angry, perhaps you should not post in order not to risk lowering your chances of getting that job.

The final point with regards to presentation of yourself on social media and making that first impression is the way that you choose to contact the company with regards to the job, particularly if you have any questions about a job that you want to apply for. Use your common sense with regards to what method of interaction with content such as social media profiles, job adverts, existing employees and recruiters is appropriate. An informal enquiry is a good way of highlighting personal skills such as being proactive. But remember that a hierarchy of ranks/jobs and responsibilities exist in any company and that it may not be (and usually it is not) appropriate to approach the company's chairperson or CEO with a question about a job that their company offers. Furthermore, it is often wholly inappropriate to send someone a direct message (DM), especially if this message is unsolicited. Therefore, when contacting a company, think: who and how?

- Who: was there a contact for an informal chat specified in the job advert?
    - If yes, contact that person.
    - If no, find out the contact for recruitment/job enquiries on the organisation's website.
- How: Was there a mode of contact (phone, e-mail, direct message) specified in the job advert?
    - If yes, use appropriate mode of contact out of those listed in the advert.
    - If no, find out the contact for recruitment/job enquiries on the organisation's website.

ONLINE SAFETY

Most people would say that the safe use of online resources, from social media to banking and shopping, is common sense. However, the number of people falling victim to online identity theft or fraud is increasing every year. Unfortunately, online job seekers are another group of people who are targeted because they will share a vast amount of personal data during a job application when they send their CV and application online.

Manchester Metropolitan University's Careers and Employability Service (www.mmu.ac.uk/careers) offers good advice for job seekers, warning applicants to be aware of:

- Disclosing financial (e.g. bank account) or personal (e.g. passport number) details before interview
- Request for sizable up-front investments or deposits to cover administrative fees
- Being forwarded to websites other than the company to which you are applying
- Things that are too good to be true: very high starting salaries for little experience
- Unsolicited job offers, which might be a way to get you to share your data.

There is also a very good website called Safer Jobs (www.safer-jobs.com), which can provide you with information on cybersecurity and your job search.

CONCLUSION

In this chapter we have covered:

- The evolution of social media and the different ways that businesses use it
- The role of social media in the recruitment process
- How to search for tourism, hospitality and event sector jobs using social media
- How to manage your social media presence and present your best social media self.

FURTHER READING

Bernstein, B. (2019) *How to Write a KILLER LinkedIn Profile… And 18 Mistakes to Avoid*. New York: Wise Media Group

Verdonck, B. Clark, M. and Storkey, C. (2019) *How To REALLY Use LinkedIn: Implementing Social Selling & Social Recruiting Projects at Scale*. Chatteris: Really Connect Ltd.

Useful resources

LinkedIn: www.linkedin.com

Twitter: www.twitter.com

Facebook: www.facebook.com

Safer Jobs: www.safer-jobs.com

26 PERSONAL BRANDING - BRAND ME

CHAPTER LEARNING OBJECTIVES

By the end of this chapter you should be able to:

- Understand what a personal brand is and articulate why it is important
- Reflect on your strengths and skills to identify areas for improvement
- Understand how to manage your personal brand
- Develop a personal brand pitch

GLOSSARY

- **Attributes:** characteristics, skills and attributes of an individual which include being having a good sense of humour, dependable, hardworking and honest
- **Personal brand:** characteristics of an individual (attributes, values, beliefs etc.) rendered into the differentiated narrative and imagery which builds a reputation on the things you want to be known for, or recognised for them
- **Values:** ideas and attitudes that guide our behaviour and shape our thoughts, feelings and actions. Personal values are those elements that are important to us; principles that motivate us, influence our decisions and guide our behaviour

INTRODUCTION

Personal branding is a means of promoting one's **personal brand** to realise career ambitions. It has also been linked to delivering greater career satisfaction (Gorbatov et al., 2019). The job market is crowded, locally, nationally and globally (Peter and Gomez, 2019); employers are often choosing between hundreds of applicants. So, how will you differentiate yourself from the millions of others worldwide with same level of qualification as you? How will you stand out from the crowd and cut through the cluttered marketplace; to be the one chosen by the employer? The answer is to build your personal brand; to communicate your individuality, recognise and exploit your strengths to make the most of future opportunities.

This chapter will require you to generate self-awareness and to self-reflect on your personality, your **values** and your skills. Throughout recruitment processes, it is important to consistently ask yourself – can I prove this? Do you have evidence to support your claim? There is little point in deceiving yourself; working out your weaknesses is just as important as identifying your strengths as this will give you areas of improvement. You will also need to focus on what makes you stand out; again, honesty is crucial which means being able to support your points with evidence. If you know that you are capable of a skill or possess a certain quality, but cannot evidence it, then work on ways you could build up evidence. This chapter will encourage you to first think about your current reputation and how others perceive you. It will then ask you to identify your skills, strengths and your areas of weakness before considering your values; reflecting on which values resonate with you and how you might align these with future job roles. It will then help you decide how you differentiate yourself from the crowd; how you can develop a favourable reputation through creating and disseminating a positive, cohesive image across multiple platforms.

PERSONAL BRAND

> Personal brand is a set of characteristics of an individual (attributes, values, beliefs etc.) rendered into the differentiated narrative and imagery with the intent of establishing a competitive advantage in the minds of the target audience (Gorbatov, Khapova and Lysova, 2018: 6).

Your personal brand is your product: who you are, what you value, what makes you stand out. For the purposes of this book, your brand is considered in terms of employability and therefore your audience and target market are potential future employers. Think about traditional marketing where branding is aimed at the consumer; those buying the product or service. Within personal branding, your consumers become those buying *into* you; potential and or future employers making decisions based on who your brand suggests you are and what you have to offer.

Within marketing, brands are the images consumers hold of an organisation based on its reputation, points of difference and knowledge consumers have on the company. If you were asked to name some of the top brands, global giants such as McDonalds, Starbucks, Hilton and Coca-Cola may come to mind. As soon as the name is mentioned, you have an image of who and what is being discussed; you may also conjure up images of the brand logo. The golden arches, for example, are a feature on many streets across the world! A brand is more than a name and a logo, however, as your brand is more than what you look like or how your voice sounds. Brand identity includes what the company values are, what they are promising consumers, what they believe in and how they behave. Similarly, your personal brand should represent your personality, your values and be reflected in how you behave.

It should communicate what you are promising to others that you can do; what are you offering to your potential employer? Your personal brand is 'about how people perceive you' (Gander, 2014: 99); it should represent your identity and therefore requires reflection on what makes you you.

PERSONAL BRANDING

If your personal brand is the product, personal branding is the process. It is the strategies and procedures involved in developing and communicating your personal brand: self-awareness, self-reflection, using feedback and performing needs analyses. Essentially, personal branding incorporates the marketing and management of your brand; the 'strategic process of creating, positioning, and maintaining a positive impression of oneself, based on a unique combination of individual characteristics, which signal a certain promise to the target audience through a differentiated narrative and imagery' (Gorbatov et al., 2018: 6).

Tom Peters first discussed the concept of personal branding in the late 1990s, applying the concepts of branding in marketing to people; how to make ourselves stand out in a crowded marketplace. Peters (1997) introduced personal branding through people being 'CEOs of our own companies: Me Inc. To be in business today, our most important job is to be head marketer for the brand called You.' As individuals we all have a personal brand; our reputation and how we are perceived by others, regardless of whether we choose to manage it or not. However, just as in marketing, a brand can produce positive or negative equity; failure to consider the importance of reputation and actions, managing how we are perceived, how we carry ourselves, and interact and communicate with others carries a risk of developing a negative personal brand. Personal branding delegates responsibility to you for your own brand – not to leave it to others to define it for you. Own it and purposefully take control of it; understand it, develop it and get it out there.

BUILDING YOUR PERSONAL BRAND

Within marketing, branding involves 'developing and consistently communicating a set of positive characteristics that consumers can relate to your name' (Lancaster and Findlay Schenck, 2014: 91). The first stage of developing a successful brand strategy is deciding on brand position by considering what these positive characteristics are: the **attributes**, benefits, beliefs and values an organisation stands for (Kotler et al., 2018). It is important at this stage to understand that within traditional marketing, branding is aimed at the consumer; those buying your product or service. Within personal branding, your consumers become those buying *into* you, including potential and future employers making decisions based on what your brand suggests you offer.

This chapter encourages you to consider the elements of a personal brand (see Figure 26.1): personality, strengths, values, passions, direction and your unique selling point. At each stage you will need to adopt the process of personal branding: self-awareness, self-reflection, feedback and needs analysis. The first stage in building your personal brand is to develop self-awareness; to consider who you are and using feedback to deliberate how others see you. You will need to reflect upon your skills, strengths, areas of improvement and your values; what do you believe in and how does this drive you? Think about your passions, what really motivates you? We rarely give ourselves the luxury of reflection, of taking the time to really think about who we are. The next stage will be to consider what you have to offer; how will you meet the needs of a future employer? The information you collate from these exercises will enable you to develop your own personal brand pitch; your brand message which can be used in impromptu networking, interviews and even application forms.

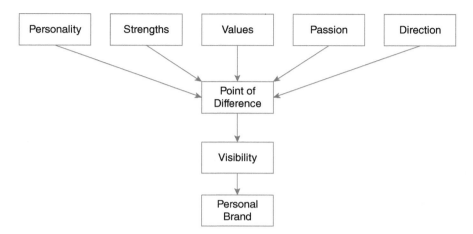

Figure 26.1   A model for building your personal brand

Sources: Developed from Gorbatov, Khapova and Lysova, 2018; Peters, 1997; PWC, n.d.

PERSONALITY

Implicit personality theories are used to make decisions about people and their behaviour. We are constantly using these, often subconsciously through making observations about people and then using these to explain or predict their behaviour.

=========== **THINK POINT** ===========

Think about the last time you were put into a group at university; what assumptions did you make about your group members? Perhaps you decided someone was boring because they wanted to sort out all the details. Perhaps you thought someone didn't understand because they were overly quiet and not contributing. Were these observations true? How do you know? Did you ever take the time to test the theory?

Building on the Think point above, it is useful to remember that a group meeting, a seminar situation or a class are just a snapshot of time with people. Think about how they behave at home, at work or socially? Perhaps their mood that day was different; perhaps they were unwell. It is estimated that we often take just 30 seconds to make a judgement about someone; to define who they are and how they are likely to behave, regardless of how well we know them. Your brand is not based on what you think of yourself, but how others perceive you; just as in traditional branding for companies, the brand is only important when being judged by others. First impressions count, however shallow they may appear. You are being judged daily by everyone you come in contact with. Day to day this may not matter to you, but in a job interview, for example, or when meeting a new contact, it can be crucial to you making a favourable impact. Therefore, it is crucial you take ownership of your own brand; to project the person you want others to perceive you as.

 ━━━ ACTIVITY ━━━━━━━━

Using OCEAN

Think about the first time you meet people; how do you think you come across? Do you think you are open? Friendly? Figure 26.2 gives you a suggestion of personality traits based on the OCEAN framework (Maltby, Day and Macaskill, 2017); **O**penness, **C**onscientiousness, **E**xtraversion, **A**greeableness, **N**euroticism. Use this to help you identify how you think you might come across during new encounters. This OCEAN mnemonic and its different elements are also discussed in Chapter 32 within the discussion on psychometric tests.

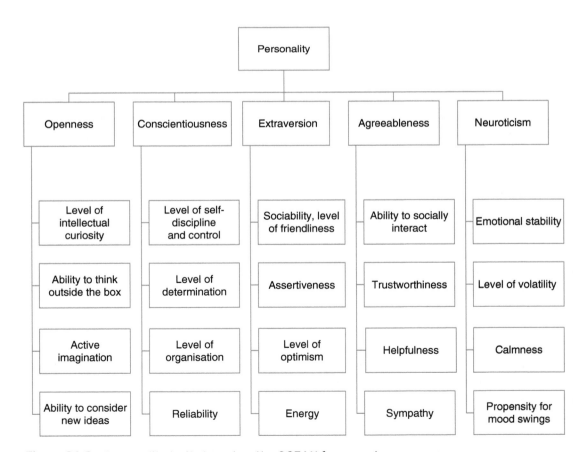

Figure 26.2 Personality traits based on the OCEAN framework

======= ACTIVITY =======

First impressions

Get together with a group of classmates (ideally six or more) to give feedback on your first impressions of each other and how each of your personalities come across.

Part I *Write*: For each person, each of you must identify the following:

- Five words to describe your first impressions of them
- Five words to describe how you see them now
- Five of their main strengths
- Five of their weaknesses
- What annoys you most about this person?

It is important to be honest; you must learn to take feedback and use this to your advantage. It is better that you learn how you come across in less formal situations, before you are going for your dream job.

Part II *Share*: Once Part I is complete, share your lists so that each person has feedback on themselves (if there are six participants, each person should have five lists).

Part III *Discuss*: Perhaps the most critical part of this activity comes after you have read the lists; you need to discuss why people felt this way. It is no good to have the answer without greater detail as often feelings are hard to describe in a single word.

Part IV *Reflect*: Once the activity is complete think about what the feedback has been; how close was this to your own reflection of how you thought others might see you? Where were there similarities? Where were there differences? Are there any immediate changes you can make or are there areas that you need more time to work on and develop? Some of these areas can be noted and used for the next activity, identifying your strengths and weaknesses.

Strengths and attributes

In order to reflect self-awareness and develop a sense of who you really are, it is important that you can recognise your key strengths and achievements, as well as acknowledge your weaker areas. Think about your capabilities and what you excel in; how can you demonstrate this? What are you most proud of? What do others think you are best at?

It is often hard to see ourselves as experts in an area but building a portfolio of examples to show our capabilities is a powerful exercise in building self-confidence and recognising our key strengths as well as areas that require improvement. For the next activity you will be able to draw upon the responses you made to activities you performed in other chapters, such as Chapter 30.

======= ACTIVITY =======

Your strengths and achievements

List your strengths and achievements. You may like to consider those you reflected on in Chapter 12 and those your peers mentioned in their feedback as well as answering some of the following:

(Continued)

- When working as a group how have you performed?
- What was the most successful project you worked on and why was there a positive outcome?
- How have you overcome any obstacles and what did you learn from these experiences?
- What are the main skills others see in you?
- What skills do you think you will use in your future career?
- What activities do you comfortably fulfil: making presentations, report writing, asking for help, working alone, working as a team, beating targets, using feedback, working under pressure, working to deadlines?

Now, from this list, rate the strengths in order with your main strengths at the top. Then for each one, give an example. The following questions may guide you towards thinking about specific examples.

Academic strengths and achievements:

Are there assignments/tasks you have excelled in?

- For new graduates or final year students, what topic did your dissertation fall into and what skills did this process give you? What did you learn?
- Have you taken on any academic responsibility at university such as mentoring or peer feedback?
- Where has feedback suggested you excel?

Professional skills, achievements and experience:

- Think about your work experience to date; this can include volunteering posts, internships and placements. Where do your strengths lie?
- What feedback have you received from work colleagues and managers?
- Have you achieved anything specific: a mystery guest score, an employee award or beaten a target?
- What tasks do you find easy?
- Think of a challenging time that you overcame; what happened?

Extra-curricular activities and achievements:

- Are you part of any societies at university; what activities have you engaged in with these?
- Are you a member of a sports team or special interest group?
- Are you a volunteer, for what cause and why?
- How do you balance your extra-curricular activities with university/work?
- What are your interests and how are these reflected in your activities?

You should now have a list of your strengths along with evidence to substantiate these.

Values

Values are ideas and attitudes that guide our behaviour and shape our thoughts, feelings and actions. Personal values are those elements that are important to us; principles that motivate us, influence our decisions and guide our behaviour. These are often abstract ideas, rather than tangible objects; chocolate does not count as a personal value! Think more about the ways you behave and the ways you view the world; what causes do you care about? You are more likely to feel happy and fulfilled if you live your life (which includes work) in accord with your personal values (Sheward, 2011).

From a recruitment perspective, top industry recruiters in tourism and hospitality frequently prioritise candidates' values and personality over qualifications and experience. Recruiters are looking for an alignment between company values and that of the candidate, but also that the candidate is an individual; that they have their own personality and can confidently project this in both one to one and group situations. Deliberating upon your values is significant when considering where you want to work and crucially who you want to work for.

═══ ACTIVITY ═══

Reflecting on values

According to Schwartz et al. (2012) there are 19 basic values. Use the examples in Table 26.1 to think about what you value.

- Which of the statements do you agree with?
- From your list note down your top five value statements
- Rank these in order of importance
- What causes could these relate to: sustainability, climate change, mental health, diversity ...?
- How do you reflect these in your everyday life?
- What *could* you do to demonstrate you have this value?

Table 26.1   Personal values

Value	Description	Examples
Self-direction thought	The importance of having your own opinions, of learning for yourself and being creative	I enjoy being creative I am motivated to learn for myself I rate originality and often have original ideas I try to improve myself
Self-direction action	The importance of being independent and having the freedom to choose what you do and how you do it	I enjoy autonomy I like to have the freedom to choose my own direction I do not enjoy being told what to do
Stimulation	The importance of excitement, new experiences and having opportunities to do diverse activities	I seek excitement New experiences are important I enjoy doing different things
Hedonism	The importance of embracing life, taking advantage of opportunities for enjoyment and having a good time	I think life is for living I love to have fun I seek opportunities to have a good time
Achievement	The importance of being successful and having people admire your achievements	I seek praise Ambition is important to me I want to be a success
Power-resources	The importance of financial wealth and status	I am motivated by money It is important to have financial wealth I like to be in a position of power

(Continued)

Table 26.1   (Continued)

Value	Description	Examples
Power-dominance	The importance of having authority and influence over others	I like people to do as I say I enjoy telling others what to do
Face	The importance of social respect and being treated with respect and dignity	I do not like to be shamed in front of others My public image is important I like to be respected by others
Security-personal	The importance of feeling secure as an individual, from where you live to where you work and socialise	I avoid situations where I might feel unsafe I am aware of danger and the need to protect myself
Security-societal	The importance of your country's security and social stability	My country should protect its citizens Social order and stability are important
Tradition	The importance of traditional and/or cultural values and beliefs, including those of family and religion	It is important to maintain tradition Cultural practices should be observed My family's views, religion and customs are important
Conformity-rules	The importance of obeying those in authority, following rules and adhering to the law at all times	Rules and regulations are important The law should always be obeyed Those in authority have the ultimate say
Conformity-interpersonal	The importance of being tactful and avoiding upsetting or irritating anyone	I do not like upsetting people I think diplomacy is important I avoid being irritating
Humility	The importance of being humble and not being arrogant or drawing attention to yourself	I do not like arrogance in people I do not enjoy being the centre of attention It is important not to brag about achievements
Benevolence-dependability	The importance of loyalty; being reliable, dependable and trustworthy	I enjoy spending time with those I can rely on I am loyal to my close friends and family
Benevolence-caring	The importance of caring for those close to you and helping them when in need	I care for my friends and family I enjoy helping those close to me
Universalism-concern	The importance of protecting vulnerable members of society and that everyone deserves to be treated fairly with equal opportunities	Equal opportunities are important for all I believe in being treated fairly, regardless of race, religion, age, gender etc.
Universalism-nature	The importance of protecting and standing up for nature	The natural environment should be protected I believe nature needs to be cared for and deserves respect
Universalism-tolerance	The importance of respecting people's views, being tolerant and promoting peace and harmony	I respect those with diverse viewpoints I listen to other's point of view even when they differ from my own I encourage peace and harmony within groups

Source: Based on details in Schwartz (2012)

Passion

Understanding your strengths is important, but knowing what you are passionate about, what motivates you and makes you excited is a crucial element of your personal brand. Passion is a major step in developing a fulfilling career. If you do not have an understanding of what makes you happy, what inspires you and what makes you want to get up in the morning, it will be difficult for you to communicate this to a future employer. Passions are often conversation starters; they help you to create your brand story and ultimately to stand out.

Many tourism and hospitality employers have developed an issue with the many CVs and cover letters containing the statement, 'I am passionate about travel.' Their issue is with the lack of substance; the limited detail which renders this a generic comment with little 'passion' demonstrated (see Chapter 29). It is easy to spot when someone is talking about their true passion; that they can articulate how this makes them feel, why they are so interested and what opportunities this has brought. Try to reflect upon your own passions; not those of your friends or your family. This can be a scary exercise; especially when you are honest with yourself, but it is crucial to allow yourself the freedom to think about what motivates and excites you. A good place to start is to reflect on what you would do if money were no object? What would you choose to be doing if money was not an issue? If all jobs paid the same, what work would you choose to do? Once you have reflected on your passion, think about how you would convince someone else this is your passion; how would you be able to demonstrate this?

========== STUDENT INSIGHT ==========

Renae, Event Management Student

As a first year Event Management students, we were tasked with developing our CVs. As with many of my friends, in my opening personal statement I put that I was passionate about events and the event industry. My tutor challenged me to answer how I could evidence this; I smartly replied that I was doing an Event Management course so what greater evidence was that?! To my annoyance at the time, her response was that for an employer, choosing a course does not necessarily represent passion, so how else could I demonstrate this. She left me alone to mull it over. Although this irritated me at the time, it struck a nerve. I realised that I, along with thousands of others, would be saying the same thing, so how could I ensure that when it came to being interviewed, my passion actually would shine?

I genuinely did have a passion for the industry; it was the only career I could imagine myself doing. So, I decided from that point on that I would pay attention to industry news, to gaining work experience, attending events such as Confex and to taking any opportunity to network within the industry. I read blogs and began to follow industry experts on Twitter and Instagram. It became my world. So, while that tutor annoyed me at the time, looking back it was the best thing she could have said to me. Now I can demonstrate my passion as I have spent the last two years living and breathing the industry!

Direction

To consider your purpose, you need to think about your vision for the future; what are you hoping to achieve? If you have no direction, your brand has no purpose; you need to be aiming for something or someone for your brand to have impact. This will also help guide you in knowing the types of job roles you are aiming for and companies you would like to work for.

ACTIVITY

Reflective exercise for visualising your purpose

Close your eyes and picture a relaxing scene and remain quiet for a few moments.

Pause

Imagine your life as you would like it to be five years from now when you have finished university.

Pause

It is morning and you have just woken up. What do you see? Where are you living? Who are you living with?

Pause

What are you doing now?

Pause

Who do you see in your workplace? What are they doing? Do you feel like you belong here?

Pause

What are your feelings about the work you are doing?

Pause

Did you feel prepared for this position?

Pause

What has been your greatest achievement?

Pause

What is next for you, career-wise? Where do you see yourself going from here?

Pause

Now take a few minutes to review your position by answering the following questions.

1. What were your most important feelings about your journey?
2. What type of work did you see yourself doing? Why?
3. Did this work make you happy?
4. What or who was important to you?
5. Did it require skills/experiences/values that you are developing now?
6. Where did you see yourself going from there?

Now that you have allowed yourself the freedom to picture your future, to see what you are working towards, you should be able to build an action plan. A combination of your strengths and evaluation of your weaker areas, your values and passions should guide the direction of your personal brand.

Your point of difference

Finally, your personal brand requires you to identify your point of distinction; what makes you different from the competition? Considering all the previous exercises, think about what you offer; what value would you add to a company? Ideally this should be a culmination of your strengths, personality, values and passion, reflected in your examples and experience. The essence of this distinction should be included in your brand message; your pitch communicating who you are and what you have to offer.

COMMUNICATING YOUR BRAND

An elevator pitch is a short, persuasive speech that would spark an interest in you; it represents your personal brand message. Think about sitting next to a CEO on a plane and after a short discussion about feeling nervous about flying or the leg room capacity, they ask about you: what you do? Where would you start? Most of us would be brief, generic and move on. What a missed opportunity! How many times have you been in a similar (perhaps less surreal) situation where you have walked away thinking, 'I wished I had said XYZ!'.

The idea of an elevator pitch is that these situations need not happen again; you would always be able to revert to your pitch, breaking the ice with a succinct, interesting and unforgettable statement about what makes you unique. The pitch should be no longer than 30 seconds to a minute; the length of an elevator (or lift in the UK) ride. Developing your pitch is useful as an introduction at conferences or post events to introduce yourself. It can be used at networking events and perhaps more importantly can help you to prepare for any interview. Ultimately the elevator pitch is a short speech about your brand; your identity and what makes you special. It should give you the confidence of knowing exactly what you are about; what you value, what you want out of life and what you can offer, and this can be a great foundation for building discussions in an interview. The word 'speech' can also be taken literally; you could develop a video version in which you verbally 'pitch' your brand.

Top tips for writing your pitch

1. Be honest: Authenticity is crucial; creating your own brand does not give you license to project the perfect image and think people will believe it. As with regular branding, your brand needs to reflect reality and to be authentic, if for no other reason than the fact that you will never be able to maintain the façade!
2. Be brief: This is not a cover letter or a personal statement. The pitch should be no more than a few lines; a paragraph in length.
3. Be compelling: The pitch should grab attention and enthuse not bore. Try thinking of it as storytelling rather than a monologue description.
4. Be relevant: You must be aware of your audience (think future employer) and know what they are looking for or what their values are before you make your pitch.
5. Be different: Show how you stand out, how you can add value beyond what they already have in employees. Organisations are not looking for replica employees; they crave diversity and those that will add a different dimension to existing teams.

6. Make it simple: Do not try to show off with over-complicated jargon or words that might not be understood by the audience. There is a fine line between appearing intelligent and coming across as arrogant.

 ACTIVITY

Taking steps to writing your pitch

1. Identify why you are writing the pitch? Is it to get a specific job role? Is it for networking purposes or to encompass all things 'you'?

2. Explain who you are; how do you want people to see you? What makes you different? Remember this is not a monologue; rather it should be a brief introduction to capture attention. It should not be a long list of 'I am this' and 'I am that'. If you are bored reading it out, the audience will be bored listening. Try to think about telling a very short story; a synopsis like the back of a book that aims to draw people in to want to know more. It is also important to be specific; saying that you value sustainability for example is not interesting; you need to make it applicable to your audience. What is the value in sustainability for a company? Try to relate ideas to operations, efficiency, revenue or cost. Instead of 'I think sustainability is really interesting and I think we should all aim to be more sustainable', think 'As an increasing number of consumers are demanding companies demonstrate sustainable behaviours, I am motivated by finding ways of establishing sustainable practice; especially as it appears to be firmly on the global agenda and increasingly that of many companies.'

3. Communicate what makes you different; how can you stand out from others? Think about a time when you have developed a solution for something or been responsible for solving a problem. How did you go about it? Think about feedback from lecturers, peers or managers; when have you been congratulated on a particular idea, behaviour or outcome? This might be customer feedback from work experience or feedback from your group when working as a team. It could simply be how your friends would describe you to others. Perhaps you can demonstrate that your combination of skills makes you different; that you can combine outwardly diverse or opposing skill sets to deliver favourable results. These can all be used to demonstrate your uniqueness.

4. Make it relevant to the audience; why should the audience care? This is where in an interview situation you should be able to confidently map your own skills, experience and values to those of the company. It might also be useful to consider trying to incorporate a question; you do not want to make the speech a one-sided sermon that ends with the person trying to escape. In order to be memorable, you need to engage the audience and to capture their attention. Adding in a question can make the process less formal and also build in a sense of humility; that you are not standing there dictating everything that makes you amazing!

5. Have a finisher; what are you trying to achieve? Remember the goal at the beginning: you need to be able to ask for that job, pay rise or interview. Make it clear what you want!

6. Practice. Seems obvious? If you cannot communicate your pitch effectively it will be wasted. Just the same as when you do a presentation in class or for an assessment; how many times are you told to practice, to make sure you run to time and that you run through the entire performance as a group? How many times have you actually done this; how many times has your feedback related to delivery? Not making eye contact, speaking too quickly, using acronyms or jargon the audience may not understand, speaking like a robot or turning your back on the audience. All of these are simple mistakes that will ruin your pitch (see Chapter 14).

PUTTING YOUR BRAND ONLINE

Now that you have developed your personal brand pitch, it is time to get your brand out there – make it visible!

Visibility

Successful brands have presence; they are out there asserting influence to gain prominence in the mind of consumers. Similarly, for your personal brand to gain credibility and to become established, it needs to be visible; you need to raise brand awareness. Remember you are carrying your brand every day; you are the brand so it is important in all your interactions that you represent brand 'you'.

Online presence

Putting your brand online may be the most effective way to increase brand awareness. It is a good idea to perform the exercises in developing your personal brand and brand pitch before you start to put your brand out there so that you develop a cohesive, holistic view of brand 'you'. As Chapters 25 and 27 point out, social media sites such as LinkedIn are valuable. Not only can you be active in demonstrating your skills, values and personality, but it is also an opportunity to display personal reviews. LinkedIn offers the facility for peers, lecturers and work colleagues to write recommendations and endorse your skills. When done properly, this can be a powerful tool; in building an impression of who you are, and ultimately in disseminating brand you. Similar to those of business organisations, your social media marketing strategy should be based on 'meaningful engagement, participation and value creation' (Qualman, 2013: p.ix).

Setting up online profiles is easy enough, but there are several things you need to consider when disseminating your brand online.

1. Consistency: Consistency is fundamental to branding; you need to make sure a consistent message is being circulated across all platforms. You should be integrating your brand across all your favoured channels albeit with varying methods and means. Try to make sure you have a visible, professional photo on each platform and that your biography is consistent across all sites. Try to view all your social media platforms as being viewed by your professional networks and this should guide you in deciding the types of pictures, posts and tags you submit. Of course, your personality needs to shine through, but in a consistent manner; try not to go to extremes.
2. Keep it clean: There are a number of points to remember here. Firstly, quite literally you need to clean up your social media history. How would you feel if a prospective employer viewed your profiles? They may well do this and not just your LinkedIn profile or the ones you add to your CV. Some employers will check over your Facebook accounts so if these have not been made private, they will be visible in their current state. While it is acceptable to have 'social' pictures of you with groups of friends, try to imagine your nan viewing your profile. Would you be happy for her to see the current content?

The second point here is to remember the global reach of the internet; once a message is posted, it is out there in the ether. Regardless of whether you delete it, the damage may be done. If you have a particular passion or view on a specific cause, you may at times make statements that appear controversial; just always have in the back of your mind that all of your networks can see this. It is easy to fall into the trap of jumping on bandwagons and liking other people's posts or being swept along by a particular cause or dispute. If you are comfortable with your boss, or your network contacts or a new employer seeing the posts then go ahead. Just think before you post!

You should also seek to keep your networks 'clean'; be purposeful with who you link to, comment on and tag in. Chapter 27 provides advice on making the most of networking, but in the context of your personal brand, make sure you are connecting with those that share similar values and passions or who may add to your strengths and provide opportunities to gain experience and overcome any weaker areas you may currently have. You should also monitor your use of hashtags; make sure you understand the content behind the hashtags and use them strategically to show your concern for an issue, your passion for a subject or your achievements in a particular field.

3. Be present: Make sure your information is current and updated regularly. It is important to be an active participant on social media; to make sure you are engaging on a regular basis. Platforms are updated by the second with new information, news stories and trends breaking online before anywhere else. This does not mean you should become a slave to your LinkedIn account or updating your profile with what you ate for lunch. Instead, you should set a time each day when you focus on your online presence; think of it as part of your daily routine.

4. Authenticity: Remember that your brand is an extension of yourself; it should represent who you are and what you do. Being authentic offers an opportunity for your personality, your values and your passions to shine through; to show who you really are. Online profiles should not be fabricated, over-exaggerated or be a sanitised version representing something you can never live up to. Just because your online presence is virtual, you are the reality and when meeting new employers, for example, in person, the reality needs to match the virtual. Be honest and transparent (Kaplan and Haenlein, 2010); never post false information or make false comments otherwise you may find these come back to haunt you later.

5. Provide content: Liking and making comments on the posts of others is an important part of networking, but in order to fully communicate your brand, you need to be generating your own content. You need detail and examples for others to develop a sense of you, your passions and values. It takes limited effort to like someone else's post, so try to demonstrate your own personality by developing your own; sharing your ideas and thoughts (professional ones, of course). A fantastic means of generating content is to use Instagram stories, hold a podcast or start a blog or vlog of your own.

Blogging and vlogging

Blogs and their video version vlogs are in essence a shared online diary. They offer a means of building your brand and raising visibility. Blogs are generally written in a conversational style and should be designed as such but should still be subject to scrutiny and proof reading. They will often carry a theme based around your interests and passions; there are those that write about food and travel, ethical travel, luxury travel, festivals and events. The options are endless, but by developing a blog on a cause, issue or subject you are in essence commanding attention as an 'expert' on the matter. Blogs also offer a deeper insight into network connections and organisations; read their blogs and add to their discussions.

══════ INDUSTRY INSIGHT ══════

Nomadic boys

After quitting their jobs in London in 2014, gay couple Stefan and Sebastien have been travelling the globe blogging about gay travel combined with their love of food. They aim to offer advice and inspiration to other gay travellers, particularly in areas where gay travel is perhaps less accepted, illegal or a major taboo. What began as an online account of their stories and photos for friends at home, has become one of the largest online LGBTQ travel websites. A combination of their values and passion for the cause has generated interest from a global community.

Source: https://nomadicboys.com/

CONCLUSION

In this chapter we have covered:

- The importance of developing and having a personal brand
- The elements that comprise your personal brand
- How to develop 'Brand Me' in terms of your employability and career development
- How to communicate your brand in effective and powerful ways, and through which media

FURTHER READING

Gander, M. (2014) 'Managing your personal brand', *Perspectives, Policy and Practice in Higher Education*, 18(3): 99–102.

Gorbatov, S., Khapova, S.N. and Lysova, E.I. (2019) 'Get noticed to get ahead: The impact of personal branding on career success', *Frontiers in Psychology*, 10 (2662). https://doi.org/10.3389/fpsyg.2019.02662

Montoya, P. (2002) *The Personal Branding Phenomenon*. Vaughan Printing: Nashville.

Sheward, S. (2011) 'Why you should identify your personal values before job-hunting'. *The Guardian*, 14 January 2011. Accessed at: www.theguardian.com/careers/careers-blog/identify-your-values-before-job-seeking.

27 EFFECTIVE NETWORKING

CO-WRITTEN WITH ROSY JONES

CHAPTER LEARNING OBJECTIVES

By the end of this chapter you should be able to:

- Explain what networks are and why they are important
- Develop a personal 'elevator pitch' that can be used at networking events and online
- Understand the principles of networking for finding work and developing contacts
- Develop an overview of the networks that are available to you
- Recognise the job roles and sectors where networking is fundamental to job success
- Develop the skills and confidence to effectively network

GLOSSARY

- **Networking:** The activity of coming together with other people to exchange information and contacts that are mutually beneficial. Mainly, but not exclusively for business purposes
- **In-person networking:** Networking face to face
- **Online network:** A network or networking event which is facilitated online often through social media. It may be concurrent (all the attendees online at the same time) or passive, where the site facilitates contacts between individuals
- **Elevator pitch:** a short speech that describes a product, service or, in this case, your own abilities. It is called an 'elevator pitch' because the concept is that the pitch should be delivered in the time it takes to ride in a lift or elevator; generally, between 60 seconds and three minutes

INTRODUCTION

The ability to network is a core skill for all people in business and is a fundamental one for those whose roles are in an industry where many people are freelancers as in tourism, hospitality and events. While some people find **networking** easy, many do not: if you are one of the more timid majority then do not worry as you will not be alone. If you go to an 'in-person' networking event, at least half the people there will be feeling a little uncomfortable, even if they don't look like it. This chapter builds on Chapter 13 on interpersonal skill development where we argue that networking is fundamental because people do business with *people* and the trust and confidence that we all have in people that we know, or have met, is a key part of our ability to agree a common goal (such as an event brief), negotiate terms and conditions and close a sale.

This chapter will give you some hints and tips about what networking is, how to use it – both online and in person – and how to make yourself more comfortable with the idea and process. It also builds on what you have learnt in Chapter 26 as it encourages you to reflect on your personal brand. You will need to reflect this 'brand' when you meet people and you will want to present yourself in the best way possible.

WHAT IS NETWORKING?

Networking is an activity where (business) people come together for a joint purpose which will include, but may not primarily be, trading ideas, widening contacts and developing skills, products and/or services. A networking event will be concurrent, i.e. meetings happen at the same time, rather than a forum where people tend to communicate asynchronously. This means at a single event there will be many conversations taking place among small groups of people at the same time, so they can be quite noisy. Networks may be structured around training, shared experiences, age of business (e.g. in start-up phase, as established businesses) or sectoral. Increasingly, networking events can be online or in-person.

Formal networks have existed for hundreds of years for the support of people and businesses. Medieval guilds or *Mysteries* were formal networks based on specific trades and were highly structured. Networks in the twenty-first century can be equally formal, semi-formal or extremely informal. For example, a network could consist of a group of friends coming together in a café and who happen to discuss aspects of their businesses.

Some studies which have formed the theoretical background around networking include the *Theory of Social Capital* (Bourdieu 1986), work by Lin (2017) and reports by the UK Behavioural Insights Team (in particular, Service et al., 2014). These theories position networking as a way to develop fellowship and knowledge by expanding the range and diversity of your contacts and learning from them. Other academic studies, such as Seibert, Kraimer and Liden (2001) discuss the value of online networking, and indeed suggest that for those that find **in-person networking** difficult, networking online has some additional benefit in order to create and develop contacts (see for example Steinfield et al., 2008).

TYPES OF NETWORKING

Fundamentally, networks underline the truism that 'people do business with people'. In the research on networks and in business practice (Service et al., 2014), it is clear that more business is done with those who are trusted and recommended than those who have little social connection, and the best way to find these connections is through personal recommendation or personal experience. Networking is a general term for defining these activities'. Thus, one can find the following:

- One to one networking: when you approach someone else to request them to introduce you to their networks
- One to many networking: generally, events where several people with some business aspect in common come together

Both these forms of networking can be either physical (in person) or online.

Structured network meetings

These take a form which is regularly repeated (e.g. weekly, monthly or even annually, though the latter is less normal). These types of networks often have a formal structure, though the interaction may be informal. They are likely to be membership groups or organisations where a regular fee is paid. Events such as these may be breakfast clubs, Chambers of Commerce or sector organisations. They range between the more- and less-explicit regarding their intra-network trading purposes. Such networks often develop socially as well, as they are likely to include people who have much in common.

Less formally structured many-to-many events are probably what we all recognise most as networking, where people with a shared interest or goal – be it small business growth or the launch of a student society – come together. These less structured events are more difficult to navigate than the membership groups but are generally more numerous and easier to access. Such events may be framed around teaching-style seminars, e.g. 'the latest accountancy rules' or 'an introduction to new software for the events industry', but they should provide a good opportunity for sector or location specific networks. The Express Food & Hospitality Trade Show in Mumbai (2020) is a prime example of a location and sector specific initiative which is promoted to clients as a platform that offers Indian and international businesses with a wide variety of opportunities to 'establish and network their businesses and brands among the top professionals in the country' (see 10times.com/times-food-wineshow).

 ━━━━ THINK POINT ━━━━━━━━━━━━━━━━━━━━━━━━━

Try and recall a time where you have attended an event where people were networking. How did you feel? Did you manage to talk to people around you? What helped you network? How did you feel?

Online networks

LinkedIn is the most obvious business network online (as covered in Chapter 25), but there are many others. The first was probably 'Friends Reunited', launched in the 1990s, but of course we now have Facebook, Weibo, Instagram and many more. **Online networks** give a rich opportunity for those who know who they would like to contact – at least by company name, and/or job description, if not necessarily by individual names. There are also online networks specifically for sectors or business types. These can be helpful when you are trying to find information or contacts from peers where advice, guidance and mutual support form the core of their use.

INDUSTRY INSIGHT

Deborah Dark, Freelance Events Manager

Deborah Dark is a freelance event manager who began working on the Isle of Wight and is now based in London. The roles that she undertakes are varied: she will work one day as a venue manager, occasionally as a venue scout and sometimes as the lead for a hospitality team. Her work is broad across industries and she has been fully self-employed for six years. Here she reflects on the value of networks.

Q: How do you find work?

A: Most of my work now comes through recommendations from people I've worked with, either clients or colleagues. There has to be a lot of trust when colleagues pass on your name as they need to be sure you're not going to 'steal' their client. Much of the trust depends on the network you've built up and the relationships you've developed.

Q: How did you start out in the business?

A: Networking was the key to finding my client base. That used to be word of mouth, but now LinkedIn is what I use most.

Q: How have you set up your LinkedIn page?

A: I post on there quite regularly. I post the kind of events I've done and the type of industry. Quite often I can't say exactly what I've been doing as its really important to be discreet. But I give a feel for the work, to show what I can do.

Q: How do you use the network?

A: Any companies I'd like to work with, I try to send them a connection. I always write a personal note. If they reply, I always follow up with an invitation for coffee or to meet up – that cements the introduction. It's been quite successful.

Q: How else have you networked to find jobs?

A: I've done a lot of work approaching people either in person or on the phone. I've called events companies or talked directly with clients. That way I found jobs I'm really interested in.

Q: Do you have any tips for people just starting out in the business?

A: I would say, don't be afraid to pick up the phone and ask for advice. People will help you to network and to join LinkedIn groups. Talk to people in the industry and find out what they do and what clients are looking for. If you've got a passion for something, then go for those types of jobs. Clients like to have people who are interested in what they are doing. Try and switch it up – try different environments, sectors. Go abroad. See what suits you best. Lastly, reach out to people. Networking can happen anywhere. Be mindful when you're talking to people as to whether you can help them. Grab any opportunity – if you turn a client down first time, they may not come back to you. Always follow up leads and remember to thank people for connections and work. People remember that.

One of the things that you need to do is to be able to find networks, online and in person. Obviously, you can type 'networking events in my area' into a search engine, and that will be effective.

Using online networking event tools: Eventbrite

One useful tool to help you network that you may not have thought of is Eventbrite. Eventbrite is an online website where people will upload any kind of event, from concerts to openings to public lectures. Registration is free and it has some useful integrations with calendars and reminders as well as being a platform through which you can book tickets for events with a charge – though many, if not most, are free. It's also a good place to promote events that you are running, so if you're not already aware of it, it's worth spending some time looking at the site.

 ━━ ACTIVITY ━━━━━━━━━━━━━━━━━━━━━━━━━━━━━━━━━━━

Using Eventbrite

STEP 1: Login

There are global sites (which you can use for looking up events if you're away or on holiday), but the UK site is at www.eventbrite.co.uk.

STEP 2: Selection

You can start by either logging in – or if you'd prefer, you can select the place, date and kind of thing that you're interested in on the first page. The drop-down list has an option for Business, but if you're interested in any other area, you could choose one of those and see if there are opportunities for networking. Hint: any group of industry-focused people will network anywhere – the only limitation being whether or not there is time to do so at an event, and the opportunity to actually hear each other speak.

STEP 3: Filter

Once you've got into the list (don't be too put off if the first page doesn't seem relevant – you can alter that), select Filter. This will again allow you to select Networking if you want to – or anything else if you think that will work. Try not to let yourself be diverted by interesting nights out. You're here – at the moment – to source work.

You can also move the map, as with many online apps, to focus on the area that you want to target and then 'search this area'. If you don't find anything right in the timescale that you have selected, just delete the time restriction. You should find plenty to be interested in.

STEP 4: Select

You can click on the event, register or send it to friends, all through the website. Once you've registered, you'll be able to add it to a calendar. It will also remain in your online account so if you need to find the tickets, you'll be able to find them once you've logged back into Eventbrite.

Speed networking

Speed networking involves structured methods and approaches which are used to encourage interaction. It originates from the concept of speed dating (attributed to Tom Jaffee) to help people meet potential partners. The key aim is to ensure there is a speedy rotation of participants at the event so that each person gets the opportunity to interact with every other person attending.

There are several models of speed networking. The three common ones are:

- the Round Robin model where you meet people in a one-on-one format, usually formed up of two lines that you move down in different directions
- the Station-based model where you meet specific participants based on a topic, or pre-activity
- the group-based model where you may meet a (smaller) pre-selected group

All of these are used in assessment centre exercises (see Chapter 33).

A standard format involves each participant being allotted a specific timeframe, say anything from 30 seconds to 5 minutes depending on the size of the group. In this time participants will usually need to introduce themselves and communicate something about themselves, whether it be business or personal in nature.

========= ACTIVITY =========

Creating your own personal networking pitches

Try the following activity when there's a few of you in the room and you've had a stab at creating your own personal networking pitches.

1. Line up in two lines, facing each other. Appoint someone as timekeeper and give them a bell, a whistle or some way of getting attention (shouting works, but won't be as effective).
2. When the whistle goes, each person has one minute to deliver an **elevator pitch** to the other. Then you switch over.
3. When the whistle goes again (perhaps after three minutes), one line moves down one person and you do it all again.

You can make the length of time longer if you think it is useful or if you want more conversation between your participants. If you want to do two pitches and have some time for actual network engagement, then try four to five minutes between moving on.

CREATING YOUR OWN ELEVATOR PITCH

As introduced in Chapter 26, the 'elevator pitch' is a short, descriptive spoken advert for whatever you are trying to promote. Entrepreneurs use them to highlight the key benefits of their business and, as a freelancer in a freelance-heavy profession, you should be able to easily promote yourself, at any time, when you have the opportunity. Although you may not be required to deliver an elevator pitch where you formally stand up in front of people and reel off a five minute summary of your background and experiences, there is a huge benefit to knowing just what to say if you see the perfect contact walking down the street, at an event – or in the elevator.

Using SPECK

SPECK is a useful mnemonic to help you assess yourself. Use this SPECK table to outline your Skills, Passions, Experience, Competencies and Knowledge to help develop your pitch and your online profile.

Table 27.1 Using SPECK

Skills	Passions
What you **can do**	What you love to talk about
What tools you can use	What you'd really want to work with
I can use MS Powerpoint	I adore Formula 1

Experience	
What you have **done**	
What you have experience in	
What you have **worked as** / where you have **worked**	
I ran the opening event for the student union environmental awareness week ...	

Competencies	Knowledge
What (nice) things people might say about you	What you **know**
How you work with people	What you have **learnt**
What **type of role** (leader, communicator, detail person) you might take in a team	
Also note down what you're less good at	
I have good communication skills	I have studied business planning ...
I am patient	I have learnt the International Regulations for the Prevention of Collisions at Sea
I'm not so good at detail	

Once you are comfortable with SPECK, try it out using the elevator pitch you developed in Chapter 26 in the activity below.

 **ACTIVITY**

Use SPECK to try out the elevator pitch you developed in Chapter 26

STEP 1: Profile your skills

Using the SPECK template (Table 27.1), outline the five areas: skills (what things you can do); experiences (where you've worked or volunteered, or club officer roles you've taken); what competencies you have (soft skills or behaviours); what passions you have (hobbies, interests, idiosyncrasies); and lastly, what you know or have learned about (your knowledge).

Be honest. Don't exaggerate, but also be fair and not modest. If you're good at something, say so and celebrate it.

STEP 2: External Validation

One of the things that is important to employers is what we might call external validation. This is why social media sites always ask you to 'Like' something or to share it. It shows everyone else that it's not only liked or approved of by one person, or that it's only one person's opinion.

Furthermore, if that validation comes from someone we respect or who has some authenticity in the field, then this is doubly comforting. This is why LinkedIn has that occasionally annoying, but generally accurate, 'do you recommend ...?' pop-up. So, collect and record quotes from supportive bosses, team-mates or happy customers. These are the things that add weight and confidence to your verbal or online pitch.

STEP 3: Examples

Try and think of examples of the skills and experiences you have noted in your table. This is particularly important in explaining your knowledge and your competencies and behaviours. Don't be scared to scribble down feedback you have had from others or when you have been invited back to work at a particular place.

STEP 4: Purpose

Now you have the raw material, you're ready to practise.

Think of a job you would like, or a person you would want to approach. What are the most appropriate parts of your experience, skills, knowledge and competencies that will fit the job? Is the sector something that you are passionate about? Try and make a short bullet-pointed card with all your notes on.

Practise telling your phone/a friend/the mirror until you are happy that you can say your pitch clearly and without a script. The reason for writing only bullet points is that trying to remember a particular script when you are at an event or on the phone can come across as wooden and unnatural; so knowing the sort of things you want to say without writing it down word for word will work better for you.

Practise again. And again. If you want to really work for a specific person or organisation, then find another one to do your first cold calling with: you can hone your skills on a less important contact. If you happen to come away with two jobs instead of one, then congratulations.

STEP 5: Go for it!

Yes, you're ready. Have a blast!

REFLECTION EXERCISE

Ask yourself the following questions:

- What areas are you really sure are your primary skills and competencies? What are the things that you think would make someone want to employ you?
- Where are you biggest weaknesses or gaps on your SPECK chart? How will you go about finding ways to reduce these weaknesses or to build your experience or knowledge?

YOUR LINKEDIN PROFILE

Once you have done all this work, you might as well use it twice. As covered in Chapter 25, LinkedIn has become the online business and networking tool and accounts for 48% of recruitment). LinkedIn's own research shows that 40% of recruits were sourced through job boards (while another 34% were found through business networks), so it is essential if you are planning to work as a freelancer or even working in an SME that you have a good LinkedIn profile and that you use the site as regularly as you would use email, WhatsApp or any other business communication tools.

LinkedIn has the facility for creating your CV as well (see example in Chapter 29), so you can download that as a pdf if you find you need to.

Step 1: Select relevant items

You have probably got lots of information from your SPECK table, including a list of your passions. You won't need everything! Mark up those which are MOST RELEVANT to the type of work you're planning to look for. These are the things that you need to upload to your profile.

Step 2: Edit

Write them up concisely and in the tone of voice that is most appropriate for the type of work you are aiming to target. For more formal work, be formal. For casual type situation, you can be a little bit chatty, but don't overdo it, and do not include emojis.

Step 3: Check the formatting

Print your webpage. If it is more than two pages, cut it down. Copy-edit it. It is essential that there are no spelling mistakes and that your grammar is appropriate. If you struggle with identifying errors in your work or have a casual approach to detail, make sure someone else checks it.

Step 4: Go

Hit the button to make your profile live, and make sure you have recorded your LinkedIn page address for your business card and/or app.

Networking through LinkedIn

Once you have a LinkedIn profile it is easy to network by using LinkedIn online. Any tourism, hospitality and events business that has any interest in networking online (which isn't necessarily all of them) *will* have a specific business LinkedIn page, which is the source of your opportunity.

Step 1: Identify the page

Login to your account and search for a business through the search box. If you don't know specifically which business you're looking for, it is worth doing a search through a search engine to narrow the field down to exact business names. Scroll down to the Company Results pages. There may be a few businesses with the same name, so make sure that you have the one you're planning on targeting.

Step 2: Search staff records

Click on the link and it will take you through to the company LinkedIn page. At the top right-hand corner there is a link to the members of LinkedIn who have this company in their profiles. It will sort them by the closest connections to yourself – not necessarily the most relevant. Make sure that the people you are selecting are currently working at your target company. You can click on Filter on the top menu bar, and this will allow you to select locations. If you put a search term in the search box, then it will search the company (and not the whole of LinkedIn). So, you could search for Events, or Recruitment or CEO depending on what your end goal is.

Step 3: Connect

Anyone for whom you have a first or second line contact, you will be able to connect with or message. For others you may need to upgrade to a premium account, so it is worth growing that network as quickly as you can, as more direct contacts mean more second line contacts, whom you can contact yourself.

Step 4: Keep in touch

Don't forget to follow up any connections that you make with a second email and perhaps an opportunity to meet up. You could suggest interning or shadowing on an event. Keep the networking going.

THE IMPORTANCE OF BEING PREPARED

While in-person networking is more difficult, it is a good exercise and the best way to keep building contacts. Here are some tips for networking events.

Choose your event carefully. If you want to go to hear a speaker, then that's fine; the networking is likely to be a secondary goal. But if you're aiming to attend just to network, decide what you want to achieve and check to see if the people you most want to talk to are likely to be there.

If you have to pay to go to the network event don't be afraid to call the organiser and find out if it suits your purpose. It may also have student discounts or a student rate.

Check the list of attendees, beforehand if possible (it is not always easy to do).

Make sure you have business cards and/or a phone app to collect and give out your details. Think about your audience and if the people you want to network with are still on paper cards, then you would be better having some.

Dress neatly and appropriately for the audience. If they are lawyers wear a suit. If tech entrepreneurs, then jeans and a smart top is usually appropriate.

Don't forget that networking is a kind of performance, and that many, many people dislike it.

Practise your elevator pitch.

Give yourself a target – either particular people or companies, or the type of contact you want to make. Don't be scared to ask people who talk to you if they can introduce you to someone you would like to meet: a) they might know them; and b) it gives your conversation a purpose if you find that they are not your core target.

Once you have met the people you wanted to meet, follow up immediately and ensure that you organise another meeting or phone call or whatever your purpose was.

Be resilient, you will come across the people who are rude or too busy to talk; do not let this put you off, it is normal part of working life. Simply move on to the next person or group.

HINTS AND TIPS TO DEAL WITH NERVES WHEN NETWORKING

Most people will feel anxious about attending a networking event, especially for the first time. It is rare to find people that feel confident about entering a room of strangers. Approaching people can feel awkward and intimidating. It can be a very uncomfortable thing to do, but here are some top tips about dealing with those inevitable nerves:

1. If you have never been to a networking event before, try and find a friend to go with
2. If you are entering into a room on your own, and there is no one you know in it, take a deep breath, smile and say hello
3. When you are introduced to someone, repeat their name ("Nice to meet you, Sarah") as this will help you remember names
4. When joining an existing group, it is easier to start by asking a question than launching into an opinion
5. Set yourself a target, e.g. at this event I will introduce myself to six people I do not know
6. Try not to get stuck talking to the 'wrong' person; you're at a networking event to network. You can avoid this by asking the host to introduce you to people you would like to meet or indeed ask anyone. It can be hard to say 'excuse me, you're really nice but I need to talk to someone else for the good of my business'. If you can pull that off, then well done. If you can't, then create a trip to the coffee, buffet or in extremis, the toilet.
7. Be polite and charming. You never know when you might meet someone who can help you – or whom you can help.
8. Don't waste your time – or anyone else's. You're there for a reason. If it becomes obvious that you won't fulfil the task you set yourself then don't be scared to leave.
9. Don't hog the bar or the cake.
10. Always, always follow up those leads.

THINK POINT

How nervous do you think you might be at your first networking event? What will you do to overcome these nerves – or, if you're confident, avoid seeming over-confident?

INDUSTRY INSIGHT

The Kingston Chamber of Commerce

Across the UK, Europe and further afield, there are Chambers of Commerce which exist to support businesses of all sizes and types, and to help them support each other. While the Chamber is there to provide business support and signposting, its principal activity is to provide networking opportunities for businesses and individual sole traders.

The Kingston Chamber of Commerce (CoC) in the Royal Borough of Kingston upon Thames organises different types of networks for different kinds of meet-ups. Lunch events tend to be sit-down and chat events; breakfast is more normal networking where you are able to get to know a number of people whom you are seated close to, and to talk about your business and opportunities.

Kingston Chamber also recognises that 'people do business with people' and so there are also social evenings such as quiz nights, pamper evenings and the inevitable Golf Day – but there are only two of those per year, and they are open to total beginners! Kingston CoC also organises the Kingston Business Expo in conjunction with Kingston University Business School which gives businesses the opportunity to promote themselves more widely than the chamber membership, and gives you the opportunity to network with them. Kingston CoC, in common with most if not all of the Chambers of Commerce in the UK, are happy for you to attend one or two meetings before joining and go out of their way to be welcoming to those who might be interested in what they do.

While a Chamber of Commerce might not be the most fertile ground for finding work as an events or hospitality freelancer, what it will give you is access to a network of business support, free or extremely good value business training and a network of people in approximately the same line of business as you are yourself, the benefit of which should not be underestimated. They also tend to offer group-negotiated discounts on useful business products and services, and a range of advice. Kingston has links to support business with start-up, marketing, law, personal law, tech and money.

 **ACTIVITY**

The key skills required for networking

Assess yourself against the key skills required for networking. Give yourself a score which ranges from 4 (comfortable) and 0 (scared). Think about what you will do to practise and develop the skill and the expected outcomes after you practise these.

Table 27.2   Assessing your networking skills

Skills required for networking	Your score – comfortable (4) to uncomfortable (0)	What you will do to practise and develop the skill?	Expected outcome after practise
I can approach people I want to talk to			
I can walk into a networking room with confidence			
I am aware of my personal impact on people			
I have developed the skills to identify the right people to talk to at a networking event			
I have resilience and persistence			
I have created my elevator pitch			
I can deliver my elevator pitch			
I am good at adapting my pitch to different situations			

THINK POINT

Where will you go first to research the best networks for your purpose? Do you think you will find them best online or as networking events?

If you are naturally turning towards the online area, don't underestimate the power of meeting someone face to face. You wouldn't do it with friends – so don't assume that you'll be able to successfully network solely by networking online.

CONCLUSION

In this chapter we have covered:

- The various types of networking events, both online and face to face
- How to approach networking and how you might overcome anxiety and nerves
- How the SPECK grid can be used to help develop a strategy to get the most out of networks
- Basic networking skills and personalised resources including an elevator pitch and a LinkedIn profile

FURTHER READING

Cummings, S., Heeks, R. and Huysman, M. (2006) 'Knowledge and learning in online networks in development: A social-capital perspective', *Development in Practice*, 16(6): 570–86.

Lin, N. (2017) 'Building a network theory of social capital', in N. Lin, K. Cook and R. Burt (eds), *Social Capital: Theory and Research*. London: Routledge, pp. 3–28.

LinkedIn (2017) *The Student's Guide to LinkedIn* (www.slideshare.net/linkedin/the-students-guide-to-linkedin).

Service, O., Hallsworth, M., Halpern, D., Algate, F., Gallagher, R., Nguyen, S., Ruda, S., Sanders, M., Pelenur, M., Gyani, A., Harper, H., Reinhard, J. and Kirkman, E. (2014) *EAST: Four Simple Ways to Apply Behavioural Insights* (www.bi.team/wp-content/uploads/2015/07/BIT-Publication-EAST_FA_WEB.pdf).

Useful resources

British Chambers of Commerce – www.britishchambers.org.uk

Kingston Chamber of Commerce – www.kingstonchamber.co.uk

The Institute of Directors – www.iod.com

The Federation of Small Businesses (FSB) – www.fsb.org.uk

EventBrite – www.eventbrite.co.uk

LinkedIn – www.LinkedIn.com

28 POSTGRADUATE STUDIES AND THE ROUTE TOWARDS AN ACADEMIC CAREER

CHAPTER LEARNING OBJECTIVES

By the end of this chapter you should be able to:

* Understand what postgraduate degrees are and the differences between taught and research degrees
* Be confident in how you can progress from your undergraduate studies to postgraduate studies
* Recognise the benefits and value of postgraduate studies for your future career as an industry professional or as an academic in tourism, hospitality and events

GLOSSARY

* **Doctorate:** the highest awarded degree by a university or other approved educational body
* **Doctor of Philosophy (PhD):** (Latin: (Ph)ilosophiae (d)octor) – a doctorate in any discipline except medicine
* **Master of Philosophy (MPhil):** a postgraduate research degree
* **Postgraduate:** a course that is taken after completing a first (undergraduate or Batchelors) degree. Usually a master's (MA or MSc) or PhD
* **Viva voce:** an oral examination where you are expected to defend your written thesis (MPhil and PhD levels of study)

INTRODUCTION

After you graduate, the outside world may seem daunting. You will need to adjust to life outside of the university bubble and you may not know what it is you want to do after your degree. So, what happens next? There are four potential routes that you may wish to take. These include searching for a graduate job (Chapter 20), enrolling on a **postgraduate** course (this chapter), set up your own business (Chapter 34), or taking a gap year (Chapters 21 and 22). Sometimes it is difficult to think about continuing your studies after studying for three or four years. However, some people enjoy studying and it is not always clear how you can progress from an undergraduate to postgraduate studies. Many study skills guides present ways in which undergraduate students can apply their skills to the workplace but how students may wish to progress to postgraduate studies and academic careers is often lacking. Therefore, this chapter presents you with ways in which you can explore postgraduate (e.g. master's) and postgraduate research (e.g. **Doctor of Philosophy (PhD)**) opportunities if you wish to pursue high-level positions such as government advisors or a career in academia such as teaching and/or researching.

WHAT ARE POSTGRADUATE STUDIES?

It is uncommon for students who study tourism, hospitality and events to require postgraduate education to access the workplace. However, this depends on the type of role and career that you wish to pursue. According to Graduate Prospects Ltd (2020a), just under 8% of graduates continue with further study in travel and tourism compared to the UK average of 21.5%. Approximately 4.5% work and study, compared to almost 75% of graduates who are employed within the sector. The top four jobs include conference and exhibition manager and organiser, marketing associate professional and travel agent.

Most postgraduate courses in tourism, hospitality and events, emphasise management skills in areas such as international tourism, hospitality, heritage and sustainability. However, some courses offer more niche and specialist subjects such as ecotourism. In some cases, it may also be relevant to study marketing, human resource management or other general business topics, as these can be applied across various disciplines (Graduate Prospects Ltd, 2020a).

WHAT ARE THE BENEFITS OF POSTGRADUATE STUDIES?

The benefits of postgraduate studies depend on your personal goals and where you want to go after your studies. There are many ways that you can study including part-time, full-time and distance learning; and there are many qualifications such as Master's degrees including MBAs, Professional Doctorates and continuing professional development (CPD) courses. You will develop and gain an important range of transferable skills, demonstrating skills of critical thinking, project management, time management, problem solving, research and data analysis. These skills can all be valuable assets from an employer's point of view.

Some courses offer you the possibility of industry experience through placements that provide you with the opportunity to network and connect with experts and employers. This was covered in Section C.

Some of the many reasons for studying a postgraduate degree include improving your employability, changing career, career progression, becoming an expert in your subject area, intellectual and personal challenge, or studying for enjoyment. These are further explained in Table 28.1. Studying at postgraduate level may open doors to careers such as environmental planner, government policy advisor, hotel and resort manager, outdoor leisure manager, regional or national tourism planner, tourism operations manager, events planner, gaming management or restaurant manager.

Table 28.1 The reasons and benefits of studying a postgraduate degree

Reasons	Associated benefits
Improving employability (see Section B of this book)	Postgraduate study can enhance your CV (Chapter 29), develop your knowledge and skills and make you more appealing in a competitive job market
Changing career	You may be a mature student wishing to change your career direction or want to learn more about another subject area. Postgraduate study can help you achieve a new and rewarding career
Career progression (see Section D)	In some cases, some jobs in the tourism, hospitality and events sector may require postgraduate qualifications. Achieving a postgraduate degree develops your skills and knowledge to a higher-level sought by employers and help to facilitate you into more senior and specialist roles. In some cases, some employers may fund your course
Becoming an expert	During your studies, you will learn from experts in your subject area and ultimately become an expert in your own right through doctoral study. Experts are made, not born! (Anders Ericsson, 2006)
Intellectual and personal challenge (see Section B of this book)	It can be very rewarding to immerse yourself in a subject that you are passionate about and develop yourself personally. Many postgraduate programmes will involve a dissertation or research project that are intellectually stimulating resulting in your deeper level of knowledge and understanding, and ability to think critically
Studying for enjoyment	Having the time and opportunity to study something that you are passionate about can be immensely rewarding

Source: Adapted from ARU, 2020a

You can progress from your bachelor's degree to postgraduate studies. The qualifications and options open to you include:

- Master's (usually Master of Arts (MA) or Master of Science (MSc))
- Master of Philosophy (MPhil)
- Master of Business Administration (MBA)
- Doctor of Business Administration (DBA)
- Doctor of Philosophy (PhD)
- Postdoctoral studies (after your PhD)

WHAT IS A MASTER'S?

Most Master's programmes are taught and include qualifications such as MA, MSc, Postgraduate Certificate (PGCert) and Postgraduate Diploma (PGDip). These courses will help you acquire more advanced skills and training for a profession or postgraduate research or a PhD (FindAMasters, 2020). Just like your bachelor's degree, you will usually be expected to attend lectures and/or seminar sessions and you will be expected to write an extended dissertation or project at most institutions. This will show future employers that you are an able researcher who is dedicated, committed and has an excellent grasp of your subject.

Studying a Master's can be an exciting prospect. The most popular reasons for studying a Master's degree, according to the Higher Education Academy's Postgraduate Taught Experience Survey (2017) are:

- Progressing current career path (58%)
- Improving employment prospects (54%)
- Developing a personal interest (46%)
- Enabling progression to a higher-level qualification (21%)
- Entering a specific profession (21%)
- Meeting the requirements of a current job (9%)

Studying a Master's degree can be intense and expensive. In some cases, some work experience may be required for entry, or a high-level bachelor's degree (for example, this may be a First or Second class honours degree in the UK). It is important that if you are considering taking on a Master's degree that you have researched the details such as costs, pre-requisite qualifications and timescales involved.

Does a Master's degree give you a competitive advantage?

Master's degrees are highly regarded by employers and increasingly popular as a way to differentiate yourself. Like your bachelor's degree, a Master's or any other postgraduate degree does not guarantee you a job immediately after graduation. However, statistically graduates and postgraduates enjoy higher employment rates than non-graduates (Graduate Prospects Ltd, 2020a).

Most postgraduates will more likely enter high-skilled professional or managerial roles. Some roles may specifically require a Master's degree as an essential entry requirement such as a clinical psychologist, lawyer, librarian, social worker or a teacher. Some may just state that a Master's degree is a highly beneficial entry requirement. In some countries, such as China, employers are insisting applicants have a postgraduate degree from a reputable university.

Applying to study for a Master's degree

As outlined above, you will usually need the equivalent of at least a 2:1 at bachelor's level. If English is not your first language, you may be required to complete a language proficiency test. These may include:

- International English Language Testing System (IELTS)
- Test of English as a Foreign Language (TOEFL)
- Pearson Test of English Academic (PTE Academic)
- Cambridge English Language Assessment

If you choose to study your Master's abroad, you may also need a language proficiency test, e.g. Brazilian universities will require you to have proficient skills in Portuguese.

If you achieve a 2:2 or Third, or have no bachelor's degree at all, you may still be accepted based on your professional experience. This will be at the discretion of the university at which you wish to study, so it is always best to contact them directly to see if you meet the requirements for acceptance onto the course. Interviews may be used as part of the recruitment process (use Chapter 31 for guidance on this).

━━━ INDUSTRY INSIGHT ━━━

Example of what is needed to secure a Master's position at a UK university

Master of Science (MSc) International Business with Tourism and Hospitality (Professional Practice) at University of Huddersfield

Entry requirements: Honours degree of 2:2 or above, or an equivalent professional qualification in Business Studies, Marketing, Management, Logistics, Accountancy or Economics. Others with appropriate professional qualifications and/or experience are considered on individual merit. Requires English Language qualification if English is not first language. Duration of study: part-time, 24 months

(*Source*: Graduate Prospects Ltd, 2020b)

Fees and funding

Postgraduate courses vary greatly in terms of fees. For a Master of Art (MA) or Social Science (MSc) degree you will pay around £6,482 per year as a UK or European Union (EU) student, although an overseas student in the UK might look to pay around £14,096 per year. Be aware though as fees can rise to over £50,000 for an MBA in a prestigious business school, sometimes over £100,000 in some top-ranking American schools.

Research Master's are often cheaper than taught Master's degrees, but they require far more independent study and less in-class teaching. For a research Master's (MRes) you are looking at around £4,000 if you are a UK/EU student or over £10,000 if you are an overseas student (FindAMasters, 2020).

There are funding options available and these can include the following:

- Postgraduate loans (UK/EU and overseas)
- Scholarships
- Erasmus fund
- Crowdfunding
- Charities and trusts
- Employer sponsorships
- Specialist MBA fund.

Postgraduate taught or a Research Master's degree?

Master's degrees can be postgraduate taught or postgraduate research degrees. One may be more suitable than the other based on your future goals and how you like to study, and what you want to learn.

Postgraduate taught degrees are like your bachelor's degree, completing a series of modules through a set timetable of seminars, lectures and other activities. These include the Master of Art (MA) and Master of Science (MSc) programmes. On the other hand, postgraduate research degrees are independent study with minimal, if any, timetabled sessions. Focus is usually on one extended project with support and guidance from a supervisor. These include Master of Research (MRes) and Master of Philosophy (MPhil). A Master of Research (MRes) will be useful preparation for a PhD, or MPhil to PhD progression is another alternative.

You may be eligible to progress to a PhD if you achieve your taught Master's in an appropriate subject area, such as Tourism Management or Events Management, and you satisfy the various entry requirements (usually a first class honours degree if you are skipping the MA/MSc).

INDUSTRY INSIGHT

Example of a Postgraduate Certificate position in a UK university

Postgraduate Certificate (PGCert) in International Events Management at Leeds Beckett University – Events, Tourism and Hospitality.

Entry requirements: Second class honours degree or equivalent professional/vocational experience. Duration of study: 6 months full-time or 18 months part-time

(*Source*: Graduate Prospects Ltd, 2020c)

POSTGRADUATE DOCTORAL RESEARCH DEGREES

There are several ways that you can achieve a **Doctorate** degree. These include an integrated PhD, Professional Doctorate, PhD (standard research route), PhD by publication, and distance learning PhD. It is worth noting that there are differences between the terms 'doctorate' and 'PhD'. A doctorate is a qualification that awards you a doctoral degree where you are required to produce advanced work that makes a significant new contribution to your chosen discipline; in your case this is in the subject field of tourism, hospitality and events. Hence, being awarded the title of 'doctor'. A PhD is a more common type of doctorate and is awarded in most academic fields of research. Essentially, PhDs are all doctorates, but not all doctorates are PhDs (FindAPhD, 2020a).

Integrated PhD: A new route to a PhD

This is a four-year qualification that involves studying a one-year research Master's degree (MRes) before progressing onto a three-year PhD. This is only available across selected UK universities and are supported by the government and the British Council. This integrated PhD combines taught materials, practical experience and advanced research. You will learn subject-specific methodologies alongside the development of transferable skills for becoming a leader in your chosen profession.

Some institutions may develop personalised integrated PhD programmes to meet your specific needs, such as a postgraduate certificate (PGCert) in Learning and Teaching (CiLT), that are beneficial, as well as a requirement, for becoming a higher education lecturer (Higginbotham, 2018).

For more information on integrated PhDs, see the UK Research and Innovation website at ukri.org.

Professional doctorates (Prof Doc)

Professional doctorates are an alternative to PhD study. These so-called 'Prof Docs' allow you to research your area of interest and expertise while you continue to work. This adds value to your organisation while enhancing your career prospects and expanding your professional network. These qualifications are usually aimed towards professional vocational sectors, such as healthcare, teaching and education.

It is structured on taught elements and requires a smaller research project compared to a PhD. They are usually studies on a part-time basis and last between two and eight years.

Even though you might not be seeking an academic job, you are still expected to contribute to theory as well as a professional practice through the real-life issues that affect your employer.

Common types of Professional Doctorate degrees include:

- Doctor of Business Administration (DBA)
- Doctor of Education (EdD)
- Doctor of Medicine (MD)

What is a Doctor of Philosophy (PhD)?

A PhD is a postgraduate doctoral degree awarded to a student who has demonstrated that they have made a significant contribution to knowledge. They originated in Germany during the nineteenth century alongside the modern university. Before the PhD was introduced, the highest level of academic degree was a Master's. However, focus shifted from mastering an existing body of scholarship to one of producing new knowledge, theories, approaches and ideas. Therefore, the PhD was brought in to recognise those who could demonstrate the necessary skills and expertise to contribute to knowledge within their academic field of study (FindAPhD, 2020a). Unlike previous degrees, a PhD is a pure research degree which is often very practical, diverse and varied with many different components.

As you progress throughout your bachelor's degree, you will notice that the first, second and third years are very similar except that you will be expected to complete modules and coursework that are a higher level as your progress to increase your level of understanding, skills and knowledge. A PhD is different to this. Instead it progresses through various systematic stages which normally involves the following:

- Reviewing existing literature to develop a literature review
- Conducting original research and generating data for findings
- Producing a thesis that concludes your research findings (usually 80,000 words)
- Writing up the thesis and submitting it as your 'dissertation'
- Defending your thesis through a **viva voce** examination

This is the common sequence of a PhD across UK universities, but some may slightly differ, as do PhDs in other countries. These stages are progressed on throughout the course of your PhD, usually between three and six years full-time, or four and eight years part-time. The common two approaches are to produce one thesis of 80,000 words or a body of published work (publication) – both will need to be defended at a viva voce (oral exam).

A PhD through published work generally suggests you have already demonstrated an independent and original contribution to knowledge, with an understanding of research methods appropriate to your field. The published work must usually have been written within the last ten years, be a continued record of publication, and be accessible in the public domain.

What will a PhD help you achieve?

Traditionally, PhDs have been viewed as a training process that helps students to develop the necessary skills to seek careers in the university sector and to undertake academic research. However, academic roles do not solely focus on research: they also involve teaching and education, enterprise and knowledge transfer, administration and leadership in roles such as 'Head of Department'.

PhDs are becoming increasingly recognised as flexible higher level qualifications outside of academia so as a consequence not all PhD students end up working within higher education. Some choose to follow other careers that are either related to their subject expertise or apply the advanced research skills that have developed throughout their PhD. Many PhD programmes recognise that these developed skills are transferable to the workplace and universities emphasise these or include specific training sessions that enable PhD students to communicate and apply their research outside and beyond the university. The portfolio of skills that you will develop as a PhD researcher are unique to you and are highly valued by potential employers. The overall view of a PhD is far more than researching and writing up a thesis. Table 28.2 shows the extra activities that you may engage in during your PhD studies that will enhance the value of your PhD regardless of your intended career.

Table 28.2   Enhancing the value of your PhD

Teaching	PhD students are often given the opportunity to become Graduate Teaching Assistants (GTAs) or Associate Lecturers (ALs) and teach undergraduate and postgraduate students. This work is usually paid and supported by training and evaluation
Conference presentation	As a PhD student, you will be at the **cutting edge** of research and other scholars will be interested in your research findings. Therefore, presenting your work at academic conferences is worthwhile for developing transferable skills in public speaking and presenting, gaining credible feedback and become recognised as an expert in your field
Publication	You may have the opportunity to publish work in academic journals, books and other media such as academic websites and blogs. This involves a robust and extensive review process of your work, but it is highly rewarding
Public engagement and communication	Many universities are involved in local events and initiatives to communicate the benefits of their research to emphasise the 'impact' of research and its wider public benefit

Source: FindAPhD, 2020

If you are interested in becoming a researcher, you might find the Researcher Development Framework (RDF) useful for developing your skills.

What is the Vitae Researcher Development Framework (RDF)?

The RDF (Figure 28.1) is a professional development framework for researcher development in 'planning, promoting and supporting the personal, professional and career development of researchers in higher education. It articulates the knowledge, behaviours and attributes of successful researchers and encourages them to realise their potential.' (Vitae, 2010: p.1). The RDF is designed for:

- Researchers for evaluating and planning their professional development
- Managers and supervisors for supporting the development of researchers under their supervision
- Trainers, developers, human resources specialists and careers advisors for the planning and provision of supporting researcher development.

For more information see the website www.vitae.ac.uk.

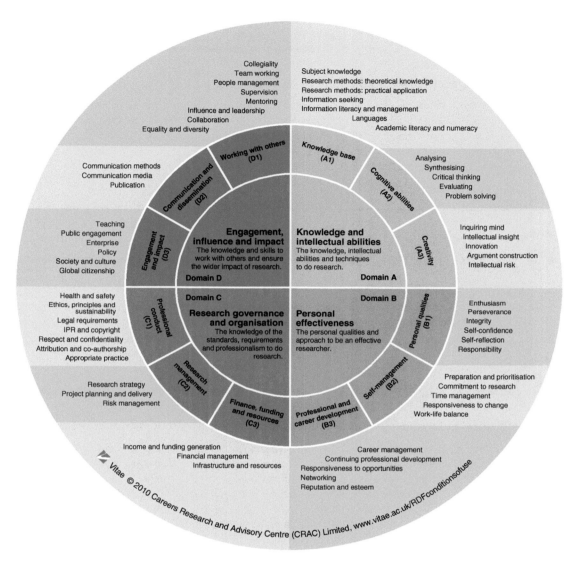

Figure 28.1 The Vitae Researcher Development Framework

Source: Vitae, © 2010 Careers Research and Advisory Centre (CRAC) Limited www.vitae.ac.uk/rdf. Permission given for reproduction.

Applying to study for a PhD

A PhD is the highest academic degree you can achieve. They are unique and based on your own research topic. You will usually need to have a relevant Master's degree to be accepted onto a PhD as otherwise you will not attain the essential level of in-depth knowledge about your subject area. Occasionally, there is a possibility of gaining entry onto a doctoral programme from a good bachelor's degree. However, as with Master's level study, entry requirements can vary between institutions. It is therefore advisable to check the specific requirements for entry (Graduate Prospects Ltd, 2020d).

INDUSTRY INSIGHT

Example of an advert for a PhD position in a UK university

Doctor of Philosophy (PhD) Planning Studies and Tourism, Hospitality and Events at London South Bank University.

Entry requirements: Expected to have a 2:1 degree as a minimum and a relevant postgraduate qualification at Master's level is beneficial. If candidate has lower-level second class honours equivalent, a postgraduate qualification at master's level is also required.

Duration of study: 36 months full-time or 60 months part-time.

(Source: Graduate Prospects Ltd, 2020e)

THINK POINT

Am I a doctor if I get a PhD?

Yes, but not in the sense of a medical doctor (a medical doctor has 'MD' after their name). You will become a Doctor of Philosophy regardless of the subject you study.

STUDENT INSIGHT

Publishing work as an undergraduate student, reflections from one of the authors

It is unusual to have published academic work during your bachelor's degree, but it is possible. As a second-year tourism management student, I was offered the opportunity to be a research assistant during the summer term to conduct interviews and transcribe interviews generating themes. I was responsible for booking and arranging interviews with small local independent businesses and entrepreneurs who participated in a local festival. This was an unpaid role but as my input was important to the study findings, I was named as a co-author on the paper. This was a major learning curve and really helped develop my skills and abilities as a researcher for later in my MPhil/PhD studies.

THINK POINT

It may be worth exploring research assistant roles while you are studying to help develop your researching skills, making you a competitive applicant for postgraduate studies.

Who should study a PhD?

A PhD is difficult and uniquely challenging, requiring at least three years of your hard work and dedication. Ensure you research this well to decide whether it is for you. There are many websites that can help you and offer useful details to help you decide. These include:

- FindAPhD
- Prospects
- StudyPortalsPhD
- University webpages

It may also be worth speaking with your undergraduate and postgraduate (if studying a Master's course) tutors and/or your major project supervisors. They will be able to advise you on what they think and offer some useful practical and personal advice.

PhDs can be lonely as much of your work is independent. It is very different to studying an undergraduate or taught Master's where you are surrounded by your peers. This does not suggest that you will not have other PhD students, university staff, supervisors and social support to hand. However, it may be these types of things that influence your decision to start a PhD.

===== STUDENT INSIGHT =====

A story of progression from an undergraduate to postgraduate student from one of the authors

I started my bachelor's degree in Tourism Management in 2013. I chose to start my degree as I was a mature student with three children and struggling to find suitable jobs. During my first year, I was really enjoying my studies and researching for my assignments and always remembered that my college tutors had told me that I was very academic and should go to university (which at the time I laughed off as I was pregnant with my second child. Yes, I waited until number three to start!).

I remember picking up the university degree course guide and searched through the postgraduate options. At this point, I clearly had high hopes and aspirations that I would successfully pass my degree and be able to start a Master's. This was without thinking about how I would pay for it!

Progressing my studies as a postgraduate was in the back of my mind until I started my second year and met one of my tutors who pulled me aside one day and advised me to seriously consider progressing onto a research degree after my undergraduate studies. I was astonished and taken aback. Me? How could I do a PhD? They explained that I displayed strong academic writing and researching skills, and these could be developed further. I had many questions as I hadn't finished my bachelor's degree and still had a year left to go. 'How would I ever afford it? How do I have the time to study a self-managed degree with three children (and a husband), just how?' However, this idea kept me focused in my bachelor's degree knowing that I need to do well in all my modules to achieve the grades required to finish my bachelor's degree with a First, or a 2:1 at the very least, for my progression to a postgraduate degree.

After much hard work and effort, I was awarded my first-class tourism management degree with honours in 2016 and applied for the scholarship of MPhil progression to PhD (MPhil-PhD) researching Rio's mega-events and the socio-economic impact on local businesses. Unfortunately, I was unsuccessful and not awarded the scholarship, so I proposed my own PhD study focusing on Rio's favela communities and the socio-cultural impacts from mega-events. I was fortunate to receive funding from the university for my tuition fees and field research and I began my research in January 2017. However, another slight issue arose. I was only registered as a Master of Philosophy, not an MPhil-PhD progression. Due to issues with student finance, I was unable to claim this as an MPhil-PhD as it was only available for Master's or MPhil studies without PhD progression. At that time, the postgraduate loan (PGL) was not available. Therefore, I had to adjust my research to ensure that I was keeping my initial focus for my PhD that I would now start after successful completion of my MPhil. I successfully completed my MPhil in July 2019 after my viva voce – yes you defend your thesis for this too!

(Continued)

I am now studying for my PhD at King's College London (KCL) as I followed my supervisor from my previous university. This is one of the best decisions I have made throughout my academic rollercoaster!

The moral to this story is: find yourself a supervisor that you can trust and who will support you and your ideas; is an expert in your field; and will be your friend throughout and always have your back. This is the most important advice that I would tell anyone wishing to pursue a PhD. It is half the battle to being successful in your studies.

HOW DO I PROGRESS TO POSTGRADUATE STUDIES?

You can search and apply for various postgraduate studies if you meet the expected criteria. Tourism, hospitality and events may fall under a range of different disciplines such as geography, marketing and economic studies, depending on the institution. Sometimes it is easier or prefererable to study at the institution in which you completed your bachelor's degree. Some universities will offer reduced fees for progressing students, so this is worth consideration.

To apply for a PhD, some universities may have specific topics that academics may want to explore further, or others may offer positions for PhDs who wish to research their own area and topic of interest. You will be expected to write a research proposal based around your chosen subject area. If you are applying for a scholarship, then you will still be expected to write a research proposal when you apply.

Commonly, a research proposal consists of an introduction to your research topic and its importance, research aim, research objectives and/or questions that you wish to address, a literature review of current and existing literature (what we know already), and a proposed methodology that consists of your research design, data generation methods and data analysis procedures, ethical considerations, limitations of your study and a timescale (how you will conduct your study). You will also need to provide references and a covering letter or complete an application form.

COVERING THE COST OF YOUR STUDIES

Some universities offer a range of scholarships and bursaries for postgraduate students. Funding is sometimes available from charities, trusts and foundations, as well as public bodies. It is important that you research all funding opportunities before you apply and accept your place as it can be very expensive. Since September 2016, the UK government have offered postgraduate funding via a Postgraduate Loan (PGL) of up to £10,000 for Master's students. This includes all Master of Philosophy (MPhil) degrees but not MPhil to PhD progression. Since September 2018, a PhD loan of up to £25,000 was also introduced. These loans are not means-tested and therefore make them appealing to help pay for yearly tuition fees, study and travel costs. It is important that you fully investigate tuition fees and study costs required to continue your studies at the time of your application.

There are many other countries that you can study for your postgraduate degree and many offer funding opportunities and scholarships. For example, Australia is a hub for research and scholarship and has much to offer in its world-class research centres and internationally ranked universities. International students will pay a higher fee than nationals who receive a state subsidy through Australian taxation; the costs for studying a PhD in Australia can be very expensive (see Table 28.3). However, it is unlikely that you will pay the full international fees as Australian universities offer scholarships and the government offer incentives as ways to attract students. Relocating abroad also means that you will need to consider your living costs.

Table 28.3 Postgraduate fees and funding in other countries

Country	PhD fees* (approximate)	Funding*	Useful links
Australia	AUD $18,000 – AUD $42,000 per year	• Australian universities – studentships and funded PhD places • Australian Government – scholarships to study in Australia • Research training programme – available for domestic and international PhD students	• Australian Government: Australian Trade and Investment Commission – scholarships to study in Australia www.studyinaustralia.gov.au/english/australian-education/scholarships • Australian Government: Department of Education, Skills and Employment – Research Training Programme. Criteria: www.education.gov.au/research-training-program-frequently-asked-questions-students (FindAPhD, 2020b)
Canada	CAD $10,000 – CAD $20,000 per year (guideline only as varies). Some supplementary costs for student services and union fees	• Canadian universities – funding for prospective international PhD students • Queen Elizabeth II Diamond Jubilee Scholarships • International Development Research Centre (IDRC) Doctoral Research Awards – for students from developing countries up to CAD $20,000 • IDRC Research Awards – for students from developing countries who receive a salary of CAD $40,000 to complete an internship • Trudeau Doctoral Scholarships – funding for international students in a range of subjects • Vanier Canada Graduate Scholarships – funding of CAD $50,000 per year for three years of PhD study in Health Sciences, Natural Sciences Engineering, Social Sciences or Humanities	• EduCanadaw05.international.gc.ca/scholarships-bourses/scholarshipnoncdn-boursenoncdn.aspx?lang=eng&menu_id=7 (FindAPhD, 2020d)
USA	Average of $12,737 but international fees are higher	• US universities – funding is offered, and it is rare for students to fully self-fund. Private universities will offer more funding than public universities, but fees are higher • Assistantships – graduate teaching assistantships (GTAs)/teaching assistants (TAs), research assistantships, administrative assistantships, fellowships	Education USA educationusa.state.gov/ (FindAPhD, 2020e)

(Continued)

Table 28.3 (Continued)

Country	PhD fees* (approximate)	Funding*	Useful links
Hong Kong	HK $90,000 – HK $265,000 per year	• Hong Kong PhD Fellowship Scheme – HK $309,600 and conference and research-related travel allowance HK $12,900 per year for up to three years • 250 fellowships available in 2020/21 academic year	• Hong Kong University Grants Committee www.ugc.edu.hk/eng/rgc/funding_opport/fellowships/hkphdfs.html (FindAPhD, 2020f; University Grants Committee (UGC), 2017)
India	No set fees but pay as little as USD $1,000 per year at some universities	• Indian universities – scholarships and fee waivers but some of these may not be available to international students • General Scholarship Scheme (GSS) – students from specific countries to study a bachelor's, master's or PhD with some restrictions • Scholarship Programmes for Diaspora Children (SPDC) – may be restricted to undergraduate programmes	• University Grants Commission www.ugc.ac.in/page/Scholarships-and-Fellowships.aspx (FindAPhD, 2020g)

Brazil	No tuition fees for Brazilian students at public universities is extended to international students.
	
	Private university fees approximately BRL 1,400 and BRL 2,400 per month. Application fees in some institutes.
	
	Health insurance for international students and student services.
		• Scholarships – available for one-year study abroad in most cases
		• Embassies, consulates and government agencies may offer bursaries
		• The Brazilian Exchange Program for Graduates (PEC-PG) – provides financial aid for master's and PhD courses for professors, researchers, professionals and graduates in developing countries
		• Fulbright program – grants for American citizens to study a PhD
		• Kleinhans Fellowship for Community Forestry Research – Latin America and various locations funding of US $20,000 stipend per year for two-years to support research projects such as:
		  ○ Social organisation and governance
		  ○ Multi-community enterprises
		• You will need to pass a Portuguese proficiency test to study in Brazil
			• The Brazilian Exchange Program for Graduates (PEC-PG) www.dce.mre.gov.br/PEC/PECPG.php (in Portuguese)
			• Fulbright Brasil fulbright.org.br/grants-for-us-citizens/
			• Kleinhans Fellowship for Community Forestry Research www.rainforest-alliance.org/careers?hh_jid=54161
			(FindAPhD, 2020c)

*Fees and information correct at time of writing

Other countries, including Hong Kong, offer many opportunities for postgraduate studies and PhD fellowship opportunities. See the 'Postgraduate Studies in Hong Kong' website for further information: www.grad.edu.hk.

You can also choose to study in developing countries, such as India and Brazil. For example, Brazil is emerging as a nation which is producing vital research in several areas with committed financial support for its public university system. However, there are some areas for consideration. If you are choosing to study in a country that does not speak your native language, then you will need proficient skills in that language to effectively complete your studies. Some appealing reasons that you may choose to study in Brazil include free tuition, language development (you can study some PhDs in English), extensive university sector (over 2,000 universities across Brazil), and unique research prospects such as rainforest and biodiversity which can be studied within the realms of tourism, hospitality and events (FindAPhD, 2020c).

A lot of hard work, effort, time and money goes into postgraduate studies so you must be confident it is the right route for you. If you want to gain a deeper level of understanding into your subject area, then postgraduate studies are for you, if you think you can withstand the many associated challenges!

You could research some PhD study events and open days across the UK or perhaps travel to the country in which you wish to pursue your PhD. These will offer useful insights for what is required for you to apply. You can find open days and study fairs on websites, such as FindAMasters.com and FindAPhD.com, and others noted throughout this chapter, including universities that you are thinking of applying to.

LIFE AS AN ACADEMIC

If you choose to continue with an academic career in tourism, hospitality and events, your roles and responsibilities may include:

- Teaching undergraduate and postgraduate students and being responsible for preparing lessons, delivery of sessions, marking and feedback
- Contribution to employer/university activities (often called 'service') which may include committees, leadership roles and supporting events
- Participation in professional activities related to the discipline such as networking and presenting at conferences, workshops or seminars
- Managing and supporting others such as supervising undergraduate and postgraduate major projects
- Undertaking research and publishing research papers and books, and wider scholarship (e.g. writing case studies, editing textbooks)
- Secure research project funding and grants related to the discipline.

An academic career is multi-dimensional, and you will be expected to take on many wide-ranging responsibilities. Therefore, it is important that you assess the requirements of the role thoroughly to ensure that this is the right career for you.

ALTERNATIVE QUALIFICATIONS

What if you want to go on to study but not do a postgraduate course? You might consider:

- Conversion courses: vocational courses designed for individuals to pursue a career that their bachelor's degree or professional career has not prepared them for. There are different types of conversion courses depending on the specific industry. See Graduate Prospects website for further information, found here: www.prospects.ac.uk/postgraduate-study/conversion-courses
- Professional qualifications: vocational training courses related to a specific industry or career path to ensure that you meet the minimum required standards of professional expertise. See Graduate Prospects website for further information, found here: www.prospects.ac.uk/postgraduate-study/professional-qualifications

CONCLUSION

In this chapter we have covered:

- The different types of postgraduate studies that you can choose from
- The differences between postgraduate taught and postgraduate research degrees
- How to progress from your undergraduate studies to postgraduate studies
- The opportunities available to you after you finish your postgraduate studies either in industry or academia
- What funding options may be available to you as a UK/European Union (EU) and overseas student

FURTHER READING

Chin, D.C.W., Law, R. and Tung, V. (2020) 'Tourism research and career: Opening the black box', *Asia Pacific Journal of Tourism Research*, 25(2): 145–156.

Denscombe, M. (2012). *Research Proposals: A Practical Guide*. Berkshire: Open University Press.

Foskett, N. and Foskett, R. (2006) *Postgraduate Study in the UK the International Student's Guide*. London: Sage Publications.

Gosling, P. and Noordam, L.D. (2011) *Mastering Your PhD: Survival and Success in the Doctoral Years and Beyond*. Dordrecht: Springer.

Ruhanen, L. and Mclennan, C. (2012) 'The learning experiences and preferences of tourism postgraduate students', *Journal of Teaching in Travel & Tourism*, 12(2): 146–164.

Useful web resources

FindAPhD.com – the world's largest database of PhD projects and programmes. They aim to help prospective PhD students find a suitable PhD and universities recruit talented PhD students. There is also advice for PhD holders looking for non-academic careers: www.findaphd.com/advice/doing/phd-non-academic-careers.aspx

FindAMasters.com – informative website for students to compare taught and research Master's courses. Offers a wide selection of advice, up-to-date funding resources, study guides and FAQs.

Graduate Prospects Ltd (2020) list leisure, sport and tourism job profiles (www.prospects.ac.uk/job-profiles/browse-sector/leisure-sport-and-tourism#top) as well as seven steps to getting started with a PhD application

(www.findaphd.com/advice/blog/2512/getting-started-with-a-phd-application-7-steps?email=1&mailshot=1113&g=a2e6b572-0f9f-47b4-bd19-9d8c8f8ac127)

Jobs.ac.uk (lists jobs, fellowships and PhD scholarships. www.jobs.ac.uk

UK Research and Innovation – www.ukri.org

SECTION E

SECURING AND ENTERING EMPLOYMENT

Level: 5 - 6

29 WRITING AND MAKING THE MOST OF YOUR CV

CHAPTER LEARNING OBJECTIVES

By the end of this chapter, you should be able to:

* Explain the role of the Curriculum Vita (CV) in the recruitment selection process
* Identify the qualities of a good CV in terms of content, structure, presentation and formatting
* Be confident in using action words to write a powerful and high-impact CV
* Write your own CV, tailored to a career in tourism, events and hospitality

GLOSSARY

* **Curriculum Vitae (CV):** a document which presents your skills, experiences and qualifications in a way that will appeal to a prospective employer
* **Competencies:** skills necessary for a job or task that might be listed in a job advert and form the basis of interviews and selection. You need to ensure your CV demonstrates relevant competencies (e.g. team-work, leadership, and communication)
* **Unconscious bias:** the social and learned stereotypes about groups of people that that are automatic, unintentional and deeply ingrained Research suggests that unconscious biases can influence shortlis-ting and interviewing candidates. Factors involved can include age, names, place of birth and even the university you went to. Some employers undertake 'blind' shortlisting in order to combat this

INTRODUCTION

This chapter introduces you to what a **Curriculum Vitae (CV)** is and what it should do for you. In some countries, it is called a résumé. By providing examples of weak and strong CVs, the chapter covers what makes a good CV, how it can be presented and structured, and how you might tailor it to your career in tourism, events and hospitality. The different rules and conventions, such as various layouts are presented to you. By the end of the chapter you should have a good idea about how to write a relevant, targeted, high-impact and strong CV.

THE ROLE OF A CV

Increasingly, employers are no longer asking for CVs and use customised (usually online) application forms. However, a CV remains a useful document to refer to when are applying for work or writing application forms. You can also use a CV for a number of other circumstances, such as when you meet an employer at a careers fair, so it is important to have an up-to-date, well-presented and suitably tailored CV. Writing a good CV takes time and it needs to be updated regularly. There are numerous online CV 'builders' and templates available, but ensure you make yours stand out as generic CVs won't get the attention you want. As Rook (2013: 100) reminds us, '80 per cent of CVs are quickly discarded within seconds, 10 per cent are dismissed after further consideration, and the remainder are considered for interview.'

LINKING YOUR CV TO 'BRAND ME'

Great CVs act as marketing tools and should not just be a list of everything you have ever done. As outlined in Chapter 26, your CV needs to ensure your unique personal brand shines out. Given that an effective CV should always be tailored to the attributes and skills needed for a specific role, it should list education and experience directly linked to the role of interest. The content should be relevant, organised and well presented, so that the short-lister can see quickly and easily how you match the role. Therefore, if you are interested in pursuing a career in THE, your CV should highlight your interest in and experience of travel (e.g. student exchanges and study abroad), organising events (e.g. student society events, or for external organisations) and any relevant work experience. Try to project a personal brand characterised by customer service, travel, organisational ability and hard work.

BASIC CONTENT AND STRUCTURE OF A CV

Although there are no fixed rules on how a CV should be presented, the standard (and expected) format includes the following headings:

- Title i.e. your name (employers know it is a CV). In some European countries, a photo may be required.
- Personal contact details i.e. postal address, email address and telephone number.
- Personal statement
- Education and qualifications

- Work experience
- Achievements and awards
- Hobbies and interests
- References

Remember that if you are applying overseas then there are different conventions. The Prospects website has useful advise on what is expecting when you are applying for work overseas: https://www.prospects.ac.uk/jobs-and-work-experience/working-abroad. If you're applying for a position in a non-English-speaking country, it is advisable to have your CV translated into the appropriate foreign language. Send both the English and the native-language version to your prospective employer.

Personal details

Ensure you include your name (as the title), your email addresses, telephone number, and contact address. The World Economic Forum (2017) reported that a study by Ryerson University and the University of Toronto found people with Chinese, Indian or Pakistani-sounding names were 28% less likely to get invited to an interview than fictitious candidates with English-sounding names, even when their qualifications were the same. Based on their study of sending 13,000 fake CVs/résumés to over 3,000 job postings, for candidates with an Asian-sounding name paired with some or all foreign qualifications, employers were between 35% (in the case of large firms) and 60% (in the case of small firms) less likely to call the candidate for an interview. Likewise in the UK, a research report in January 2019 found levels of discrimination against black Britons unchanged for over fifty years. Researchers at the Centre for Social Investigation at Nuffield College, University of Oxford, found applicants from minority ethnic backgrounds had to send 80% more applications to get a positive response from an employer than a white person of British origin.

To protect yourself from unconscious bias (as introduced and discussed in Chapter 24) we suggest that it's not a good idea to include your date of birth on a CV. We also suggest you don't include your marital status, nationality, or health status. This kind of data should not be required by an employer, and indeed should not be asked for at any point in the recruitment process until you are offered a position (this is another reason why employers in the UK tend not to request photos on your CV).

Personal statement

A personal statement is your first chance to sell yourself to an employer in a short, focused paragraph, summing up your skills and experience that make you ideal for the job. You need to highlight your suitability and convince the recruiter to read on.

These kinds of statements and profiles at the top of your CV are debated across the industry, with some people claiming you need to get noticed (a study revealed that on average recruiters spend 8.8 seconds looking at your CV (Eleftheriou-Smith, 2015) and others saying they are a waste of time and space. Lepore (2020) claims recruiters spend an average of 'six seconds before they make the initial 'fit or no fit' decision' on candidates. This short time employers look at CVs has been compared to the online dating app, *Tinder* (an app where you simply swipe left or right based on a photo). You don't *need* to have a personal statement, but if you have experiences or qualifications that you are proud of and worry might not be immediately apparent to someone reading your CV for the first time, then think about highlighting them in this way.

Statements are usually 4–6 sentences in length, 50–150 words. You might think about covering who you are, what you can offer the company, and your career goals. You might also want to consider whether it's best in the first or third person. Writing in the third person can make you seem more objective (e.g. 'Tourism graduate seeking… skills include…') or the first person can feel more personal ('I am a final-year events management student seeking… My skills are…'). You may also want to consider using bullet points (see the Activity below). If you can, start sentences throughout your CV with a verb rather than using pronouns (such as 'I'). Avoid passive terms such as 'I had to', 'I was involved in', 'I was required to', in favour of statement that make you sound more engaged in the process you are describing ('I lead', 'I suggested', 'I decided' etc.).

Positive action words: keywords, not buzzwords

Picking up and reflecting back keywords from the job description (but not buzzwords) can be a useful technique. Keywords are specific terms that appear in the job advert, whereas buzzwords can be generic and meaningless. The Head of Talent at Credit Karma UK exclaims, 'It seems the world is full of disruptors, gurus and ninjas', so you need to avoid these kinds of buzzwords that will make your statement feel empty and lacking in substance. According to a survey by LinkedIn, the top 10 overused buzzwords used in LinkedIn Profiles in the US are below. What do they mean to you? What are they trying to say?

- Extensive experience
- Innovative – most common word in France, Germany, Italy, and the Netherlands
- Motivated – most common word in the UK
- Results-oriented
- Dynamic – the most common word in Brazil, India, Spain
- Proven track record
- Team player
- Fast-paced
- Problem-solver
- Entrepreneurial

Sometimes digital recruitment software uses keywords to filter candidates, looking for CVs that use terms relevant to the job, like 'events' or 'tourism'. It will then rank the suitability of each CV according to the keywords and role criteria. For instance, if a charity events officer is being sought, then keywords might include 'charity', 'NGO' or 'not for profit'.

When you are writing your CV or application, try to use positive action words such as those in Figure 29.1 below.

Adapted	Enforced	Performed
Advised	Enhanced	Persuaded
Analysed	Established	Prepared
Arranged	Expanded	Presented
Assigned	Explained	Produced
Attained	Explored	Motivated

Authored	Facilitated	Negotiated
Briefed	Gathered	Organised
Clarified	Hosted	Oversaw
Classified	Identified	Proposed
Collated	Implemented	Provided
Communicated	Improved	Recommended
Compiled	Incorporated	Recruited
Composed	Increased	Reduced
Consulted	Influenced	Replaced
Contributed	Informed	Reported
Created	Initiated	Restored
Critiqued	Interpreted	Revised
Decreased	Instructed	Served
Delegated	Lead	Solved
Demonstrated	Leveraged	Streamlined
Designed	Liaised	Stimulated
Developed	Located	Strengthened
Directed	Maintained	Structured
Drafted	Managed	Studied
Edited	Mapped	Supervised
Enabled	Monitored	Verified

Figure 29.1   Action words for your CV

The University of Hertfordshire careers team drew up a list of the 10 top words with which to make a good impression in applications:

- Achievement
- Active
- Developed
- Evidence
- Experience
- Impact
- Individual
- Involved
- Planning
- Transferable skills

Some examples from effective CVs are as follows:

- Provided excellent customer service: assessed guests' needs, suggested upgrades to enhance experience and solved concerns or issues.
- Performed research study on effectiveness of interpretation in museums through surveys, interviewing visitors and analysing data; findings helped visitor engagement manager to develop a new strategy for educating visitors.
- Collaborated with six colleagues to create a social responsibility agenda; we implemented a charity food bank donation point, enabled 25 school visits to the restaurant and chose a monthly charity to support where money raised totalled £1250 in a year.
- Trained and developed 20 members of staff in both front and back of house standards and progression opportunities; enabling the progression of five team members from entry level positions to supervisors and two being accepted to the organisation management programme.
- I worked with clients to develop a plan for the event and an agenda. This meant I had to work under pressure and showed I have good interpersonal skills and people management skills.

 THINK POINT

Put yourself in the mind of an employer – what skills and experiences would you want to see in a future employee? Why? How can you evidence these?

 ACTIVITY

Write a personal statement in 50–100 words

Most CVs will have a brief statement at the top giving a snapshot of who you are in terms of your passions, skills and experience. This brief statement should be catchy, focused and enticing. Here is an example, in the first person:

'I am a final year events management student expecting a 2:1 degree. I have developed an excellent eye for detail due to my leadership role in running three large events for university, on top of achieving high grades in all my assignments. I would like to build on my volunteering placement experience, where I developed charity events, to pursue *a challenging career in events management that utilises my creative knowledge, enterprising approach to events, and my passion for people.*'

Here is another example written in the third person:

'A recent tourism management graduate with a 2:2 honours degree from the University of X, looking to secure a graduate level position in the travel industry. Fluent in French and German so keen to secure an internationally-orientated career that builds on extensive travel, marketing work experience and database development skills.'

Or, you may want to try writing it in bullet points:

Bullet 1: Qualifications and credentials

Bullet 2: What you bring to the employer

Bullet 3: Your career goals and how they fit with the employer/role

- Recent ambitious graduate with a degree in tourism and hospitality from University X.
- Brings knowledge of social media marketing gained from work experience as the former editor of the University's online student guide and blog
- Eager to build career in the hotel industry where I can develop customer service skills gained from two years (part time) as front of house staff at boutique hotel in X

A bad example would be something like 'I would like a job in the events industry. I am a dynamic individual with excellent team-working and communication skills.' What makes this a weak statement?

Write 50–100 words about yourself that you can use at the top of a CV. Think about:

1. What makes you different to others?
2. What are you passionate about?
3. How might others describe the way you work and what you have achieved?

Education and qualifications

You should provide a list of the educational institutions you have attended since secondary school. List these with the most recent first. Ensure there are no unexplained gaps in your employment, making sure that the dates are clear. Our advice is to give all the grades but pick out the most relevant subjects e.g. '10 GCSEs grades A-C, including A for Maths, B for English and A for Geography'. Leaving out the grades altogether suggests that the grades are poor. If you studied overseas, give the UK equivalent in terms of level, credit and grades (see www.naric.org.uk, a database of all internationally recognised and verified qualifications).

Obviously if you have a tourism, events or hospitality degree it should be obvious how your education links to your application in this sector, but if you have a degree in a different subject, then you might wish to name specific modules or projects you undertook to make a more explicit link to the role you are applying for.

Example: The education section of your CV might look something like this:

2018	MA Hospitality and Event Management (with Merit)
	University of Wolverhampton, UK
2015	BSc Event Management, 2:1 (Hons)
	University of Central Lancashire, UK
2011–2013	A levels
	English, Geography and Maths

Work experience

In this section, you should include all relevant paid and voluntary work experience, highlighting those most relevant to the job (See Chapters 21 and 22). In THE, some employers prioritise this over formal qualifications. According to C&M Travel Recruitment sales manager Barbara Kolosinska (cited in Travel Weekly 2008) notes, 'Travel industry experience is more important than qualifications. It's important to put qualifications down but they definitely should not be first on your CV.' Again, list your experience in reverse chronological order (most recent first). Ensure you include your main duties and responsibilities. You might care to use the job advert and the essential and desirable criteria to do structure this section.

Be specific about any relevant experience, specialist knowledge and training you have undertaken, and ensure you use language they recognise. If you don't have anything you can put in this section, think about volunteering at a local event or part-time work at a hotel or restaurant. In the tourism sector, there are more opportunities over the peak tourist season (summer), so make the most of your university holidays. If this section is empty, employers are unlikely to consider you.

Achievements and awards

If you haven't won any relevant awards, leave this section out. Make sure any scholarships or prizes are relevant and recent: don't include things like swimming badges awarded when you were a child, but do consider things like a Duke of Edinburgh Award, scholarships or university awards (e.g. highest module mark, best intern etc.). For example, 'during my two years at Trailfinders, sales increased by 15% in my team and I received an "Award for Excellence" in recognition of my role in this success.'

Hobbies and interests

Only list hobbies that are relevant to the job you are applying for and link them wherever you can to the **competency**-based skills you have developed. You might have had a role such as a young leader, or race coordinator, or led charity events and these would be worth highlighting in terms of the leadership, coordination, project management skills you developed. For a tourism and travel related application, be sure to include all the countries you have visited and what you did there. If you were there for work or study (as opposed to a holiday), be sure to say so. You might also want to list additional skills such as foreign language skills or if you have a clean driving licence.

References

If you are just leaving university, give details of a referee who knows you well such as a personal tutor or course leader, and a professional referee (your line manager or work experience manager). It is always advisable to ask your referees when you use their name, as something companies will contact them without notifying you first. If there have been a few years between university and your job application, then include two professional referees' details (unless of course you are applying for a university position). If you do not wish your current line manager to know you are applying for a job or if the person you would ideally like to write your reference may not be available (e.g. on annual leave or maternity leave), or if you haven't been able to ask their permission before the application deadline), then simply write 'References on request' in this section.

ACADEMIC CVs

If you are intending to apply for an academic role in a university, you should also include headings such as 'Research Publications', 'Conference Papers', 'Research Income' and 'Teaching Responsibilities' (see Chapter 28 for further advice on pursuing an academic career).

Matching your CV to the vacancy

You should update and tailor your CV every time you apply for a role, showing how your skills address the needs of the organisation by carefully matching what they are looking for in their job description to your CV.

Online and digital CVs

Increasingly, CVs are now written, submitted and viewed online. There are also online platforms that 'host' CVs, and you should think about whether this is right for you, and if so, which platform suits you best. For example, a platform like WordPress.com will allow you to embed and link images, video and media files more effectively. In some cases, companies will want to ensure they appoint someone with digital skills (e.g. digital marketing officer for an events company or travel agent). The way you format and present your CV is a skills test in its own right. Although the content will resemble the standard CV, a digital CV will allow you to insert hyperlinks to external sources, such as your own or current company's website, blogs, social media (e.g. LinkedIn or Twitter) and your Skype address; insert signposts and cross references within the CV so the reader can jump around the CV in a way that you feel best presents your skills; and be more creative (for example, see those on https://weare.guru/creative-cvs/) with images, text and fonts.

Some people use LinkedIn as their CV. Below is an example of such a CV a few years after Karolina completed her MA Travel and Tourism.

Adopting a skills-based structure

Some people chose to highlight their skills in their CV, rather than the more traditional CV organised by time i.e. you could list your skills using the skills listed in the job advertisement criteria and then provide evidence against each one.

What is Karolina's top skill?

Help us identify relevant opportunities and content for your connections

×

| Event Planning | Social Media | Research | Tourism |

Your response is anonymous and will not be directly shared with your connections or other LinkedIn members. Learn more

None of the above

Highlights

27 mutual connections
You and Karolina both know Maria Jurvelius, Dr. Nazia (Naz) Ali, and 25 others

About

An articulate and highly motivated Tourism & Travel graduate with strong analytical and interpersonal skills; accustomed to working under pressure and using own initiative in customer service industry. Highly computer literate, fluent in English and Polish. Currently aspiring to join and start a challenging career with a high profile company that ... see more

Experience

Freelance Translator
Various online and print publications
Jun 2019 – Present · 4 mos
Luton, United Kingdom

easyJet
7 yrs 9 mos

Cabin Crew
Jan 2012 – Present · 7 yrs 9 mos
Luton, United Kingdom

Performing variety of personal services conducive to safety and comfort of airline passengers during flights.

Payroll Assistant
Nov 2016 – Aug 2017 · 10 mos

Receptionist
Lea Vale Clinic
Oct 2011 – Jan 2012 · 4 mos
Luton, United Kingdom

Receiving, assisting and directing patients in accessing the appropriate service or healthcare professional in a courteous, efficient and effective way.
Providing general assistance to the practice team and projecting a positive and friendly image to patients and other visitors, either in person or via the telephone.

G Casino
3 yrs 4 mos

Team Coach
Sep 2011 – Jan 2012 · 5 mos
Luton, United Kingdom

Helping with ongoing, long-term improvement of employees' skills, enabling them to fulfil their potential within the organisation.

Receptionist - Front Desk
Oct 2008 – Jan 2012 · 3 yrs 4 mos
Luton, United Kingdom

Dealing with customers and enquiries; answering the telephone and handling other general administrative duties, such as typing and filing.

Education

The University of Bedfordshire 2008 - 2011
BA with Honours, 1st Class, Travel and Tourism
2008 – 2011

University of Bedfordshire
Travel and Tourism

Skills & Endorsements

 Customer Service · 14

 Endorsed by Timothy Cakebread, who is highly skilled at this

 Endorsed by Ismael Noorally and 6 other mutual connections

Figure 29.2 An example of a LinkedIn CV. Example provided courtesy of Karolina, travel and tourism graduate, 2008–2011

ACTIVITY

Matching skills to your experience

1. List of all the significant activities you would like to include on your CV
2. Next to them list all the skills you think you have developed and demonstrated through each of those activities
3. Slot these into your CV structure

Things not to put on a CV

Do not include the following information:

- Your date of birth
- Your Facebook, Instagram or social media accounts (except for LinkedIn if you are confident in your online profile)
- Some European employers like to see a photo, but increasingly employers will be blind-screening to avoid issues of unconscious bias
- Unprofessional or silly email addresses
- References. Unless you have published a paper or book yourself, there is no need to reference or cite research
- Apart from the personal statement at the start, do not use paragraphs.

STUDENT INSIGHT

Cassie applying for a travel agent role

Cassie studies in the US. She loves travel and has just completed her tourism management bachelor's course. She thought she would like to work as a travel agent. When she downloaded the job description, she found it asked for various types of skills and experience. She applied, but did not secure an interview. The feedback was that she lacked skills. She decided to look again at her CV to see what skills she was missing, comparing it to the job advert.

- ✓ Degree in Hospitality, Travel, Tourism, Business or relevant field
- ✓ Excellent knowledge of computer reservations systems, GDS systems and e-travelling
- ✓ Fluency in English; multilingualism is a plus
- ✓ Strong sales skills and commercial awareness
- ✓ Ability to interact, communicate and negotiate effectively
- ✓ Sound knowledge of domestic and international travel trends
- ✓ Personal travel experience will be considered an advantage

Cassie signed up for an evening class on Galileo, the world's most widely-used computerised reservation system (GDS) at her local college to fill this gap in her skills. For $240, she studied one evening per week for 12 weeks and got her GDS qualification. She applied again once she got this, and secured an interview

 THINK POINT

What are the top skills that employers are looking for in the tourism/events/hospitality industry? Why?

How might the industry seek to further reduce bias in applications? Are there examples of positive action to address discrimination against people from ethnic minority backgrounds?

TOP TIPS FOR CV PRESENTATION AND FORMATTING

Length: for graduate level CVs, no more than two pages (this will expand as you go through your career). Many academic CVs are pages long as they include publications, grants and awards. Ensure you align the text (justify left) so it is consistent in its format, easy to read and looks neat.

Bullet points: outlining some of your key responsibilities and duties is an effective way to present information.

Bold, underlines and italics: avoid using these in mid-sentence. Use bold sparingly, for headings only.

Font type and size: use a sans serif font such as Arial, Calibri or Verdana, and the text should be at least 11pt in size and spaced at 1.5 lines.

Colour: a pale background is advised, and black text. The only exception is if you are applying for a creative job such as brochure designer or marketing design, in which case you might showcase some of your skills here.

Level of detail: less is more. Be succinct and focused.

Spelling and punctuation: Ask other people to read it and if you have time to get it proofread (by either a friend, colleague or a professional editor), do so. Spelling errors are an immediate concern for employers as it indicates a lack of effort and poor attention to detail.

Tone and voice: avoid colloquial phrases, informal language or acronyms. Avoid contractions and write in simple, clear words and sentences. Be confident and avoid phrases such as 'I believe' and 'I think' as they may suggest doubt.

COMMON ERRORS THAT MAY CAUSE YOUR CV TO BE REJECTED

1. Bad grammar
2. Spelling mistakes
3. Poor formatting
4. CV longer than two pages (if graduate level job) unless told otherwise
5. Casual tone and colloquial words
6. Use of jargon and excessive use of acronyms

7. Unusual or inconsistent font style or size
8. Irrelevant exam grades listed in full
9. Generic interests listed, such as cooking or reading
10. Lack of activities related to personal development

According to the University of Kent, 60% of CVs are sent to the wrong person (usually the managing director). Applicants who addressed their application to the correct person were 15% more likely to get a letter of acknowledgement and 5% more likely to get an interview.

Example 1: An example of a good CV of a tourism graduate seeking a role as a tour leader

---

ALI AHMED

12 Travel Grove, Bristol, England BS3 ***, Mobile: 072984 982**

Email: ali.ahmed@myemail.com Twitter: @AAhmedTravels

PERSONAL STATEMENT

A recent tourism graduate (2:1, University of Westminster) with two years' summer holiday experience as a tour guide in Jordan and one summer as a research intern. Experience in coordinating tour schedules, adhering to event times and keeping everything running smoothly for diverse groups of customers. Highly organised, friendly and skilled. Would be an enthusiastic and hard-working addition to the tourism team.

EDUCATION AND QUALIFICATIONS

2018	BSc Tourism Management (2:1) with Honours
	University of Westminster, London • 10,000 word dissertation on sustainable tourism in Jordan, mark of 80. • Communication and team-working skills: group work assignments where I led the team on CSR (75), visitor management (82) and pro-poor tourism (68).
2014	A levels
	English, History and Geography

WORK EXPERIENCE

January 2016–Sept. 2018

Tour Guide (summer holiday, 8-week period), for Jordan Tour Company, Jordan

• Handle registration and transportation.
• Plan routes with rest stops, hotel and meal reservations, shops, sightseeing and entertainment.
• Resolve guest complaints.
• Develop long-term relationships with regular customers, which often turns into repeat business.
• Negotiate contracts with hotels and buses for tour packages.

Sept 2018–May 2019

Tourism researcher (part-time over summer)

- Worked as intern for lecturer in tourism to research tourism development in Middle East
- Took over centre's website in December 2018
- Co-delivered conference paper with Professor Brown
- Analysed data (qualitative and quantitative)

AREAS OF EXPERTISE

• Bilingual English & Arabic	• Innate logic and problem-solving skills
• Management expertise	• Excellent time management
• Strong communicator	• Skilled at multitasking
• Natural leader	• Research skills

HOBBIES

Travelled to over 30 countries, mainly trekking and walking including an ascent of Kilimanjaro. Experienced orienteering lead.

REFERENCE

Available on request

Reflection on this example

You will note that Ali has followed some of the advice outlined in the next chapter about a sensible email address and appropriate structure, for example. Ali has tried to highlight the skills and experience he has that are most clearly aligned to the travel industry. You will note that for most students and graduates, 'Education' comes before your work experience, but if you have a lot of relevant industry experience, you might choose to swap these sections around.

Ali has focused on the elements of his degree that he feels are most relevant to the job, including his dissertation on Jordan and group work assessments to demonstrate his team-working skills. This CV also draws on his relevant part-time jobs and volunteering to give evidence of the skills the employer is looking for. Add a third-party endorsement if you can (e.g. grade, promotion, or as listed here added responsibility when he took over the website in December 2018).

Example 2: An example CV for an events job

EVELYN YU

24 Tree and Leaf Street, York, YO1 ***, Mobile: 07254 625645
Email: yu_evelyn@gmail.com

(Continued)

PERSONAL STATEMENT

Just completing the BA Event Management (due to graduate July 2020 with a 1st class honours). Having run over ten different events, I have demonstrated that I am self-motivated with a strong drive for success. I believe I will be well suited to an events officer role as I have proven myself to be a very capable student in all event modules whilst displaying the ability to work to deadlines, and work with others to achieve successes.

EDUCATION AND QUALIFICATIONS

2017-2020	BA Event Management with Honours
	University of Hertfordshire • Put on ten events as part of course and as Student Union events rep • Raised £5000 for charity by putting on student ball
2017	A levels
	Art, Geography, Politics and Maths

WORK EXPERIENCE

2018-2020	Events Planning Assistant (weekends), Cancer Research • Supported marketing team with administration of events • Provided social media support to promote events • Collated and distributed even materials • Developed event schedule and delegated activities

AREAS OF EXPERTISE

- Social media
- Administrative support
- Project management
- Research
- Multi-tasker
- Operate well under pressure

HOBBIES

- Love to travel: visited Botswana, Malaysia, and Zambia in the last year
- Completed three peaks challenge in 2018
- Pottery and art – attend weekly art classes
- Cross-country running – won York 10km (women's) run two years in a row

REFERENCE

Available on request

Reflection on this example

Evelyn has been explicit about her desire to secure an events officer role. She has highlighted relevant skills and work experience, which not only shows she is serious about this sector, but has the right experience and skills for this kind of role. The information about how much she has helped raised for charity through events is particularly impressive. Use your time at university to see what you can do that has this kind of impact.

 REFLECTION EXERCISE

Reflecting on your CV

What is your CV missing? What experience, qualifications or skills might you want to develop and build?

CONCLUSION

In this chapter we have covered:

- The importance of getting your CV right in a climate where employers spend very little time deciding whether to shortlist you or not
- How your CV should be structured to create a good first impression
- The kinds of positive words and phrases you should be using in your CV
- The importance of tailoring your CV to each post and keeping your experiences and skills up to date.
- The kinds of information you need to include for a job in the tourism, events or hospitality industry

FURTHER READING

Prospects – CVs and Cover Letters: https://www.prospects.ac.uk/careers-advice/cvs-and-cover-letters
REED – https://www.reed.co.uk/career-advice/how-to-write-a-cv/
Student Jobs – application tips for your CV: https://www.studentjob.co.uk/application-tips/cv-example
Travel Weekly – how to write a good travel industry CV: http://www.travelweekly.co.uk/articles/26758/how-to-write-a-good-travel-industry-cv

Useful web resources

CV Library – https://www.cv-library.co.uk/career-advice/cv/how-to-write-a-cv-tips/

Institute for Student Employers – https://ise.org.uk/

The University of the Arts London have tips on how to write a creative CV.

Creative CV Guide (http://careerweb.leeds.ac.uk/downloads/file/262/creatuve_cv_guide) by Jan Cole to find samples and tips for writing CVs in the creative sector

The University of Leeds Careers Centre has some sample CVs in different job sectors: http://careerweb.leeds.ac.uk/info/19/cvs

The University of Kent has a lot of good advice on CVs: https://www.kent.ac.uk/ces/cv/cv.html

30 APPLICATION FORMS AND COVERING LETTERS

CHAPTER LEARNING OBJECTIVES

By the end of this chapter you should be able to:

- Understand the rationale for covering letters and application forms
- Write an appropriate covering letter and application form
- Recognise the importance of research within the application process
- Confidently and successfully complete application forms for any job role
- Demonstrate your experiences and examples using the STAR matrix

GLOSSARY

- **Shortlisting:** The process of selecting candidates to enter the next phase of the application process, usually via an assessment day or interview

INTRODUCTION

Covering letters and application forms are a crucial part of any job application process. They are often the first points of contact you will have with an employer and therefore need to set the correct tone and communicate the right messages to make an eye-catching first impression. This chapter will provide you with an insight into the role of covering letters and application forms, their role in the overall application process and how to prepare yourself for completing them. Using examples and top tips, this chapter will provide you with advice on developing an effective covering letter and how to fill out an application for the best chance of success.

It is important to recognise that your career planning can begin well in advance of when you start to apply for vacancies. You may have had a part-time job or volunteering experience while you were at school or college, so your portfolio of experience can be built from there. If you start the process early, you not only allow yourself the time to reflect, but it means you will have done a lot of the hard-work so writing covering letters and completing application forms become less onerous tasks!

PREPARATION IS KEY

Preparation is fundamental to applying for any job role, be it work experience, an internship or a graduate position. A proportion of this preparation will take place after you have identified a vacancy you wish to apply for. However, groundwork can begin as early as the first year of your degree. Your CV, for example, can be developed and then amended regularly with progression including any new experience or achievements. You can perform a skills audit to identify your strengths and weaknesses and highlight areas where personal development is required. The skills audit will provide a basis from which you can develop an evidence base of examples for these skills; consider how you can demonstrate that you possess these skills.

With each piece of experience, you can start to develop a portfolio of examples around key skills: customer service, management, teamwork, time management, communication, flexibility and problem solving. This can then be added to and amended throughout your degree journey. Starting these processes and preparation early will not only give you a solid platform from which to build future applications but reflecting on your abilities and where you feel you lack skills may encourage you to seek experiences that challenge these weaknesses.

It is tempting when you have found an appealing job vacancy to apply immediately using your current CV and a covering letter you have used before. Similarly, it may make sense to canvas several job vacancies and make multiple applications using the same CV with a cut and pasted covering letter. A word of warning is that organisations will recognise if you have not done any research on their company and will likely reject applications that have not been tailored to them individually and relate your skills explicitly to the job role offered. Each job application will therefore require three steps:

1. An inspection of the specific job role criteria and the person specification
2. A reflection of how your current skills and experience meet these requirements
3. Wider research on the organisation itself

Your covering letter should be tailored to the specific company and job role being considered. Similarly, application forms should evidence significant knowledge of both the company and industry being applied for.

UNDERSTANDING THE JOB DESCRIPTION AND PERSON SPECIFICATION

Within the tourism, hospitality and events sectors, there are several common characteristics and skills, such as customer service, managerial ability and flexibility, that may be applicable to a variety of roles (as discussed throughout Section B). However, no organisation is identical and each job role will be developed to meet specific needs resulting in a unique combination of skills and experience required from candidates looking to apply for the position. The tasks and responsibilities expected of the role are laid out in the job description which you should use to assess whether you want the position. The personal qualities, skills and experience required for the job are stated in a person specification; it is for candidates to demonstrate how well they meet these criteria.

For both covering letters and applications forms, the job description and person specification are crucial and should be used to develop the content of both. The person specification will provide a list of essential and desirable criteria which you should use to map your skills against and develop evidence-based examples to corroborate each. These are the criteria against which you are initially being assessed; often if you do not demonstrate that you meet the essential criteria you will not be shortlisted for successive stages of the process. Therefore, as outlined in the previous chapter, it is crucial that you explicitly show how you meet each of these criteria through evidence communicated in your covering letter, CV and application form.

Before you begin the filling out your form or writing your covering letter, you must go over the person specification thoroughly and map out your examples to evidence each criterion. It is a good idea to draw up a table with the job criteria down one column and your examples laid out in a second column. This will help to focus your thoughts and help prepare you for answering competency-based questions in the application form, develop your personal statement if required and eventually to answer interview questions. Demonstrating a good understanding of the job description and person specification will also help you to write a more effective covering letter.

EFFECTIVE EXAMPLES: USING THE STAR FRAMEWORK

It is not enough to say you possess a skill or have certain experience; you need to be able to evidence and communicate this effectively. The examples you include should be detailed; recruiters often suggest an effective way to achieve this is to follow the STAR framework: **S**ituation, **T**ask, **A**ction, **R**esult:

Situation: This section provides context for the example. Where were you? What were you doing? What had happened? Essentially you set the scene here for someone who was not there.

Task: Now you address the specific task; what were you asked to do? What was your role?

Action: This section covers what you did; how did you meet the task?

Result: A crucial area is to make it clear what the outcome was. What happened as a consequence of your action(s)?

==== **INDUSTRY INSIGHT** ====

STAR examples

S: 'In my previous role as a restaurant shift supervisor, our branch had received two mystery guest scores that fell below company average and had brought our previously high average score of 95% to below 60%.'

T: 'I was given responsibility for ensuring the team achieved a score of above 80% in the subsequent guest visit.'

A: 'I reviewed both reports to identify where the issues were and where improvements could be made. Low scores related to front of house staff and customers not being asked certain questions; namely if the customer would like a second drink, desserts and tea or coffee. As these were all part of our steps of service, I had a discussion with my manager and we decided to hold a staff meeting for waiters to reiterate these steps. I developed a quiz as a fun way to check knowledge and then to make sure these areas were a priority. I suggested a staff incentive: a prize for the largest increase in second drinks and desserts sold over a two-week period.'

R: 'The next two mystery guest scores were above 90% and as a bi-product, sales also increased resulting in us having a record sales week. Additionally, staff motivation and engagement also improved; the informal competition galvanised the team and created a spirited atmosphere.'

An academic example:

S: 'In my third year at university I undertook a Tourism Marketing module as part of my course.'

T: 'I needed to work as part of a group to prepare a pitch to an organisation that owned a newly renovated country house and gardens that sought ideas on increasing visitor numbers and widening current visitor demographics.'

A: 'I took the role of team leader, needing to co-ordinate a team of five students all of different nationalities. This required intercultural communication and ensuring that the brief had been fully understood. We each performed an element of research which we then brought together to discuss potential areas for improvement. As a team we decided our focus would be on recommendations for improving accessibility for those with disabilities and the addition of an onsite café. I brought together these ideas to develop our pitch presentation to make sure there was a unified voice.'

R: 'The organisation was impressed by our ideas so consequently our team won the pitch. I was given an A as a result and we saw our pitch be included as part of the organisation's strategy for the following year.'

THE SIGNIFICANCE OF RESEARCH

In a recent interview with a leading UK tour operator, when asked for their top tips for completing an application form, their response was 'research, research, research'. In fact, ensuring candidates perform research was the single unified piece of advice given in several interviews with a number of global tourism and hospitality employers including tour operators and hotel, restaurant and visitor attraction recruiters. These recruiters expect candidates to do their due diligence and have a good understanding of the organisation, its successes, strategy and overview of business operations. The same interviewee that gave research as her triple bottom line then went on to add reflection to her advice: 'research, research, research and reflection'. Research alone will not necessarily make you stand out; it is your reflection on that research that will show your ability to consider the consequences of action and the potential for organisational strategic success and direction in the future.

Your research should consider the following questions:

- How is the industry performing overall? What are the current industry trends?
- What does the organisation do and where do they operate? There are numerous stories of candidates not actually knowing what the company does, let alone where are their operational locations. Are there opportunities for future expansion? Can you identify areas that offer potential for future operations?
- What are the company values and how do you feel your own values fit with these? Many recruiters are keen to see how you align with their organisational values. What are their values around sustainability and corporate social responsibility (see more on this in Chapter 17)?
- Who are their competitors? What do they do better than their competitors? What is their Unique Selling Point (USP)? How are their competitors performing?
- What is their organisation strategy? Are there plans for future development or expansion? Are there any projects due to begin or coming to an end?

USEFUL SOURCES OF INFORMATION

There are numerous sources of information you should consult:

- *The organisation's website*: it is expected at a minimum that you will check out their website. This will give you information on what the company does, an insight into its target audience and allow you to consider who their competition might be. It is a good idea to look at both the customer facing and corporate webpages if they have them as corporate pages are more likely to provide the company strategy, vision, recent achievements and future plans, including expansion. Remember that employers know what information is on their website; if you want to stand out, you need to demonstrate that you have done more than looking at their webpages.
- *Social media content*: these platforms will likely give you the most up to date information on the company and particularly on their communications. LinkedIn will provide you with more professional and operational related content, including recent achievements, recruitment drives and examples of operational excellence.
- *Competitor websites*: it is a good idea to understand the key organisation competitors to demonstrate your understanding of competitive advantage and the significance of competitor analysis.
- *Industry websites and literature*: it is important that you are able contextualise information within the overarching industry. What are the current industry trends, developments, opportunities and challenges? How do you feel the organisation is performing against these? ABTA, Big Hospitality, Insider, Skift, Travel Daily News, Travel Pulse, Travel Weekly, World Tourism Organisation (UNWTO) and World Travel and Tourism Council (WTTC) are a good place to start.

- *Travel blogs and travel writers*: given the significance of influencers and bloggers within the industry, these offer a gateway into the minds of consumers; what are the trends, tastes, opinions and behaviours of travellers themselves.
- *Newspapers and documentaries*: wider research beyond the organisation itself is important for you to be able to discuss current issues and reflect upon these in the context of the industry. BBC News, CNN International, *The Guardian, The Independent, The Telegraph* and *The Times* all have travel sections but also report on other world news.
- *Conferences, events and guest speakers*: industry research can be gathered at more informal opportunities throughout your degree and at seminars you attend at conferences or events such as Confex or World Travel Market. Make contacts with any guest speakers your university hosts; make the effort to introduce yourself to them and take their business card.

THE VALUE AND IMPORTANCE OF THE COVERING LETTER

'As an employer I find these really help me understand why the person has applied to work for my company. We all understand in this day and age that candidates are applying for multiple roles – but equally as employers we are screening hundreds of CVs so your covering letter needs to make us feel special; that you have specifically chosen our company to work for.'

(Visitor Services Manager, Leisure industry, 2019)

A covering letter enables you to formally and professionally introduce yourself and your accompanying CV to a potential employer. These letters have two main objectives. Firstly, they allow you to develop some of the main points of your CV; to highlight what makes you stand out. Secondly, and perhaps more importantly, they give you a chance to communicate why you have chosen to apply for the specific job role and company. Essentially, the covering letter is your opportunity to personalise your application.

Covering letters are mutually beneficial; for companies it gives greater insight into each candidate including their ability to write an effective piece of communication. The benefit for candidates is the scope to add value to your application; to communicate your knowledge of the company and understanding of the role and demonstrate how well you meet the person specification criteria. According to some employees within the tourism, hospitality and events sectors, this is significant if you are over-qualified for a role. It gives you the opportunity to explain your reasoning for applying for the role in the letter, as prospective employers may automatically discount you from the selection process if you are applying for a role that does not match your qualifications.

The covering letter should not be confused with a personal statement; it should not represent a lengthy document detailing all your experience and skills. Employers suggest the length should be brief; around half a page and certainly no more than one full A4 page. According to the *Guardian* newspaper (2018) a recruiter will often spend an average of 30 seconds to read a CV with some estimates being as little as 6 seconds. Therefore, the covering letter should be designed to be succinct yet grab attention. It should not merely replicate your CV; it should enhance it but not regurgitate what is already there. A good point to note is that if the covering letter is being sent electronically via email, it should form part of the main email body rather than being sent as an attachment which may be detected by spam filters and end up in junk mail.

STUDENT INSIGHT

Faye – Taking a step back to leap forward

Faye was a graduate hospitality student who had worked in a management role within a global hotel chain, but decided she was more interested in events and event planning. Despite her experience within hospitality, she found it difficult to gain an equivalent level role in event management without more specific experience. Therefore, she decided to take a step back in terms of pay, even though she saw this as a step forward in terms of her career and apply for more junior roles. Having sought feedback on rejected applications, it became clear that employers were unable to match her professional and academic experience with the roles being applied for and therefore she had been consistently overlooked for **shortlisting**.

On one occasion, the feedback suggested she could have discussed in her covering letter the reasons why she was keen to gain such a position (even though it was lower down the career ladder) and how she felt this would contribute to a change in career. She ended up getting the next job she applied for and after just two years is now a successful event planner for a London-based event management firm. A change in career or a sideways move should not be considered a step back; employers are increasingly searching for people with a breadth of experience in a diversity of areas as it demonstrates versatility and extensive understanding rather than being bound to linear progression in a field you may have fallen into but have limited passion for. The key is to use your covering letter to demonstrate the move is part of a well thought out, wider career plan.

Some simple covering letter do's and don'ts to consider are:

- Do tailor it to each company
- Do make it relevant to the job
- Do highlight your relevant skills and experience with examples
- Do point out your unique selling points
- Do be clear and to the point; avoid generalised statements
- Do format it effectively and get it proofread
- Don't duplicate your CV
- Don't exceed a single A4 page
- Don't include a photograph
- Don't include overly personal details
- Don't send it as an attachment in an email

WRITING THE COVERING LETTER

Before writing the covering letter, it is important to have the following information to hand:

- The company and job role you are applying for
- A copy of the job description and person specification if available
- The name and contact of the person to whom you are addressing the letter

To whom should I address the letter?

Where possible your covering letter should be addressed to a named person. If the job advert provides details of where to send the application, then these should be adhered to fully. This means that you make sure you have the name correct and their title should be accurate; make sure you get the gender right and do not mistake Ms. for Mrs. or vice versa. This is the first impression of you the employer will get; mistakes at this stage are likely to impede the application. If there is no named contact on the advert, then attempt to find the designated person via their website or call the organisation. Failing that, the correct way to address the letter would be 'Dear Sir/Madam'.

What content should I include in a covering letter?

While there is no one best way to write a covering letter, there are certain sections that should be included regardless of the template you adopt. The format of the letter should include:

- *An opening statement*: this should set out the reason for writing the letter. Begin by stating the position you are applying for, where you saw it advertised and include a reference number for the job if advertised. This is where it is crucial that you have proofread your covering letter to make sure the company and job role are correct.
- *Suitability for the job*: the most detailed section should focus on your skills, expertise and experience that suggests your suitability for the role. It should cover your interest in working for the company and importantly what you can offer the organisation, while highlighting relevant experience and demonstrating how your skills match the specific requirements of the person specification.
- *Additional skills relevant to the position/company interests*: there is an opportunity to briefly mention any achievements or experience that you feel would add value to the role or company but may not be included in the person specification. Following your research on the company, you should now be able to identify any areas you feel you could contribute outside the job role or job description requirements. This also demonstrates your interest in working specifically for this company. This could be anything from a common value, a common interest or a common belief in a certain policy or opportunity in the sector.
- *A closing statement*: you should conclude your letter by reiterating your interest in the role and indicating your availability for interview. Finish by say that you're looking forward to hearing from them to continue the conversation and that you are looking forward to receiving a response. When signing off the letter, make sure if you have sent it to a named contact that the sign off is 'Yours Sincerely'. If you have addressed it to an anonymous contact, i.e. Dear Sir/Madam, then you sign off 'Yours Faithfully'.

A fundamental error that candidates make is not tailoring covering letters to the potential employer. Do not send a copy and pasted version of a generic letter for all applications. You may well be making multiple applications, but each one should be built around the individual job role and company. Broad statements in your letter that cover multiple companies show little effort so should be avoided. What really grates is when people are sending out multiple applications and forget to amend it to your business and reference a different employer!

As with CVs, there are a number of resources online that provide guidelines and examples of covering letters including Prospects, Targetjobs and Reed. The following section provides an example of a covering letter (Figure 30.1) and another for those making a speculative application (Figure 30.2), so you can consider how you might develop and write your own version.

It is important to make sure your email address is professional. Examples of addresses to avoid: bunnyhop@hotmail.com, fluffyfoo@outlook.com, biggdubz@gmail.com

123 The Road
MyTown
LW23 6RF
J.Smith@google.com
0777711133

Grace Tebbutt
The Hotel
The Lane
MyTown
LW23 8AA

Make sure you have the person's title correct; is it Mrs, Miss or Ms? Have you made sure you have the right gender; is it Mr or Ms? Are there any special prefixes i.e. Dr?

2nd December 2020

Make sure that you have the correct job title and accurate company name here. If the application is via email then say the CV is attached; if you are posting then say enclosed.

Dear Ms. Tebbutt

I wish to apply for the role of **xxxxx** currently being advertised on **xxxxx**. As requested, please find my CV enclosed/attached for your consideration.

As you can see from my attached CV, I have over **xxxx** years of experience in the **tourism/hospitality/events/leisure** industry, and I believe the knowledge and skills built up during this time make me the **right/perfect** candidate for the role.

Make sure you use the job description for this section to highlight relevant skills

In my **current/most recent** role as a **[job title]** at **[employer name]**, I **have been/was** responsible for **[Insert a notable achievement/s – quantified where possible i.e. managing a team of 20; increasing sales by 10%; achieving 100% in guest satisfaction]**, which when coupled with my **xxxxx [insert skills relevant to the role – usually found in the job description/person specification]**, has helped the business to **[measure of success – be at the top of the area; fall within the top 10 within the company; receive an outstanding achievement award]**.

I am confident that I can bring this level of success with me to your organization and help **[organization name]** build upon their reputation as **[state their position in market - learned through your research]**. With my previous experience and expertise, I believe my contribution will have an immediate impact on the business.

Thank you for your time and consideration. I look forward to meeting with you to discuss my application further.

Yours sincerely/Yours faithfully,

Dear Ms. Tebbutt: Yours Sincerely if you have named the person

Dear Sir/Madam: Yours Faithfully

[Signature - if desired]

Jade Smith

Figure 30.1   An example of a covering letter

Source: adapted from Reed.co.uk

Jade Smith
23 The Road
MyTown
LW23 6RF
j.smith@google.com
0777711133

Grace Tebbutt
The Hotel
The Lane
MyTown
LW23 8AA

> The first paragraph should note your interest in a particular area of the sector, as well as demonstrating your research on the organization itself. It might be that you saw them at a conference or exhibition (i.e. WTM). Perhaps you have read their blog or read about their plans for expansion. Something that makes you stand out and them feel special.

2nd December 2020

Dear Ms. Tebbutt

I am writing to explore whether an opportunity might exist to join The Hotel in a graduate level management role. As a tourism and hospitality student, I have been following The Hotel for many years now, and your recent success in achieving Best International Sustainable Hotel at the International Hotel awards 2019 makes you stand out against the competition, particularly in such a significant yet challenging category. Your commitment to sustainability and future climate change action is commendable and testament to your work ethic. I would welcome the opportunity to work with you during such an exciting phase.

> The subsequent sections should demonstrate your skills and experience relevant to the type of role/ organization you are applying to. It can also be an opportunity to highlight a particular achievement; this could be anything from volunteering to writing your own blog or winning an award. Make sure you make explicit the relevance of the example as well as the outcome/consequence or learning gained from it.

I am in the final year of an International Tourism and Hospitality degree and have maintained a 2:1 average to date. The course has given me a strong grounding in tourism and hospitality management where modules have included intercultural communication, sustainable tourism management and marketing for tourism, hospitality and events. The degree has involved significant independent research, requiring initiative, self-motivation, time management and strong administration skills. Last summer I secured work experience within a global hotel chain as a receptionist during which time I engaged with and managed large volumes of guests, used Cloudbeds software and trained new members of staff to meet quality and process standards. Impressed by my work ethic, my manager gave me responsibility of a project to improve efficiency in the check-in and check-out process. From analysing the areas of inefficiency across the entire process, I managed paperwork needs and staff rotas, streamlining to create a more productive check-in/out system. The new process has now been rolled out across all hotels in the chain.

I believe that the skills I have gained from my academic and work experience, which include skills in dealing with guests, problem solving, using professional judgement, working effectively in a team and being able to work independently would assist me when working within hospitality management. In addition, I bring a positive, can do attitude and enthusiasm; noted through my experience as student representative and recent accolade as Student of the Year 2019 voted by staff and peers.

I am committed to developing a career within hospitality management and feel confident that I would make an effective contribution to your current management team. I have attached my CV for your perusal and would welcome the opportunity to discuss any possible openings with you.

I look forward to hearing from you.

Yours sincerely,

> The final section should include a reinforced statement of interest, a call to action and availability for interview if needed. Remember to sign off 'Yours sincerely' if using a named recipient and 'Yours faithfully' if using 'Dear Sir/Madam'.

Figure 30.2 Example of a speculative cover letter template

SPECULATIVE APPLICATIONS

It is estimated that as many as eight in ten job vacancies are not actually advertised. This means there may be situations where job descriptions do not exist. Instead you may be sending out a speculative application, meaning there may not be an actual job vacancy, but rather you are sending out a note of interest in case something is available or becomes available in the future. This includes times when seeking opportunities for voluntary work or an internship; these types of vacancies may also not always be advertised, but welcomed nonetheless.

Even though the application is speculative, the content should be well thought out and thoroughly researched for it to make an impact and be worthy of a response. The first point to consider is what it is that you want; remember by sending this out, you are essentially asking for something so you must be clear on what it is that you want!

ADVICE FOR INTERNATIONAL STUDENTS

It is important for international students and those applying for positions outside their country of residence that research is undertaken on visa procedures and work permit restrictions within the employer country prior to application. This information should then be included in the covering letter acknowledging the requirements in the region of the world where you are applying for work. A section should be added such as:

> I am committed to working in the UK and I see from your website that [company name] has a number of international employees and a sponsorship license.

> I am available for interview via Skype or telephone, before coming to the UK. I look forward to hearing from you.

Source: Adapted from Christian (2019)

Further advice for international students can be gained from your university careers department, international office or from websites such as Student Circus. Student Circus was set up by a team of international graduate students after their own experiences gaining work experience in the UK. Their platform now offers advice and guidance for international students in careers, internships and work placements: see www.studentcircus.com.

UNDERSTANDING APPLICATION FORMS

Application forms enable companies to build specific questions around the job role and description. Essentially, they give firms the opportunity to delve deeper into you; to see the types of skills you have, how well you can identify and communicate these and how well you meet the needs of the role. This all sounds rather daunting and merely a way for employers to pitch you against other candidates. In a sense, of course, this is the point as employers must find ways to shortlist candidates. However, it is not all one sided: application forms are also an opportunity for you, the candidate. You should try to view the application form as your chance to shine; to sell yourself.

Your CV provides a snapshot of who you are and an overview of your work and academic history (as outlined in Chapter 29), but the application form allows you to showcase your skills set, to flesh out the points on your CV and to demonstrate your ability to meet the requirements of the job description and person specification. It enables you to add in some of your personality and gives you the opportunity to make the case for why you should be hired; why are you right for the job role? Think about your CV; what does it tell employers about you? There is limited space to move beyond the facts, the bullet points of your work experience and academic history. At most you have the short personal statement to add some personality and reveal who you are, but is this possible in a few sentences? So, start to see the application form in a different light; rather than a hassle, see it as a positive. If you can master this frame of mind now, completing them becomes a whole lot easier.

Application forms are an opportunity for you to shine but they are not a free for all. It is not just an opportunity to talk at length about everything that makes you special and about what an amazing employee you would be. Instead, all your discussions should be firmly based around a reflection of the job role you are applying for. You must demonstrate how well you meet the criteria of the person specification.

ONLINE APPLICATIONS

Most applications are now completed online with forms that can be accessed and completed via any smart mobile device. Although this may facilitate ease of form completion, it should not mask the substantial amount of effort required in terms of research, consideration and reflection.

For most organisations you will be required to create a log in which enables you to complete the form over a period. Forms will allow you to 'save and continue' or 'save and exit' so a good tip is to download the questions (or copy and paste them) to a separate document to give you the time to reflect and answer as fully and competently as possible. It also gives you the time to proofread, spell check, format your work and monitor the word count before cutting and pasting answers back into the form.

WHAT WILL I BE REQUIRED TO DO?

Many employers are seeking to streamline the application process and develop diverse ways of short-listing candidates, embracing diversity whilst minimising potential bias. Application forms may therefore constitute a less traditional format where you may be required to complete basic information such as contact details, education and experience and then take an online ability and/or personality test. Others may follow a more conventional format and require details of your contact information, education, work experience and then ask you to competency-based questions like those you might get at an interview.

Competency-based questions

These require you to provide real-life examples as the basis for your answers, to evidence your skills and experience. Answers should reflect why decisions were made and what the outcomes were. Do not be afraid to mention when a task was unsuccessful, providing you can demonstrate what you learned from it consequently. The good news is that if you prepare for these types of questions during the application process, it will be easier to prepare for the interview. There are some examples below, with sample answers.

1. Why do you want to work for [company]?

The employer is trying to find out your motivation and commitment to the role. You need to be specific here and show your research on the organisation and job role.

'Having stayed in a Myhotel property in Thailand, I have first-hand experience of the impressive care and attention to detail staff provide guests. Having spent over two years providing excellent customer service myself, assessing guests' needs, suggesting upgrades to enhance experience and solving issues, I feel well placed to enhance the calibre of your team.

The organisation's commitment to sustainability are commendable; particularly the impact you have on local communities and the dedication demonstrated to employee training and development. I have similar values, demonstrated by my current role as shift supervisor where I developed a social responsibility agenda for the restaurant; implementing a charity food bank donation point, enabling 25 school visits to the restaurant and raising £1250 in charitable donations in a year.'

2. Outline your skills and experience that make you suitable for this role.

The employer will be looking to see that you can match your skills to the person specification. Highlight any transferrable skills that you feel may be relevant to the role or wider organisational goals.

'Excellent interpersonal and people management skills whilst working under pressure demonstrated through liaising with clients to develop event plan and agenda and negotiating with suppliers; ensuring deadlines were met and events were a success.'

The following types of questions provide an opportunity to put the STAR framework to use. For all of these, make sure you give the context of the issue (situation), what you were required to do (task), what you actually did (action) and what the outcome was (result).

3. What is the biggest challenge that you've faced and how did you handle it?

If you have work experience then draw upon an example from that, but if not, then try to think outside the box for another example that could meet the brief; it could be dealing with a difficult situation at university, handling a group member or completing an activity such as the marathon.

'Last year a friend was unfortunately diagnosed with cancer. A group of my friends and I decided to complete the National Three Peaks challenge to raise money for a cancer charity. This involved climbing the three highest mountains in England, Wales and Scotland. I had never completed anything this strenuous and had to train hard while studying at university and working part-time. The challenge demonstrated my tenacity and although it was a challenge to train after a long day at work, my dedication and commitment paid off; we successfully completed the challenge and raised over £3000 in the process.'

4. Give an example of where you made a positive contribution to a team.

You do not always need to demonstrate being a team leader, but rather that you are able to work as part of a team.

'During my time as a member of the university tourism and events society, we regularly held events for charity. My role was to develop ideas for raising money so we could host these events. I organised fundraising opportunities from car washing to cake and bake sales. Over the course of a year we successfully raised £3800 which helped fund events including a tea party for the elderly in the community, a black-tie dinner and an auction night.'

5. Describe a time when you were faced with a stressful situation that demonstrated your ability to deal with pressure.

'As a shift manager at a restaurant I often had to deal with customer complaints. On one occasion a waiter had unfortunately spilt a tray of drinks over a table, some of which had splashed onto a lady's jacket. The guest was understandably furious but was making a scene and threatening to walk out without paying. To diffuse the situation I went straight over, apologised and encouraged her to come to the bathroom to dry off. Having removed her from the restaurant floor, I was able to calm her down and offered her a scarf to use for the remainder of her meal. She accepted my offer of paying for dry cleaning and once she returned to the table, the waiter took over a complimentary drink. Making sure I paid her table attention throughout, by the time she left she had paid in full for the meal, thanked me and even complimented me on my service and attention; the complaint was not escalated, and the customer was happy.'

6. Give me an example of when you showed initiative.

'During my time at university I volunteered at the local tourism office where we were often asked for recommendations for day trips to within the local area. After a month of being asked the same question I took the initiative to build a set of suggested itineraries built around grouping activities by interest; from food and culture to sport and adventure. The destination development manager was suitably impressed and not only had the itineraries printed but subsequently added them in a downloadable format to the website.'

Personal statements

Often at the end of an application form you will be asked to submit a personal statement outlining your skills, experience and communicating your overall suitability for the role. There will most likely be a word count; use this as a guide as this will dictate the level of detail expected in your response. The personal statement can often read as a lengthier covering letter; it should:

- provide a strong opening statement and explanation of why you are applying
- map your relevant experience, knowledge and skills to the job description and person specification
- discuss any additional interests or experience that you feel may complement or add value to the role or overall organisation
- provide a concluding statement that sums up your suitability and what you have to offer

The main point to remember, as with covering letters and answers in application forms, is relevancy to the role; demonstrate how your skills, experience and knowledge meet the requirements of the job.

Proofreading of application material

As with every aspect of the application process including covering letters and CVs, it is crucial that you proofread your application form before submitting or sending if by post. Check the following things:

- That the company name is correct and spelt correctly
- Spellings: use spellchecker to make sure you have not made errors. Check also for errors that the spellchecker will miss e.g. 'form' when you mean 'from'; 'through' when you mean 'thorough' and so on
- Try reading it aloud, giving it to someone else and ideally running it past a professional.
- Grammatical errors: full stops at the end of sentences with a capital at the beginning of a new one, and commas to break separate items in a sentence or join two clauses together
- Tenses: make sure you have been consistent with your tenses and are not leaping between tenses unnecessarily
- Paragraphs: that you have structured the work using paragraphs and that a new subject or discussion indicates the beginning of a new paragraph
- Word count: that you have met the requirements for length of answer and word count
- Font style and size: all documents should be submitted in the same font and size. Keep to professional styles, such as Times New Roman, Arial or Calibri rather than Bradley Hand ITC or Magneto. Font size should be 12 or larger to meet accessibility criteria. This also means you can't fit more on the page by just reducing the font size!

Referees

You will most likely be asked to provide at least two referees. These should be as current as possible and include your current or most recent employer if you are or have previously been working; if you do not use a current or past employer as a reference it may send a warning signal that you are trying to hide something. There is usually an option to click that references will not be contacted until you have been offered the position so there is no risk that a current employer will be contacted unexpectedly. The second referee should be another person that knows you in a professional or academic capacity. This could be a university lecturer, personal tutor or volunteer manager. It is not recommended to use a friend or family member as a reference.

WHAT TYPE OF ROLE ARE YOU LOOKING FOR?

This is crucial to gaining a response as it shows you have thought about the details and gives employers a specific point on which to respond. While a job description may not exist if there is no position advertised, you should demonstrate knowledge of the type of job role you are seeking.

- Look at previous/similar job role descriptions for the types of skills and experience you may need

- Visit your university careers department to see what types of job roles exist and whether the university has any contacts with recruiters
- Look at recruitment pages of various organisations: Centre Parcs, Hilton, Intercontinental Hotels Group (IHG), Marriott International, Merlin Entertainments, TUI and Whitbread are a good place to start

=== ACTIVITY ===

What do you have to offer?

Note down the job roles that interest you and some bullet points about each role and the types of skills and experience you would need.

Think about your current skills set; what do you have to offer? Why would you be suitable for these positions? How would you add value? What could you bring to the team? What experience do you have? What are your strengths?

Now make a list of your key assets in terms of both skills, experience and achievements. Have an example prepared as evidence for each one.

Reflect upon what makes you different? What are your values? What are your interests? What makes you stand out? Employers are increasingly recruiting for diversity; this goes beyond the traditional sense of demographic difference (age, gender, ethnicity) towards diversity in mindset, skills and experiences. Companies do not want replicas of what they already have in staff. They want recruits to add value to the current employee profile.

Write down what you think your competitive edge is; what makes you unique?

Think about which areas of tourism, hospitality and events you want to work in. Why?

Which companies are you interested in working for? Who are the major employers? Do any of these companies offer the types of job roles you have noted down above? Are there any graduate schemes available? Do they meet any of the criteria you developed above?

Write down a list of criteria that you would consider as: a) essential; and b) desirable in a company you would like to work for.

=== ACTIVITY ===

Aligning your skills to employers and companies

Write down your list of ideal employers and research each company in depth. How are they performing? Who are their competitors? Are there any plans for expansion? Do they have any forthcoming plans or strategies for development? You may choose to follow them on social media or add as a contact via LinkedIn.

Consider how your strengths and values align with these companies. Go back over your skills, experience and competitive advantage analysis above. How would your strengths and expertise benefit the company? How/where could you add value?

You will need to do some additional research to find the best contact to send your application to; a name and contact details (ideally in recruitment) for each. Some larger recruiters such as TUI have a recruitment section on their website with addresses of contacts in different areas of the business. Smaller companies may list the managing director's details or head of department. LinkedIn is a valuable resource for making contacts within individual companies and networks. Social media sites may also offer a platform for asking questions about recruitment or where to find contacts in recruitment.

REACHING OUT TO YOUR NETWORKS

This should not conjure up thoughts of awkward meet and greet opportunities in a pre- or post-business meeting environment. It is much more than this; it should be a part of a focused plan to find your next career opportunity. A great example is LinkedIn; a fantastic case of e-networking where you can connect with people you would perhaps never have met in daily life. It is also providing a platform for you to learn: what are companies doing, how they are performing, what do they have an interest in; essentially, what makes them tick? It is also a great way to learn about opportunities, where there might be potential opportunities or where you see you could add value to a company and therefore send a speculative application. Read more about online networks in Chapter 25.

- Think about what makes you different; what are your values? What are your interests? What makes you tick?
- Map out your networks; consider who you already have in your networks, who do you consider your closest network contacts to contact first and who should you approach last? Are there any opportunities to make new contacts based on your industry specialism, job choice and interests?
- Write a 'reach out' message (see below for guidelines and example)
- Proofread message and check with peers for message effectiveness and communication (see below)
- Send out to chosen networks; keep a record of who you send the message to and when; this will give you an accurate reference for who to follow up with

Network message examples

Read Message A below. What do you think a network contact would do with this message?

Message A

'I'm looking for a new job, but no clue as to what I want to do! That being said, I'm pretty desperate so really, I'm prepared to take anything that comes along. Can you help?'

Does it prompt action? Does it inspire you to help? The message shows little effort and no attempt has been made by the writer to think about that task themselves. The sender has left the responsibility to the receiver to do the work. The sub-text of the message is 'I cannot be bothered to do any research, so I hope you can help me find a fantastic job that requires minimal effort!' It screams of lack of effort; so why would anyone recommend such a lazy person for a position? You must show that you have clear plan, that you have done some research, know what you are looking for and know your field. Now read Message B. How is this different?

Message B

'I'm looking for the next challenge in my career. I want to use my networking, communication and project management skills to help an events company grow and tap into new markets. I'd ideally be looking for a job within event sales or as an event manager. I'm hoping you might be able to help me find opportunities or introductions to anyone you think could help in finding a role at a respected events-based company. Some of my ideal targets include Clearwater events, IE Live Event Services, MCL Create, TBA or The Events Company. Please could you email me with any opportunities or connections you might be able to make.'

This not only sounds more professional, but the sender sounds driven, well researched and informed. It shows they have thought about their career trajectory and have knowledge of key industry players. It gives prompts for a network connection to respond to; do they know anyone at these companies? Do they know anyone looking for someone in any of these positions? Here, the sender has done the hard work and has asked targeted questions that make it easy for a receiver to respond to.

Check for message impact

Once you have developed your message, share it with a close friend or family member for feedback. Is it clear? Does it deliver the right message? Does it make a clear and concise call to action, i.e. does it make a clear request for a response?

Once you are happy that the message is clear, concise and effective, you are ready to share it with your network. At this point a word of warning: if you are currently in a job role, be careful with whom you are requesting help. It is important to maintain professionalism and not share with your current CEO, for example! That does not mean that you should not reach out to competitors. Moving companies after a period for new opportunities is natural; so long as your message includes a rationale, i.e. the desire for progression or development.

Following up speculative applications

This is where you need to develop a thick skin. The response rate to speculative applications may be low, but you must learn not to take this personally. Firstly, if you have made the effort to apply to a certain company or reach out to contacts for information on developing networks and finding prospective job roles, you need to be willing to follow up. Remember that while this application may be significant to you, the receiver is likely to have a very busy agenda of their own. The message may have been forgotten or the application passed on to another member of staff. Be tenacious while refraining from being annoying! A follow-up call or email one or two weeks after the application or network message is acceptable and indeed shows your commitment to your application.

CONCLUSION

In this chapter we have covered:

- The importance of preparation and early planning when you are applying for employment
- The value of fully understanding the job description and person specification and undertaking research to ensure you can tailor your application to the role and company
- What should be contained within a covering letter and application, and what should be avoided
- How to approach a speculative application

FURTHER READING

Morgan, P. (2017). *The Business Student's Guide to Study and Employability*. London: Sage (especially Chapter 16 on CVs and application forms)

Leigh, J. (2013). *How to Write: Successful CVs and Job Applications*. Oxford: Oxford University Press

Rook. S. (2013). *The Graduate Career Guide Book*. Basingstoke: Palgrave Macmillan (especially Chapter 11)

Useful web resources

Albany appointments: www.albany-appointments.co.uk

Association of Event Organizers: www.aeo.org.uk/recruitment

At Your Service: www.atyourservice.co.uk

Career Scope: careerscope.uk.net

Caterer.com: www.caterer.com

Event Job Search: www.eventjobsearch.co.uk

Events: www.ukdirectory.co.uk/business/conference-and-events

Hosco: www.hosco.com

Hotel Employers Group: www.jobsinhotels.co.uk

HQ Theatres and Hospitality: hqtheatres.com/about/careers

Live Recruitment: www.live-recruitment.co.uk

Prospects: www.prospects.ac.uk

Targetjobs: www.targetjobs.co.uk

Travel Weekly: jobs.travelweekly.co.uk

Travel and accommodation: www.ukdirectory.co.uk/travel-and-accommodation

31 SELECTION INTERVIEWS

CHAPTER LEARNING OBJECTIVES

By the end of this chapter you should be able to:

- Differentiate between the different types of selection interviews that exist
- Align your preparation activities to interview type
- Identify own strengths and weaknesses, and develop an interview strategy

GLOSSARY

- **Person-organisation fit:** how well your values align with those of an organisation (Cable and Judge, 1996; see Chapter 24)
- **Person-job fit:** the match between your abilities and the demands of a specific job
- **Recruitment:** the process of generating an optimal pool of applicants capable of performing a role or roles
- **Selection:** using reliable, fair and valid instruments to choose from a pool of applicants
- **Selection tool:** the type of interview used
- **Selection approach:** underpinning interview philosophy adopted in a selection process

INTRODUCTION

According to the CIPD (2020) people are an organisation's best asset but are also the most expensive resource. High employee turnover causes stress, work overload, low job satisfaction, and poor staff retention (Deery, 2008). Furthermore, failure to appoint the right person can be very costly in terms of poor performance and the time take to address this. Thus, **recruitment** and **selection** are often considered a means to:

* gain competitive advantage, especially in skilled areas;
* attract and retain high-calibre employees with the potential to develop; and
* reduce undesirable costs, such as those associated with customer dissatisfaction.

The tourism, hospitality and events (THE) sectors need to ensure that the recruitment and selection of staff is compliant with the legal requirements relating to employment, equal opportunities and the recommended codes of practice in place to ensure fair treatment to all applicants/candidates (Mullins, 2017). Since many individuals prefer to work for organisations that reflect their personal views, selection practices should be considered as a way for both parties to observe each other: the organisation evaluates candidates for a role, and the candidate considers the organisation as a prospective employer (as detailed in Chapter 24). Interviews are widely used as they provide the employer with an opportunity to explore a candidate's experience, assess their ability to perform in a role, clarify the employers proposition (culture, values, expectations of the role) and promote the organisation as a good employer. For the candidate, an interview provides an opportunity to ask questions about the role and the organisation, such as career developmental and progression opportunities, flexible working practices, and in some cases, relocation fees.

As we move towards a more digital world, the way in which we conduct interviews is changing via artificial intelligence. The need for cost-effective objective selection systems that reduce conscious and unconscious bias is reflected in increasing numbers of companies using 'content and structure-based analytics to hire and manage employees' (McCarthy et al., 2017: 1705). In practice this means that you would submit a CV online (see Chapter 29), which would be assessed using content analytics. At this point you could be rejected or progressed to the next stage of the recruitment cycle, and so on until the final selection procedure, when you may have the first 'human' contact (face-to-face or virtually) with your future employer. This remote (almost dehumanised) part of the selection process is challenging for most people but particularly for students and graduates who are just entering the market who may be inexperienced at applying for jobs. Despite the growth in digital recruitment practices, interviews remain a popular option for many employers.

TYPES OF SELECTION INTERVIEWS

Interviews are daunting for most people and feelings of anxiety are not unusual (McCarthy et al., 2017). As a student entering the THE job market (whether this is for a work placement or a permanent position), there are many types of selection interviews that you may be invited to attend. The choice of **selection tool** (interview type) is based on what the interviewer considers to be the most effective way of assessing a candidate's potential for a role. Some of the more common interview types that linked to graduate employability include the following:

- *Online aptitude tests*, which are ideal for self-assessment and identifying areas of strength and weaknesses (see Chapter 32)
- *Telephone interviews* are usually pre-arranged and you may be given an indication of the sort of questions that may be asked. They last between 35 and 60 minutes and can happen at any stage of an application process
- *Structured interviews*, which assess whether a candidate has the experience, skills and knowledge to be successful in a role. Structured interviews incorporate the following:

  o   A standardised set of pre-planned questions asked to all candidates
  o   Answers scored according to agreed rubrics (set marking criteria) (Taylor, 2010: 239)

- *Presentations* provide candidates with the opportunity to show a company what they can do. For example, if you are applying for a front of house position, you may be asked to present on reception desk customer care. Quite often you will be allowed to use software such as PowerPoint but you may be asked to present without any supporting material other than a few notes. The rationale for this is to observe how you approach discussions, explain and articulate your arguments (see Chapters 7 and 33)
- *Technical tests* (written, numeracy, customer care) assess practical (applied) skills and knowledge
- *Practical assessments* such as in-tray exercises are designed to see how you will cope with the real-world stresses of diary management and prioritisation, and test a particular set of key competencies, such as your delegation skills, your readiness to share problems with others, your independence, or your affinity with or aversion to procedures.
- *Personality questionnaires* are used to help recruiters make inferences about an individual's psychological make-up (Taylor, 2010: 258) (see Chapter 32)
- *Assessment centres* involve a half or whole day during which candidates will participate in numerous activities (see Chapter 33). An example of this multidimensional approach is used by the Marriott Graduate Scheme which works closely with Student Ladder on assessment centre activities (www.studentladder.co.uk/job/marriott-graduate-scheme/)
- *Gamification* is growing in popularity as a means to assess teamwork, problem-solving and emotional intelligence (Armstrong, Landers and Collmus, 2015)

══════════ REFLECTION EXERCISE ══════════

Selection interviews

Look at the various types of selection interviews, consider which one would suit you best? What do you think are the pros and cons of these different approaches?

HOW DO INTERVIEWS WORK?

Interviews often start with a broad question, and then use more focused questions to drill down into a deeper understanding of the person's knowledge, skills and behaviours. This process of the interview question funnel is shown in Figure 31.1.

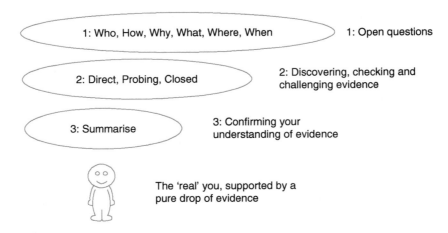

Figure 31.1   The Interview Question Funnel

Whilst the typology of selection interviews appears to be quite broad, even outside a formal assessment centre, it is not unusual for one recruitment process to include a combination of selection strategies with each element assessing specific skills sets. For example, the case study below details the multiple assessment points that an undergraduate events student experienced as part of securing her professional placement year with a large hotel in London.

 **STUDENT INSIGHT**

Ann, a tourism Professional Placement Student (Level 4), Monash University, Australia

I remember in my cover letter highlighting my passion for making people happy, which aligned with the Hilton values. There were several competency tests following the first round of recruitment (numeracy skills, literacy skills, verbal reasoning skills, analytic skills etc.) so there were some basic requirements that must be met before I really had an opportunity to demonstrate my attitude towards work and personality. This was a pre-recorded interview where a question would pop up on screen and I had 10 seconds to answer via webcam – I could show a bit more of my personality than in the test elements and I could explain a few items on my CV in more detail and in my own words. I then went through to the final interview stage (face-to-face interview with my boss). Teamwork is important in the hospitality industry (even in corporate) so it's important to be approachable and communicate well with your team. My boss mentioned that she liked that I had lots of volunteering on my CV as it proved I had a good, strong work ethic and that when speaking about my previous jobs, I spoke about them with a smile on my face and could pinpoint examples of challenges I had overcome, my greatest achievement and my fondest memories of working in the service sector.

Given the diverse nature of selection interviews, the underpinning philosophies (the **selection approach**) are also very different. For example, a biographical interview will focus on a person's past record of achievement but may not readily identify a person's potential, whereas a stress interview or stress questioning will deliberately place a candidate in a position of contradiction or conflict in order to observe first-hand reactions to stressful or uncomfortable situations. Instead of being subject to a traditional interviewing process that focuses on alignment of the applicant with job descriptions and person, you may find yourself being invited to a competency-based interview. The differences between the two approaches are shown below.

Table 31.1   Traditional vs competency-based interviews

Traditional	Competency-Based
• Matching the characteristics of an 'ideal' person to fill a defined job • Use job descriptions and person specifications • Selection based on knowledge, skills, and personal qualities	• Focus on identifying the abilities needed to do the job well • Recruit 'flexible' workers • Look at potential as well as actual skills or competences • Recruitment to team requirements rather than a specific job

WHAT IS A COMPETENCY?

In simple terms, a competency is about the way we do things or 'behaviours' we use. Competencies are the result of a mixture of skills, abilities and knowledge. A *competency-based interview* is one in which each candidate is asked similar questions designed to ascertain the match between the candidate's competencies and those required for the role. The panel will examine the examples you give in more detail, asking a series of probing questions. In view of this, it is important to use good, solid examples, about which you recall plenty of detail. It is perfectly acceptable to use examples from your personal life as well as from your professional activities. The evidence-based responses provided will then allow the panel to 'match' the individual to the job.

Table 31.2   Competency-based selection Interviews

Competency	Definition
Customer Service	• To have a good knowledge and understanding of your customers, their needs and to find the most effective way to deliver a high standard of service. • To communicate effectively with colleagues and customers to deliver an efficient service.
Decision-Making & Problem-Solving	• To make effective decisions on a day-to-day basis, taking ownership of decisions and demonstrate sound judgement in escalating issues where necessary. • To analyse situations, diagnose problems, identify the key issues, establish and evaluate alternative courses of action and produce a logical, practical and acceptable solution.
Teamwork	• To work co-operatively and flexibly with other members of the team, with a full understanding of the role to be played as a team member, to achieve a common goal. • To build relationships with others and show consideration, and to present the key points of an argument persuasively so as to convince others.
Planning & Organisation	• To organise own time effectively, create own work schedules, prioritise and prepare in advance, and set realistic timescales.

(Continued)

Table 31.2   (Continued)

Competency	Definition
Continuous Improvement	• To get things done well, setting and meeting challenging targets. • To be aware of own shortfalls and take charge of personal development.
Business Awareness	• To appreciate the commercial impact of role on the business
Management and Leadership	• To inspire individuals to give their best to achieve a desired result, and to maintain effective relationships with individuals and the team as a whole.
Change Management and Resilience	• To adapt and work effectively in different situations • To carry out a variety of tasks, and remain calm and level-headed under pressure, keep positive and put difficulties in perspective.

Examples of the type of questions that you might be asked in a competency-based interview for a customer focused role are listed below:

Focus of the role:

- To have a good knowledge and understanding of your team's customers, their needs and to find the most effective way to deliver a high standard of service.
- To focus on the needs of the customer in conducting your role.
- To communicate effectively with colleagues and customers to deliver an efficient service.

Questions that might be asked:

- How would you define excellent customer service?
- Give an example of a difficult customer situation you have had to handle?
- *Tip: Explain the situation and the approach you took*
- Describe a time when you have delivered excellent service to a customer?
- *Tip: What was the outcome?*
- Explain how you know when you are meeting a customer's requirements.
- *Tip: Give a specific example.*

Describe a time when you have worked with another department to deliver a quality service to customers. How important was this to you? How successful was the relationship? What do you believe makes effective communication?

 **ACTIVITY**

One of the most useful things you can do to prepare for an interview is to undertake an audit of your experiences to date, and to identify case studies and activities that you can use as examples of your abilities. Using the Making the Most of Me (M3) grid, plan your responses using the STARR guidelines.

STARR

- **S**ituation   What is the context?
- **T**ask   What was achieved and what was your role?
- **A**ctivity or **A**ction   What was the process used to achieve the task?
- **R**esult   What was the outcome?
- **R**eflection   What did you learn? What would you do differently?

The **R**esult may also be considered to be the '*So what?*' question in that you need to be able to explain why the task was important. You should also consider

- What hurdles or obstacles did you face?
- What was your specific role?
- Why did you behave the way you did?

PRE-INTERVIEW: MAKING THE MOST OF ME (M³ GRID)

The aim of the M³ grid is to provide you with a structure on which you can map your experiences against a job description. The example is of a generic administrator role in the THE industries, but of course you can use it for any job.

Themes	Examples of achievements to date (as a student and in work)
Customer Service	S
	T
	A
	R
	R
Adaptability	S
	T
	A
	R
	R
Problem-Solving	S
	T
	A
	R
	R

(Continued)

Figure 31.2 (Continued)

Themes	Examples of achievements to date (as a student and in work)
Teamwork	S
	T
	A
	R
	R
Planning and Organisation	S
	T
	A
	R
	R
Change Management and Resilience	S
	T
	A
	R
	R

Online Tests:	1)	Practice different types of aptitude tests
	2)	If going to a test location, arrive in good time so you can relax
	3)	Be aware of the time as you work through questions
	4)	Don't spend too long on a question that you are struggling with (but don't abandon a question prematurely if you are close to solving it)
	5)	Avoid wild guessing
Presentations:	1)	Read the brief carefully, and make sure your presentation answers it
	2)	Avoid 'death by PowerPoint' at all costs, and work on the principle that 1 slide = 1 message
	3)	Try and avoid animation overload – whizzy bits and words flying across pages can distract from the key points you are trying to make
	4)	Avoid reading off slides verbatim, but weave a narrative around the slides. Not only will this be more engaging for your audience, it will also give you an opportunity to show your personality
	5)	Practice your timing (and make sure you leave time for questions)
Interviews:	1)	Do some background work on the company and read the job description thoroughly
	2)	Give real, specific examples
	3)	When answering questions, focus on what **you** did ('I'). You may feel awkward doing this, or indeed as if you are boasting or showing off, but you are simply positioning and presenting your skills and experience and taking ownership of your achievements
	4)	Focus on what actually happened
	5)	Re-read the job description and person specifications. Try and imagine yourself in the job

Gamification	1)	Read the instructions
	2)	Practice before hand
	3)	Try different scenarios
	4)	Ensure you have a good internet connection
	5)	Be prepared, find a quiet place where you can relax and not be interrupted
Assessment Centres	1)	Re-read at your application
	2)	Check your invitation from the employer
	3)	Remember first impressions matter (follow the dress code, watch your posture and how you present yourself)
	4)	Do some background checking on the company (website, social media, LinkedIn, commercial awareness)
	5)	Remember that you are being assessed all day (as you arrive and as you leave)

Figure 31.2   Making the Most of Me (M³) interview preparation grid

Below is some practical advice about how to cope with the interview situation, and how you can TARGET your energies.

- **T**ry not to fiddle
- **A**llow yourself to be nervous
- **R**emember interviews are a two-way process
- **G**o there early and take your time when talking
- **E**xhale
- **T**ry not worry if you make a mistake

LEARNING FROM FAILURE

Quite often candidates will hear that they are qualified and experienced enough to do the role 'on paper', but the interviewers need to see if they 'fit' the organisation. This type of feedback is difficult to accept because 'organisational fit' is intangible and difficult to articulate. Other types of feedback offer real opportunities for development and so it is important to deal with rejection well and learn from it. It is important not to lose confidence when you get a rejection. Competition for jobs (and especially graduate jobs) is very high in some sectors, in which case getting an interview is a major achievement.

Some companies will automatically offer you feedback or an opportunity to discuss your performance. When receiving feedback follow these basic rules:

1. Listen to the feedback, no matter how uncomfortable
2. Try not to be defensive because you may hear that:
   a. you were not specific enough
   b. you did not come across as being very interested or
   c. you did not appear to know enough about the job or the company
3. Take notes, do a gap analysis, identify your weaknesses and develop a plan to address them

If the company does not automatically offer a feedback opportunity then it is reasonable to contact them and say something like, 'I am disappointed that I wasn't chosen and would appreciate some honest feedback. I value your insight and opinion about how I could improve my performance and employability prospects.'

CONCLUSION

In this chapter we have covered:

- Some of the key approaches to recruitment and selection
- How the advent of digital recruitment practices has changed the recruitment process
- How selection interviews demand robust evidence to support your claims
- The importance of preparing properly for interviews
- The TARGET approach to overcome your nerves.

FURTHER READING

CIPD (2015) *A Head for Hiring: The Behavioural Science of Recruitment and Selection.* [Research Report, August 2015] London: CIPD

CIPD (2020) *Selection Methods. Factsheets.* London: CIPD https//www.cipd.co.uk/fundamentals/people/recruitment/selection-factsheet. [Accessed 20 February 2020]

Deery, M. (2008). 'Talent management, work-life balance and retention strategies'. *International Journal of Contemporary Hospitality Management,* 20 (7): 792-806.

Edwards, J.R. (1991) 'Person-fit: A conceptual integration, literature review, and methodological critique'. In: Cooper, C.L. and Robertson, I.T. (eds). *International Review of Industrial and Organisational Psychology. Volume 6.* Chichester: John Wiley, pp 283-357

Sharma, B. (2019) 'Review of human resource practices in hospitality and tourism'. *Journal of Hospitality,* 1(1), 15–30

Taylor, S.(2010) *Resourcing and Talent Management.* London: CIPD

Useful Web Resources

- Team Technology: Free Personality Test: www.metarasa.com/mmdi/questionnaire
- Human Metrics: Jung Typology Test: www.humanmetrics.com/cgi-win/jtypes2.asp
- Student Ladder: Steps to Success: www.studentladder.co.uk/assessment-centres/
- The Graduate Job Hunters Guide to gamification: https://targetjobs.co.uk/careers-advice/psychometric-tests/453607-the-graduate-job-hunters-guide-to-gamification
- Arctic Shores: Advice for candidates (www.arcticshores.com/candidates) – tips from Arctic Shores, providers of game-based assessments for several graduate employers.

32 PSYCHOMETRIC TESTS

CHAPTER LEARNING OBJECTIVES

By the end of this chapter, you should be able to:

- Articulate what psychometric tests are and why employers use them in recruitment
- Identify the different types of psychometrics tests and what they are designed to assess
- Outline the most common psychometric tests used for graduate recruitment in the tourism, events and hospitality industries
- Reflect on your own strengths and weaknesses in relation to the skills assessed by psychometric tests and understand how you might improve your performance
- Be confident in undertaking some of the most common tests used for recruitment
- Discuss the common problems and mistakes people make with psychometric tests
- Develop personal strategies to better prepare yourself for tests

GLOSSARY

- **Aptitude test:** assesses a candidate's abilities to perform specific tasks, identify skills, knowledge and personality and assess how someone reacts to a range of different situations relevant for a specific role or job
- **Predictive validity:** the extent to which a score in a test predicts scores on some criterion measure
- **Psychometric:** literally 'measure of the mind', the concept comes from a field of study concerned with the theory and technique of psychological measurement. When employers use the term 'psychometric test' they are generally referring to aptitude tests

INTRODUCTION

This chapter looks at how skills and personality are assessed and tested in the recruitment process. Drawing on examples and case studies, this chapter presents and defines what **psychometric** testing is, its associated benefits, why employers use these types of tests and outlines the contexts in which they are most commonly used. Alongside the different types of test (including verbal, numeric, and reasoning tests), it provides examples for you to try out for yourself. This chapter also provides insights into how and where you might find opportunities to access and practice tests so you feel better prepared. It particularly focuses on the common tests used for graduate recruitment in the THE sectors and the types of companies that use them. It will also provide an overview of some of the problems with psychometric tests and provide advice on how to avoid some of the more common mistakes.

WHAT ARE PSYCHOMETRIC TESTS?

Tests are often used as part of an assessment centre recruitment exercise (see Chapter 33). In the initial stages of an assessment process, tests are often run online before you are invited in person. Psychometric tests are a way for a potential employer to get to know you and your abilities. They are used in recruitment and staff development, to assess your true abilities in areas like numerical reasoning and logical reasoning.

WHO USES PSYCHOMETRIC TESTS?

According to the job website Prospects (2019b), graduate psychometric tests,

> [h]elp to identify your skills, knowledge and personality. They're often used during the preliminary screening stage, or as part of an assessment centre. They're objective, convenient and strong indicators of job performance – making them very popular with large graduate recruiters.

The Association of Graduate Recruiters found that 67% of the largest employers were using some form of psychometric test. There are a few leading test companies that have an international reputation because companies tend to use tests that have a high **predictive validity** to ensure they are reliable.

HOW TO PREPARE FOR PSYCHOMETRIC TESTS

The very word 'test' can trigger anxiety. Houston and Cunningham (2015) suggest that we might consider tests we enjoy. What kinds of test do you enjoy? This might mean Sudoku, computer games or puzzles. The most useful and constructive way to prepare for them is to understand them and prepare thoroughly. Very few of the tests mentioned in this chapter require formal revision (i.e. learning facts), but you should revise how to undertake them, and in some cases, how to work out basic mathematical calculations such as percentages, ratios and currency conversions.

On the day of the test itself, you need to ensure you are hydrated, have eaten well and slept well the night before. If you are conducting the tests at home online, be sure to pick a place and time that will be quiet, free of distractions and with a reliable internet connection. If your house is busy, consider undertaking the test at your university or a local library.

If you are attending an assessment centre to undertake the tests, ensure you know exactly where you are going, and how to get there. Arrive on time as latecomers will generally be excluded from the process (see Chapter 33 for more details).

DIFFERENT PSYCHOMETRICS TESTS AND WHAT THEY ASSESS

As outlined above, many tests are conducted online, but some employers still use paper versions as part of in-person assessment centres. In general, there are two main types of test: **aptitude tests** (sometimes called ability tests) and personality tests. Aptitude tests will generally be under exam conditions, often adopting a multiple-choice format. You are often scored on the number of right answers and your level of accuracy within a given timeframe. This means that it is unwise to spend too much time on one question you might be stuck on: the best approach is to leave it and then come back if you have time. However, be reassured that usually more questions are set than an employer would expect most applicants to answer. In contrast, personality tests are often completed in your own time. There is no right or wrong with these types of test: they assess your potential 'fit' with the organisation and focus on your approach to work, your interests and motivations. You should always answer these as 'you', rather than giving the answers you think are being sought.

The tests most commonly used are outlined below in Table 32.1. For more information, see www.assessmentday.co.uk, www.practiceaptitudetests.com, or www.graduatesfirst.com.

Table 32.1   Common types of psychometric tests: aptitude and personality

The two main types of psychometric tests

Aptitude/ability tests	Common personality tests
Abstract reasoning (also called Diagrammatic reasoning)	Myers Briggs Type Indicator MBTI
Numerical reasoning	Cubiks In-Depth Personality Questionnaire
Verbal reasoning	The SHL Occupational Personality Questionnaire (OPQ) – measures of workplace behavioural styles (www.shl.com)
Spatial reasoning	16PF® assessment of 16 personality factors https://www.16pf.com
Error checking	Cappfinity Strengths - www.cappfinity.com
In tray tests (prioritisation)	
Critical thinking tests (e.g. arguments, deductions, assumptions, inferences)	

For graduate level jobs in the tourism, hospitality and events sectors, there will be a range of ability tests that employers use. The most common are numerical and verbal tests as well as critical thinking and situational judgement assessments. An example from the TUI Graduate Scheme is provided as an employer insight.

The use of psychometric tests in graduate recruitment for the TUI Analytics Graduate Programme

TUI have a number of graduate pathways with different selection requirements. Note that the second stage involves verbal and numerical tests to filter applicants.

The First Stage – Online Application

Apply online via our website. This will include uploading your CV and answering a series of questions.

The Second Stage – Online Tests

If you meet the criteria, we will ask you to complete online verbal and numerical and inductive tests which will assess your ability to analyse business-related information.

The Third Stage – Video Interview

Candidates who have successfully completed the online tests will be invited to take part in a video interview. In this interview we would like to gain an understanding of your motivation for the application. You will also be asked competency-based questions.

The Final Stage – Assessment Day

If you pass the video interview, you will be invited to join us at our unique assessment centre in Luton. We will spend the whole getting to know each other. The assessment days, including a number of one-to-one and group-based activities, will give you the chance to demonstrate your skills. You will also have the opportunity to meet some of our current graduates, to find out more about us, our culture, our organisation and our Graduate Programme.

Source: http://tuijobsuk.co.uk/work-at-tui-travel/graduates/ (2019)

APTITUDE/ABILITY TESTS

Abstract reasoning (also known as Diagrammatic Reasoning) tests

These tests assess how quickly you can learn things, identify patterns and apply rules to new situations. Common abstract reasoning tests use images that change slightly, asking you to identify the pattern and state which picture should follow in the sequence. These kinds of tests tend to be multiple choice exercises. With all such tests, the best approach is practice, however there are three strategies that should help you correctly answer these kinds of questions:

I.   Commonality: look at what the symbols have in common. It might be their colour, size, shape, or symmetry.
II. Pattern: is there a repeated sequence, say every second or third? Are they in groups of two, three or four? Are the symbols repeated? If the sequence is displayed in a shape other than a line, is this repeated horizontally or vertically?
III. Prediction: you will need to predict the next symbols in a series.

=========== **ACTIVITY 1** ===========

Test yourself with abstract reasoning

Using input and outputs

A typical test with questions like this might last around 15–30 minutes. In this example the questions have an input diagram, one or more 'operators', and an output. You will need to study the impact of the operators on the shapes and then decide which option gives the best answer.

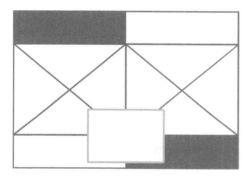 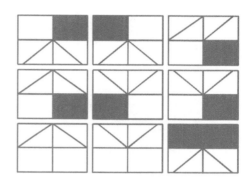

1   What replaces the missing section?

A   B   C   D   E

2   Which one replaces the question mark?

A

B

C

D

E

(Continued)

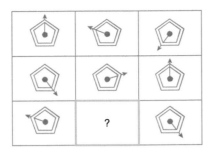
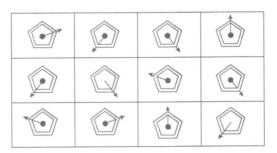

3   What replaces the question mark?

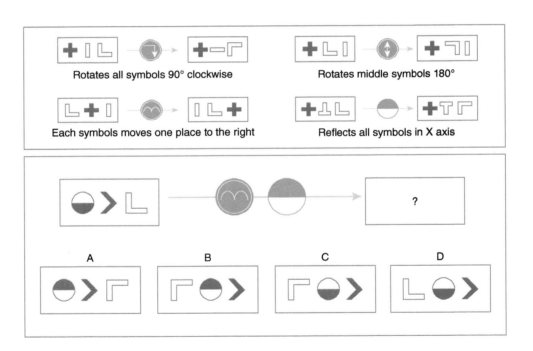

4   Which diagram replaces the question mark?

A

B

C

D

Set A

Set B

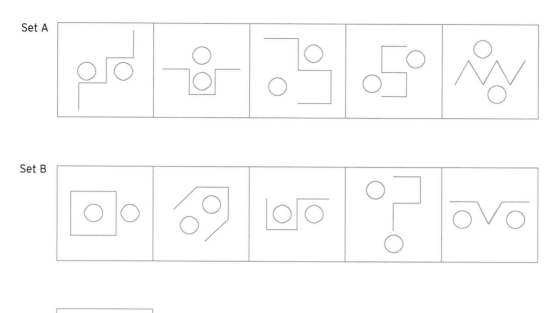

5   Which set does the figure belong to?

A. Set A
B. Set B
C. Neither set A nor set B

Credit: Abstract Diagrammatic Reasoning Tests kindly provided by Assessment Day (www.assessmentday. co.uk)
    The solutions can be found at the end of the book (Chapter 36).

Numerical reasoning

Being able to deal with numbers and data quickly, accurately and confidently is necessary for many roles in THE. Consequently, these kinds of tests will often ask you to look at some data and then interpret them. It could take the form of raw data, or charts, graphs and tables. Most tests for graduate level roles will test your skills with basic calculations which might include working out percentages, ratios and currency conversions. For example, you might be asked something like this: 'The ages of a group of people are: 29, 47, 53, 17, 48, 59, 22 and 33. What percentage are over 40 years of age? A: 60% B: 50% C: 40% D: 10% E: 4%.'

As an applicant, you will need to demonstrate an ability to draw conclusions from numerical data quickly and accurately. Examples may include performance figures, financial results and analysis reports. You will also be expected to show a capacity to monitor performance and progress using numerical metrics and numerical performance indicators. Test yourself with some examples, given below.

ACTIVITY 2

Test yourself with numeric reasoning test

There are four numerical questions that follow. They are multiple choice questions. You are expected to look at the data presented and then calculate the answer for each question.

Example of numerical tests

Example Test 1

Here is a test of building energy usage

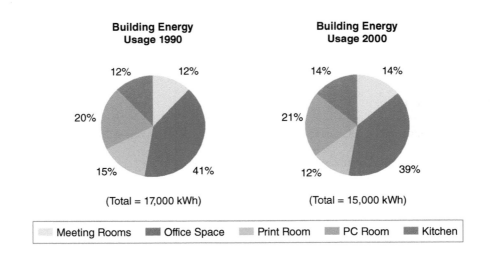

1   If the Building Energy Use today is 6% less than it was in 2000, by what percentage is today's Building Energy Use lower than that of 1990?

    (A) 82.9%
    (B) 17.1%
    (C) 17.8%
    (D) Cannot say

Example Test 2 Numerical Reasoning

Men and women working in different employment sectors

Sector	Male	Female
Voluntary Work	41,000	67,000
IT	121,000	107,000
Engineering	398,000	105,000
Legal Services	273,000	251,000
Healthcare	227,000	271,000
Business Services	186,000	124,000
Self-Employed	45,000	62,000
Unemployed	52,000	43,000
Total	1,343,000	1,031,000

2   If it is predicted that the number of females employed in IT will rise by 10% every year, but the number of males stays the same, what percent of IT employees would be female after a three year period?

(A)   54.1%
(B)   53.5%
(C)   85.0%
(D)   45.5%

Example Test 3

Share Prices

Share Prices

Company	Today's Price (€)	Change from previous day (%)	Past 12 months	
			Maximum price (€)	Minimum price (€)
Huver Co.	1,150	1.10	1,360	860
Drebs Ltd	18	0.50	22	11
Fevs Plc	1,586	-9.00	1,955	1,242
Fauvers	507	-1.00	724	464
Steapars	2,537	1.00	2,630	2,216

Dividend paid per share (€)	Huuver Co.	Drebs Ltd	Fevs Plc	Fauvers	Steapars
Interim Dividend	0.83	0.44	0.34	0.09	0.48
Final Dividend	1.75	1.12	1.25	0.32	0.96

Note: the total annual dividend paid per share is the sum of the interim dividend and the final dividend

(Continued)

3   What was yesterday's cost difference between 50 shares in Fevs plc and 100 shares in Steapars?

    (A)   €164,726
    (B)   €251,163
    (C)   €172,577
    (D)   €164,045
    (E)   None of these

Example Test 4

Question: Spending by the Legal Sector

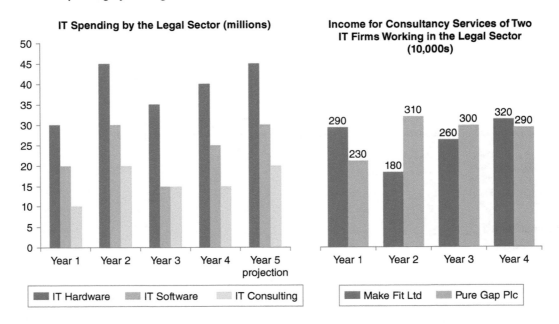

4   Legal sector spending on IT hardware, IT software and IT consulting are all set to increase by the same amounts in Year 6 as they did from Year 4 to Year 5. Assuming this is the case, what would be the total legal sector spending in Year 6 on these three IT areas combined?

    (A)   £75 million
    (B)   £85 million
    (C)   £95 million
    (D)   £105 million
    (E)   £110 million

The solutions can be found at the end of the book (Chapter 36).
   Credit: Numerical tests kindly provided by Assessment Day (www.assessmentday.co.uk)

Verbal logical reasoning tests

These test your ability to comprehend words and written information, as well as test your spelling, grammar and knowledge of the written word. You should be able to show you can assimilate written materials such as company reports and manuals, instructions, and policies. The tests tend to be based on short passages of text followed by a set of questions to assess your comprehension. Many roles in tourism, hospitality and events will require an ability to use written information to develop arguments, summarise information, and provide accurate and clear statements.

====== ACTIVITY 3 ======

Test yourself with a verbal logical reasoning test

Read the information given to you, and then work out whether the statement given is true, false or you cannot say for certain based on the information provided.

Verbal reasoning tests

Example Test 1

Analysis of the Department of Tourism Infrastructure – reading Profit & Loss sheets

> The project was ambitious in its size, complexity, triparty nature, and in its pioneering of the Private Finance Initiative. This difficulty was unavoidable and contributed to the project's failure. However, a more thorough estimate of the unknown difficulties and timescales would have enabled the Department of Tourism Infrastructure to better prepare for the project and increase its chances of success.
>
> In December 1997, XSoft, the company tasked with completing the project on behalf of the Department of Tourism Infrastructure, had asked for an extension of the deadline because they could already see that the project would not meet the promised January 1998 deadline and would not be completed until June 1999, at the earliest. If the Department had known from the start the true scale of the project, it is likely they would have chosen another smaller project. Accountants have reported that the delay has already had negative effects on the Profit & Loss sheets for both parties.

1   If more care had been put into estimating the difficulties, it is less likely the project would have failed.

  True   False   Cannot say

2   XSoft withheld information from the Department regarding how long the project would take.

  True   False   Cannot say

Example 2: Financial statements verbal test

Questions

> The first problem with financial statements is that they are in the past; however detailed, they provide just a snap-shot of the business at one moment in time. There is also a lack of detail in financial statements, giving little use in the running of a business. Financial statements are provided for legal reasons to meet with accounting regulations and are used mainly by City analysts who compute share prices and give guidance to shareholders. Accounts often have hidden information and may also be inconsistent; it is difficult to compare different companies' accounts, despite there being standards, as there is much leeway in the standards.

3   Financial statements are useful for businesses to understand their financial activities.

  True   False   Cannot say

(Continued)

4   If account reporting standards were tightened, it would be easier to compare the performance of different companies.

True   False   Cannot say

The solutions can be found at the end of the book (Chapter 36).

    Credit: Numerical tests kindly provided by Assessment Day (www.assessmentday.co.uk)

    More practice verbal reasoning tests can be found here: https://www.assessmentday.co.uk/aptitudetests_verbal.htm

Critical thinking tests

Critical thinking can be defined as 'the ability to consider a range of information derived from many different sources, to process this information in a creative and logical manner, challenging it, analysing it and arriving at considered conclusions which can be defended and justified' (Moon, 2008: 30).

One of the most common types of this test is the Watson-Glaser Critical Thinking Appraisal (W-GCTA) and details can be found at Watson Glaser (www.talentlens.co.uk/product/watson-glaser). This appraisal is the most popular measure of critical thinking ability with recruitment teams at law firms. Their tests are said to be good predictors of future success in roles that require clarity of understanding from multiple perspectives and the ability to reason with fact versus assumption. The decisions you make in the test must solely be based on the information givens. The five types of test within this category are:

I.   Assumptions: decide if an assumption has been made in making the statement.

II.   Analysing arguments: you will be provided with a given scenario (e.g. 'Should cities have a tourist tax?') and a list of arguments for or against, presented in terms of whether the argument is strong or weak, based on how relevant it is and how well it addresses the question.

III. Deductions: you will be presented with some information and asked to evaluate a list of deductions made based on that information (example below).

IV. Inferences: you will be given some information and a list of possible inferences. You then need to say whether the inferences are true, false, possibly true, possibly false or whether it is not possible to say.

V.   Interpreting Information: some text will be given to you with a list of possible conclusions. You will need to decide if each conclusion is possible based on the presented information.

 ACTIVITY ON DEDUCTIONS

Test yourself with a critical thinking test

For each question, you are presented with two statements or premises and your task is to identify which one conclusion from a series of five possible conclusions must be true, based solely on those premises.

Critical Reasoning Example Tests

For each question you will be presented with two premises and your task is to identify which one conclusion from a series of five possible conclusions must be true based solely on those premises. Some statements might seem a little abstract, but must still be treated as fact during the test.

1 Which one of the following conclusions is definitely true based on the statement?

All events are live. All conferences are events.

A.   All conferences are live
B.   No conferences are live
C.   Some conferences are live
D.   Some conferences are not live
E.   No valid conclusion

The answer is A. If all conferences are events, and all events are live, then it follows that all conferences are live.

2. Which one of the following conclusions is definitely true based on the statement?

All hotel managers are senior leaders. No senior leaders are part time staff.

A.   All part time staff are hotel managers
B.   No part time staff are hotel managers
C.   Some part time staff are hotel managers
D.   Some part time staff are not hotel managers
E.   No valid conclusion

3. Which one of the following conclusions is definitely true based on the statement?

No events staff are accountants. All finance staff are accountants.

A.   All finance staff are events staff
B.   No finance staff are events staff
C.   Some finance staff are events staff
D.   Some finance staff are not events staff
E.   No valid conclusion

4. Which one of the following conclusions is definitely true based on the statement?

All new customers are eligible for a discount. Some new customers are tourists.

A.   All tourists are eligible for a discount
B.   No tourists are eligible for a discount
C.   Some tourists are eligible for a discount
D.   Some tourists are not eligible for a discount
E.   No valid conclusion

5. Which one of the following conclusions is definitely true based on the statement?

Some women are hard working. Some hotel staff are women.

A.   All hotel staff are hard working
B.   No hotel staff are hard working
C.   Some hotel staff are hard working
D.   Some hotel staff are not hard working
E.   No valid conclusion

The solutions can be found at the end of the book (Chapter 36).
   A useful resource for more examples is https://www.assessmentday.co.uk/watson-glaser-critical-thinking.htm.

Another type of critical reasoning test is based on strong and weak arguments.

 ━━━━ ACTIVITY ━━━━━━━━━━━━━━━━━━━

Test yourself with 'strong and weak' critical thinking tests

Assuming the argument is true, state whether you think each of the five arguments below are strong or weak. These are examples from some of the harder levels of a test.

Statement: Is the value of a tourism, hospitality or events degree decreasing?

1. Yes, as starting salaries in this sector are not keeping pace with inflation and are traditionally in lower paid areas

2. Yes, there are a lot more graduates in these fields now than 20 years ago

3. No, the number of opportunities for graduate level work in the tourism, hospitality and events area has increased over the past few years

4. No, education is always valued and is vital for the global economy

5. Yes. more graduates are now taking other degrees and moving into this field of work at a later stage, for example marketing, business or the sciences and making the field more competitive

You can find the answers at the end of the book.

There are some free downloadable tests available at: https://www.assessmentday.co.uk/watson-glaser-critical-thinking.htm

---

Situational judgement

These tests assess how you approach a hypothetical situation in the workplace. How well can you make decisions about what to do? More sophisticated tests might ask you to rank responses, explain what you have chosen the options you have and perhaps even identify the least appropriate response.

 ━━━━ ACTIVITY ━━━━━━━━━━━━━━━━━━━

Situation test — working in an events company

You have started a new job at an events company. The marketing department's team is currently under-staffed, so you have been asked to join the team temporarily. However, you have received almost no training and you are struggling to keep up. Although this position is temporary, it is likely you will need to remain in this role for at least a year. You should:

1) Intentionally deviate from marketing procedures, ensuring you are transferred back to your own events team.
2) Take no further action. If you make mistakes, blame the marketing team for providing insufficient training.
3) Request additional training to bring you up to speed.
4) Request to be assigned an experienced marketing professional as a mentor to guide you through the work and processes.

Think about your answers and if they are likely to be 1) Very Ineffective, 2) Ineffective, 3) Fairly Ineffective, 4) Fairly Effective, 5) Effective or 6) Very Effective.

In tray/e-tray exercises

This assesses your ability to plan your work, prioritise, delegate and carry out tasks. It helps recruiters see how well you cope with a real-life office environment in terms of diary management, stresses of juggling competing tasks and your efficiency, assessing your time management, adherence to process and general attitude to the work. The test simulates a work environment, usually set at a fictitious company. You will be given a set of documents as your 'in-tray'. The number of documents will vary but can be around 10–30 items provided in a variety of formats. The documents and tasks might include emails, complaints, reports, telephone calls, or may be a more relevant task for an events, hospitality or tourism position such as planning an event which will involve bookings, marketing, and liaison.

The way you will be tested will vary, but often it will involve explaining your decision-making and actions in terms of time commitments, urgency, people, diary clashes and company priorities. These exercises are often online. It is key to note how you approached the task, why you took the decisions and actions you did, and think carefully about your answers.

Top tips for success in these tests:

- Work out the overarching theme or focus of the work – the fictitious company will often have a story behind it that may be useful
- Ensure you know what you are being tested for. For example, does the role you have applied for involve working independently, or as part of a team?
- Read everything in your in-tray before you answer the questions.
- Ensure you keep notes on the process you used.
- Don't waste time, but also don't rush.
- Keep your desk and working space tidy and organised (if doing this in person and being observed). You should lay items out in a logical order that works best for you.
- Ensure you keep notes on what has already been done, by you or others.
- Check dates on documents. Are there deadlines? Have some tasks been waiting a long time?
- Think about the logistics. For example, if you are planning a tour or a large event, then you need to ensure there is time for delegates or visitors to get from one place to another.
- Consider who is asking for the work to be done. How senior are they? Who should be prioritised?

Once again, the best way to prepare is to practice. An example of a typical question is provided below. Another example can be found in Chapter 33. There is also an example of an e-tray test in the next chapter on Assessment Centres that you may wish to try.

 ACTIVITY

In-tray exercise

Dealing with the prospect of legal action

Scenario: you are in a junior manager position and receive an email from Travel Legal, your company's legal advisers.

Subject: Potential legal action by Smithson of Tourism

We have been informed that the travel company Smithson of Tourism is considering taking legal action as a result of your recent launch of the 'Events4you' app. It appears that the name 'Events4you' was registered

(Continued)

as a website by Smithson of Tourism four years ago. It has been growing in popularity and has over 2 million registered users. Smithson of Tourism is very unhappy that a new app has been launched under the same name as they have plans in place to launch an app to accompany their website.

What do you do?

A – Immediately forward email to your senior managers to action

B – Reply to email seeking legal advice, 'cc'-ing it in your senior managers

C – Reply to email seeking legal advice

Answers:

A)   Immediately forward email to your managers for them to action

This is not the best approach. It is important to inform senior staff but you should be expected to take action and develop a plan to deal with the situation rather than just forward problematic issues.

B)   Reply to email seeking legal advice, 'cc'-ing it your managers.

Good answer. This legal action could have major implications for your company so it is good that you get back immediately to your legal advisors and find out what should be done. It is, however, important that you also keep your managers informed.

C)   Reply to email seeking legal advice

Maybe, but given the seriousness of the potential action, you should ensure your senior managers are made aware of the situation.

Finding errors and checking accuracy

This is an important test and something you should have practiced numerous times when you proofread your assignments. Attention to detail is crucial for some roles. Data checking tests measure how quickly and accurately you can detect errors. They are common for clerical and data input vacancies. Fault-diagnosis tests, meanwhile, test your ability to approach problems logically.

Skills being assessed

Table 32.2 summaries the kinds of skills that the different tests are designed to test. Most of these skills are essential to work in the tourism, hospitality and events industries.

Table 32.2   Matching skills to tests

Test type	Skills being assessed
Abstract reasoning and diagrammatic reasoning	Analytical ability
	Decision-making
	Logical and abstract reasoning
	Critical thinking
	Problem-solving

Test type	Skills being assessed
Numerical reasoning	Numerical ability Problem-solving Dealing with numbers quickly
Verbal logical reasoning	Analytical ability Ability to think logically Decision-making Critical thinking Problem-solving
Critical thinking tests	Analytical ability Decision-making Critical thinking Problem-solving
Situational judgement	Analytical ability Problem-solving Decision-making Interpersonal skills Critical thinking
In-tray/e-tray	Adaptability Analytical ability Decision-making Managing ambiguity Prioritisation and time management
Finding errors and checking accuracy	Ability to be methodical Accuracy and ability to check information Attention to detail

Common problems and mistakes (and how to avoid them)

As outlined above, it is important to practice undertaking tests, there is no substitute for practice. Some of the common reasons given for poor performance are outlined here. We have provided some words of advice on how to mitigate against these problems.

- Panic and anxiety – think about when you have taken other tests with positive outcomes. Ensure you sleep, eat and drink well. Try listening or watching some mindfulness videos. Remember, everyone is feeling the same way about these.
- Carelessness and not reading the question carefully – take time to read it, and read it again. It is better to take more time to do this than rush and get the whole test wrong.

- Being interrupted (especially those completed at home) – ensure you find somewhere warm, quiet and appropriate to complete the online tests.
- Unfamiliarity with the test – practise as many as you can, and practise some more
- Lack of ability – practice should help you overcome concern that you don't have the skills to complete the tests
- Confidence – everyone is in the same position as you. If you have practised the tests, then you are ready! Undertake the reflection exercise below.
- Timeframe (rushing and making mistakes or taking too long) – breathe and take time to read the instructions carefully and do not dwell on one question for too long.

 ═══ REFLECTION EXERCISE ═══════════════════════════

Think about the problems you had with the example test questions. Develop a plan to try and address these concerns:

What type of test did you find most challenging? Why? What can you do to better prepare yourself for it? List at least three things.

Personality tests

Personality tests assess if your personality matches the job role and skills required. These tend to take the form of questionnaires, which then calculate a 'type'. All such tests have their critics and employers should employ them cautiously (Baez 2013). Baez suggests that 'the link between personality and emotional intelligence to job performance is compelling' (2013: 1) but adds employers must be aware of their weaknesses and use 'valid, reliable and legally sustainable tests in hiring employees' (2013: 8). Most are self-reporting tests that rely on you deciding what to reveal about yourself.

According to the Institute of Psychometric coaching, employers seeking THE graduates looking for the following characteristics (see www.psychometricinstitute.com.au/Graduates-Hospitality-Tourism. html):

- Focus on excellence and results attainment
- Strategic thinking and ability to get 'over and above' the situation at hand
- Emotional resilience
- Drive, determination and a positive attitude
- Social confidence (friendly and highly engaged in any social situation)
- Considerate of others
- Stress tolerance
- Able to take personal responsibility and accountability
- Structured, planned and calculated approach to solving problems
- Conflict resolution skill

There are numerous tests that are used to assess such characteristics, some of which are outlined below, starting with Myers Briggs Type Indicator.

THINK POINT

Take each of the characteristics above and think about why it might be important in this sector. Can you demonstrate this personality trait?

Myers Briggs Type Indicator (MBTI)

The Myers Briggs questionnaire is based on the theory that personality is characterised by four criteria (extroversion/introversion, sensing/intuition, thinking/feeling, and judging/perceiving, i.e. EISNTFJ and P). The test has its origins in the work of Carl Jung and seeks to apply his theory of psychological types to the workplace. The MBTI tool was developed in the 1940s by Isabel Briggs Myers and the original research was done in the 1940s and '50s. More details can be found at www.myersbriggs.org where you can also take your own test (for a small fee). There are 16 different personality types, which emerge from various combinations of EISNTFJ and P. Try the reflective exercise in this chapter. You may also like to try a number of freely available tests online, one of which is offered by Human Metrics: www.humanmetrics.com/cgi-win/jtypes2.asp#questionnaire.

REFLECTION EXERCISE

Myers Briggs Type Indicator (MBTI)

Read a little more about the personality types at https://www.myersbriggs.org. What combination of the four criteria do you think you are? Put a (mental) mark on where you think you are on the scale and jot down the letter you are closest to.

* Where you focus your attention
  Extraversion (E) --- Introversion (I)

* The way you take in information
  Sensing (S) --- Intuition (N)

* How you make decisions
  Thinking (T) -- Feeling (F)

* How you deal with the world
  Judging (J) --- Perceiving (P)

What does this say about the kind of work you might be suited to? Are there any surprises?

CUBIKS IN-DEPTH PERSONALITY QUESTIONNAIRE

Cubiks is an international consultancy that has developed tests based on the 'Big 5' personality dimensions of OCEAN (Digman 1990). As introduced in Chapter 26, this mnemonic stands for Openness,

Conscientiousness, Extraversion, Agreeableness, and Neuroticism (another way to remember them is CANOE). McCrae and Costa (1999) suggested that the big five traits are fairly universal, finding that people from more than 50 different cultures presented the same five dimensions in their personality, as follows:

- Openness: this is about imagination, insight and creativity. People high in this trait tend to have many interests and are adventurous and creative. People low in this trait are often more traditional and may struggle with abstract thinking and resist new ideas.
- Conscientiousness: people with high levels of this trait demonstrate thoughtfulness, good impulse control, and tend to be organised and mindful of details. They plan ahead and consider deadlines. They attend to detail and like schedules. Those low in conscientiousness will procrastinate and dislike structure.
- Extraversion: social, talkative and assertive, enjoying being the centre of attention, making friends easily and feeling energised by social situations. If you are low in extraversion (i.e. introverted) you will be reserved and have less energy to expend in social settings, preferring solitude and disliking the idea of being the centre of attention.
- Agreeableness: kind, affectionate, and sympathetic. People with this trait tend to show trust, altruism, and kindness. They feel empathy for others and enjoy helping them. Those low in this tend to take little interest in others and might manipulate others to get what they want.
- Neuroticism: this is also known as emotional stability. If you score high on this, then you tend to experience stress, worry and get upset easily. Those low in this trait tend to be more stable, deal well with stress, don't worry much and are emotionally resilient.

 THINK POINT

Think about your own personality and how you might score on these Big 5. What traits would a potential employer be looking for? It is unlikely they want someone neurotic, so how might you address this if you think you have this trait?

Take the Big 5 test for free. A number of websites offer free tests, including https://www.123test.com/personality-test/. Tests are always being updated and more recently we have seen a six-factor model known as HEXACO, which adds honesty-humility to the original five traits to incorporate ethical behavior into the mix.

THE SHL OCCUPATIONAL PERSONALITY QUESTIONNAIRE (OPQ)

Developed by Saville and Holdsworth Ltd (SHL), the OPQ is known as the SHL personality test or OPQ32. It is widely used as a measure of behavioural styles and measures 32 specific personality characteristics that predict future performance at work. These tests are also based on the Big Five Personality Traits at their core, but the three building blocks are relationships with people, thinking style and feelings and emotions.

Within these three categories, you are assessed across 32 dimensions of personality. The test is therefore sometimes referred to as OPQ32. The OPQ is taken online and has several formats. You are most likely to take what is called the OPQ32r which has 104 questions. It contains groups of three statements, from which you choose the one that sounds most like you and the one which sounds the least like you. Remember, there is no 'wrong' kind of personality. For example, you might be asked to choose one most true and one least true statement from the following:

- I enjoy the companionship of others
- I try out new activities
- I look to the future

(*Source*: https://service.shl.com/docs/OPQ_Fact_Sheet.pdf)

You should seek to present your personality accurately. Think about your preferred approach in terms of your relationships with people (are you a leader, or do you prefer to follow?), thinking style (are you laid-back or do you like structure and organisation?) and feelings (do you often feel anxious? Are you competitive?). You should also carefully research the company and the role. Think about which characteristics they may be looking for and how you fit the criteria. If you understand how your personality corresponds with the characteristics required, this will likely come across in your test result.

16PF® ASSESSMENT OF 16 PERSONALITY FACTORS

This test is about the 16 'personality/primary factors' and is structured around the 'Big Five' factors of personality. According to 16PF (www.16pf.com), the model was developed from Raymond Cattell's (1956) research on second-order factor analysis, which identified five broad dimensions of personality. The five global factors give a useful overview of an individual's personality, while the 16 Primary Factors provide better information for predicting behaviour and performance.

The test includes forced-choice questions in which you must choose one of three different alternatives. Personality traits are then represented by a range and the individual's score falls somewhere on the continuum between highest and lowest extremes. So, rather than asking respondents to self-assess their personality like other methods (e.g. 'I am a warm and friendly person'), they ask about specific situations, e.g. 'When I find myself in a boring situation, I usually "tune out" and daydream about other things' or 'when a bit of tact and convincing is needed to get people moving, I'm usually the one who does it'. The 16 personality dimensions described by Cattell (1956) are as follows:

- Abstractedness: imaginative/practical
- Apprehension: worried/confident
- Dominance: forceful/submissive
- Emotional Stability: calm/highly-strung
- Liveliness: spontaneous/restrained
- Openness to Change: flexible/attached to the familiar
- Perfectionism: controlled/undisciplined
- Privacy: discreet/open
- Reasoning: abstract/concrete
- Rule-Consciousness: conforming/non-conforming
- Self-Reliance: self-sufficient/dependent
- Sensitivity: tender-hearted/tough-minded.
- Social Boldness: uninhibited/shy

- Tension: impatient/relaxed
- Vigilance: suspicious/trusting
- Warmth: outgoing/reserved

Try one of the free 16PF tests for yourself at: https://openpsychometrics.org/tests/16PF.php. This one consists of 164 statements about yourself, for each you need to indicate how accurate it is on the scale of (1) disagree (2) slightly disagree (3) niether agree nor disagree (4) slightly agree (5) agree. It will take about ten minutes to complete.

Finally, we turn to Cappfinity, which is increasingly popular among employers.

INDUSTRY INSIGHT

Strengths Profile by Cappfinity

What Cappfinity recruiters say about strengths:

Organisations and recruiters use strengths-based assessments to authentically find out what their candidates love to do, do well and might be good at in the future – they are focused on finding the right people for the right role. Strengths-based assessments measure natural engagement and motivation, which are just as important as capability when it comes to creating the best fit between an individual and the role they have applied for.

Research has shown that only one in three people can naturally say what their strengths are without having taken a strengths-based assessment beforehand. When people talk about strengths, most people think about the things they are good at. That's right to an extent, but there is much more to strengths. A strength is defined by three key areas: *performance* (how well you perform when using these strengths), *energy* (how energised you are by using these strengths) and *use* (how often you use these strengths).

The Strengths Profile assessment identifies and breaks down our strengths into four action-based quadrants: realised strengths, unrealised strengths, learned behaviours and weaknesses (see below). the Strengths Profile is a product by Cappfinity, who specialise in authentic assessment, development and transformation.

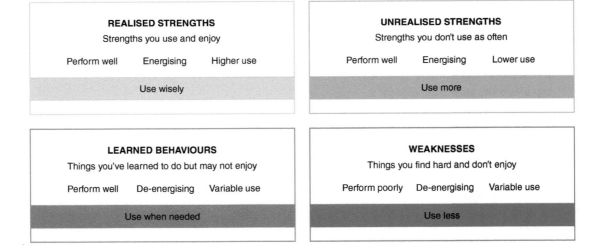

Figure 32.1 Strengths profile

Source: Kindly provided and permission given by Lauren Scarlett, Cappfinity

Companies such as Legal and General, Deloitte, EY and Grant Thornton use Cappfinity tests, aimed at assessing how accurate you are and applying numerical, verbal and critical reasoning tests. The methods they use include editing passages of text, ranking multiple choices and drag-and-drop passages. The case study outlines their approach. More information on these tests can be found at www.assessment day.co.uk/capp-verbal.htm.

CONCLUSION

In this chapter we have covered:

- The main types of aptitude and personality tests you may have to undertake as part of securing a graduate role in the THE sectors
- What different tests are looking for and how they are used by employers
- How best to prepare yourself for psychometric tests in terms of practice, research and mental preparation

FURTHER READING AND USEFUL WEB RESOURCES

de Raad, B. E., & Perugini, M. E. (2002). *Big Five Assessment*. Hogrefe & Huber Publishers.

Houston, K and Cunningham, E. (2015) *How to Succeed at Assessment Centres*. London: Palgrave Macmillan.

Useful web resources

Assessment Day provides an excellent set of free downloadable resources and examples: https://www.assessmentday.co.uk/

Institute of Psychometric Coaching https://www.psychometricinstitute.com.au/Psychometric-Guide.html.

Mathcentre – www.mathcentre.ac.uk. Useful site to help you update and refresh your numerical skills.

Prospects (2019) https://www.prospects.ac.uk/careers-advice/interview-tips/psychometric-tests

Psychometric Success – http: Psychometricsuccess.com

33 ASSESSMENT AND RECRUITMENT CENTRES

CHAPTER LEARNING OBJECTIVES

By the end of this chapter you should be able to:

- Articulate how assessment centres work and what recruiters are looking for
- Describe the kinds of tests, exercises and processes used in an assessment centre, especially those in the tourism, events and hospitality sectors.
- Plan your preparation to attend and succeed at an assessment centre
- Reflect on how you might improve your own performance at an assessment centre and in the various tests you will face
- Draw on examples and case studies to identify some successful strategies

GLOSSARY

- **Assessment centre:** a series of tests undertaken as part of a recruitment exercise and not a physical location
- **E-tray:** similar to the 'in-tray' exercise mentioned in Chapter 32, this is an electronic 'in-tray' e.g. emails and online files
- **Ice-breakers:** activities designed to warm candidates up, used to introduce people to each other in a fun yet constructive way
- **Interpersonal skills:** how you relate to and engage with people i.e. listening skills, persuasion, diplomacy, mediation, composure and patience

INTRODUCTION

This chapter looks at the role of **assessment centres** in the recruitment of employees in the THE sectors (Nickson, 2013). Around two-thirds of employers use an assessment centre process to recruit graduate-level staff (mainly the larger employers). Assessment centres aim to assess your skills against key job competencies and give employers an insight into your abilities and personality. This chapter will ensure you feel prepared for an assessment centre, covering the format and structure of them and providing an overview of the different types of tests including presentations (how to give a good one, building on Chapter 7), role play, **e-tray** exercises and business scenarios. This chapter includes insights from THE employers who use assessment centres and includes case studies from graduates. This chapter should be read in conjunction with Chapter 31 on interviews and Chapter 32 on psycho-metric tests, as a large part of succeeding at assessment centres relies on getting through several aptitude and personality tests.

WHAT IS AN ASSESSMENT CENTRE AND WHY ARE THEY USED?

Given that interviews and application forms often only just provide a snapshot rather than holistic assessment, employers need a way to select the best candidate and use methods that provide a more rounded picture of potential employees. Increasingly, assessment centres are regarded as a fair way of assessing a candidate (Houston and Cunningham, 2016). Potential employers will assess various aspects of how you work and your skill set so it is advisable to be aware of your skills and those you need to develop (covered in the chapters that make up Section B).

GETTING TO THE ASSESSMENT CENTRE

Recruiters use a number of different ways to shortlist applicants. The standard methods are through application form, CV and letter, and online tests (Chapters 29–32), but some of the more unusual tasks used to shortlist candidates for an invite to an assessment centre include:

* Social media activity: e.g. write ten Tweets about yourself (Houston and Cunningham 2016: 18)
* Create a brief YouTube clip about a destination of your choice, demonstrating how you undertake research, communicate ideas and engage in basic marketing techniques
* Leave recruiters a brief telephone message about why you want the job (this tests how you might communicate with customers)
* Psychometric tests (see Chapter 32)

WHAT TO EXPECT DURING AN ASSESSMENT CENTRE

Assessment centres are expensive to run, so they usually happen at the end of the recruitment pro-cess. You are likely to have been asked to complete a few online psychometric tests (Chapter 32) before you are invited to an assessment centre. You should practice these tests, as you may also be expected to undertake some on the assessment day. The more common ones to be held in person will be ability or aptitude tests (numerical and verbal reasoning), critical thinking and personality tests. Most assessment centres will follow a similar format over a day or two. They will start with introductions to the assessors and other candidates. The day will be split into sections and after each section, unsuccessful candidates might be asked to leave. Usually you will be split into small groups and then asked to work in these groups for discussions, and activities. Don't regard other candidates as your competition (although they are!): you will feel more comfortable if you make friends and work together.

STUDENT INSIGHT

Jeannie's experience of an assessment centre

Jeannie was invited to attend an assessment centre for a graduate-level sales position for an international travel company. She was anxious about doing well and recalls her first experience and what helped put her at ease.

'I was scared about what to expect for the day. I didn't know anyone else there and had stayed overnight near their office to ensure I was there on time. I would recommend doing this if you live far away from where the assessment centre is taking place. When I arrived and checked in, I was one of the first and sat in a waiting room. The receptionist was lovely and tried to put me at ease but I felt incredibly anxious and had not been able to eat that morning.

'Thankfully, another women came to sit near me and smiled. I introduced myself and she asked if I was here for the recruitment day. She said that she was feeling really worried about it all. It was lovely as she felt exactly the same as me, and I was able to reassure her that we would be fine – who would have thought I would be able to do that, as I was so worried too! She told me what university she was from, and we really hit it off. To my surprise we were later put in the same group for a team exercise and because we had chatted in the waiting room already, we were able to get on immediately and felt at ease. I think the task was so much easier already having someone I knew in the group. I would advise other students facing these kinds of centre so be friendly and say "hi" to people as it really put me at ease too.'

Some of the more common activities that are used in recruitment to tourism, hospitality and event sectors include the following:

- Written report under timed conditions
- In-tray or prioritisation exercise
- Group exercises and discussions
- Presentations (see Chapter 7)
- A research activity (e.g. analysis of data)
- Role play with a focus on customer service
- A panel interview (see Chapter 31)

It is likely that you will have to complete individual and group exercises. The most common individual tests will be an interview (Chapter 31), psychometric tests (Chapter 32), a timed written report (Chapter 6), and an in-tray exercise. You should ensure you do your research about the company and the role (Rook, 2013).

===== ACTIVITY =====

What exercises would you expect at a recruitment centre for a role as an Events and Hospitality Officer?

Think about the skills and knowledge you might need to demonstrate for the role of 'Events and Hospitality Officer' below. What tests might you expect at an assessment centre? Think about the skills and knowledge required and then match them with the tests from the list above and those in Chapter 32. Complete a table like the one below.

Table 33.1   Skills and knowledge mapped to assessment method

	Potential assessment/test method
Skills to be tested	
Knowledge to be tested	

Advert: We are looking for a highly competent, well organised, customer-focused graduate to help organise and develop our events and hospitality business. This is an exciting opportunity for someone who has online marketing skills and enjoys direct contact with customers to deliver an enjoyable experience. You must have excellent marketing, organisational and communication skills, with a highly customer-focused approach. A good working knowledge of Microsoft Office applications is essential. The main responsibilities are as follows:

Marketing

- Support the implementation of the promotion of all events and tourism initiatives.
- To keep the website updated and oversee website development and social media accounts.
- To analyse and present website use statistics to the senior team.
- To help in the design and print of marketing materials
- To help organise and attend marketing events to showcase facilities to relevant market sectors.

Event Delivery

- To help the Events Manager deliver events and be the main point of contact for customers.
- To coordinate all suppliers during the event and ensure that the event runs smoothly
- To be responsible for the security and safety of the guests and the site.

Sales and administration

- To help in the production of the budget and report on financial performance to the senior team
- To deal with enquiries and respond efficiently with relevant information and literature.
- To meet potential clients on site, discuss their requirements and show them the facilities.
- To co-organise the ongoing maintenance required to the wedding and event facilities.
- To manage the events diary and manage customer database and update as necessary

UNDERTAKING A WRITTEN REPORT OR CASE STUDY EXERCISE IN TIMED CONDITIONS

You should try to remember the principles of writing a report outlined in Chapter 6. These kinds of tests are partly to ensure the work you produce is your own and to test how well you can write, analyse and process information in a limited time period. While working in THE, you may have to respond to a crisis such as the need to evacuate a ship or hotel, or deal with customer complaints. In the assessment centre, you may be asked to respond to a case study or scenario, such as being given materials to read about a hotel, destination or travel company and answer questions, perhaps in response to a recent news event such as the collapse of Thomas Cook.

 ━━━━ ACTIVITY ━━━━━━━━━━━━━━━

A brief analysis of why you think Thomas Cook collapsed in 2019

You will be expected to have a good knowledge of current affairs, particularly relating to the sector in which you hope to work. You might be asked to write around 1000 words on such a scenario. Sketch out a plan or Mind Map on how you might approach this question. Things you should consider including when approaching this writing task might include:

- A very brief history of Thomas Cook
- Financial mis-management and excessive executive pay including for their CEO, pension deficit and mounting debts
- The disastrous merger in 2007
- Increasing competition from the internet market and online travel agents where people now pull their own packages together
- Rise of low-cost airlines, political unrest and terrorism
- Prospect of a hard Brexit put some customers off booking
- Weather issues – climate change and a heatwave in 2018 meant customers delayed holidays or stayed at home
- In the end, Thomas Cook was unable to secure a £200m lifeline from the banks

Other similar questions you might be asked:

- What can other travel agencies learn from the collapse of Thomas Cook?
- What could have Thomas Cook done differently to prevent it collapsing?
- How should CEOs be held account for the collapse of the company?

IN-TRAY OR E-TRAY EXERCISE

Although you may have completed an exercise like this online to secure the assessment centre invite (see Chapter 32), you may also be asked to perform a prioritisation task in person. A simple but effective way to think about such tasks is the 'do, delegate, delay' sequence (Houston and Cunningham, 2015: 158.). An example might be an email inbox you have to cover for another colleague. You need to decide what requires immediate action or escalation, and what emails should be prioritised. It is important to check the dates and think about the people involved and their potential influence. To practice an e-tray or in-tray exercise try the following websites:

- https://www.assessmentday.co.uk/e-tray-exercise.htm
- https://www.jobtestprep.co.uk/free-in-tray-exercise
- https://targetjobs.co.uk/careers-advice/assessment-centres/275463-what-are-in-tray-exercises

Try the example in the activity below.

ACTIVITY

Dealing with the email inbox

There are eight emails you need to consider and action when you start at an events management company. Rank them (1–10) in order of priority with 1 being the highest priority and then explain why you have ranked them in this way

Table 33.2   E-tray exercise

	Email	Priority (1-10)	Justify your rank and the action required
A	Your line manager needs 50 copies of the business plan by the end of the day for a client briefing		
B	A company wishes to arrange a meeting with a view to employing the company to run an event in the summer		
C	The launch event venue for Friday has fallen through. A new event venue needs to be found for 100 guests		
D	A colleague has fallen ill and is unable to cover a presentation today		
E	You need to complete your induction training from HR within a month		
F	The team have asked when you are free this week to have a social drink		
G	You have not received your contract from HR		
H	The catering firm is now unable to make the event that your company is responsible for tomorrow		

This could be a very stressful situation so read them through carefully and think what needs to be done now and what has the most significant impact on the company's reputation and the business. In events, unexpected problems can arise such as the catering pulling out or venues being suddenly unavailable. You also need to know what to delegate. For example, being new you are unlikely to be able to cover a presentation – but who can? Get them on it ASAP! These issues need to be your priority given the potential impact on the business. The socials, future bookings, your HR issues and training can wait until after the immediate client problems are addressed because if an event doesn't run, it can spell disaster for an events company!

UNDERTAKING GROUP EXERCISES AT AN ASSESSMENT CENTRE

Group exercises are used at assessment centres to measure how you engage with teamwork and behave in a group. High Fliers research (2014) found 79% of graduate recruiters use group exercises. THE courses are often assessed with group work and although sometimes unpopular, this should give you an excellent insight into how you might tackle such exercises. As with most assessment exercises at university or college, you are not usually assigned a particular role as part of the assessment will be based on how a leader is chosen, who develops the ideas, who organises the team and the roles (see Chapter 15). The kinds of skills group exercises seeks to test

- Communication skills
- Leadership and influence
- Team working ability
- Decisiveness and critical thinking ability
- Business acumen
- How you perform tasks under pressure
- Your social skills and confidence (sometimes the dinners and lunches will also be used to assess how you interact with people)
- How skills and behaviour link to the role
- **Interpersonal skills** (how you engage with other people)

 REFLECTION EXERCISE

Group exercise skills

How do you rate yourself against these group exercise skills? What might you need to improve?

Often you will be put into a group of around 6–16 people and given tasks to complete. During a group exercise, you are likely to find yourself in group of diverse individuals, potentially from around the world. One approach you could take is to encourage the quieter ones to share their views and the louder and more overbearing ones to listen to the other candidates. If someone is quiet or reserved during your group exercise, make a point of asking their opinion. It will help if you learn people's names and refer to them by name during the exercise. Skills of diplomacy and influence that demonstrate skills of collaboration will certainly be noted by the assessors. It is not about who speaks the most, but how you tactfully encourage people to contribute. If you want to make a good and relevant point for the task, make sure you articulate it to the group but don't seek to dominate the conversation. Consider your body language (Chapter 14) as people will want to engage with someone who seems open, friendly and approachable. On the flip side, some of the things you need to avoid in a group scenario are not listening to others, speaking over people, not taking the exercise seriously (but also taking it too seriously!), and not speaking or contributing much.

BREAKING THE ICE

It is likely that you will be expected to get to know your team and ice-breaker activities may be used for this. Although they are used to help facilitate introductions, they can also be part of the assessment, so be prepared. You may be expected to share something interesting about yourself, so come prepared with a couple of interesting things to say about yourself! You won't have long for the exercise so rather than spending the whole time thinking of memorable and unusual examples, have them at the forefront of your mind so you can share them confidently. This is your chance to make a good first impression with your group and the assessors!

═══ ACTIVITY ═══

Ice-breaker example

Everyone is given ten minutes to think about what animal best represents their personality and why. Then you will need to illustrate this in a drawing you can show to the other candidates via a short presentation
How might you tackle this exercise? What will you say? What will you draw?

Other industry-relevant **ice-breakers** might include choosing a country you would like to work in and saying why, or naming three things a hotel must offer and why. After the ice-breakers, you may be given a number of group tasks which could range from a business scenario to work through or problem to solve, to a group challenge which has little to do with the company or sector (but everything to do with assessing how you rise to the challenge with others).

BUSINESS SCENARIO EXERCISE

Your group may be given a fictional scenario and asked to collaborate on something like creating a business plan to set up a new hotel in a new destination, planning an event, or working out the best location for a new restaurant. Remember the recruiter is looking at how you developed the final plan, rather than whether it is 'right' or not.

DEALING WITH COMPLAINTS AND PROBLEMS

In service-focused sectors, you will be customer facing and although it will be greatly rewarding, it is likely you will have to deal with customer problems, complaints and issues. The assessment centre is likely to want to know how you and your group deal with these kinds of situations. Think about the two scenarios below and how you might approach them:

═══ ACTIVITY ═══

A letter of complaint

Imagine you are a hotel manager and receive this complaint letter. As a group, outline how you would respond. You have 30 minutes.

(Continued)

'Dear Hotel Manager

I recently stayed at your hotel and am now writing to raise some serious concerns. I am always very careful to undertake research before booking where to stay and your website is beautifully presented with wonderful photos of the hotel. I was impressed that there are many positive reviews and you have been awarded four stars, which convinced us that this was the place to stay for our annual holiday.

I was also reassured by a number of our friends who have stayed with you that this was a wonderful place and they highly recommended your hotel. During the booking process, I specifically requested a sea view room and your colleagues informed me that we would be placed in the North Wing, which is quieter and guaranteed a sea view room. Unfortunately, when we checked in, we were told this information was not on your records and the North Wing was full. We were therefore given a different room, which was not quiet and did not have a sea view! The room and bathroom were very dirty and smelt damp, so much so that we had to keep the window open all night to get rid of the smell. The pillows and bedding seemed extremely old and worn and when we called to ask for different bedding, the reception said they were unable to help until the morning! When morning came, the pillows and duvet we were offered were just as worn, including a stain on one!

I complained, but the front of house staff did not seem to take my concern seriously. It was noisy most nights with people coming and going outside until 2am and the bathroom pipes made a constant dripping sound inside the walls. I am astonished that the website and reviews we read are of the same hotel! Given our terrible experience, I would like a refund for our total stay as you should have records of me raising issues with your staff from day one.

Yours faithfully,

Mrs Customer'

As outlined in Chapter 20, another possible scenario is a natural disaster.

 **ACTIVITY**

Crisis on an island resort

As a group you will need to agree what your priorities should be in this scenario.

'Your group are resort managers of an island resort hotel that is cut off from the mainland by a hurricane. You need to deal with the loss of communications to the mainland, rationing of supplies (food), and a medical emergency.'

What kinds of actions should you undertake and why? Are you confident you have read enough about what similar island resorts have done? What emergency plans are in place at these kinds of resorts?

Adapted from Armstrong (2003)

ROLEPLAY

Armstrong (2003) finds that role-playing in tourism management is an effective learning tool and High Fliers (2014) found 35% of graduate recruiters use this method of assessment. In a roleplay exercise, you will usually be assigned roles, such as tourist, marketing director, or business owner. Try to put yourself in the mindset of your role and work to get the best outcome for your character and for the group. This kind of exercise aims to test how well you can see a situation from different perspectives. A good tip offered by the AssessmentDay (2020) recruitment team is 'to focus the group's attention on the objectives set by the exercise. It's easy to go along with the flow and lose track of the objectives. A gentle reminder to the group, along with an awareness of time, will show that you are focused on the objectives that have been set.'

As an individual, you might be asked to make a phone call to a supplier or customer and this might be a roleplay with an assessor. In this case, keep calm and ensure you read all the information provided before you embark on the test. Be calm, clear and professional. In a group, a typical scenario might be that a hotel company wants to build a new hotel in an environmentally sensitive area. It is likely to bring jobs and income to the local people. You might take one of the following roles and argue for/against the development:

- A local tour operator
- The hotel developer
- An international tourist
- Local fisherwomen
- The mayor or member of local government
- Conservationist
- Wildlife photographer

TEAM CHALLENGES AND MORE PHYSICAL TASKS

Although in some ways these are the most fun, they also reveal how people work together. They are designed to assess your influencing skills, how you communicate with others and whether you take the lead or facilitate others. The kinds of activities you might be asked to undertake are to build something, move something using unusual objects, or develop a 'dream team' using historical or fictitious figures.

 REFLECTION EXERCISE

Building a tower to balance a sweet

You are put in a group of five candidates and asked to build the tallest tower you can out of straws and balance a large sweet at the top. What do you think assessors are looking for? What sort of person do your assessors want to work with?

PRESENTATIONS AT ASSESSMENT CENTRES

In an assessment centre scenario you will have very little time to prepare a presentation (see Chapter 7), unlike at university when you may have had weeks to prepare. There is a number of potential presentation types used here:

- Prepared individual presentation – the topic is sent to you in advance as part of your invitation;

- Unprepared individual presentation – you are given the topic during the assessment centre exercise; and
- Group presentation – you are allocated a group and topic and are expected to work with your group.

If you have to provide an individual presentation, remember that the short preparation time is part of the test – they will want to see you adapt to the situation and embrace the challenge. You might be asked not to use PowerPoint or visual aids, so ensure you read the instructions carefully. If you can use visuals, then consider an alternative to PowerPoint, which can be overused – think about a flipchart, a video or artefact (e.g. something relevant from your travels). It is important that text is large, uses a sans serif font and keeps diagrams simple. Ensure you research the company and role, as it likely you will be expected to reflect this in your presentation. It is also useful to ensure you are up to speed with current affairs and perhaps have a few statistics in your head about the size and scale of the industry. Regardless of whether the presentation is planned or not, remember the simple rules of giving a short presentation:

- Dress smartly and smile
- Introduce yourself to the audience and think about to engage with them
- Speak clearly and keep good eye contact
- Make it memorable: the assessor will be reviewing a few during the day so make sure they remember you for the right reason!
- Less is more, so use the format of an introduction, three main points and then a summary
- Vary the delivery in terms of pace, visuals, music, data, quotes, stories. Sometimes silence is very powerful
- Practice it (even if it is a surprise on the day, you should mentally rehearse it in your head or in a quiet space). You need to avoid reading from a script and timekeeping is key.

BEING OBSERVED: WHAT ARE ASSESSORS LOOKING FOR IN GROUP WORK?

Assessors will generally have a scorecard to complete for each member of the group, linked to several skills and competencies. Before you start your assessment, you should think about what these competencies might be based on the job description. In the THE industries, assessors will want to see collaboration and good teamwork, how you influence others, your organisational skills, working under pressure, listening skills, analytical skills, assertiveness and how creative you are in terms of solutions to tasks. Do remember that usually assessors are not looking for the person who shouts the loudest or talks the most.

Do ensure you remember the kinds of approaches mentioned in Section A about critical and reflective thinking. You need to demonstrate that you have independence of mind, and you can weigh up issues, evidence and challenges. Employers will want someone who can think for themselves and challenge the status quo.

 ━━━ EMPLOYER INSIGHT ━━━━━━━━━━━━

Virgin Holidays, Head Office Roles

Virgin Holidays use assessment centres as part of their graduate recruitment process, and state that 'you can expect to be with us for all or part of a day and they're made up of a number of different exercises.

We appreciate that it can seem a long process for an all-day interview, but we often receive feedback on how candidates have enjoyed the day and made new friends!'

Virgin Holidays assessment centres usually include a group discussion, roleplay, ability tests, presentations and behavioural and biographical interviews.

Virgin note that, 'Effective team working is vitally important in all areas of our business, so a group discussion can be a useful tool to help us see how you relate to one another when you work as a team. We'll give you a topic to discuss in a given time and then our assessors will observe the group for the duration of the exercise. Don't be put off by assessors making notes, we are purely writing observations of the behaviours we see you demonstrate throughout the exercise.'

In terms of roleplays, they expect you to re-enact a scenario you might find yourself in as part of the role. It gives assessors 'a good insight into how you may handle certain challenges that might happen in your role. We are aware that sometimes the role you have applied for might be a completely different step in your career direction so we'll ensure you have all the tools that you'll need to complete this exercise.'

In behavioural interviews, you will be asked to think of examples of specific work-based situations you've been in. They ask that you 'tell us how you handled it and what the outcome was. It might be worth thinking about this before your interview. The more detail you can recall, the better.' A biographical interview involves a discussion about your CV and employment history, outlining what you've done, what your achievements are and why you've made certain career choices. It might help you to bring an up-to-date copy of your CV to the interview with you. They state, 'our philosophy is that interviews are a two-way process, so it's just as important for you to find out about life at Virgin Holidays and if we are the right fit for your career as it is for us to find out more about you.'

More details available from: https://careers.virginholidays.co.uk/head-office

Table 33.3   Preparing for an assessment centre

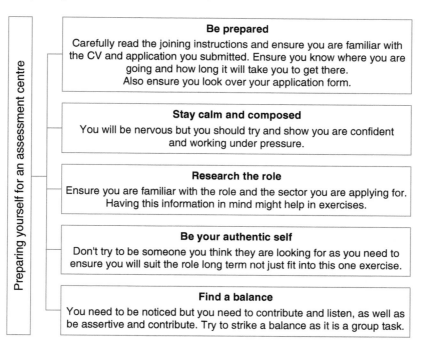

GETTING PREPARED

As Houston and Cunningham (2016: 10) point out, although assessment centres are seen as a fairer way to assess candidates, 'the stress is magnified because you have to "perform" well throughout an extended time period'. Therefore, you need to prepare yourself thoroughly. Here are five top tips for preparation.

DEALING WITH SETBACKS

Inevitably, some candidates will be unsuccessful. If this is you, then do not despair. It is hard to re-energise yourself after a knockback and it can be hard not to take it personally. One of the main attributes that universities and colleges try to build in their students is resilience and employers in hospitality and sales specifically want candidates who can show resilience given the long hours and levels of stress involved (Targetjobs.ac.uk, 2019b).

It is important that you ask for feedback from the employer and evaluate your own performance. It is useful to write down how you think you could have performed better after the assessment centre (even if you get the role!), and what you did well. See the setback as an opportunity to think about the career you want, the skills you need to develop further, and use it as an example when you are asked about how you bounce back in a future interview. You might want to give yourself a break after a rejection to ensure you are in the right mindset to apply for another role.

CONCLUSION

In this chapter we have covered:

- Why assessment centres are used in graduate recruitment
- The kinds of tests and activities you may be requested to complete at an assessment centre (individual and group)
- how you might tackle some of the more common assessment tasks
- advice on helping you prepare for an assessment centre
- examples of some THE employers that use assessment centres and considered what they may be looking for from you
- how to deal with setbacks and reflect on your own performance

FURTHER READING

Armstrong, E. K. (2003). 'Applications of role-playing in tourism management teaching: An evaluation of a learning method'. *Journal of Hospitality, Leisure, Sport and Tourism Education*, 2(1), 5–16.
Houston, K., and Cunningham, E. (2015). *How to Succeed at Assessment Centres*. London: Palgrave Macmillan International Higher Education.
Rook, S. (2013). *The Graduate Career Guidebook*. London: Palgrave Macmillan International Higher Education.

Useful web resources

There are also some useful assessment centre resource sites available on university career pages:

- The University of Sydney (they have an assessment centre tool): https://sydney.edu.au/careers/students/applying-for-jobs/assessment-centres.html
- University of Birmingham Assessment Centre pack – downloadable pdf
- University of Bradford – https://www.bradford.ac.uk/careers/applications/assessment-centres/
- University of Oxford – http://www.careers.ox.ac.uk/assessment-centres/

Prospects: https://www.prospects.ac.uk/careers-advice/interview-tips/assessment-centres

Monster.co.uk: https://www.monster.co.uk/career-advice/article/what-is-an-assessment-centre

Grad Australia: https://gradaustralia.com.au/interviews-and-assessments/how-to-ace-assessment-centre-day

Glassdoor: https://www.glassdoor.co.uk/blog/how-to-succeed-at-an-assessment-centre/

SECTION F

YOUR OWN WAY? ENTREPRENEURSHIP AND EMERGENT OPPORTUNITIES

Level: 6

34 DEVELOPING IDEAS AND CONCEPTS FOR A NEW BUSINESS

== CHAPTER LEARNING OBJECTIVES ===========

By the end of this chapter you should be able to:

- Understand and explain the terms entrepreneur, enterprise, start-up business and business plan
- Expand and develop your own skills set as an entrepreneur, especially in the tourism, hospitality and events market
- Confidently explore a suitable business idea that is right for you
- Create a viable business plan

== GLOSSARY ===========

- **Entrepreneur:** a person who sets up and develops business ideas, using creativity, knowledge and their skills and talents
- **Business plan:** the document that you create before starting the business to outline and explain all the important areas of the business idea
- **Financial statement cash flow forecast:** an outline of the financial position of your business, including income, expenses investment, projected sales and projected profit
- **Start-up business:** a new business or potential business that has just opened or is about to open

INTRODUCTION

When thinking about **entrepreneurs**, some famous names come to mind: Jeff Bezos (founder of Amazon), Oprah Winfrey (founder of OWN), Bill Gates (founder of Microsoft), Mark Zuckerberg (founder of Facebook), Ratan Tata (founder of Tata Steel), Anita Roddick (founder of The Body Shop) or Ariana Huffington (founder of The Huffington Post and CEO of Thrive Global), Jack Ma (founder of Alibaba), Sir Richard Branson (founder of Virgin), Steve Jobs (founder of Apple) and Michael Sual Dell (founder of Dell Technologies). However, there are many more entrepreneurs who have been successful, on a smaller scale, but are still equally as enterprising and entrepreneurial. Many of these are in the tourism, hospitality and events sector. Examples include Darrell Wade who co-founded Intrepid Travel, or Grace Lee founder and CEO of WishPoints (an app that records travel wishes).

This chapter will explore entrepreneurship, developing new ideas and concepts and the areas that need to be covered when thinking of setting up a new business. Every business relies on selling something (a product or a service). An entrepreneur is someone who can look at an existing or new product and/or service and identify a gap in the market that they can exploit. We explore what is meant by the term 'entrepreneur' and how you can start developing the skills you will need to become one in the THE sector (Rimmington et al., 2009; Sotiriadis, 2018). The chapter then shows you how to evaluate your current skills and identify where and how you can build the skills you need. Additionally, you will learn how to identify a suitable business opportunity and create a **business plan**. This chapter uses activities, case study insights and Think points throughout, as well as theory and practical examples to help you develop your understanding of setting up a new venture.

WHAT IS AN ENTREPRENEUR?

An entrepreneur is someone that starts up a business, often organising and running it entirely in the early stages. They take on the risk associated with the start-up of a new business, including the financial risk, in the hope that they will benefit from the eventual profits. Entrepreneurs have an entrepreneurial mind-set through which they demonstrate enterprising skills, behaviours and attitudes across a diversity of concepts (Kuratko, 2014). These include intuitive decision-making, the capacity to make things happen autonomously, networking, initiative, the ability to identify opportunities, creative problem-solving, strategic thinking and self-efficacy (Stokes, 2010). An entrepreneur focuses on the application of these enterprising skills and the entrepreneurial mind-set in setting up a new venture, developing/growing an existing venture or designing an entrepreneurial organisation. Stokes suggests that an entrepreneur 'can break through the resistance to change that exists in society' (Stokes, 2010: 14) to challenge the status quo and tradition to implement new ideas or ways of doing things. The context might be business, social or charitable enterprise, non-governmental organisations or public sector bodies. They are innovators, creating and exploiting opportunities, resulting in better products and services, systems and ways of managing people and organisations. The successful pursuit of innovation is a function of individual enterprising endeavour and entrepreneurial organisation capacity. Entrepreneurship is a necessary pre-condition for innovation.

Entrepreneurs see things differently (Gibb, 2011), they are able to identify something unique that others have not offered i.e. an unique selling point (USP). They are excellent at seizing the opportunity and making it happen, rather than just sitting on it or waiting for someone else to see it. Additionally, they follow their interests. It is much easier to be passionate about something if you are already interested in that product or service. There are many virtual and very successful entrepreneurs using YouTube or similar platforms, for example.

CAN YOU DEVELOP ENTREPRENEURIAL SKILLS?

There are many theories on whether you can develop the skills needed to be an entrepreneur. Research has shown that entrepreneurship can be taught effectively (Kaplan & Waren, 2010; Henry et al., 2005; Stokes, 2010) and that all individuals have some capacity for entrepreneurial behaviour. Skill can develop these with practice, but you may find some of the relevant skills more difficult than others. Firstly you need to identify the skills you have and which ones need development.

EVALUATE YOUR BUSINESS SKILLS AND KNOWLEDGE

Complete the activities below to assess where you need to develop entrepreneurial skills. This is a reflective practice activity (see Chapter 10).

 ACTIVITY

How entrepreneurial are you?

Answer yes or no to the questions below and think about how you might develop these skills if you answer 'no' to any of the questions.

Table 34.1   How entrepreneurial are you

Entrepreneurial Attribute	Y/N	Entrepreneurial Behaviour	Y/N	How can you develop these skills?
Are you self-confident?		Do you look for opportunities?		
Are you ambitious?		Do you take the initiative or lead in situations where it is needed?		
Are you hardworking and dedicated to succeed?		Do you grasp opportunities?		
Are you action-orientated?		Will you take calculated risks if needed?		
Are you able to work independently (autonomously)?		Do you welcome the opportunity to solve problems in a creative way?		
Are you able to listen and not jump to conclusions or action?		Do you take on the advice of others and consider its merit?		

 ACTIVITY

Creative Attribute: do you allow yourself to be creative?

Table 34.2　Creative Attributes

Creative Attribute: do you allow yourself to be creative?	Y/N	What can you do to help you develop these skills?
Are you open to new experiences? Being open to new experiences allows you to experience new things and understand and develop new and creative solutions		
Are you observant? When you observe a situation well, you are more likely to see both positive and negative issues, which allows you to explore how to improve the situation		
Do you have a curiosity and an interest in making changes to improve things?		
Are you willing to take calculated risks when you have identified a solution to a problem or situation? You need to be confident in implementing your creative solution		
Do you give yourself the time to think creatively, or do you rush into a decision? Without giving yourself the time to think, it is difficult to be creative. You will find that you are reacting rather than reflecting		
Do you give yourself permission to fail? Fear of failure inhibits creativity		
Are you open-minded and able to listen to others?		
Do you have good communication skills? Good communication skills are important if you want people to take you seriously		

Once you have identified the areas that require further development, you can find ways to develop these skills. It may be a short course, an entrepreneurial society at your university, an online course, a module that teaches enterprise and entrepreneurship at your university or researching on the internet and identifying useful self-help websites. Here are some websites and YouTube videos you might like to visit to help you develop your skills:

- www.business.com/articles/12-business-skills-you-need-to-master/
- www.business.qld.gov.au/running-business/employing/staff-development/business-skills-planning/develop-skills
- www.impactfactory.com/library/business-skills
- www.youtube.com/watch?v=Ihs4VFZWwn4
- www.youtube.com/watch?v=dulBMqkuHes

THINK POINT

We all have skills and talents. Sometimes we take them for granted or are just not aware of them. Think about the skills that you have that makes you stand out from other people. Do you have an outgoing personality, a good head for figures, or a large capacity for hard work? How could you use the skills you already have to develop your business idea?

STUDENT INSIGHT

Michael, recent events management student and now an entrepreneur

As a student in my second year I believed that I wasn't a creative person. This was a worry for me, as I wanted to start up my own events planning business. Without the skills to set the business up and make the business unique to the customers, I thought this was only ever going to be a dream. I happened to talk to a lecturer one day who taught enterprise and entrepreneurship, as he was covering for one of our tourism lecturers who was off sick. He introduced himself at the beginning of the class and I thought he would be an ideal person to chat to. He had a lot of experience, not only as a lecturer but also as a small business-owner and a consultant for small business start-ups. I really do believe that this chance meeting, changed my life. After the class I asked him if we could meet up and have a chat about an idea I have. He was more than willing to make the time and we met up.

At the meeting I told him my fears and concerns that I did not have the skills needed to start up a business. The first thing he said to me was, 'you might not know you have them, or you might not have them, but that doesn't mean you can't have them'. He put it into perspective for me by saying, 'do you think that a brain surgeon is born with the skills to operate on a brain? They have to learn these skills, practice them, build their confidence in them before they put them into practice on a person. This is no different to the skills that you will need to run your own business. You learn some of them as you go along, and others you can learn here.' He advised me to join the Entrepreneur's Society, get involved with other enterprise initiatives, like the 'Big Pitch', to help meet like-minded people. We continued to talk for a little while longer and then he sent me off with a small project. He provided me with a simple template on creating a business plan and asked me to complete as much of the template as possible and then meet up with him again. This gave me the opportunity to think about things I had not considered before and also areas that I needed to find solutions for. It also helped me understand that I could be creative and I could learn the skills I needed to be an entrepreneur. Over the next couple of months we met up regularly, and I learnt so much from him about business and planning.

I left university four years ago and set up my business about 9 months after leaving. I now have a successful events management business, dealing with both corporate and private events and clients. I have seven people working for me fulltime and thirty people working for me part-time or temporarily. My advice to anyone who doubts themselves would be to not leave things to chance. Seek out the right people to talk to, join the local societies and groups available to you. Take a module on enterprise and entrepreneurship if you can, as all these will help you develop your skills. I learn every day from my business and face new challenges every day. I now have the confidence to deal with these. This confidence didn't happen overnight: I learnt to be confident as my skills developed. I now spend some of my time mentoring other young people who want to be entrepreneurs, I learn from them and pay forward the kindness and support that the stand-in lecturer gave to me.

HOW TO FIND THE BUSINESS IDEA THAT BEST SUITS YOU

There are many areas to start a business in, but you must choose one that suits your skills and interests. The following are a few areas that you can use as sources to help you think about the sort of business you would like to open.

 ACTIVITY

Working with the things you enjoy

Make a list of all the things that you enjoy: these can be hobbies, sports or work. From that list identify, which of these areas you might like to work in, the kind of businesses you could run and how viable you think they might be. Apply your ideas to the information below.

EXISTING BUSINESSES

Look at a business that you admire in an area that you are interested in. What is it that makes them successful? Do they offer anything that other businesses in their area do not? There are numerous opportunities in the tourism and hospitality areas, as demonstrated by recent entrepreneurs using apps to help book flights or hotels. For example, Scott Keyes who launched Scott's Cheap Flights (https://scottscheapflights.com); Yulia Denisyuk's Nomad and Jules which is a small group travel company (www.nomadandjules.co); or Natastasia Yakoub with Dame Traveller, a travel platform for women (www.dametraveler.com). The gaps in the market might include a need for better or different modes of customer service, cheaper products, more value for money or a unique product or service. Once you have identified why they are successful, consider whether you have something to add that customers want/need that is not already provided.

FRANCHISES

Franchises can be a great way to set up a 'business out of a box'. There are many benefits to opening a franchise (Kuratko, 2014), including ongoing training and guidance, a respected brand that already has appeal and brand-recognition, a proven track record for success, ongoing financial assistance and advice. However, there are also disadvantages to the franchise model, such as fees, franchisor control (i.e. you can not deviate from the set protocols and rules laid down by the franchise) and complex franchise law (Kuratko, 2014; Deakins, 2012). The ultimate source of your idea is your interest and your craft. This is especially true for YouTube, Pinterest, Instagram and Facebook entrepreneurs. They have taken their interests, hobbies and knowledge and have built successful business around their videos, from endorsements, advertising and sponsorship. Other ways to generate and find ideas include:

• A problem that someone has faced to which they could not find a solution, but which you think you have identified

- An unmet need of a customer that you have discovered at a previous place of employment or through your research
- Changes to the environment or the law – for example, climate change is at the forefront of people's minds now. How can you develop an idea that lessens the impact of tourism and hospitality on the world?
- Changes in consumer tastes and spending that have not been identified by others
- Changes in technology, including inventions or improvements that have not been implemented or exploited.

===== ACTIVITY =====

Developing ideas

Once you have had an idea, consider the following questions:

- Why is it a good idea?
- What are the assumptions about the idea?
- What type of customer will buy it or use the service?
- Why will they buy it or use the service?
- List four reasons why it will work.
- List four reasons why the idea will NOT work

If you cannot answer these questions, ask yourself why. Do you need to do more research? Is it a fundamentally unsound idea, or simply not right for you? Don't let your heart rule your head.

HOW TO GET YOUR IDEA(S) OFF THE GROUND

Once you already have an idea, and you have defined the product or service that will be offered, you should clearly, precisely and unambiguously define a market that will be served with these products or services. The activity below will help you to define these areas and give you a clear understanding of your proposed business.

===== ACTIVITY =====

Sketching out a proposed business

- Clearly define in a short paragraph what your business idea offers
- How is your business unique from other businesses in a similar area?
- In which market will you offer the product or service (local, city wide, region, country or worldwide)?
- Who will your target market be (tourists, young, middle or older people, wholesale or direct to public etc.)?
- What are the features of these consumers (sex, gender, income, ethnicity, families etc.)?

PUTTING TOGETHER A BUSINESS PLAN

There are many reasons for writing a business plan. It can be the foundation of your business and help you to keep on track. Additionally, it can be presented to a lender if you are looking for finance or investment. It can provide staff with an understanding of the mission of the business, as well as showing you and others that the business is a sound idea. The business plan outlines the company's expected course of action for the short, medium and long term. The business plan should be in the context of the industry, market, products, policies, capacity and resources relating to your business idea. It should not be a one-off exercise, but a document that is regularly used and revised. Its purpose is to help the business and the owner(s). You may find that you need more than one business plan depending on the intended audience. For example, you wouldn't want to share detailed financial information if you are showing it to the employees; equally, you wouldn't want to include staffing issues or problems that you have identified to someone you are hoping will invest in the business (Finch, 2016; Russell-Jones, 2014; Butler, 2012).

 INDUSTRY INSIGHT

Jenni's jewellery start-up

I was very lucky when I was at university, as my Travel and Tourism course had a module covering starting up a new small business. My hobby had always been making jewellery, which I sold to friends and family, although I did have a lot of pieces that I had made stored in boxes in my house. One of the assignments for the module was to create a business plan for a new **start-up business** and I decided to do mine on my jewellery business. The plan was fun to put together, although it did take me longer to complete than I thought, as I had to do a lot of research in areas that I thought I already knew about, like finding out what others were doing, what they were selling and the prices they sell at, plus I needed to know where and who my target customers would be.

I decided to set my small business up while still at university and sell some of the stock I still had and also the items that I would continue to make. It would have been impossible and far too expensive for me to open a physical shop, so I decided to open a virtual shop using Etsy and Amazon. I really thought that the plan I had put together would work and that I would be inundated with orders and make my fortune. I was disappointed at first. I hadn't been as honest with myself with the amount of sales I would get: I thought of a number and put it in without really giving it too much thought. My heart was ruling my head with the numbers. I was extremely disappointed with the sales, as people were just not visiting my virtual shops. I wasn't going to let this get me down and stop me from selling my jewellery, however. I decided that I needed to market the business differently. I wanted to show people how I made some of the jewellery so that they could see how much work and effort went into the pieces and also how each piece was unique. After doing my research, I realised that YouTube would be the best way to do this. It took a while for the YouTube channel to take off, but now I have a lot of subscribers. I film the making of the jewellery and post the videos on YouTube. My subscribers and viewers are then directed to my Etsy and Amazon stores when they watch the videos. This approach has worked really well.

I am struggling to keep up with orders, and also I make money from the advertising on YouTube. I make an excellent living, enough to put down a deposit on a house and buy a car. I have also been approached by a craft TV channel to provide a couple of sessions demonstrating on their channel. I have also been asked to write a how to book on making jewellery. I can't tell you how happy I am being my own boss. It can be stressful at times, but I enjoy the autonomy that I have with the business. My advice to anyone would be, don't be too over optimistic with your sales at the start. You need to generate interest and sales in the best way you can. Also, never give up. If you have a sound business plan and know it will work, keep looking for ways to make that happen.

WHAT SHOULD BE INCLUDED IN THE BUSINESS PLAN?

These are the key areas that you should cover in your business plan:

- At the front of your plan, include a one-page concise summary of your business and what you hope to achieve. What is the aim?
- A mission statement
- Target customers
- Date that you propose to start in business
- Names of the founders, and the functions they perform
- Address, telephone and e-mail of the enterprise
- Number of employees
- Information on current investors or sources of funding
- Brief summary of goals and plans for the future
- Time frame. Business planning can either be short term (what is to happen over the coming month, 3 months, 6 months), medium term (what is to happen over 1–2 years), or long term (what is to happen over the coming 2–5 years). Long-term planning is also often referred as strategic planning.
- Analysis of the current situation. Where are we now? What is our legal identity and location?
- Key people: management team, experience, knowledge, skills
- Future needs: training and recruitment
- Nature of the business: description, application, product/service and USP
- Market research: defining target markets, trends in the marketplace, needs of customers, benefits offered to the customers
- Competition: identify competitors' strengths and weaknesses and your own competitive edge

THINK POINT

What are the development stages for the business and the key decision points? Have you satisfied stakeholders' expectations? What are the financial assumptions and projections for the business? Who is involved in the business and how does the team work? How the ownership of the business structured? How do you expect this to change to achieve funding? How have you researched competitors?

INDUSTRY INSIGHT

Setting up a dark tourism business

When I was a student, I had many ideas about the type of business I wanted to set up. I had been working in a city renowned for its tourism and I had identified several gaps where the tourists were not being served that I believed I could fill. I had undertaken a module on Enterprise and Entrepreneurial management that taught me the fundamentals of planning and developing my business ideas. I finally chose one area that I wanted to focus on and started to develop a business plan.

(Continued)

Dark tourism was something that I was really interested in. The city I live in is medieval and there were several high-profile murders carried out in it throughout history, supposed hauntings, executions and other local crimes that people wanted to learn about. I set up a city tour business that catered for those tourists that were interested in these areas. Initially it was just me, so I had to offer different tours covering each of the areas I have mentioned. That was three years ago. I now have more than twenty-five people working for me who provide tours. The tours are specialised and often fully-booked weeks before the tour date. This has been the best experience of my life and I wouldn't want to do anything else.

The best piece of advice I can give someone who is looking at setting up their own business is to make sure you have done your research fully and created a clear business plan, setting yourself objectives and targets. It is hard work, and the business is not going to come to you initially. You have to go out and get the business and make contacts with people who can help your business grow. There are many things that you need to keep on top of when you are starting and running a business, so you need to be organised. Above all, you must deliver what you promise and give the customer what they have paid for and more if you can. An unhappy customer is someone who can damage your business. There are so many websites and social media platforms that an unhappy customer can use to destroy your hard work. Equally, these are the same areas in which a happy customer can help promote your business. A lot of my business is repeat business or from word of mouth because of the excellent service I provide.

DEFINE YOUR MAIN COMPETITORS

The next key element after the product/service and the market is your competition. Do not make the mistake of underestimating your competitors, because the success of your business in large part will depend on their performance. Here are some questions to consider:

- What are the five largest market players in the industry in which your business idea is categorised?
- What, where and how do those five major market players offer their products and services?
- What are the features of their products or services?
- What are the benefits that they provide to the market with their products or services?
- What is the resistance of the market to entry of new competitors and how difficult is it likely to be for you to enter the market?

FINANCIAL PLANNING

1. *Working capital.* This is the capital you have available today. This is determined by subtracting current liabilities from current assets. A rule of thumb says you should have £1 ($1.30) to £2 ($2.60) of current assets for every £0.75 ($0.96) of current liabilities *(exchange rate £1 sterling to $USD was 1.28 at time of publication).*
2. *Revenues.* Know your sales on a monthly, quarterly and year-to-date basis. Compare these to your plan to see if you are behind or ahead.
3. *Gross profit.* Revenues less the direct costs of producing your product represents your gross profit. In most cases, there should be 50% or more of your sales volume left over after you subtract your direct costs (cost of goods sold).
4. *Profit margin.* Subtract your general and administrative expenses from your gross profit, then divide that number by your sales. This will tell you how profitable the business is. If the number is negative, you are losing money. Some research may be needed to find out how other

businesses like yours are doing and if you find that that the typical profit margin in your industry is 12% and yours is 5%, you are not managing your business as well as your competitors.

It is also important to include a Cash Flow Forecast in a business plan (Table 34.3). This is a simple process, but a valuable one. It allows you to quickly identify where you are, if you are hitting targets and the level of your cash flow.

Table 34.3 Cash flow forecast

					Month							
Income	1	2	3	4	5	6	7	8	9	10	11	12
Capital introduced												
Loans												
Sales (inc VAT)												
Sales (0% VAT)												
Total Income												
Expenses												
Rent												
Business Rates												
Partners' Drawings												
Salaries												
Supplies (inc Vat)												
Supplies (0% VAT)												
Electricity												
Gas												
Telephone												
Water												
Internet												
Advertising												
Stationery												
Miscellaneous												
Total Expenses												
Total Income												
(Minus) Expenses												
Balance												

CONCLUSION

In this chapter we have covered:

- Entrepreneurship and other areas related to setting up your own business
- The meaning of the word 'entrepreneurship', how you can develop the skills required to become an entrepreneur and think like an entrepreneur, the importance of making sure you undertake your research and creating a real, honest business plan
- Case studies, which show that it is not always easy at first, but determination will help you succeed
- How to identify your skills

FURTHER READING

Butler, D. (2012). *Business Planning*. Hoboken: London: Taylor & Francis.

Deakins, D. (2012). *Entrepreneurship and Small Firms*. London: McGraw-Hill Higher Education.

Finch, B. (2016). *How to Write a Business Plan*. [e-book] (5th ed.) London: Kogan Page.

Leitch, C., Hill, F., and Henry, C. (2005). 'Entrepreneurship education and training – can entrepreneurship be taught? Part 1'. *Education and Training, 47*, 158-169.

Kapalan, J. M. and Warren A. C. (2010). *Patterns of Entrepreneurship Management* (3rd ed.) MA, USA: John Will & Sons.

Rimmington, M., Williams, C., and Morrison, A. (2009). *Entrepreneurship in the Hospitality, Tourism and Leisure Industries*. London: Routledge.

Russell-Jones, N. (2014). *Business Planning Pocketbook* (3rd ed.). [e-book] Alresford, Hampshire: Management Pocketbooks.

Sotiriadis, M. (2018). *The Emerald Handbook of Entrepreneurship in Tourism, Travel and Hospitality: Skills for Successful Ventures*. West Yorkshire: Emerald Publishing Limited

Stokes, D. (2010). *Entrepreneurship*. Andover, Hampshire: Cengage Learning EMEA

35

EMERGENT OPPORTUNITIES AND THE FOURTH INDUSTRIAL REVOLUTION

CHAPTER LEARNING OBJECTIVES

By the end of this chapter you will be able to:

* Describe what is meant by the terms 'Fourth' Industrial Revolution, Industry 4.0, and Tourism 4.0.
* Outline the kinds of career opportunities that might soon exist in the tourism, hospitality and events sectors
* Articulate some of the potential innovations in the industry in terms of digitally-supported personality and customisation, artificial intelligence and big data
* Identify the skills, attributes, and behaviours you will need to respond to the rapidly evolution of the THE industries

GLOSSARY

* **Blockchain technology:** a structure that stores transactional records (the block) in several databases (the chain) in a network connected through peer-to-peer nodes. It offers a distributed and decentralised ledger that records the provenance of a digital asset
* **Fourth Industrial Revolution:** a period of new digital industrial technology made possible through technology advances building on advances in human working from the first, second and third industrial revolutions
* **Industry 4.0:** a time of new digital industrial technology as processes move towards automation and seamless data exchange, which includes aspects such as the artificial intelligence, the internet of things, big data analysis and cloud computing.
* **Internet of Things:** the interconnection of digital devices in which technology is embedded in everyday objects that enables them to exchange data
* **Tourism 4.0:** the transformation of the tourism and hospitality industry using key enabling social and technological developments

INTRODUCTION

This chapter explores some of the careers opportunities that are emerging in the tourism, hospitality, and events (THE) sectors, particularly in relation to the **'Fourth Industrial Revolution'**. Whilst there are some opportunities already emerging in response to societal and technological changes, and it is also possible to predict some future ones there are some future jobs and careers that we cannot yet envisage. In many ways universities are trying to prepare students for jobs that do not yet exist. This makes it a very interesting time to be a THE student.

The chapter begins by explaining briefly what the 'Fourth Industrial Revolution' is and what its impact means for us as a global society. It then goes on to explore the key aspects of the Fourth Industrial Revolution in the context of tourism (i.e. **Tourism 4.0**), giving you an overview of the current Tourism 4.0 trends in tourism, hospitality and events, so that you have a clear idea of the environment you are graduating into and how this might impact your future career. This chapter refers back to several earlier chapters, to highlight how some of the skills and employability guidance offered throughout the text might apply to the new world of work and employment.

THE FOURTH INDUSTRIAL REVOLUTION

We are currently in the midst of the what is being labelled the 'Fourth Industrial Revolution' or '**Industry 4.0**', a period of fast-paced change in the way we communicate, live and work. The technological advances are merging the physical, digital and natural worlds in ways that 'create both huge promise and potential peril' (World Economic Forum, 2020). However, Industry 4.0 is about more than technological change: it is an opportunity to improve the lives of individuals, families, communities and organisations. The end goal of Industry 4.0 is not technological advancement, but how it can be used to enhance human lives and experiences (Chartered Institute of Tourism and Hospitality South Africa, 2020).

TOURISM 4.0

The term Tourism 4.0 describes the changes that Industry 4.0 is bringing about in the THE sectors. Whilst it is worth noting that this happening now and the future potential and impact of Tourism 4.0 is hard to predict. It is generally accepted that tourism has always responded to changes affecting society and technology, and now Tourism 4.0 is about adaptation to the digital age (Starc Peceny, 2019; Starc Peceny et al., 2019). The aim of Tourism 4.0 is to 'reduce the negative effects of tourism' (IGI-Global, 2020). Work by Çeltek (2020) reflects not only how tourism can utilise new technological advances, but how society can benefit from them. As outlined in Chapter 17, the negative effects of tourism include a negative environmental impact in terms of the increased consumption of resources, the production of large amounts of waste, population overcrowding (residents and visitors), and poor accessibility. The economy can suffer as the price of land and housing increases, as well as the cost of goods and services, alongside employment becoming temporary and seasonal, and regions become overly reliant on tourist income. Socially, tourism can result in human trafficking, illegal activities, over-commercialisation, and a loss of a sense of place and local cultural identity (Starc Peceny et al., 2019). Furthermore, Tourism 4.0 aims 'to see the effects of the use of technology in the tourism sector and to develop cooperation models in partners' (IGI-Global, 2020). Starc Peceny et al. (2019) frame this aim in terms of exploring the value added to tourism through innovation, knowledge, technology and creativity. Both the concepts and tools of Industry 4.0 should be applied to create more personalised tourism and visitor experiences utilising ICT, and to ensure tourism becomes more sustainable. Finally, Starc Peceny et al. (2019) argue that the impact of these applications is that tourism will become more collaborative, accessible, technology-focused and sustainable.

It is anticipated that technology will be harnessed to bring together stakeholders in tourism to work in collaboration (Ramos, Ribeiro de Almeida and Fernandes, 2020). Whilst data are key to the future of tourism, collaboration is hugely important. Data are of no use if collected in independent sets, rather than shared to help organisations make sound strategic decisions. Technology can also be utilised to help aid the sharing of knowledge and skills and there are already projects being implemented to harness technology and encourage collaboration. An example in Slovenia is below.

THINK POINT

Can you subscribe to the principles of Tourism 4.0?

INDUSTRY INSIGHT

The Tourism 4.0 Partnership in Slovenia (Starc Peceny et al., 2019)

The Slovenian Tourism 4.0 Partnership was established to allow global stakeholders to take part in tourism research and development. The partnership brought together relevant industrial partners with leading tourism and ICT research organisations to create a forward-looking partnership forum. The project has a website (tourism4-0.org) that functions as a virtual creative lab, connection point, and information hub for anyone interested in smart tourism. One of the outcomes of this infrastructure is that smaller organisations can access knowledge and expertise they might not otherwise be able to engage with.

An interesting aspect of the project is that there is a real appreciation for the history and existing knowledge of Slovenian tourism, whilst innovation in tourism takes place via the digital platform. Communication and collaboration are being enhanced and thus important knowledge is not lost. The aim of the platform is to have a live mechanisation for collaboration that will allow stakeholders to develop new tourism products and services that link to the aims of Tourism 4.0, with a particular focus on communities, quality of local life within tourism areas, less environmental damage, and stronger economies.

The project is underpinned by the Collaboration Impact Model that motivates and rewards positive behaviour by tourists, and aims to reduce negative behaviours by educating tourists about low-impact activities they can engage in. This system is based on data about the area and profile-driven data about the user, and aims to help with problems like overcrowding. The rewards for positive actions that benefit local communities and the environment use **blockchain technology**, offering tourists the opportunity to collect digital currency in the form of Collaboration Impact Tokens. Online safety and data protection are considered within the project through encryption of information.

The tourism industry was fast to adopt digitalisation, with online booking systems for flights, hotels, and tourism experiences (Dredge et al. 2019; Ramos et al. 2020). The focus on technology has been how to innovate and create a physical and digital environment where those working in tourism can create personalised experiences for tourists. Technology such as the **Internet of Things**, Big Data, blockchain technology, artificial intelligence, and virtual and augmented realities help to gain a good understanding of what tourists know, expect and have experienced, to build new services, products, and 'end user devices' that ultimately help to increase tourist satisfaction and improve the visitor and tourist experience (Jafari and Xiao, 2016). This is called 'Smart Tourism' (Buhalis and Amaranggana, 2015) and is based on digital, intelligent and virtual technology in which information communication technologies are applied across all travel-related activities and experiences.

Examples of some of the technological advances already introduced that make our travelling experiences better include biometric technology at airports, hotels and travel agents using artificial intelligence to created more personalised experiences for tourists, blockchain technology being utilised for loyalty programmes, luxury brand management offering seamless on and offline experiences, and smart hotel rooms where the technology is voice-controlled by the guest (Chartered Institute of Tourism and Hospitality South Africa, 2020). These kinds of innovations are presented by Yeoman (2012) as he considers tourism in the year 2050. Consider a world where a contact lens can work like a smart device and camera, perhaps where all travel will be hypersonic and solar-powered, or where we are served by robotic butlers. One only has to look at new restaurants using robot waiters in Tokyo to see the future world is already partly here.

THINK POINT

What do you think tourism, hospitality and events will look like in 2050? How might we be travelling? How might we be enjoying events?

EMPLOYER INSIGHT

The Aloft Hotel Experience by Marriott (from Marriott, 2020 and One Mile at a Time, 2020)

The Aloft Hotel Experience is a luxury one, whose marketing clearly identifies the target audience as young, affluent, brand-conscious, and seeking new experiences. Their website clearly sets out what their hotels are about: freedom, people and technology-enhanced experiences.

> Aloft Hotels is open in space and spirit. Fresh, purposeful environments and vibrant spaces that bring people together. We are the next generation of hotel, using technology and design to enhance experiences and move at the pace of our guests. (Marriott, 2020)

Technology includes being able to register online to go keyless, using your smart phone or Apple Watch to check in and unlock your room. Marriott also have the Marriott Bonvoy app for the Apple Watch. The app provides you with your booking confirmation number, directions to the hotel, the ability to not have to manually check in and as mentioned above it allows your watch to act as your room key. Once you are in your room, you are able to voice-activate the technology in your room and an iPad with an Aloft app on it is provided for guests to control their in-room features. This means guests can use Siri to adjust the room temperature, select pre-set lighting options for different times of day or fit in with activities like reading or watching television. There are also Siri-activated music options for the shower if you have iTunes, and a virtual concierge to help you to explore the local area.

These technological features offer guests an integrated booking, check-in and room access service, which is convenient and unobtrusive. The in-room features allow guests to personalise their experience and all of these things should equate to more satisfied customers. However, it is highly dependent on Apple technology and requires the guest to be an Apple user to get the most out of the experience.

Source: https://onemileatatime.com/aloft-voice-activated-hotel-rooms/ and https://aloft-hotels.marriott.com/hotel-technology/

TOURISM 4.0 AND THE UNITED NATIONS SUSTAINABLE DEVELOPMENT GOALS

The concept of sustainability in relation to Tourism 4.0 is important given the dramatic increase expected in tourist numbers. Small changes can have a big impact on society and the planet. This idea is reflected in the way the United Nations World Tourism Organisation (UNWTO) has started to link tourism to the United Nations Sustainable Development Goals (see Chapter 17). Technology plays an important role in sustainability because it can be used to develop mechanisms for controlling tourist flow and numbers, which could impact positively on local communities and climate change. These ideas link to the concept of 'conscious travel', which is centred on the idea of compassion and social consciousness. With concerns such as over-tourism (Jacobsen, Iversen and Hem, 2020), technology has the potential to advise people when to use public transport systems or visit attractions, or to experience a fragile site virtually, using their smart phones to show historical environments through augmented reality. An example of this is in the activity below on the Spanish network of smart cities.

=== ACTIVITY ===

The Spanish Network of Smart Cities

Spain has a public network of smart cities across the country who work together on a range of challenges related to tourism, including sustainability. Their primary function is to exchange knowledge (EU Smart Cities Group, 2020). In March 2020, an online portal promoting better cities through collaboration across Europe reported on some activities of two members of the group (provided below). As you read the article highlight important points and take notes to answer the questions below:

1. How do the activities mentioned embody the principles of Tourism 4.0?
2. How has the city of Santander benefitted from being a smart city?
3. What is the outcome of this activity: utilisation of technology or benefitting people?
4. How do you think the Smart Citizen project (an open data project looking at parking, traffic intensity, environment, irrigation etc.) based on the Internet of things could contribute to sustainability? For more information on the project visit https://synchronicity-iot.eu/project/santander/

Murcia borrows smart city ideas from Santander

Murcia is looking into ways to implement smart city solutions and know-how, borrowing ideas from Santander. This was made clear last week, following a promising meeting between city representatives from both administrations in Santander.

(Continued)

A decade of intelligent transformation in Santander

The delegation from the City of Murcia, headed by the deputy mayor and councillor for Urban Development and Modernisation of the Administration José Guillen Parra, visited the Smart City demonstration centre in Pronillo. They were accompanied by the local mayor, Gema Igual and the councillor for Innovation, Javier Ceruti. During the meeting, the mayor recalled the early 2010s, when the City Council of Santander began to position itself as an intelligent city and started to be recognised as an international urban laboratory for the validation of technologies, services and applications in the field of smart cities.

As the municipal website points out, ever since, they have carried out research and 27 EU-funded projects. As a partner in them, the city collaborated with a total of 325 institutions, companies and centres of technology. 'This generated important benefits for the city, which allowed us to position ourselves and continue researching in the field of new technologies,' said Gema Igual, quoted by Santander.es. This enabled the City Council to enter a sector with a potential niche market to create employment, she added.

Open Data in the Spanish city

The importance of open data was also highlighted as a means to help companies by giving them important raw material and enabling them to incorporate the projects of private entities. Igual has highlighted the technological innovations in all public services and emphasised that, thanks to having adequate technology, Santander has been distinguished as DTI (Intelligent Tourist Destination). Finally, the mayor of Santander highlighted the two Smart City projects developed with Telefónica and Nec, involving an investment of €1.7 million. Also mentioned was the Smart Citizen initiative, which has been running since last year with a budget of €6.7 million that conceives the citizen in the centre of municipal management.

Source: www.themayor.eu/ga/murcia-borrows-smart-city-ideas-from-santander

---

THE FUTURE OF CAREERS IN THE SECTORS

The OECD (2020: 3) claim that, 'The digital economy is having a profound impact on the tourism sector, transforming the process of communicating with tourists and marketing tourism services, and opening up new and creative ways to deliver tourism services and enhance the visitor experience.' The evolution of the THE sectors will inevitably create a more personalised, technology-led experiential route, feeding the growth in online booking companies and technology-enhanced experiences (Hansing, 2020). The focus on innovation, co-creation, and technological collaboration means that there is much more scope to work with other industry sectors in creative and enterprising ways. Most THE degrees include core business modules such as human resource management, economics, accounting and international business, which students sometimes struggle to see the value and importance of. However, Tourism 4.0 means that graduates in THE will need to understand business functions outside of tourism to be able to work effectively with partners. It is likely you will collaborate with people from a diverse range of experience, backgrounds and cultures, requiring you to be culturally sensitive. As outlined in Chapter 16, you will also need effective communication and language skills, and will need to be able to present yourself confidently and professionally in different formats and contexts (see Chapters 12 and 13). You will need to be able to talk and write about your sector in an accessible way to people who might not have a background in the same area as you, and be willing to learn from people about things outside your current sphere of knowledge.

As a natural extension of 'transformative travel', which empowers the traveller to make meaningful changes to their lives, future graduates in the hospitality sector will need to think about how to strike the right balance between developing automated solutions and human interaction. These decisions might be about using technology to personalise hotel rooms, offering real time translation to communicate with guests in their language, using virtual reality to help future customers tour their hotel room before they leave the house, and in marketing terms may involve systems such as beacon technology that encourages guests to use hotel services via promotional offers sent direct to their phones.

Likewise, in events we might see more chatbots being used to answer customer questions and provide a more effective service. Artificial intelligence technology may be used to create more personalised event experiences and increase attendee engagement. Events will certainly need to be more sustainable and seek to reduce waste at every point of the supply chain; increased data quality and privacy will be required to overcome sophisticated hacking systems; virtual tours will help event planning; gamification will undoubtedly help delegates engage with sponsors; and experiential marketing methods will allow more sharing, targeting and interaction.

THINK POINT

How do you prepare for a job that doesn't yet exist? How does your degree programme prepare you for a career in the context of Tourism 4.0? What skills, experience, and attributes do you think you will need to develop whilst at university to be successful working in the context of Tourism 4.0?

Human capital will still impact significantly on the quality of the product, service, or experience (Hansing, 2020). This means that graduate jobs are very unlikely to be replaced by technology. All the potential changes outlined above will require you as a graduate to be able to think creatively, critically and innovatively in your approach to problem-solving to develop new services and products that meet customer demand and expectations (see Chapter 19). Whilst AI can collect and manage data, you are going to need to employ critical thinking and decision-making skills to continue to develop and work with innovation.

You will need to maintain a good understanding of the mission and quality standards of your organisation and will need excellent customer services and communication skills to be successful. Digital marketing and branding will continue to be important in destination marketing and management, and whilst you will not be expected to be able to do the technical work, you will be expected to understand trends and data relating to key aspects of your role and the sector. You may be required to contribute to a range of communication from formal text to blogs, video uploads, newsletter, e-promotions, social media and gamification. You therefore need to have a wide range of communication skills and experience of using different platforms (Chapter 13).

As argued in Chapter 17, above all else, sustainability is only going to become more important as the sector develops. Understanding the challenges that the THE sectors faces in relation to sustainability will be key, along with being able to work with data and technology to solve problems such as over-tourism, pollution, congestion and damage to fragile destinations. You will need to be able to contextualise the role of THE within the UN SDGs, have a strong moral compass, and think about your work and role in the context of social, economic, and environmental factors. Above all you will need to be able to recognise and implement ideas that benefit local communities as well as tourists.

CONCLUSION

In this chapter we have covered:

- What the Fourth Industrial Revolution is and what it means for us as a global society
- The concept and application of Tourism 4.0 and explored the skills, knowledge, experience and attributes you will need to have a successful career within this context.
- The links between Tourism 4.0, hospitality, events and sustainability

FURTHER READING

Dredge, D., Phi, G. T. L., Mahadevan, R., Meehan, E., and Popescu, E. (2019). *Digitalisation in Tourism: In-depth Analysis of Challenges and Opportunities*. Aalborg, Denmark: Executive Agency for Small and Medium-sized Enterprises (EASME), European Commission: Available from: https://vbn.aau.dk/ws/portalfiles/portal/296441087/REPORT_TourismDigitalisation_131118_REV_KB_EM_4_.pdf

Ramos, C. M.Q.; Ribeiro de Almeida, C., and Fernandes, P.O. (eds) (2020). *Handbook of Research on Social Media Applications for the Tourism and Hospitality Sector*. Hershey PA, USA: IGI Global.

OECD (2020) *Tourism Trends and Policies 2020*. Available from: http://www.oecd.org/cfe/tourism/2020-Tourism-Brochure.pdf.

Yeoman, I. (2012). *2050 – Tomorrow's Tourism* (Vol. 55). Bristol: Channel View Publications.

36 CONCLUSION

REFLECTING ON WHAT WE HAVE COVERED

This book was divided into five thematic sections. Section A took you through the essential study skills that THE students should be developing. We believe these chapters are also relevant for the study of any-related business degree programme. We hope introducing some aspects of a university education and typical teaching methods and approaches have given you the confidence to progress with your studies. Researching the sector (Chapter 3), finding relevant and appropriate sources (Chapter 4), and academic writing skills (Chapter 5) should be the core pillars of your studies. After all that researching, studying and writing comes the inevitable assessment and you should now feel confident in tackling both written assessments (essays, reports) and more online methods (Chapter 6), as well as feeling ready to prepare for presentations in all their different formats and types (Chapter 7). As we have said in this same section, you should practice your reflective and critical thinking

(Chapters 8 and 10), as well as ensure everything you write is secure, backed up and organised (Chapter 9). Throughout your time studying and ensuring assessments are completed well, don't forget to plan your time to avoid last minute panic and uncertainly – time management skills are crucial and you will certainly need these as you move into the workplace. The THE sectors are unpredictable and intense at times, so you will need to be able ride the waves of uncertainty with resilience and a positive attitude.

Section B introduced personal development and employability skills. We guided you through the value of developing skills for life and work (Chapter 12). The ability to communicate effectively with people and build strong interpersonal skills will allow you to tackle interactions and social engagement in and out of the workplace (Chapter 13). As you will have noted, good communication is more than talking: in fact, your body language can say more than any verbal communication (Chapter 14). Working out what the body language of others means, and how you can express yourself physically, is crucial for nurturing healthy, constructive and positive relationships with others. Learning how to work effectively as a team and lead others (Chapter 15), in a sensitive way that demonstrates cultural competence and global awareness (Chapter 16), will ensure you stand out in assessments, and in the workplace. Our aim in this book was to cover skills that are not often found in such texts, but that are highly relevant for working in THE. Therefore, Chapter 17 on social responsibility and sustainability provided insights into how the industry is handling global issues and asked you to reflect on how you might contribute to an organisation's CSR objectives and the value of considering the global sustainable development goals in your work. The issues you will have to consider working in an ever-changing international sector will be complex. Consequently, we hope that the advice we provide on project management (Chapter 18) and creative problem-solving (Chapter 19) will support you to stay calm and resourceful.

As outlined at the very beginning of this book, the global employment market is competitive, with ever-increasingly numbers of graduates entering the labour market. However, it is also worth remembering that the sector is growing, worth $8.8 trillion and was responsible for 319 million global jobs in 2018. To help you get ahead of other graduates, Section C provides graduate employment ideas, insights and opportunities (Chapter 20) on gaining work experience through internships (Chapter 21) and volunteer work (Chapter 22).

By Section D, we hope you have developed a good sense of your skills, and the kind of graduate career you might want to pursue, and this section aims to help you successfully transition into the world of work (Chapter 23). You need to understand how the selection process works (Chapter 24) and how you put your best self forward (Chapter 25 and 26) through effective searching and networking (Chapter 27). You might even be thinking about postgraduate study or contemplating an academic life (Chapter 28). To secure that opportunity, you will need a CV that stands out (Chapter 29), alongside outstanding and memorable applications and covering letters (Chapter 30). We want you to ace the interview (Chapter 31), perform brilliantly in psychometric tests (Chapter 32) and shine at the assessment centre (Chapter 33). Finally, if you fancy being your own boss, Chapter 34 was for you. Being an entrepreneur is massively rewarding, but incredibly challenging and hard work (at least at first). The insights and reflections offered in that chapter should help you decide if that path is for you. There are emerging opportunities in tourism, hospitality and events every day (Chapter 35) and we hope you will look to the future with confidence, taking control of your life, and shaping your future. We hope this book, and our employers and students through their personal and professional insights, have provided (and will continue to provide) company along the way.

ANSWERS TO SOME ACTIVITIES IN PREVIOUS CHAPTERS

Chapter 2

In Chapter 2 we asked you to develop some brief definitions for some terms so here are a few suggestions and we have used the Open University Innovating Pedagogy report (2020) to provide some suggested answers (www.open.ac.uk/blogs/innovating).

- *Playful learning*: learning through play for adults
- *Learning with robots*: intelligent software and robots can help you learn by engaging you in an exercise or conversation
- *Decolonising learning*: universities are challenging the view that white European/Western traditions of learning and writing are the most valuable in terms of knowledge and approaches to learning. Curricula need to reflect a more diverse and inclusive world view and recognise academic thought and ways of seeing the world that exist in Africa, India, the East and other areas
- *Drone-based learning*: using drones enriches the exploration of spaces and provides a way of engaging in three-dimensional learning and ways of seeing the landscape
- *Learning through wonder*: using visual cues that elicit an emotional response such as rainbows, sunsets or natural landscapes to trigger interest and foster curiosity
- *Action learning*: small groups of diverse people work together to solve a real-world problem to offer new perspectives and possible solutions
- *Virtual studios*: using online environments to recreate the interaction of a physical teaching space
- *Place-based learning*: using places and spaces to inspire learning and move learning out of classrooms
- *Making thinking visible*: using visual concepts and Mind Maps (see Chapter 4) to express ideas and arguments

Chapter 32

ANSWERS TO ACTIVITY 1 IN CHAPTER 32

Abstract Reasoning Tests

1

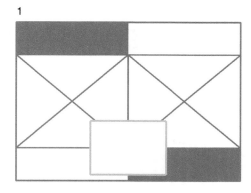
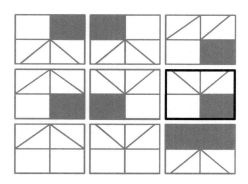

(Continued)

2

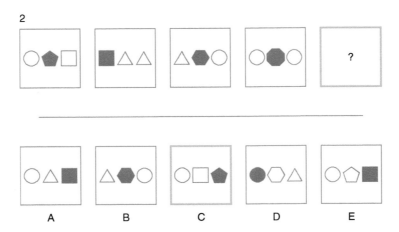

Rule 1: The left hand symbol rotates 90° clockwise each time.

Rule 2: The centre and right hand symbols rotate 90° counter clockwise each time.

Rule 3: The shaded symbol moves one place to the right each time.

3

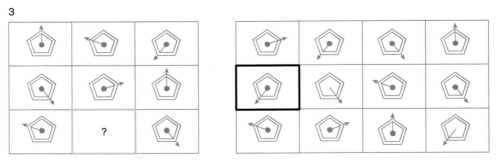

Rule 1: From left to right, the arrow moves one place counterclockwise around the pentagon each time. This pattern continues onto the next row.

Rule 2: From left to right, the arrow alternates between being in front of and behind the pentagon. This pattern continues onto the next row.

4

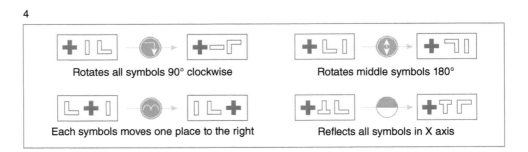

The circle with the top semi-circle blank and the bottom semi-circle shaded is in position 1 of 3. The symmetrical arrow shaded black pointing right is at position 2 of 3. Lastly, the L-shape not shaded is at position 3.

The first operation is defined by the wide 'm' shape indicates that each symbol must move one position to the right. So, after performing this operation, the circle shall be at position 2, the arrow at position 3 and the L-shape, as given in the example operation for the 'm'-shape shall move to position 1.

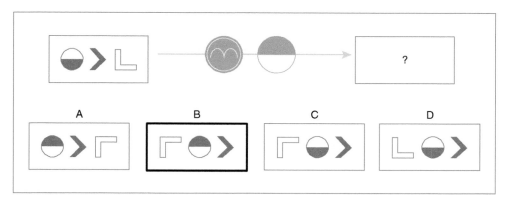

The second operation is to reflect all shapes in the x-axis, so the L-shape now at position one will flip to resemble more of an 'r'-shape, the circle shall flip to have the shaded semi-circle at the top and the blank semi-circle on the bottom. The arrow is symmetrical along the x-axis so there will be no visible change here.

Answer option B is the correct option because the shapes are in the correct position and have been reflected correctly.

A more visual explanation of each operation performed successfully is shown here.

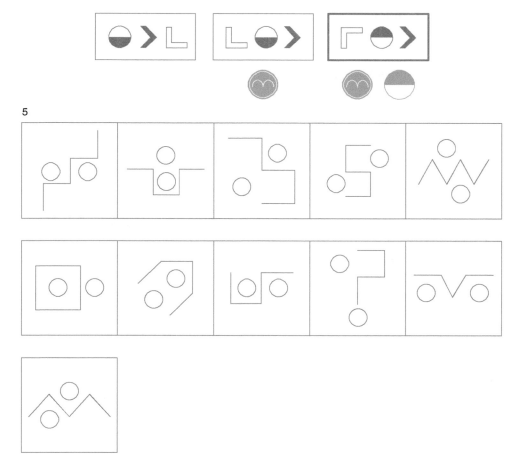

B – The Figure contains four lines and two circles, as does each box in Set B, whereas each box in Set A contains five lines and two circles.

ANSWERS TO ACTIVITY 2 IN CHAPTER 32

Example of numerical tests

Example Test 1

1   If the Building Energy Use today is 6% less than it was in 2000, by what percentage is today's Building Energy Use lower than that of 1990?

    (A) 82.9%
    (B) 17.1%
    (C) 17.8%
    (D) Cannot say

Step 1 – *Total energy usage in 2000 = 15,000kWh, so today's at 6% less is 15,000 x 0.94 = 14,100kWh. This compares with 1990 levels of 17,000kWh.*

Step 2 – *To work out the reduction from 17,000 to 14,100, calculate (14,100 ÷ 17,000) = 0.8294, which is a reduction of (1-0.8294 = 0.17059) 17.1%.*

Thus, the correct answer is (B) 17.1%.

Example Test 2

Men and women working in different employment sectors

2   If it is predicted that the number of females employed in IT will rise by 10% every year, but the number of males stays the same, what percent of IT employees would be female after a three year period?

    (A) 54.1%
    (B) 53.5%
    (C) 85.0%
    (D) 45.5%

Step 1 – *Number of female IT employees to start with is 107,000 from the table.*

Step 2 – *If the number of female employees rises by 10%, that gives 142,417 employees after three years (107,000 x 1.10 x 1.10 x 1.10 = 142,417).*

Step 3 – *The number of male IT employees is still 121,000, so the total in IT is now 142,417 + 121,000 = 263,417. So 142,417 out of 263,417 IT employees is 54.07%.*

Tip – With this question, where we are dealing with number of people, you should end up with integers in the working since it is not possible to have part of a person. If you start to get decimals, consider whether you have made a mistake.

Thus, the correct answer is (A) 54.1%.

Example Test 3

3   What was yesterday's cost difference between 50 shares in Fevs plc and 100 shares in Steapars?

    (A) €164,726
    (B) €251,163
    (C) €172,577
    (D) €164,045
    (E) None of these

The information that we need is shown in the table Share prices.

Step 1 – *Calculate yesterday's share price for each share:*
Fevs plc = 1,586 ÷ 0.91 = 1,742.86
Steapars = 2,537 ÷ 1.01 = 2,511.88

Step 2 – *Calculate the cost difference between 50 Fevs and 100 Steapars shares yesterday:*
50 x 1,742.86 = 87,143
100 x 2,511.88 = 251,188
Difference = 251,188 - 87,143 = 164,045

Tip: *Percentage increases and decreases catch out a lot of people. For this question, think about what's happening. The percentage change from yesterday to today in the case of Fevs is a 9% decrease. So that means (today's price) ÷ (yesterday's price) = 0.91 (a 9% decrease). Using algebra we can recast this as yesterday's price = today's price ÷ 0.91.*

Thus the correct answer is (D) €164,045

Example Test 4

4   Legal sector spending on IT hardware, IT software and IT consulting are all set to increase by the same amounts in Year 6 as they did from Year 4 to Year 5. Assuming this is the case, what would be the total legal sector spending in Year 6 on these three IT areas combined?

(A)   £75 million
(B)   £85 million
(C)   £95 million
(D)   £105 million
(E)   £110 million

The information that we need is shown in the graph IT spending by the legal sector.

Step 1 – *Calculate the increases in each IT spending category*
IT hardware = 45 (increase of £5 million from Year 4)
IT software = 30 (increase of £5 million from Year 4)
IT consulting = 20 (increase of £5 million from Year 4)

Step 2 – *Calculate the total for the year after the projected year 5. Since there is an even increase the same increase of £5 million will occur in IT hardware, software and consulting.*
Total = 45 + 30 + 20 + (3 x 5) = £110 million

Thus the correct answer is (E) £110 million

ANSWERS TO ACTIVITY 3 IN CHAPTER 32

Verbal reasoning tests

Example Test 1

The project was ambitious in its size, complexity, triparty nature, and in its pioneering of the Private Finance Initiative. This difficulty was unavoidable and contributed to the project's failure. However, a more thorough estimate of the unknown difficulties and timescales would have enabled the Department of Infrastructure to better prepare for the project and increase its chances of success.

(Continued)

> In December 1997, XSoft, the company tasked with completing the project on behalf of the Department of Infrastructure, had asked for an extension of the deadline because they could already see that the project would not meet the promised January 1998 deadline and would not be completed until June 1999, at the earliest. If the Department had known from the start the true scale of the project, it is likely they would have chosen another smaller project. Accountants have reported that the delay has already had negative effects on the Profit & Loss sheets for both parties.

1   If more care had been put into estimating the difficulties, it is less likely the project would have failed.

   True   False   Cannot say

True – Since more thorough can be considered equivalent to giving more care, this is stated as true in the following excerpt 'a more thorough estimation of the unknown difficulties and timescales would … increase its chance of success'.

2   XSoft withheld information from the Department regarding how long the project would take.

   True   False   Cannot say

Cannot say – We are told XSoft requested more time, and the passage implies the Department did not know how long it would take at the beginning, but the passage does not tell us if XSoft did or did not withhold time information.

Example 2: Financial statements verbal test

> The first problem with financial statements is that they are in the past; however detailed, they provide just a snap-shot of the business at one moment in time. There is also a lack of detail in financial statements, giving little use in the running of a business. Financial statements are provided for legal reasons to meet with accounting regulations and are used mainly by City analysts who compute share prices and give guidance to shareholders. Accounts often have hidden information and may also be inconsistent; it is difficult to compare different companies' accounts, despite there being standards, as there is much leeway in the standards.

3   Financial statements are useful for businesses to understand their financial activities.

   True   **False**   Cannot say

False – The passage says that financial statements have 'a lack of detail in financial statements, giving little use in the running of a business', which is supported by other critical statements such as 'the first problem with financial statements is that they are in the past' means they cannot be considered useful for businesses to understand their financial activities.

4   If account reporting standards were tightened, it would be easier to compare the performance of different companies.

   True   False   **Cannot say**

Cannot say – The last sentence in the passage says, 'it is difficult to compare different companies' accounts, despite there being standards, as there is much leeway in the standards'. Though this implies that if there were less leeway in the standards, it would be easier to compare different companies' accounts, this is only an inference. Thus, it can only be asserted as a probability rather than a certainty. Since the passage does not expressly say, we require more information. Therefore, it is Cannot say.

ANSWERS TO ACTIVITY ON DEDUCTIONS IN CHAPTER 32

Critical Reasoning Example Tests

1. Which one of the following conclusions is definitely true based on the statement?

    All events are live. All conferences are events.

    The correct answer is A: All conferences are live.

2. Which one of the following conclusions is definitely true based on the statement?

    All hotel managers are senior leaders. No senior leaders are part time staff.

    The correct answer is B: No part time staff are hotel managers

3. Which one of the following conclusions is definitely true based on the statement?

    No events staff are accountants. All finance staff are accountants.

    The correct answer is B: No finance staff are events staff

4. Which one of the following conclusions is definitely true based on the statement?

    All new customers are eligible for a discount. Some new customers are tourists.

    The correct answer is C: Some tourists are eligible for a discount

5. Which one of the following conclusions is definitely true based on the statement?

    Some women are hard working. Some hotel staff are women.

    The correct answer is E: No valid conclusion

In Chapter 32 you were given the opportunity to try some critical thinking tests (from the Activity: Test yourself with 'strong and weak' critical thinking tests on page 498):

*   Q1, 3 and 5 are strong answers as they focus on the question of value.
*   Q2 and 4 might sound plausible, but don't address the specifics of the question (more graduates do not mean less value).

REFERENCES

Abdelmotaleb, M. and Saha, S. (2013) 'Academic Self-Efficacy and Student Academic Performance', *Journal of Education and Learning*, 2(3): 117–29.

ACAS (2020) Checklist for Inducting New Staff into a Business (www.acas.org.uk/checklist-for-induction-of-new-staff).

Adair, J.E. (1973) *Action-Centred Leadership*. London: McGraw Hill.

Adebisi, J.F. (2013) 'Time Management Practices and its Effect on Business Performance', *Canadian Social Science* 9 (1): 165–8.

Advance HE (2018) Equality in Higher Education: Statistical Report 2018 (www.advance-he.ac.uk/knowledge-hub/equality-higher-education-statistical-report-2018).

Advance HE (2020) Flipped Learning (www.heacademy.ac.uk/knowledge-hub/flipped-learning-0).

Agorni, M. (2018) 'Cultural Representation through Translation: An Insider-Outsider Perspective on the Translation of Tourism Promotional Discourse', *Altre Modernità: Rivista di Studi Letterari e Culturali*, 20: 253–71.

Akhtar, M. (2008) 'What is Self-Efficacy? Bandura's 4 Sources of Efficacy Beliefs', *Positive Psychology UK* (positivepsychology.org.uk/self-efficacy-definition-bandura-meaning/).

Albright, S.C. (2015) *Business Analytics: Data Analysis and Decision Making*. Stamford, CT: Cengage Learning.

Alexander, E.C., Mader, D.R.D. and Mader, F.H. (2019) 'Using Social Media during the Hiring Process: A Comparison between Recruiters and Job Seekers', *Journal of Global Scholars of Marketing Science*, 29(1): 78–87.

Alipour, H. and Arefipour, T. (2020) 'Rethinking Potentials of Co-management for Sustainable Common Pool Resources (CPR) and Tourism: The Case of a Mediterranean island', *Ocean and Costal Management*, 183: 1–14.

Alshaibani, E. and Bakir, A. (2017) 'A Reading in Cross-Cultural Service Encounter: Exploring the Relationship between Cultural Intelligence, Employee Performance and Service Quality', *Tourism and Hospitality Research*, 17(3): 249–63.

Anderson, C. (2013) 'How to Give a Killer Presentation', *Harvard Business Review* (hbr.org/2013/06/how-to-give-a-killer-presentation).

Anderson, R.D. (2004) *European Universities from the Enlightenment to 1914*. Oxford: Oxford University Press.

Anderson, R.D. (2006) *British Universities Past and Present*. London: Bloomsbury.

Anglia Ruskin University (ARU) (2019) University Library: Guide to Harvard Style of Referencing (libweb.anglia.ac.uk/referencing/files/Harvard_referencing_201718.pdf).

ARU (2020) Types of Degree we Offer (aru.ac.uk/research/postgraduate-research/degrees-we-offer).

Armstrong, E.K. (2003) 'Applications of Role-Playing in Tourism Management Teaching: An Evaluation of a Learning Method', *Journal of Hospitality, Leisure, Sport and Tourism Education*, 2(1): 5–16.

Armstrong, M.B, Landers, R.N. and Collmus, A.B. (2015) 'Gamifying Recruitment, Selection, Training and Performance Management: Game Thinking in Human Resource Management', in D. Davis and H. Gangadharbatla (eds) *Handbook of Research Trends in Gamification*. Hershey, PA: Information Science Reference. pp. 103–124

Ashforth, B.E., Saks, A.M. and Lee, R.T. (1998) 'Socialization and Newcomer Adjustment: The Role of Organizational Context', *Human Relations*, 51(7): 897–926.

Assessment Day (2020) Assessment Centre Guide (www.assessmentday.co.uk/assessmentcentre/).

Association for Project Management (2019) Association for Project Management – The Chartered Body for the Project Profession (www.apm.org.uk/about-us).

Aubrey, K. and Riley, A. (2019) *Understanding and Using Educational Theories*. London: Sage Publications.

Australian Institute of Project Management (AIPM) (2019) *Annual Report* (www.aipm.com.au/documents/aipm-key-documents/annual-reports).

Ayala, J.C. and Manzano, G. (2018) 'Academic Performance of First-Year University Students: The Influence of Resilience and Engagement', *Higher Education Research & Development*, 37(7): 1321–35.

Baez H. (2013) 'Personality Tests in Employment Selection: Use with Caution', *Cornell HR Review* (digitalcom mons.ilr.cornell.edu/chrr/59).

Baker, H. and Feldman, D. (1990), 'Strategies of Organizational Socialization and their Impact on Newcomer Adjustment', *Journal of Managerial Issues*, 2(1): 198–212.

Balaji, S. and Sundararajan Murugaiyan, M. (2012) 'Waterfall Vs Agile: A Comparative Study on SDLC', *International Journal of Information Technology and Business Management*, 2(1): 26–30.

Bandura A. (1997) *Self-efficacy: The Exercise of Control*. New York: W.H. Freeman & Company.

Barker, M. (ed.) (1990) *Orientated for Success*. Australia: Australian Government Publishing Service.

Bartlett, J. E. (2002). 'Analysis of Motivational Orientation and Learning Strategies of High School Business Students'. *Business Education Forum*, 56(4), 18–23.

Baska, M. (2019) 'One in Five Graduates Not "Workplace Ready", Research Finds', *People Management* (www.peoplemanagement.co.uk/news/articles/graduates-not-workplace-ready).

Bass, B.M. (1990) 'From Transactional to Transformational leadership: Learning to share the Vision', *Organisational Dynamics*, 18(3): 19–31.

Battelle For Kids (2019) Framework for 21st Century Learning (static.battelleforkids.org/documents/p21/P21_Framework_Brief.pdf).

Baudrillard, J. (1994) *Simulacra and simulation*. Michigan: University of Michigan Press.

BBC News (2019) 'Coldplay to Pause Touring until Concerts Are "Environmentally Beneficial"' (www.bbc.co.uk/news/entertainment-arts-504907001)

Beeton, S. (2005) 'Understanding Film-induced Tourism', *Tourism Analysis*, 11(3): 181–8.

Belbin, R.M. (2010) *Management Teams: Why they Succeed or Fail*. London: Routledge.

Bello, F.G., Kamanga, G. and Jamu, E.S. (2019) 'Skills Gaps and Training Needs in the Tourism Sector in Malawi', *African Journal of Hospitality, Tourism and Leisure* (www.ajhtl.com/uploads/7/1/6/3/7163688/article_25_vol_8_4__2019_malawi.pdf).

Bender, T. (2012) *Discussion-Based Online Teaching to Enhance Student Learning: Theory, Practice and Assessment*. [e-book] Sterling: Stylus Publishing, LLC.

Berger, D. and Wild, C. (2016) '*Refining the Traditional Flipped Classroom Model: Teaching Students HOW to Think and Not WHAT to Think*', unpublished paper presented at the British and Irish Law Education and Technology Association Annual Conference, Law School, Hatfield.

Berger, P. (1963) *Invitation to Sociology*. Harmondsworth: Penguin Books.

Berkeley Graduate Division (2020a) Cognitive Constructivism (gsi.berkeley.edu/gsi-guide-contents/learning-theory-research/cognitive-constructivism/).

Berkeley Graduate Division (2020b) Social Constructivism (gsi.berkeley.edu/gsi-guide-contents/learning-theory-research/social-constructivism/).

Bethal, E. (2014) *Posters and Presentations, Pocket Skills Guide*. Basingstoke: Palgrave Macmillan.

Beyer, A.M. (2011) 'Improving Student Presentations: Pecha Kucha and Just Plain PowerPoint', *Teaching of Psychology*, 38(2): 122–6.

Bhowmik, M., Banerjee, B. and Banerjee, J. (2013) 'Role of Pedagogy in Effective Teaching', *Basic Research Journal of Education Research and Review*, 2(1): 1–5.

Biggs, J. (2003) Aligning Teaching and Assessment to Curriculum Objectives (www.advance-he.ac.uk/knowledge-hub/aligning-teaching-and-assessment-curriculum-objectives).

Birdwhistell, R.L. (1970) *Kinesics and Context: Essays on Body Motion Communication*. 2nd edn. Philadelphia: University of Pennsylvania Press. (1st edn, 1952.)

Blake. R.R. and Mouton, J.S. (1964) *The Managerial Grid*. Houston: Gulf Publishing.

Blake, R.R., Mouton, J.S., Barnes, L.B. and Greiner, L.E. (1964) 'Breakthrough in Organization Development', *Harvard Business Review* (https://hbr.org/1964/11/breakthrough-in-organization-development)

Bloom, A. (n.d.) Critical Thinking in Buddhism: The Kalama Sutta (bschawaii.org/shindharmanet/critical/).

Bloom, B. (1956) *Taxonomy of Educational Objectives*. New York: David McKay Ltd.

Bloxham, S. and Boyd, P. (2007) *Developing Effective Assessment in Higher Education: A Practical Guide*. Maidenhead: Open University Press.

Booking com (2019) Booking.com reveals Key Findings from its 2019 Sustainable Travel Report (globalnews. booking.com/bookingcom-reveals-key-findings-from-its-2019-sustainable-travel-report/).

Boorstin, D.J. (1962) 'From Traveler to Tourist: The Lost Art of Travel', in D. Boorstin (ed.) *The Image, or, What Happened to the American Dream*. New York: Atheneum. pp. 77–117.

Boud, D., Keogh, R. and Walker, D. (1985) *Reflection: Turning Experience into Learning*. London: Kogan Page.

Bourdieu, P. (1986) 'The Forms of Capital', in J. Richardson (ed.), *Handbook of Theory and Research for the Sociology of Education*. Westport, CT: Greenwood. pp. 241–58.

Bowdin, G., Allen, J., O'Toole, W., Harris, R. and McDonnell, I. (2011) *Events Management*. 3rd edn. Oxford: Butterworth-Heinemann.

Bozick, R. (2007) 'Making It Through the First Year of College: The Role of Students' Economic Resources, Employment, and Living Arrangements', *Sociology of Education*, 80(3): 261–85.

Bracher, L. (1998) 'The Process of Poster Presentation: A Valuable Learning Experience', *Medical Teacher*, 20(6): 552–7.

Braid, K. (ed.) (2017) *Functional Skills ICT, Study and Text Practice*. Broughton-in-Furness: Coordination Group Publications Ltd.

Brigham Young University (2017) Meta Analysis of Flipped Classroom (http://jur.byu.edu/?p=21807).

Brockner, J. and Higgins, E.T. (2001) 'Regulatory Focus Theory: Implications for the Study of Emotions at Work', *Organizational Behavior and Human Decision Processes*, 86(1): 35–66.

Brookfield S. (2015) 'Speaking Truth to Power: Teaching Critical Thinking in the Critical Theory Tradition', in M. Davies and R. Barnett (eds), *The Palgrave Handbook of Critical Thinking in Higher Education*. New York: Palgrave Macmillan. pp. 529–43.

Brotherton, B. (2015) *Researching Hospitality and Tourism*. London: SAGE.

Brown, K. (2020) '5 Global Issues to Watch in 2020', United Nations Foundation (unfoundation.org/blog/post/5-global-issues-to-watch-in-2020/).

Brown, S. (2002) *Lecturing: A Practical Guide*. London: Kogan Page.

Brown, S. (2014) *Learning, Teaching and Assessment in Higher Education: Global Perspectives*. London: Macmillan International Higher Education.

Brown, V.R. and Vaughn, E.D. (2011) 'The Writing on the (Facebook) Wall: The Use of Social Networking Sites in Hiring Decisions', *Journal of Business and Psychology*, 26(2): 219–25.

Buhalis, D. and Amaranggana, A. (2015) 'Smart Tourism Destinations Enhancing Tourism Experience through Personalisation of Services', in I. Tussyadiah and A. Inversini (eds.), *Information and Communication Technologies in Tourism*. Cham: Springer, pp. 377–89.

Bulwer, J. (1644) *Chirologia: or the Natural Language of the Hand*. London: Thom. Harper and Henry Twyford.

Busby, G.D. and Gibson, P. (2010) 'Tourism and Hospitality Internship Experiences Overseas: A British Perspective', *Journal of Hospitality, Leisure, Sport and Tourism Education*, 9(1): 4–12.

Butler, D. (2012). *Business Planning*. [e-book] Hoboken: Taylor & Francis.

Butler, R. (1980) 'The Concept of a Tourist Area Cycle of Evolution: Implications for Management of Resources', *The Canadian Geographer*, 24(1): 5–12.

Butler, S. (2019) 'Zero-hours Workers May Get Compensation for Cancelled Shifts', *The Guardian* (www.theguardian.com/uk-news/2019/jul/19/zero-hours-workers-may-get-compensation-for-cancelled-shifts).

Buzan, T. and Buzan, B. (2003) *The Mind Map Book*. Harlow: BBC Active.

Buzan, T. and Buzan, B. (2010) *The Mind Map Book: Unlock your Creativity, Boost your Memory, Change your Life*. Harlow: BBC Active.

Cable, D.M. and Judge, T.A. (1996) 'Person-Organization Fit, Job Choice Decisions, and Organizational Entry', *Organizational Behavior & Human Decision Processes*, 67(3): 294–311.

Cambridge Assessment (2020) Active Learning (www.cambridgeinternational.org/Images/271174-active-learning.pdf).

Cambridge Dictionary (2019) (dictionary.cambridge.org).

Cameron, S. (2010) *The Business Student's Handbook: Skills for Study and Employment*. 5th edn. Harlow: Pearson Education Limited.

Canavan, B. (2017) 'Narcissism Normalisation: Tourism Influences and Sustainability Implications', *Journal of Sustainable Tourism*, 25(9): 1322–37.

Canterbury Christ Church University (CCCU) (2019) Culture Kent Research Programmes (www.canterbury.ac.uk/social-and-applied-sciences/human-and-life-sciences/research/tourism-events-hub/culture-kent-research-programme.aspx).

Cape Town Declaration on Responsible Tourism (2002) The Cape Town Conference on Responsible Tourism in Destinations (responsibletourismpartnership.org/cape-town-declaration-on-responsible-tourism/).

Carayannis, E.G., Kwak, Y-H. and Anbari, F.T. (2005) *The Story of Managing Projects: An Interdisciplinary Approach*. Westport: Praeger Publishers.

CareerBuilder (2012) Thirty-seven Percent of Companies Use Social Networks to Research Potential Job Candidates (www.careerbuilder.com/share/aboutus/pressreleasesdetail.aspx?id=pr691&sd=4%2F18%2F2012&ed=4%2F18%2F2099).

Carless, D. (2015) *Excellence in University Assessment: Learning from Award-Winning Practice*. London: Routledge.

Carless, D. and Boud, D. (2018) 'The Development of Student Feedback Literacy: Enabling Uptake of Feedback', *Assessment & Evaluation in Higher Education*, 43(8): 1315–25.

Cattell, R.B. (1956) 'Second-order Personality Factors in the Questionnaire Realm', *Journal of Consulting Psychology*, 20(6): 411-418.

Çeltek, E. (2020) *Handbook of Research on Smart Technology Applications in the Tourism Industry*. Hershey, PA: IGI Global.

Chartered Association of Business Schools (CABS) (2015) The Academic Journal Guide 2018: The Purpose of the Academic Journal (charteredabs.org/academic-journal-guide-2018/).

Chartered Institute of Tourism and Hospitality South Africa (2020) From Industry 4.0 to Tourism 4.0 (www.ith.org.za/4ir-future-of-south-african-tourism/).

Chase, M., Magyar, T. and Drake, B. (2005) 'Fear of Injury in Gymnastics: Self-Efficacy and Psychological Strategies to Keep on Tumbling', *Journal of Sports Sciences*, 23(5): 465–75.

Chemers, M.M., Hu, L-T. and Garcia, B.F. (2001) 'Academic Self-Efficacy and First Year College Student Performance and Adjustment', *Journal of Educational Psychology*, 93(1): 55–64.

Chen, J.S. and Hsu, C.H.U. (2000) 'Measurement of Korean Tourists' perceived Images of Overseas Destinations', *Journal of Travel Research*, 38: 411–16.

Cheng, L., Ritzhaupt, A.D. and Antonenko, P. (2019) 'Effects of the Flipped Classroom Instructional Strategy on Students' Learning Outcomes: A Meta-Analysis', *Education Technology Research Development*, 67: 793–824.

Cheung, C., Law, R. and He, K. (2010) 'Essential Hotel Managerial Competencies for Graduate Students', *Journal of Hospitality & Tourism Education*, 22(4): 25–32.

Chivers, B. and Shoolbred, M. (2007) *A Student's Guide to Presentations*. London: Sage Publications.

Choy, S. (2001) *Students Whose Parents Did Not Go to College: Postsecondary Access, Persistence and Attainment*. Washington, DC: National Center for Education Statistics.

Christian, S. (2019) 'Cover Letter by an International Graduate', *Prospects* (www.prospects.ac.uk/careers-advice/cvs-and-cover-letters/cover-letters/cover-letter-by-an-international-graduate).

Chung, G. and Chung, D. (2018) 'WOW the Hospitality Customers: Transforming Innovation into Performance Through Design Thinking and Human Performance Technology', *Performance Improvement*, 57(2): 14–25.

CIPD (2015) *A Head for Hiring: The Behavioural Science of Recruitment and Selection*. London: CIPD.

CIPD (2020) Selection Methods: Factsheets (www.cipd.co.uk/fundamentals/people/recruitment/selection-factsheet).

Clarke, A. (1973) *Profiles of the Future: An Inquiry into the Limits of the Possible*. London: Pan Books.

Clegg, B. (2007) *Instant Creativity: Simple Techniques to ignite Innovation & Problem Solving*. London: Kogan Page.

Clutch (2018) What Causes Workplace Ghosting? (clutch.co/hr/resources/what-causes-workplace-ghosting).

Cohen, E. (1988) 'Authenticity and Commoditization in Tourism', *Annals of Tourism Research*, 15(3): 371–86.

Cole, S. (2014) 'Tourism and Water: From Stakeholders to Rights Holders, and What Tourism Businesses Need to Do', *Journal of Sustainable Tourism*, 22(1): 89–106.

Collier, P., Elliott, H., Hoeffler, A., Reynal-Querol, M. and Sambanis, N. (2003) *Breaking the Conflict Trap: Civil War and Development Policy*. Washington, DC: World Bank.

Collis, J. and Hussey, R. (2014) *Business Research: A Practical Guide for Undergraduate and Postgraduate Students*. Hampshire: Palgrave Macmillan.

Cone Communications (2017) CSR Study (www.conecomm.com/2017-cone-communications-csr-study-pdf).

Connell, J., Page, S.J. and Meyer, D. (2015) 'Visitor Attractions and Events: Responding to Seasonality', *Tourism Management*, 46: 283–98.

Cottrell, S. (2015) *Skills for Success: Personal Development and Employability*. Basingstoke: Palgrave Macmillan.

Cottrell, S. (2013). *The Study Skills Handbook*. London: Macmillan.

Cottrell, S. (2019) *The Study Skills Handbook*. London: Macmillan. 5th edition.

Creme, P. and Lea, M.R. (1997) *Writing at University: A Guide for Students*. Buckingham: Open University Press.

Cronen, V. and Shuter, R. (1983) 'Forming Intercultural Bonds', in W. Gudykunst (ed.), *Intercultural Communication Theory: Current Perspectives*. Beverley Hills, CA: Sage. pp. 34–45.

Cuddy, A., Wilmuth, C.A., Yap, A. and Carney, D.A. (2015) 'Preparatory Power Posing Affects Nonverbal Presence and Job Interview Performance', *Journal of Applied Psychology*, 100(4): 1285–95.

Cullinane, C. and Montacute, R. (2018). Pay as you go? Internship Pay, Quality and Access in the Graduate Jobs Market (cdn.ymaws.com/ise.org.uk/resource/resmgr/files/knowledge_reports/diversity/pay_as_you_go.pdf).

Cummings, S., Heeks, R. and Huysman, M. (2006) 'Knowledge and Learning in Online Networks in Development: A Social-Capital Perspective', *Development in Practice*, 16(6): 570–86.

Cuocci, S. (2015) The Importance of Cross-Cultural Training for Tourism Employees (trainingmag.com/importance-cross-cultural-training-tourism-employees/).

Curren-Everett, D. (2019) Every Presentation is a Performance (journals.physiology.org/doi/full/10.1152/advan.00118.2019).

Dacre Pool, L. and Qualter, P. (2018) *An Introduction to Emotional Intelligence*. Chichester: Wiley & Sons.

Daher, T.A. and Kiewra, K.A. (2016) 'An Investigation of SOAR Study Strategies for Learning from Multiple Online Resources', *Contemporary Educational Psychology*, 46: 10–21.

Dalhousie University (n.d.) The Evolution of Critical Thinking (cdn.dal.ca/content/dam/dalhousie/pdf/faculty/medicine/departments/core-units/DME/critical-thinking/OnePager-EvolutionofCriticalThinking.pdf).

Dashper, K.L. (2013) 'The "Right" Person for the Job: Exploring the Aesthetics Of Labor Within the Events Industry', *Event Management*, 17(2): 135–44.

Davidson, K. (2016) Employers Find 'Soft Skills' Like Critical Thinking in Short Supply, Wall Street Journal (www.wsj.com/articles/employers-find-soft-skills-like-critical-thinking-in-short-supply-1472549400).

Dayal Chauhan, B., Rana, A. and Sharma, N.K. (2017) *Impact of Development Methodology on Cost & Risk for Development Projects*, Sixth International Conference on Reliability, Infocom Technologies and Optimization (Trends and Future Directions) (ICRITO). pp. 267–72.

Deakins, D. (2012) *Entrepreneurship and Small Firms*. London: McGraw-Hill Higher Education.

De Bono, E. (2009). *Six Thinking Hats*. London: Penguin.

Deery, M. (2008) 'Talent Management, Work-Life Balance and Retention Strategies', *International Journal of Contemporary Hospitality Management*, 20(7): 792–806.

De Groot, J. I. M. and Steg, L. (2008) 'Value Orientations to Explain Beliefs Related to Environmental Significant Behavior', *Environment and Behaviour*, 40(3): 330–54, Sage Publishing [Online]. Available at: http://0-eab.sagepub.com.brum.beds.ac.uk/ (Accessed 21 June 2019).

Denman, B.D. (2009) 'What Is a University in the 21st Century?', *Higher Education Management and Policy*, 17(2): 9–28.

Department for Digital, Culture, Media and Sport (DCMS) (2019) Department for Digital, Culture, Media and Sport (www.gov.uk/government/organisations/department-for-digital-culture-media-sport).

de Raad, B.E. and Perugini, M.E. (2002) *Big Five Assessment*. Boston, MA: Hogrefe & Huber Publishers.

Dessler, G. (2016) *Human Resource Management*. Harlow: Pearson Education.

Devine, A., and Devine, F. (2012) 'The Challenge and Opportunities for an Event Organiser during an Economic Recession', *International Journal of Event and Festival Management*, 3(2): 122–36.

Digman, J.M. (1990) 'Personality Structure: Emergence of the Five-factor Model', *Annual Review of Psychology*, 41(1): 417–40.

Discenza, R. and Forman, J.B. (2007) *Seven Causes of Project Failure: How to Recognise Them and How to Initiate Project Recovery*. Paper presented at the PMI Global Congress 2007. Atlanta, GA: Project Management Institute.

Disegna, M. (2016) 'Tourists' Expenditure Behaviour: The Influence of Satisfaction and the Dependence of Spending Categories', *Tourism Economics*, 22(1): 5–30.

Dryden, L., Hyder, T. and Jethwa, S. (2003) 'Assessing Individual Oral Presentations', *Investigations in University Teaching and Learning*, 1(1): 79–83.

Du Boulay, D. (2011) *Study Skills for Dummies*. Chichester: John Wiley & Sons.

Earley, P.C. and Mosakowski, E. (2016) 'Cultural Intelligence', in *HBR's 10 Must Reads on Managing Across Culture*. Boston, MA: Harvard Business Review Press. pp. 1–16.

EBSCO (2020) Hospitality and Tourism Complete (www.ebsco.com/products/research-databases/hospitality-tourism-complete).

ECPAT (2016) In Brief: Volun-tourism (www.ecpat.org/wp-content/uploads/2016/10/Volun-tourism.pdf).

Edgell, D. (2016) *Managing Sustainable Tourism*, 2nd Edition. Oxfordshire: Routledge.

EducationData.Org (2020) Number of College Graduates Per Year (educationdata.org/number-of-college-graduates/).

Egeland, B. (2018) Lessons Learned from the Inconsistent Project Manager (www.apm.org.uk/blog/lessons-learned-from-the-inconsistent-project-manager/).

Ekman, P. and Friesen, W. (1978) *Facial Action Coding System: A Technique for the Measurement of Facial Movement*. Palo Alto: Consulting Psychologists Press.

Eleftheriou-Smith, L.M. (2015) 'Employers sifting through Applications likened to swiping through Tinder as Research shows People spend 8.8 seconds looking at a CV', *The Independent* (www.independent.co.uk/news/uk/home-news/employers-sifting-through-applications-likened-to-swiping-through-tinder-as-research-shows-people-9988512.html).

Entz, S. (2007) 'Why Pedagogy Matters: The Importance of Teaching in a Standards-Based Environment', *Forum on Public Policy Online*, 2. (files.eric.ed.gov/fulltext/EJ1099138.pdf).

Epler Wood, M., Milstein, M. and Ahamed-Broadhurst, K. (2019) 'Destinations at Risk: The Invisible Burden of Tourism', *The Travel Foundation* (s3-eu-west-1.amazonaws.com/travelfoundation/wp-content/uploads/2019/03/09153642/Tourisms-Invisible-Burden.pdf).

Equality Challenge Unit (2013) Unconscious Bias and Higher Education (s3.eu-west-2.amazonaws.com/assets.creode.advancehe-document-manager/documents/ecu/unconscious-bias-and-higher-education_1579011683.pdf).

Ericsson, K.A. (2006) 'The influence of experience and deliberate practice on the development of superior expert performance', *The Cambridge Handbook of Expertise and Expert Performance*, 38, pp. 685–705.

EU Smart Cities (2020) Spanish Network of Smart Cities (eu-smartcities.eu/group/1970/description).

Everett, S. (2016) Food and Drink Tourism: Principles and Practice. London: Sage.

EY (2019) The Economic Impact of Yorkshire 2019: Harrogate Impact Study Findings (www.harrogate.gov.uk/downloads/file/5470/uci_road_world_championships_impact_study).

Facebook (2019a) How Do I Find and Apply to a Facebook Page's Job Post? (www.facebook.com/help/1644821235823585?helpref=uf_permalink).

Facebook (2019b) Company Information (newsroom.fb.com/company-info/).

Facione, P.A. and Facione, N.C. (2007) 'Talking Critical Thinking', *Change: The Magazine of Higher Learning*, 39(2): 38–45.

Faus, J. (2020) This is How Coronavirus Could Affect the Travel and Tourism Industry (www.weforum.org/agenda/2020/03/world-travel-coronavirus-covid19-jobs-pandemic-tourism-aviation/).

Feldman, D. (1981) 'The Multiple Socialization of Organization Members', *Academy of Management Review*, 6(1): 309–18.

Ferreira, D. (2019) 'Research on Big Data, VGI, and the Tourism and Hospitality Sector: Concepts, Methods, and Geographies', in M. Sigala, R. Rahimi and M. Thelwall (eds), *Big Data and Innovation in Tourism, Travel, and Hospitality*. Singapore: Springer. pp. 77–85.

Fiedler, F.E. (1967) *A Theory of Leadership Effectiveness*. New York: McGraw-Hill.

Fil, C. and Turnbull, S. (2016) *Marketing Communications: Discovery, Creations and Conversations*. 7th Edn. Harlow: Pearson Education.

Firth, M. (2019) *The Employability and Skills Handbook for Tourism, Hospitality and Events Students*. London: Routledge.

FindAMasters (2020). Taught vs Research Masters – Which is Right for Me? (www.findamasters.com/advice/finding/taught-vs-research.aspx).

FindAPhD (2020a) PhD Study – What is a PhD? (www.findaphd.com/advice/finding/what-is-a-phd.aspx).

FindAPhD (2020b) PhD Study in Australia – A Guide for 2020 (www.findaphd.com/study-abroad/aus-nz/phd-study-in-australia.aspx).

FindAPhD (2020c) PhD Study in Brazil – A Guide for 2020 (www.findaphd.com/study-abroad/america/phd-study-in-brazil.aspx).

FindAPhD (2020d) Study in Canada (www.findaphd.com/study-abroad/america/phd-study-in-canada.aspx).

FindAPhD (2020e) PhD Study in USA (www.findaphd.com/study-abroad/america/phd-study-in-usa.aspx).

FindAPhD (2020f) PhD Study in Hong Kong (www.findaphd.com/study-abroad/asia/phd-study-in-hong-kong.aspx).

FindAPhD (2020g) PhD Study in India (www.findaphd.com/study-abroad/asia/phd-study-in-india.aspx).

Finch, B. (2016). *How to Write a Business Plan*. [e-book] 5th edn. London : KoganPage (1st edn, 2001)

Fisher, J. (2018). The Beauty of Blue Sky Thinking (ideadrop.co/beauty-blue-sky-thinking/).

Flint, A. (2018) Higher Education Teachers as Pedagogic Researchers (www.heacademy.ac.uk/blog/higher-education-teachers-pedagogic-researchers).

Foer, J. (2012) *Moonwalking with Einstein: The Art and Science of Remembering Everything*. London: Penguin.

Foley, G.N. and Gentile, J.P. (2010) 'Non-verbal Communication in Psychotherapy', *Psychiatry*, 7(6): 38–44.

Forbes (2013) How Social Media Can Help (Or Hurt) You in Your Job Search? (https://www.forbes.com/sites/jacquelynsmith/2013/04/16/how-social-media-can-help-or-hurt-your-job-search/#76aad9497ae2).

Fowler, Jie G., Reisenwitz, Timothy H. and Carlson, Les (2015) 'Deception in Cosmetics Advertising: Examining Cosmetics Advertising Claims in Fashion Magazine Ads', *Journal of Global Fashion Marketing*, 6(3): 194–206.

Gale, T. and Parker, S. (2014) 'Navigating Change: A Typology of Student Transition in Higher Education', *Studies in Higher Education*, 39(5): 734–53.

Gallagher, K. (2013) *Skills Development for Business and Management Students: Study and Employability*. Oxford: Oxford University Press.

Gander, M. (2014) 'Managing your Personal Brand', *Perspectives, Policy and Practice in Higher Education*, 18(3): 99–102.

Gaumer Erickson, A.S. and Noonan, P.M. (2018) 'Self-Efficacy Formative Questionnaire', *The Skills that Matter: Teaching Interpersonal and Intrapersonal Competencies in any Classroom* (www.researchcollaboration.org/uploads/Self-EfficacyQuestionnaireInfo.pdf).

Getz, D. (2002) 'Event Studies and Event Management: On Becoming an Academic Discipline', *Journal of Hospitality and Tourism Management*, 9(1): 12–23.

Getz, D. (2005) *Event Management and Event Tourism*. 2nd edn. New York: Cognizant Communication Corporation. (1st edn, YEAR?.)

Gibb, A. (2011). 'Concepts into Practice: Meeting the Challenge of Development of Entrepreneurship Educators around an Innovative Paradigm', *International Journal of Entrepreneurial Behaviour & Research*, 17(2): 146–65.

Gibbs, G. (1988) *Learning by Doing: A Guide to Teaching and Learning Methods*. Oxford: Further Education Unit.

Gilbert, S.J., Bird, A., Carpenter, J.M., Fleming, S.M., Sachdeva, C. and Tsai, P.C. (2020) 'Optimal Use of Reminders: Metacognition, Effort, and Cognitive Offloading', *Journal of Experimental Psychology*, 149(3): 501–17.

Godwin, J. (2019) *Planning Your Essay (Pocket Study Skills)*. London: Macmillan/ Red Globe Press.

Goleman, D. (2006) 'The Socially Intelligent', *Educational Leadership*, 64(1): 76–81.

Goodwin, H. (2016) *Responsible Tourism: Using Tourism for Sustainable Development*. 2nd edn. Oxford: Goodfellow Publishers. (1st edn, YEAR?.)

Goodwin, H. (2019) Overtourism: Causes, Symptoms and Treatment (responsibletourismpartnership.org/wp-content/uploads/2019/06/TWG16-Goodwin.pdf).

Gorbatov, S., Khapova, S.N. and Lysova, E.I. (2018) 'Personal Branding: Interdisciplinary Systematic Review and Research Agenda', *Frontiers in Psychology*, 9: Article 2238.

Gorbatov, S., Khapova, S.N. and Lysova, E.I. (2019) 'Get Noticed to get Ahead: The Impact of Personal Branding on Career Success', *Frontiers in Psychology*, 10: Article 2662.

Gordon, S. (2018) ISE Research: Internships help tackle Skills Gaps (ise.org.uk/page/blogInternships?).

Graduate Prospects (2019a) Assessment Centres (www.prospects.ac.uk/careers-advice/interview-tips/assessment-centres).

Graduate Prospects (2019b) Psychometric tests (www.prospects.ac.uk/careers-advice/interview-tips/psychometric-tests).

Graduate Prospects Ltd (2020a) Higher Education Academy's Postgraduate Taught Experience Survey 2017 (www.prospects.ac.uk/postgraduate-study/masters-degrees/should-i-do-a-masters).

Graduate Prospects Ltd (2020b) International Business with Tourism and Hospitality MSc (www.prospects.ac.uk/universities/university-of-huddersfield-3786/huddersfield-business-school-13751/courses/international-business-with-tourism-and-hospitality-msc-125061?keyword=tourism%20&featuredCourses=124923%2C107686&size=20&page=0).

Graduate Prospects Ltd (2020c) International Events Management (www.prospects.ac.uk/universities/leeds-beckett-university-3812/events-tourism-and-hospitality-10901/courses/international-events-management-124074?keyword=tourism%20&featuredCourses=124923%2C107686&size=20&page=0).

Graduate Prospects Ltd (2020d) What is a PhD? (www.prospects.ac.uk/postgraduate-study/phd-study/what-is-a-phd).

Graduate Prospects Ltd (2020e) Planning Studies and Tourism, Hospitality and Events (www.prospects.ac.uk/universities/london-south-bank-university-3984/social-and-policy-studies-11198/courses/planning-studies-and-tourism-hospitality-and-events-52697?keyword=tourism%20&featuredCourses=&size=20&page=0&qualifications=21368).

Graduate Prospects (2000f) Museum/gallery Exhibitions Officer (www.prospects.ac.uk/job-profiles/museum-gallery-exhibitions-officer)

Greetham, B. (2018) *How to Write Better Essays* (Macmillan Study Skills). London: Macmillan.

Gregory, A. (2010) 'Teacher Learning on Problem-Solving Teams', *Teaching and Teacher Education*, 26(3): 608–15.

Grieve, R. (2019) *Stand Up and Be Heard: Taking the Fear Out of Public Speaking at University*. London: Sage Publications.

The Guardian (2017) How to Use Social Media in Your Job Search (jobs.theguardian.com/article/how-to-use-social-media-in-your-job-search/).

The Guardian (2018) Does Your CV Pass the 30 Second Speed Test? (jobs.theguardian.com/article/does-your-cv-pass-the-30-second-speed-test-/).

The Guardian (2019) UK 300 (viewer.zmags.com/publication/d545e52b#/d545e52b/1).

Hall, C.M. and Page, S. (2010) 'The Contribution of Neil Leiper to Tourism Studies', *Current Issues in Tourism*, 13(4): 299–309.

Hall, E.T. (1963) 'A System for the Notation of Proxemic Behavior 1', *American Anthropologist*, 65(5): 1003–26.

Hall, E.T. (1966) *The Hidden Dimension*. New York: DoubleDay.

Hall, E.T. (1976) *Beyond Culture. Garden City*, New York: Anchor/Doubleday.

Han, H., Meng, B., Chua, B-L., Ryu, H.B. and Kim, W. (2019) 'International Volunteer Tourism and Youth Travellers – An Emerging Tourism Trend', *Journal of Travel & Tourism Marketing*, 36(5): 549–62.

Hansing, D. (2020) The Future of Careers in Travel Tourism (theknowledgereview.com/future-career-opportunities-travel-tourism/).

Hattie, J. (1999) Influences on Student Learning. Inaugural Lecture (cdn.auckland.ac.nz/assets/education/about/research/documents/influences-on-student-learning.pdf).

Healey, M., Flint, A. and Harrington, K. (2014) Engagement through Partnership: Students as Partners in Learning and Teaching in Higher Education (www.advance-he.ac.uk/knowledge-hub/engagement-through-partnership-students-partners-learning-and-teaching-higher).

Hedges, K. (2013) The Five Best Tricks to Remember Names (www.forbes.com/sites/work-in-progress/2013/08/21/the-best-five-tricks-to-remember-names/#7dd1d4f501f6).

Henry, C., Hill, F. and Leitch, C. (2005) 'Entrepreneurship Education and Training: Can Entrepreneurship be taught? Part I', *Education and Training*, 47: 158–69.

Hernandez-Maskivker, G., Lapointe, D. and Aquino, R. (2017) 'The Impact of Volunteer Tourism on Local Communities: A Managerial Perspective', *International Journal of Tourism Research*, 20: 650–9.

Higginbotham, D. (2018) '4 Routes to getting a Doctorate', Graduate Prospects Ltd (www.prospects.ac.uk/postgraduate-study/phd-study/4-routes-to-getting-a-doctorate).

Higher Education Authority (HEA) (2008) Employable Graduates for Responsible Employers: Research on the links between sustainability and employability in the graduate job market in relation to higher education teaching and learning (s3.eu-west-2.amazonaws.com/assets.creode.advancehe-document-manager/documents/hea/private/esd-employable-graduates-responsible-employers_1568036713.pdf).

Higher Education Statistics Agency (HESA) (2019), Higher Education Student Statistics: UK, 2017/18 – student numbers and characteristics (www.hesa.ac.uk).

HESA (2020) Higher Education Student Statistics: UK, 2018/19 – Qualifications achieved (www.hesa.ac.uk/news/16-01-2020/sb255-higher-education-student-statistics/qualifications).

High Fliers (2014) The Graduate Market in 2014 (www.highfliers.co.uk/download/2014/GMReview14.pdf).

High Fliers (2019) The Graduate Market in 2019: Annual Review of Graduate Vacancies & Starting Salaries at the UK's Leading Employers (www.highfliers.co.uk/download/2019/graduate_market/GMReport19.pdf).

Hitchcock, D. (2017) 'Critical Thinking as an Educational Ideal', in D. Hitchock, *On Reasoning and Argument: Essays in Informal Logic and on Critical Thinking*. Dordrecht: Springer, pp. 477–97. doi:10.1007/978-3-319-53562-3_30.

HM Government (2017) Higher Education and Research Act (www.legislation.gov.uk/ukpga/2017/29/contents/enacted/data.htm).

Ho, G. and McKercher, B. (2015) 'A Review of Life Cycle Models by Plog & Butler from a Marketing Perspective', in M. Kozak and N. Kozak (eds), *Destination Marketing: An International Perspective*. Abingdon: Routledge. pp. 145–54.

Hoag, A. and T.F. Baldwin (2000) 'Using Case Method and Experts in Inter-University Electronic Learning Teams', *Education Technology and Society*, 3(3): 337–48.

Hofstede, G. (1991) *Cultures and Organizations: Software of the Mind*. London: McGraw-Hill.

Hofstede, G. (1994) 'The Business of International Business is Culture', *International Business Review*, 3(1): 1–14.

Hofstede, G. (1997) *Cultures and Organizations: Software of the Mind*. London: McGraw-Hill.

Hofstede Insights (n.d.) Country Comparison (www.hofstede-insights.com/country-comparison/australia, new-zealand,the-uk,the-usa/).

Holden, A. (2016) *Environment and Tourism*. Oxfordshire: Routledge.

Holden, A. and Fennell, D.A. (2017) *The Routledge Handbook of Tourism and the Environment*. Abingdon: Routledge.

Holdsworth, S., Turner, M. and Scott-Young, C.M. (2018) 'Not Drowning, Waving. Resilience and University: A Student Perspective', *Studies in Higher Education*, 43(11): 1837–53.

Hollander, S.A. (2002) 'Helping Students Prepare Poster Presentations', *College Teaching*, 50(3):103

Holmes, D.E. (2017) *Big Data: A Very Short Introduction*. Oxford: Oxford University Press.

Honey, P. (1994) *Teams and Leaders: Trainer's Guide*. London: Melrose Film Productions.

Hong Kong University (2020) Critical Thinking (philosophy.hku.hk/think/critical/ct.php).

Hook, C., Jenkins, A. and Foot, M. (2015) *Introducing Human Resource Management*. Harlow: Pearson Education Limited.

Hounsell, D. (1984) 'Essay Planning and Essay Writing', *Higher Education Research & Development*, 3(1): 13–31.

Houston, K. and Cunningham, E. (2015) *How to Succeed at Assessment Centres*. London: Palgrave Macmillan International Higher Education.

Houston, K. and Cunningham, E. (2015) *How to Succeed at Assessment Centres*. London: Palgrave Macmillan.

Howard, S. and Johnson, B. (2000) 'What Makes the Difference? Children and Young People and Teachers Talk About Resilient Outcomes for Students at Risk', *Educational Studies*, 26(3): 321–7.

Huber, J.A. (2004) 'A Closer Look at SQ3R', *Reading Improvement*, 41(2): 108–13.

Hwang, G., Lai, C. and Wang, S. (2015) 'Seamless Flipped Learning: A Mobile Technology-Enhanced Flipped Classroom with Effective Learning Strategies', *Journal of Computers in Education*, 2(4): 449–73.

IATA (2018) IATA Forecast Predicts 8.2 billion Air Travelers in 2037 (www.iata.org/en/pressroom/pr/2018-10-24-02/).

ICEF Monitor (2019) More than Eight Million Graduates from Chinese Universities This Year (monitor.icef.com/2019/07/more-than-eight-million-graduates-from-chinese-universities-this-year).

IFLA (2020) How to Spot Fake News (www.ifla.org/files/assets/hq/topics/info-society/images/how_to_spot_fake_news.pdf).

IGI Global (2020) What is Tourism 4.0 (www.igi-global.com/dictionary/technological-developments/81655).

Illumine Ltd (2019) How to Make a Mind Map (www.illumine.co.uk/resources/mind-mapping/how-to-make-a-mind-map).

Indeed (2016) Volunteering and the Workplace: Hands up for New Skills (www.london.gov.uk/sites/default/files/indeed_report_-_final_version.pdf).

Institute of Leadership & Mana (2007). *Achieving Objectives Through Time Management Super Series*. Burlington: Taylor & Francis.

International Labour Office (ILO) and Walk Free Foundation (2017) Global Estimates of Modern Slavery: Forced Labour and Forced Marriage (www.ilo.org/wcmsp5/groups/public/---dgreports/---dcomm/documents/publication/wcms_575479.pdf).

International Journal for Students as Partners (IJSaP) (2020) *International Journal for Students as Partners* (mulpress.mcmaster.ca/ijsap).

Iso-Ahola, S.E. (1982) 'Toward a Social Psychological Theory of Tourism Motivation: A Rejoinder', *Annals of Tourism Research*, 9(2): 256–62.

Jack, K., Stansbie, P. and Sciarini, M. (2017) 'An Examination of the Role played by Internships in nurturing Management Competencies in Hospitality and Tourism Management (HTM) Students', *Journal of Teaching in Travel and Tourism*, 17(1): 17–33.

Jacobsen, J.K.S., Iversen, N.M. and Hem, L.E. (2019) 'Hotspot Crowding and Over-Tourism: Antecedents of Destination Attractiveness', *Annals of Tourism Research*, 76(1): 53–66.

Jairam, D., and Kiewra, K.A. (2009) 'An Investigation of the SOAR Study Method', *Journal of Advanced Academics*, 20(4): 602–29.

Jafari, J. and Xiao, H. (eds) (2016) *Encyclopedia of Tourism*. Cham: Springer Publishing Company.

Jago, L.K. and Shaw, R.N. (1998) 'Special Events: A Conceptual and Definitional Framework', *Festival Management and Event Tourism*, 5(1–2): 21–32.

Jairam, D. and Kiewra, K.A. (2009) 'An Investigation of the SOAR Study Method', *Journal of Advanced Academics*, 20(4): 602–29.

Jasper, M. (2013) *Beginning Reflective Practice*. Andover: Cengage Learning.

Jayatunge, R.M. (2018) The Buddhist Philosophy and Critical Thinking (www.dailynews.lk/2018/01/31/features/141439/buddhist-philosophy-and-critical-thinking).

JISC (2016) Virtual Learning Environments (VLE) (www.jisc.ac.uk/guides/technology-and-tools-for-online-learning/virtual-learning-environments).

Jones, G.R. (1983) 'Psychological Orientation and the Process of Organizational Socialization: An Interactionist Perspective', *Academy of Management Review*, 8(3): 464–74.

Jones, R. and Sant, R. (2013) The Solent Capital Compass Model of Employability (http://ssudl.solent.ac.uk/2567).

Jucan, C.N. and Jucan, M.S. (2013) 'Travel and Tourism as a Driver of Economic Recovery', *Procedia Economics and Finance*, 6(1): 81–8.

Kapalan, J.M. and Warren, A.C. (2010) *Patterns of Entrepreneurship Management*. 3rd edn. London: John Willey & Sons. (1st edn, 2009.)

Kaplan, A.M. and Haenlein, M. (2010) 'Users of the World, unite! The Challenges and Opportunities of Social Media', *Business Horizons*, 53: 59–68.

Kaynardağ, A.Y. (2019) 'Pedagogy in HE: Does It Matter?', *Studies in Higher Education*, 44(1): 111–9.

Kazemek, E. (1991) 'Ten Criteria for Effective Team Building', *Healthcare Financial Management*, 45(9): 15.

Kendrick, T. (2015). *Identifying and Managing Project Risk: Essential Tools for Failure-Proofing Your Project*. 3rd edn. San Carlos, CA: American Management Association. (1st edn, 2003)

Khaleeli, H. (2017) 'From Barcelona to Malia: How Brits on holiday have made themselves unwelcome', *The Guardian* (www.theguardian.com/travel/shortcuts/2017/jan/17/from-barcelona-to-malia-how-brits-on-holiday-have-made-themselves-unwelcome).

Kiewra, M. (2005) 'Iterative Discovering of User's Preferences Using Web Mining', *International Journal on Computational Science and Applications*, 2(2): 57–66.

King's College London (KCL) (2019) Library and Collections: Citing References (libguides.kcl.ac.uk/ld.php?content_id=32466479).

Knowles, E. (2019) Getting the most out of Lectures and Seminars (https://www.prospects.ac.uk/applying-for-university/university-life/getting-the-most-out-of-lectures-and-seminars).

Knox, J. (2012) 'Just in Time Management Information Helps Drive Business', *Automotive Industries*, 191(3): 58–59.

Koch, T., Gerber, C. and De Klerk, J.J. (2018) 'The Impact of Social Media on Recruitment: Are you Linkedin?', *SA Journal of Human Resource Management* (sajhrm.co.za/index.php/sajhrm/article/view/861/1437).

Kolb, D. (1984) *Experiential Learning: Experience as the Source of Learning and Development*. New Jersey: Prentice Hall.

Kolb, A.Y. and Kolb, D.A. (2009) 'Experiential Learning Theory: A Dynamic, Holistic Approach to Management Learning, Education and Development', in Steven J. Armstrong and Cynthia V. Fukami (eds), *The SAGE Handbook of Management Learning, Education and Development*. London: Sage Publications. pp. 42–68.

Kolosinska, B. How to Write a Good Travel Industry CV (http://www.travelweekly.co.uk/articles/26758/how-to-write-a-good-travel-industry-cv).

Kotler, P., Armstrong, G. and Opresnik, M.O. (2018) *Principles of Marketing*. 17th edn. Harlow: Pearson.

Krechowiecka, I. (2003) Welcome to the World of VLEs (www.theguardian.com/education/2003/nov/18/elearning.technology11).

Kristof-Brown, A.L. (2000) 'Perceived Applicant Fit: Distinguishing Between Recruiters' Perceptions of Person-Job and Person-Organization Fit', *Personnel Psychology*, 53(3): 643–71.

Kuhnke, E. (2015) *Body Language for Dummies*. Chichester: Wiley & Sons

Kuratko, D.F. (2014) *Entrepreneurship: Theory, Process, Practice.* 9th edn. Australia: South-Western. (1st edn, 2004)

Lancaster, P. and Findlay Schenck, B. (2014) *Small Business Marketing for Dummies.* Chichester: John Wiley and Sons.

Lavietes, S. (2003) F. William Free, 74, Ad Man Behind 'Fly Me'. (www.nytimes.com/2003/01/08/business/f-william-free-74-ad-man-behind-fly-me.html).

Lee, Z., Chan, T., Balaji, M. and Chong, A. (2018) 'Why People Participate in the Sharing Economy: An Empirical Investigation of Uber', *Internet Research,* 28 (3): 829–50.

Lee-Davies, L. (2007) *Developing Work and Study Skills.* London: Thomson.

Lehdonvirta, V. (2018) 'Flexibility in the Gig Economy: Managing Time on Three Online Piecework Platforms', *New Technology, Work and Employment,* 33(1): 13–29.

Leiper, N. (1979) 'The Framework of Tourism: Towards a Definition of Tourism, Tourist, and the Tourist Industry', *Annals of Tourism Research,* 6(4): 390–407.

Lenzen, M., Sun, Y., Faturay, F., Ting, Y.P., Geschke, A. and Malik, A. (2018) 'The Carbon Footprint of Global Tourism', *Nature Climate Change,* 8: 522–8.

Lepore, M. (2020) 'You Have 6 Seconds to Make an Impression: How Recruiters See Your Resume', *The Ladders* (www.theladders.com/career-advice/you-only-get-6-seconds-of-fame-make-it-count).

Leslie, D. and Russell, H. (2006) 'The Importance of Foreign Language Skills in the Tourism Sector: A Comparative Study of Student Perceptions in the UK and Continental Europe', *Tourism Management,* 27: 1397–1407.

Lewin, K., Lippitt, R. and White, R.K. (1939) 'Patterns of Aggressive Behaviour in Experimentally Created Social Climates', *Journal of Social Psychology,* 10: 271–301.

Lin, N. (2017) 'Building a Network Theory of Social Capital', in N. Lin, K. Cook and R. Burt (eds) *Social Capital: Theory and Research.* London: Routledge, pp. 3–28.

LinkedIn (2017) The Student's Guide to LinkedIn (www.slideshare.net/linkedin/the-students-guide-to-linkedin).

LinkedIn Learning (2018) Workplace Learning Report: The Rise and Responsibility of Talent Development in the New Labor Market (learning.linkedin.com/content/dam/me/learning/en-us/pdfs/linkedin-learning-workplace-learning-report-2018.pdf).

London School of Economics (2020) Oral Presentations (https://info.lse.ac.uk/staff/divisions/Eden-Centre/Assessment-Toolkit/Assessment-methods/Oral-presentations).

Lovelock, B. and Lovelock, K.M. (2013) *The Ethics of Tourism: Critical and Applied Perspectives.* London: Routledge.

Luka, I. (2015) 'Enhancing Employability Skills for Tourism and Hospitality Industry Employees in Europe', *Acta Prosperitatis,* 6 (1) 75–95.

Luo, L., Kiewra, K.A. and Samuelson, L. (2016) 'Revising Lecture Notes: How Revision, Pauses, and Partners Affect Note Taking and Achievement', *Instructional Science,* 44(1): 45–67.

Lumley, M. and Wilkinson, J. (2013) *Developing Employability for Business.* Oxford: Oxford University Press.

Lynch, M. (2016) Social Constructivism in Education (www.theedadvocate.org/social-constructivism-in-education/).

Lyneham, S. and Facchini, L. (2019) 'Benevolent Harm: Orphanages, Voluntourism and Child Sexual Exploitation in South-East Asia', *Trends and Issues in Crime and Criminal Justice* (eds.b.ebscohost.com/eds/pdfviewer/pdfviewer?vid=1&sid=92dcedba-3d87-46dc-9a9e-d96e26c705a3%40pdc-v-sessmgr05).

MacCannell, D. (1976) *The Tourist: A New Theory of the Leisure Class.* London: Macmillan.

MacCannell, D. (1999) *The Tourist: A New Theory of the Leisure Class.* Revised edition. Berkeley: University of California Press. (1st edition 1976.)

Mackenzie, A. (1990). *The Time Trap.* New York: AMACOM.

Mackenzie, A. and Nickerson, P. (2009) *The Time Trap.* 4th edition New York: AMACOM. (1st edition 1990.)

Mair, J. and Whitford, M. (2013) 'An Exploration of Events Research: Event Topics, Themes and Emerging Trends', *International Journal of Event and Festival Management,* 4(1): 6–30.

Malia Kana'iaupuni, S., Ledward, B. and Malone, N. (2017) 'Mohala I ka wai: Cultural Advantage as a Framework for Indigenous Culture-Based Education and Student Outcomes', *American Educational Research Journal*, 54(1S): 311S–39S.

Marston, R. (2018) 'Can your Social Media Profile Kill your Job Prospects?', *BBC* (www.bbc.co.uk/news/business-42621920).

Marx, E. (1999) *Breaking Through Culture Shock*. London: Nicholas Brealey.

Mayer, J.D., Caruso, D.R. and Salovey, P. (2016) 'The Ability Model of Emotional Intelligence: Principles and Updates', *Emotion Review*, 8(4): 290–300.

McCabe, V.S. (2008) 'Strategies for Career Planning and Development in the Convention and Exhibition Industry in Australia', *International Journal of Hospitality Management*, 27(2): 222–31.

McMillan, K. and Weyers, J. (2011) *How to Succeed in Examinations and Assessments*. Harlow: Pearson.

McMillan, K. and Weyers, J. (2012) *The Study Skills Book*. 3rd edn. Harlow: Pearson Education Limited (1st edn, 2009)

Massachusetts Institute of Technology (2019) Effects of the Flipped Classroom: Evidence from a Randomized Trial by Elizabeth Setren, Kyle Greenberg, Oliver Moore, and Michael Yankovich. SEII Discussion Paper #2019.07 (seii.mit.edu/wp-content/uploads/2019/08/SEII-Discussion-Paper-2019.07-Setren.pdf).

Mayer, J. D. and Salovey, P. (1997) 'What Is Emotional Intelligence?', in D.J. Sluyter (ed.), *Emotional Development and Emotional Intelligence: Educational Implications*. New York: Basic Books. pp. 3–34.

Mayer, R.E. (2010) *Applying the Science of Learning*. Upper Saddle River: Pearson.

Mehrabian, A. (1971) 'Nonverbal Communication', *Nebraska Symposium on Motivation*, 19: 107–61.

Mehta, S.S., Newbold, J.J., and O'Rourke, M.A. (2011) 'Why Do First-Generation Students Fail?', *College Student Journal*, 45(1): 20–36.

Mei, X.Y. (2019) 'Gaps in Tourism Education and Workforce Needs: Attracting and Educating the Right People', *Current Issues in Tourism*, 22(12): 1400–4.

Mercer-Mapstone, L., Dvorakova, S.L., Matthews, K., Abbot, S., Cheng, B., Felten, P., Knorr, K., Marquis, E., Shammas, R. and Swaim, K. (2017) 'A Systematic Literature Review of Students as Partners in Higher Education', *International Journal for Students As Partners*, 1(1): https://doi.org/10.15173/ijsap.v1i1.3119.

McCarthy, J.M., Bauer, T.N, Truxillo, D.M, Anderson, N.R., Costa A.C. and Ahmed, S.M. (2017) 'Applicant Perspectives During Selection: A Review Addressing "So What?", "What's New?", and "Where to Next?"', *Journal of Management*, 43(6): 1693–1725.

McCrae, R.R. and Costa, P.T., Jr. (1999) 'A Five-Factor Theory of Personality', in L.A. Pervin and O.P. John (eds), *Handbook of Personality: Theory and Research*. New York: Guilford Press. pp. 139–53.

McLeod, S. (2019) What Is Constructivism? (www.simplypsychology.org/constructivism.html).

McKie, F. (2019) Flipping Great? The Case For and against Flipping the Classroom (www.timeshighereducation.com/news/flipping-great-case-and-against-flipping-classroom).

Mikkelsen, R. (2015) Person-Job-Fit: Finding the Right Candidate for Each Position (workology.com/person-job-fit-finding-the-right-candidate-for-each-position/).

Mogelonsky, L. (2016) 'Are Tattoos Taboo In Hospitality?', *HospitalityNet* (www.hospitalitynet.org/opinion/4080041.html).

Mohanty, S. and Mohanty, S. (2019) 'A Skill-gap Study: An Analytical Approach with a Special Focus on Tourism Education and the Tourism Industry in Odisha', *African Journal of Hospitality, Tourism and Leisure* (www.ajhtl.com/uploads/7/1/6/3/7163688/article_10_vol_8_3__2019.pdf).

Moon, J. (2008) *Critical Thinking: An Exploration of Theory and Practice*. London: Routledge.

Morgan, P. (2017) *The Business Student's Guide to Study and Employability*. London: Sage.

Morgan-Thomas, M. (2015) 'Acting Out in Class: The Group role-play Advantage over PowerPoint Presentation', *Journal of Legal Studies in Business*, 19(1): 118–28.

Mössenlechner, C. (2017) 'ePortfolio Task Design: A High-Impact Tool for Higher Education Teaching in Tourism', in Pierre Benckendorff and Anita Zehrer (eds), *Handbook of Teaching and Learning in Tourism*. Cheltenham, Edward Elgar Publishing. pp. 173–89.

Moynihan, R. (2020) How Can We Help Students Transition into Graduate Life? (wonkhe.com/blogs/how-can-we-help-students-transition-into-graduate-life/).

Mullins, L. (2017) *Management and Organisational Behaviour.* 8th edn. Harlow: Financial Times/Prentice Hall.

Murray, J. (2019) 'How to Use Twitter to Find a Job in 2020', *Save The Student* (www.savethestudent.org/student-jobs/how-to-get-a-job-using-twitter.html).

National Cyber Security Centre (2018) Top Tips for Staying Secure (www.ncsc.gov.uk/collection/top-tips-for-staying-secure-online).

National Research Council (1999) *The Impacts of Natural Disasters: A Framework for Loss Estimation* (doi.org/10.17226/6425).

Neary, M. (2010) 'Student as Producer: Bringing Critical Theory to Life through the Life of Students', *Roundhouse: A Journal of Critical Social Theory*, 1, 36–45.

Neugebauer, J. and Evans-Brain, J. (2009) *Making the Most of Your Placement.* SAGE: London.

Neville, C. (2010) *Complete Guide to Referencing and Avoiding Plagiarism.* New York: McGraw-Hill Education.

Newham, A. (2013) 'Mascara Ads Craw Criticisms', *New York Times* (www.nytimes.com/2013/11/14/fashion/Mascara-Ads-Draw-Criticisms.html).

Newstrom, J.W. and Davis, K. (1993) *Organizational Behavior: Human Behavior at Work.* New York: McGraw-Hill.

Nghia, T. L. H. and Duyen, N. T. M. (2018) 'Internship-related Learning Outcomes and Their Influential Factors: The Case of Vietnamese Tourism and Hospitality Students', *Education and Training*, 60(1): 69–81.

Nguyen-Truong, C., Davis, A., Spencer, C., Rasmor, M. and Dekker, L. (2018) 'Techniques to Promote Reflective Practice and Empowered Learning', *Journal of Nursing Education*, 57(2): 115–20.

NHS (2020) Mindfulness (www.nhs.uk/conditions/stress-anxiety-depression/mindfulness/).

NHTI (2014) SQ3R (www.nhti.edu/student-resources/where-can-i-get-help-my-studies/study-solutions-lab/reading-and-learning-sq3r).

Nickson, D. (2013) *Human Resource Management for the Hospitality and Tourism Industries.* Abingdon: Routledge.

Nottingham Trent University (2020) SCALE UP (www.ntu.ac.uk/about-us/academic-development-and-quality/innovations-in-learning-and-teaching/scale-up).

NUS (2019) Sustainability Skills Survey: Research into Students' Experiences of Teaching and Learning on Sustainable Development (sustainability.nus.org.uk/resources/nus-sustainability-skills-survey-2018-2019).

Nye, J. (2005) 'Soft Power and Higher Education', *Educause* (library.educause.edu/-/media/files/library/2005/1/ffp0502s-pdf.pdf).

Oberg, K. (1960) 'Cultural Shock: Adjustment to New Cultural Environments', *Practical Anthropology*, 7(4): 177–182.

Odgers Berndtson (2018) Launching Women into Hospitality Senior Leadership (www.odgersberndtson.com/en-gb/insights/launching-women-into-hospitality-senior-leadership).

OECD (2020) Tourism Trends and Policies 2020 (www.oecd.org/cfe/tourism/2020-Tourism-Brochure.pdf).

Office for Students (2009) Continuation and attainment gaps (www.officeforstudents.org.uk/advice-and-guidance/promoting-equal-opportunities/evaluation-and-effective-practice/continuation-and-attainment-gaps).

Open University (2019) Innovating Pedagogy (www.open.ac.uk/blogs/innovating/).

Open University (2020) Active Reading (help.open.ac.uk/active-reading).

Oxford Economics (2012) Global Talent 2021: How the New Geography of Talent will Transform Human Resource Strategies (www.oxfordeconomics.com/Media/Default/Thought%20Leadership/global-talent-2021.pdf).

Padesky, C. and Greenberger, D. (1995) *Clinician's Guide to Mind over Mood.* New York: Guildford Press.

Padgett, R.D., Johnson, M.P. and Pascarella, E.T. (2012) 'First-generation Undergraduate Students and the Impacts of the first year of College: Additional Evidence', *Journal of College Student Development*, 53(2): 243–66.

Page, S.J. (2013) *Tourism Management.* London: Routledge.

Payne, E. and Whittaker, L. (2006) *Developing Essential Study Skills.* Harlow: Pearson Education Limited.

Pease, A. and Pease, B. (2004) *The Definitive Book of Body Language.* London: Orion.

Pecha Kutcha (2020) Pecha Kutcha (www.pechakucha.com).

Perraudin, F. (2018) 'How Tattoos went from Subculture to Pop Culture', *The Guardian* (www.theguardian.com/fashion/2018/oct/26/how-tattoos-went-from-subculture-to-pop-culture).

Peter, J. and Gomez, S.J. (2019) 'Building Your Personal Brand: A Tool for Employability', *The IUP Journal of Soft Skills*, 8(2): 7–20.

Peters, T. (1997) 'The Brand Called You', *Fast Company* (*www.fastcompany.com/28905/brand-called-you*).

Petrone, P. (2019) The Skills Companies Need Most in 2019 – And How to Learn Them, LinkedIn Learning (learning.linkedin.com/blog/top-skills/the-skills-companies-need-most-in-2019--and-how-to-learn-them).

Phelan, K. V., Mejia, C. and Hertzman, J. (2013) 'The Industry Experience Gap: Hospitality Faculty Perceptions of the Importance of Faculty Industry Experience', *Journal of Hospitality & Tourism Education*, 25(3): 123–130.

Picton, C., Kahu. E.R. and Nelson, K. (2018) 'Hardworking, Determined and Happy': First-year Students' Understanding and Experience of Success', *Higher Education Research & Development*, 37(6): 1260–73.

Pine, B.J. and Gilmore, J.H. (2011) *The Experience Economy*. Updated edition. USA: Harvard Business School. (1st edn, 1999.)

PMI (2013a) *A Guide to Project Management Body of Knowledge*. 5th edn. Newton Square, PA: Project Management Institute. (1st edition 2000)

PMI (2013b) *Pulse of the Profession In-Depth Report: The Essential Role of Communications*. Newton Square, PA: Project Management Institute.

PMI (2017a) Pulse of the Profession In-Depth Report. *The High Cost of Low Performance: The Essential Role of Communications*. Newton Square, PA: Project Management Institute.

PMI (2017b) Pulse of the Profession In-Depth Report. *Success Rates Rise: Transforming the High Cost of Low Performance*. Newton Square, PA: Project Management Institute.

Poon, A. (1993) *Tourism, Technology and Competitive Strategies*. Wallingford: CABI.

Pope, K. (2019) '22 Places to Write When You're Tired of Working at Home', *The Write Life* (thewritelife.com/22-places-to-write/).

Psychology Today (2020) Memory (www.psychologytoday.com/gb/basics/memory).

Prince, M. (2004) 'Does Active Learning Work? A Review of the Research', *Journal of Engineering Education*, 93(3): 223–31.

Probst, G. (2014) *Tackling Complexity: A Systematic Approach for Decision Makers*. Sheffield: Greenleaf Publishing.

Proctor, V. (2019) Learning Lessons from VLEs (edtechnology.co.uk/latest-news/learning-lessons-from-vles/).

Purdue University (2020) Historical Perspectives on Argumentation (owl.purdue.edu/owl/general_writing/academic_writing/historical_perspectives_on_argumentation/toulmin_argument.html).

Puschra, W. and Burke, S. (eds) (2012) 'Sustainable Development in an Unequal World: How Do We Really Get "the Future We Want?"', *Friedrich Ebert Stiftung* (library.fes.de/pdf-files/iez/global/09371.pdf).

PWC (2016) Economic Impact of Air Traffic Control Strikes in Europe Prepared for A4E Airlines for Europe (www.politico.eu/wp-content/uploads/2016/10/ATCimpactreportA4E.pdf).

Qualman, E. (2013) *Socialnomics*. New Jersey: Wiley & Sons.

Queen's University (2020) Active Learning (www.queensu.ca/teachingandlearning/modules/active/04_what_is_active_learning.html).

QS (2019) QS World Rankings 2019 (www.qs.com/rankings/).

Race, P., Brown, S. and Smith, B. (2005) *500 Tips on Assessment*. London: Routledge.

Ramos, C.M.Q., Ribeiro de Almeida, C. and Fernandes, P.O. (eds) (2020) *Handbook of Research on Social Media Applications for the Tourism and Hospitality Sector*. Hershey, PA: IGI Global.

Reisinger, Y. & Turner, L.W. (2011) *Cross-Cultural Behaviour in Tourism: Concepts and Analysis*. London: Routledge.

ReThink Orphanages (2018) Responsible Volunteering Abroad: How to be a Responsible Volunteer? (rethinkorphanages.org/individual-orphanage-volunteering/responsible-volunteer-checklist).

Riahi, S. and Riahi, A. (2018) 'The Pedagogy of Higher Education: How to Evaluate the Quality of Training in Morocco to Improve it', *International Journal of Engineering Pedagogy*, 8(1): 92–108.

Robinson, F.P. (1941) *Effective Study*. New York: Harper & Row.

Robinson, F.P. (1946) *Effective Study*. 2nd edn. New York: Harper & Row. (1st edn, 1941.)

Robinson, P., Heitmann, S. and Dieke, P.U.C. (eds) (2011) *Research Themes for Tourism*. Wallingford: CABI.

Roche, M. (2000) *Mega-Events Modernity: Olympics and Expos in the Growth of Global Culture*. London: Routledge.

Rojek, C. and Urry, J. (eds) (1997) *Touring Cultures*. London: Routledge.

Rook, S. (2013) *The Graduate Career Guide Book*. Basingstoke: Palgrave Macmillan.

Rothstein, R., Wilder, T. and Jacobsen, R. (2007) 'Balance in the Balance', *Educational Leadership*, 64(8): 8–14.

Rozhdestvenskaya, N.A. (2017) 'The Activity Approach to the Psychological Support of the 1st Year University Students', *National Psychological Journal*, 3: 113–20.

Ruffle, B.J. and Shtudiner, Z.E. (2014) 'Are Good-Looking People More Employable?' *Management Science*, 61(8): 1760–76.

Russell-Jones, N. (2014) *Business Planning Pocketbook*. 3rd edn. Alresford: Management Pocketbooks. (1st edn, 1998.)

Ryals, J. (2011) Leaving Lectures Behind (news.ncsu.edu/2011/09/leaving-lectures-behind/).

Sackstein, S. (2015) *Teaching Students to Self-Assess: How Do I Help Students Reflect and Grow as Learners?* Danvers, MA: ASCD Arias.

Sagan, C. (1980) *Cosmos: A Personal Voyage*. Public Broadcasting Service, United States, aired 14/12/1980.

Salazar, N.B. (2014) 'Culture Broker, Tourism', in J. Jafari & H. Xiao (eds), *Encyclopedia of Tourism*. Basel: Springer International Publishing, pp. 1–2.

Salit, C. (2017) 6 Secrets From the Theater For Giving Great Presentations (That Anyone Can Use) (performanceofalifetime.com/2017/09/6-secrets-from-the-theater-for-giving-great-presentations-that-anyone-can-use/).

Sambell, K., McDowell, L. and Montgomery, C. (2012) *Assessment for Learning in Higher Education*. London: Routledge.

Sambell, K., Brown, S. and Graham, L. (2017) *Professionalism in Practice: Key Directions in Higher Education Learning, Teaching and Assessment*. London: Springer.

Save the Children (2017) The Truth about Voluntourism (www.savethechildren.org.au/Our-Stories/The-truth-about-voluntourism).

Schwartz, S.H., Cieciuch, J., Vecchione, M., Davidov, E., Fischer, R., Beierlein, C., Ramos, A., Verkasalo, M., Lönnqvist, J.E., Demirutku, K., Dirilen-Gumus, O. and Konty, M. (2012) 'Refining the Theory of Basic Individual Values', *Journal of Personality and Social Psychology*, 103: 663–88.

SCImago Journal and Country Rank Journal (SJR) (2007–2020) Journal Rankings: Tourism, Leisure and Hospitality Management (www.scimagojr.com/journalrank.php?category=1409&country=GB).

Seibert, S., Kraimer, M. and Liden, R. (2001) 'A Social Capital Theory of Career Success', *Academy of Management Journal*, 44(2), 219–37.

Sendmail (2013) Sendmail, CPP Survey: 64% Cite #Email as Source of #Workplace Confusion, Resentment (www.prnewswire.com/news-releases/sendmail-cpp-survey-64-cite-email-as-source-of-workplace-confusion-resentment-211802791.html).

Service, O., Hallsworth, M., Halpern, D., Algate, F., Gallagher, R., Nguyen, S., Ruda, S., Sanders, M., Pelenur, M., Gyani, A., Harper, H., Reinhard, J. and Kirkman, E. (2014) *EAST: Four Simple Ways to Apply Behavioural Insights* (www.bi.team/wp-content/uploads/2015/07/BIT-Publication-EAST_FA_WEB.pdf).

Seyitoglu, F. and Yirik, S. (2015) 'Internship Satisfaction of Students of Hospitality and Impact of Internship on the Professional Development and Industrial Perception', *Asia Pacific Journal of Tourism Research*, 20(1): 1414–29.

Sharpley, R. and Telfer, D. J. (eds) (2014) *Tourism and Development: Concepts and Issues*, 2nd Edition. Bristol: Channel View Publications.

Sheward, S. (2011) 'Why You Should Identify Your Personal Values before Job-Hunting', *The Guardian* (www.theguardian.com/careers/careers-blog/identify-your-values-before-job-seeking).

Shine (2020) Build your Tourism Marketing Strategy and Planning (www.shinepeopleandplaces.co.uk/).

Shiva Foundation (2018) Charting a Course for Collective Action: Addressing Slavery in the Hotel Industry (www. shivafoundation.org.uk/wp-content/uploads/2018/03/01_Charting-a-Course-for-Collective-Action.pdf).

SHRM (2015) Using Social Media for Talent Acquisition (www.shrm.org/hr-today/trends-and-forecasting/ research-and-surveys/pages/social-media-recruiting-screening-2015.aspx).

Sindik, J. and Božinoviⵒ, N. (2013) 'Importance of Foreign Languages for a Career in Tourism as perceived by Students in Different Years of Study', *Journal of Economic & Politics of Transition*, 15(31): 33–45.

Singh, T. (2018) 'Is Over-Tourism the Downside of Mass Tourism?', *Tourism Recreation Research*, 43(4): 415–6.

Smale, B. and Fowlie, J. (2015) *How to Succeed at University*. London: Sage Publications.

Smith, J. (2013) 12 Tips for Transitioning to an Office Job (www.forbes.com/sites/jacquelynsmith/2013/11/22/12-tips-for-transitioning-to-an-office-job/#6ece703b4dbe).

Smith, J. (2019a) Internships (www.prospects.ac.uk/jobs-and-work-experience/work-experience-and-internships/internships).

Smith, J. (2019b) Work Placements (www.prospects.ac.uk/jobs-and-work-experience/work-experience-and-internships/work-placements).

Smith, R. and Welton, R. (2016) 'Enabling and Embedding the Oath Project into Student Learning and Ethical Career Pathways', in K. Ogunyemi (ed.), *Teaching Ethics across the Management Curriculum: Principles and Applications*. New York: Business Expert Press, pp. 35-52.

Smith, V. (2001) 'The Culture Brokers', in V. Smith and M. Brent (eds), *Hosts and Guests Revisited: Tourism Issues of the 21st Century*. Elmsford: Cognizant, pp. 275–82.

Social Media Today (2019) LinkedIn Growth (www.socialmediatoday.com/news/linkedin-engagement-continues-to-rise-as-per-microsofts-latest-performanc/565802/).

Sonntag, S. (2010) *Teaching, the Hardest Job You'll Ever Love: Helpful Ideas for Teachers In and Out of the Classroom*. Lanham: R&L Education.

Sperry, Richard C. and Jetter, Antonie J. (2019) 'A Systems Approach to Project Stakeholder Management: Fuzzy Cognitive Map Modelling', *Project Management*, 50(6): 699-715.

Standing Committee for Economic and Commercial Cooperation of the Organisation of Islamic Cooperation (COMCEC) (2014), 'Enhancing the Capacity of Tourism Workforce in the OIC Member Countries For Improved Tourism Service Quality' (https://www2.gwu.edu/~iits/Qatar/References/Enhancingthe CapacityofTourismWorkforce.pdf)

Starc Peceny, U., Urbančič, J., Mokorel, S., Kuralt, V. and Ilijaš, T. (2019) 'Tourism 4.0: Challenges in Marketing a Paradigm Shift', in M. Reyes (ed.), *Consumer Behaviour and Marketing*. London: InTechOpen Limited, doi: 10.5772/intechopen.84762.

Starc Peceny, U. (2019) Tourism 4.0. Addressing the Challenges of the Modern Tourism (destinationhealth-mag.co.uk/tourism-4-0-addressing-the-challenges-of-the-modern-tourism/).

Statista Research Department (2018) Terrorism Impact on the Travel Industry in Europe - Statistics & Facts (www.statista.com/topics/3329/terrorism-impact-on-the-travel-industry-in-europe/).

Statista Research Department (2020) Skills important to the hospitality and tourism industry future in the United Kingdom (https://www.statista.com/statistics/302449/skills-important-to-the-hospitality-and-tourism-industry-future-in-the-united-kingdom/)

Steg, L., Bolderdijk, J. W., Keizer, K. and Perlaviciute, G. (2014a) 'An Integrated Framework for Encouraging Pro-environmental Behaviour: The Role of Values, Situational Factors and Goals', *Journal of Environmental Psychology*, 38, pp.104–15, Science Direct [Online]. Available at: http://0-www.sciencedirect.com.brum.beds.ac.uk/science/article/pii/S027249441400005X (Accessed 20 May 2015).

Steg, L., Perlaviciute, G., van der Werff, E., and Lurvink, J. (2014b) 'The Significance of Hedonic Values for Environmentally Relevant Attitudes, Preferences, and Actions', *Environment and Behaviour*, 46(2): 163–192, Sage Publishing [Online]. Available at: http://0-eab.sagepub.com.brum.beds.ac.uk/ (Accessed 4 September 2015).

Steinfield, C., Ellison, N.B. and Lampe, C. (2008) 'Social Capital, Self-esteem, and Use of Online Social Network Sites: A Longitudinal Analysis', *Journal of Applied Developmental Psychology*, 29(6): 434–45.

Stokes, D.R. (2010) *Entrepreneurship*. Mason, Ohio: South-Western Cengage Learning.

Stop Slavery Hotel Industry Network (2017) Framework for working with Suppliers: Mitigating Risk of Modern Slavery (www.shivafoundation.org.uk/wp-content/uploads/2018/03/04_FrameworkForWorkingWithSuppliers.pdf).

Su, A.J. (2016) 'How to Calm Your Nerves Before a Big Presentation', *Harvard Business Review* (hbr.org/2016/10/how-to-calm-your-nerves-before-a-big-presentation).

Sucher, W. and Cheung, C. (2015) 'The Relationship between Hotel Employees' Cross-Cultural Competency and Team Performance in Multi-National Hotel Companies', *International Journal of Hospitality Management*, 49: 93–104.

Sullivan, L.E. (ed.) (2009) *The SAGE Glossary of the Social and Behavioral Sciences*. London: Sage Publications.

Swan, K., Shen, J. and Hiltz, S.R. (2006) 'Assessment and Collaboration in Online Learning', *Journal of Asynchronous Learning Networks*, 10(1): 45–62.

Taiwo, A.A. and Afolami, J.A. (2011) 'Incessant Building Collapse: A Case of a Hotel in Akure, Nigeria', *Journal of Building Appraisal*, 6: 241–8.

TargetJobs (2019a) Top Ten Tools for Getting a Graduate Job in the Hospitality Industry (targetjobs.co.uk/career-sectors/hospitality-leisure-and-travel/320903-top-ten-tools-for-getting-a-graduate-job-in-the-hospitality-industry).

TargetJobs (2019b) Resilience: The Ability to Cope with Setbacks (targetjobs.co.uk/careers-advice/skills-and-competencies/452729-resilience-the-ability-to-cope-with-setbacks).

Tarlow, P. (2020) Unique Forms of Tourism – Thinking Outside the Box? (www.hotel-online.com/press_releases/release/unique-forms-of-tourism-thinking-outside-the-box/).

Taylor, S. (2010) *Resourcing and Talent Management*. London: CIPD.

Taylor, S. (2015) *You're a Genius: Using Reflective Practice to Master the Craft of Leadership*. New York: Business Expert Press.

Team Based Learning Collaborative (2020) Team Based Learning (www.teambasedlearning.org/definition/).

TES (2020) What is Pedagogy? (www.tes.com/news/what-is-pedagogy-definition).

TEDx Talks (2014) Volunteerism – Best Platform for Personal and Professional Development: Tuan Nguyen at TEDxUOttawa (www.youtube.com/watch?v=xJ7_0d_etKg).

The Foundation for Critical Thinking (2019) A Brief History of Critical Thinking (www.criticalthinking.org/pages/a-brief-history-of-the-idea-of-critical-thinking/408).

Thomas, D. (2019) 'Tattoos at Work: Are They Still an Issue?', *BBC* (www.bbc.co.uk/news/business-48620528).

Thomas, G. (2011) *Doing Research (Pocket Study Guide)*. Basingstoke: Palgrave Macmillan.

Times Higher Education (2019) World University Rankings, 2019 (www.timeshighereducation.com/world-university-rankings/2019/world-ranking).

Timming, A. R., Nickson, D., Re, D. and Perrett, D. (2017) 'What Do You Think of My Ink? Assessing the Effects of Body Art on Employment Chances', *Human Resource Management*, 56(1): 133–49.

Todorov, A., Baron, S.G. and Oosterhof, N.N. (2008) 'Evaluating Face Trustworthiness: A Model Based Approach', *Social Cognitive and Affective Neuroscience*, 3(2):119–27.

Tomić, M. and Čolić, D. (2019) 'The Importance of Intercultural Competence in Foreign Language Teaching, with References to Tourism Curricula in Higher Education', *TIMS Acta*, 13: 99–105.

Tomlinson, M. and Holmes, L. (eds) (2017) *Graduate Employability in Context: Theory, Research and Debate*. London: Palgrave Macmillan.

Tracy, B. (2014) *Time Management*. New York: AMACOM.

TravelMole (2019) Air New Zealand Will Allow Crew to Have Visible Tattoos (www.travelmole.com/news_feature.php?news_id=2037843#).

Travel Weekly (2006) Mentoring in the Travel Industry (www.travelweekly.co.uk/articles/22054/mentoring-in-the-travel-industry).

Travel Weekly (2019) Special Report: Future Skills in Travel and Tourism (www.travelweekly.co.uk/articles/336040/special-report-future-skills-in-travel-and-tourism-seminar).

Tuckman, B. W. (1965) 'Development Sequence in Small Groups', *Psychological Bulletin*, 63(6): 384–99.

TUI (2017a) TUI Group Sustainability Survey Global Insights 2017 (www.tuigroup.com/damfiles/default/tuigroup-15/de/nachhaltigkeit/berichterstattung-downloads/2018/TUI-Group-Sustainability-Survey-2017/2017_TUI-Sustainability_Results-JA.pdf-cbbef94d1e83d193ea7bd4e933f63ba8.pdf).

TUI (2017b) Caring for a Better World Strategic Plan 2017-2020 (www.tuicarefoundation.com/damfiles/default/PDFs/170720-TCF-Strategic-plan-2017-2020.pdf-d3d6fbae04bae9bebee37f83004d0153.pdf).

Tümkaya S., Aybek, B. and Aldağ, H. (2009) 'An Investigation of University Students' Critical Thinking Disposition and Perceived Problem-Solving Skills', *Egitim Arastirmalari-Eurasian Journal of Educational Research*, 36(1): 57–74.

Tylor, E.B. (1871) *Primitive Culture*. Cambridge: Cambridge University Press.

Uber Grosse, C. (2004) 'The Competitive Advantage of Foreign Languages and Cultural Knowledge', *The Modern Languages Journal*, 88(3): 351–73.

Ulrey, K.L. and Amason, P. (2001) 'Intercultural Communication Between Patients and Health Care Providers: An Exploration of Intercultural Effectiveness, Cultural Sensitivity, Stress and Anxiety', *Journal of Health Communication*, 13(4): 449–63.

UN (1948) Universal Declaration of Human Rights (www.ohchr.org/EN/UDHR/Documents/UDHR_Translations/eng.pdf).

UN (2011) Guiding Principles on Business and Human Rights: Implementing the United Nations "Protect, Respect and Remedy" Framework (www.ohchr.org/documents/publications/guidingprinciplesbusinesshr_en.pdf).

UN (2015) Transforming Our World: The 2030 Agenda for Sustainable Development (www.un.org/pga/wp-content/uploads/sites/3/2015/08/120815_outcome-document-of-Summit-for-adoption-of-the-post-2015-development-agenda.pdf).

UN (2018) State of the World's Volunteerism Report: The Thread that binds, Volunteerism and Community Resilience (unv-swvr2018.org/files/51692_UNV_SWVR_2018_WEB.pdf).

UN (2019) Global Sustainable Development Report 2019: The Future is Now – Science for Achieving Sustainable Development (sustainabledevelopment.un.org/content/documents/24797GSDR_report_2019.pdf).

University College London (2019) Active Learning (www.ucl.ac.uk/teaching-learning/publications/2019/aug/active-learning).

University Grants Committee (UGC) (2017) Hong Kong PhD Fellowship Scheme (www.ugc.edu.hk/eng/rgc/funding_opport/fellowships/hkphdfs.html).

University of Birmingham (2020) Tips for Effective Presentation (www.birmingham.ac.uk/schools/metallurgy-materials/about/cases/tips-advice/presentation.aspx).

University of Leicester (2020a) Critical Writing (www2.le.ac.uk/offices/ld/all-resources/writing/writing-resources/critical-writing).

University of Leicester (2020b) Delivering an Effective Presentation (www2.le.ac.uk/offices/ld/all-resources/presentations/delivering-presentation).

University of Oxford (2019) OSCOLA: Oxford University Standard for the Citation of Legal Authorities (www.law.ox.ac.uk/sites/files/oxlaw/oscola_4th_edn_hart_2012.pdf).

University of Queensland (2017) Flipped Classroom Project (https://itali.uq.edu.au/about/projects/flipped-classroom-olt).

University of the Sunshine Coast (2020) What Is the Difference between a Lecture, Tutorial, Workshop and Lectorial? (usc.custhelp.com/app/answers/detail/a_id/16/~/what-is-the-difference-between-a-lecture%2C-tutorial%2C-workshop-and-lectorial%3F).

University of Sussex (2020) Critical Thinking (www.sussex.ac.uk/skillshub/?id=277).

Universities UK (2018) Regulation of Higher Education (www.universitiesuk.ac.uk/policy-and-analysis/Pages/regulation.aspx).

Universities UK (2019) Black, Asian and Minority Ethnic Student Attainment at UK Universities (www.universitiesuk.ac.uk/policy-and-analysis/reports/Pages/bame-student-attainment-uk-universities-closing-the-gap.aspx).

United Nations World Tourism Organisation (UNWTO) (2011) Tourism Towards 2030 / Global Overview (www.e-unwto.org/doi/book/10.18111/9789284414024).

UNWTO (2017) 2nd UNWTO Report on Gastronomy Tourism: Sustainability and Gastronomy (www.unwto.org/archive/global/press-release/2017-05-17/2nd-unwto-report-gastronomy-tourism-sustainability-and-gastronomy).

UNWTO (2019) Tourism for SDGS: A Platform developed by UNWTO (http://tourism4sdgs.org/).

UNWTO (2020a) Tourism and Coronavirus Disease (COVID-19) (www.unwto.org/tourism-covid-19-coronavirus).

UNWTO (2020b) World Tourism Barometer No.18 January 2020 (www.unwto.org/world-tourism-barometer-n18-january-2020).

UNWTO (2020c) Impact Assessment of the Covid-19 Outbreak on International Tourism (www.unwto.org/impact-assessment-of-the-covid-19-outbreak-on-international-tourism).

UNWTO, Centre of Expertise Leisure, Tourism & Hospitality, NHTV Breda University of Applied Sciences and NHL Stenden University of Applied Sciences (2018) 'Overtourism'? – Understanding and Managing Urban Tourism Growth beyond Perceptions (doi.org/10.18111/9789284420070).

Urry, J. (1992) 'The Tourist Gaze "revisited"', *American Behavioral Scientist*, 36(2): 172–86.

van Alten, D.C., Phielix, C., Janssen, J. and Kester, L. (2019) 'Effects of Flipping the Classroom on Learning Outcomes and Satisfaction: A Meta-Analysis', *Educational Research Review*, 28: 1–18.

van Der Wagen, L. and White, L. (2014) *Human Resource Management for the Event Industry*. London: Routledge.

van Emden, J. (2010) *Presentation Skills for Students*. Basingstoke: Palgrave Macmillan.

van Maanen, J. and Schein, E.H. (1979) 'Toward a Theory of Organizational Socialization', in B.M. Staw (ed.), *Research in Organizational* Behavior. Greenwich: CT. pp. 209–64.

Vanneste, D., Huyghe, S., Vandensavel, K. and Vanginderachter, K. (2009) 'Languages and Aspects of Tourism Education and Training in Flanders', *Scottish Languages Review*, 19: 25–34.

Verdonck, B., Clark, M. and Storkey, C. (2019) How to REALLY Use LinkedIn: Implementing Social Selling & Social Recruiting Projects at Scale. Chatteris: Really Connect Ltd.

Vitae (2010) Vitae Researcher Development Framework (RDF) 2011 (www.vitae.ac.uk/vitae-publications/rdf-related/researcher-development-framework-rdf-vitae.pdf/view).

Walter, R. (n.d.) Using Social Media in the Recruitment Process (www.robertwalters.co.uk/hiring/campaigns/using-social-media-in-the-recruitment-process.html).

Warren, K. (2018) How to use LinkedIn to Find a Job (www.businessinsider.com/how-to-use-linkedin-to-find-a-job-2018-8?r=US&IR=T).

Watkins, R., Corry, M., Dardick, W. and Stella, J. (2015) 'Note-taking Habits of Online Students: Value, Quality, and Support', *Quarterly Review of Distance Education*, 16(3): 1–12.

Watson, D. (2002) 'What Is University For?', *The Guardian* (www.theguardian.com/education/2002/jan/15/highereducation.news).

Watson, D. (2015) Is Critical Thinking a Western Concept? (www.britishcouncil.org/voices-magazine/critical-thinking-western-concept).

Way, A. (2011) Deconstructing a $1 Billion Disaster. The Project PERFECT White Paper Collection. *Thinking Big Partners* (http://www.projectperfect.com.au/downloads/Info/white-paper-deconstructing-a-one-billion-disaster.pdf)

Wearing, S., Young, T. and Everingham, P. (2017) 'Evaluating Volunteer Tourism: Has It Made a Difference?', *Tourism Recreation Research*, 42(4): 512–21.

Weedon, C. (2014) *Responsible Tourist Behaviour*. Abingdon: Routledge.

Weyers, J. and McMillan, K. (2011) *How to Write Essays & Assignments (Smarter Study Skills)*. London: Prentice Hall.

Whistance, D. and Campbell, S. (2019) 'Investigating the Impact of a Careers Development Model', *Prospects Luminate* (luminate.prospects.ac.uk/investigating-the-impact-of-a-careers-development-model).

Wiggins, B. (2016) Effective Document and Data Management. *Unlocking Corporate Content*. London: Routledge.

Wiggins, G. (1990) 'The Case for Authentic Assessment. Practical Assessment', *Research & Evaluation*, 2(2): 1–6.

Williams, K. (2011) *Time Management*. Basingstoke: Palgrave Macmillan.

Williams, K., Woolliams, M. and Spiro, J. (2012a) *The Reflective Practitioner: How Professionals Think in Action*. New York: Basic Books.

Williams, K., Woolliams, M. and Spiro, J. (2012b) *Reflective Writing*. Basingstoke: Palgrave Macmillan.

Willingham, D.T. (2008) 'Critical Thinking: Why Is It So Hard to Teach?', *Arts Education Policy Review*, 109(4): 21–32.

Wood, M. (2017) 'Not Getting Any Job Offers? Your Social Media Activity Could Be The Reason', *Forbes* (www.forbes.com/sites/allbusiness/2017/06/22/not-getting-any-job-offers-your-social-media-activity-could-be-the-reason/#5d543aa6374b).

World Economic Forum (2017) Here's Why You Didn't Get That Job: Your Name (www.weforum.org/agenda/2017/05/job-applications-resume-cv-name-descrimination/).

World Economic Forum (2020) Fourth Industrial Revolution (www.weforum.org/focus/fourth-industrial-revolution).

World Travel and Tourism Council (WTTC) (2013) A Career in Travel & Tourism: Chinese Undergraduate Perceptions (www.wttc.org/-/media/files/reports/policy-research/human_capital_report_chinese_final.pdf).

WTTC (2015) Global Talent Trends and Issues for the Travel & Tourism Sector (www.wttc.org/-/media/382b-b1e90c374262bc951226a6618201.ashx).

WTTC (2019a) Economic Impact 2019 (www.wttc.org/-/media/files/reports/economic-impact-research/regions-2019/world2019.pdf).

WTTC (2019b) Travel & Tourism Continues Strong Growth above Global GDP (www.wttc.org/about/media-centre/press-releases/press-releases/2019/travel-tourism-continues-strong-growth-above-global-gdp).

Yeoman, I., Ali-Knight, J., Robertson, M., Drummond, S. and McMahon-Beattie, U. (eds) (2004) *Festival and Events Management: An International Arts and Culture Perspective*. Abingdon: Routledge.

Yeoman, I. (2012) *2050 – Tomorrow's Tourism*. Bristol: Channel View Publications.

Yiu, M. and Law, R. (2012) 'A Review of Hospitality Internship: Different Perspectives of Students, Employers and Educators', *Journal of Teaching in Travel & Tourism*, 12(4): 377–402.

Yorke, M. (2006) 'Employability in Higher Education: What It Is – What It Is Not', *Advance HE* (www.advance-he.ac.uk/knowledge-hub/employability-higher-education-what-it-what-it-not).

Zhang, T., Bufquin, D. and Lu, C. (2019) 'A Qualitative Investigation of Microentrepreneurship in the Sharing Economy', *International Journal of Hospitality Management*, 79: 148–57.

Zopiatis, A. (2007) 'Hospitality Internships in Cyprus: A Genuine Academic Experience or a Continuing Frustration?', *International Journal of Contemporary Hospitality Management*, 19: 65–77.

Zopiatis, A. and Constanti, P. (2012) 'Managing Hospitality Internship Practices: A Conceptual Framework', *Journal of Hospitality & Tourism Education*, 24(1): 44–51.

APPENDIX

CHAPTER 18 SPECTRE SKILLS AUDIT TABLE

SKILLS	SCORE
Specialist: Management Skills	
1. I can influence and secure stakeholder buy-in	
2. I am positive and resilient under pressure	
3. I stand by my values, have integrity and can be trusted	
4. I can foster a common vision, set objectives and follow them through to completion	
5. I delegate and empower colleagues and ensure a wide range of views and perspectives are considered during the project life cycle	
6. I lead by example	
Participatory: Team Working Skills	
1. I recognize the skills, knowledge, strengths and weaknesses of others, and ensure appropriate support and guidance is available where necessary	
2. I ensure others are provided with the information they need to do their jobs in a timely manner	
3. I encourage transparency, interaction and collaboration (knowledge sharing) among team members	
4. I recognize and celebrate individual and team successes	
5. I can chair and/or lead group meetings effectively	
Environmental: Technical Skills	
1. I am a competent user of MS Word, Excel, PPT, Projects and/or similar packages	
2. I know how to ensure that data management practices are compliant with legal regulations, e.g. GDPR (General Data Protection Regulation (EU) 2016/679)	
3. I can create and use GANTT charts to assign tasks and monitor who is working on what	
4. I can create financial plans and budget forecasts, including monitoring and reporting on progress against expenditure	
5. I understand procurement processes and can ensure a project is compliant with legal requirements	
Communication: Interpersonal Skills	
1. I listen to feedback and ask questions	

(Continued)

(Continued)

SKILLS	SCORE
2. I do not require direct line management of an individual/team and am able to secure commitment and/or resources through negotiation and influencing skills	
3. I have excellent verbal and written communication skills	
4. I can make complex problems accessible to a wide range of audiences	
5. I am comfortable managing conflicts of interest or differences of opinion	

Time: Organizational Skills

1. I am a skilled time-manager	
2. I can manage conflicting priorities	
3. I can identify project actions and develop work packages and delivery schedules	
4. I ensure that stakeholders have regular and timely updates	
5. I understand risk management, and work with the project team and key stakeholders to agree, monitor and review the effectiveness of interventions	

Resource: People Management

1. I encourage and support team building activities	
2. I recognize the importance of motivating individuals and teams	
3. I monitor team and individual performance and provide constructive feedback to help improve skills and capabilities	
4. I consider that cultural competence and diversity awareness is critical to effective project management and success	
5. I promote respect through ensuring that all team members recognize and value what each other brings to the team	

Entrepreneurialism: Soft Skills

1. I am flexible and comfortable dealing with uncertainty and ambiguity	
2. I ensure my decisions are informed by evidence	
3. I use, and encourage others to use, creative thinking to solve complex problems	
4. I can be opportunistic when required	
5. I can multi-task	

INDEX

Please note that page numbers in italics *direct the reader to photographs, tables, diagrams or other images.*